MAGILL'S SURVEY OF AMERICAN LITERATURE

Revised Edition

MAGILL'S SURVEY OF AMERICAN LITERATURE

Revised Edition

Volume 2

Cisneros—Guare

Edited by

Steven G. Kellman
University of Texas, San Antonio

SALEM PRESS, INC.
Pasadena, California   Hackensack, New Jersey

Editor in Chief: Dawn P. Dawson

Editorial Director: Christina J. Moose	*Production Editor:* Joyce I. Buchea
Project Editor: Tracy Irons-Georges	*Acquisitions Editor:* Mark Rehn
Copy Editors: Sarah M. Hilbert	*Research Supervisor:* Jeffry Jensen
Elizabeth Ferry Slocum	*Research Assistant:* Rebecca Kuzins
Editorial Assistant: Dana Garey	*Graphics and Design:* James Hutson
Photo Editor: Cynthia Breslin Beres	*Layout:* William Zimmerman

Cover photo: Emily Dickinson (The Granger Collection, New York)

Library of Congress Cataloging-in-Publication Data

Magill's survey of American literature / edited by Steven G. Kellman. — [Rev. ed.].
    p. cm.
Includes bibliographical references and index.
ISBN-10: 1-58765-285-4 (set : alk. paper)
ISBN-13: 978-1-58765-285-1 (set : alk. paper)
ISBN-10: 1-58765-287-0 (vol. 2 : alk. paper)
ISBN-13: 978-1-58765-287-5 (vol. 2 : alk. paper)
  1. American literature—Dictionaries. 2. American literature—Bio-bibliography. 3. Authors, American—Biography—Dictionaries. I. Kellman, Steven G., 1947- II. Magill, Frank Northen, 1907-1997. III. Title: Survey of American literature.
  PS21.M34 2006
  810.9′0003—dc22

2006016503

First Printing

CONTENTS

CONTENTS

COMPLETE LIST OF CONTENTS

Volume 1

Volume 2

Volume 3

Volume 4

Volume 5

Volume 6

Magill's Survey of American Literature

Revised Edition

SANDRA CISNEROS

Born: Chicago, Illinois
December 20, 1954

Cisneros was one of the first United States Latina writers to win a wide reading audience outside the Latino community.

© Rubén Guzmán

BIOGRAPHY

Sandra Cisneros was born in Chicago, Illinois, on December 20, 1954, the only daughter in a family of seven children. Her mother, Elvira Cordero Anguiano, was a self-educated Mexican American who kindled her children's enthusiasm for reading by taking them to libraries. Her father, Alfredo Cisneros Del Moral, was a Mexican upholsterer who regularly moved the family between Chicago and Mexico City.

In Chicago Catholic schools, where expectations for Mexican American girls were low, Cisneros was a below-average student, but she read voraciously and began writing early. After graduating from Loyola University in Chicago in 1976, she earned a master's degree at the prestigious Iowa Writers' Workshop, where she learned "what I didn't want to be, how I didn't want to write."

Upon returning from graduate study to Chicago, she awakened to what she called the "incredible deluge of voices" that has become the hallmark of her writing. Her stories and poems reveal a variety of voices, Mexican American voices mainly, telling their stories in an exuberant mixture of English and Spanish.

Her writing career started slowly. She earned her living as a teacher, college recruiter, arts administrator, writing teacher, and lecturer. Her

choice to remain poor in order to write puzzled her father and brothers and often caused her to wonder whether she was betraying her beloved Mexican American culture by choosing a nontraditional life. She wrestled with the problems of how to be a liberated woman and remain a Latina.

Cisneros's fiction and poetry are widely anthologized, and *The House on Mango Street* is frequently taught in schools and colleges. Random House issued a one-volume selection from her fiction and poetry, *Vintage Cisneros*, in 2004. She has won a number of honors, including two National Endowment of the Arts Fellowships for fiction and poetry (1988, 1982), a MacArthur Foundation Fellowship (1995), and a Texas Medal of the Arts (2003). She has received several grants and guest lectureships, and honorary degrees from Loyola University, Chicago (2002), and the State University of New York at Purchase (1993). *Caramelo* (2002) was named a notable book of the year in several newspapers, including *The New York Times*, the *Los Angeles Times*, the *San Francisco Chronicle*, and the *Chicago Tribune*.

Cisneros has a Web site with biographical information and images and links to reviews and interviews. In June, 2003, Cisneros wrote at her Web site, "I currently earn my living by my pen. I live in San Antonio, Texas, in a violet house filled with many creatures, little and large." In interviews, she reports that in San Antonio she found a rich source of voices for her stories and poems as well as an increasing independence that confirmed her in the choice of a nontraditional life, which she described as being "no one's mother and nobody's wife." Cisneros has come to see a main purpose of her writing as helping people to see their lives more clearly. This help often takes the form of showing that "we can be Latino and still be American."

467

ANALYSIS

In a 1991 interview, Cisneros spoke of the "deluge of voices" she heard upon returning to Chicago after studying in the Iowa Writers' Workshop. She said she was "fascinated by the rhythms of speech." Both her fiction and her poetry may be described as a deluge of voices, for virtually all of her fiction and some of her poems take the general form of the dramatic monologue.

A dramatic monologue is a literary work that consists of a speech such as one might hear in ordinary conversation, or especially in a play. A good example is "*Los* Boxers," in which a talkative widower in a laundromat explains to a young mother how he has learned to do his laundry systematically, effectively, and cheaply, without any perception of the irony of his giving this information to a Latina—for whom such work is traditionally a life sentence and who presumably still knows a good deal more about doing laundry than he does.

Cisneros's stories more often take the form of an internal monologue. The reader follows the speaker's inner thoughts as if he or she were saying them out loud in a distinctive voice; often the speaker is engaged in some specific actions while thinking. An example is "My Friend Lucy Who Smells Like Corn," a story that communicates the joys of youthful friendship in a poor neighborhood. The speaker breathlessly describes her friend while recounting past and current activities and adventures, including snatches of dialogue. She reveals her pleasures in playing at Lucy's house with her friend's eight sisters and tells of her wish for sisters of her own so that she could sleep with them "instead of alone on a fold-out chair in the living room."

Almost every story and many poems seem to be spoken aloud, even if there is not a specific dramatic situation. Even when a story clearly consists of recorded writing, as opposed to speech, Cisneros emphasizes a particular writing voice. For example, in "Little Miracles, Kept Promises," she presents notes left at shrines, notes thanking or making requests of various saints. Each note is a story told in a unique voice that reveals the personality of the writer, his or her situation and cultural background, and the writer's conception of the addressed saint as a listener. Though forms of the dramatic monologue and closely related letter forms are favorites for Cisneros, she occasionally tells stories in the third-person voice, and many of her poems seem to be in her own voice, describing her own family and acquaintances.

Readers will recognize similarities between characters in her stories and members of her family. The Reyes family of *Caramelo* and the Cordero family of *The House on Mango Street* are based on her own family. While these novels and several of her stories contain autobiographical elements, Cisneros points out that these always are fictionalized and not literal stories from her life.

Cisneros's main themes include the position of women in Latino culture, the problems of Latinas who want to live independent lives, and the complex relations between Anglo-Americans, Mexican Americans, and Mexicans. She also gives considerable attention to religious themes, reflecting her ambivalence toward her family's Catholicism and her eventual conversion to Buddhism, which she says allowed her to maintain her devotion to the Virgin of Guadalupe. Although Cisneros has clear political concerns that appear in virtually all of her work, her stories and poems are rarely political or moral tracts. Even the parable "There Was a Man, There Was a Woman" presents portraits without explaining the meanings readers should see in the depiction of the two characters.

As Cisneros has said in interviews, one of her purposes as an artist is to change the way in which people see their world. Her works thus often present a picture of Latino life from a point of view that reveals aspects that ordinarily might be hidden. For example, in "*Los* Boxers," there is no moralistic voice that points out the irony of a middle-aged widower telling a mother how to do laundry. The man simply talks, and the irony is left for the reader to discover. As one thinks about such a story, with its new point of view on "women's work," further discoveries about political meanings in the story may emerge, such as, for example, what it means that a man finds the problems of doing laundry interesting to think and talk about.

Furthermore, in the context of traditional Latino culture—in which the ideal woman passively serves men, obeying her father and then her husband, giving her life to housekeeping and motherhood—the story of a Latino advising a Latina about laundry takes on another dimension. For example, "*Los* Boxers" opens with a child dropping and breaking a bottle of soda, setting up a situation in which the mother, following orders, cleans up the glass and mops away the spill, while the man watches and lectures. He never thinks of helping her; in his culture, this is unthinkable, even for a man who has learned to do his own laundry. Because Cisneros usually avoids overt political statement, confining herself to pointed description or letting her characters speak, readers are encouraged to explore implicit meanings of the presented experience.

THE HOUSE ON MANGO STREET

First published: 1984
Type of work: Novella

In a mid-twentieth century Chicago barrio, a Latina enters her teen years, struggling to become the person she envisions herself being.

The House on Mango Street is Cisneros's best-known work. Though it is made up of stories and sketches, some of which have been published separately, the collection has the unity of a novella. Cisneros has described the book as a connected collection, "each story a little pearl. . . . the whole thing like a necklace." In her own mind, Esperanza Cordero, the narrator, has one main problem: She wants to have a house of her own. As the story develops, the meaning of having a house of her own grows richer and more complex, until finally, she understands that she wants not only a literal house but also "a home in the heart." Furthermore, her one problem connects with many other problems that are clearer to the reader than to Esperanza, especially problems related to the roles and treatment accorded women in her culture and the problems of being Mexican American in U.S. culture.

Esperanza is the older of two daughters and has two brothers. Her wish for a house grows out of the family desire that is realized when they buy the house on Mango Street. This turns out not to be the home of which they have dreamed, with a large yard and many bathrooms, but the house they can afford, in a neighborhood being transformed into a ghetto. Esperanza's disappointment sparks her wish. She also realizes after moving to Mango Street that she does not want to live her life as do most women whom she knows. She is named after her great-grandmother, a woman who refused to marry: "Until my great-grandfather threw a sack over her head and carried her off. Just like that, as if she were a fancy chandelier. . . . And the story goes she never forgave him."

Having inherited her great-grandmother's name, Esperanza believes that she also has inherited her nature, a determination to be strong and to live independently. After young Esperanza is sexually assaulted at a carnival, she decides that she wants a house that belongs to her alone, not to any man. Her own bad experience confirms what she sees everywhere: that many women are seen as servants and property, their power and imagination imprisoned in houses that belong to husbands and fathers.

To Esperanza, a house comes to mean not only freedom from sexual oppression but also the freedom to pursue her vision of herself as an artist. Several times, Esperanza receives mysterious messages from seemingly spiritual sources that reveal what she must do to become an artist. Elenita, a medium, tells her mysteriously that she will have "a new house, a house made of heart." At the wake for her friend Lucy's baby sister, Esperanza meets three elderly sisters who see something special in her. They take her aside and tell her to make a wish. Seeming to know that Esperanza has wished to go away, they tell her, "When you leave you must remember to come back for the others. A circle, understand? You will always be Esperanza. You will always be Mango Street. . . . You must remember to come back. For the ones who cannot leave as easily as you."

These messages tell Esperanza that she is destined to be a writer, to create an imaginary home out of the materials of her heart, which she will take with her wherever she goes and which will call her back to help those who are unable to leave. Near the end of the book, Esperanza's friend Alicia asks her a question: If she does not return to make Mango Street better—presumably a better place for women and for Latinos—then who will do so? Esperanza then begins to see that, as a poet and storyteller, she will have a mission, to return not necessarily literally but certainly in her heart and mind, to make her people better known to themselves, to each other, and to the rest of U.S. culture.

Sandra Cisneros

"Woman Hollering Creek"

First published: 1991 (collected in *Woman Hollering Creek, and Other Stories*, 1991)
Type of work: Short story

A young Mexican woman is disillusioned by her marriage to a Mexican American man.

In "Woman Hollering Creek," Cisneros describes the experiences of an ideal Mexican wife, Cleófilas. Having grown up with her father, six brothers, and no mother, Cleófilas learns how to be a woman by watching *telenovelas* on television. She learns to expect that passion will fill her life. This passion will be the great love of her life, which will give it direction and meaning, so that "one does whatever one can, must do, at whatever the cost." This, she believes, is how life should be, "because to suffer for love is good. The pain all sweet somehow. In the end." To be complete as a woman, she need only wait for her lover to appear and carry her away into "happy ever after."

Her husband, Juan, carries her away from Mexico to Seguin, Texas, where she finds no community or family to support her, living in a comparatively isolated home and without independent

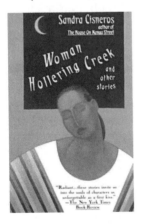

means of transportation. Aware of the role of a good wife, she learns how to fit gracefully in with Juan's life. She cares for his house and bears a son, Juan Pedrito. Both she and Juan, however, are foreigners in Seguin. His work is menial and does not pay well enough for the minimum standard of life in Texas. By the time she is pregnant with their second child, he has taken to beating her regularly, partly as a way of dealing with his frustration and powerlessness.

As their relationship deteriorates, Cleófilas comes to realize that this marriage does not contain the passion she learned about in the *telenovelas*. She thinks about her situation while sitting next to Woman Hollering Creek, her baby in her lap; she sometimes wonders whether the woman after whom the creek is named cries out in pain or in rage. She finally realizes that she can do nothing herself to make the marriage right, and she wonders whether the arroyo was named after *La Llorona*, the weeping woman who drowned her own children, in the stories of her childhood.

Finally, she returns to her father, disillusioned but still the passive woman depending upon men to care for her. To make her escape, she gets help from a woman who provides a glimpse of another way to live. Felice gives her a ride in her truck on the first part of her escape. That Felice lives alone, takes care of herself, and owns a truck—in short, that she lives much as a man does in Cleófilas's experience—astonishes Cleófilas. She continues to think about Felice long after her return to Mexico, and she tells others about this woman who, when they crossed the creek upon leaving Seguin, hollered like Tarzan: "It was a gurgling out of her own throat, a long ribbon of laughter, like water."

"Little Miracles, Kept Promises"

First published: 1991 (collected in *Woman Hollering Creek, and Other Stories*, 1991)
Type of work: Short story

A collection of notes left at saints' shrines, ending with a long letter from a young woman who has achieved faith in herself.

"Little Miracles, Kept Promises" is a catalog of Cisneros's strengths and appeals as a fiction writer. The collection of notes left at saints' shrines may recall the letters of Nathanael West's *Miss Lonelyhearts* (1933), but the tone of these is more consistently comic, showing well the witty and humorous side of Cisneros that appears in many of her stories and poems. For example, Barbara Ybañez threatens to turn the statue of San Antonio de Padua upside down until he sends her "a man man. I mean someone who's not ashamed to be seen cooking or cleaning or looking after himself."

Rubén Ledesma somewhat reluctantly, yet desperately, appeals to San Lázaro, who was "raised from the dead and did a lot of miracles," to help him deal with his "face breaking out with so many pimples." These letters are especially rich in the variety of voices and tones they present, from the devout who speak to their saint as a friend, to the pious who lapse into almost meaningless formulas, to the inexperienced who are uncomfortable addressing a person they do not know personally, to the irreverent and skeptical.

These many voices lead finally to that of a young woman, Rosario, who has cut off a braid of hair that has never before been cut and pinned it by the statue of the Virgin of Guadalupe. Rosario is an image of Cisneros, the young Latina artist rebelling against the restrictive roles of women in her culture, especially as they have been reinforced by the massive cultural authority of the Catholic Church. She says that she has resisted religious belief until her discovery that the Virgin is not simply a passive sufferer but also one manifestation of woman as goddess, the powers of fertility, healing, creative energy. This discovery made it possible for Rosario to love the Virgin, to stop being ashamed of her mother and grandmother, and, finally, to love herself.

Of Rosario, Cisneros said, "That's me. . . . I'm very, very much devoted to the Virgin of Guadalupe, but not exactly the same figure celebrated in Church."

CARAMELO

First published: 2002
Type of work: Novel

A Latina tells the painful and humorous story of her family at the request of her dead grandmother.

In the first part of *Caramelo*, Celaya Reyes remembers a summer trip from Chicago to visit her grandparents in Mexico City in about 1962. With rich imagery and humor and from the perspective of a five-year-old, Celaya introduces her extended family and the culture of Mexico City in the mid-twentieth century.

In the second part, with the ghost of her grandmother, Soledad, watching over her shoulder and commenting, an older Celaya recounts Soledad's life. This is a story of suffering and hardening against the epic backdrop of twentieth century Mexican history. Celaya explains how Soledad—repeatedly abandoned by parents and her husband—turned into "the Awful Grandmother," hated and feared by Celaya and her mother because of her fierce possessiveness toward her son, Celaya's father, Inocencio.

In the final part, Celaya, from a teenager's perspective, recounts Soledad's final years, after her husband's death, when she continued to sow discord in her son's family. She returns from death to haunt Celaya and threaten Inocencio. In a struggle over Inocencio's hospital bed after his heart attack, Celaya and the ghost strike a bargain. If Celaya will tell Soledad's story—as she does in the second part—Soledad will not carry her father away to be with her. Soledad wants her story told because she is suffering alone; she cannot pass on to the next life until those she has hurt can understand her and forgive her.

Soledad's cruelest act was telling the truth at a carefully chosen moment. Knowing that Inocencio had an illegitimate daughter with her laundress, Soledad brings both mother and child to work in her house while Celaya's family is visiting. While on an outing, Soledad reveals the truth to Celaya's mother, hoping that she will leave Inocencio. Celaya does not understand this treachery fully until after her father's illness, and yet she still is willing to bargain with this "Awful Grandmother" for her father's life.

In an interview with Ray Suarez of the Public Broadcasting Service (PBS) network, Cisneros said that in a story, she has the opportunity to think deeply about her characters and to be more forgiving than people are normally. *Caramelo* is, in part, about forgiveness. Her characters often discuss truth and "healthy lies." Soledad attempts to destroy Celaya's family by telling the truth. Repeatedly Celaya and various characters find reasons to tell what they call "healthy lies," usually the kinds of stories that help people to be kind to one another

DISCUSSION TOPICS

- Sandra Cisneros says that one purpose of her stories is to help readers to see one another more sympathetically and so to be more forgiving. What are some examples of stories and incidents that serve this purpose?

- *Caramelo* opens with this statement: "Tell me something, even if it is a lie." Think of examples of characters telling stories about themselves and others, whether they are true or false. In which examples is the storytelling hurtful and in which is it helpful? What makes the difference?

- Many of Cisneros's stories offer comparisons between two or more cultures, especially Anglo-American, Mexican American, and Mexican. What features stand out as distinctive in each culture? What points of comparison does Cisneros emphasize?

- Cisneros's female characters, especially in *The House on Mango Street* and *Caramelo,* often struggle for self-realization against the expectations for women in traditional Mexican culture. What does traditional Mexican culture expect of women? Consider the motives of her main female rebels against tradition. What factors make their rebellions difficult and painful? What factors go into a successful rebellion?

- Cisneros's Mexican and Mexican American characters often seem ambivalent about their American Indian ancestry. What are some examples of these ambivalent feelings? What reasons does Cisneros suggest for this ambivalence?

- In several of her stories, Cisneros mixes a good deal of Spanish in with the English. How does this mixing of languages affect the reading experience for an English-speaking reader? Why do you think Cisneros does this? For one example, what themes emerge when one studies the meanings and uses of the word "caramelo," in *Caramelo?*

when closeness is more important than knowing the facts.

Caramelo also develops Cisneros's typical theme of the young Latina struggling toward becoming an artist within a family and culture that frowns on women choosing nontraditional lives. Celaya's aspirations are almost thwarted by the values Soledad seems to represent, but finally, they are affirmed when Soledad finds she needs Celaya's storytelling abilities to free her own voice and ask for mercy.

SUMMARY

While Cisneros's themes often concern race, gender, and class, her stories and poems are not narrowly political. Rather than focusing on specific social problems and their remedies, Cisneros tries to be part of a more general solution, calling attention through lively and entertaining stories to how life is experienced, especially by Mexican American women. In *Caramelo,* she emphasizes family as a model for humanity, and storytelling as the central means by which universal human interdependence and connectedness become visible. In her stories, she works at changing the ways her readers look at their worlds, helping them to imagine better ways to live. In these ways, her work is related to that of major local color writers of the nineteenth century, such as Sarah Orne Jewett.

Terry Heller

BIBLIOGRAPHY

By the Author

LONG FICTION:
The House on Mango Street, 1984
Caramelo, 2002

SHORT FICTION:
Woman Hollering Creek, and Other Stories, 1991

POETRY:
Bad Boys, 1980
The Rodrigo Poems, 1985
My Wicked, Wicked Ways, 1987
Loose Woman, 1994

CHILDREN'S LITERATURE:
Hairs = Pelitos, 1984

MISCELLANEOUS:
Vintage Cisneros, 2004

About the Author

Brackett, Virginia. *A Home in the Heart: The Story of Sandra Cisneros.* Greensboro, N.C.: Morgan Reynolds, 2005.

Cisneros, Sandra. "The Authorized Sandra Cisneros Web Site." http://www.sandracisneros.com/home .html.

_____. "From a Writer's Notebook: Ghosts and Voices—Writing from Obsessions, Do You Know Me? I Wrote *The House on Mango Street.*" *The Americas Review* 15 (Fall/Winter, 1987): 69-73, 77-79.

Jussawalla, Feroz, and Reed W. Dasenbrock, eds. *Interviews with Writers of the Post-Colonial World.* Jackson: University Press of Mississippi, 1992.

Kevane, Bridget A., and Juanita Heredia. "A Home in the Heart—An Interview with Sandra Cisneros." In *Latina Self-Portraits: Interviews with Contemporary Women.* Albuquerque: University of New Mexico Press, 2000.

Olivares, Julián. "Sandra Cisneros' *The House on Mango Street* and the Poetics of Space." In *Chicana Creativity and Criticism: Charting New Frontiers in American Literature,* edited by Maria Herrera-Sobek and Helena María Viramontes. Houston: Arte Publico Press, 1988.

Petty, Leslie. "The 'Dual'-ling Images of la Malinche and la Virgen de Guadelupe in Cisneros's *The House on Mango Street.*" *Melus* 25 (Summer, 2000): 119-132.

Rodriguez-Aranda, Pilar E. "On the Solitary Fate of Being Mexican, Female, Wicked, and Thirty-Three: An Interview with Writer Sandra Cisneros." *The Americas Review* 18 (Spring, 1990): 64-80.

Tompkins, Cynthia. "Sandra Cisneros." In *American Novelists Since World War II, 4th Series,* edited by James and Wanda Giles. Vol. 152 in *Dictionary of Literary Biography.* Detroit: Gale, 1995.

Valdéz, Maria Elena de. "The Critical Reception of Sandra Cisneros's *The House on Mango Street.*" In *Gender, Self, and Society,* edited by Renate von Bartelben. Frankfurt: Peter Lang, 1993.

TOM CLANCY

Born: Baltimore, Maryland
April 12, 1947

Credited for creating the "techno-thriller," Clancy combines state-of-the-art military technology and superpower or terrorist confrontation in his best-selling novels.

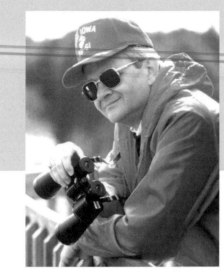

John Earle

BIOGRAPHY

Thomas L. Clancy was born in Baltimore, Maryland, in 1947. His father, a mailman, and his mother, who worked in a department-store credit office, provided him with a middle-class upbringing. Toys, particularly toys featuring military technology, fascinated the young Clancy; he also became and remained a voracious reader.

Educated in Roman Catholic schools, Clancy attended Loyola College in Baltimore, majoring in English. He later said that he always wanted to see his name on a book, although he never imagined that he would become a best-selling author. While in college, he was a member of the Reserve Officers' Training Corps (ROTC), but poor eyesight kept him out of the regular military, much to his regret. He married Wanda Thomas in 1969, shortly after leaving college, and the need to support his growing family of eventually four children led him away from a literary career and into a more immediately financially rewarding occupation as an insurance agent, and he eventually joined his wife's grandfather's insurance agency in rural Maryland.

Clancy never abandoned his quest to become a writer. He had a science-fiction story rejected, and in the early 1970's, he began plotting a novel, a work that contained characters that would eventually populate his published books. During those years he also continued his extensive reading, particularly in science fiction and military manuals. Al-

though he did well in business, by the end of the decade he again turned to the task of getting his name on a book jacket.

In 1976, a naval mutiny occurred on a Soviet frigate, the mutineers hoping to defect to Sweden. The mutiny failed, but the incident gave Clancy the inspiration for his first published novel. Written during several months in late 1982 and early 1983, the unknown author's *The Hunt for Red October* was published in 1984 by the Naval Academy's Naval Institute Press, which had recently decided to publish works of fiction, an unlikely publishing house to produce one of the best sellers of the year. Clancy said that he thought the work might sell 5,000 or 10,000 copies, but eventually 300,000 copies were sold in hardback and two million in paperback. Film rights were purchased for $500,000, and the motion picture, which starred Sean Connery as a defecting Soviet submarine captain, was a popular hit. Several of his other novels, including *Patriot Games* (1987) and *The Sum of All Fears* (1991), have also become successful films, and his works have been adapted to profitable video games.

The fame of *The Hunt for Red October* reached the upper levels of the political and military establishment in Washington. President Ronald Reagan called it "the perfect yarn." Defense Secretary Caspar Weinberger reviewed it favorably in *The Times Literary Supplement*. Clancy was invited to the White House, and the Pentagon gave him access to some of its major weapons systems; he spent time on a nuclear submarine and a naval frigate and drove an M-1 tank. All these experiences became grist for future works.

The books came rapidly. In 1986, Clancy published *Red Storm Rising*, about a third world war fought in Europe between North Atlantic Treaty Organization (NATO) forces and the Soviet Union. In 1987, he wrote *Patriot Games*, a story of terrorists from Northern Ireland. A highly placed Russian official who spied for the Central Intelligence Agency (CIA) was the focus of *The Cardinal of the Kremlin* (1988), followed by *Clear and Present Danger*, involving the Colombian drug trade, in 1989. *The Sum of All Fears* pivoted around an international terrorist plot to explode a nuclear weapon during the Super Bowl game. *Without Remorse*, which returned to the era of the Vietnam War in the early 1970's, appeared in 1993, followed by *Debt of Honor* (1994), in which a Japanese terrorist pilots a 747 into the Capitol building, killing the president and most members of Congress. *Executive Orders* (1996) centered upon a biological terrorist attack on the United States. *The Bear and the Dragon* (2000) featured an invasion of Russia by Communist China. In *Red Rabbit* (2002), Clancy returned to the early 1980's and a plot to assassinate Pope John Paul II. A new generation of Clancy characters entered the canon in *The Teeth of the Tiger* (2003), which featured Jack Ryan, Jr., as a CIA recruit. Clancy has also written several other fictional works as well as numerous nonfiction military studies, often with a coauthor. In addition, Clancy became a newspaper columnist and a popular lecturer. His continuing best-seller status saw the one-time insurance agent become one of the most recognized authors of the day, both in the United States and abroad.

Clancy's first marriage ended in 1998. The following year, he married Alexandra Llewellyn, the daughter of a wealthy Philadelphia businessman and the niece of General Colin Powell, the secretary of state in George W. Bush's first administration.

ANALYSIS

Clancy has stated that he does not like to analyze the themes of his books. "A theme to me is a question that a high-school English teacher asks," he told an interviewer, explaining that his literary concerns were with more essential matters. "In the real world, and that's what I try to write about as basically as I can, somebody has to get the job done." Nevertheless, there are obvious themes in Clancy's works. Clancy claims that, like most Americans, he is entranced with technology, and "the military

happen to have the best toys." If so, it is not surprising that *The Hunt for Red October* became a best seller. From the opening paragraph, the reader is caught up in the world of men at war, a world about which Clancy seems exceptionally knowledgeable. The attempt of the Soviet captain Mark Ramius to turn his nuclear submarine over to the Americans shows both sides caught in a web of circumstances that could lead to nuclear war between the superpowers. The author's expertise in military technology and in the minds and mores of those who fight—or, to use Clancy's words, those who must get the job done—is compelling and convincing.

The harnessing of the latest military technology to a plot in which a nuclear war is a possible outcome is a combination likely to attract many readers. Clancy, however, denies that he either invented what has been called the techno-thriller or that his writings should be so labeled. Clancy claims that he aims merely to be as accurate as possible; because he is writing about war and terrorism in the late twentieth and early twenty-first centuries, technology must play a central role.

Technology, however, is not the master of humanity in Clancy's fiction. The machines can do only what men and women would have them do. Obviously, technology can be used for destructive and immoral purposes. Underneath the violence, there are pervasive elements of good and evil in Clancy's novels. Evil generally results from corrupt institutions, false ideologies, and immoral values. Although the author was strongly opposed to the Soviet Union and what it stood for—*The Hunt for Red October*, *Red Storm Rising*, and *The Cardinal of the Kremlin* all depict the Soviets as the mortal enemies of American values and institutions—many of Clancy's Soviet characters are sympathetically drawn.

The Soviet world portrayed in Clancy's novels, however, is not morally or spiritually equal to the West. In Clancy's works, the Soviet system devalues traditional religious and spiritual values; humans are no better than animals, and international terrorists are no more than common killers. Morality and immorality are opposing foes in Clancy's novels, and the good always win in the end. Neither pacifism nor neutrality, however, can preserve the West and its Judeo-Christian ethic; in Clancy's literary world, military values and strengths are necessary and imperative. Fortuitously for him, his early publications coincided with a political generation eager to shake off the perception of American weakness and debility that followed the Vietnam War. It is no wonder that the Reagan White House found in Clancy a kindred spirit.

Clancy, though, has little respect for most politicians; too often they are amoral, committed to their own careers. The unnamed president in *The Hunt for Red October* and *The Cardinal of the Kremlin* is often too pragmatic, but ultimately he makes the correct and necessary decisions. The same president is diminished in *Clear and Present Danger* because of his concern with his coming reelection campaign. President Fowler, his liberal successor, is worse, combining ignorance and arrogance, and he almost starts World War III by threatening to use nuclear weapons against the Soviets in *The Sum of All Fears*. Individual politicians may have vision and competence, but most of Clancy's are simply concerned with keeping their offices at any cost. In *Executive Orders*, when his protagonist, Jack Ryan, becomes president after a terrorist attack kills the incumbent president, Ryan appoints successful businessmen as his close advisers because, unlike self-serving politicians, they have amassed great fortunes while serving the common good through their private enterprise accomplishments. Although Clancy's books are populated by military figures, his alter ego in his novels is Jack Ryan, a civilian. Ryan, who has a doctorate in history and has made a small fortune in the stock market, saves the heir to the British throne in *Patriot Games*, becomes a consultant to the CIA and the national security adviser, and finally ascends to the presidency itself. Ryan is not a superman—he has a fear of flying and a weakness for cigarettes—but in the convoluted plots of Clancy's books, Ryan is forced into the world of terror and war. He then becomes the man who, in Clancy's phrase, gets the job done.

Ryan is not the leading figure in all Clancy's books; however, he is the thread that ties the many subplots and numerous characters together. Clancy's works can thus be read as a whole. Not only Ryan but many other figures also appear and reappear, sometimes as major characters, other times in smaller parts. A character such as John Clark plays only a small—although crucial—role in *The Cardinal of the Kremlin*, but he has a much larger part in *Clear and Present Danger* and the lead role in *Without Remorse*.

Reviewers have criticized the lack of character development in Clancy's novels. While the dialogue is generally satisfying, many of his characters are indeed one-dimensional figures. Clancy is writing largely about desperate crises; action, not introspection, is perhaps expected. The character of Ryan, however, does evolve from novel to novel. By the time that *The Sum of All Fears* was published in 1991, Ryan was in his forties, working too hard at the CIA, neglecting his family, worrying about his inability to take his young son to a baseball game, and drinking too much. Even his marriage seemed in danger. The centrality of the family is an underlying theme in Clancy's works; Ryan's own family is the model modern family.

The ultimate crisis of *Patriot Games* sees Ryan defending his family and home from a terrorist assault. The family personifies and preserves the moral and religious values crucial to society. It is a deeply conservative and traditional view that is undoubtedly related to the author's middle-class Catholic background; that synthesis of traditional values with the latest technology and the threat of total war explains his great popularity.

THE HUNT FOR RED OCTOBER

First published: 1984
Type of work: Novel

A Soviet submarine captain attempts to defect to the United States.

Clancy's first published novel, *The Hunt for Red October*, became a runaway best seller. Writing at a time of heightened Cold War tensions, Clancy touched a deep chord. Soviet submarine captain Mark Ramius is disillusioned by the communist system and the Soviet state. His wife, a former ballerina, died on an operating table at the hands of a drunken doctor who, because of his Communist Party connections, was not punished for his misdeed. The leading Soviet expert in submarine tactics, Ramius decides to defect to the United States.

A number of themes common to Clancy's work appear in *The Hunt for Red October*. His knowledge of submarine technology and tactics carries the reader into an underwater world that, because of the technological framework, seems more fact than fiction. The Soviets do not want a nuclear war, but they might resort to war to recapture Ramius and his submarine, and power divorced from morality could well destroy the world. Ramius, driven by family feelings and moral considerations, transcends a system that has proved to be an evil failure.

On the other side is Jack Ryan, a consultant to the CIA. Because he is only a professor of history, he lacks the authority government office might give him; he is neither a high-ranking military figure nor a politician. Ryan is an Everyman who is willing and able to do what is necessary. Eventually, Ryan boards the *Red October* and is forced to kill a committed young communist who has been or-

dered to sink the submarine rather than have it fall into American hands. Although his submarine is damaged, Ramius sails his ship into an American port. Ryan has received an education in the necessity of using power, political and military, to maintain the good society: It is not enough merely to write about history.

As in all of his stories, Clancy brings together a number of subplots and numerous major and minor characters. Even if the politicians are not always dependable, the officers and men of the military invariably excel. Well trained and motivated, they work together for the greater good of their unit and their country. Clancy makes numerous comparisons between the Soviet system and the freedoms to be found in the West. The book is not so much a story of "good guys" and "bad guys" as a contest between a system that has failed and one that, in spite of individual human weaknesses, is the last best hope of humankind.

PATRIOT GAMES

First published: 1987
Type of work: Novel

A young American historian runs afoul of Irish terrorists after foiling their attack upon the Prince and Princess of Wales.

Because of its success as a film, *Patriot Games* is one of Clancy's best-known novels. He began writing it before *The Hunt for Red October,* but it was not published until after his second hit novel, *Red Storm Rising* (1986). *Patriot Games,* however, relates the earliest part of Jack Ryan's fictional biography. Clancy has admitted that in creating Ryan he has projected an idealized version of himself.

In a departure from his other novels, in *Patriot Games* technology plays only a secondary role. The story opens in London. Ryan and his family are enjoying a working vacation; his wife and daughter sightsee and shop while he researches his next work of history. At the end of the day, Ryan meets his family in a peaceful London park, but an explosion a few yards away aborts the plans for a pleasant evening. A radical Irish republican faction of dedicated Marxists has just attacked the automobile carrying the Prince and Princess of Wales.

Ryan, a former Marine officer, reacts instinctively, killing one terrorist and disarming another. Ryan himself is shot. For his heroism, he is given an honorary knighthood. The terrorists vow revenge, however, and eventually attack Ryan and his family after they have returned to the United States.

There are fewer subplots than in Clancy's other novels; Ryan remains the focus of the work. While still in a London hospital recovering from his wounds, Ryan is visited by the Prince of Wales, who feels guilty that he was unable to personally protect his wife. In American fashion, Ryan bucks up the prince, giving him renewed confidence in himself. In *Patriot Games* the importance of the family and all that it represents takes center place. The Windsors, who later visit the Ryans' home for dinner while on a tour to the United States, are presented as holding the same values and morals as Ryan and his wife, Cathy. They might be royalty, but underneath they are just like the people next door. In contrast, the terrorists, rootless and homeless and driven by perverted philosophies and blind hatreds, lack those necessary societal values. Clancy—and Ryan—are Irish Americans, but neither has any sympathy for radical Irish terrorists.

Clancy has the ability to touch the concerns of his readers. Cold War fears and the threats of terrorism were headline issues and events when his novels appeared. In *Patriot Games*, he capitalized on America's fascination with Britain's Prince Charles and Princess Diana. With Everyman Jack Ryan becoming a knighted hero battling ruthless villains, the novel was guaranteed to be a best seller and a hit film.

THE SUM OF ALL FEARS

First published: 1991
Type of work: Novel

> *An international terrorist group explodes a nuclear device during the Super Bowl.*

One of the strengths of Clancy's novels is their timeliness. *The Sum of All Fears*, published in 1991, reflects the immediate post-Cold War world. The Berlin Wall has fallen; the Soviet Union is no more. Yet the world is not necessarily safer. New tensions and old rivalries have replaced superpower antagonisms. International terrorism is obviously not new—Clancy himself wrote about it in *Patriot Games*—but without the restraining influence of the Cold War, terrorism could well pose a greater threat than in the past.

Ryan has risen to a position of authority in the CIA. Unfortunately, the new president, Jonathan Robert Fowler, a liberal, and his national security adviser, Elizabeth Elliot, a leftist academic, see such agencies as the CIA as incompetent and as relics of history that can be ignored. Ryan, who is not a politician, does little to avoid alienating Fowler and Elliot. The conservative Clancy holds no brief for their liberal politics, but even worse than their politics is their lack of morality. When Fowler and Elliot become lovers, it becomes obvious to the reader that they are destined to be Ryan's foes.

In *The Sum of All Fears*, the terrorists are a mixed group of German Marxists, radical Muslims, and an American Indian. Each has different motives, but all are wedded to ideologies foreign to Western values and institutions. As in most of Clancy's novels, technology plays a key role. The technological focus revolves around an Israeli nuclear weapon lost during the 1973 war with Syria. Rediscovered years later in a farmer's garden, the rebuilt weapon is secretly shipped to the United States, trucked to Denver, and explodes during the Super Bowl game.

In the aftermath, President Fowler loses control of himself, almost declaring war on the Soviets, whom he suspects of setting off the device. When it is learned that the plot originated in the Middle East, possibly at the instigation of an Iranian Muslim cleric, Fowler issues the order to bomb the cleric's hometown, the holy city of Qum, an act that would kill tens of thousands of innocent people. At the crucial point, Ryan steps in and vetoes the presidential order, and the vice president replaces Fowler. Although thousands have died in Denver, a world conflagration is narrowly avoided.

In this novel, Clancy brings together all the themes that make his books so popular. There is the struggle between good and evil. Technology is central to the story. The threat of nuclear weapons, a fear since the end of World War II, is shown to be a potential reality. Eternal vigilance is necessary, and someone must do what is required in spite of all obstacles. In the course of *The Sum of All Fears*, Ryan, driving himself too hard at work, almost destroys his own family through drink and inattention. At the end, he puts his family at the center of his life and resigns from the CIA. Someone must do the job, but the human costs can be high.

EXECUTIVE ORDERS

First published: 1996
Type of work: Novel

> *Unexpectedly assuming the presidency, Ryan faces an international attempt to bring down the United States through the use of biological terror weapons, orchestrated by the Ayatollah of Iran.*

In *Debt of Honor* (1994), in an event in which art anticipates eventual reality, a deranged Japanese terrorist crashes a 747 into the Capitol, killing the president, all of the members of the Supreme Court, as well as most members of Congress. In *Executive Orders*, Jack Ryan, who had been sworn in as vice president after the resignation of the elected vice president (who was accused of sexual battery), survives the destruction and assumes the presidency. This is an office that he did not desire, but as a patriot, he accepted the responsibility. Ryan guides the creation of a new national government, while facing numerous challenges, both domestic and international.

The Ayatollah Daryaei, the radical Islamic leader of Iran, arranges for the assassination of neighboring Iraq's Saddam Hussein, and quickly unifies Iran and Iraq in the United Islamic Republic. Daryaei's long-term goal is to invade and capture Saudi Arabia and Kuwait and create a single Islamic state throughout the Middle East and Central Asia. An outbreak of Ebola fever in Africa allows Daryaei's clique to develop Ebola as a terror weapon, importing it secretly into the United States in aerosol shaving cream cans, which are eventually released simultaneously into the air in convention halls in many American cities. The same Iranian group also plots to kidnap Ryan's youngest daughter from her preschool and possibly kill her, as well as to have a secret service bodyguard, a Muslim, assassinate Ryan himself. In typical Clancy fashion, the convoluted but page-turning plot also involves

the prime minister of India and officials from the People's Republic of China, who support the Iranians in a concerted attempt to weaken the United States, the world's sole superpower after the collapse of the Soviet Union.

A no-nonsense, nonpolitical president, Ryan leads the American counterattack, but in *Executive Orders*, it is a different Ryan than readers are used to. As president, Ryan is at the center, making the decisions and giving the orders, but those orders are carried out by others, many of whom are characters from previous Clancy novels, such as John Clark. Ryan himself is largely a passive figure, complaining about having

to deal with politicians and wasting time and energy in what he considers irrelevant matters, and, in Hamlet-fashion, worrying about his abilities and responsibilities. However, good again triumphs over evil. The kidnapping attempt fails; the Ebola attack, which Ryan interprets as a weapon of mass destruction, kills only a few thousand Americans instead of the massive numbers hoped for by Daryaei; and the assassination attempt is foiled. Daryaei's United Islamic Republic of Iran and Iraq invades neighboring Saudi Arabia, but backed by the technology and expertise of a relatively small American military contingent, the invasion fails, thus ending the "Second Persian Gulf War." Issuing an executive order, Ryan orders the death of Daryaei, accomplished by a single missile attack on the Ayatollah's residence in Tehran.

THE BEAR AND THE DRAGON

First published: 2000
Type of work: Novel

When the People's Republic of China invades Russia in the quest for oil and gold, President Ryan supports the Russians.

Ryan, the nonpartisan citizen president, has been reelected, but his negative attitude toward career and typical politicians has not softened. His major advisers, the secretaries of the treasury and defense, are wealthy self-made businessmen, who bring their private enterprise acumen to their departments. Early in the novel, a Japanese American secret CIA agent, whose cover is selling Japanese computers in the People's Republic of China, has seduced the secretary of Fang Gan, a member of the Chinese Communist politburo or governing council, dominated by Zhang Han San, thus giving the CIA access to the inner workings and conversations of China's despotic governing elite.

Communist China has been rapidly building up its military, purchasing weapons and other war materials from abroad, but the Chinese economy, in spite of its many exports, verges on bankruptcy, although the members of the politburo are only dimly aware of the impending crisis. Fortuitously, a lifeline appears. Massive amounts of gold and enormous oil reserves are discovered in Russia's Siberia, the oil reserves alone potentially larger than in the oil-rich Middle East. The gold and oil promise to invigorate and modernize Russian society, struggling since the collapse of the Soviet Union a decade earlier. To the Chinese leadership, the solution to China's problems is to invade Russia and forcibly seize those valuable resources. Prior to the Chinese military invasion, an attempt is made to assassinate Sergy Golovko, the chief adviser to the Russian president and one-time nemesis of Ryan (but now a friend), as well as the Russian president himself. Both plots fail, however.

From the White House, President Ryan observes the machinations of the Chinese, helped in large part by the CIA's access to politburo conversations. Militarily, Russia is unprepared for a major invasion of its territory. Old foes of Ryan from the Soviet era are now allies, and Ryan makes the obvious decision to assist Russia against Communist China aggression. As in *Executive Orders*, the war takes up several hundred pages of *The Bear and the Dragon*, from the Chinese mobilization to the Russian defensive preparations to the arrival of American forces to the ultimate defeat of the Chinese. The dramatic denouement of the novel results from a decision to eliminate China's nuclear missiles in fear that they would be used in order to prevent final defeat. However, one missile, aimed at Washington, D.C., was not destroyed. Following prearranged plans for such a disaster, President Ryan is ordered to leave the district, but instead joins the crew on a docked Aegis antimissile ship, which, at the last possible minute, destroys the incoming nuclear weapon, thus saving America's capital. In China, university students, reacting angrily to the corrupt and despotic nature of the Communist leadership, gather in Tiananmen Square, march to the party headquarters, and confront the politburo. Zhang and the rest of the hardliners are arrested and Fang assumes leadership, with the implication that a more democratic China will emerge.

SUMMARY

Clancy is only one of many writers who have used the background of the Cold War, the threat of nuclear conflict, international terrorism, and other contemporary concerns to attract a wide reading audience. Clancy, however, has joined those fears to military technology in a manner that his rivals have not; he might deny it, but he does write "techno-thrillers." His first story was science fiction, and it was rejected. In a sense, though, he has been writing science fiction ever since—although it is science fiction that reflects the modern world rather than a future world. However, Clancy's wars, in spite of his reliance on cutting-edge military technology, are not always realistic. There is no fog of war, and the Americans invariably know where the enemy is and what it will do. Clancy's wars are invariably brief wars, with few casualties. It is not surprising that in 2004, Clancy became a vocal critic of the United States war against Iraq: The war did not follow his expected script of how wars should be fought and won.

Eugene Larson

BIBLIOGRAPHY

By the Author

LONG FICTION:
The Hunt for Red October, 1984
Red Storm Rising, 1986
Patriot Games, 1987
The Cardinal of the Kremlin, 1988
Clear and Present Danger, 1989
The Sum of All Fears, 1991
Without Remorse, 1993
Debt of Honor, 1994
Op-center, 1995 (with Steve Pieczenik)
Executive Orders, 1996

Tom Clancy's Power Plays: Politika, 1997 (with Martin Greenberg)

Rainbow Six, 1998

Tom Clancy's Power Plays: Ruthless.com, 1998 (with Greenberg)

The Deadliest Game, 1999 (with Pieczenik)

Tom Clancy's Net Force, 1999 (with Pieczenik)

Night Moves, 1999 (with Pieczenik)

Tom Clancy's Power Plays: Shadow Watch, 1999 (with Greenberg)

Virtual Vandals, 1999 (with Pieczenik)

The Bear and the Dragon, 2000

Net Force: Hidden Agenda, 2000 (with Pieczenik)

Private Lives, 2000 (with Pieczenik)

Shadow of Honor, 2000 (with Pieczenik)

Red Rabbit, 2002

The Teeth of the Tiger, 2003

NONFICTION:

Submarine: A Guided Tour Inside a Nuclear Warship, 1993

Armored Cav: A Guided Tour of an Armored Cavalry Regiment, 1994

Fighter Wing: A Guided Tour of an Air Force Combat Wing, 1995

Marine: A Guided Tour of a Marine Expeditionary Unit, 1996

Airborne: A Guided Tour of an Airborne Task Force, 1997

Into the Storm: A Study in Command, 1997 (with Fred Franks, Jr.)

Carrier: A Guided Tour of an Aircraft Carrier, 1999

Every Man a Tiger, 1999 (with General Chuck Horner)

Future War: Non-Lethal Weapons in Modern Warfare, 1999 (with John B. Alexander)

Special Forces: A Guided Tour of U.S. Army Special Forces, 2001

Shadow Warriors: Inside the Special Forces, 2002 (with Carl Stiner)

Battle Ready, 2004 (with Tony Zinni and Tony Koltz)

DISCUSSION TOPICS

- From his novels, is it possible to ascertain Tom Clancy's political views?

- Is Jack Ryan a surrogate for Tom Clancy?

- What are the possible reasons that Clancy criticized the Iraq War in 2004?

- Discuss the pros and cons as to whether Jack Ryan is a "constitutional" president in *Executive Orders* and *The Bear and the Dragon.*

- Are Clancy's religious beliefs reflected in his novels?

- What are the possible factors that explain Clancy's great popularity as an author?

- Compare *The Hunt for Red October* and *Patriot Games* with two of Clancy's later novels, such as *Executive Orders* and *The Bear and the Dragon.* Has Clancy's work changed or evolved, considering his themes or literary style?

- Are Clancy's novels popular because of his extensive use of military technology or in spite of it—that is, can there be too much of a good thing?

About the Author

Anderson, Patrick. "King of the 'Techno-Thriller.'" *The New York Times Magazine,* May 1, 1988, 54.

Cowley, Jason. "He Is the Most Popular Novelist on Earth." *New Statesman* 130 (September 24, 2001): 2.

Greenberg, Martin H., ed. *The Tom Clancy Companion.* New York: Berkley Books, 1992.

Grossman, Lev. "Ten Questions for Tom Clancy." *Time* 160 (July 29, 2002): 8.

Phillips, Christopher. "*Red October*'s Tom Clancy: After the Hunt." *Saturday Evening Post* 263, no. 6 (September/October, 1991): 16-19.

Ryan, William F. "The Genesis of the Techno-Thriller." *Virginia Quarterly Review* 69, no. 1 (Winter, 1991): 24-41.

Struckel, Katie. "A Conversation with Tom Clancy." *Writer's Digest* 81 (January, 2001): 20.

Terdoslavich, William. *The Jack Ryan Agenda: Policy and Politics in the Novels of Tom Clancy—An Unauthorized Analysis.* New York: Forge, 2005.

"The Tom Clancy Effect?" *The Atlantic Monthly* 294 (November, 2004): 59.

JAMES FENIMORE COOPER

Born: Burlington, New Jersey
September 15, 1789
Died: Cooperstown, New York
September 14, 1851

One of the nineteenth century's most popular storytellers, Cooper presented a simplified, idealized view of America's westward migration.

Courtesy, New York State Historical Association

BIOGRAPHY

James Fenimore Cooper (the Fenimore was added to his name in 1826) was born on September 15, 1789, in Burlington, New Jersey. The twelfth of thirteen children born to William and Elizabeth (Fenimore) Cooper, James was only fourteen months old when his father moved the family to Cooperstown, a village he had founded on Otsego Lake, the source of the Susquehanna River and the model for Glimmerglass of the Leatherstocking Tales.

A descendant of English Quakers, William Cooper played a great part in the developing prosperity of the newly settled area and enjoyed the fruits of his hard work. His popularity and wealth allowed James to enjoy many urban comforts during his childhood at Otsego Hall, a beautiful brick mansion. Elizabeth, who detested the frontier, introduced young James to cultural refinements that she had brought in from Albany, Philadelphia, and New York City. It was during these early years that James also developed his lifelong love of the wilderness.

After a few years at a local academy, young James was sent in 1801 to a preparatory school in Albany run by the Reverend Thomas Ellison, an Episcopal clergyman. In 1803, thirteen-year-old James entered Yale College, only to be expelled two years later for playing pranks.

In 1806, Cooper's father sent him to sea as a common sailor, and later Cooper sailed the Medi-terranean Sea on a merchant ship. Two years later he was issued a midshipman's warrant in the U.S. Navy. His three years in the Navy made him an expert on naval warfare and provided the raw material for his sea novels.

His father was killed by a political opponent in 1809. Cooper inherited $50,000 and a portion of his father's $700,000 estate. In 1811, he resigned from the Navy and married Susan Augusta De Lancey, the daughter of a wealthy and renowned family in Westchester County. After a few years of moving between Cooperstown and Westchester, the couple settled on De Lancey land in Scarsdale, where Cooper led the life of a gentleman farmer and pillar of the community. During this period, five daughters were born to the couple, one of whom died.

In 1819, Cooper became the head of the family after the death of the last of his five elder brothers. As a result of high living and speculation, most of the family fortune had been lost, and the estate taken charge of by Cooper was heavily in debt. On a dare from his wife, he wrote *Precaution* (1820), a novel about English life that was very imitative of Jane Austen's work and not successful. It was published anonymously, a great deal of animosity having arisen between Cooper and the publisher over a rash of printer's errors.

In 1821 Cooper published *The Spy*, a novel set in the revolutionary American colonies but endowed with the spirit of an English romance. The book went through three editions, was translated into several languages, and was even adapted for the stage. Cooper was on his way to success. *The Spy* was quickly followed by *The Pioneers* (1823), the first of the Leatherstocking Tales. His fame was such that the novel sold three thousand copies on the first day. All was not well, however; his son Fenimore died, and his household goods were seized to cover outstanding debts. Only his revenues from writing saved him from financial ruin.

A year later, again on a dare, he wrote *The Pilot* (1824), the first of eleven nautical tales he would produce over the following three decades. His experience in the Navy and with the whalers he had sailed on allowed him to challenge Sir Walter Scott's latest romance with a tale of the sea that was accurate (Cooper claimed Scott's work was not) in its nautical detail. In 1826, he continued his explosion of writing with *The Last of the Mohicans* and, with his financial situation stabilized, sailed for Europe after a gala send-off by a host of celebrities and politicians, all eager to attest Cooper's talent.

The trip to the Continent provided an education for the family, a chance for Cooper to improve his failing health, and an opportunity for the author to thwart the many pirated European editions of his works while ensuring that the authorized edition became more profitable. During the two years the family spent in Paris, Cooper was introduced into the high life of the international social set. He published *The Prairie* (1827) while there.

In 1828, the Cooper family left Paris for the grand tour of Europe, a trip that the prolific writer would chronicle in five books of European travels. Also in 1828, he published in London *Notions of the Americans,* a book intended to correct European views of the United States. It was found offensive by both British and American critics.

On his return to Paris in 1830, Cooper became embroiled in French politics in an attempt to aid his old friend the Marquis de Lafayette. In the following three years before he left Paris, Cooper wrote three political novels about Europe. In addition, he published *A Letter of J. Fenimore Cooper to General Lafayette* (1831), a book on American finance that won for him disapproval at home for meddling in foreign affairs. Before returning to the United States he became embroiled in a transatlantic squabble with the New York press over a review of one of his novels that effectively damaged his reputation with the press, editors, and the public.

In 1833, Cooper returned to the United States and seclusion in Cooperstown. His reputation in decline, he yearned to live a life of privacy, but his next few years were spent in various controversies with neighbors over land and property rights. In 1838, he published *The American Democrat*, a defense of his political and social philosophy, and two novels, *Homeward Bound* and *Home as Found.* The next year he followed with the two-volume *The History of the Navy of the United States of America* (1839). His latest period of productivity saw him publish the last two novels in the Leatherstocking Tales, *The Pathfinder* (1840) and *The Deerslayer* (1841).

In 1842, he won judgments in two of the seemingly countless libel suits he filed against newspapers during the bitter later years of his career. The following year he edited *Ned Myers: Or, A Life Before the Mast,* the autobiography of a shipmate from his earlier merchant seaman days. Between 1845 and 1846 he published a fictional trilogy concerning the Anti-Rent Wars in New York State; in 1850 he published *The Ways of the Hour,* his last novel. Cooper died in Cooperstown on September 14, 1851.

ANALYSIS

To appreciate Cooper's accomplishments, one must understand the literary and historical climate of the early nineteenth century United States. In the 1820's, American fiction was much scorned by the European literati. One British critic went so far as to ask, "Who reads an American book?" Before Cooper's work, few people outside the United States had; after his widespread acceptance, many did.

A related and much-debated question often troubled early nineteenth century American writers: Was there sufficient material in the United States for a truly American book in terms of form and themes? Until Cooper, most American writers borrowed their subject matter and literary styles from Europe, especially the great English writers. Cooper proved that such imitation was not necessary. By utilizing American history—specifically the French and Indian War, the American Revolution, and the westward migration—he became a role model for the so-called Columbian Ideal. It might be said that in his thirty-two novels, he (along with Washington Irving) truly wrote the American literary declaration of independence.

Moreover, by gaining international fame, Cooper proved that an American could make a living being a full-time writer.

In 1850, for a new edition of the combined Natty Bumppo quintet, Cooper penned a preface to the Leatherstocking Tales that is absolutely indispensable in understanding his style and purpose. He labeled his five novels "romances," not realistic fiction. Since Mark Twain's stinging criticism in "Fenimore Cooper's Literary Offences," critics have pointed out that Natty Bumppo is as pure as a saint, his diction is often too poetic for a man not formally educated, and his adventures are marred by improbabilities and coincidences. Cooper, however, was self-admittedly writing romances, and in that form everything is subordinate to the book's didactic purpose.

As the author claims: "It is the privilege of all writers of fiction, more particularly when their works aspire to the elevation of romances, to present the *beau-ideal* of their characters to the reader." In other words, Natty Bumppo is not meant to be read as a mirror of any real person or persons but instead as a moral paragon, a character who "possessed little of civilization but its highest principles."

In Natty Bumppo, Cooper also created a character whose life parallels the growth of the United States, a national hero in every sense of the term. The young Natty is a resourceful hunter living in the woods. Just as the United States matured and cut its umbilical cord with its mother country, Natty must deal with the eighteenth century switchover to an agrarian economy, the westward expansion, and the creation of a civilized legal system. The five Leatherstocking Tales, then, constitute an elaborate initiation story, the favorite pattern in American literature.

Natty begins in *The Deerslayer* as a callow youth who must determine whether it is right under any circumstances to take another's life, and he dies in *The Prairie* having learned that justice and the march of civilization are inevitable. Along the way, he comes to an understanding of women and love in *The Pathfinder* and the necessity of the law in *The Pioneers*.

Of course, as a romancer, Cooper was primarily interested in Natty's code, his ethical system for living. Essentially, his hero embodies the spirit that formed America, a trait that would later be called rugged individualism. Natty's code, though triangulated by the Christianity of the Moravian missionaries who raised him, the laws of civilization (as shown with their flaws and attributes in the characters of Judge Marmaduke Temple and Ishmael Bush), and Indian customs, is Natty's own creation. Natty is finally a rebel whose life is his own.

This is not to say that Cooper was wholly original. Although he did use the matter of America as his subject, his manner was often that of the English novelists, especially Sir Walter Scott. Admittedly, some of Cooper's novels justify his epithet "the American Scott" (in one novel, Cooper has the mounted Indians jousting like characters out of Scott's 1819 novel *Ivanhoe*). As Natty Bumppo journeys across the ever-expanding countryside, encountering America's heroic past with his faithful companion Chingachgook, Cooper's hero is not unlike Don Quixote and his squire. Cooper obviously read a great many historical, gothic, and sentimental romances.

Why were the Leatherstocking Tales so popular? As noted earlier, Cooper was able to adapt the popular English styles of the moment while tapping into America's archetypal character. He gave the American public what it desperately wanted—a national hero whose history was theirs. In his aforementioned preface, Cooper predicted that if anything of his would endure, it was "the series of the Leatherstocking Tales." Another reason Natty Bumppo came alive was that he kept popping up; he was America's first popular recurring character in fiction. Even Cooper's desultory writing for the series worked to his hero's popularity, for after his death in 1827 (in *The Prairie*), two more Natty Bumppo novels were published, suggesting a certain immortality to Leatherstocking.

With his didactic purpose, Cooper mined that religious vein that ran deep throughout early American history. The majority of the colonies were founded for religious reasons, especially in the Northeast, the country's literary center during the early nineteenth century. Since its beginning, America had been described as the New Eden, an image pattern Cooper continued. As Natty Bumppo, for example, wrestled with the Christian ideal "Thou shalt not kill" in *The Deerslayer*, he was everyone in the United States trying to translate abstract Christianity into a practical moral system. Natty Bumppo became one of the first examples of the American Adam—the basically good man in American literature.

Even today, some of these reasons endure. If nothing else, Cooper knew how to tell an adventure story, with his clear-cut good guys fighting against obvious evil. Cooper provided a link in the popular writing chain that went from the Indian captivity narratives of writers such as John Smith through him to the dime novels and Western tales. In fact, Natty Bumppo—with his eye for detail, his ability to track friend or foe, his survival skills, and his refusal to follow the conventional mores of civilization blindly—is the prototype for that distinctly twentieth century American literary invention, the hard-boiled private investigator.

Despite critics such as Twain, then, Natty Bumppo remains one of the true originals of American fiction. Paradoxically, he is simultaneously the antihero and the mythic representation of American national character. For readers today and for Cooper's contemporary audience, the Leatherstocking Tales present a simpler version of American history, a nostalgic journey to a more innocent time where gray had not begun to shade good and evil, and a place where individual action is not only possible but is also rewarded.

THE DEERSLAYER

First published: 1841
Type of work: Novel

In his first warpath, a young man comes to terms with taking a life as well as with the corrupt values of civilization and the Indians.

The Deerslayer, a prequel (the last published but the first in the hero's chronology of the Leatherstocking Tales), introduces Cooper's youthful protagonist. Natty Bumppo, a young man in his twenties, has come to Glimmerglass (Otsego Lake) in upper New York State to help his blood brother, Chingachgook, rescue the Delaware chieftain's betrothed, Hist. In this idealized natural world of the 1740's, these two noble savages must formulate a practical morality somewhere between abstract Christianity, Indian savagery, and corrupt civilization's values.

The Deerslayer is a good example of a romance, that nineteenth century version of the novel. In order to ensure its didactic intent, the romance presents a simpler view of reality. Characters are clearly good or bad. Natty, Chingachgook, and Hist are basically heroic representatives of civilization and the Indian world, while Hurry Harry, Tom Hutter, and Rivenoak are their evil counterparts. Similarly, the Delaware Indians are good; the Hurons, bad. Natty is the moral paragon, refusing, for example, to take scalps as Hurry Harry and Tom Hutter do. Appropriate for a man caught between ethical codes, Natty is part white and part Indian as well as part Christian and part savage.

The highly episodic plot follows the popular novel pattern of pursuit, capture, and escape. There are no surprising reversals, and the ending is pure deus ex machina, complete with the king's troops arriving for a nick-of-time rescue. Good defeats evil, though the happy ending is partially diluted by Natty turning down the charms of the beautiful Judith Hutter. Cooper even foreshadows the familiar Western theme by suggesting that ultimate happiness is found in nature and that the male-male bond (Natty and Chingachgook) is often greater than that between a man and a woman. As with most romances, the setting is manipulated. Cooper conveniently narrows and deepens the river when it suits his needs, and the idyllic Glimmerglass, in reflecting the heavens, becomes the ultimate moral symbol in the book.

The human moral model is Natty himself, and the novel's focus is implied in its subtitle, *The First Warpath*. Known at the beginning of the story as the Deerslayer, Natty is given a morally symbolic sobriquet by the enemy. Natty is forced to kill a Huron/Mingo when he spots a rifle leveled at him, and as he gives water to his dying foe, the Indian nicknames him Hawkeye. It is this eye of the hawk that allows Natty to pierce the false philosophies of both civilization and savagery to see God's law applicable in the wilderness. The ultimate test of Natty's superior ethical code comes when Rivenoak, the Huron chieftain, grants Natty, after having captured him, a day's furlough to act as a go-between for the Indians and the white settlers. Though it means certain death, at the end of the twenty-four hours Deerslayer returns, as promised, to his captors.

Cooper's success in *The Deerslayer*, then, comes

from his successful blending of several popular English novel types and setting the action in America. He borrowed some of the techniques of Sir Walter Scott and adapted the historical romance; Cooper also used elements of the gothic novel. In the middle of Glimmerglass lies the Hutter castle as well as a damsel in distress. Hutter himself has a dark secret, a hidden crime (he was once a pirate). Realists, including Twain, have criticized the book's language and the implausibility of some action (especially the Indian attack on the ark), but it is the very simplicity of the tale, from its characters and plot to its moral stance, that has provided its lasting appeal.

THE LAST OF THE MOHICANS

First published: 1826
Type of work: Novel

In this adventure story, Cooper emphasizes that people of all races must work together and try to understand one another.

The Last of the Mohicans, the second of the Leatherstocking Tales published and also the second in the hero's chronology, picks up the story of Natty Bumppo and Chingachgook in 1757, some fourteen years later. In this, the most popular of the quintet, the scene has moved northward in New York State to Glen Falls and Lake George. The plot centers on a true historical event, the British surrender of Fort William Henry to the French and their massacre by Indians immediately following. Cooper explores the themes of miscegenation, the expansion of America, and the decline of the Indians' power and domain. Although the story is based on fact, Cooper fictionally realigns the Indians' true historical alliances to the French and English in order to suit his storytelling needs.

The Last of the Mohicans is first and foremost an adventure story in the tradition of the historical romance. The Delaware are the good Indians; the Huron/Mingoes, treacherous. While Natty, now known as Hawkeye, and Chingachgook remain the moral center of the book, Cooper offers two new creations in his good-evil dichotomy. Uncas, the son of Chingachgook and Hist (who has died), is a

living example of physical and moral perfection. Ironically (and appropriately) Uncas's death occurs because he violates his noble instincts and rushes ahead of the rescue party to save Cora, the woman he loves.

Like *The Deerslayer, The Last of the Mohicans* is a pursuit, capture, and escape story. Hawkeye spends most of the novel either trying to free Alice and Cora Munro from their Indian captors or trying to escape the evil Huron, Magua. Magua, probably Cooper's best-drawn villain, is portrayed as a once-noble savage whose life has been corrupted by civilization, especially its particular form of poison, alcohol. Magua is actually motivated in his pursuit of Cora Munro by his desire for revenge—he was whipped for showing up for work drunk, and he lost his natural honor. Cooper also borrows from the sentimental romance with the many disguises donned, the comic relief in the form of the crazy Yankee psalmodist (David Gamut), the courtship of Major Heyward and Alice Munro, and the pathos-filled ending, wherein the Indians suggest that the spirits of Cora and Uncas will be united in the afterlife.

Perhaps the main thrust of the novel is the usually overlooked national theme that is often hidden by the critics' overconcern for the more controversial miscegenation theme. Leslie Fiedler and D. H. Lawrence, in particular, have suggested that the secret theme of *The Last of the Mohicans* is interracial marriage. Uncas, an Indian, and Cora, of black and white heritage, are undeniably attracted to each other, and even Hawkeye considers this match in the context of its naturalness. In a larger sense, though, the novel has a sociological purpose. Having represented the three main races in America at the time, Cooper seems to be asking whether the country as melting pot is a viable concept. By killing off both Uncas and Cora, Cooper perhaps indicates that the creation of a new race may be a utopian dream.

Just as important, however, he states that the whites and Indians can live in harmony—shown by the prototypal relationship of Hawkeye and Chingachgook. Their friendship endures, foreshadowing future literary endeavors such as Herman Melville's *Moby Dick* (1851) and Mark Twain's *Adventures of Huckleberry Finn* (1884).

Ultimately, *The Last of the Mohicans* should be read as more than simply a boy's book or an adventure story. The novel is Cooper's prediction of the United States' future success and, just as important, the passing of the Indian. As Tamenund, the old chief, remarks at the conclusion, "The palefaces are masters of the earth, and the time of the redmen has not yet come again."

THE PATHFINDER

First published: 1840
Type of work: Novel

Cooper's hero must choose between conventional courses of action and his true calling.

The Pathfinder, the fourth of the Leatherstocking Tales published (the third in Deerslayer's chronology), is an often-overlooked part of the quintet; its protagonist seems to act more like a Sir Walter Scott hero than the famed frontiersman.

Deerslayer, now called Pathfinder, is two years older than in *The Last of the Mohicans* and, with Chingachgook, has moved westward to Lake Ontario. This novel also has a historical backdrop, taking place during the French and Indian War. The focus of the novel, however, is not on the usual pursuit, capture, and escape plot, the westward migration, or even the simplistic moral view (good Indian against bad Indian, Deerslayer against bad white men), but on Deerslayer himself as a vulnerable human being.

With his interest in the person of Deerslayer, Cooper is content to reuse many elements from *The Last of the Mohicans.* Once again the author disregards fact and has the Iroquois (Mingoes, to Deerslayer) historically allied with the British, as the villains. Mabel Dunham, like the Munro sisters, is a woman traveling through the wilderness to visit her British military father at a fort. The Indian guide—Arrowhead, in this case—is, like Magua, a treacherous Iroquois leading the group into an ambush. Also like Magua, he falls for a white woman. This party also runs into Deerslayer and Chingachgook, who again save them. Instead of Uncas, a red paragon of natural virtue and strength, Cooper offers a white version, frontiersman and seaman Jasper Western, who emerges as second best to Deerslayer. Instead of multiple land battles with the Indians being the major action, Cooper draws on his sea background to show Jasper as a master mariner. There is also an element of espionage, as Lieutenant Muir turns out to be a French spy.

Some critics have labeled the Leatherstocking Tales fictional hagiography and referred to Deerslayer as a secular saint. The real strength of *The Pathfinder* is that it deeply humanizes Deerslayer to such a degree that Cooper could never decide whether he thought this novel or *The Pioneers* was his finest.

The Pathfinder is constructed around the familiar love triangle of the sentimental romance. Deerslayer is attracted to Mabel Dunham, the daughter of an old friend (who wants Deerslayer to marry his daughter). Mabel is attracted to, respectful of, and honored by Deerslayer's eventual proposal, but she truly loves Jasper. Jasper returns this love, but he is best friends with Deerslayer. Ultimately Deerslayer realizes all these relationships and, knowing that Jasper is younger and more educated (and that Mabel truly loves the young man), bows out. There is a saintliness about Deerslayer when Mabel kneels before him for his blessing, but more important, there is also a full-blooded human being, a man vulnerable from the fact that he has considered love, marriage, and all that such a relationship entails.

At the end of *The Pathfinder,* Deerslayer and Chingachgook set out westward once again. Though tempted by civilization and romantic love, Deerslayer remains true to his code, to his vocation. Jasper becomes a successful merchant, thus fulfilling the Horatio Alger aspect of the American Dream. Deerslayer, perhaps the last autonomous man, is less concerned with "things" and more with the original American Dream.

THE PIONEERS

First published: 1823
Type of work: Novel

In the clash between the communal agrarian economy and the individual freedom of the hunter, progress will be served.

The Pioneers, the first published of the Leatherstocking Tales (but the fourth in Deerslayer's chronology), though containing some of the usual Scott influences, is essentially a mirror of American history. Deerslayer, now known as Leatherstocking, has advanced to his early seventies, and the action takes place in 1793 and 1794. The setting is Templeton, which Cooper identifies in his introduction to the novel as representing the customs and inhabitants of early Cooperstown. Although the plot concerns the Temple-Effingham feud (complete with Romeo and Juliet lovers, Oliver and Elizabeth), the novel's strength is its re-creation of daily scenes from late eighteenth century American life (such as lake fishing and a turkey shoot) and its central theme of economic change and the law.

Cooper's basic conflict is still between two differing ways of life, but this time they are not the Indians' and whites'. Templeton is a farming community that survives by cutting trees, planting crops, and turning hunting grounds into pastures. As such, it represents the new American agrarian economy. In order to prosper, it has to create a new system of laws as, in a larger sense, the United States must.

The living embodiment of this emerging system is Judge Marmaduke Temple (modeled upon Cooper's father), who, though fallible, tries to apply these laws equitably. Built into the system are its flaws, including political patronage and the sometime destruction of personal freedom for the greater good. Opposing this new system is that of Leatherstocking. As the hunter, he lives in a cabin on the outskirts of the community. He represents the old America whose day, at least in the East, is slowly fading. Cooper uses the time passage in the novel—from opening on Christmas Eve to closing in autumn—to suggest such change is both natural and inevitable.

The community conflicts with the hunter. Lacking the time to learn to kill game with a single ball, the farmers have resorted to mass slaughter and waste of the forest denizens, In April, the Templetonians shoot thousands of pigeons that are migrating in sky-darkening flocks, In counterpoint, Leatherstocking kills the one bird he needs and calls the townsfolk sinful for their waste. In chapters 23 and 24, the townspeople employ a huge seine to catch fish, also slaughtering more than they need.

Leatherstocking spears only one fish. Ultimately he kills a deer, but the townspeople have created a new law that claims he has done so out of season. When they come to arrest him, he forcibly opposes them. Leatherstocking is convicted of assault and battery as well as resisting a search warrant. For this crime he is imprisoned and fined, but not before burning his long-standing home so that it cannot be entered against his will.

Another theme-reinforcing subplot involves Leatherstocking's oldest companion: Chingachgook has become Christianized by civilization and given the name John Mohegan. Civilization has also provided him with alcohol and turned him into a hopeless drunk. Finally, after donning his battle garb, the once-noble chief is killed by an exploding canister of gunpowder—another product of civilization. *The Pioneers*, then, concludes with the only possible resolution of the major conflict. Unable to triumph against inevitable progress, Leatherstocking heads westward to the new frontier; the future belongs to the Templetons and Judge Temple. *The Pioneers* has been called the first genuinely American novel.

THE PRAIRIE

First published: 1827
Type of work: Novel

As civilization and justice come to the frontier, the day of the hunter and pure individual freedom are over.

The Prairie, the third published novel of the Leatherstocking Tales but the last in Deerslayer's chronology, depicts Leatherstocking, now known as the trapper or the old man, in his final days. The set-

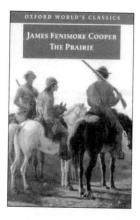

ting is the edge of the Great Plains, the time is 1805, and the hero is in his eighties—his maturation and movement have paralleled that of the United States. Although Cooper himself never traveled to this locale, he researched his subject well. Unfortunately, with the familiar good against bad Indians dichotomy (this time the Pawnee and Sioux, respectively), wise sayings that sound more like platitudes, and the stock romance pursuit, capture, and escape plot, Natty Bumppo's exit is not as memorable as his entrance.

The Prairie offers Natty one last chance to return to his glory. Reduced in his last days to mere trapping, he has the opportunity to be a scout once again with the arrival of the Bush party of squatters. By way of continuity, Cooper also has Natty run into Captain Duncan Uncas Middleton, the grandson of Duncan Heyward and Alice Munro Heyward of *The Last of the Mohicans*; moreover, the captain's middle name is that of Chingachgook's son. Much of this novel, though, reads like a rehash. The evil Sioux chieftain, Mahtoree, is a lesser copy of Magua (from *The Last of the Mohicans*, which Cooper had written the year before). The narrative is laden with tricks, some improbable and some clichéd. Dr. Obed Bat (like David Gamut) exists only to provide comic relief; the scholarly naturalist uses Latin names for everything, but he knows less about the frontier than Natty (and probably Natty's dog).

One of the true strengths of the novel is the character of Ishmael Bush. As patriarch of the Bush family, he is in charge of moving them West. Ironically, for a man in conflict with the law, Bush, when all the chase is over, must preside over a makeshift frontier court. He rules on white and Indian cases, doling out justice fairly even when it means sentencing his wife's brother to die. As *The Pioneers* suggests, justice eventually comes to the frontier.

The final days of Natty Bumppo, then, are a return to his roots. In the new frontier of the West he goes to live among the Indians—with the Pawnee and Hard-Heart, his adopted son. Although he is offered quarters in civilization, he chooses the freedom of nature. The legend concludes as Natty, knowing his time has passed, dies among the tribe, facing the setting sun.

SUMMARY

In the Leatherstocking Tales, Cooper created one of the earliest, one of the most representative, and one of the best American heroes. Natty Bumppo, like young America, is an orphan who must forge his destiny on the edge of civilization. A moral man, he sorts through his Christian background, the mores of civilization, and the laws of the Indians to create his individual code of behavior.

Cooper brought this vision not only to the United States but also to the world. At a time when American literature was devalued, he offered hope by weaving a tapestry of America's past and presenting it in a popular form, the romance, for all to see.

Hal Charles

BIBLIOGRAPHY

By the Author

LONG FICTION:
Precaution: A Novel, 1820
The Spy: A Tale of the Neutral Ground, 1821
The Pioneers: Or, The Sources of the Susquehanna, 1823
The Pilot: A Tale of the Sea, 1823
Lionel Lincoln: Or, The Leaguer of Boston, 1825
The Last of the Mohicans: A Narrative of 1757, 1826

The Prairie: A Tale, 1827
The Red Rover: A Tale, 1827
The Wept of Wish-Ton-Wish: A Tale, 1829
The Water-Witch: Or, The Skimmer of the Seas, 1830
The Bravo: A Tale, 1831
The Heidenmauer: Or, The Benedictines—A Tale of the Rhine, 1832
The Headsman: Or, The Abbaye des Vignerons, 1833
The Monikens, 1835
Homeward Bound: Or, The Chase, 1838
Home as Found, 1838
The Pathfinder: Or, The Inland Sea, 1840
Mercedes of Castile: Or, The Voyage to Cathay, 1840
The Deerslayer: Or, The First War-Path, 1841
The Two Admirals: A Tale, 1842
The Wing-and-Wing: Or, Le Feu-Follet, 1842
Wyandotté: Or, The Hutted Knoll, 1843
Le Mouchoir: An Autobiographical Romance, 1843 (also known as *Autobiography of a Pocket Handkerchief*)
Afloat and Ashore: A Sea Tale, 1844
Miles Wallingford: Sequel to Afloat and Ashore, 1844
Satanstoe: Or, The Littlepage Manuscripts, a Tale of the Colony, 1845
The Chainbearer: Or, The Littlepage Manuscripts, 1845
The Redskins: Or, Indian and Injin, Being the Conclusion of the Littlepage Manuscripts, 1846
The Crater: Or, Vulcan's Peak, a Tale of the Pacific, 1847
Jack Tier: Or, The Florida Reef, 1848
The Oak Openings: Or, The Bee Hunter, 1848
The Sea Lions: Or, The Lost Sealers, 1849
The Ways of the Hour, 1850

NONFICTION:
Notions of the Americans, 1828
A Letter to His Countrymen, 1834
Sketches of Switzerland, 1836
Gleanings in Europe: France, 1837
Gleanings in Europe: England, 1837
Gleanings in Europe: Italy, 1838
The American Democrat, 1838
Chronicles of Cooperstown, 1838
The History of the Navy of the United States of America, 1839 (2 volumes)
Ned Meyers: Or, A Life Before the Mast, 1843
Lives of Distinguished American Naval Officers, 1845
New York, 1851
The Letters and Journals of James Fenimore Cooper, 1960-1968 (6 volumes; J. F. Beard, editor)

DISCUSSION TOPICS

- What is James Fenimore Cooper's explanation for the feeble state of American literature when he began writing? What is the basis of his conviction that American literature would become a powerful influence in the world?

- Cooper was one of the earliest exponents of several subgenres of the novel other than that represented by the Leatherstocking Tales. These include the spy novel, the sea novel, and the novel of political satire. Which works exemplify his achievements in these modes of fiction?

- Explain how the stages of Natty Bumppo's life mirror changes in American society over several decades.

- Is Cooper's Chingachgook a plausible character?

- In what respects is Mark Twain's essay "Fenimore Cooper's Literary Offences" unfair to Cooper?

About the Author
Barker, Martin, and Roger Sabin. *The Lasting of the Mohicans: History of an American Myth.* Jackson: University Press of Mississippi, 1995.
Clark, Robert, ed. *James Fenimore Cooper: New Critical Essays.* Totowa, N.J.: Barnes & Noble Books, 1985.

Darnell, Donald. *James Fenimore Cooper: Novelist of Manners.* Newark: University of Delaware Press, 1993.

Dyer, Alan Frank, comp. *James Fenimore Cooper: An Annotated Bibliography of Criticism.* New York: Greenwood Press, 1991.

Fields, W., ed. *James Fenimore Cooper: A Collection of Critical Essays.* Boston: G. K. Hall, 1979.

Frye, Steven. *Historiography and Narrative Design in the American Romance: A Study of Four Authors.* Lewiston, N.Y.: Edwin Mellen Press, 2001.

Long, Robert Emmett. *James Fenimore Cooper.* New York: Continuum, 1990.

McWilliams, John. *The Last of the Mohicans: Civil Savagery and Savage Civility.* New York: Twayne, 1995.

Newman, Russell T. *The Gentleman in the Garden: The Influential Landscape in the Works of James Fenimore Cooper.* Lanham, Md.: Lexington Books, 2003.

Peck, H. Daniel, ed. *New Essays on "The Last of the Mohicans."* New York: Cambridge University Press, 1992.

Ringe, Donald A. *James Fenimore Cooper.* Updated ed. New York: Twayne, 1988.

Verhoeven, W. M., ed. *James Fenimore Cooper: New Historical and Literary Contexts.* Atlanta: Rodopi, 1993.

ROBERT COOVER

Born: Charles City, Iowa
February 4, 1932

Coover's novels, plays, and short stories stress the importance of narrative while experimenting with narrative forms, historical texts, and popular culture.

National Archives

BIOGRAPHY

Robert (Lowell) Coover was born in Charles City, Iowa, on February 4, 1932, to Maxine (Sweet) Coover and Grant Marion Coover, but as a child of nine moved to Bedford, Indiana, and then later to Herrin, Illinois. At Herrin he was president of his high school class, edited school newspapers as "Scoop" Coover, and wrote a column called "Koover's Korner." In high school he avidly followed baseball and played tabletop baseball as well; the sport figures prominently in his second novel, *The Universal Baseball Association, Inc., J. Henry Waugh, Prop.* (1968). Coover attended Southern Illinois University from 1949 to 1951, where he worked as a reporter for the college newspaper, the *Egyptian*. In 1951 he transferred to Indiana University, from which he graduated in 1953 with a bachelor of arts degree in Slavic studies.

Until graduation he wrote for the *Herrin Daily Journal*, of which his father was managing editor. Coover's first novel, *Origin of the Brunists* (1966), would feature the character of a small-town newspaper man. Shortly after graduation, Coover enlisted in the Navy and served as a lieutenant from 1953 to 1957. Most of his Korean War service was in Europe.

In the summer of 1957, Coover spent a month at Rainy Lake, Minnesota, where he began writing the innovative stories of his second book, *Pricksongs*

and Descants (1969), including "The Magic Poker," which mentions Rainy Lake. He discovered Samuel Beckett that summer, whose work influenced him profoundly. He later published an essay on Beckett, "The Last Quixote."

In 1958, Coover began graduate studies at the University of Chicago, which he attended until 1961. He received an M.A. in general studies in the humanities in 1965. He traveled in Spain between 1958 and 1959. In June of 1959, he married María del Pilar, whom he had met while on a Mediterranean tour during his Korean War service. The couple honeymooned in southern Europe, traveling by motorcycle. Coover's first publication arose from these travels: "One Summer in Spain: Five Poems" appeared in *Fiddlehead* in 1960.

Back at the University of Chicago, Coover was deeply influenced by Richard McKeon, a professor of philosophy and classics to whom he dedicated his first work, the novel *Origin of the Brunists*. McKeon's courses suggested that the world was undergoing a tremendous transition which required new ways of thinking. This worldview informs much of Coover's writing.

Coover began to publish short stories in the early 1960's, such as "The Second Son," which would later figure in *The Universal Baseball Association, Inc., J. Henry Waugh, Prop.* He lived in Spain from 1962 to 1965, in his wife's hometown of Tarragona, where he worked on his first two novels and some short stories. He also read deeply in ancient literature, including the Bible, *Alf layla wa-layla* (compiled fifteenth century; *The Arabian Nights' Entertainments*, 1706-1708), and Ovid's *Metamorphoses* (c. 8 C.E.; English translation, 1567), developing a lifelong interest in myth as narrative structures by which humans organize the universe and, ultimately, by which they live.

Though rejecting Christianity—and even seeing dogma as dangerous—Coover embraced biblical narrative and Christian myth as structural concepts, ways of ordering experience and belief. As a writer, he plays with myth at all levels, whether the folk tale of Little Red Riding Hood reinterpreted in "The Door: A Prologue of Sorts," in *Pricksongs and Descants*, or religious belief in the short stories "J's Marriage" or "The Brother" from the same collection, or the novels that depend on interpretations of Christian belief, *Origin of the Brunists* and *The Universal Baseball Association, Inc., J. Henry Waugh, Prop.*

In 1965, Coover began teaching at Bard College in New York, which brought him some financial security. *Origin of the Brunists* came out the following year. Though he had most of the "fictions" for *Pricksongs and Descants* written prior to *Origin of the Brunists*, Coover believed it was necessary to establish himself as a skilled writer in the traditional vein of the realist, chronological novel before venturing out with the metafictions–or fictions about writing fiction–of his first collection of short stories.

He taught at the University of Iowa in 1967 and the following year was a writer in residence at Wisconsin State University. In 1969, he won a Rockefeller Foundation Fellowship, was Writer in Residence at Washington University in St. Louis, and received the Brandeis Creative Arts Award. In 1971, he won his first Guggenheim Fellowship and in 1974 his second. In 1972, he taught at Princeton University and published a collection of four one-act plays, *A Theological Position*. He taught at Virginia Military Institute in 1976 and published *The Public Burning* in 1977.

He visited Barcelona in 1978 and then lived in England until returning to the United States in 1979, when the Coover family settled in Providence, Rhode Island, where Coover became a professor at Brown University. He published his second collection of short stories, *A Night at the Movies: Or, You Must Remember This* in 1987, winning the Rea Award for the short story that same year. He has published more than twenty books, including his 2004 novel, *Stepmother*, and a third collection of short stories, *A Child Again* (2005), both firmly fixed in the tradition of the fairy tale.

He remains on the faculty as adjunct professor of English in the graduate program in literary arts, teaching standard writing workshops as well as workshops on electronic, or hypertext, writing and mixed media. He has reached far beyond the classroom and beyond the text, organizing festivals and conferences on literature, including "Unspeakable Practices" (1988), which brought together postmodernist writers; "Unspeakable Practices II" (1993), which highlighted the early days of hypertext fiction; and "Unspeakable Practices III" (1996), which brought together print and hypertext writers from many nations.

ANALYSIS

Coover sees the world as constructed of fictions. Societal belief systems, whether organized religion or the civil religion of the state, are narratives by which most people live. The writer's role is both to question, deconstruct, and dismantle established fictions and to construct new fictions, new and better narratives by which to live. The writer's role is to "demythologize," to strip accepted myths of their meaning and replace them with new myths, myths appropriate to the current age. Such interests naturally lead Coover to metafiction, or fiction about fiction, fiction that analyzes or exposes the fiction-making process, just as demythologizing exposes the mythic impulse.

All of Coover's work is in some way revisionist. Even his most traditional work, *Origin of the Brunists*, though traditional in a structural sense, chronologically ordered, and essentially a realist novel, questions basic Christian beliefs. If a prophet, Bruno, can arise simply as a consequence of (miraculously?) surviving a mining disaster, and be the object of a cult, the Brunists, how can the reader not see the parallels with Christianity? Like many of Coover's fictions, the novel bristles with biblical allusions, including many epigraphs from Revelation, or the book of the apocalypse.

Pricksongs and Descants may be Coover's most revisionist work. He had written many of the "fictions" prior to *Origin of the Brunists*, but he believed that only after releasing a so-called standard novel could he safely publish the innovative texts of his first short-story collection. In *Pricksongs and Descants* Coover showcases most of the themes and techniques visible throughout his career.

Coover rewrites fairy tales. In "A Door: A Prologue of Sorts," he revises the traditional children's tales of "Little Red Riding Hood" and "Jack and the Beanstalk." (They are more clearly erotic, for example.) In "Panel Game," he reconfigures the popular game show and iconic writer William Shakespeare. In "J's Marriage" and "The Brother," Coover rewrites biblical text (or stories, or Christian myths): J (Joseph) is not happily married to the Virgin Mary and drinks himself to death, while Noah abandons his brother and his brother's pregnant wife to the floods that destroyed the world—even though the brother helps Noah build the boat that will save him and a select few.

"The Babysitter" and "The Elevator" are stories told through numerous short fragments, like individual cards that together create a whole deck. Which story is the true one? Such fragmented fictions present multiple possibilities, some seemingly more "real" than others, though of course all are inventions.

Similar themes surface throughout Coover's work. *Ghost Town* (2000) takes the cliché of the Western and reinvents it. *Stepmother* reimagines the tradition of the fairy tale. *A Child Again* (2005) is a collection of short stories in which Casey is again at the bat, Red Riding Hood returns, and the Pied Piper still plays his pipe. Whether writing a short story or a novel, Coover is a master craftsman of language.

THE UNIVERSAL BASEBALL ASSOCIATION, INC., J. HENRY WAUGH, PROP.

First published: 1968
Type of work: Novel

J. Henry Waugh creates a table-top baseball game, complete with players, teams, and fifty-five seasons of play but then loses control of the world he has created.

Henry is a lonely, middle-aged accountant who invents a fantasy baseball game based on dice and complex charts. Henry becomes more and more involved with the game, creating biographies for the players, factoring in crowd reactions. The game is infinitely more interesting than his real life and gradually takes over. Henry becomes more alien-

ated from his job and his colleagues, arriving at work late and carrying his players in his imagination at all times. After lengthy play, Henry begins to get bored, but a talented rookie, Damon Rutherford, saves the game, and Henry's interest surges.

Henry is particularly attached to Damon, who is like a son to him. Then a throw of the dice dictates Damon's death, when a ball strikes him in the head and kills him. Henry is devastated by his loss, and for the first time changes the rules of the game, cheating so that Jock Casey, whose pitch killed Damon, also dies by a roll of the dice. Thanks to Casey's sacrifice, the game itself has been saved. The novel's first seven chapters are narrated in the third-person voice, from Henry's point of view; in the final, eighth chapter, Henry does not appear. Rather, the last chapter details the yearly ritual of "Damonsday," something like a passion play in which players reenact the games in which Rutherford and Casey died. The characters Henry created now have lives of their own; they have been set free from their maker.

The Universal Baseball Association, Inc., J. Henry Waugh, Prop. manifests many biblical parallels. The structure of the novel reflects the seven days of creation, with a final chapter to suggest the Apocalypse. J. Henry Waugh reminds one of Yahweh, or God the Creator, and Henry does, in fact, create a world. His absence from that world reflects the modern world, in which God's existence is contested, affirmed, denied, and ultimately unprovable.

THE PUBLIC BURNING

First published: 1977
Type of work: Novel

A ribald retelling of the Rosenberg case includes famous historic figures, such as Richard Nixon, among its characters.

The most political of all of Coover's works, *The Public Burning* is a complex, carnavalesque investigation into the case of Ethel and Julius Rosenberg, a Jewish couple with young children, executed in 1953 for allegedly sharing atomic secrets with the Soviets. The novel's publication was delayed because of its controversial nature.

Coover's text, based on extensive historical research and sometimes weaving in snippets of historical documents, suggests that the Rosenbergs may have been innocent victims of a bloodthirsty American public which needed scapegoats during the fearful Cold War period. Perhaps more controversial, the figure of Richard Nixon, "Tricky Dicky," alive at the time and later to be president of the United States, is a narrator and main character. Nixon's first-person narration alternates with that of an anonymous third-person narrator.

The novel contains twenty-eight chapters, divided into four seven-part sections by three "*intermezzos.*" It opens with a "newsreel" prologue and ends with an epilogue in

which Nixon is raped by Uncle Sam. The action occurs principally in the last two and half days before the Rosenbergs' execution. Characters range from Nixon to Uncle Sam to Gary Cooper playing a Western hero to a real Western hero, Wild Bill Hickok. Settings range from Sing Sing Prison to Times Square, where the Rosenbergs are executed in a carnival-like atmosphere which draws an immense audience. Nixon is a young, inexperienced politician, Uncle Sam the folksy image of America.

A third main character is the Phantom, representing chaos and disorder, who threatens the myth of America which Uncle Sam exemplifies. The Phantom is responsible for the Korean War, anti-American demonstrations around the world, and a temporary stay of execution for the Rosenbergs. As the plot develops, it becomes clear that the execution of the Rosenbergs is essential to the identity of the United States. Their execution is a public burning (electrocution), made into an "event" by the media, a national circus that draws

together all members of "the tribe" and solidifies American group identity during a time of tremendous global uncertainty.

"THE BABYSITTER"

First published: 1969 (collected in
Pricksongs and Descants, 1969)
Type of work: Short story

A babysitter arrives, the parents leave for a party, and a multiplicity of possible, often contradictory, events occur at the parents' home and at the party they attend.

Perhaps Coover's most anthologized story, "The Babysitter" exemplifies the notion behind the title of the collection: a "pricksong," or main theme, with "descants," or variations on that theme. Using a series of one hundred and seven sections, the shortest containing only nineteen words and the longest nearly two-thirds of a page, "The Babysitter" takes the "pricksong" of an extremely ordinary event and transforms it with the descant of infinite possibility.

The main events can be summarized simply: At 7:40 P.M. a babysitter arrives to care for three children (Jimmy, Bitsy, and "the baby"); the parents, Harry and Dolly Tucker, leave for a party; the babysitter bathes the children, puts them to bed, and watches television; at 10:00 P.M. the parents return home. The action of the story occurs simultaneously in four locations: the Tucker household; a drugstore, where the babysitter's boyfriend Jack plays pinball with his friend Mark, whose anonymous parents are hosting the party; the party itself; and on television.

There is a chronology of sorts in the story. The babysitter arrives at 7:40, ten minutes late. Over the next twenty minutes the parents leave; the sitter feeds, bathes, and wrestles with the children; Jack and Mark play pinball; and the characters on television dance in formal clothes. During the hour from 8:00 to 9:00 P.M. the children resist going to bed, Harry Tucker (at the party) imagines having sex with the sitter and imagines her having sex with her boyfriend, Dolly Tucker worries that the sitter is not trustworthy, Jack and Mark rape the sitter,

Jack defends the sitter against rape, she willingly has sex with them, she refuses to let them come over, she innocently watches television with them, she takes a bath, she lets Jimmy wash her back, a Western and then a spy movie are on television, and the sitter vacillates between watching television and doing her homework.

The final hour of the story, from 9:00 to 10:00 P.M., reveals more variations on previous events: Harry Tucker is at home, at the party Dolly Tucker cannot get back into her girdle and several guests try to stuff her back into it, at the Tucker home the two boys drown the babysitter and the babysitter suffocates the baby and, through negligence, lets the baby drown.

The final two sections of the narrative provide alternative endings to a text of nearly endless possibility. In the first, the television is on at the party, there has been news of "a babysitter," but the sports scores claim Harry's Tucker's attention. Dolly Tucker gets up off the floor, and Harry says he will drive her home, where she notices that the dishes have been washed. In the last section, ending Two, the hostess apologizes, noting that her husband is gone and the children and the sitter murdered. Her only response is to see what the late-night movie is. The third-person narration of the story switches from one event and locale to another, much as a television viewer changes channels. Most of these events are mutually exclusive; the baby, for example, cannot be killed twice. "The Babysitter" is a dazzling display of metafictional creativity that mixes fantasy and reality and thus reveals the arbitrariness of narrative, which is, after all, only the creation of its author.

SPANKING THE MAID

First published: 1981
Type of work: Novella

A maid repeatedly enters her master's bedroom to clean, but her attempts at order are frustrated; her work displeases her master, who punishes her.

Originally published in *The Iowa Review* in 1979 as a long short story, *Spanking the Maid* was collected in *Best American Short Stories* of 1981 and *Best Ameri-*can *Short Stories of the 1980's* under the title "A Working Day." It was later published with only minor changes as a novella as *Spanking the Maid* (with illustrations in 1981 and without illustrations in 1982).

Spanking the Maid describes a day in the life of a maid, "she," and her employer or "master," "he." They are the only two characters in a single setting: the master's bedroom, which the maid comes to clean. The story is told through a series of thirty-nine fragments much like scenes in a stage play or a film.

In the first fragment, the maid enters and then enters again, much as an actor might exit the stage to redo a scene. The bed is empty, the master not present. The second fragment is told from the master's point of view. In general, the remaining sections alternate point of view from servant to master and back again. The actions, though essentially the same, change and expand incrementally with each new fragment. The maid clearly seeks to do her duty, to clean the master's bedroom suite properly, with proper demeanor. Sometimes the room is empty, sometimes the master is in bed or in the shower. The two talk, or they do not.

She seeks, and cannot attain, perfection. For that, she must be punished, and just as her attempts at cleaning reiterate themselves but change over time, so too does her punishment. He uses a belt, a rod, his hand, a whip, a switch, a leather strap, a hairbrush, according to the instructions in "the manuals." The manuals in question refer to Victorian guides for domestic servants on which Coover based this story, though he has taken the repetition of those guides to new extremes. Indeed, the repetition and its variations end only because the text ends. There is no resolution. The characters are doomed to repeat endlessly their assigned roles and tasks. The reader, too, is contained within the paradox of the text and is unable to distinguish between what is fantasy and what is reality.

SUMMARY

Beginning with his earliest publications, Coover has challenged the American literary and cultural status quo. He also challenges the reader. Coover mixes realism with the fantastic, interrogates history, and rewrites the sacred texts of world culture, whether Bible stories, children's stories, myths, fairy tales, or folk tales. He dismantles the accepted and the expected to create the unexpected, to move his readers from the past to the future.

Linda Ledford-Miller

BIBLIOGRAPHY

By the Author

LONG FICTION:
The Origin of the Brunists, 1966
The Universal Baseball Association, Inc., J. Henry Waugh, Prop., 1968
Whatever Happened to Gloomy Gus of the Chicago Bears?, 1975, expanded 1987
The Public Burning, 1977
Hair o' the Chine, 1979 (novella/screenplay)
A Political Fable, 1980 (novella)
Spanking the Maid, 1981 (novella)
Gerald's Party, 1985
Pinocchio in Venice, 1991
Briar Rose, 1996 (novella)
John's Wife, 1996
Ghost Town, 1998
The Adventures of Lucky Pierre: Directors' Cut, 2002

SHORT FICTION:
Pricksongs and Descants, 1969
The Water Pourer, 1972 (a deleted chapter from *The Origin of the Brunists*)
Charlie in the House of Rue, 1980
The Convention, 1981
In Bed One Night and Other Brief Encounters, 1983
Aesop's Forest, 1986
A Night at the Movies: Or, You Must Remember This, 1987
The Grand Hotels (of Joseph Cornell), 2002 (vignettes)

DRAMA:
The Kid, pr., pb. 1972
Love Scene, pb. 1972
Rip Awake, pr. 1972
A Theological Position, pb. 1972
Bridge Hound, pr. 1981

SCREENPLAYS:
On a Confrontation in Iowa City, 1969
After Lazarus, 1980

About the Author

Andersen, Richard. *Robert Coover*. Boston: Twayne, 1981.
Cope, Jackson. *Robert Coover's Fictions*. Baltimore: Johns Hopkins University Press, 1986.
Evenson, Brian. *Understanding Robert Coover*. Columbia: University of South Carolina Press, 2003.

DISCUSSION TOPICS

- What is the function of repetition in Robert Coover's work?

- In what ways does Coover suggest that everything—including literature and life itself—is a fictional construct?

- How does Coover incorporate popular culture into his work?

- Coover is considered a postmodern writer. How is postmodernism exemplified in his work?

- Why does Coover mix "invented" characters with "historical" figures as characters?

- What is the role of the reader who engages Coover's fiction?

Robert Coover

Gado, Frank. *First Person: Conversations on Writers and Writing.* Schenectady, N.Y.: Union College Press, 1973.

Gordon, Lois G. *Robert Coover: The Universal Fictionmaking Process.* Carbondale: Southern Illinois University Press, 1983.

Kennedy, Thomas E. *Robert Coover: A Study of the Short Fiction.* New York: Twayne, 1992.

McCaffery, Larry. "As Guilty as the Rest of Them: An Interview with Robert Coover." *Critique* 42, no. 1 (Fall, 2000): 115-125.

———. *The Metafictional Muse: The Work of Robert Coover, Donald Barthelme, and William H. Gass.* Pittsburgh: University of Pittsburgh Press, 1982.

Maltby, Paul. *Dissident Postmodernists: Barthleme, Coover, Pynchon.* Philadelphia: University of Pennsylvania Press, 1992.

Pughe, Thomas. *Comic Sense: Reading Robert Coover, Stanley Elkin, Philip Roth.* Berlin: Birkhäuser Verlag, 1994.

Robert Cormier

Born: Leominster, Massachusetts
    January 17, 1925
Died: Boston, Massachusetts
    November 2, 2000

Cormier has contributed several important works to the new realism genre of young-adult fiction.

Courtesy, Delacourt Press

BIOGRAPHY

For a writer who has dealt with a number of extreme subjects—including death, the occult, and terrorism—Robert Cormier lived a rather quiet and unassuming life. Born in Leominster, Massachusetts, into a large French Canadian family, Cormier lived most of his life in that small town some thirty miles from Boston. After a year at Fitchburg State College, he began work at a radio station in nearby Worcester before working at newspapers, first in Worcester and then in Fitchburg. At Fitchburg newspapers he was a reporter, editor, and columnist, until he left to write full-time in 1978; during that period, he won several awards for his stories and columns. "John Fitch IV" was his pseudonym as a newspaper columnist.

Throughout his adult life, Cormier continued to produce fiction. His stories have appeared in *Redbook, McCalls,* and other popular publications, and he published a short-story collection, *Eight Plus One* (1980) as well as four adult novels—*Now and at the Hour* (1960), *A Little Raw on Monday Mornings* (1963), *Take Me Where the Good Times Are* (1965), and *Heroes* (1998). His literary career dramatically changed when his agent convinced Cormier that *The Chocolate War* was really a young-adult title. Pantheon Books agreed, and the novel was an instant success. Since its publication in 1974, Cormier has become known primarily as a writer for young people.

During his career, Cormier and his wife raised four children and maintained as normal a life in Leominster as a writer can manage in the United States. They lived for years at the same Main Street address, and Cormier even listed his phone number in one of his novels. He was always been accessible to his readers, and young people called and wrote to him regularly to ask about his novels and his career as a novelist.

In many ways, Cormier was an autobiographical writer. The settings of his novels resemble the Massachusetts locales near where he lived in Leominster in a number of significant details, and the action of his fiction often has a personal origin. *The Chocolate War,* for example, began in an incident during his son Peter's parochial school chocolate sale. *Fade* (1988) retells much of Cormier's own French Canadian family history and Roman Catholic background. Yet Cormier's novels are not really as autobiographical as they appear, for once his settings and characters have been established, what takes place in his fiction has a terrifying life of its own that ranges far beyond the rather mundane details of his own quiet life in Leominster. Cormier died of a blood clot in late 2000.

ANALYSIS

In 1974, when Cormier agreed to allow Pantheon to market *The Chocolate War* as a young-adult novel, the little-known journalist who had been writing adult fiction for several decades became almost instantly one of the most popular and respected writers in the young-adult field. This novel about a teenager fighting almost alone against the evil at a Catholic boys' school—and apparently losing—caused an immediate sensation and controversy.

Cormier's novels since *The Chocolate War* have continued to take as their subjects extreme, often violent, acts. *I Am the Cheese* (1977) is a mystery thriller about a young boy trying to learn his family history before the killers pursuing his parents and himself catch them all. *After the First Death* (1979) is a violent novel about terrorists taking over a schoolbus full of children. *The Bumblebee Flies Anyway* (1983) is a bleak depiction of a young boy trying to find out why he is in a hospital with terminally ill children. *Beyond the Chocolate War* (1985) continues some of the same themes of Cormier's first young-adult novel, but it focuses on different characters. *Fade* concerns several generations of a family tragically gifted with the power of invisibility. Cormier produced some of the most vivid and compelling works in the young-adult field, but his subjects are often grim and his treatment rarely sentimental.

Approximately every three years, Cormier contributed another important, if unsettling, work to the canon of young-adult fiction. Not only are his novels set in the same general location, in various urban, suburban, or rural locales in northeastern Massachusetts, but they are also linked by a careful formal technique. The point of view in each novel, for example, is usually multiple or complex and aids in the suspense that builds throughout the work. The language of the novels is not difficult for younger readers and is usually recognizable for its metaphorical intent (the religious symbolism in *The Chocolate War*, for example). Characterization is facile and at times two-dimensional, but the tense structure of each work keeps the action moving quickly. Cormier's novels highlight his unique protagonists in their struggles with forces more powerful than themselves.

Cormier's novels resemble one another most significantly in their themes. All of his young-adult works focus on an individual struggling to survive in a society dominated by evil and defined by violence. The individual has few chances against the system or the institution he or she faces but usually manages to bring meaning to these struggles for survival. Most of Cormier's heroes are male, but Kate Forrester, the schoolbus driver who dies trying to save the children from the terrorists who hold them, is the real heroine of *After the First Death*.

In spite of the similarity of his subjects, Cormier's novels are hardly formulaic, and each one has its own special appeal. If each is somehow bleak or depressing, it is also compelling in its own way.

Cormier's novels are not didactic; his protagonists face their situations without benefit of authorial moralizing. Yet his heroes often leave readers with a real sense of courage: Young people, in the face of almost overwhelming odds, somehow manage to carve meaning out of their desperate lives. In a culture in which young people are often seen as soft or cynical, Cormier's is an inspiring model.

Cormier had noted that his focus is on the individual versus the system. The institutions which represent this "system" change from novel to novel—from the Catholic prep school in *The Chocolate War* to the corrupt government agencies in *I Am the Cheese* to the impersonal hospital in *The Bumblebee Flies Anyway*—but the focus tends to remain on innocent individuals struggling against these evil agencies. In one sense, then, Cormier was a very political writer, for he was concerned with the power relationships among individuals and institutions and with the ways that those institutions (and the people who run them) misuse their power. The villains in his novels are not institutions but the authoritarian individuals acting in their names (Brother Leon in *The Chocolate War*, Dr. Lakendorp in *The Bumblebee Flies Anyway*) without regard for individual human need.

Like many political novelists, Cormier was at heart a moralist. He applauded those individuals (such as Jerry Renault in *The Chocolate War*) who stand up against the system and are martyred in their battles with it. Cormier's connections to Henry David Thoreau, Mark Twain, Ken Kesey, and other American writers in this tradition of social protest are clear.

Cormier's success as a writer can be gauged by the number of awards he garnered over the length of his career, both as a newpaperman and as a writer for young people. When *The Chocolate War* was first published in 1974, the American Library Association's *Booklist* journal gave the novel a black-bordered review, indicating an obituary for naïve optimism. Prior to this work, even the most realistic young-adult novel had left its protagonists on an upbeat note. After *The Chocolate War*, the young-adult novel was capable of true tragedy. More than any other single writer, Cormier was responsible for having broadened the possibilities of the young-adult genre.

THE CHOCOLATE WAR

First published: 1974
Type of work: Novel

Jerry Renault learns much during his freshman year at a Catholic boys' school and gains his own identity.

The Chocolate War is an unrelentingly bleak account of life in a Catholic boys' school, from its opening line ("They murdered him.") to the closing defeat of its young protagonist and the reascendancy of the school's evil forces. Yet the novel is also an important example of the realistic quality of much young-adult fiction, and it is certainly Cormier's strongest effort in this field.

Set in a small New England city, the novel could take place in any urban academic setting—at least in any school where the pressures of grades, conformity, and repressed sexuality create an unhealthy and competitive atmosphere. Trinity is a school where privacy is nonexistent, where teachers intimidate students, and where students brutalize one another. Cormier's view of Trinity is singularly gloomy, but few readers would argue that it is totally unrealistic.

The story in this short, fast-paced novel is neither complex nor difficult. Jerry Renault is in his first year at Trinity and is trying to become a quarterback on the football team. He needs this success badly, for his mother has died the previous spring, and Jerry is living in an apartment with his father, who sleepwalks through his days. Jerry wants desperately to fit in, but a contrary impulse also motivates him. In his school locker, Jerry has a poster that shows

a wide expanse of beach, a sweep of sky with a lone star glittering far away. A man walked on the beach, a small solitary figure in all that immensity. At the bottom of the poster, these words appeared—*Do I dare disturb the universe?* By [T. S.] Eliot, who wrote the Waste Land thing they were studying in English. Jerry wasn't sure of the poster's meaning. But it had moved him mysteriously.

In the course of *The Chocolate War,* Jerry will discover the full import of the poster's message.

Jerry accepts an "assignment," or school stunt, from the powerful Vigils secret society to refuse to sell chocolates in the annual Trinity sale, but when the ten days of his prank are up, Jerry continues his rebellion, in protest now against the authoritarian tactics of Brother Leon, the acting headmaster, and against Jerry's own isolation at the school. He gains a new identity through his rebellion: "I'm Jerry Renault and I'm not going to sell the chocolates," he declares to Brother Leon and his homeroom. The Vigils, enlisted by Brother Leon, however, whip up school support for the chocolate sale and ensure that every student has sold his fifty boxes—every one except Jerry.

Emile Janza, a school bully who badly wants to get into the Vigils, gathers a gang of younger kids to beat up Jerry, and when Archie, the leader of the Vigils, arranges a boxing match in front of the whole student body between Jerry and Janza, Jerry accepts. The fight has been arranged so that Jerry cannot win, and in fact the young hero loses the very individuality he had earlier gained in his protest. In the end, as Jerry is being treated for a possible broken jaw and internal injuries, he is advising his friend Goober not to "disturb the universe," and the Vigils and Brother Leon are even more firmly in control of Trinity.

The meaning of *The Chocolate War* is complex and, for many readers, depressing—the makers of the 1989 film of the novel created a more upbeat ending—but it is an important novel for young people. As with any work of this complexity, there are a number of subthemes: loss, violence in its many forms, and power—how it is maintained in human society and the hatred and brutality that its misuse breeds. *The Chocolate War* is a novel of initiation in which the young protagonist, like the reader, learns a number of crucial lessons about the adult world—most of them negative.

Like all Cormier's novels, the central theme of

The Chocolate War is the relation of the individual to society and the price one pays for conformity or (the other side of this theme) the greater sacrifices one must make in order to realize one's individuality. Jerry's protest is not easy for him to carry out, but he gains a new identity through his actions. What this idea becomes in the novel is the concept of being true to oneself and standing up to the evil that one perceives in the world.

The only character who is true to himself in the novel is Jerry—but at a terrible price. Goober tries to emulate Jerry but, in a crucial test, caves in. When the Vigils make sure that a "50" is posted after his name in the auditorium, representing boxes of chocolates sold, Goober does not have the courage to challenge it and tell the truth. The situation raises all kinds of questions, in the novel as in society: Which is more important, loyalty to oneself or to the group? Which takes more courage? What are the real consequences of conformity? How can evil be stopped except by heroic individual human action?

In the end, Jerry did disturb the universe: He stood up against peer pressure and teacher intimidation to protest the evil he recognized in the world, and his example is a model of courage in the face of cowardice and conformity. He is, in the true sense of the word, a martyr, and, if he gives in at the end, that action only makes the novel more psychologically realistic and his earlier courage even greater. The evil at Trinity can only be defeated if more people speak up. The power of *The Chocolate War* is this social and psychological realism: The novel shows what can happen to people who stand up for their rights in a totalitarian system.

There are several stylistic elements that distinguish *The Chocolate War* from most young-adult novels and that distinguish Cormier as a writer. For one thing, the multiple points of view in the novel provide a much more complex structure than that of most adolescent novels. The language in the book is not very difficult, but the honest and mature matter in which its subjects are treated may cause problems for some readers. The students here act like real teenagers—they swear and frequently think about sex. Irony plays a large part in the novel, and readers will notice the double meanings that pepper *The Chocolate War.*

There is also rich religious symbolism. On one level, Jerry is a Christ figure who tries to change the world but is metaphorically crucified in the attempt. Trinity is a religious school, but evil there dominates any kind of Christian love or spirit. The complex religious symbolism in the novel underscores the themes that Cormier is raising: Must someone else be crucified before the evil is banished? Finally, as a powerful psychological novel, *The Chocolate War*'s characterization is realistic if unremittingly grim.

I AM THE CHEESE

First published: 1977
Type of work: Novel

In this mystery thriller a young boy tries to determine his family's history and fate.

Cormier's next novel, *I Am the Cheese*, was a departure from his first success in a number of ways. The multiple points of view of the first novel become, in the second, a mosaic of perspectives that challenge the reader and build the tension in the novel until its very last word.

Even the innocuous opening of the novel—"I am riding the bicycle and I am on Route 31 in Monument, Massachusetts, on my way to Rutterburg, Vermont, and I'm pedaling furiously"—raises mysteries: Who is riding, and why? The second chapter only adds to readers' confusion, for it starts with a transcript of what appears to be a counseling session between a boy, Adam Farmer, and a psychiatrist. Is Adam trying to recall his own lost history, or is his interrogator trying to get information from him?

What is slowly revealed, as Adam uncovers his past for the reader and for the mysterious Brint, is that his father had been a reporter for a small New York State newspaper who discovered evidence of government corruption and testified in Washington about what he knew. When attempts were made on his life, Anthony Delmonte joined a witness protection program, and he and his wife and small son, Paul, were given new names and identities and moved to Monument, Massachusetts. The new identities do not shield them, however; Grey, the government contact responsible for the family, is apparently a double agent. The family is forced to flee Monument, and Adam's parents are killed. In the stunning shock of the last chapter, it is revealed that Adam/Paul's "furious" bike ride has only been around the grounds of a hospital where he is a so-called patient, and where some malevolent and mysterious government agency has confined him, after murdering his parents, until they can decide what is to be done with him or (as the last paragraph reveals) "until termination procedures are approved."

This is no simplistic young-adult work; rather, it

is a thriller in which the reader is left hanging until the very end—and beyond, in fact, for the boy's fate is intentionally unresolved. Similarly, it is no didactic novel: If there is a lesson here, it is the same one as in many adult thrillers, to trust no one, not even—or especially not—the government. Like *The Chocolate War,* however, there is also the theme of the young innocent trying to establish his identity in a violent world where the authorities (government agents here, school officials in the earlier novel) are doing everything they can to destroy the will of the young protagonist. The novel was chosen one of the best books of the year for young readers by both *The New York Times Book Review* and the Young-Adult Services division of the American Library Association.

As with all Cormier titles, the literary technique is prominent and facilitates meaning and power. The point of view and plot are both structured so that the tension of the novel is increased until the very last page. (The film that was made of the novel in 1983 only turned the suspense into confusion.) As in *The Chocolate War,* the literary language and imagery reinforce meaning. The title comes from the children's song, "The Farmer in the Dell." Adam is himself the "farmer," at least in one of his identities, but in the end he does "stand alone," like the cheese of the last line of the song.

THE BUMBLEBEE FLIES ANYWAY

First published: 1983
Type of work: Novel

Young Barney Snow tries to discover why he is in a hospital with terminally ill young people.

The Bumblebee Flies Anyway has another institutional setting (a hospital, as in *I Am the Cheese*), but there is perhaps a larger glimmer of hope, for the focus of the novel is on the meaning that the individual can make of his own life, in spite of overwhelming odds—in this case, imminent death.

As in *I Am the Cheese,* the tension is almost unbearable. Barney Snow is in "the Complex," his name for a hospital for the incurably ill, but he does not know why he is there, for he is clearly not ill. All he knows for certain is that he is part of an experiment, as are the other young patients around him, and is being administered drugs under the careful supervision of the person he calls "the Handyman," Dr. Lakendorp. The story of the novel is Barney's attempt to piece together his past and with it the reasons that he is there.

His story is also tied up with the lives of the other terminally ill patients in his ward, such as Mazzo, Billy, and others. Barney falls in love with Mazzo's sister, Cassie, who comes to visit her twin brother but who uses Barney for her own ends, and the relationship actually provides some relief from the clinical setting. Barney is also fascinated with "the bumblebee," a wooden mock-up of a sports car that sits in a lot next to the hospital. When Barney finally discerns the truth—that he is just as ill as all the other patients there and is a victim of medical experiments to make him forget his past, including his earlier hospitalization—he gets the car to the roof of the hospital and makes elaborate plans to give Mazzo one last ride.

Mazzo dies in Barney's arms, however, and Barney lets the bumblebee fly off the roof empty, in the dramatic high point of the novel and in a conclusion that gives readers some release from the gloom that has preceded it. The flight of the car becomes Barney's transcendence from this life and from the pain and suffering that surround him.

Although *The Bumblebee Flies Anyway* resembles

I Am the Cheese and *The Chocolate War* most in its bleak setting and mood, it also resembles them in its theme, the struggle of the individual to stay alive and to beat the system in even the most dire circumstances. In an institution that (under the guise of scientific experimentation to lessen suffering) is actually playing callously with human life, Barney frees himself and perhaps others; he cannot beat death (as no one can), but he helps his friend Mazzo, and his own end is clearly brightened by what he has been able to accomplish. Like Randle P. McMurphy in Ken Kesey's *One Flew over the Cuckoo's Nest* (1962), another novel about men trapped in inhuman institutions, Barney Snow leaves a heroic echo for readers.

Cormier's gift is his ability to sustain the tension, and reader interest, amid subjects so morbid and themes so heavy. There are problems with the novel—with characterization, for example; Cassie never really comes alive for readers as she so clearly does for Barney, and Dr. Lakendorp remains a monster instead of a human being throughout the book. Most of the elements in the novel, however, help to reinforce the powerful and poignant story. Like the most significant of contemporary adult titles, *The Bumblebee Flies Anyway* brings up significant social problems, not only the issue of death, for example, but also the question of medical ethics.

FADE

First published: 1988
Type of work: Novel

The gift of becoming physically invisible is a curse to several generations of a New England family, as Paul Moreaux discovers.

Fade is possibly the blackest of Cormier's realist young-adult novels, and there is some question whether it is a young-adult work at all. Cormier seems to be aspiring to the popular adult genre (popular with teenagers, as well) presided over by such writers as Stephen King and V. C. Andrews. The sex, the violence, and, more than anything, the tone of this supernatural story raise questions about its appropriateness for the teenage audience.

The summary printed on the publishing information page (a common practice in young-adult novels) only hints at the violence of the novel: "Paul Moreaux, the thirteen-year-old son of French Canadian immigrants, inherits the ability to become invisible, but this power soon leads to death and destruction," The novel itself is broken into five uneven parts.

In the first, Paul Moreaux narrates the story of his realization in 1938, at the age of thirteen, of his fateful power. Paul discovers, from his Uncle Adelard, that every generation of this fated family produces a member with the supernatural power to become invisible. The nomadic Adelard has it; now he identifies it in his nephew Paul. The power seems to be a teenager's fantasy come true: to be able to go into houses unseen and spy on lives. What Paul witnesses while in "the fade," however, hardly brings him joy: He sees only the evil, including his own, of which humans are capable, especially behind closed doors. In particular, he witnesses two sexual acts (cunnilingus and incest) and spies on and lusts after his own Aunt Rosanna.

The power of the first half of the novel lies not only in Paul's story of his newfound invisibility but also in the broader background of Paul's history. In no earlier Cormier novel has there been such a rich historical setting: the French Canadian family struggling to survive in late 1930's America, the labor struggles of a depressed New England factory town, and the violent strike that ends the struggle. Paul sees personal evil in the fade, but in his normal self he witnesses the evil that socioeconomic conditions produce.

The second half of the novel is much choppier. In the next segment, and in present fictional time, a young female cousin of Paul works with his literary agent in New York trying to determine if the manuscript fragment that is the first half of *Fade* is really the work of the famous "Paul Roget," the novelist who died at age forty-two in 1967. The third and fourth sections continue the manuscript, as Paul discovers who has the "fade" in the next generation and tracks him down. This is where the "death and destruction" begin, for the thirteen-year-old Ozzie Slater, the abandoned son of Paul's sister Rose, has become a psychopathic killer who is terrorizing the small Maine town where he lives. In the novel's final violent scene, the older fader must kill his successor.

What bothers some critics and reviewers of young-adult fiction about this Cormier novel is more than its sex and violence. The sexuality in the first part is certainly adult, and is sickening to the young Paul. In the second half of the novel, the sex disappears and is replaced by grisly violence, in a supernatural story that rivals those of Stephen King and other practitioners of this adult genre. What is most bothersome is that there is no serious theme to balance the sex and violence; rather, the focus of the novel is on the effects themselves, and the author's aim seems to be to startle and frighten the reader.

Many of the elements in the novel are autobiographical, but Cormier seems to be unable to find the lessons from his story that have been the strengths of all his earlier works. The simplest contrast is to *I Am the Cheese*, as both novels are suspenseful thrillers with violent endings. In the earlier work, however, Adam Farmer seemed to be trying to make sense of his past and to resist the forces threatening him in the present. Paul Moreaux's life, on the contrary, has no such inherent meaning (except perhaps involving how to cope with the "fade"), and the juxtaposition of the secondary plot in the present time mitigates what meaning there may be in his story.

SUMMARY

Cormier became the premier novelist of young-adult new realism in a few short years, and his works challenge readers with their grim, often violent subjects. He also offers important messages about the ability of the individual to battle the system. Until *Fade*, at least, Cormier's novels are distinguished by depressing subjects but transcendent themes, and his writing is characterized by tense stories that are full of literary language and multiple points of view that intensify their suspense. Few young-adult writers have been able to match Cormier in his ability to keep younger readers entranced in a story with an important message.

David Peck

DISCUSSION TOPICS

- How do Robert Cormier's adult novels differ thematically or stylistically from his young adult fiction?
- What effect does setting have on the themes of Cormier's fiction?
- Compare the way Cormier presents his characters to the methods used by one or more other young adult writers.
- Compare the ways Cormier presents institutions in two of his novels.
- Cormier's novels have frequently been the targets of censorship. What qualities in his fiction attract such controversy?
- Does Cormier's view of conformity vary from novel to novel?
- Why is it necessary for *The Chocolate War* to be told from several points of view?
- Why is Adam's fate left unresolved at the end of *I Am the Cheese*?

BIBLIOGRAPHY

By the Author

CHILDREN'S/YOUNG-ADULT LITERATURE:
The Chocolate War, 1974
I Am the Cheese, 1977
After the First Death, 1979
The Bumblebee Flies Anyway, 1983
Beyond the Chocolate War, 1985
Fade, 1988
Other Bells for Us to Ring, 1990
We All Fall Down, 1991

Robert Cormier

Tunes for Bears to Dance To, 1992
In the Middle of the Night, 1995
Tenderness, 1997
Frenchtown Summer, 1999

LONG FICTION:
Now and at the Hour, 1960
A Little Raw on Monday Mornings, 1963
Take Me Where the Good Times Are, 1965
Heroes, 1998

SHORT FICTION:
Eight Plus One, 1980

NONFICTION:
I Have Words to Spend: Reflections of a Small Town Editor, 1991

About the Author

Campbell, Patricia J. *Presenting Robert Cormier*. Boston: Twayne, 1985.

Coats, Karen. "Abjection and Adolescent Fiction." *JPCS: Journal for the Psychoanalysis of Culture & Society* 5 (Fall, 2000): 290-300.

Gallo, Donald R. "Reality and Responsibility: The Continuing Controversy over Robert Cormier's Books for Young Adults." In *The VOYA Reader*. Metuchen, N.J.: Scarecrow, 1990.

Hyde, Margaret O. *Robert Cormier*. Philadelphia: Chelsea House, 2005.

Ishandert, Sylvia Patterson. "Readers, Realism, and Robert Cormier." *Children's Literature* 15 (1987): 7-18.

Karolides, Nicholas J., ed. *Censored Books, II: Critical Viewpoints, 1985-2000*. Lanham, Md.: Scarecrow, 2002.

Keeley, Jennifer. *Understanding "I Am the Cheese."* San Diego: Lucent, 2001.

Myers, Mitzi. "'No Safe Place to Run To': An Interview with Robert Cormier." *The Lion and the Unicorn: A Critical Journal of Children's Literature* 24 (September, 2000): 445-464.

Tarr, C. Anita. "The Absence of Moral Agency in Robert Cormier's *The Chocolate War*." *Children's Literature* 30 (2002): 96-124.

Veglahn, Nancy. "The Bland Face of Evil in the Novels of Robert Cormier." *The Lion and the Unicorn: A Critical Journal of Children's Literature* 2 (June 12, 1988): 12-18.

HART CRANE

Born: Garretsville, Ohio
July 21, 1899
Died: Gulf of Mexico
April 27, 1932

A consummate lyric poet, Crane was also one of the few of his time who wrote against modernist despair, sharing Walt Whitman's invincible hope for the American people's future.

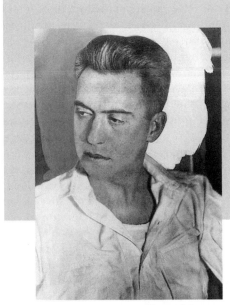

Library of Congress

BIOGRAPHY

Harold Hart Crane was born in Garretsville, Ohio, on July 21, 1899, the son of Clarence and Grace Hart Crane. He was an only child, stuck between incompatible parents who each demanded his allegiance. His father, a successful businessman who founded what became a prosperous candy company, wanted his son to follow in his footsteps. His mother, who resented her husband's absences and abuse, pressed the boy to develop in a more artistic direction.

When he was nine, the family recriminations exploded so fiercely that his mother had a nervous breakdown and entered a sanatorium, while Crane was sent to live with his grandmother in Cleveland. Eventually the whole family relocated to Cleveland, where Crane went to East High School. He was an introverted adolescent, occupying his free time in voracious reading or taking long walks alone. His high school years were punctuated by a trip to visit his grandmother's plantation on the Isle of Pines, Cuba. Although the trip was ruined by family discord, it introduced Crane to the tropical regions to which he would return and which he would picture so magically in his last poems.

In November, 1916, Clarence Crane moved out, and his wife filed for divorce. Their marriage was over. The young Crane, who had been viewing the Greenwich Village arts explosion from a distance

and had a few months previously had his first poem published in one of its small magazines, *Bruno's Weekly*, quit high school and set off for New York City. Over the following few years he would get to know many literary figures, such as Allen Tate and Waldo Frank. Although Crane was to achieve a measure of success and even become associate editor of another small magazine, *The Pagan*, he never seemed able to commit himself to poetry or to one place.

Certainly, it was no easy task to be a poet in the United States in the 1920's. Many writers settled in Europe, where literary pursuits were more respected; in France and Italy, particularly, one could live more cheaply than in the United States. Crane chose to stay largely in his own country, restlessly moving back and forth from the Midwest to the East Coast and from job to job. He was handicapped by his lack of education but found work in advertising, as a salesman for his father, and as a traveling secretary for a stockbroker. He was further handicapped by an ever-growing alcoholism and the type of homosexuality that led to a fascination with sailors and a constant involvement in barroom brawls.

Throughout these years, he kept publishing and polishing his verse, often, when unemployed, staying with friends and receiving financial aid from his father. In 1925, he obtained a degree of recognition when a wealthy arts patron gave him money to continue work on his book-length poem *The Bridge* (1930). His first book of poems, *White Buildings*, was published in 1926. As was the case with all of his work, reviews of the book were mixed.

507

Most reviewers recognized and applauded the unmatched lyrical intensity, but there were also many complaints of obscurity and density. Meanwhile Crane was plowing ahead on the larger canvas of *The Bridge*, which was to occupy him for seven years and would range over America's geography and history. Working sporadically, he, too was ranging; in the years between 1925 to 1930 (the year this second book was published), he moved from New York to Cuba, then to New Jersey, California, Majorca, and Paris.

With the publication of *The Bridge*, again to mixed reviews, Crane received a Guggenheim Fellowship to work on a project in Mexico. In Mexico, he stayed at an artists' colony and had as fellow members such luminaries as the American novelist Katherine Anne Porter and the Mexican muralist David Siqueiros, who painted a portrait of Crane. In the spring of 1932, Crane decided to sail back to the United States on the SS *Orizaba* to help settle his father's estate. Depressed and drinking heavily on the voyage, on April 27, near noon, Crane committed suicide by jumping overboard.

ANALYSIS

If his late poems, brilliant but few in number, are set aside, Crane's poetry can be divided into two phases. The first is that of apprenticeship, when he was composing the poems to go into the volume *White Buildings*. "Apprenticeship" should not be taken in this case to denote any immaturity or lack of mastery but rather that in the individual short lyrics of this book he developed a language and outlook and worked with a variety of poetic forms that in his second period he would weld into one vast, multifaceted commentary on the United States in his long poem *The Bridge*.

In his first phase, he tried many forms: epithalamions, elegies, and love cycles as well as many types of versification, such as free verse, quatrains, and heroic couplets. He could work within highly constricted metrical structures naturally, never showing off this aspect of his poetry, never using this formal mastery for attention-getting effects. The most outstanding of his technical skills was his command of rhythm. Paralleling the content of his poems, which generally would describe a persona moving from a flaccid, uninspired, ordinary moment to one of heaven-sent revelation and uplift, the rhythmic movement would begin sluggishly, bogged

down with caesuras (pauses in the middle of lines) and multiple uses of parataxis (clauses arranged with no apparent subordination), but the pace would gradually increase, building to an impassioned forward flow at the close.

What many readers experienced as the difficulty of entering a Crane poem is not only attributable, however, to the purposely stumbling meter at the beginning but also to both the poem's language and manner of linking concepts. Crane had a voracious love of words from all levels of discourse, and he mixed into his poems such things as racy slang, scientific terms, everyday speech, and advertising slogans. Such combinations were common in the poetry of the day, but Crane's approach was unusual. Where poets such as T. S. Eliot and Ezra Pound juxtaposed high and low vocabulary to make a comment on modern vulgarity, Crane was trying to create a fused compound, almost a new tongue, where many lexical fields would blend together for a unified effect. His usage here paralleled his belief that the United States was, or rather would be, great because of its ability to meld together all the world's races.

What caused even greater difficulties for readers was his presentation of a startling, allusive sequence of concepts. Many serious readers could not follow the leaps of this argument and imagined that his writing was the product of some sort of poetic frenzy. In actuality, his texts exhibited incredibly compressed and subtle trains of thought that recall the lightning-like logical discussions appearing in poems of John Donne and other seventeenth century British metaphysical poets, whom Crane much admired.

To illustrate the uncomprehending reception accorded his works, one could consider the response of Harriet Monroe, editor of *Poetry*, one of the most prestigious magazines of the period, who chided him about a submission: "Your poem reeks with brains. . . . [T]he beauty which it seems entitled to is tortured and lost." She consented to publish the poem only with Crane's explanation appended. In his clarification, Crane outlined his doctrine of the "logic of metaphor." He argued that "emotional dynamics are not to be confused with any absolute order of rationalized definitions." He went on to ask: "Isn't there a terminology something like shorthand as compared to usual description . . . which the artist ought to be right in trusting as a reasonable connective agent toward fresh concepts, more inclusive evaluations?" That is, in order to depict accurately the flickering play of emotions as they intersect with intellection and the objects of feelings, what is needed is a style of writing that moves associatively and quickly inside language.

As mentioned, the theme of these shorter poems is transcendence. More specifically, and in keeping with his youth, Crane's poems centered on such adolescent themes as appreciation of other writers or artists from whom the poet had learned, in pieces such as "Chaplinesque" (1921) and "At Melville's Tomb" (1926), or of longing for experience, in such poems as "Repose of Rivers" (1926). The writer may (for example, in "Chaplinesque") begin by meditating disconsolately on the nature of life but then see suddenly how great art finds and gives importance to the small victories that are still possible.

In his monumental *The Bridge*, Crane again must work his way from despair to hope, but in this work his melancholy turns on the sorry state of the crass, materialistic United States—a country which the writer eventually sees revealed, in an apotheosis, as the center of light and democracy that it could be, symbolized in the image of a bridge. His final poems, darker and yet still as lyrically intense—poems such as "The Broken Tower" (1932)—portray a bid for elevation that fails as the poet's own force seems insufficient for renewing vision.

"AT MELVILLE'S TOMB"

First published: 1926 (collected in *The Complete Poems and Selected Letters and Prose of Hart Crane*, 1966)
Type of work: Poem

The poet visualizes nineteenth century American novelist Herman Melville sadly meditating on the destructive force of the ocean but then rising toward acceptance.

"At Melville's Tomb" is the poem that caused *Poetry* editor Harriet Monroe such trouble in interpretation and called forth Crane's famous reply in which he expounded his theory of composition.

The sixteen-line poem pays homage to the nineteenth century American novelist Herman Melville. In the manner of many poems by young writers addressing their forebears, it manages both to praise the older writer and to suggest that he shares the younger writer's outlook.

Crane pictures Melville as meditating on one of Crane's favored themes, the dual nature of the sea, beginning the lyric with the imaginative depiction of the novelist watching breakers roll onto a beach. Certainly Melville, a sailor, wrote knowingly about the sea, but his major novel, *Moby Dick* (1851), to which Crane alludes, is little concerned with this topic and centers on fraternal and hierarchical relations in a small community of men on a whaling ship.

As Crane depicts the ocean that Melville is observing, it is a place both of death and of eventual resurrection as men overcome their fears and create a faith in something higher. Water has traditionally been viewed as connected to rebirth in baptism and other rituals. As Melville looks into the surf, he sees "the dice of drowned men's bones" and thinks of the wrecks and lost lives in the depths. His thought rises up, though, to a vision of men at sea finding a spiritual solace in the sky as "silent answers crept across the stars."

The poem is written in four-line stanzas in iambic pentameter. The strict meter and stanzaic form play against an irregular rhyme scheme that is used to reinforce the argument. The only heroic couplet (consecutive rhyming lines), for example, occurs in the climactic lines at the end of the third stanza, where Melville finds metaphysical rest.

The terrific condensation of image and argument make the poem difficult to read easily, and this difficulty starts with the title. "At Melville's Tomb" suggests that the piece to be presented will describe the poet pondering the novelist's tombstone. Yet from the first line, setting the poem on a deserted beach, it becomes evident that the "tomb" denoted by the title is not one in which Melville is buried but the place where many of his characters, such as the crew of the *Pequod* in *Moby Dick*, are buried—that is, the bottom of the sea. This redirection of the reader from an individual grave to broader resting place can be seen as symbolizing the way an artist redirects a reader's gaze from his or her own personal problems to the universality of the human condition.

"FOR THE MARRIAGE OF FAUSTUS AND HELEN"

First published: 1926 (collected in *The Complete Poems and Selected Letters and Prose of Hart Crane*, 1966)

Type of work: Poem

Crane presents mythic characters from the Trojan War as embodiments of human energies that can still be unearthed in humankind's midst by the poet-seer.

It would be appropriate to begin the analysis of "For the Marriage of Faustus and Helen" with its title. The reader will search in vain for any mention of a marriage or of Faustus in the three-part piece; however, a study of the title leads directly into an understanding of Crane's ideas about historical correspondence. He wrote that in this poem he was trying to find "a contemporary approximation to an ancient human culture." In the case of Helen, considered the most beautiful woman in the classical world, Crane sought to reconstruct in "modern terms . . . the basic emotional attitude toward beauty that the Greeks had." Thus, in the poem's first part, the narrator sees Helen in modern garb stuck in rush-hour traffic.

This attitude toward the past offers a strong rebuff to the outlook of Crane's pessimistic contemporaries. An example of this more prevalent, darker attitude is to be found in Ezra Pound's *Cantos* (1917-1970). In this work, the poet, disavowing the present, imaginatively envisions previous times in history, in Renaissance Italy or feudal China, for example, when one could combine writing verse with living a socially and politically active life. Crane refuses to follow Pound in entering the past as a refuge but insists that every possibility for heroic life that could be found in other periods is still to be found.

As if to prove this assertion, his poem finds modern equivalents for specific events in the life of the mythological Helen of Troy, mentioned in the poem's title. In the original myth, Helen had been kidnapped from her Greek husband, Menelaus, by Paris, son of the king of Troy, which precipitated a war between the two countries. In the first section of Crane's poem, the narrator locates the modern Helen in a streetcar: "some evening," he muses, "I might find your eyes across an aisle." In the next part, he finds the contemporary version of the revels at Menelaus's court in a hot jazz club. Then, in the last part, he depicts a modern version of the Trojan War in the bombings and dogfights of World War I.

Even after all of this, however, the reference in the title to Helen marrying Faustus remains to be explained. The poem's epigraph is from an Elizabethan playwright, which suggests that the story Crane is recalling is not the Homeric epic but this tale as it is refracted through Christopher Marlowe, who wrote *Doctor Faustus* (c. 1588). If Helen is the ideal of beauty, Faustus, in this play, is the ideal of learning and scholarship, who, though he has to sell his soul to the devil to obtain his desires, is able to call up Helen of Troy from hell to be his paramour.

In Crane's poem, Faustus is never clearly identified, or even mentioned, but it is implied that he is represented by the narrator, who has drawn Helen out of the hell of a modern traffic jam. The narrator's ability to recognize the woman who embodies beauty and offer her "one inconspicuous, glowing orb of praise" indicates that he, a poet, is the modern equivalent of Doctor Faustus, who should be rewarded with the highest prize, her hand, and that the world owes him gratitude for his ability to perceive something valuable—her beauty—that is unrecognized.

In its view of the poet's function, then, this piece can be seen as an extension of themes in Crane's earlier Melville poem. There the writer wrested meaning from drowned men's bones, here from a tarnished modern world where "The mind has shown itself at times too much the baked and labeled dough," too willing to accept pat answers rather than seeking truth for itself. Crane's use of words from different levels of language parallels his work on myths. The poet shows both that a woman as beautiful as Helen is in our midst and that modern American English, even the vulgarized words of advertising copy, if properly combined with other words, can yield delightful harmonies.

"VOYAGES"

First published: 1926 (collected in *The Complete Poems and Selected Letters and Prose of Hart Crane*, 1966)
Type of work: Poem

In a dual movement, the poet describes his deep, conflicting feelings toward a friend and the sea.

The six-part poem "Voyages" holds the last place, a position considered most important by Crane, in his first volume, *White Buildings*. In many of his shorter lyrics and in sections of *The Bridge*, the central figure is scarcely individuated, a near anonymous observer who undergoes a visionary experience rooted in the coming to a deeper appreciation of language and the human lot but not involving any biographical self-exposure. In "Voyages," however, Crane strikes a more intimate note, dealing with the pain of parting and being apart from someone loved.

Given the scandal that would have accompanied a writer's admission of homosexuality in this period, Crane's reticence about given intimate details of his life in his works and his indirection in speaking about the objects of his affection are understandable. In this piece, two stylistic traits compound the difficulty of comprehending, while adding to the originality of the description of, his relation to his friend on which the poem is centered.

It is expected that a poem of friendship will be addressed to the friend, but Crane adds to such addresses numerous apostrophes. The literary use of apostrophe occurs when a poet speaks to an inanimate object as if it were a human interlocutor. Thus Crane writes, "O rivers mingling toward the sky// . . . let thy waves rear/ More savage than the death of kings." The reader may notice in this passage the ascription of a personal pronoun, "thy," to the water. The poet also grants the rivers a human will, indicating that he believes they can alter the height of their waves to answer his entreaties. By this apostrophizing practice, the love for his friend and his feeling for the sea are mingled in a complex web.

Not only are the sea and other bodies of water

put into a human dialogue, but water is humanized with anthropomorphic descriptions as well. Crane depicts the Caribbean Sea by saying, "Mark how her turning shoulders wind the hours." The "shoulders" are the waves that move in predictable tides.

It is in the many passages of description in the poem that the second stylistic feature mentioned occurs (a feature that is even more prominent in *The Bridge*). This involves the presenting of a number of adjectival clauses, ambiguous in reference, before the noun they modify in such a way that until that noun appears it is difficult to identify the description's object. The first stanza of the second section, for example, speaks of "this great wink of eternity" and "her undinal vast belly" before identifying that it is the ocean that these clauses are describing.

One effect of this usage is that, combined with the apostrophes and anthropomorphic references, the water and the poet's missing friend are easily confused, which suggests there is some equivalence between the two. Crane is not arguing that the sea is actually partially human but rather the profound point that one's feelings toward nature and one's fellows may hold similar depths of emotion.

It has already been suggested that Crane's poems characteristically move from a feeling of disconnectedness and melancholy to a realization of underlying integration. In this piece, by adopting almost a pantheistic position—that is, the belief that the world as a whole has a single soul and so is necessarily one—Crane seems to be prejudging his case. If the world is united in substance with the human, then it is easy to find resemblances between the two. The poet is not writing a philosophical argument, and it is not necessary for him to prove anything, but it might seem that the reason for his stress on this unifying underpinning is so that he can shift attention to another disturbing disharmony, not between humanity and nature but within each.

In plumbing his feelings, he finds that he has a love/hate relationship with both his friend and the ocean. His friend, after all, has left him; the sea, after all, is what separates him from this friend, who is pictured watching the receding waters on a ship. The very first section of the poem presents this duality. The narrator is observing children playing and feels it necessary to warn them that the "bottom of the sea is cruel."

This simple contrast between two features of the sea is expanded through the rest of the poem. Crane, for example, explores how the ocean is more than a place for children to swim; it is freighted with a symbolic and linguistic history that has played a part in the narrator's life and friendships. The movement of the poem is through a continual deepening of material. The narrator's social and psychic connections to water are uncovered until the ending note, which affirms poetry as the one vehicle that can convey such a complex emotional and intellectual intertwining.

THE BRIDGE

First published: 1930
Type of work: Long poem

The poet finds that the United States, if it will be nourished on its own myth and history, can overcome its contemporary doldrums.

The book-length poem *The Bridge* far surpasses in scope anything else Crane attempted. In "For the Marriage of Faustus and Helen," he had indicated how the energies of ancient mythic symbols still exist in modern times. In this larger work, he attempts to explain how primary American myths are embedded in current consciousness and, further, how these myths are basically emancipatory, pointing the United States to a future of ethnic harmony and a valuing of artistic achievement.

One thing that spurred Crane to the creation of this work was his reading of Eliot's *The Waste Land* (1922). In looking at the work, Crane was both awed by Eliot's technical mastery and irritated by his hopelessness. Eliot, too, drew on mythology to create his work, turning to agrarian cultures for his theme. In those cultures, there was often a myth of a king or hero who died in the autumn but who was reborn in spring with the new crops. Eliot, as his title suggests, stopped the unfolding of this story halfway, depicting modern society as one that had lost all of its legitimate authorities and was stuck in a winter without hope of resurrection.

A look at the manner in which Crane treated the story of Rip Van Winkle in the second part of his

poem will indicate his contrasted approach. The folktale is presented in a way that is both wittily irreverent and personal. It is not called up in a portentous meditation but by recalling how it first was learned by the author in a primary school lesson, where the pupil "walked with Pizarro in a copybook." The story is interpreted positively, as charting the capacities of the human mind.

Rip Van Winkle woke up in a confused state, in which events that for him occurred yesterday had actually taken place twenty years before. Crane presents his mature narrator effortlessly, vividly recalling his school days, and so indexes Van Winkle's juxtaposition of time periods to the human ability to recapture the past. This point validates, in turn, the broader project of the poem, which argues for the centrality of memory. If, the poem argues, the United States' historical and mythic apprehension were fully used, the nation would be regenerated.

It should not be thought that Crane's fervent optimism meant that he underestimated the problems of America. Two of its major defects, as he diagnosed them, propelled his work. The country had lost touch with its past, he says, and this is shown in a number of ways. For one, the omnipresent clamor of advertising and other distractions, as described in the opening of "The River" section, tricks the people into a pointless immersion in contemporary ephemera.

A related point is that the lack of historical circumspection has undercut an appreciation of who really built the country. "The River" section casts light on the lives of transient workers, roustabouts, and ne'er-do-wells who worked the farms and factories. He speaks of "hobo-trekkers that forever search/ An empire wilderness of freight and rails" as the true elders of the country. This group has come to know the physical terrain of the nation in a way the comfortable never could—by their daily harsh contact with it.

A second fault that Crane spies is the United States' mistreatment and ignorance of the Ameri-

Instead, he moved to New York to seek his fortune; more specifically, he moved to his brother Edmund's house in Lake View, New Jersey, close enough for forays—job-hunting, adventuring, observing urban life—into the city. During this period, as throughout his adult life, he was destitute much of the time; his frequent malnourishment probably contributed to his early death. With the death of his mother on December 7, 1891, he was more than ever on his own.

He tried salaried journalism (much of his life's work would consist of features, notably war correspondence, for newspapers) but, in early 1892, lost a briefly held job with the *New York Herald.* Straight reporting bored him, and he did not get along well with reporters. Whatever his intentions at the time, he was essentially serving a literary apprenticeship. His explorations of the Bowery, the most notorious New York slum of the time, gave him the material for *Maggie: A Girl of the Streets,* and in 1893 he began *The Red Badge of Courage.* He had *Maggie* privately printed because no one—given its prostitute heroine, its (rather mild) profanity, and its lurid scenes of slum life—was bold enough to publish it. Few read it, but one who did and greatly admired it was William Dean Howells, foremost American novelist and champion of realism of his day. Crane thus gained a crucial friend and ally.

Crane continued to write: the poems that would go into *The Black Riders and Other Lines* (1895), and *George's Mother* (1896), another novella of slum life. Excerpts from *The Red Badge of Courage* published in 1894 by the Bacheller Syndicate gained for him some notoriety. During the next year, the syndicate sent him west as a correspondent, providing him with background for some of his finest stories. In October, 1895, *The Red Badge of Courage* was published; by December, Crane was an international literary celebrity. Unfortunately, from this point on, his life went steadily downhill.

He became the subject of envious, malicious gossip, especially as a result of his defense—against the corrupt New York police—of Dora Clark, who may or may not have been a prostitute. He fled this uncomfortable atmosphere in November, 1896, for Jacksonville, Florida, to report on the Cuban insurrection; there he met the madam of a brothel, Cora Taylor, who (though she was married to a husband who would not divorce her) would become his domestic partner. In January, 1897, he was ship-

wrecked from the steamer *Commodore* off the Florida coast, an experience which led him to write his masterful short story "The Open Boat" (1897), collected in *The Open Boat, and Other Tales of Adventure* (1898).

In 1897 he moved to England with Cora, traveled to Greece to report the Turkish war, then, in 1898, returned to the United States to volunteer for service in the Spanish-American War; he was turned down, probably because of a diagnosis of pulmonary tuberculosis, but went anyway as a correspondent. He thrust himself into danger at every opportunity, perhaps even seeking his own death. From Havana, in 1899, he returned to England, where he lived in Brede Place, an ancient manor house that Cora had found; he wrote frantically in a losing effort to generate income that would keep up with Cora's extravagance. At Christmas he suffered a massive tubercular hemorrhage; that spring, Cora took him to Badenweiler, Germany, where he died at the age of twenty-eight on June 5, 1900.

ANALYSIS

Crane might best be regarded as an inexplicable literary phenomenon: a brief, bright comet, brilliantly distinct from every other writer of his time. Such an approach, however—metaphorically throwing up one's hands and standing back in wonder—is not very satisfying to literary critics, who have expended vast amounts of energy attempting to fit Crane into various pigeonholes. Thus the student of Crane will soon wander into a bewildering maze of theory: The author is referred to as naturalist, realist, impressionist, and ironist. It may be useful to discuss these concepts, then, before examining Crane's principal theme and the lasting value of his fiction.

Literary naturalism was imported to the United States from Europe, mainly by way of the French novelist Émile Zola, and found its chief American expression, around the beginning of the twentieth century, in the novels of Theodore Dreiser and Frank Norris. It is a literary concept based on the idea that the physical world is all that exists; it denies the supernatural. The novelist's approach is that of the scientist: to examine phenomena, rigorously and objectively, with a view to proving a thesis about the human condition. Typically, this thesis is that people are indistinguishable from animals—

can Indian. This represents another loss of the country's past, for, in conceiving of America, Crane is thinking not primarily of the history of the United States since the thirteen colonies but of the history of the geographical land mass. His sensitivity in examining the symbolic, personal, and interpersonal connotations of the Caribbean Sea in "Voyages" had prepared him for the similar examination he carries out in this work of his own country's topography. In studying this terrain, he repeatedly finds evidence of a layer of history and myth left by the Indians. The section "The Dance" focuses on Indian ceremonials and beliefs, which he reveals need to be acknowledged and integrated into his country's awareness.

With themes as powerful as these handled with such boldness and lyricism, it is not surprising (or pretentious on Crane's part) that he was to compare his poem to the Roman epic poem by Vergil, *The Aeneid* (c. 29-19 B.C.E.). In the most elementary of ways, *The Bridge* is not an epic, as it lacks both a straightforward narrative and an epic hero, but it does employ a number of epic devices and is guided by an epic theme.

A standard epic poem begins with an invocation of the muse, the goddess of poetry who the writer hopes will provide inspiration on this high venture. Crane, believing in no gods, calls on the image of the Brooklyn Bridge, which he could see close at hand from his window during some of the time he was writing this work. He calls to it, "Unto us lowliest sometime sweep, descend." The Brooklyn Bridge is one of the most beautiful bridges in the world and so reveals to the poet that America can, on rare occasions, use its mechanical, pragmatic genius for the construction of lovely objects.

A second important device Crane reemploys is the epic guide. In Dante's *La divina commedia* (c. 1320; *The Divine Comedy,* 1802), for example, the poet narrator is led through hell by the ghost of his predecessor, Vergil. In the "Cape Hatteras" section of Crane's poem, the shade of Walt Whitman, nineteenth century American poet, appears. Whitman also had seen his country on the rack, having served as a male nurse in the Civil War, and yet had felt the country's promise, as Crane does. The poet of *The Bridge* feels his vigor renewed by contact with this earlier giant.

Finally, epic poems are often concerned with the founding of cultures or countries. *The Aeneid*

DISCUSSION TOPICS

- What claims does Hart Crane make for the role of poetry in American culture?

- What features of Crane's early poetry exemplify a conservative approach to poetic form?

- What is anthropomorphism? Discuss its employment in Crane's *Voyages.*

- Both Walt Whitman and Hart Crane wrote poems honoring means of crossing New York's East River. What resemblances in tone, imagery, and poetic style generally do you see in Whitman's "Crossing Brooklyn Ferry" and Crane's *The Bridge?*

- *The Bridge* seems to be made up of a series of rather disparate parts. What unifying element or elements do you see in the poem?

- Several writers contributed to the discovery of Herman Melville's genius in the 1920's, mostly in biographical and critical prose. What made Crane's "At Melville's Tomb" a distinctive addition to this process of discovery?

ends with the founding of Rome. John Milton's *Paradise Lost* (1667) concludes with the origins of the Christian world in the Garden of Eden. *The Bridge* sets out to reform America by pondering its origins. The first section of the poem, "Ave Maria," concerns Christopher Columbus's discovery of America for the Europeans. The next section, "Powhatan's Daughter," however, undercuts the finality of Columbus's so-called discovery, both by discussing the Indians, who came to the land long before Columbus, and by noting that it was anonymous workers and farmers, not the well-known, who did most of the work of discovery.

The following sections develop the narrator's own sense of the past and explore how the past is sedimented in every landscape. In "Quaker Hill," for example, Crane's visit to the New Avalon Hotel, a building that had once been a Quaker meeting house, leads to reflections on the political and spiritual changes one area of New England has undergone in its history. The last section, "Atlantis," returns to the Brooklyn Bridge, playing off the multiple associations of its architecture to dream of what happiness the future will hold if only the nation can follow the lead of its poets in grasping hold of its own myth and life history.

SUMMARY

It is easy to imagine that writing, for Crane, was strenuous, even painful, for what he demanded of his verse was both lyrical intensity and intellectual density. At the core of his thought was a depiction of transcendence, a bursting of the bonds of received perception that led to a fuller recognition of how the past and myth were entwined with the present moment. He argued that the United States, addled in the 1920's by materialism, could be regenerated by an increase in self-knowledge that could be gained by listening to its poets.

James Feast

BIBLIOGRAPHY

By the Author

POETRY:
White Buildings, 1926
The Bridge, 1930
The Collected Poems of Hart Crane, 1933 (Waldo Frank, editor)

NONFICTION:
The Letters of Hart Crane, 1952 (Brom Weber, editor)

MISCELLANEOUS:
The Complete Poems and Selected Letters and Prose of Hart Crane, 1966 (Brom Weber, editor)
O My Land, My Friends: The Selected Letters of Hart Crane, 1997 (Langdon Hammer, editor)

About the Author
Berthoff, Warner. *Hart Crane: A Re-introduction*. Minneapolis: University of Minnesota Press, 1989.
Bloom, Harold, ed. *Hart Crane: Comprehensive Research and Study Guide*. Philadelphia: Chelsea House, 2003.
Cole, Merrill. *The Other Orpheus: A Poetics of Modern Homosexuality*. New York: Routledge, 2003.
Fisher, Clive. *Hart Crane*. New Haven, Conn.: Yale University Press, 2002.
Hammer, Langdon. *Hart Crane and Allen Tate: Janus-Faced Modernism*. Princeton, N.J.: Princeton University Press, 1993.
Leibowitz, Herbert A. *Hart Crane: An Introduction to the Poetry*. New York: Columbia University Press, 1968.
Mariani, Paul L. *The Broken Tower: A Life of Hart Crane*. New York: W. W. Norton, 1999.
Rehder, Robert. *Stevens, Williams, Crane, and the Motive for Metaphor*. New York: Palgrave Macmillan, 2004.
Unterecker, John. *Voyager: A Life of Hart Crane*. New York: Farrar, Straus and Giroux, 1969.

STEPHEN CRANE

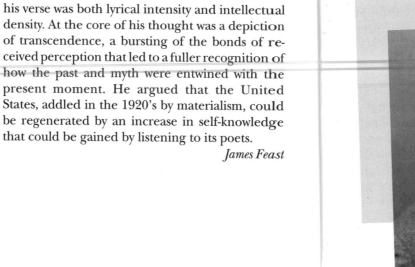

Library of Congress

Born: Newark, New Jersey
November 1, 1871
Died: Badenweiler, Germany
June 5, 1900

Despite his short life and small output, Crane was a [...] American fiction writer, crucial in the development of mo[...] psychological realism.

BIOGRAPHY

Stephen Crane was born November 1, 1871, in Newark, New Jersey, the fourteenth and last child of the Reverend Jonathan Townley Crane and Mary Helen Peck Crane. Dr. Crane was an eminent Methodist ecclesiastic, one consequence of which was that the family moved frequently: in 1874, 1876, and finally, in 1878, to Port Jervis, New York, a town that would figure in Stephen Crane's late fiction as Whilomville (*Whilomville Stories*, 1900). Dr. Crane died suddenly in 1880.

One plausible source of Stephen Crane's universal skepticism is rebellion against his religious upbringing. His rootlessness and death-haunted fiction may have been influenced by the crucial events of his early childhood. On the positive side, Crane grew up exposed to good books. Though few specific details of his reading are known, clearly he absorbed enough to give him the literary background he needed, despite a weak formal education.

In 1883, Crane's mother took him to Asbury Park, a resort town established by the Methodists on the beaches of southern New Jersey. Here among her co-religionists, Mrs. Crane established her family as best she could. Asbury Park had a "sin-

ful" side, however—prostitution, liquor, [...] bling were all present—and Crane, by no [...] lescent, was pulled in two directions. Pr[...] he remained innocent of "bad women'[...] rarely able to portray women convincin[...] fiction). Primarily an observer, he neverth[...] with a fast, sporting crowd; he developed [...] for baseball and took up smoking.

His mother, having lost control of h[...] rebel, attempted the traditional solution: [...] him away to school. He went first to Pe[...] Seminary, of which his father had been [...] before the Civil War, then, in early 188[...] Hudson River Institute in Claverack, N[...] This military school was weak academica[...] gave Crane some background (and pre[...] from the Civil War veterans on the staff, [...] him with some anecdotes) that would pro[...] when he came to write *The Red Badge of Co[...] Episode of the American Civil War* (1895).

In September, 1890, he entered Lafay[...] lege as an engineering student; he failed [...] tered Syracuse University in January, 1[...] played catcher and shortstop on the vars[...] ball team; his first published story appeare[...] *University Herald*, and he probably began [...] *Maggie: A Girl of the Streets* (privately printe[...] published, 1896). That summer he r[...] Asbury Park news for his brother Townl[...] owned a news agency, and for the *New York*[...] He met Hamlin Garland, a writer well kn[...] his realistic stories of midwestern farm life[...] fall Crane did not return to Syracuse; his for[...] ucation was over.

that their lives are strictly governed by heredity and environment, making them essentially victims of biological and social forces which they are helpless to oppose.

Probably the most readable works of American naturalism are Norris's *McTeague* (1899) and Dreiser's *Sister Carrie* (1900). Crane's fiction has some naturalistic elements, in that it is skeptical, probably agnostic, and generally pessimistic. Yet even in *Maggie*, the work to which the term most readily applies, it is not clear that the characters are purely victims of their environment. At key turning points they are offered opportunities to act kindly—to change the course of Maggie s life—but fail to take them. Nor is the deep moral outrage that pervades the story typically naturalistic. Crane knows what good is and takes his stand for it, even if the realist in him sees that, in the Bowery, the good generally fails.

Realism in its most basic form refers simply to getting things right—careful observation and rendering of detail. For example, the realist Mark Twain felt that a famous American romantic novelist, James Fenimore Cooper, had made egregious errors of detail that robbed his work of conviction. In this sense Crane is certainly a realist; he was an expert reporter, and the details of his work ring true. Much of his writing, though by no means all, centers on probable and everyday occurrences. In this aspect he stands firmly in the camp of such leading realists as Hamlin Garland and William Dean Howells.

Crane was more concerned than either of those writers, however—and herein lies a clue to his greater significance for most modern readers—with inner reality: not merely with what happened, but with how it felt and why it mattered. Thus, his realism is more subjective. He describes Civil War battles not as they might appear to a disembodied observer floating above them, but as they looked and sounded to a terrified soldier in the middle of them. His method is, in turn, affected. In *The Red Badge of Courage*, in particular, the narrative is far more disconnected and the imagery more dreamlike than in the social realism of Garland and Howells. It is these qualities that have caused some critics to refer to Crane as an impressionist. Impressionism, an extremely vague term as applied to literature, suggests an attempt to render the subjective aspects of a scene, as opposed to the verifiable

events—what could be filmed by a documentary filmmaker, for example—that make it up.

The greatest fiction writers are able to view events from multiple perspectives, a quality readily apparent in Crane's best work. He is at once the frightened correspondent in "The Open Boat," concerned only with survival from moment to moment, and the survivor observing the foibles, pretensions, and ultimate helplessness of humankind. He is both the runaway soldier wallowing in self-justification and the dispassionate witness. It is out of this multiplicity of vision that Crane's pervasive irony arises.

His is not to be confused with a simple irony of tone, a kind of sarcasm whose purpose is to proclaim the author's distance from and superiority to the people and events he or she is describing. Instead, it expresses a complex, deeply imagined and unsentimental vision. If humans need their illusions to survive in an indifferent universe, in a state of war with one another and with the natural world, let them have them; nevertheless, let them back off from time to time and see those illusions for what they are. It is only in such moments of clarification that human beings, understanding their true place in the scheme of things, come together as brothers and sisters.

In Crane's universe, everyone is indeed at war: The statement is a critical commonplace and is self-evident to any reader once alerted to it. Usually ("The Open Boat" is a notable exception) the enemy is human, and the cause of the conflict is human blindness—failure of observation and imagination, leading to an inability to see others as sentient beings capable of suffering. It is difficult to shoot down another person, face to face, but in *The Red Badge of Courage* the Confederate soldiers are cogs in a war machine that has been aimed at another war machine. To the Swede, in "The Blue Hotel" (1899), the other characters are murderers out of pulp adventure fiction.

Rarely do Crane's characters connect in any significant way; all too often they lash out blindly to save whatever is precious to them, whether self-image, social status, or life itself. Crane's vision, then, is essentially tragic. His stories do not necessarily make comforting reading. They are passionately honest, however, revealing an integrity found only in the finest fiction. They have much to say to a world that remains at war.

MAGGIE: A GIRL OF THE STREETS

First published: 1896 (privately printed, 1893)

Type of work: Novella

Cast out by her family and abandoned by her lover, a young woman comes to a sad end.

Maggie: A Girl of the Streets presents more difficulties to modern readers than other major work by Crane. The heavy dialect and outmoded slang can be distracting, but a more central problem lies in the characterization, or lack of it, of the protagonist. The harrowing pictures of life in a New York slum, however, still ring true.

The fundamental law of life in the Bowery is revealed in the opening scene and depicted as absolute throughout the story. Maggie's brother Jimmie Johnson appears as a small boy fighting a group of boys from Devil's Row "for the honor of Rum Alley." As he is about to be overwhelmed, an older boy, Pete, happens along and pitches in on his side. With the enemy routed, Jimmie goes home to a family also at war; here the mother is victorious, the father driven out to drown his sorrows in a neighboring saloon. So it goes throughout: The powerful prey on the powerless and are preyed upon themselves in turn. Power may stem from physical prowess, from socioeconomic position, or from sexual desirability. Whatever its source, however, power is universally exploited for pleasure or vindication.

Because the characters lack any vestige of self-knowledge or empathy, inevitably their behavior is revealed as at best futile, at worst destructive. Jimmie fights for the "honor" of Rum Alley, but Rum Alley has no honor. The mother ultimately banishes Maggie in the name of conventional respectability, but she herself is a ranting and raving alcoholic. The streets and tenements that make up the urban jungle are strewn with victims. Maggie, from the first scene in which she appears, is only one of many.

Maggie: A Girl of the Streets consists of nineteen brief sections; in the first four, Maggie and Jimmie are children. In these sections, Crane is highly successful in evoking the milieu. It is in the fifth—with Maggie grown and engaged in near-slave labor as a seamstress—that he begins to run into trouble. She has become "a most rare and wonderful production of a tenement district, a pretty girl." As additional characterization, Crane reveals that "when a child, playing and fighting with gamins in the street, dirt disgusted her." That statement essentially marks the limit of his conception of Maggie. For the story to rise above pathos, its heroine would have to reveal some divine spark, or, in practical terms, considerable spunk in her attempts to make a new life for herself. The potential for triumph or tragedy is present in the situation; unfortunately, however, the protagonist, in her timid passivity, remains nothing more than a victim of circumstances.

Her good looks and vulnerability make her a natural target for Pete, Jimmie's rescuer in the opening scene, who has become a bartender and a swaggering man about town. He begins squiring her about—more because she is a decorative prop to his ego than out of any real feeling—and Maggie, naturally enough, falls in love with him. Thus, ominously, the power is all on Pete's side. Interspersed with scenes of the courtship are scenes with Jimmie, now a truck driver and minor-league swaggerer himself, and Maggie's mother, widowed but unchanged in her alcoholic, sanctimonious violence.

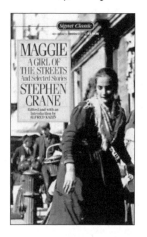

At the end of section 9, the midpoint of the story, the mother throws Maggie out. With nowhere to go except with Pete, Maggie now (it is indicated discreetly) loses her virginity—she is "ruined." The sexual double standard comes into darkly ironic focus: Jimmie, who has been "ruining" girls for years, proclaims that "Maggie's gone teh d' devil." The mother responds with a curse biblical in intensity but with imagery straight from the Bowery: "May she eat nothin but stones and deh dirt in deh street. May she sleep in deh gutter an' never see deh sun shine again."

After a dramatic scene in a saloon, in which a fight between Jimmie and Pete over Maggie's honor escalates into a riot, the beginning of the end for Maggie comes quickly. By now, with no one else to turn to, her "air of spaniel-like dependence had been magnified and showed its direct effect in the peculiar off-handedness and ease of Pete's ways toward her." In a dance hall they meet Nell, "a woman of brilliance and audacity" whom Pete had known previously, and whom he wants more than she wants him. As a result of this shift in the balance of power, Maggie is very soon abandoned. Her mother refuses to take her back in, effectively condemning her to a life of prostitution.

To this point Crane's techniques have been realistic. Now, in section 17, Maggie's remaining life is foreshortened into a few pages, as she is shown first well-dressed in a brilliantly lit theater district, then walking down darker, grimier streets, being rejected finally by boys and drunks, coming at last to the river, into which she will deliver up her life. How much time has passed cannot be determined exactly, but it is presumably several years. The power of this section depends on the extent to which the reader has come to identify with Maggie in the earlier, more fully developed ones; many will find it more puzzling than anything else.

After a scene depicting the downfall of Pete, *Maggie: A Girl of the Streets* ends with the announcement to her family of her death. In the last line of the story, her mother, utterly unconscious of what she has done to her daughter in her vindictive failure of love, screams "Oh, yes, I'll fergive her! I'll fergive her!" It is one of the most harrowingly ironic endings in all of fiction and anticipates the greatness of the work to come.

THE RED BADGE OF COURAGE

First published: 1895
Type of work: Novel

In the course of a series of Civil War skirmishes, a young Union soldier is initiated into manhood.

The Red Badge of Courage is hard to classify, as is Crane's work in general. It is a war story in the sense that the major external action consists of clashes between opposing armies, but certainly it is

unconventional in what it omits. No geographical place names are given, except for a single casual mention of the Rappahannock River, so that the action—all the more surreal for this reason—cannot be located on a map. Similarly, no dates are given; it is impossible to tell what strategic significance, if any, the series of inconclusive actions might have had.

In fiction that is intended to justify one side in a war, much is generally made of the justice of the cause; moreover, the soldiers on "our side" are portrayed as brave and noble, the enemy as evil. In *The Red Badge of Courage*, on the other hand, the cause is never described, and, though the enemy remains mostly faceless, it becomes clear at last that the only difference between Union and Confederate soldiers is the color of their uniforms. The novel is distinctly modern in this sense, much in the spirit of the  fiction engendered by the Vietnam War. In its vivid depiction of the futile suffering brought about by war, it is an antiwar novel.

It is also, and perhaps primarily, a coming-of-age story. According to traditional readings, Henry Fleming, the young protagonist, moves in a series of stages from boyhood, marked by his cowardly flight from his first battle, to manhood, marked by his leading a charge and capturing a rebel flag. In the fiction of Crane, however, as ironic a writer as ever lived, nothing is ever quite that simple. The question of just what it is that Henry learns (and in turn, just what it is that war teaches any of those condemned to fight in it) remains open, to be answered by each reader by closely following the details of the story.

The Red Badge of Courage moves back and forth between traditional realism, partly from Henry's point of view and partly from Crane's ironical one, and the surreal, disjointed imagery of nightmare. Thus, in the opening paragraph, from the camp of Henry's untested regiment one can see "the red, eyelike gleam of hostile campfires set in the low brows of distant hills"—a picture of a war monster.

Next the story turns to a matter-of-fact description of camp life, including small domestic arrangements, quarrels, and the inevitable buzz of rumor. By these varied techniques, Crane accurately expresses the flavor of Henry's existence—mostly ordinary, a life dominated by trivial events and emotions but always haunted by the specter of the fearful unknown.

At length, the regiment begins its march to action. Before any fighting actually occurs, Henry begins to feel his helplessness to alter the onrushing course of events. His regiment "inclosed him. And there were iron laws of tradition and law on four sides. He was in a moving box." It is this kind of statement that has caused some critics to describe *The Red Badge of Courage* as naturalistic and Henry as simply a victim of historical forces. Yet it is important to remember that these are Henry's perceptions, not Crane's, and that Henry is often self-deluded. A moment later, he reflects that he "had not enlisted of his free will," when in fact he had. He made that choice and, like the characters in "The Blue Hotel," will have others to make as well.

His first crisis occurs when his regiment has to withstand an infantry charge. At first he "suddenly lost concern for himself, and. . . . He became not a man but a member. . . . He felt the subtle battle brotherhood more potent even than the cause for which they were fighting." This is reminiscent of the brotherhood in "The Open Boat," but it is ironically undercut by its arising from war (Henry's state is described as "battle sleep") and by its being so very short-lived. Soon, when a few men run, Henry runs too.

He runs blindly, without conscious volition, and his adventures while away from his regiment, chapters 6 through 12 of the twenty-four in the book, make up the dramatic heart of the novel. He pictures himself initially as being pursued by dragons and shells with "rows of cruel teeth that grinned at him." Soon, as he calms down, he begins to justify his flight: Because his regiment was about to be swallowed, running was an intelligent act. Yet when he overhears some officers saying that the regiment held, he feels more than ever isolated: He grows angry at his comrades for standing firm and actually thinks of them as his enemy.

Throughout the novel, in typical adolescent fashion, Henry undergoes wild mood swings that color the ways he sees the external world. Distanced for a time from the fighting, he enters a forest and comes to "a place where the high, arching boughs made a chapel. . . . There was a religious half light." Then, in a type of violent juxtaposition that Crane uses frequently, Henry sees that he is "being looked at by a dead man," a decaying corpse Crane describes in graphic detail. Henry disintegrates: "His mind flew in all directions," matching the chaos of the day's events. It is when he comes to a road filled with wounded men that he most acutely feels his shame, hence the need for a wound of his own, a "red badge of courage."

He falls in with a "tattered man" who befriends him and with a "spectral soldier," a dying man he recognizes with horror as Jim Conklin, formerly known as the "tall soldier" of his own company. Henry and the tattered man accompany Jim on his death walk as he searches, seemingly, for the right place to die. At his death occurs the most famous and controversial image of the novel: "The red sun was pasted in the sky like a wafer." One prominent critic has interpreted this sun to be a metaphor for a communion wafer, and an elaborately worked-out system of religious references as giving the book its underlying structure. Others, probably with better reason, discount the religious element and see the source of the image as the red seals that were commonly pasted on envelopes.

Henry, in his shame, now abandons the badly wounded tattered man. As he frantically questions a soldier in a routed mass of Union infantry, the man hits him on the head with his rifle, thus bestowing on him a profoundly ironic red badge. As the day ends Henry staggers on into the dark, only to be rescued by a mysterious "cheery man" whose face he never sees. This cheery man, with almost magical prowess and rare good will, restores him to his regiment.

It is typical for heroes of epic myth to make a trip to the underworld, a trip which explores their own deepest fears and from which they are reborn to a higher self. Henry has now completed such a journey; when he wakes the next morning, "it seemed to him that he had been asleep for a thousand years, and he felt sure that he opened his eyes upon an unexpected world." The difficulty with this sort of mythic reading, however, is that in many ways Henry seems unchanged and continues to behave badly.

Wilson, a comrade formerly known as the "loud

soldier," has been genuinely humbled; there have been models of brotherhood in the tattered man and the cheery soldier, and of heroism in the dignity of Jim Conklin's death. Yet Henry never tells the truth about his wound, and he is not above wanting to humiliate Wilson for having revealed his fears. At the end, he is tormented not by having abandoned the tattered man but by his fears of being found out. It is as though whatever meaning the mythic story might have had for Crane was overwhelmed by his clear-eyed realism.

Henry does become heroic, or at least stalwartly successful, in conventional military terms, and he turns at the end to "images of tranquil skies, fresh meadows, cool brooks—an existence of soft and eternal peace." On the face of it, there is a happy ending. Henry has basked euphorically in nature before, however, only to be brought up short by a rotting corpse. The war is by no means over; there is little peace to be had, and there is no convincing evidence that Henry will experience unbroken inner peace. So the meaning of the ending remains decidedly ambiguous. Exactly what lessons has Henry Fleming learned—that appearance matters more than reality, or that peace of mind is best attained by internalizing the values of society? If so, *The Red Badge of Courage* is a darker book than has generally been recognized.

"THE OPEN BOAT"

First published: 1898 (collected in *The Open Boat, and Other Tales of Adventure*, 1898)
Type of work: Short story

Four men shipwrecked in a ten-foot dinghy struggle to survive.

"The Open Boat" is considered by some critics to be Stephen Crane's masterpiece. Summarizing the rudimentary plot—the struggle of four shipwrecked men to survive in a rough sea in a ten-foot dinghy—suggests little of the story's abiding interest. At its center lies not the question of who will survive, ultimately revealed as a matter of chance anyway, but rather the progressively revealed nature of human life and the place of humanity in the universe. The theme is not presented as an abstract philosophical statement; it emerges, rather, from a brilliantly compelling rendition of life in an open boat, vividly portrayed and psychologically exact.

The events immediately preceding those of "The Open Boat" are recounted in "Stephen Crane's Own Story," published January 7, 1897—five days after the *Commodore* sank—in the *New York Press*. The short story can be appreciated without reading the journalistic narrative, though knowing the context is useful as background. It is instructive, nevertheless, to compare the openings. "Stephen Crane's Own Story" begins, after the dateline, "It was the afternoon of New Year's. The Commodore lay at her dock in Jacksonville"—functional journalistic prose, whose sole purpose is the objective presentation of facts. The opening of "The Open Boat," on the other hand—"None of them knew the color of the sky" is one of the most famous sentences in modern literature. Arrestingly, with the utmost concision, it reveals the essentials of life in a ten-foot dinghy: One's world is reduced, one's attention is focused solely on survival from moment to moment. What the men know about, in frighteningly intimate detail, is the waves that threaten to swamp the boat.

The four men in the dinghy are the captain of the *Commodore*; the oiler, who worked in the engine room; the ship's cook; and the correspondent, Stephen Crane himself. They have come together by accident, strangers whose names—except for the oiler's, given incidentally in dialogue—are not even mentioned. This deliberate omission comes to suggest, by the end, that the men are Everyman, that everyone, in a symbolic separated sense, lives in an open boat without knowing it.

They are separated from the sea by "six inches of gunwale." The correspondent rows and wonders "why he was there"—in that boat, in that particular place and time—but the wonderment is also about his life and about human life in general. Many of the details in the story have a similar double significance, coming as they do from two different angles: The correspondent is sitting in the boat six inches from the waves, and is at the same time reflecting on the events afterward as he writes the story.

The surface structure of "The Open Boat" is that of the journey itself; an almost random movement as the boat, sometimes controlled by the struggling oarsmen, sometimes by wind and waves, works its way up and down the Florida coast. Land and safety are within sight but are unattainable because of the pounding surf. A more significant movement lies in the rapidly altering perspectives of the men as they experience hope and fear, confidence and despair, anger, puzzlement, and love for one another in the brotherhood of the boat—a lifetime's range of emotions. Ultimately, however, the controlling factor is irony: In the contract between what humanity is and what it thinks it is, layer after comforting layer of illusion is stripped away.

The source of the ironic revelations that, by the end, make the men think "that they could then be interpreters" is a radically altered perspective. From the open boat, everything looks different. A seagull, ordinarily harmless and indeed afraid of people, tries to land on the captain's head; if he tries to shoo it away he might swamp the dinghy. The men see people on the shore but cannot make their need understood; the people on the beach, the purported lords of the earth, are not merely ineffectual but ludicrous.

Night falls, and the correspondent, the only man awake in the boat, learns something about real power from a shark: "It cut the water like a gigantic and keen projectile." In the end, as the boat founders in the surf, it is the oiler, the strongest swimmer of the four, who drowns. Human strength and resourcefulness are no match for the power of a universe that has revealed itself to the correspondent as "flatly indifferent."

Yet the philosophy that emerges from "The Open Boat" is not unmitigatedly dark. For all the hardship, fear, and disillusionment, the correspondent recognizes "even at the time" that his boat ride is "the best experience of his life." The wellspring of this paradox is love, "the subtle brotherhood of men." Brotherhood is no hedge against mortality, but it does make life in the open boat, life without illusions, worth living. "The Open Boat" is a timeless and moving tale of struggle, not merely for physical survival but also for understanding and acceptance of humanity's fate.

"THE BLUE HOTEL"

First published: 1898 (collected in *Great Short Works of Stephen Crane*, 1968)

Type of work: Short story

A quarrel over a card game in a storm-bound Nebraska hotel leads to tragedy.

In "The Blue Hotel," a group of strangers comes together in a small isolated hotel, a refuge from the storm outside. Isolating characters in this way is a common plot device in both mainstream and mystery fiction—and Crane's story is a suspense thriller, whatever its larger meanings. People in such a situation, unconstrained by the laws and traditions of a larger society, become a society in themselves; under the additional pressure imposed by unfamiliar and unpredictable events, they reveal their truest and deepest values. In this story, as in "The Open Boat," the implications are universal.

"The Palace Hotel at Fort Romper was painted a light blue . . . screaming and howling in a way that made the dazzling winter landscape of Nebraska seem only a gray swampish hush." What is the significance—beyond the spelled-out realistic one that it makes the hotel visible to travelers—of the unusual color? Bright primary colors, as in *The Red Badge of Courage* and "The Bride Comes to Yellow Sky," appealed to Crane. Here the color occurs again later, when the characters go outside to fight: "The covered land was blue with the sheen of an unearthly satin." The suggestion is fundamental to an understanding of the story: The blue hotel is no refuge from the storm, because the characters carry the storm—uncontrolled violence and hatred—within them.

The three guests who come to the hotel owned by Pat Scully, and run by him with the help of his son Johnnie, are "a tall bronzed cowboy," "a silent little man from the East," and a "shaky and quick-eyed Swede"—characters from widely spaced places who, as in "The Open Boat," are never given names. That the hotel is anything but a safe harbor, a place of peace and love, is revealed at once; the small room "seemed to be merely a proper temple for an enormous stove, which, in the center, was humming with godlike violence." Johnnie Scully is playing cards and quarreling with an old farmer. Pat Scully loudly "destroys the game of cards," sending his son up with the baggage. The guests then hear his "officious clamor at his daughters."

The potential for violence, then, is already present. It is the Swede, who sits silently "making furtive elements of each man in the room," who provides the catalyst. The others play cards and again quarrel. The Swede, who is badly frightened by his own preconceptions of the Wild West, at length speculates—to everyone's astonishment—that "there have been a good many men killed in this room." No one is able to reassure him, and at length, in his growing hysteria, he bursts out with "I suppose I am going to be killed before I can leave this house!" In his literal insanity—he has fabricated a world which connects with reality hardly at all—he carries within him the seeds of his own death.

Scully finally does manage to placate him, whereupon the Swede turns into an arrogant bully. He views all human relationships in terms of power; interpreting Scully's overtures as signs of weakness, he concludes that the power is on his side now, and, as the characters do in *Maggie: A Girl of the Streets*, he abuses it. He joins the card game, accuses Johnnie of cheating, and the two go out into the storm to fight. The scene that follows is full of animal images: Scully turns on the Swede "panther-fashion"; the combatants watch each other "in a calm that had the elements of leonine cruelty in it"; they collide "like bullocks." Meanwhile, the cowboy, whose animal nature has surfaced as well, urges Johnnie: "Kill him."

The Swede wins, however, and walks into town, goes into a bar, and arrogantly attempts to browbeat a group of men into drinking with him. In a brief melee, and more or less in self-defense, one of them, a quiet, respectable gambler, stabs him: "[A] human body, this citadel of virtue, wisdom, power, was pierced as easily as if it had been a melon." The dead Swede lies with his eye on a sign on the cash register: "This registers the amount of your purchase." By his failures of "virtue, wisdom, power," he has bought his death.

If the story ended here, as it logically might, it would be naturalistic, portraying humans revealed as animals, helpless in the grip of their bestial emotions. Crane added a kind of coda, however, a scene later between the cowboy and the easterner. The easterner reveals that Johnnie really was cheating

at cards; he himself was too cowardly to reveal what he knew and forestall the fight, while Scully permitted it and the cowboy fueled it with his rage. All of them, in a sense, collaborated in the murder; all could have made different choices that would have prevented it. Naturalism, with the characters in the grip of forces too great for them to oppose, cannot rise above pathos; "The Blue Hotel," on the other hand, is tragic. The characters have the chance to live up to their highest human potential. Because they fail, a man needlessly dies.

"THE BRIDE COMES TO YELLOW SKY"

First published: 1898 (collected in *Great Short Works of Stephen Crane*, 1968)
Type of work: Short story

A showdown in a Western town concludes with a comic twist.

"The Bride Comes to Yellow Sky," half the length of "The Blue Hotel" and "The Open Boat," lacks the narrative density and philosophical depth of either. Instead it debunks some pervasive myths of the American West, with wonderfully comic effect. In the generally grim catalog of Crane's work, this story offers a refreshing change of pace.

In the most primitive kind of Western story, the characters lack identifiable human characteristics. They are robotlike, standing for largely meaningless abstractions of good or evil; everything leads up to, and the interest of the story lies in, the climactic showdown. Marshal Jack Potter of Yellow Sky, Texas, on the other hand, is all too human. As he rides home on the train from San Antonio, his new bride beside him, he is thinking not of confrontations with bad guys but, anxiously and distractedly, of what the town will think of him in his new married state. This is a rite of passage in more than the ordinary sense. It marks Jack's transition from Old West lawman, the stereotypical hero of the American frontier, to solid married citizen of the New West, the self-conscious hero of domestic comedy. To mark the occasion, he has left his gun at home.

Meanwhile, back in Yellow Sky, the Old West

seems alive and well in the person of Scratchy Wilson. In a scene out of any number of dime Westerns (the kind of story that fatally terrified the Swede in "The Blue Hotel"), a young man appears at the door of a saloon and announces that Scratchy is drunk and on the rampage. Nobody is tempted to become a dead hero; doors and windows are bolted and barred, and everyone awaits the return of the marshal, whose job is to fight Scratchy. It seems that he has fought him before (a detail which, to the experienced reader of Westerns, might seem odd—in the classic showdown, someone invariably dies).

In the next section, Scratchy himself appears, a criminal with some details comically askew: His flannel shirt is "made principally by some Jewish women on the East Side of New York. . . . And his boots had red tops with gilded imprints, of the kind beloved in winter by little sledding boys on the hillsides of New England." On the streets of the deserted village there is no one to fight. He chases a dog to and fro with bullets, nails a scrap of paper to the saloon door as a target—and misses it by half an inch.

As Jack Potter and his new bride walk "sheepishly and with speed" toward their house, then, everything is set for the climax. Scratchy points his revolver at the unarmed marshal and sets out to play with him like a cat with a mouse; the only possible outcomes, seemingly, are tragedy or implausible heroism. Scratchy is enraged to discover that the marshal has no gun—what fun is that? When he asks why, Jack replies that it is because he is married. The stunned Scratchy is "like a creature allowed a glimpse of another world"—as indeed he has been—and it is a new world with no place for him in it. In the showdown between old and new, Scratchy is armed with his six-guns, Jack with his wife. Jack wins handily: Scratchy turns and walks away, leaving "funnel-shaped tracks in the heavy sand." Time and the prairie wind will soon efface them, and the Old West will be no more.

SUMMARY

Crane is a crucial transitional figure in American literature. The psychological depths of Henry James, the master realist of Crane's lifetime, went virtually unrecognized at the time; the dominant

DISCUSSION TOPICS

- Does classifying *Maggie: A Girl of the Streets* as a naturalistic novel facilitate or hinder the reader's understanding of the novel?

- What lessons does Henry Fleming learn in *The Red Badge of Courage?* Do they, as has been suggested, make the novel a "dark" one?

- What qualities in *The Red Badge of Courage* have kept this novel alive despite the fact that the nature of warfare has changed so much since it was written?

- Stephen Crane called one of his books of poetry *War Is Kind,* an obviously ironic title. A famous Civil War general said, "War is hell." Explain why no simple formulation is adequate to explain Crane's attitude toward war as expressed in his fiction and poetry.

- By what means does Crane unify "The Open Boat"?

- What does Crane mean by his statement at the end of "The Open Boat" that the survivors "felt that they could then be interpreters"?

- Discuss the unconnectedness of human beings as a theme in Crane's fiction.

figure was William Dean Howells, most of whose genteel social realism is unread today except by scholars. It was Crane who made the great leap inward—who, in *The Red Badge of Courage,* exhumed buried feelings to which the public responded with a shock of recognition. Such a response to a work so radically new is almost unheard of in the history of literature. For an instantaneous success to continue to speak to later generations is rarer still. Crane's fiercely unconventional honesty, above all, makes of his small body of fiction a treasure.

Edwin Moses

BIBLIOGRAPHY

By the Author

LONG FICTION:
Maggie: A Girl of the Streets, 1893
The Red Badge of Courage: An Episode of the American Civil War, 1895
George's Mother, 1896
The Third Violet, 1897
Active Service, 1899
The Monster, 1898 (serial), 1899 (novella; pb. in *The Monster, and Other Stories*)
The O'Ruddy: A Romance, 1903 (with Robert Barr)

SHORT FICTION:
The Little Regiment and Other Episodes of the American Civil War, 1896
The Open Boat, and Other Tales of Adventure, 1898
The Monster, and Other Stories, 1899
Whilomville Stories, 1900
Wounds in the Rain: War Stories, 1900
Last Words, 1902

POETRY:
The Black Riders and Other Lines, 1895
A Souvenir and a Medley, 1896
War Is Kind, 1899
The University Press of Virginia Edition of the Works of Stephen Crane, 1970 (Volume 10)

DRAMA:
The Blood of the Martyr, wr. 1898?, pb. 1940
The Ghost, pr. 1899 (with Henry James; fragment)

NONFICTION:
The Great Battles of the World, 1901
The War Dispatches of Stephen Crane, 1964

About the Author

Benfey, Christopher E. G. *The Double Life of Stephen Crane*. New York: Knopf, 1992.

Berryman, John. *Stephen Crane: A Critical Biography*. New York: Cooper Square Press, 2001.

Cady, Edwin H. *Stephen Crane*. Rev. ed. Boston: Twayne, 1980.

Davis, Linda H. *Badge of Courage: The Life of Stephen Crane*. Boston: Houghton Mifflin, 1998.

Gullason, Thomas A., ed. *Stephen Crane's Literary Family: A Garland of Writings*. Syracuse, N.Y.: Syracuse University Press, 2002.

Hayes, Kevin J. *Stephen Crane*. Tavistock, Northumberland, England: Northcote House in association with the British Council, 2004.

Johnson, Claudia D. *Understanding "The Red Badge of Courage": A Student Casebook to Issues, Sources, and Historical Documents*. Westport, Conn.: Greenwood Press, 1998.

Monteiro, George. *Stephen Crane's Blue Badge of Courage*. Baton Rouge: Louisiana State University Press, 2000.

Robertson, Michael. *Stephen Crane: Journalism and the Making of Modern American Literature*. New York: Columbia University Press, 1997.

Weatherford, Richard M., ed. *Stephen Crane: The Critical Heritage*. Boston: Routledge & Kegan Paul, 1973.

Wertheim, Stanley. *A Stephen Crane Encyclopedia*. Westport, Conn.: Greenwood Press, 1997.

ROBERT CREELEY

Born: Arlington, Massachusetts
May 21,1926
Died: Marfa, Texas
March 30, 2005

Working in the modernist mode of Ezra Pound and William Carlos Williams, Robert Creeley's exceptional sensitivity to language and rhythm made him a notable literary figure throughout the world and one of America's leading poets.

© Bruce Jackson/Courtesy, New Directions

BIOGRAPHY

Robert White Creeley was born in Arlington, Massachusetts, on May 21, 1926, two weeks before the birth of Allen Ginsberg in Newark, New Jersey. His parents were both from families that had been living in New England for generations, and his sister Helen was four years old when Oscar Slate Creeley, a physician married for the third time, and Genevieve Jules Creeley had their second child. When Dr. Creeley took his two-year-old son for a drive in an open car, a piece of coal shattered the windshield and a shard of glass cut Robert's eye, leading to a series of infections which culminated in the removal of the eye when the young boy was five—one year after his father's death. His mother moved to West Acton and became a public health nurse when Dr. Creeley died, and for the remainder of his childhood, Robert was raised in the care of aunts, grandmothers, and a maid named Theresa.

In 1940, Creeley entered Holderness School, a small boarding school in Plymouth, New Hampshire, where he published articles and stories in the *Dial*, the school literary magazine, which he edited in his senior year. Upon graduation in 1943, he entered Harvard University. After two years, Creeley joined the American Field Service and drove an ambulance in Burma and India; he then returned to Harvard for a second try. In 1946, he helped to edit the Harvard *Wake*'s special E. E. Cummings issue and published his first poem, "Return," there. During this year, his schoolmates at Harvard included the poets Robert Bly, Frank O'Hara, Kenneth Koch, and John Ashbery.

Creeley had just married Ann McKinnon, however, and one semester short of his degree in 1947, he left school and moved to a chicken farm in New Hampshire. His son David was born in October, 1948. His wife's trust fund provided a meager subsistence, and he raised pigeons and chickens for additional income. His first public poetry reading took place in 1950 on Cid Corman's radio program "This Is Poetry," and Creeley began to gather manuscripts from contemporary writers for an alternative magazine to be called *Lititz Review* (for Lititz, Pennsylvania, the home of his coeditor Jacob Leed). Corman told Creeley about Charles Olson, the poet who was about to publish his groundbreaking "Projective Verse" essay. It moved that free verse poetry should embed itself in the process of one perception leading to deeper perceptions in order to attain a heightened sense of compositional energy. Creeley and Olson began a mammoth correspondence in which they both worked out the fundamental strictures of their poetic philosophies, and although the material for the magazine was not used immediately, Creeley placed some of it in *Origin I* and *Origin II* in 1951, including the first poems of Olson's *Maximum* sequence.

Creeley and his family (now including three children) lived in France from 1951 to 1952 and then on the Spanish island of Mallorca from 1952 to 1955. His first book of poems, *Le Fou,* was published in 1952, and in 1953 he started the Divers Press, publishing his second book of poems, *The Kind of Act Of,* and publishing his first book of short fiction, *The Gold Diggers,* in 1954. In December of 1953, Olson, now the rector of Black Mountain College in North Carolina, asked Creeley to edit the *Black Mountain Review.* Creeley's first issue of the influential magazine appeared in March, just before he arrived to teach at the college.

Creeley returned to Mallorca to try to repair his marriage but came to North Carolina to teach and edit the review in 1955 after his divorce. That same year, his volume of poems *All That Is Lovely in Men* was published by Jonathan Williams. Creeley resigned from Black Mountain College in 1956, traveling to San Francisco, where he met Allen Ginsberg, Jack Kerouac, Gary Snyder, and other members of the San Francisco renaissance. Later in the year, he moved to Albuquerque, New Mexico, to teach in an academy for boys and was presented with a B.A. by Olson from Black Mountain.

Creeley met and married Bobbie Louise Hoeck in 1957, began an M.A. at the University of New Mexico, and became the father of a daughter, Sarah, in November. Continuing his studies, he presented for his M.A. thesis a collection of poems and was granted the degree in 1960. He won the Levinson Prize from *Poetry* magazine for a group of ten poems and was included in Donald Allen's landmark anthology *The New American Poetry, 1945-1960* (1960). He remained at the University of New Mexico through 1962 as a visiting lecturer, and in 1962, his first book of poems to gain national attention, *For Love: Poems 1950-1960,* was published. In 1962-1963, he lectured at the University of British Columbia, then returned to New Mexico, remaining there from 1963 to 1966. In 1963, after completing the spring semester, he contributed to the Vancouver Poetry Festival, which brought together Olson, Robert Duncan, Ginsberg, Denise Levertov, and others Creeley had met while he edited the *Black Mountain Review.*

Late in 1963, his novel *The Island* was published, and in 1964, he received a Guggenheim Fellowship. His friend Olson had begun to teach at the State University of New York, Buffalo, and Creeley participated in the Buffalo Arts Festival in 1965. In the following year, he accepted a position as a visiting professor at Buffalo, and in 1967, he was appointed professor of English there, a position he held until 1978.

Scribners published his second major collection of poems, *Words,* in 1967, and in 1968, Creeley returned to the University of New Mexico as a visiting professor for one year. Scribners published his next collection, *Pieces,* in 1969; a book of early and uncollected poems, *The Charm,* was issued by the Four Seasons Foundation in that year. Creeley also recorded two readings of his work. He spent the 1970-1971 academic year as a visiting professor at San Francisco State College and took part in poetry festivals in Texas and Belgium. In an attempt to conclude a peripatetic existence that had gone on for more than two decades, Creeley established a permanent residence in Buffalo in 1973 and began to take a very active interest in the cultural affairs of the city, working against the prevailing academic disinclination to bring literature to a wider segment of the population.

Continuing to travel extensively, Creeley took part in a poetry festival in Toronto in 1975 and spent the spring of 1976 reading his work in Fiji, New Zealand, Australia, the Philippines, Malaysia, Japan, and Korea, sponsored by the United States Information Agency (USIA). Scribners published a volume of his *Selected Poems* in 1976; *Mabel: A Story and Other Prose* was published by Marion Boyars in London, an indication of his growing international reputation. At the end of the year, he was divorced from his second wife, and in 1977, he married Penelope Highton.

In 1979, Creeley began to publish poetry with the innovative, pioneering New Directions Press, founded and run by James Laughlin. Their association began with *Later* (1979), a volume that marked a ripening, more reflective turn in Creeley's style. Creeley returned to the University of New Mexico as a visiting professor in 1979, 1980, and 1981. In 1980, Black Sparrow Press published the first two volumes of his historic correspondence with Olson, an exchange of letters that was both a record of a special friendship and an epistolary analysis of postmodern poetry and poetics.

His son William Gabriel was born in 1981, the same year Creeley received the Shelley Memorial Award from the Poetry Society of America, a further indication of how much his work had become a part of the main current of American poetry. In 1982, he augmented his position as a major figure in American literature with the publication of *The Collected Poems of Robert Creeley, 1945-1975*, a book that Creeley regarded as a coherent expression of his work which had "a sense of increment, of accumulation . . . that is very dear to me." New Directions followed this volume with Creeley's work over the next four years in *Mirrors* (1983), and in December of that year his daughter Hannah Highton was born.

Creeley spent the winter of 1983-1984 in Berlin on a Berlin Artists Program Grant, then served on the National Endowment for the Arts (NEA) Literature Fellowship Panel in 1984. In that year, he turned again toward his New England origins by establishing a residence in Waldoboro, Maine, behind his sister Helen's house.

In 1986, his third collection from New Directions, *Memory Gardens*, was published, a book which offered many reflections about members of his immediate family. The seventh and eighth volumes of Creeley's correspondence with Olson were published in 1987, and two years later, the University of California Press issued *The Collected Essays of Robert Creeley*, a companion volume to the *Collected Poems* and a book which, in gathering most of Creeley's theoretical, critical, autobiographical, and occasional prose into one collection, provided further evidence of the weight and influence of his thinking about literature. In 1990, New Directions published *Windows*, Creeley's eleventh book of poetry. Creeley continued to teach at the State University of New York, holding the Samuel P. Capen Professorship of Poetry and Humanities, and he was honored by his community with the title New York State Poet for 1989-1991. He was elected a Chancellor of the Academy of American Poets in 1999 and joined the faculty at Brown University in 2003. He died of pneumonia while in residence in Marfa, Texas, on March 30, 2005. He was seventy-eight.

ANALYSIS

Among the poets who took it as an obligation to explain the poetics of the evolving modernist continuation of the tradition in American literature which began with Walt Whitman and was developed by Ezra Pound and William Carlos Williams, Creeley may have been the most lucidly articulate as well as the most challengingly imaginative. With his friend and poetic brother Charles Olson, whose own theoretical suggestions (especially his "Projec-

tive Verse" essay of 1950) led to what Gilbert Sorrentino called "an encouragement for all young writers who felt themselves to be disenfranchised," Creeley accepted the task of demonstrating that his differences from the established strictures of the New Critics (such as John Crowe Ransom and Cleanth Brooks) were not failures of form but a different approach to the entire question of what form might be.

In his essays and interviews, Creeley responded to the need for "the dignity of their own statement" felt by writers who shared his concerns, and although he rarely used his own poetry as an example of his theories in argument, preferring to cite the work of many colleagues he admired, his poems may be most clearly understood in the context of his own observations about the nature of writing.

Creeley's work has adhered to the nature of form and writing so fully that many poets commit his famous comment about form to memory. As quoted by Olson, Creeley once remarked that "form is never more than an extension of content," a direct refutation of the idea common to academic criticism in the first half of the twentieth century that a poem should be a container of a specific design into which the poet arranged his words and images. Creeley has stressed the idea that, as Olson put it, "there's an appropriate way of saying something inherent in the thing to be said." That is, each specific occasion from which a poem emerges requires the suitable form and language of its particulars. Organizing such a principle can be both tedious and second-nature, and Creeley was so intent on this mode of poetic practice that he once said of the poet's subject: "Try not to describe *it*. But if one can, somehow, enter *it*."

Creeley claimed to feel "a rhythmic periodicity in the weight and duration of words to occur in the first few words, or first line, or lines, of what I am writing." Therefore, the crucial choice in the poem's opening established a measure—a much wider and subtler determinant than meter—to which the poet was compelled to respond as the poem continued. Put in another way, Creeley drew a parallel between a farmer plowing a field and a poet composing a poem. The first line, or furrow, determines direction; the second line solidifies it. Creeley saw the literal root of the word "verse" as a furrow, or a turning, just as the line turned in accordance with the requirements of emphasis, stress, breath units, and other elements inherent in the language as it was employed.

While it is clear from Creeley's work that he was very much aware of the entire history of poetry in the English language (and that he regarded it as "rather regrettable and a little dumb not to make use of the full context of what's been done"), he was also interested in the "possibilities of coherence . . . other than what was previously the case." Or, as he explained in his essay expressing his basic credo, "I'm *given* to write poems," he believed that it requires all of his intelligence to "follow the possibilities that the poem 'under hand' as Olson would say, is declaring."

Another crucial component of Creeley's poetic style is his use, in the spirit of Williams's arch claim that his poetic language came from "the mouths of Polish mothers," of the colloquial, with which he feels "very at home." Following the pioneering example of Williams's work, Creeley attempted to engage language at a level he regarded as both familiar and active, so that the poem is an "intensely *emotional* perception," no matter how evident the poet's intelligence and education may be. This insistence on emotion recalls Walt Whitman's dictum, "Who touches this book touches a man," and is a part of Creeley's determination to resist the academic theorists who emphasized an ironic distance that was part of a habit of diction that excluded many modes of speech as inappropriate for poetry.

The use of a "commonly situated vernacular," however, does not mean that Creeley neglected craft in the shaping of the language into a poem. One of the most distinctive aspects of his style is his precise arrangement of words so that a minimum of material is concentrated to produce an often complex series of meanings; a compact, even sparse poem—unadorned with rhetorical touches that mainly call attention to themselves—that answers Pound's insistence on condensation and compression.

Because Creeley's poetry has removed some of the accumulated verbiage of previous conceptions of the "poetic," it has been described as "thin," whereas it is more accurately lean or trim, with implication replacing unnecessary explanation. As Creeley pointed out, it is not that Williams restricted himself to a colloquial language which never uses words that are less frequently spoken. "What is common is the *mode* of address," Creeley

observed, while the "sense of source in common speech" leads to an authenticity that supports Creeley's ideas that "the local is universal" and that language is the most basic instrument in permitting a poem to "exist through itself," as Olson insists.

While Creeley's poetics remained relatively consistent during the course of their development, the poems he wrote over four decades evolved in terms of their perception of his personal experiences. His first significant book, *For Love: Poems 1950-1960*, contains lyrics, many patterned after classical antecedents, which concentrate on the nature of love, but on a "strained, difficult love relationship" (as John Wilson remarks) in which Creeley, contrary to more recent social developments, attests a kind of primitive maleness endemic in American life.

The conditions that drew the poems, often in pain, from the poet's life are captured in language that seethes with erotic intensity while maintaining a decorum that elevates the work beyond mere confession. The poems are rife with wit, directed at the poet himself as frequently as at the world, but beyond the dark comedy of a man who called an earlier collection a "snarling garland," there is a gentleness, a poignancy that is very affecting.

Poems such as "Ballad of the Despairing Husband" or "The Ball Game" use a comic mood to keep chaos at bay, while "I Know a Man" is "the poem of the decade . . . on a world gone out of control," according to Robert Hass, but beyond these, poems such as "The Name" (addressed to his daughters) or the extraordinary "The Rain" have a depth of feeling produced by words absolutely appropriate for the occasion.

Creeley's next collection, *Words*, moved further from the demands of formal concerns, employing a method Creeley called "scribbling" or "writing for the immediacy of the pleasure." Some of the most severe critical reactions Creeley suffered were directed at poems such as "A Piece," which reads in its entirety:

> One and
> one, two,
> three.

Creeley's concern here was to focus on the process of his thinking and to use both the rhythms of jazz and the techniques of a painter such as Jackson

Pollock, whose paintings reflect the artist's actual placement of paint (words) on the canvas (the page) independent of specific representation. In addition to the poems which emphasize the singular effect of each word, there are longer, more intricate arrangements which move beyond the play of individual units of meaning to the human dimension.

Pieces moves even further in the direction of abstraction but from the position that the poet is interested in establishing a harmony with the natural world. The structural openness that is declared in this collection and which marks Creeley's writing for the next ten years (through the collection *Hello: A Journal, February 29-May 3, 1976*, published in 1978) tends to break the "boundaries of individual poems (as John Wilson observes) so as to emulate what Louis Zukovsky called "continuing *song*." Creeley, in quoting Robert Lowell, mentioned that he moved back to a "more deliberate organization" at the point where he sensed he was at the "edges of incoherence."

In *Pieces* and in other poetry written during the 1970's, Creeley depended on the pacing and rhythms to provide scraps of information; at times, a kind of minimalist reduction became so pervasive that Creeley was, as Louis Martz put it, "at the taut edge of poetic existence."

The poems that appear in his next significant collection, *Later*, do not contradict Creeley's original intentions but give him a wider field for operation. The poetry of the first part of the 1970's used a method Creeley called "a continuity rather than a series of single instances," while *Later* and then *Mirrors* move again toward the strengths of the single poem, although always in the context of the other poems surrounding it. The major change in *Later* is a turn toward the reflective, as Creeley's characteristic expression of immediate thought and feeling in a very specific present is tempered by the reflection of a man who can see his own life as history combining occasion into pattern.

Creeley remarked that he felt *Later* was "a really solid book," and he stopped writing for nearly two years after its publication to take a "breathing space." Realizing in 1981 that he still had "a lot that I wanted to get out," he wrote the poems that were published in *Mirrors* in 1983. In this book, the poetry has a reflective range that does not lessen the impact of Creeley's "luminous austerity" but

merges or mingles it with a new feeling of quiet acceptance. There is a troubled awareness of fatigue, failure, and aging in the poems, but the frustration and confusion expressed in "Age," in which the poet says

> He thinks he'll hate it
> and when he does die
> at last, he supposed
> he still won't know it,

is balanced, even countered, with the sentiments in "Oh Love": "Oh love / like nothing else on earth!"

The strain of philosophical consideration, often presented with Creeley's dry humor, continues in *Memory Gardens*. The book has four sections, the first two containing many terse statements such as "I'll Win," in which the poet reviews his strategy of "being gone / when they come" and summarizes its effect by saying mordantly, "Being dead, then / I'll have won completely."

Such "cryptic epigrams" (as Dudley Fitts called Creeley's earliest poems) alternate with poems specifically written for various friends and several translations/adaptations (or as Creeley put it, "free play on sounds and occasionally understood words") of poems by Richard Anders, whom he met in Berlin. The third section is Creeley's most comprehensive examination of his family background to this point in his life. This group includes meditations about his early life and poems about his parents, such as the deeply affecting "The Doctor," in which images, like fragments of memory, recall the father he hardly knew. The poem closes with the poet's memory still charged with desire to uncover more information.

After the psychic exhilaration and strain of the mental excursion into the realm of his past, Creeley again shifts to a more contemplative mood in section 4, in which a philosophic calendar with a poem for each month matches the spirit of the season to a specific kind of insight. This twelve-part sequence, with some variants on poets such as Thomas Wyatt and Ralph Waldo Emerson, leads toward Creeley's next book, *Windows* (1990), which is a display of virtuosity offering many of the most successful examples of Creeley's voice from previous collections in fresh and vital new poems.

There is a lyric intensity in "Broad Bay," structural compactness in "Tree," explications of language in "Sight," considerations of relationships in "You," terse and penetrating philosophical discourse in "Age," more cryptic epigrams in "Improvisations," linguistic density in "Here," and the familiar sense of the poet working toward versions of his life as occasions of place. This collection seemed to suggest that Creeley's future work would maintain the vigor and clarity of what Charles Molesworth calls "the hard-won specificity of his voice, its timbre, its tremors," which is "like nothing else on earth."

"THE RAIN"

First published: 1962 (collected in *For Love: Poems, 1950-1960*)
Type of work: Poem

The poet, in a contemplative mood at night while listening to rain falling, wishes his love were content in his company.

Among his lyrics that use an image from the natural world as an occasion for an emotional revelation, "The Rain" is one of Creeley's most poignant and successful efforts. It opens with the direct, lean language that is Creeley's special signature:

> All night the sound had
> come back again,
> and again falls
> this quiet, persistent rain.

It then proceeds to a psychological correlative, where the poet asks "What am I to myself" and considers whether "hardness" is permanent, whether he is to "be locked in this/ final uneasiness" that even "rain falling" cannot alleviate.

Then the poem moves beyond observation (of the self in the context of the phenomena of nature) to a fervent declaration of necessity:

> Love, if you love me,
> lie next to me.
> Be for me, like rain,
> the getting out
>
> of the tiredness, the fatuousness, the semi-lust of intentional indifference.

The plague of human frailty, which he condemns in three multisyllabic constructions that stand in stark contrast to the poem's other diction, is a part of the common affliction that dismembers relationships. As a remedy, Creeley then instructs his "love" to "Be wet/ with a decent happiness." The joining of rain, its properties of liquidity and fluidity, with a desirable human attribute unifies everything, and the mixture of the modestly hopeful and the idealistic in the last line perfectly captures the reserved or cautious optimism that is one of Creeley's most appealing features.

"I KEEP TO MYSELF SUCH MEASURES . . ."

First published: 1967 (collected in *The Collected Poems of Robert Creeley, 1945-1975*, 1982)
Type of work: Poem

Concerned about the nebulous nature of language, the poet seeks tangible coordinates with which to measure his perceptions.

The nature of language and its relationship to the physical world and the individual self ("speech is a mouth," Creeley exclaims with audacity in "The Language") is the subject of the poem "I Keep to Myself Such Measures." The title, which is completed in the second line by the very personal " . . . as I care for," is an expression of the poet's interest in dimensions both in his art and in his daily life.

The completing line of the first stanza, "daily the rocks/ accumulate position," uses a concrete object to stand for the accretion of experience, but then, in a dramatic reversal, Creeley qualifies the particularity of the rocks by observing, "There is nothing/ but what thinking makes/ it less tangible," expressing one of his most basic principles: the

Robert Creeley

concern that language is nebulous and that the thought it renders can never be precise or final. Nevertheless, a position is established through the direction ordered by experience, even though that position is never so solid that it cannot be shaken.

The consequence of Creeley's perception that "thinking makes/ it less tangible" compromises sanity itself, leading to uncertainty as a principle of existence:

> The mind
> fast as it goes, loses
>
> pace, puts in place of it
> like rocks simple markers,
> for a way only to
> hopefully come back to
>
> where it cannot.

The "simple markers" to which Creeley refers are the mental coordinates that prove unsatisfactory as permanent guidelines because of the motion—external and internal—that is the source of change in every form of life. The realization that the mind "cannot" come back to a previous position is the burden and fascination of the entire process of perception.

Creeley's attempts to deal with this transitory universe are the focus of his measuring; his creation of the measures in his poems is a figure for a method of seeing that requires a measuring of everything in the personal realm. The "rocks" or "simple markers" cause him to say "My mind sinks" because measure is both a restriction and a point of reference, but because there is no alternative (if the mind is to be maintained at all as a functioning entity), Creeley concludes that "I hold in both hands such weight/ it is my only description." The word "such" retains the ambiguity of the shifting process of measuring, but the tangibility of "both hands" reinforces the importance of the process itself for the man and the poet.

"THERESA'S FRIENDS"

First published: 1979 (collected in *Later,* 1979)

Type of work: Poem

The poet's recollections of his youth are informed by the Boston Irish cultural community that is his heritage.

Creeley was raised by several women after his father died, including his mother, his grandmother, and a slightly retarded woman named Theresa whom his father had brought home to work as a maid. Creeley came to think of her as an "emotional ally" who was not as severe as his family and who needed his friendship in her alien condition. Among the poems Creeley wrote about his family, "Theresa's Friends" is a reminiscence that excludes some of the complex emotional intensity that sometimes almost overwhelms the poet so that here he can enjoy his reflections without feeling forced to wring nuance from every particle of memory.

"From the outset," he recalls, he was "charmed" by the soft, quick speech of Theresa's friends. Typically, it is their use of language that captivates him, the "endlessly present talking" that gave him his first sense of being Irish, which included the cultural mix of "the lore, the magic/ the violence, the comfortable/ or uncomfortable drunkenness." Each of these features is a source of recollective pleasure, not an element to be worried over, and as the poem narrows in focus, an ironmonger is depicted patiently telling the young man "sad, emotional stories/ with the quiet air of an elder." This is a feature of the oral tradition that informs Creeley's work as a poet of sound and speech, and the relaxed, conversational pace of the poem—more like a narrative than most of Creeley's works—sets the structure for a concluding insight that is especially dramatic because of its sudden increase in emotional pitch.

After the gradual preparation he has received from Theresa's friends concerning his cultural heritage, Creeley's mother tells him "at last when I was twenty-one" that "indeed the name *Creeley* was Irish," including him officially in the community of tale and mood toward which he has been drawn. The information comes with the effect of revelation, certifying all that Creeley had instinctively sensed about his origins, his destiny, and his gifts. In an unusually traditional concluding stanza, Creeley raises the level of language to inform and convince the reader/listener fully of the depth of his feeling:

> and the heavens opened, birds sang,
> and the trees and the ladies spoke
> with wondrous voices. The power of the glory
> of poetry—was at last mine.

"THE EDGE"

First published: 1983 (collected in *Mirrors,* 1983)
Type of work: Poem

Uncertainty about everything plagues the poet, who continues to explore the world in language that is itself tentative and uncertain.

The insistent inspection and dissection of linguistic possibility for which Creeley was known reaches a kind of peak in "The Edge." The very short, elliptic word-unit common to Creeley's style throughout his writing life is fused into compact three-line stanzas, which are linked by a continuing focus on edges or boundaries in thought and action, poetry and life. Each stanza has a tentative hold, and then a release into the next one; a hesitancy that occurs after almost every unit of meaning.

Creeley suggests that the poem itself is unclear in its way or course, "this long way comes with no purpose," just as the life it expresses seems unsure of its direction as the poet continues seeking, experimenting, testing, trying, and measuring language and form. Uncertainty does not preclude action, however; the poem's tentativeness is not an indication of paralysis but of an effort to discover a true course after many missteps. The poem itself expresses the poet's desire to construct or discover meaning through the repetition of small actions:

> I take the world and lose it,
> miss it, misplace it,
> put it back or try to, can't
>
> find it, fool it, even feel it.

There is no end to this, and the poem does not have an ending, only another thrust further into being, as the poet proclaims "This must be the edge/ of being before the thought of it! blurs it." As Charles Molesworth aptly observes, poems such as this one are "a dramatization of the limits of Creeley's existential, improvisatory stance," statements where language and thought shift perception even as it occurs.

"FATHERS"

First published: 1986 (collected in *Just in Time: Poems, 1984-1994,* 2001)
Type of work: Poem

The poet is drawn into the difficulties of paternal lineage and the uncertainties that infuse many family histories.

As noted already, one of Creeley's greatest talents as a poet was his ability to reshape language and writing. Whereas many early twentieth century poets prided themselves in clear, sharp images and poignantly articulated rhetoric, Creeley diverged from them in his creative lack of punctuation and syntactical ambiguity. "Fathers" is a prime example of these artistic differences as such, and it can be a difficult poem to understand because of this. Moreover, the form of the poem, its look on the page, its lack of stanza breaks, and its length are somewhat uncharacteristic of Creeley's earlier works. What must be remembered is that the voice of this poem is an interior voice; speaking in to the self rather than out the world, per se.

All of these formalistic nuances, however, are at best a testament to the speaker's need to engage a personal rhetoric in his attempt to rediscover paternal lineage and family history. The first line, "Scattered, aslant"—as in many of Creeley's works— should immediately key us in to the awkward nature of lineages as the poem addresses them. One begins to read on, and by the end of the poem, what little we know of the poet's familial past, let alone his ability to conclude *anything* concrete about it, becomes the penultimate concern for us. It is a poem of images, of "place[s] more tangible" and of "graves" that never give up their most valuable secrets.

The ambiguity of personal definition via a historical reckoning is more finely the point of the poem, and this too can be difficult for readers to grasp. What can clue us in to this notion in the poem itself, however, are the last four lines: "his emptiness, his acerbic/ edge cuts the hands to/ hold him, hold on, wants/ the ground, *wants* this frozen ground." In short, "this resonance" of past lives (from line 20) finds itself, much like the speaker, at a loss for anything other than the "acerbic edge" that refutes and cuts off any satisfactory knowledge of the self in relation to the progenitors that came before us.

"PLAGUE"

First published: 1990 (collected in *Just in Time: Poems, 1984-1994*, 2001)
Type of work: Poem

The poet sees the isolation of patients at a leper hospital as a symbol of human loneliness and reaches for the consolation of human decency to avoid despair.

Although doubt and uncertainty are the climate of much of Creeley's poetry, there is a hard-won hope based on the trials of experience that resists despair or cynicism. In "Plague," a poem written in terse two-line units which are like semidiscrete couplets that lean into each other, the world is described in those times when it has become "a pestilence! a sullen, inexplicable contagion" for the poet. Creeley reaches back toward the medical imagery of his father's life to form a figure for mental disorder, a figure which conveys the feeling of "a painful rush inward, isolate"—akin to a time in his own childhood when he saw "lonely lepers" he knew to be social pariahs "just down the street,/ back of shades drawn, closed doors."

The closeness of the afflicted, the people damned by disease, reminds Creeley of how near to disaster all people are. In times of mental pressure or pain, the poet realizes, anyone may be similarly ravaged, forced to submit to a kind of universal aloneness in which the individual is transformed into an alien "them." "No one talked to them, no one/ held them anymore," he laments soberly. For

a poet who was a master of the considered relationship, this complete absence of even the possibility of love is chilling to contemplate. However, as in an earlier poem in which Creeley called on the rain to inspire "decent happiness," here he reaffirms the reaching, sympathizing impulse in the human spirit in a symbolic evocation of "the faint sun":

> again, we look for the faint sun,
> as they are still there, we hope,
> and we are coming.

A poem such as "Plague" shows how the pared-down, lean lines and the open interconnected images produce "movingly rich emotional testaments" that are impressive explorations of language and self-consciousness—the kind of poetry that Creeley made his own.

"AGE"

First published: 1990 (collected in *Just in Time: Poems, 1984-1994*, 2001)
Type of work: Poem

The poet contemplates old age, its effects on the physical body, on experiences in the past and present, and the self's inevitable journey toward death.

As one can see in much of Creeley's later poetry, age and, more specifically, death take center stage. Of course, there is no fear in the poet's voice. Rather, there is a conscious attempt to define and question the sorts of estrangement one comes to in old age. The first line, "Most explicit," alone makes readers aware of the speaker's devotion to adequately exploring his aged condition. The following nine or ten lines make up the metaphorical significance of that condition "as a narrowing/ cone one's got/ stuck into," and "any movement/ forward simply/ wedges once more." In other words, time and age only move forward, and humankind must move with them despite any reticence to do so.

This realization naturally leads to further questions and eventually, in lines 20-34, the speaker meets a sort of communicative hopelessness; that is, how can the young, who are on the "other side all/ others live on," ever be made aware of the harsh realities and health struggles they too will have to face in life? There is no way to exactly address such communication or answer such a question, as signified in the ellipsis at the end of line 34. Lines 35 through 45 move readers away from such personal experience into a wider, albeit more difficult realm of thinking: the solitary nature of knowing one's own mortality. Oddly enough, these lines usher Creeley's audience into the more hopeful aspects of the poem's subject matter, the companionships one is graced with in life: "*you, you, you/* are crucial," the poet professes to his "love." What matters more than "fears when I may/ cease to be me," however, regards how one comes to any conclusion on such morbid matters through "talks and talks" in the last line.

"Age" is, at length, much less cryptic than many of Creeley's later poems. Some critics argue that "Age" is narrative based rather than language based, as most of his poetry is. Regardless of such arguments, however, it is a poem that is at once frightening and drastically realistic. Creeley was noted as saying, "The world is our physical lifetime." There are few other quotes that can accurately describe the attitude of Creeley's later works and of this poem in particular.

SUMMARY

In one of the best reviews of Creeley's work, the poet and critic Robert Haas said that Creeley's way "has been to take the ordinary, threadbare phrases and sentences by which we locate ourselves and to put them under the immense pressure of the rhythms of poetry and to make out of that what dance or music there can be." In a threefold pattern, Creeley used the postmodern reliance on process (language in action) to reduce the chaos of abstraction, applied the analytic power of the mind to draw specific shape out of the promise of the process, and then applied the core instincts of the human heart striving for love to prevent the analytic reductions of the demands of form from turning all to abstraction again. Often difficult and even irritating, Creeley's poetry at its finest is, as many commentators have pointed out, unlike anything else in the language or literature of the twentieth century.

Leon Lewis; updated by David R. Howell

DISCUSSION TOPICS

- Consider the statement made by Robert Hass that Robert Creeley's way "has been to take the ordinary, threadbare phrases and sentences by which we locate ourselves and to put them under the immense pressure of the rhythms of poetry and to make out of that what dance or music there can be." How would you reconcile what Hass refers to as "the ordinary, threadbare phrases" used in everyday life with the odd rhythms and line breaks in Creeley's verse that seem anything but "ordinary"? What does this mixture suggest about the individuality of Creeley's poetic voice?

- Creeley lost his left eye very early in his life. Is it possible that this physical loss affected Creeley's intellectual take on the world around him? How might such a notion influence the way readers view his poems?

- How do the poems "Plague" and "Age" build upon each other as works focused on taboos? Do they move readers to think solely of mortality and how to deal with it on a daily basis, or does each poem serve to alleviate the fears that society commonly associates with death, loss, and aging?

- Creeley is best known for his experimental uses of rhythm and language. Choose three of his poems and discuss how they differ in form from one another and from other poets from Creeley's era.

- Creeley's most famous statement is, arguably, "form is never more than an extension of content." Discuss this statement as it may pertain to the poems you have read. How do form and content influence each other in any work or art?

- The bulk of Creeley's best-known poetry was written during the 1960's and 1970's. How does his work handle or deal with the historical changes that took place in American society during these years?

Robert Creeley

BIBLIOGRAPHY

By the Author

POETRY:
For Love: Poems, 1950-1960, 1962
Words, 1967
Pieces, 1969
A Day Book, 1972 (includes poetry and prose)
Robert Creeley: An Inventory, 1945-1970, 1973
Hello, 1976, expanded 1978 (as *Hello: A Journal, February 29-May 3, 1976*)
Selected Poems, 1976
Later, 1979
The Collected Poems of Robert Creeley, 1945-1975, 1982
Mirrors, 1983
Memory Gardens, 1986
Window: Paintings, 1988 (paintings by Martha Visser't Hooft)
Selected Poems, 1991
Life and Death, 1993, expanded 1998
Echoes, 1994
So There: Poems, 1976-1983, 1998
For Friends, 2000
Drawn and Quartered, 2001 (with Archie Rand, artist)
Just in Time: Poems, 1984-1994, 2001
If I Were Writing This, 2003

LONG FICTION:
The Island, 1963

SHORT FICTION:
The Gold Diggers, 1954, expanded 1965 (as *The Gold Diggers, and Other Stories*)
Mabel: A Story and Other Prose, 1976

NONFICTION:
A Quick Graph, 1970
Presences, 1976
Charles Olson and Robert Creeley: The Complete Correspondence, 1980-1996 (10 volumes)
Collected Essays, 1989
Day Book of a Virtual Poet, 1998

EDITED TEXTS:
Mayan Letters, 1953 (by Charles Olson)
Selected Writings of Charles Olson, 1966
Selected Poems, 1993 (by Olson)
The Best American Poetry, 2002, 2002
George Oppen: Selected Poems, 2003

MISCELLANEOUS:
The Collected Prose, 1984 (novel, stories, radio play)

About the Author
Allen, Donald, ed. *Contexts of Poetry: Interviews with Robert Creeley, 1961-1971.* Bolinas, Calif.: Four Seasons, 1973.

Clark, Tom. *Robert Creeley and the Genius of the American Commonplace.* New York: New Directions, 1993.

Edelberg, Cynthia. *Robert Creeley's Poetry: A Critical Introduction.* Albuquerque: University of New Mexico Press, 1978.

Faas, Ekbert, and Maria Trombaco. *Robert Creeley: A Biography.* Hanover, N.H.: University Press of New England, 2001.

Ford, Arthur. *Robert Creeley.* Boston: G. K. Hall, 1978.

Foster, Edward Halsey. *Understanding the Black Mountain Poets.* Columbia: University of South Carolina Press, 1995.

Fox, Willard. *Robert Creeley, Edward Dorn, and Robert Duncan: A Reference Guide.* Boston: G. K. Hall, 1989.

Oberg, Arthur. *Modern American Lyric: Lowell, Berryman, Creeley, and Plath.* New Brunswick, N.J.: Rutgers University Press, 1977.

Rifkin, Libbie. *Career Moves: Olson, Creeley, Zukofsky, Berrigan, and the American Avant-Garde.* Madison: University of Wisconsin Press, 2000.

Terrell, Carroll, ed. *Robert Creeley: The Poet's Workshop.* Orono, Maine: National Poetry Foundation, 1984.

Wilson, John, ed. *Robert Creeley's Life and Work: A Sense of Increment.* Ann Arbor: University of Michigan Press, 1987.

COUNTÉE CULLEN

Born: New York, N.Y., or Louisville, Ky., or Baltimore, Md.
May 30, 1903
Died: New York, New York
January 9, 1946

Cullen was a major figure in the Harlem Renaissance, a literary movement associated with African American writers in New York City in the 1920's. Though primarily a poet who wrote in standard forms, Cullen also wrote a novel, plays, and children's literature.

BIOGRAPHY

The early life of Countée Cullen is shrouded in mystery. His birthplace was probably Louisville, Kentucky, but New York City and Baltimore have also been suggested. He may have been raised by his paternal grandmother, but at age fifteen, he was adopted by the Reverend and Mrs. F. A Cullen, though the adoption may never have been made official. Reverend Cullen was minister of Salem Methodist Episcopalian Church, a large congregation in Harlem, New York.

Cullen attended DeWitt Clinton High School in New York City, a school famous for its excellence. In 1922, he entered New York University. In 1925, he was elected to Phi Beta Kappa, won first prize in the Witter Bynner Poetry Contest, published *Color* (an impressive volume of poems), and entered Harvard University. In 1926, he completed a Master of Arts degree at Harvard and accepted a position as assistant editor at *Opportunity*, a magazine for which he wrote a regular poetry column.

Some critics argue that Cullen's later works did not fulfill the promise of his early writings, but he published widely and regularly: *Copper Sun* (1927); *The Ballad of the Brown Girl: An Old Ballad Retold* (1927); *Caroling Dusk* (1927); *The Black Christ, and Other Poems* (1929); *One Way to Heaven* (1932); *The Medea, and Some Poems* (1935); *The Lost Zoo (A Rhyme for the Young, but Not Too Young)* (1940); *My Lives and How I Lost Them* (1942).

In 1934, he accepted a teaching position at Frederick Douglass Junior High School in New York City, where he taught primarily African American children, including James Baldwin, who himself became a well-known writer two decades later.

Like his early life, Cullen's personal life was mysterious. In 1928, he married Yolande Du Bois, the daughter of distinguished intellectual W. E. B. Du Bois, but soon after the marriage he traveled to France without his wife. The couple divorced in 1930. Some scholars suggest that Cullen may have had a homosexual relationship with fellow writer Harold Jackman, but no substantiation of this observation exists. In 1940, Cullen married Ida Mae Roberson. In 1946, he died of uremic poisoning.

ANALYSIS

Orderliness is a hallmark of Cullen's work. In "Yet Do I Marvel," Cullen's faith in the orderliness of God's inexplicable creation is reinforced by the orderliness in the design of the poem, which is a sonnet. The first eight lines present apparent difficulties for human comprehension; the next four lines postulate that God's ways, when seen from the mortal frame, are seemingly unjust, but if God's ways could be seen from God's perspective, then his justice would be clear. The final two lines give the problem poignancy, but faith in God is assured by the wonder of God's creation. All lines are neatly and naturally rhymed (*ababcdcdeeffgg*), and the poem is executed in iambic pentameter. Thus Cullen's poem pits the orderliness of writing against any questions about the orderliness of God's creation, and the fact that Cullen, an African American poet, is singing eloquently, proves that "Yet Do I Marvel" is a poem of affirmation.

Beyond metrical patterns and rhyme schemes, Cullen in "Yet Do I Marvel" provides a range of literary references. He begins with common references, citing the mole and the human. Cullen elevates the discussion through classical allusions, citing the story of Tantalus, who stole nectar and ambrosia from the gods and was condemned to starve while food was just beyond his reach. In addition, Cullen alludes to the myth of Sisyphus, who sought to elude eternity, but faced eternal frustration in his efforts to ascend stairs (or, in some accounts, to push a boulder up a hill).

Although orderliness is a key factor in Cullen's work, in "To John Keats, Poet. At Spring Time," Cullen shows that the poem, like springtime, can be a vibrant combination of regularity and variety. Four stanzas of varying lengths (ten lines, fourteen lines, twelve lines, and ten lines) seem to proceed in four-line units with alternating rhyme, but couplets end the stanzas. In the second stanza, perhaps in tribute to Keats, the rhyme scheme exhibits flashes of freedom (*ababaccdcdeeff*).

"To John Keats, Poet. At Spring Time" opens with an apostrophe as Cullen addresses John Keats, a person who cannot literally respond to Cullen's address. Spring is personified as Cullen suggests that spring has a voice, cheeks, breasts, and shoulders. In the concluding stanza, dramatic irony is at work because Cullen allows the reader to know more than the observers who think that Cullen's response to spring is strange. Unlike the observers, readers have the privilege of knowing the force of Keats in Cullen's mind and can share Cullen's delight in springtime and Keats's voice.

In "Heritage," Cullen adopts a swift pace that underscores the idea of thoughts racing through the poet's mind. The rhymed couplets, which prevail in the poem with few exceptions, reinforce the sense of alternation in thinking between African heritage and African American identity. The persistence of the problem of heritage is brought out through the four-line refrain, which ends, "What is Africa to me?" The intensity of the recurring thoughts is made clear through italicized lines. Perhaps the subtlest effects in "Heritage" arise from irony. Cullen's description of African heritage creates an ironic discrepancy between the realities of

African culture and the stereotypical impressions of jungles and heathens. Cullen ironically toys with his reader, testing the reader's awareness of African identity. Even greater irony emerges in Cullen's use of the word "civilized." An ironic discrepancy arises between the presumed refinement and education of the poet's world and the presumed barbarism of African heritage. In the end, a society that includes hatred, cruelty, war, and lynching can be no more civilized than a land of lions, snakes, and heathens. The fact that the choice between these alternative worlds is tormenting to the poet should ultimately be no surprise to the reader.

In "Uncle Jim," Cullen resorts to the orderliness of the ballad, with alternation of tetrameter and trimeter in four-line stanzas. In each of the four stanzas, the second and fourth lines rhyme. By quoting Uncle Jim, the speaker reveals African American idiom, but the reply from the speaker displays haughty sophistication. Irony provides the basis for the conclusion as the educated speaker begins to realize that Uncle Jim, not the educated speaker, had the most accurate view of the world of race.

In all, Cullen is a traditional poet who writes eloquently in traditional forms, revealing the influence of John Keats and A. E. Housman. Though Cullen explores the difficulties of African American identity, he is sometimes set aside by readers who insist that African American writers should write in their own idiom and express themes related to their own culture instead of following the models of classic white predecessors.

"YET DO I MARVEL"

First published: 1925 (collected in *Color,* 1925)
Type of work: Poem

In "Yet Do I Marvel," Cullen explores the problem of justifying the ways of God to humankind.

"Yet Do I Marvel" opens with a declaration of faith in God's ways, and this faith is sustained through the first twelve lines. God is "good, well-meaning, kind," and he does not need to explain his creation or his actions to humankind; however, if God were to "stoop" to humankind's level, he could explain why the mole must be blind; why humans, who are made in God's image, are mortal; why Tantalus is perpetually baited and left unsatisfied; why Sisyphus must experience futility in his efforts to ascend. Nevertheless, to those in the mortal world, God's ways are beyond explanation because the petty distractions in immediate surroundings leave the universal picture beyond view.

The concluding couplet in Cullen's poem, despite the affirmation of faith in the first twelve lines, raises a problem that at first inspection seems to go beyond faith: why does God "make a poet black," thereby making him or her endure endless injustices and distress, if God intends that the black poet should also "sing"? This creation seems beyond human comprehension, but Cullen's reaction is not anger or frustration; indeed, faith is heightened by a "curious thing" that causes the poet to "marvel." In the end, the example that seems furthest from possible explanation stands out as the greatest affirmation of faith.

"TO JOHN KEATS, POET. AT SPRING TIME"

First published: 1925 (collected in *Color,* 1925)

Type of work: Poem

In "To John Keats, Poet. At Spring Time," Cullen describes the emotional excitement he feels as he witnesses the arrival of spring; Cullen pays tribute to John Keats, the immortal poet whose writings reveal an extraordinary sensitivity to spring's power to awaken the earth and the human spirit.

Countée Cullen in "To John Keats, Poet. At Spring Time" speaks to Keats as if he were alive. For Cullen, Keats's response to the beauty of spring cannot be extinguished or suppressed, even in death. Keats is the author who is most sensitive to beauty, and as Cullen beholds the magnificent spring of 1924, he cannot stifle his feeling that the spirit of Keats is coexistent with the grandeur of the season.

Spring arrives with a "tocsin call," and blossoms are so abundant that they seem to envelop the "breast" of spring with "drifts of snow." The dormancy of winter is at an end: white birds flit about the "shoulders" of spring and "kiss her cheeks." Lilacs bloom and contribute to the scene with fragrance and varied colors.

The resurgence of life in spring makes Cullen sense the resurgence of Keats's voice. True, Keats lies as dust in his grave, but for Cullen, Keats's spirit runs with the sap in maple trees and makes music in the leaves, just as the wind blowing through the strings of an Aeolian harp makes wondrous sound. For Cullen, the call of spring is so strong that Keats, the great dead poet, renews his life.

In contrast to Cullen, others cannot sense the vibrant spirit of Keats. When Cullen bows his head in reverence to Keats's "full insistent cry," others find that Cullen's behavior is "strange" and believe that an ecstasy prompted by the simple arrival of a new season is an unwarranted response, perhaps even a sign of insanity. However, these observers lack the privilege of Cullen, who not only savors spring's gorgeous arrival, but also delights in the vibrant company of Keats.

"HERITAGE"

First published: 1925 (collected in *Color,* 1925)

Type of work: Poem

"Heritage" explores the questions of ancestry and national identity for the African American individual in the twentieth century.

"Heritage" opens in the interrogative, posing a question about the significance of the African continent to Cullen, offering hypothetical answers that have their basis in myths and stereotypes. For the young African American poet, is Africa a blend of colors, including copper, scarlet, bronze, and black? Is Africa a jungle or an Eden? Does Africa have special stars, paths, and scents? Is Africa the poet's royal birthplace? The speculation returns the poet to his original question, now repeated in italics for emphasis: "*What is Africa to me?*"

In the second stanza, the poet admits that he would prefer not to hear "wild barbaric birds" and "massive jungle herds," that he would prefer not to envision "tall defiant grass" and "young forest lovers"; however, even as he stops his ears with his thumbs, "drums throbbing" fill his mind. The predicament of the African American poet is that "pride," "distress," and "joy" combine in his consideration of African ancestry.

The third stanza reveals weariness with the responsibility to know ancestry. A book on African culture induces sleep, not interest, and the details of bats, predatory cats, shiny snakes, and dangerous flowers seem remote and without significance. Like a tree that in previous seasons blossomed, bore fruit, and was a home for wildlife, the African American poet "must forget" the past and work with what the present offers in a new season.

Despite the claim that African heritage is remote and uninteresting, the question of heritage haunts the poet. If the poet seeks rest, he can "find no peace" because within himself he feels the pounding of feet on a jungle path. At night an extraordinary rain implores him to be naked and "dance the Lover's Dance!"

The struggle with ancestry reaches a peak with the question of religion. On one hand, the poet considers "outlandish heathen gods," and on the other hand, he measures his own devotion to Jesus Christ. He concludes, "Heathen gods are naught to me." Even with this conclusion, the poet admits that he plays a "double part." Jesus Christ, in the poet's imagination, is white, and in being white, Christ is insufficiently satisfying. If Jesus were black, the poet would have a "kindred woe" and following Jesus would be easier. For this questioning of Christ, the poet appeals for indulgence: "Lord forgive me if my need/ Sometimes shapes a human creed."

The final stanza, set in italics to convey intensity, reaches a conclusion that returns to the theme of the "double part." Within the poet's "heart or head," a potential exists for a full reversion to African ancestry; the poet must satisfy "pride" and moderate the heat in his "blood," because, as he as-

serts in closing, he, his heart, and his head have yet to realize that they "are civilized."

"UNCLE JIM"

First published: 1927 (collected in *Copper Sun*, 1927)
Type of work: Poem

In "Uncle Jim," Cullen presents the contrast between the experienced African American, who has learned the ways of white people, and the inexperienced African American, who insists that white people are not all alike and that some are worthy of friendship.

Uncle Jim declares, "White folks is white," and the grammatical deficiency of his sentence seems to show his ignorance. The speaker of the poem dismisses Uncle Jim's remark, insisting that milk and the foam on beer are also white. Not pleased to be rejected, Uncle Jim smokes his pipe and in reply seems to insist that with time the young man will see that Uncle Jim knows what he is talking about.

In the third stanza, the poem turns to a friend of the poet—a drinking partner who commiserates with the young African American. Apparently the friends drink to excess, even as the drinking partner raises toasts to the speaker's "joy," because the companions are soon "face-in-the-grass."

The emptiness of this friendship and the activity connected with it teach a moral lesson. Perhaps the speaker is not made fully wise, but something about the friendship or the friend apparently dawns on the speaker, whose mind turns to Uncle Jim.

SUMMARY

Countée Cullen was an accomplished artist whose work in standard forms modeled by famous literary artists, such as John Keats, earned him a bright reputation at an early age. He published in distinguished literary magazines, demonstrating an ability to function in both black and white literary circles and drawing praise from critics across the racial spectrum. His distinguished academic career led to sustained literary production in various forms, but *Color*, his first volume of poems, brings together most of his memorable works, including "Yet Do I Marvel," "Heritage," and "To John Keats, Poet. At Spring Time."

Cullen retains an important place in literary history as part of the Harlem Renaissance, but some critics lament that Cullen relied too heavily on white literary predecessors and did not go far enough in establishing African American idiom and culture in his works.

William T. Lawlor

BIBLIOGRAPHY

By the Author

POETRY:
Color, 1925
The Ballad of the Brown Girl: An Old Ballad Retold, 1927
Copper Sun, 1927
The Black Christ, and Other Poems, 1929
The Medea, and Some Poems, 1935
On These I Stand: An Anthology of the Best Poems of Countée Cullen, 1947

LONG FICTION:
One Way to Heaven, 1932

DRAMA:
Medea, pr., pb. 1935 (translation of Euripides)
One Way to Heaven, pb. 1936 (adaptation of his novel)
St. Louis Woman, pr. 1946 (adaptation of Arna Bontemps's novel *God Sends Sunday*)
The Third Fourth of July, pr., pb. 1946 (musical)

CHILDREN'S LITERATURE:
The Lost Zoo (A Rhyme for the Young, but Not Too Young), 1940
My Lives and How I Lost Them, 1942

EDITED TEXT:
Caroling Dusk, 1927

About the Author

Cullen, Countée. *My Soul's High Song: The Collected Writings of Countée Cullen, Voice of the Harlem Renaissance.* Edited by Gerald Early. New York: Anchor Books, 1991.
Fetrow, Fred M. "Cullen's 'Yet Do I Marvel.'" *Explicator* 56, no. 2 (Winter, 1998): 103-106.
Goldweber, David E. "Cullen, Keats, and the Privileged Liar." *Papers on Language and Literature* 38, no. 1 (Winter, 2002): 29-49.
Lomax, Michael L. "Countée Cullen: A Key to the Puzzle." In *The Harlem Renaissance Re-examined,* edited by Victor A. Kramer. New York: AMS Press, 1987.
Powers, Peter. "'The Singing Man Who Must Be Reckoned With': Private Desire and Public Responsibility in the Poetry of Countée Cullen." *African American Review* 34, no. 4 (Winter, 2000): 661-679.
Shucard, Alan R. *Countée Cullen.* Boston: Twayne, 1984.
Turner, Darwin T. "Countée Cullen: The Lost Ariel." In *In a Minor Chord: Three African American Writers and Their Search for Identity.* Carbondale: Southern Illinois University Press, 1971.

DISCUSSION TOPICS

- How do rhyme, meter, and stanzaic patterns reinforce the themes of Countée Cullen?
- In "Heritage," what problems does Cullen face as he tries to reconcile African heritage with African American identity?
- What arguments exist for and against the claim that Cullen is a literary hero for African Americans?
- In "Yet Do I Marvel," how does Cullen present racial injustice as part of God's orderly creation?
- Why does John Keats earn the admiration of Cullen?
- Why are some things about Cullen easy to explain, while other things remain a mystery?

E. E. CUMMINGS

Born: Cambridge, Massachusetts
October 14, 1894
Died: North Conway, New Hampshire
September 3, 1962

Though he is recognized as a writer whose poetic experiments added significantly to the development of modern literature, E. E. Cummings also contributed to the development of other forms of literature, including autobiography.

BIOGRAPHY

The first of two children born to Edward Cummings and Rebecca Haswell Clarke, E. E. Cummings was raised in a curious milieu for a rebel poet. He virtually grew up in Harvard Yard and was surrounded by the most traditional aspects of Cambridge culture. His father, an instructor in sociology who later became a Unitarian churchman, instructed his son to pass the collection plate during certain church services. One of the few deviations from this elite, exclusive upbringing was E. E. Cummings's time in public high school, the result of one of his father's democratic ideas.

In 1911, Cummings entered Harvard University. He lived at home during the first three years of his university education. He wrote for the *Harvard Monthly*, publishing his first poems in that journal in 1912. He graduated from Harvard magna cum laude in 1915, and he delivered the commencement address, titled "The New Art." During his undergraduate years at Harvard, Cummings demonstrated a revolutionary and rebellious attitude toward traditional, conventional art and literature, an attitude that would be characteristic of Cummings throughout his life.

After receiving his M.A. from Harvard in 1916, Cummings moved to New York City and spent three months in an office job. The following year he sailed for France as a volunteer in the Norton Harjes Ambulance Corps of the American Red Cross. His four-month imprisonment by French authorities on suspicion of disloyalty provided the basis for his first autobiography, *The Enormous Room*, published in 1922. Released from prison on New Year's Day, 1918, Cummings returned to New York City, where he lived in Greenwich Village.

In 1920, Cummings made his first major appearance in *The Dial*, a literary magazine that was a vehicle for most of the leading artists of the time. From 1921 to 1923, he made his first trip to Paris, where he met many leading avant-garde figures who found Paris to be a lively and stimulating place for art and artists. Cummings lived in Paris intermittently throughout the 1920's and made numerous trips abroad throughout his life. When he returned to the United States in 1923, he took up permanent residence in New York City, spending the summers at Joy Farm, his family's summer home, in Silver Lake, New Hampshire. His return to New York coincided with the publication of the first of twelve volumes of poetry, *Tulips and Chimneys* (1923), all of which revealed Cummings's effort to experiment with language, structure, and ideas.

Cummings was married three times: first to Elaine On in 1924, then to Anne Barton in 1927, and finally to Marion Morehouse in 1932. While he was dealing with these personal changes, he wrote prolifically: nearly eight hundred poems, plays, ballets, fairy tales, and autobiographies. He also produced a number of drawings and watercolors, having his first major showing of paintings at the Painters and Sculptors Gallery, New York City, in 1931. Other shows were held at the American British Art Center and the Rochester Memorial Art Gallery.

During his life, E. E. Cummings was recognized for both the quantity and quality of his work. He was awarded two Guggenheim Fellowships, the first in 1933—the year his book *Eimi*, based on a trip to Russia, was published—and the second in 1951. He was also awarded a fellowship of the American Academy of Poets in 1950 and a National Book Awards special citation in 1955. In 1957, Cummings received the Bollingen Prize in Poetry as well as the Boston Arts Festival Award.

Despite this public recognition of his work and despite his position as the Charles Eliot Norton Professor at Harvard during 1952-1953, Cummings was a private person. Toward the end of his life he made few public appearances except for a series of lectures at Harvard and readings of his poetry to mostly undergraduate audiences. He became partly crippled by arthritis and wore a brace that forced him to conduct these readings while sitting in a straight-backed kitchen chair. He would read for a half hour, rest, then return to finish the program, charming audiences with his poetry and personality. Cummings died in 1962, having worked to the last day of his life.

ANALYSIS

Because of his idiosyncratic punctuation and typography, E. E. Cummings is often labeled an experimentalist, and indeed his art is innovative and revolutionary. One of the most curious aspects of Cummings's work, however, is that it combines experimentation with tradition, a point Gertrude Stein noted in her book *The Autobiography of Alice B. Toklas* (1933):

> Gertrude Stein who had been much impressed by *The Enormous Room* said that Cummings did not copy, he was the natural heir of the New England tradition with its aridity and its sterility, but also with its individuality.

In all of his works—prose, poetry, drama, and autobiography—Cummings celebrated this quality of individuality, seeing it as the legacy of his New England upbringing and also as the outstanding characteristic of modernism. For Cummings, individuality was both a theme and a technique. Thematically, it was a faith in a world in which the inde-

pendent, alive, living individual struggled against the cerebral, joyless nonindividual. Cummings celebrated the existence of the individual and satirized the boring, mechanistic lives of nonindividuals. Technically, individuality was at the core of Cummings's experiments with word coinings, free verse, innovations with typography and punctuation, and other strategies that make his literature, especially his poetry, look and sound different from almost any other artist's work, especially those who preceded him. Thematically and technically, then, Cummings was committed to individuality, a dedication he made clear during one of his six "nonlectures" at Harvard: "Let us pray always for individuals; never for worlds."

The individuals for whom Cummings prays and about whom he writes inhabit a particular kind of universe. It is, first of all, a place that is natural, not created by human beings, and it is a place in which nature is process, not product. To understand this place and the people within it requires intuition and imagination, not mere intellectualizing. Thus Cummings is constantly criticizing those who believe they can rely only upon reason, while he praises those who try to understand with their hearts and their emotions.

Cummings's true individuals are lovers, artists, clowns, circus people, or adolescents—those who, in his view, challenge both society and labels. They are connected by their freedom—their vital need to be independent—and they typically demonstrate that independence by challenging those who embody convention, tradition, and mechanization. Politicians, soldiers, bureaucrats, and "Cambridge ladies" are targets of their assaults, for all those individuals not only represent categories themselves but they also attempt to label, and thus limit, the freedom of others.

In his poetry, Cummings uses several strategies to explore his ideas about individuality. He coins words so that nouns are made of verbs, creating a sense of nonstop motion and forcing the reader to become actively involved in the poem. He also distorts the syntax of sentences so that it is impossible to read his works in a traditional way of identifying subject-verb-object. Still another strategy is visual—setting up the poem on a page so that it looks different from the traditional, linear lyric, thus compelling the reader to move back and forth within the poem, making meaning out of the motion of reading as well as out of the words being read. Taken together, these strategies emphasize process: the process of being alive—a hallmark of a true individual—and the process of reading.

His other literary forms demonstrate this same celebratory stance. In his autobiographies—*The Enormous Room* and *Eimi*—Cummings honors the individuals who transcend the boundaries of society. Whether they are the prisoners in the French army camp or citizens in Russia, individuals who listen to and learn from their hearts and who are independent and self-reliant are the objects of Cummings's praise. In his plays and ballets and other works, the same kind of people are honored, and, by contrast, their opposites are parodied and satirized.

THE ENORMOUS ROOM

First published: 1922
Type of work: Autobiography

A self-portrait in which Cummings describes his captivity in a French prison during World War I.

The Enormous Room is Cummings's autobiographical narrative of the time he spent in La Ferté Mace, a French concentration camp a hundred miles west of Paris. Cummings and a friend, both members of an American ambulance corps in France during World War I, were erroneously suspected of treasonable correspondence and were imprisoned from August, 1917, until January, 1918. In this book, Cummings describes the prisoners with whom he shared his captivity, the captors who subjected their victims to enormous cruelty, and the filthy surroundings of the prison camp.

Written in the form of a pilgrimage and modeled after John Bunyan's *Pilgrim's Progress* (1678), Cummings's narrative also shows the influence of early American black autobiographies. Like Christian in *Pilgrim's Progress* and the slaves who wrote their own stories, the narrator in Cummings's self-portrait faces an arduous journey to freedom, a voyage not unlike the ones described in many early black autobiographies also modeled on Bunyan's classic. In Cummings's voyage, the autobiogra-

pher emphasizes and celebrates his belief in individuality, especially as it is seen in the characters of the prisoners, including the gypsy dubbed Wanderer, the childish giant named Jean le Nègre, and the clownish captive called Surplice.

In *The Enormous Room*, the reader follows the enslaved Cummings along three legs of his journey: first, the period before La Ferté Mace; then, the period beginning with the second day in the enormous room; and finally, the departure from the French prison. During the first part of the autobiographical journey, Cummings appears as a rebellious American soldier parodying the rhetoric of wartime communication in his description of dissension within the ranks:

To borrow a characteristic-cadence from Our Great President: the lively satisfaction which we might be suspected of having derived from the accomplishment of a task so important in the saving of civilization from the clutches of Prussian tyrany [sic] was in some degree inhibited, unhappily, by a complete absence of cordial relations between the man whom fate had placed over us and ourselves. Or, to use the vulgar American idiom, B. and I and Mr. A. didn't get on well.

Rebellious and independent, the young Cummings quickly learns the price of asserting these two qualities: He is imprisoned and joins a multitude of other captives who try desperately, and usually successfully, to retain their individuality despite their captors' efforts to rob them of this quality.

Enclosed in the space he calls "the Enormous Room," Cummings is entrapped in an oblong room eighty feet by forty feet. This room in La Ferté Mace both restricts and unites an international menagerie of humanity (Dutch, Belgian, Spanish, Turkish, Arabian, Polish, Russian, Swedish, German, French, and English), including the American animal, E. E. Cummings. Among the most memorable of these fellow prisoners is Surplice—the court jester of the enormous room, the fool, the scapegoat, the eternal victim—who occupies an important spot in both the prison and the world, as Cummings notes: "After all, men in La Misère as well as anywhere also rightly demand a certain amount of amusement; amusement is, indeed, peculiarly essential to suffering; in proportion as we are able to be amused we are able to suffer." Cummings's description of this classic notion of scapegoating is especially poignant because he is describing himself as well as his readers: "I, Surplice," says Cummings, "am a very necessary creature after all."

Another memorable prisoner with whom Cummings shares his space is Zulu, thus called, says Cummings, partly because he looks like something Cummings had never seen, partly because the sounds of the two syllables appeared to relate to his personality, and partly because Zulu seemed to like the name. Cummings is particularly attracted to this prisoner because Zulu embodies the qualities that Cummings cherishes: individuality, vitality, emotion, and timelessness. Zulu is "A Verb; an IS," according to Cummings, meaning that he is an example of life and action—as a verb represents action—not a victim of passivity, the quality Cummings associates with nouns.

His insights into scapegoating and verbs are two of the many lessons Cummings learns during his captivity; they are lessons that contribute to the changes that occur within him and that result in his being a different person when he leaves La Ferté Mace. Having entered the prison as a youthful soldier who flippantly used language to parody wartime rhetoric and officials, he leaves the prison as a more thoughtful individual, one who sees the power of language to celebrate the wonders of life and individuality. As he prepares to leave the prison, he writes a poem, not only the first stanza of a ballad, as he had done in the beginning of his journey, when he had hoped that the next day he would write the second, the day after, the third, and the next day, the refrain—never having done any of it.

On the boat to America, Cummings is surrounded by strangers, and when he arrives in New York he is struck by the image of anonymous Americans, hurrying about in a frenzy of activity. He sees New York differently from the time he left it because he himself is different. This final scene in *The Enormous Room*, a picture of separateness yet potential connectedness, reflects the basic lesson that

Cummings learned from his education in prison: He can neither completely nor permanently unite himself with others. He can, however, celebrate his individuality, his sense of self, and his gratitude for being alive and able to use language to describe his journey into and out of La Ferté Mace and the trips that lie ahead of him.

One of the strengths of *The Enormous Room* is that it explores several important issues, including war, society, and language. In the tradition of war novels, it protests the war, but it is more of a parody than a protest, as Cummings uses humor to present his view of people. Thus one has the *plantons*, the cruel jailers, whom Cummings depicts with a mixture of mockery and sympathy, and the prisoners, whom Cummings describes with humor and joy as they find ways to remain individuals despite the efforts of their captors to dehumanize their innocent victims.

The Enormous Room is a book about society insofar as it protests society's tendencies toward dehumanization, nonreflection, mechanization, and overintellectualizing. Amid his descriptions of prisoners and jailers, Cummings inserts his protestations about education, government, and religion, suggesting that these institutions rob people of their individuality.

The Enormous Room is also about language, the vehicle that Cummings manipulates for two reasons: to show the dangers of empty rhetoric and to help readers see the world in a new way. Like other artists during and after World War I, including Ernest Hemingway, who objected to the lofty words that frequently concealed reality, Cummings protests the politicians' words that, in his view, were largely responsible for the "Great War." Cummings uses language as art—art that is intended to help people see in a new way. Thus he describes the prisoners, whom he calls Delectable Mountains, in poetic terms that force the reader to see these characters as beautiful individuals, not as dirty criminals.

Finally, *The Enormous Room* is about Cummings, the prisoner who begins his captivity as a young Harvard graduate and who grows through the process so that he is able to transcend his Cambridge roots and connect with prisoners whose lack of education and sophistication taught him who he was and wanted to be. At the conclusion of the book, when Cummings returns to New York, he is a different person, one who has recaptured the joy of childhood and the importance of being an individual who celebrates humanity, life, and love.

"IN JUST-"

First published: 1920 (collected in *Tulips and Chimneys*, 1923)

Type of work: Poem

This lyric is about the time that immediately follows winter.

One of Cummings's most famous poems, "in Just-" reveals the poet's typically experimental approach, avoiding all punctuation to emphasize the nonstop vitality of a season he describes as "mud-/ luscious" and "puddle-wonderful." A goat-footed balloonman whistles; children play hopscotch, jump-rope, and marbles; and the world celebrates the season that can only be described as "Just-spring."

The poem is divided into five sections, with a format that matches the sense of dance and music that are described in the lyric. Contrasts are important—the slow tune of "Just-/ spring" and "mud-/ luscious" is juxtaposed with the speed of "and eddieandbill come/ running from marbles and/ piracies and it's/ spring." The poem, like the season, is a mixture of contrasts, from old balloonman to young children, from the slow, quiet time of growth to the rapid, explosive moments of ecstasy. Taken together, these contrasts describe a season which has no word in the English language except for Cummings's coined phrase: "Just-spring."

"ALL IN GREEN WENT MY LOVE RIDING"

First published: 1923 (collected in *Tulips and Chimneys*, 1923)

Type of work: Poem

The myth of Diana slaying Actaeon is recreated.

"All in green went my love riding" is an example of Cummings's use of an ancient myth to communicate his message to a modern audience. The poem

is about courtly love, and it alludes to the Roman and Greek myth in which Diana or Artemis, goddess and protectress of wildlife, is challenged by the hunter Actaeon. The goddess changes Actaeon into a stag, whereupon Actaeon's own hounds attack and kill him. Cummings retells this story, using fourteen stanzas, each of which paints a graphic picture that chronicles a part of this chase.

The poem is replete with colors: the green garb of a lover, the golden color of the horse, the silver dawn, the redness of the roebuck, the whiteness of water. It is equally specific in other details, such as numbers: There are four hounds and four deer. These and other details paint a picture that combines beauty with terror; the beauty of the place and the lover are enveloped in the ominous atmosphere of death.

Told from the view of Diana or Artemis, this poem describes the chase, beginning with Actaeon's departure and concluding with his death and Diana's swoon. Though the poem ends with these images, it is not a lyric about finality or mortality. On the contrary, it is about vitality and life, for the lovers are united in their ecstasy, just as the poem is united by its repetition (with the variation in the final line) of the first and last two stanzas. Thus the color green, the color of life, connects the lovers, who themselves are joined in the cycle of life and death.

"THE CAMBRIDGE LADIES WHO LIVE IN FURNISHED SOULS"

First published: 1923 (collected in *Collected Poems*, 1938)

Type of work: Poem

This poem satirizes people whom Cummings viewed as aristocratic snobs.

A sonnet, "the Cambridge ladies who live in furnished souls" attacks a broad group of people who, Cummings believed, populated Cambridge, Massachusetts, and many other locales. These faculty wives, church women, and literary society ladies are described in careful detail, beginning with the first line, in which they are seen in terms of the stuffy Victorian rooms in which many of them reside.

They have "comfortable minds," suggesting their lack of individuality and originality, and daughters who are like themselves: "unscented shapeless spirited."

These Cambridge ladies believe in Christ and the American poet Henry Wadsworth Longfellow, "both dead." They themselves are also dead, unaware that, above their stuffy rooms and beyond their stuffy lives, the "moon rattles like a fragment of angry candy." Isolated in their artificial world, they engage in meaningless banter, oblivious of the wonders of the natural world within and around them.

"I SING OF OLAF GLAD AND BIG"

First published: 1931 (collected in *W: Seventy New Poems*, 1931)
Type of work: Poem

The poem sings the praises of Olaf, a conscientious objector.

The opening line of "i sing of Olaf glad and big" announces the poet's intention: to sing, to celebrate, the greatness of an individual who bravely defies convention and who heroically dies because of his act of rebellion. Olaf's "warmest heart recoiled at war," so he became a conscientious objector, subjecting himself to cruel harassment at the hands of a "trig westpointer"—a graduate of the United States Military Academy at West Point. Like the Delectable Mountains in *The Enormous Room*, Olaf stands his ground and announces to his tormentor that he will not kiss the flag that he represents.

Described as "a conscientious object-or," Olaf becomes an "object" to the officers who treat him as cruelly as the *plantons* treated the prisoners in La Ferté Mace. Olaf continues in his opposition to war, however, and is thrown into prison for his defiant stance. His tragic, heroic death causes the poet

to sing his praises and to question conventional notions of courage: "unless statistics lie he was/ more brave than me: more blond than you."

"ANYONE LIVED IN A PRETTY HOW TOWN"

First published: 1940 (collected in *Fifty Poems*, 1940)
Type of work: Poem

In the town depicted, humanizing and dehumanizing forces coexist.

"Anyone lived in a pretty how town" is a poem in which Cummings's wordplay is especially effective. The poem contrasts "anyone" and "noone" with "someones and everyones," the first pair being the hero and heroine who love each other, the second pair being the anonymous mass of nonbeings who live lives of quiet desperation, as another New Englander, Henry David Thoreau, once lamented. Eventually "anyone" and "noone" die, but their lives have been meaningful and enriching; the rest of the townspeople—the "someones and everyones"—continue to live, though their existences, like those of the Cambridge ladies, are characterized not by life but by living death.

In the first stanza, Cummings reveals a number of technical innovations. In addition to his inventive use of the pronoun "anyone," he plays with the phrase "a pretty how town," suggesting that the saying—"how pretty a town"—conceals something not so pretty after all. The second line is a syntactical jolt: "(with up so floating many bells down)." It is followed by a line in which four words, without punctuation, imply the tolling of those bells to signify the passing of time: "spring summer autumn winter." The final line of this first stanza returns to the first line and anyone, who "sang his didn't he danced his did."

Unaware of and unconcerned about the "someones and everyones" who "cared for anyone not at all," the hero of the poem falls in love with "noone," whose celebration of life rivals that of her lover. As they live life and the rest of the town lives death, the cycle of nature continues. Bells continue to toll, children continue to be born, and the townspeople continue to say not their prayers but their "nevers." While these nonbeings "slept their dream," the lovers anyone and noone lived their dream, ultimately dying and being buried side by side, just as they had lived their full, vital lives.

After their deaths, the "pretty how town" continued exactly as it always had, with "Women and men (both dong and ding)" pursuing their meaningless lives; they "reaped their sowing and went their came/ sun moon stars rain." Though dead, anyone and noone are alive because at least they once were alive; by contrast, someones and everyones, though still breathing, are merely existing, surviving the seasonal change. Clones of one another, they are untouched by the individuality and vitality of their neighbors who loved and died singing their "didn'ts" and dancing their "dids."

"PITY THIS BUSY MONSTER,MANUNKIND"

First published: 1944 (collected in *1 x 1*, 1944)
Type of work: Poem

The natural world is preferable to the restless unsatisfying human world of "progress."

"Pity this busy monster,manunkind" is a poem that emphasizes Cummings's belief in nature and his opposition to those things—science, technology, and intellectual arrogance—that he believed attack the purity of nature. In the opening lines, Cummings makes it clear that man is un-kind—as opposed to being "mankind"—when he or she engages in "progress." In this case, "Progress is a comfortable disease, one which uses electrons and lenses to "deify one razorblade/ into a mountain-range;lenses extend/ unwish through curving wherewhen till unwish/ returns on its unself." For Cummings, progress contrasts with nature, as he suggests when he writes, "A world of made/ is not a world of born."

The speaker in this poem, as revealed in the last line, represents progress but suggests the promise of nature; "We doctors," he or she says, "know a hopeless case." Hopelessness is the human-made cycle of progress, scientific progress. There is a way out, however, as the speaker points out in the concluding lines of the poem: "listen:there's a hell/ of a good universe next door;let's go." Unlike this universe, composed of negative Cummings-created words such as "unwish" and "unself," the next-door universe consists of wishes and selves—that is, real emotions and real individuals. Those realities, for Cummings, are the true realities.

SUMMARY

Cummings's works are testimonies to the self and the natural world which nurtures that self. They speak of the need to experience the world, not control it; they remind their readers of the importance of the present moment. They celebrate the individual over society, the self over selves. They honor emotion over intellect, feeling over thought. In Cummings's works, one hears a voice that speaks clearly and loudly to the modern world, a voice that both warns and celebrates. That combination of sounds is, in itself, one of Cummings's most significant contributions.

Marjorie Smelstor

BIBLIOGRAPHY

By the Author

POETRY:
Tulips and Chimneys, 1923
&, 1925
XLI Poems, 1925
Is 5, 1926
W: Seventy New Poems, 1931
No Thanks, 1935
1/20 Poems, 1936

Collected Poems, 1938
Fifty Poems, 1940
1 x 1, 1944
Xiape, 1950
Poems, 1923-1954, 1954
Ninety-five Poems, 1958
One Hundred Selected Poems, 1959
Selected Poems, 1960
Seventy-three Poems, 1963
E. E. Cummings: A Selection of Poems, 1965
Complete Poems, 1913-1962, 1968
Etcetera: The Unpublished Poems of E. E. Cummings, 1983, revised and expanded 2000 (George James Firmage and Richard S. Kennedy, editors)

DRAMA:

Him, pb. 1927
Tom: A Ballet, pb. 1935
Anthropos: The Future of Art, pb. 1944
Santa Claus: A Morality, pb. 1946

NONFICTION:

The Enormous Room, 1922
CIOPW, 1931 (drawings)
Eimi, 1933
i: six nonlectures, 1953
Adventures in Value, 1962 (photographs by Marion Morehouse)

TRANSLATION:

The Red Front, 1933 (a selection of poems by Louis Aragon)

DISCUSSION TOPICS

- In what ways did E. E. Cummings's prison camp experience help to preserve him from the elitist attitude that a privileged upbringing such as his can easily foster?

- Cummings can express both childlike and childish attitudes in his writing. What is the difference? Exemplify each.

- What is traditional in Cummings's sonnets and what unique?

- "Anyone lived in a pretty how town" is a relatively short lyric poem that implies but compresses a love story. Explain the suggestions of the story.

- Cummings is also a satiric poet. What satirical techniques does he bring to a poem such as "I sing of Olaf glad and big"?

- What does Cummings mean by his reference to the Cambridge ladies' "furnished souls"? To what exactly is the poem objecting? Comfort? Complacency? Some other unstated quality in their lives?

- Choose one of Cummings's grammatically unconventional poems and explain how it challenges you to think productively about the poem.

About the Author

Ahearn, Barry, ed. *Pound/Cummings: The Correspondence of Ezra Pound and E. E. Cummings*. Ann Arbor: University of Michigan Press, 1996.

Bloom, Harold, ed. *E. E. Cummings: Comprehensive Research and Study Guide*. Philadelphia: Chelsea House, 2003.

Dumas, Bethany K. *E. E. Cummings: A Remembrance of Miracles*. London: Vision Press, 1974.

Kennedy, Richard S. *E. E. Cummings Revisited*. New York: Twayne, 1994.

Kidder, Rushworth M. *E. E. Cummings: An Introduction to the Poetry*. New York: Columbia University Press, 1979.

Lane, Gary. *I Am: A Study of E. E. Cummings' Poems*. Lawrence: University Press of Kansas, 1976.

Norman, Charles. *The Magic Maker: E. E. Cummings*. Rev. ed. Indianapolis: Bobbs-Merrill, 1972.

Sawyer-Lauçanno, Christopher. *E. E. Cummings: A Biography*. Naperville, Ill.: Sourcebooks, 2004.

Wegner, Robert E. *The Poetry and Prose of E. E. Cummings*. New York: Harcourt, Brace & World, 1965.

EDWIDGE DANTICAT

© Arturo Patten

Born: Port-au-Prince, Haiti
January 19, 1969

Danticat has achieved both popular and critical acclaim for her novels and collections of short stories, which weave together the culture and landscape of her native Haiti with portrayals of the immigrant experience in New York City.

BIOGRAPHY

Edwidge Danticat was born in Port-au-Prince, Haiti, in 1969. Like many Haitian children of her generation, she was born into a poor family and was left in the care of relatives when her parents emigrated to the United States in search of better opportunities. Danticat's father left first, when she was two years old; her mother followed two years later. Danticat's parents settled in Brooklyn, New York, and found work—her father as a cab driver, her mother as a textile worker. They had two more children, both boys, before sending for their older children in Haiti. In 1981, when Danticat was twelve years old, she and her younger brother were reunited with their parents in Brooklyn.

As a child in Haiti, Danticat spoke Haitian Creole, or Kreyol, a language that is based mainly on French but includes influences from West African languages as well. Creole is still the language that Danticat speaks at home with her parents in Brooklyn. Danticat recalls that storytelling was one of the favorite pastimes in Haiti when she was young. Older relatives would ask "Krik?" to inquire whether the children were ready to hear stories, and the children would reply "Krak!" to indicate that they were ready to listen. Danticat believes that her love of writing stems from her immersion in the culture of storytelling as a child.

When Danticat arrived in Brooklyn, she spoke no English. In school in Haiti, she had learned to read and write in French. English was her third language, which she learned in bilingual classes at Brooklyn's Intermediate School 320. Her teen years were difficult. Danticat felt like an outsider at school, because she was very shy, and her Haitian background made her feel different from most of her classmates. In addition to adjusting to living in a new country, Danticat had to adjust to living with her parents again after eight years of separation. Although she was glad to be reunited with them, she did not remember them well, and it took some time to get to know them again.

During her first few years in Brooklyn, Danticat spoke very little, partly out of shyness, partly because she was ashamed of her accent. She quickly learned to read and write English, however, and she found consolation in the world of books at her local public library. Some of her favorite authors were Alice Walker, Richard Wright, and James Baldwin. Danticat began writing during her adolescence, at first keeping journals, later writing for a high school publication, and even starting on the book that would become her first novel, *Breath, Eyes, Memory* (1994).

Danticat's parents hoped that she would become a nurse, and she enrolled in a special high school for students planning to enter the health professions. To her parents' disappointment, though, Danticat was much more interested in writing than nursing. Her parents worried that writing would not help Danticat earn a living. However, Danticat attended Barnard College and excelled in writing. Some of the stories in her first collection of short stories, *Krik? Krak!* (1995), were written while she was at Barnard. After graduating from college in 1990, Danticat enrolled at Brown University and earned an M.F.A. degree in creative writing in 1993.

Returning to Brooklyn, she published her first two books in 1994 and 1995 and quickly achieved both popular and critical success. She was named by *Granta* magazine as one of the twenty "Best of American Novelists" in 1996, a remarkable accomplishment for a writer in her twenties. Several of her books have won literary awards. In 1998, Danticat's first novel, *Breath, Eyes, Memory* was selected for the Oprah Winfrey Book Club and became a bestseller. Later, Danticat published the novels *The Farming of Bones* (1998) and *The Dew Breaker* (2004).

Danticat is easily the best-known Haitian American writer. However, she is not comfortable with the idea that her writing "represents" the experience of Haitian Americans. In an interview with Garry Pierre-Pierre for *The New York Times*, Danticat said, "I don't really see myself as the voice for the Haitian American experience. . . . There are many. I'm just one."

ANALYSIS

All of Danticat's works draw on her Haitian background and her immigrant experience. Many of her characters' lives are shaped by the fact that they live "in between" two worlds, as immigrants often do, belonging to neither world completely. Amabelle, the main character in *The Farming of Bones*, is a Haitian woman in her twenties living in the Dominican Republic in the 1930's. (Haiti and the Dominican Republic are two different countries which share one small island, Hispaniola.) Orphaned as a child, she was adopted by a Dominican family and raised almost as a sister to Señora Valencia, who is the same age as Amabelle.

However, even though Amabelle feels at home with Valencia and her father, even calling the father "Papi," she is not quite "family." Her position in the household is that of a servant, and Valencia remarks frequently that Amabelle's skin color is darker than that of her Dominican family. As an immigrant, she lives between two physically separate countries, but she also lives between two different roles in her household—sister and servant—and between two different social classes, as identified by skin color.

The constraining power of social class is a theme

repeated in many of Danticat's other tales. In "A Wall of Fire Rising," a story in *Krik? Krak!*, a young couple living in poverty in Haiti dream of a better life for their young son, a gifted student. However, they disagree strenuously about what "a better life" means. The boy's father, who works intermittently at best and has always dreamed of a permanent job at the local mill, wants to place his son on the waiting list for mill work so that "maybe by the time he becomes a man he can be up for a job." The boy's mother, on the other hand, is opposed to this; to her, a better life means education and a life beyond mill work and poverty. Placing the boy on the waiting list, she feels, will condemn him to a life of mill work. This conflict in their marriage ultimately turns tragic: The boy's father kills himself by leaping from a hot-air balloon, symbolically demonstrating to his wife what he thinks will happen to the boy if she aims too high for him.

Danticat frequently places her characters in real historical settings that depict the often violent political situation in Haiti and the Dominican Republic. A particular strength of her writing is the skill with which she portrays the effect of political violence on individual lives. In *The Farming of Bones*, Amabelle loses her lover, Sebastien, and almost loses her own life in the great massacre of 1937, a historical event in which almost twenty thousand Haitians were murdered in the Dominican Republic and thousands of others were driven out of the country.

The Dew Breaker looks at Haitian political violence from another perspective. It tells the story of a Haitian man who was a "dew breaker"—a torturer—but then emigrated to Brooklyn and established a new, peaceful life as a barber and family man. In a series of interrelated stories, the novel explores the lives of several people affected by the dew breaker's violence. Although it provides no straightforward answers, the novel raises the question of whether a person can be forgiven for a brutal past.

The importance of the mother-daughter relationship is another common theme in Danticat's work. Often in her fiction, daughters lose their mothers to death, emigration, or prison. Inevitably, daughters are damaged by being motherless. Amabelle (of *The Farming of Bones*) is disturbed by recurring dreams and nightmares about her mother's life and death. In "Nineteen Thirty-

Seven," a story in *Krik? Krak!*, Josephine becomes mute when her mother is imprisoned for having witch-like powers. Marie, the main character in *Krik? Krak!*'s "Between the Pool and the Gardenias," is unable to have children of her own after her mother dies. Instead, she finds a dead baby girl lying in a gutter and carries its body home, taking care of it like a living baby until it starts to decompose.

The damage of being motherless can be overcome, however. After a terrible ordeal, Amabelle finds solace in the home of an older woman, a stranger who takes her in and gives her motherly care. Josephine encounters an older woman who helps her come to terms with her mother's death in prison. In "The Missing Peace," from *Krik? Krak!*, Lamort is a teenager whose name means "death" because her mother died giving birth to her. After she meets and helps a woman who is searching for her own missing mother, Lamort gains confidence and decides to change her name to Marie Magdalène, after her mother, symbolically claiming her own life. In Danticat's writing, no other relationship can quite compare to the tenderness of the mother-daughter bond, but healing can be found in friendships with surrogate-mother figures.

KRIK? KRAK!

First published: 1995
Type of work: Short stories

These nine stories center on relationships during difficult times—relationships between lovers or family members strained by political violence, poverty, or other forces beyond their control.

Krik? Krak! opens with the story "Children of the Sea," which consists of an "exchange" of letters between two young lovers. Hauntingly, the letters are written, but never actually exchanged, because the young man is on a small boat with a group of people who are trying to escape Haiti, where they are wanted by the police for speaking out against the government. The reader learns at the end of the story that the young man is being forced to throw his letters overboard to make the boat lighter, be-

cause it has sprung a leak. The reader also suspects that the boat and its inhabitants will not survive this journey. For all its tragedy, this story has a tender side. In their writing, the young lovers reveal the depth of their feelings for each other, the unconditional love that the young woman's parents have for her, and the young man's commitment to justice despite its cost.

Many of the other stories in *Krik? Krak!* are similarly bittersweet. The prostitute in "Night Women" dreads the night, when her "suitors" come to visit. Yet, to protect her young son from the truth about her work, she invents magical stories about visiting angels to explain why she dresses up and puts on make-up at night when she is not planning to go out. "Nineteen Thirty-Seven" also transforms tragedy into tenderness. Josephine's mother's "crime" is purportedly being a witch and having the ability to fly. Josephine is devastated by her mother's imprisonment, and she finds that she cannot talk when she visits her mother. When her mother dies, Josephine, nurtured by a friend, realizes that the mother-daughter bond is not broken even by death, and that she might one day be reunited with her mother.

The most complicated story in *Krik? Krak!* is "A Wall of Fire Rising," in which Lili and Guy's young son, a good student, is chosen for the lead role in a school play. In their pride over their son's accomplishments, the parents dream of a better life for him than the poverty, hunger, and unemployment that mark their lives.

Ironically, the son's school play is about Boukman, a leader of the slave rebellion that won Haiti its independence from France in 1804. In the play, Boukman's passionate speeches about freedom are written not in the Creole dialect of native Haitians but by a European who has the slave speak in "European phrasing." As the symbol of the boy's aptitude for learning, the play hints that Lili's dreams of an education for her son will make him less Haitian and more European. Most tragically, the reader learns in a later story that Lili "killed herself in old age because her husband had jumped out of a flying balloon and her grown son left her to go to Miami."

THE FARMING OF BONES

First published: 1998
Type of work: Novel

Amabelle, a Haitian orphan, is raised in a Dominican family but forced back to Haiti during the great massacre of 1937, in which she loses her lover and almost loses her own life.

The main character in *The Farming of Bones*, Amabelle, is a young Haitian woman living with her adoptive family in the Dominican Republic in the 1930's. Orphaned at the age of eight when her parents drowned, Amabelle is haunted by dreams and nightmares about her childhood. In the happy dreams, she recalls the tender memories of family life with loving parents, but in the nightmares, she relives the moment when her mother reached out to her as she was drowning. Amabelle is never sure whether her mother was motioning for her to enter the river to die with her parents or warning her to stay back.

As a child, Amabelle was taken in by a Dominican widower and his small daughter, Valencia. Although Amabelle calls her adoptive father "Papi" and feels almost like part of the family, she also realizes that her role is that of a servant. Now in her twenties, she has found a lover, Sebastien, who is also a Haitian living in the Dominican Republic. Sebastien's patience and soothing presence help Amabelle heal the scars of her childhood.

However, soon after the couple has become engaged to be married, violence erupts in the Dominican Republic. The Dominican dictator, General Trujillo, has incited his people to force the Haitians out of the country. In the ensuing chaos, Amabelle and Sebastien become separated from each other, and Amabelle makes her way to the border without him. There, she is brutally beaten and barely makes it across the Massacre River alive. However, she is nursed back to health by Man Rapadou, a friend's mother, and she settles into Man Rapadou's household much like she once set-tled into Papi and Valencia's household. This time, though, she is in a Haitian household, with a surrogate-mother figure, and she is an equal, not a servant.

Amabelle spends the next years searching for some scrap of information about Sebastien, but to no avail. When she finds the priest with whom Sebastien was last seen, she is hopeful that she will find out for sure whether Sebastien died or survived the massacre. The priest, however, has gone insane as a result of being tortured, and all he can do is babble the racist words of the dictator: "Our motherland is Spain; theirs is darkest Africa. . . . We, as Dominicans, must have our separate traditions and our own ways of living." Because these words are uttered in a priest's voice, it is as if even God has abandoned the Haitians.

In late middle-age, Amabelle journeys back to the Dominican Republic, both to revisit the place where she knew Sebastien and to try to find additional information about him. She visits Valencia during this trip, but now they are "neither strangers nor friends." Although she learns nothing about Sebastien's fate, she visits the waterfall where she used to meet him, and this brings her a sense of closure. On the way back to Haiti, Amabelle enters the Massacre River once again, symbolically reliving the massacre but also undergoing a rebirth of sorts. "The water was warm for October, warm and shallow, so shallow that I could lie on my back in it with my shoulders only half submerged. . . . cradled by the current, paddling like a newborn in a washbasin."

THE DEW BREAKER

First published: 2004
Type of work: Novel

A Haitian man known as a "dew breaker"—a torturer under Haitian dictator François Duvalier—emigrates to Brooklyn and begins a new life, keeping his brutal past a secret from his daughter.

It is not entirely accurate to call *The Dew Breaker* a novel. It is really a collection of interrelated stories. Each story has its own plot, setting, and group of characters. Each story also sheds light on the main character of the novel, a mild-mannered Haitian American barber and family man who had been a "dew breaker," or torturer, during the dictatorship of François Duvalier during the 1960's. (These

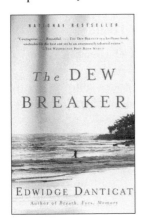

torturers were known as "dew breakers" because they made their arrests very early in the morning, breaking the dew on the grass with their footsteps.)

The book opens with an encounter between Ka Bienaimé, a sculptor and teacher, and her father, the dew breaker. Ka has grown up believing that her father was once a prisoner in Haiti, and that his scarred face is a result of torture. She has created a sculpture of her father in which she has tried to capture his experience as a prisoner, and a famous Haitian American actress has expressed interest in purchasing the sculpture. However, just before Ka is to deliver the sculpture, her father suddenly disappears with it. He returns some hours later, saying that he has dumped the sculpture into a lake because he does not "deserve a statue" and confessing the truth to his daughter: He was never in prison. He was a torturer who killed and maimed people and rounded them up for prison. His scar is the result of a fight with a prisoner whom he murdered.

The chapters that follow let the reader glimpse the perspectives of several people whose lives were changed by the dew breaker. Dany, a Haitian immigrant to Brooklyn, returns to Haiti after ten years to tell his aunt that he has met the man who blinded her and killed his parents. At first, Dany wants to kill the dew breaker, but this desire fades with time, and Dany realizes that what he really wants is to know "why one single person had been given the power to destroy his entire life." Dany gains some insight into the dew breaker's character when he gets to know Claude, a young Haitian American who, at the age of fourteen, killed his parents for drug money and spent time in prison. Upon hearing Claude's story, Dany says, "I'm sorry," but Claude responds, "Sorry? . . . I'm the luckiest f——er alive. I've done something really bad that makes me want to live the rest of my life like a f——ing angel now."

In another chapter, "The Bridal Seamstress," the reader meets Beatrice, another character whose life is uprooted by the dew breaker. Now an old woman living in Brooklyn, Beatrice was once arrested and beaten in Haiti by the dew breaker simply because she refused to date him. Since moving to Brooklyn, Beatrice still lives in fear because she sees the dew breaker everywhere she goes and thinks he is looking for her. She does not know that he has reformed, and she plans to move away so that he will not be able to find her.

In the end, after hearing the truth about her father, Ka asks her mother, "How do you love him?" but she also asks, "Is there more?" expressing her willingness to hear another side of her father's story. After all, her father's brutal past scarred not only his victims but his own face as well. The book does not leave the reader with any answers about whether such brutality can be forgiven. At the very least, it leaves open the possibility that a person can make the transformation from a monster to a human being.

SUMMARY

Danticat's fiction is informed by her own experiences as a Haitian American and as an immigrant. But she infuses her experience with a compelling voice and well-drawn characters that illustrate the complex themes that are woven into her work. Her writing explores how people can "live between two worlds," how social class and color exert powerful forces on people's lives, how the major upheavals of history affect individuals, and how the mother-daughter relationship resonates throughout the lives of women. Most of all, Danticat's work centers on relationships and the ways that relationships are affected by difficult times. To be certain, many of her characters undergo great hardships and tragedies. Most of the time, the bitterness is tempered with a share of sweetness or tenderness.

Karen Antell

BIBLIOGRAPHY

By the Author

LONG FICTION:
Breath, Eyes, Memory, 1994
The Farming of Bones, 1998
The Dew Breaker, 2004

SHORT FICTION:
Krik? Krak!, 1995

DRAMA:
The Creation of Adam, pr. 1992
Dreams Like Me, pr. 1993
Children of the Sea, pr. 1997

NONFICTION:
After the Dance: A Walk Through Carnival in Jacmel, Haiti, 2002

EDITED TEXT:
Butterfly's Way: Voices from the Haitian Dyaspora in the United States, 2001

CHILDREN'S LITERATURE:
Anacaona: Golden Flower, 2005

About the Author

Brown, Mariel. "Finding Her Way Home." *Caribbean Beat* 64 (November/December, 2003).

Danticat, Edwige. "An Interview with Edwidge Danticat." Interview by Bonnie Lyons. *Contemporary Literature* 44, no. 2 (Summer, 2003): 181-198.

Pierre-Pierre, Garry. "At Home with Edwidge Danticat." *The New York Times,* January 26, 1995, p. C1.

Shea, Renee H. "The Dangerous Job of Edwidge Danticat: An Interview." *Callaloo* 19, no. 2 (1996): 382-389.

Valbrun, Marjorie. "Haiti's Eloquent Daughter." *Black Issues Book Review* 6, no. 4 (July/August, 2004): 42-43.

Wucker, Michele. "Edwidge Danticat: A Voice for the Voiceless." *Américas* 52, no. 3 (May/June, 2000): 40-45.

DISCUSSION TOPICS

- Many of Edwidge Danticat's characters are immigrants. What are some of the ways that her characters change in response to a new culture? What are some of the ways that they retain their old culture?

- The mother-daughter relationship is important in Danticat's fiction. Discuss the similarities and differences among several of the motherless daughters in her works—for instance, Amabelle and Valencia from *The Farming of Bones,* Josephine from "Nineteen Thirty-Seven," Lamort from "The Missing Peace," and Marie from "Between the Pool and the Gardenias" in *Krik? Krak!*

- In Danticat's fiction, characters' names often shed some light onto their traits or experiences. For instance, in *The Dew Breaker,* the main character's last name is Bienaimé, which translates roughly as "love well" in French. What is the significance of other character's names—for instance, Ka from *The Dew Breaker,* Amabelle and Valencia from *The Farming of Bones,* and Marie from "Between the Pool and the Gardenias" in *Krik? Krak!*?

- "Magical Realism" is a term sometimes applied to Danticat's works. Find and discuss several passages that could be considered Magical Realism.

- Danticat's characters often suffer violence from political or social clashes. How do her characters achieve emotional healing from this kind of violence? Is forgiveness part of their healing?

GUY DAVENPORT

Born: Anderson, South Carolina
       November 23, 1927
Died: Lexington, Kentucky
       January 4, 2005

Widely recognized as one of American literature's most sophisticated postmodern short-story writers, Davenport is also known as a literary critic, translator, poet, and editor.

BIOGRAPHY

Guy Davenport was born on November 23, 1927, in Anderson, South Carolina. His father, Guy Mattison Davenport, spent most of his working life as a shipping agent in Anderson. His mother, Marie Fant Davenport, was a housewife. Although Guy Davenport kept his private life very private, he seemed to have had a happy childhood and recalled with pleasure summer days when he and his father scoured the South Carolina forest looking for Indian arrowheads.

Davenport attended Duke University, where he studied literature and languages, including French, Latin, and Greek, graduating with honors in 1948. He then moved on to Oxford University's Merton College as a Rhodes Scholar and earned a B. Litt. degree in 1950. He subsequently served in the United States Army Airborne Corps for the following two years. He taught at Washington University in St. Louis, Missouri, from 1952 to 1955, moving on to further graduate studies at Harvard University from 1956 to 1961. He earned a Ph.D. in modern literature from Harvard in 1961. He taught at Haverford College in Philadelphia from 1961 to 1963 and accepted a permanent position at the University of Kentucky, where he remained for the rest of his academic career. He retired from Kentucky in 1991 after receiving a prestigious MacArthur Grant.

Besides teaching at the University of Kentucky, where he taught courses in modern literature, Davenport traveled extensively throughout Europe, especially France, gathering material for his stories and his scholarly essays. In addition to his many literary essays and more than sixty short stories (some the length of novels), he wrote literary criticism and book reviews for many journals and magazines. He reviewed books for *National Review* for eleven years and also for *Life, The New York Times Book Review, Hudson Review, Poetry, Book Week, The New Criterion,* and the *Los Angeles-New York Times Book Review Service.* He died in early 2005 of cancer.

ANALYSIS

The key to understanding the complex literary world of Davenport is his commitment to understanding and using the lessons of the past in both his stories and his literary criticism. In his seminal essay "The Symbol of the Archaic," he most clearly articulates the need for humanity to save itself from the encroaching destructive effects of industrialization and mechanization by reawakening a passion for the "archaic," a passion that manifests itself in "a longing for something lost, for energies, values, and certainties unwisely abandoned by an industrial age."

Davenport's project of reclaiming the ameliorating lessons of the past closely resembles similar efforts of other modernist writers such as Ezra Pound, James Joyce, and Charles Olson, and visual artists such as Pablo Picasso, Max Ernst, and Georges Braque. Davenport envisions these modernists as seriously trying to use the wisdom of the ancient Greeks, in particular, to heal the fragmentation in Western civilization resulting from the disastrous destructiveness of both World War I and World War II. Those wars, and the subsequent rise of fascism and communism that followed them, obliterated any remaining cohesive structures that had previously kept Western Europe unified. The artists and writers in whom Davenport is most interested are those who attempted to forge new literary and aesthetic methods and models to deal with and understand the fragmentation of the post-World War I era.

Davenport's most persuasive and brilliant essays on various aspects of the loss of a spiritual center that is grounded in the archaic imagination can be found in a number of essays in both *The Geography of the Imagination* (1981) and *Every Force Evolves a Form* (1987). In many of these essays, his persistent theme is the damage that an overly mechanistic society inflicts upon the feeling life and imaginations of human beings who have been cut off from the healing energies of geographical, cultural, and spiritual origins.

Davenport used the same principles in formulating his uniquely compelling stories and novellas, which he collected in books beginning with *Tatlin!* in 1974. Few short-story collections have been so praised; most reviewers confessed that they had seen nothing remotely like these six stories, which are united around the common theme of flight, both physical and spiritual, from the life-denying energies of Stalinism and capitalist industrialization. Davenport called his highly individual use of collage "assemblages of history and necessary fiction," a modernist method that juxtaposes images of the past with the present to demonstrate the emptiness and aesthetic and spiritual poverty of the modern age. He acknowledged that his stories, particularly in *Tatlin!*, "are lessons in history."

Davenport also used the ideogrammatic techniques of poets Ezra Pound and William Carlos Williams and frequently combined them with the cinematic techniques of the experimental filmmaker Stan Brakhage, replacing traditional narrative and documentary methods with images that form a structure of their own as they accumulate throughout the stories. Davenport clearly asserts his view of what distinguishes human beings from the animal and vegetable world: the imagination, which he further defines as "what mankind makes of things." He explained that

> My theory of the imagination is this: that in the evolution of man this was the moment in which we became what we call human. That is, it's an amazing ability to see something with your eyes closed. Which is what imagination is . . . a power of com-

munication so high that I can't think of humanity doing any better.

Concurrent with Davenport's reverence for the creative power of the human imagination was his persistent use of the theme of the "Fall." All of his stories throughout his six short-fiction collections could be said to treat, in one form or another, the consequences of humankind's Fall from a preternatural condition of Edenic happiness and ignorance into experience, time, and knowledge. His fictions attempt, then, to regenerate, fictively, an Edenic innocence that has been destroyed by the dehumanizing powers of so-called civilization and the Western obsession with rationality.

Davenport's second collection, *Da Vinci's Bicycle* (1979), persuasively documents the ways in which people habitually marginalize, overlook, or ignore unique geniuses who are later discovered. He cites such figures as Leonardo da Vinci, the idiosyncratic Swiss poet and novelist Robert Walser, and Davenport's greatest philosophical influence, the French Utopian sociologist and philosopher Charles Fourier, to whom he dedicated his fourth collection of stories, *Apples and Pears, and Other Stories* (1984). Indeed, the longest and most intricately structured story in *Da Vinci's Bicycle* is "Au Tombeau de Charles Fourier" (at the tomb of Charles Fourier), which is an homage to the genius of Fourier as a visionary whose planned communities, such as Brook Farm, were tried in various parts of the United States but failed as a result of a lack of consistent and dedicated community support.

Davenport's next collection, *Eclogues* (1981), moves back in time to compare ancient Greek stories, with special emphasis on the "pastoral" elements in the eclogues of Virgil, Theocritus, and Plutarch, to modern Edenic pastoral communities of a fictional Dutch philosopher, Adriaan van Hovendaal. Van Hovendaal continues his attempt to regenerate a Utopian community in the Netherlands, a project that he first began in the longest story in *Tatlin!*, "The Dawn in Erewhon." Next to Fourier, Davenport's most crucial intellectual and spiritual influence was Samuel Butler, the English Utopian novelist whose *Erewhon* (an 1872 satire on Victorian society the title of which is an anagram of "nowhere") becomes the subtext for Davenport's long story about the need for human beings to free themselves of sexual guilt and shame.

Apples and Pears, and Other Stories is considered by many critics to be Davenport's most brilliant collection, especially the 233-page title novella which constitutes most of the book. *Apples and Pears* is a treatise organized along the lines of Fourier's favorite four-part structure, which he used in his major work, *Théorie des quatre mouvements and des destinées générales* (1808; *The Social Destiny of Man: Or, Theory of the Four Movements*, 1857). The main character is, again, the Dutch philosopher Adriaan van Hovendaal, whose Fourierist group has grown to eight members. Under van Hovendaal's gentle leadershp, the young members of the group spend their time enjoying camping trips in the forests and developing their artistic and intellectual powers.

Nowhere does Davenport devote as much space in detailing the activities available to young people to enlarge both their physical as well as their mental and spiritual capacities as in *Apples and Pears*. The apples and pears as objects also symbolize the Fall and redemption, respectively, that take place in the Old and New Testaments. This work becomes Davenport's most important chapter in what he called his "history of affection," as all the exercises of the adolescents throughout the story are aimed at deepening and enlarging their feeling for one another within the natural landscape around them.

Davenport's fifth collection of short stories is titled *The Jules Verne Steam Balloon* (1987). The setting has moved from the sensually alluring Netherlands to a more northerly idyllic place, Denmark. Adriaan van Hovendaal has been replaced by a less sensual leader, Hugo Tvemunding, a doctoral student in theology and a teacher of classics in a Danish folk high school. A new moral note enters Davenport's fiction in this collection, especially in "The Bicycle Rider," a story that features a young man who is suffering from drug addiction and who finally dies because of his inability to participate in the rich emotional life around him. Davenport also invites his readers to compare the vocation of the artist to that of a religious leader insofar as both are involved in attempting to transcend the limitations of the mundane by the liberating power of the imagination.

Davenport's sixth collection of short fiction is titled *The Drummer of the Eleventh North Devonshire Fusiliers* (1990). Of the five stories in the volume, the longest, "Wo es war, soll ich werden" (where it was,

there I must begin to be), examines the ways in which adolescents view life around them in its simplest terms and how the self-consciousness of adulthood destroys that purity of vision. These fictions are Davenport's clearest statements of his increasing concern over Western civilization's penchant for involving itself in potentially self-destructive political and military projects.

TATLIN!

First published: 1974
Type of work: Short stories

The six stories in this collection demonstrate Davenport's unique way of developing a story by means of collage and juxtaposition.

Tatlin! is the collection of short stories that made Davenport one of the most admired and studied fiction writers in modern American literature. Most of the reviewers who commented on the volume when it appeared admitted that they had seen nothing like these highly sophisticated and polished stories, either in subject matter or technique. The stories range from the title piece, about the founder of Constructivism and Russian Formalism, to a story about young boys who stumble on the Paleolithic cave paintings of Lascaux, France, in "Robot," and move through the deep Greek past in "Herakleitos" to an imaginary past of the writer Edgar Allan Poe in "1830." The volume ends in an imaginative descent into Holland as a sensual "netherland" or underworld, where a Dutch philosopher attempts to regenerate an earthly Eden by means of the body.

The second story in the collection, "The Aeroplanes at Brescia," was actually the first story that Davenport published and concerns a famous air show at Brescia, Italy, in 1909 in which most of the world's renowned pilots took part. The construction of the story has become as famous as the story itself; Davenport initially began it as an essay on writer Franz Kafka, but in the midst of his research, he discovered that Kafka's first published newspaper story was titled "The Aeroplanes at Brescia." Though Kafka's story was a piece of journalism, Davenport views it as a typical Kafka short story and uses, in his own story, every sentence that Kafka wrote. However, Davenport makes important changes to suit his own style. Accompanying Kafka was Max Brod, a character in Davenport's story as well as Kafka's first biographer. Davenport also used

every sentence of Brod's report of the air show at Brescia in his story. Again, he rearranges both Kafka's and Brod's sentences in highly imaginative ways to produce a composite narrative that fuses all of their perspectives into a typical Davenport story.

Davenport employs similar methods in many of the other stories in *Tatlin!*. In the title narrative, he tells the story of the difficult life of Vladimir Tatlin, founder of Constructivism, an engineer, designer, painter, sailor, teacher, and folk musician—a veritable modern Renaissance man whose genius was crushed by the life-denying strategies of communism. Davenport, also a highly respected artist, interweaves his own drawings of Joseph Stalin, Vladimir Ilich Lenin, and Tatlin throughout the story, creating an intertextual collage of visual images and written passages.

The charming story "Robot" records the accidental discovery of the caves of Lascaux by six French peasant boys in 1941. The story is titled "Robot" because that was the name of the dog of one of the boys who actually discovered the caves while chasing a rabbit. This story dramatically illustrates Davenport's persistent concern for the submerged archaic wisdom that lies hidden beneath modern civilization, waiting for discovery. Because of this important discovery, it became clear that Western humanity had attempted to express itself through imaginative forms at a much earlier date than anyone had ever suspected.

The longest story in *Tatlin!* is "The Dawn in Erewhon." The story's title connects it to the famous English Utopian novelist Samuel Butler and his book *Erewhon*, an anagram of "nowhere." The fictional Dutch philosopher Adriaan van Hovendaal attempts to escape his overly intellectual propensities by creating an Edenic community of three, with a teenage boy and girl, Bruno and Kaatje.

They travel to idyllic forests, carefully dividing up duties and enjoying themselves in clean but sensual activities. "The Dawn in Erewhon" is Davenport's first attempt to present the social ideals of Fourier in a fictional form. Feelings and the claims of the body take precedence over all intellectual duties or exercises in the longest story in the collection.

ECLOGUES

First published: 1981
Type of work: Short stories

The eight stories in this collection illustrate the concept of societal unity as embodied in the pastoral tradition of ancient Greece.

As a translator of classical Greek and Latin texts, Davenport found great affinity with the classical concept of pastoralism as a way of creating and enacting an Edenic society. Davenport harked back to the classical pastoral poetry of Theocritus and Virgil and of English pastoral poets such as William Shakespeare, Christopher Marlowe, and John Milton. All the stories contain a shepherd figure who helps to keep order and direction within the group and who maintains the beauty and structure of Arcadian society. There are humorous stories about the Greek philosopher Diogenes, who respects no one, not even Alexander the Great, whom he chides for blocking "his" sunlight.

The most charming and intricately developed story, and the longest, is the concluding one, "On Some Lives of Virgil." The setting, the southwestern French city of Bordeaux, is key to understanding the theme of how geography influences the imagination and produces local aesthetic geniuses. In this story, the shepherd is the classical scholar Tullio, who leads his charges, again French teenagers who constantly experiment with innocent sexual pleasures, to examine some ancient French caves just outside Bordeaux. He teaches his students that true history is actually "the history of attention" and that they must pay attention to all forms of narrative, both written and oral, to understand and appreciate the complete historical canvas. "The Death of Picasso" finds Adriaan van

Hovendaal and a student, Sander, discussing the significance of the painter's death in light of the fact that Picasso helped to create "modernism" as an amalgamation of the ancient and the contemporary.

THE JULES VERNE STEAM BALLOON

First published: 1987
Type of work: Short stories

Though the Fourierist communities have moved from the Netherlands to Denmark, a new moral note enters this collection, and evil is confronted and challenged.

This collection contains nine highly diverse stories that range from the pastoral Greek tale "Pyrrhon of Elis" to the avant-garde dramatic fragment "We Often Think of Lenin at the Clothespin Factory." Adriaan von Hovendaal is replaced by the Danish theology student Hugo Tvemunding, who also teaches at a high school and who is featured in "The Bicycle Rider," "The Jules Verne Steam Balloon," and "The Ringdove Sign." Davenport employs unusual narrative structures throughout the collection, such as a pastiche of quotations from the schoolbooks of Nazi children in "Bronze Leaves and Red" and a botanical listing of the components of Eden in "The Meadow."

The three longest stories concern themselves with Hugo's gradually emerging knowledge that he should not pursue his calling to the Lutheran ministry but should rather follow his leanings toward his vocation as an artist. He boldly confronts evil in the drug addiction of one of the more attractive young men, known as the Bicycle Rider, who eventually dies of an overdose because he has lost the ability to respond on a human level to his fellow companions. It is in this story that Hugo realizes fully what the purpose of art is and that an artist's first duty is to respond to the world as authentically as he can, regardless of how demanding those responses may become. The title story presents three male sprites, Tumble, Buckeye, and Quark, as messengers from beyond who come down to earth in their steam balloon to remind humankind that salvation lies in the ability to use imagination to transform the mundane into forms of visionary experience.

SUMMARY

Guy Davenport's fictions are variations on the theme of the loss of innocence—the Fall from a childlike vision of the world into the adult world of experience and knowledge. The villains are always the mechanistic and dehumanizing forces in Western society, which continually threaten to eradicate the joyous and childlike sense of the marvelous that transforms boredom into celebration. The source of that energy has always existed and resides in the continuous rediscovery of the archaic—that is, of the wisdom found in the great art and literature of the ancient Greeks and Romans. Davenport wanted nothing less than a new Renaissance, imitative of the fifteenth century one that transformed Europe from a dark ages society into one of the greatest and richest civilizations in existence.

Patrick Meanor

BIBLIOGRAPHY

By the Author

SHORT FICTION:
Tatlin!, 1974
Da Vinci's Bicycle: Ten Stories, 1979
Eclogues: Eight Stories, 1981
Apples and Pears, and Other Stories, 1984
The Jules Verne Steam Balloon, 1987
The Drummer of the Eleventh North Devonshire Fusiliers, 1990
A Table of Green Fields: Ten Stories, 1993

Guy Davenport

The Cardiff Team: Ten Stories, 1996
Twelve Stories, 1997

POETRY:
Flowers and Leaves, 1966
Thasos and Ohio: Poems and Translations, 1986

NONFICTION:
Pennant Key-Indexed Study Guide to Homer's "Odyssey," 1967
Pennant Key-Indexed Study Guide to Homer's "Iliad," 1967
The Geography of the Imagination, 1981
Every Force Evolves a Form, 1987
A Balthus Notebook, 1989
Charles Burchfield's Seasons, 1994
The Hunter Gracchus, and Other Papers on Literature and Art, 1996
The Geography of the Imagination: Forty Essays, 1997
Objects on a Table: Harmonious Disarray in Art and Literature, 1998

TRANSLATIONS:
Poems and Fragments, 1965 (of Sappho)
Herakleitos and Diogenes, 1979
Archilochos, Sappho, Alkman: Three Lyric Poets of the Late Greek Bronze Age, 1980
Anakreon, 1991
Seven Greeks, 1995
The Logia of Yeshua: The Sayings of Jesus, 1996 (with Benjamin Urrutia)

EDITED TEXTS:
The Intelligence of Louis Agassiz: A Specimen Book of Scientific Writings, 1963
Selected Stories, 1993 (of O. Henry)

MISCELLANEOUS:
The Death of Picasso: New and Selected Writing, 2003

DISCUSSION TOPICS

- Are the themes of Guy Davenport's essays also apparent in his fiction or poetry?
- How does visual imagery enhance Davenport's fiction or poetry?
- How is one Davenport short story an attack upon the dehumanizing effects of society?
- What does *Da Vinci's Bicycle* seem to be saying about the nature of genius?
- What is the role played by nature and landscape in "Apples and Pears"?
- How does the theme of flight link the stories in *Tatlin!*?
- Compare Davenport's treatment of the loss of innocence in two stories.

About the Author

Bawer, Bruce. "Guy Davenport: Fiction á la Fourier." In Diminishing Fictions. St. Paul, Minn.: Graywolf Press, 1988.
Furlani, Andre. "Postmodern and After: Guy Davenport." Contemporary Literature 43 (Winter, 2002): 709-735.
Kenner, Hugh. "A Geographer of the Imagination." Harper's 263 (August, 1981): 66-68.
Meanor, Patrick. "The Fourierist Parables of Guy Davenport." In Postmodern Approaches to the Short Story, edited by Farhat Iftekharrudin and Joseph Boyden. Westport, Conn.: Praeger, 2003.
Olsen, Lance. "A Guidebook to the Last Modernist: Davenport on Davenport and 'Da Vinci's Bicycle.'" Journal of Narrative Technique 16 (Spring, 1986): 148-161.
Sullivan, John Jeremiah. "Guy Davenport: The Art of Fiction CLXXIV." Paris Review 163 (Fall, 2002): 43-87.
Vandiver, Elizabeth. "Fireflies in a Jar." Parnassus: Poetry in Review 21 (Winter, 1995): 59-76.

ROBERTSON DAVIES

© Jerry Bauer

Born: Thamesville, Ontario, Canada
August 28, 1913
Died: Toronto, Ontario, Canada
December 2, 1995

Although he was also a successful playwright and critic, novelist Robertson Davies is chiefly known for his three loosely conceived trilogies of novels which explore the archetypal relationships between contemporary life and various mythic frameworks.

BIOGRAPHY

William Robertson Davies was born in Thamesville, Ontario, and spent his earliest years there. His father was the owner and editor of the town's newspaper. Davies' career as a writer seems to owe much to the early influence and encouragement of his parents, and a journalistic interest in community life is evident in many of his best novels. Davies read voraciously from an early age and wrote his first newspaper article at the age of nine. His family was also active in the Presbyterian Church, and Davies seems to have been sensitive to the denominational diversity found even in the smallest communities.

When Davies was twelve, the family moved to Kingston, where they lived in a supposedly haunted house. Kingston was a large enough community to offer Davies much greater exposure to the worlds of art, drama, and music. At the age of fifteen, he earned a scholarship to a prestigious boys' school in Toronto, where he distinguished himself through his unconventional mode of dress and behavior. Academically unsuccessful, he began to be known as a conversationalist and actor and availed himself of Toronto's many theaters. In 1932, his father took him on a summer trip to Great Britain, where Davies was able to immerse himself in drama from William Shakespeare to the contemporary period, giving him at a young age a remarkable grounding in his chosen trade. He continued his dramatic endeavors as a special student (nondegree seeking) at Queen's University, including directing an outdoor production of *A Midsummer Night's Dream*, which seems to have contributed significantly to the events in his 1951 novel *Tempest-Tost*. Davies continued his formal education at Oxford's Balliol College, where he became active in the Oxford University Dramatic Society, stage-managing several successful performances. During this period, Davies became familiar with the works of Sigmund Freud and converted from Presbyterianism to the Anglican faith. He earned his bachelor of literature in 1938.

By this time, Davies was writing. He published his thesis, *Shakespeare's Boy Actors*, in 1939 to good reviews, and in December of that year, he joined the Old Vic Company, one of London's most venerable and prestigious theater companies, where he acted, lectured, and was encouraged to write. In the early days of World War II, Davies proposed marriage to his Australian colleague Brenda Ethel Mathews, bringing her back to Canada in 1940.

Back in Ontario, Davies was rejected twice for military service because of his poor eyesight. He tried his hand at journalism with a series of newspaper columns published under the pseudonym Samuel Marchbanks. These columns prefigured many of the themes and subjects of his later novels. Soon he became literary editor of a weekly journal, *Saturday Night*, and a prominent figure in Canadian literary life.

By 1960, Davies had written more than two dozen dramatic pieces and was known as one of

Canada's leading playwrights. In 1950, he began *Tempest-Tost*, the first novel in the Salterton Trilogy (the other two are *Leaven of Malice* and *A Mixture of Frailties*). He remained active in the theater and was an influential early supporter of the Stratford Festival, becoming a member of its board of governors and publishing three books that drew attention to the dramatic accomplishments of the festival.

In 1961, Davies was appointed Master of Massey College, a newly formed residential college for graduate students within the University of Toronto, the first of its kind in Canada. He would hold the position for the next twenty years. He had already begun planning his well-known novel *Fifth Business*, but his teaching and scholarly and administrative duties would delay its completion until 1970. *Fifth Business*, *The Manticore* (1972), and *World of Wonders* (1975) are together known as the Deptford Trilogy. Davies stepped down from his post as Master of Massey College in 1981.

In the years following his retirement from his academic appointment, Davies addressed himself to his career as a writer with renewed vigor, writing opera librettos for the Canadian Children's Opera Chorus and collecting ghost stories into a book called *High Spirits* (1982). He was also hard at work on the novels that would become the Cornish Trilogy: *The Rebel Angels* (1981), *What's Bred in the Bone* (1985), and *The Lyre of Orpheus* (1988). Davies died in 1995 at the age of eighty-two.

ANALYSIS

Any understanding of Robertson Davies' literary achievement must begin with an acknowledgment of the significance of his nationality to his art. Canada plays a vitally important role in Davies' fiction. His complicated, even contradictory attitude of pride in his country and concern over its provincialism are significant and persistent threads that bring many of his novels together. Early twentieth century life in small-town Ontario is seldom idealized in Davies' novels; instead, he scrupulously depicts it as difficult and insular. The squabbling and petty insecurities of the members of the Salterton Little Theatre are presented for comic effect in *Tempest-Tost*, but Davies, who had real-life experience working with such groups and in promoting the arts in places such as the fictional Salterton, would certainly have disdained such pretensions.

Provincial attitudes reign in Davies' fictional small towns, along with rumor and gossip, and the protagonists who hail from these places seem eager to leave their limited worlds behind and reluctant to return. In terms of religion, interdenominational distrust and rivalry are recurring themes. When protagonists do return to visit their hometowns, the visits are frequently brief and uncomfortable, as when Dunstan Ramsay returns from the Great War in *Fifth Business*. However, Davies is fair; he willingly showcases the best things small towns have to offer, neighborly charity chief among them. Moreover, lest it be thought that Davies did not care for Canada, his record of support for the promotion of a Canadian national drama speaks eloquently against that interpretation.

Indeed, the uses to which Davies puts satire are varied, and small Ontario towns certainly receive their fair share. However, Cornish provincialism is treated very similarly in *What's Bred in the Bone*, and urban pseudo-sophistication is also examined. The foibles of amateur actors are mocked in *Tempest-Tost*, but their goal of presenting Shakespeare to their own hometown is admirable. Protagonists are by no means immune to the satire either. Mackilwraith, the *unfortunate* math-teacher-turned-Shakespearean-actor in *Tempest-Tost*, is clearly an object of satirical amusement. Dunstan Ramsay and Francis Cornish are not satirical, exactly, but each goes through his respective story with an ironic lack of awareness of his role in the grand scheme of things. The wealthy and pretentious fare even worse in Davies' novels. The upwardly mobile Boy Staunton is shown to be shortsighted, dishonest even with himself.

Another significant aspect of Davies' fiction is his preoccupation with the visual and performing arts. His lifelong interest in the stage, which was his first passion, is evident in *Tempest-Tost* and elsewhere. Though his depiction of the production clearly shows a satirical bent, Davies is also applauding the dramatic and artistic aspirations of the working-class and middle-class residents of Salterton. No one is more aware than Davies that a tremendous amount of time and effort goes into any successful dramatic production, and he pays homage to that fact in the novel. While *Fifth Business* is more concerned with hagiography than with drama, the title comes from an operatic term, and conjuring (stage magic)—itself a kind of performance art—does play a significant role. The authorship of an opera libretto is also the subject of *Lyre of Orpheus*, one of Davies' later novels. In *What's Bred in the Bone*, the subject of artistic authenticity is analyzed, and while painting is the nominal subject, the significance is actually much broader.

Religion, in particular the conflicts and disagreements between religious denominations, also figures prominently in Davies' novels. In *Fifth Business*, Davies describes in humorous terms Presbyterian attitudes toward Baptists, Anglicans, and Roman Catholics. Later, the Protestant protagonist develops an unusual preoccupation with saints and sainthood, and in the process becomes involved with the Jesuit order of the Catholic priesthood.

In *What's Bred in the Bone*, the difficulty of synthesizing conflicting religious viewpoints is an important issue in Francis Cornish's young life. He is raised Catholic in a home where his father is violently anti-Catholic, and his nursemaid is an evangelical Protestant, an enthusiastic uniformed member of the Salvation Army. In Davies' work, no religion or denomination is portrayed as holding all the answers.

The key to Davies' persistent but not proselytizing interest in religious matters lies, perhaps, in his interest in psychology. In the 1930's, he read Freud with interest, but later he discovered the writings of Freud's onetime disciple and later rival, C. G. Jung. Two important concepts commonly associated with Jung are the collective unconscious and archetypes. The collective unconscious is, for Jung, an inherited body of cultural—or species—knowledge that links the individual with everyone else, living or dead. Archetypes, located within the collective unconscious, are patterns and tropes that manifest themselves in mythology, religion, literature, and life. These concepts play significant roles throughout much of Davies' fiction, but they are discussed most explicitly in *Fifth Business*.

Taken together, the novels of Davies offer a particular and yet full picture of twentieth century life in Canada and beyond. His concerns are at once the commonplace and the cosmic, as he frequently depicts the solitary individual's flirtation with the eternal. His tone, frequently satirical but generally sympathetic, allows him to depict human shortcomings and successes with equal mastery. His three loosely connected trilogies afford his writing a scope that transcends that of many comparable writers, and his journalistic eye and ear permit him to report his subject matter in a way that is at once artful and honest.

TEMPEST-TOST

First published: 1951
Type of work: Novel

A mathematics teacher auditions for a community theater production of Shakespeare's play The Tempest *and becomes infatuated with a young cast member.*

Davies' first novel, *Tempest-Tost*, draws heavily on his own involvement in community theatrical productions. While the novel uses multiple points of view, its protagonist is clearly Hector Mackilwraith, a lonely mathematics teacher who bravely chooses to vary the routine of his day-to-day existence by auditioning for a part in the Salterton Little Theatre production of *The Tempest*. Though he admonishes himself to "do nothing foolish," the thought that he may soon be leaving Salterton for a different job encourages him to take the chance. His audition for the part of Gonzalo is not excellent, but he suggests that if he is not given a part, he will no longer serve in his essential role as treasurer of the Salterton Little Theatre. This production will be the company's first outdoor production, to be performed at St. Agnes's, an estate owned by George Alexander Webster.

Other important characters include Freddy (Fredegonde) Webster, the fourteen-year-old daughter of George Alexander Webster, and Griselda, her eighteen-year-old sister, with whom Hector becomes infatuated. As in a Shakespearean comedy, there are several other characters and relationships that provide a perspective on the story's main action. Some characters involved with the Salterton Little Theatre seem designed to allow Davies to highlight, satirically, certain aspects of small-town life, and the conflicts, artistic and otherwise, that arise in local theater groups. Indeed, Salterton bears considerable resemblance to Kingston, Ontario, where the author spent much of his younger life, and several of the novel's characters can be traced to individuals that Davies encountered there and in his earlier theatrical endeavors.

The fuller characters are the ones whom Hector perceives as threats to his future with Griselda. Solly Bridgetower is the wise-cracking young assistant director who is dominated by his mother, and he is the man in whom Griselda is actually interested. Roger Tasset is the play's leading man, a womanizer who eventually fights with Solly. The play's director is thirty-six-year-old Valentine Rich, a professional director who has taken on the Salterton Little Theatre production as a favor. She is also in town to settle the estate of her grandfather, Dr. Adam Savage.

Conflict arises as Hector, a very shy man but one who nonetheless has set his mind and heart on Griselda, begins to perceive Solly and Roger as romantic rivals. Griselda is moderately interested in Solly, who is sincerely attracted to her; Roger is only interested in her money and in winning her away from Solly, and declares his intention of taking her to the June Ball.

Hearing this, Hector decides to attend the ball as well, obtaining a ticket through shady means. Solly attends as the escort of Pearl Vambrace, the professor's shy and sheltered daughter, who is smitten by Roger. At the ball, Griselda rejects Roger after he kisses her passionately. Hector witnesses only the kiss and assumes that a seduction is inevitable.

The novel's climax comes with the performance of *The Tempest*. Before it opens, Solly declares his love for Valentine, who is flattered and accepts his statements as a compliment. Midway through the play, a despondent Hector attempts to hang himself in the shed that serves as the backstage area. Valentine berates him for endangering the performance and plays his role through the remainder of the play. At the end of the novel, order is restored when Hector comes to his senses and seems prepared to move past this episode.

FIFTH BUSINESS

First published: 1970
Type of work: Novel

Dunstan Ramsay, a history teacher with an interest in saints, describes his lifelong interactions with a disturbed, saintly woman and others whose lives she touched.

Taking the form of a first-person memoir, *Fifth Business* is the life story of Dunstable (later Dunstan) Ramsay, a retired school teacher whose life has been guided by the conviction that there are saints in the contemporary time period, and that his childhood neighbor is one such person. The novel's title refers to a figure in an opera who is not directly involved in the action but exists only to observe and comment on it; clearly, Ramsay is such a figure. His story begins when, at the age of ten, he dodges a snowball thrown by Percy Boyd Staunton; the snowball hits Mary Dempster, the wife of the Baptist minister. The incident sends her into labor, and Paul Dempster is born eighty days early. Young Ramsay feels himself responsible.

The snowball and emergency childbirth bring about a change in Mrs. Dempster. She becomes unhealthily generous, disgracing her husband by having sex with a tramp. Later in the novel it is revealed that this act brings about a miraculous transformation in the tramp, who becomes an inner-city missionary. Her other miracles entail apparently bringing Willy Ramsay back from the point of death and, years later, appearing to Dunstable Ramsay on a statue of the Virgin Mary in a World War I battlefield. These miracles lead Ramsay to the belief that Mary Dempster is a saint.

Young Ramsay develops an interest in conjuring—stage magic—and introduces the art to Paul Dempster. Later, while Dunstable is fighting in the war, Paul runs away with a circus, eventually becoming a world-famous stage magician. Ramsay's interest in magic connects with his interest in sainthood; his curiosity about saints has less to do with Christianity than with the supernatural in general. In fact, the New Testament is associated in his mind with the tales of the Arabian Nights. In Jungian fashion, he traces the parallels between Mary Magdalene and many similar figures in pseudohistory and mythology in search of their archetypal significance.

Ramsay returns from the war severely injured—

he has lost a leg, and his body is scarred from burns. He is also a decorated hero. A girlfriend rechristens him Dunstan, after a saint who allegedly twisted the devil's nose with a pair of tongs. He reconnects with his friend Percy Boyd Staunton, who has also renamed himself Boy Staunton; thus they are both "twice-born," which in mythological terms sets them apart somewhat from normal people.

After earning two degrees, Ramsay becomes a teacher in a boarding school and takes annual "saint-hunting" trips to Europe; eventually he writes several significant books on saints and earns a reputation as a hagiographer. On one such trip, he visits a traveling carnival, where he is reunited with Paul Dempster, now a magician.

Many years later, Ramsay encounters Dempster yet again, this time under the stage name Magnus Eisengrim. The magician's closing illusion dramatizes the union of Sacred and Profane Love in the Eternal Feminine. Ramsay agrees to travel with the show and write Eisengrim's (Dempster's) fictional autobiography. He has an encounter with the show's backer, Liesl, that significantly parallels St. Dunstan's encounter with the devil.

Eventually he introduces Boy Staunton to Dempster and tries to make Staunton accept responsibility for throwing the snow-covered stone that induced Mary Dempster's early labor and apparently triggered her madness. Staunton and Dempster leave Ramsay's home together, and the next morning, Staunton is found in his submerged automobile with the stone in his mouth, the implication being that Dempster, a hypnotist and an escape artist, has encouraged him to commit suicide, as he must have unconsciously wanted to do.

WHAT'S BRED IN THE BONE

First published: 1985
Type of work: Novel

Francis Cornish is exposed to a variety of childhood influences and leads an extraordinary life as an artist and collector.

One of the distinguishing characteristics of *What's Bred in the Bone* is the use of a double frame. The novel tells the story of Francis Cornish but opens with Arthur Cornish, Francis's nephew, arguing with his own wife, Maria, and Francis's erstwhile friend Simon Darcourt over whether Darcourt should complete the biography of Francis Cornish he has begun. Arthur has turned up evidence that Francis "faked" paintings, producing a masterpiece that has passed for a previously unknown Renaissance painting. The second, more playful framing device is an ongoing conversation between Francis Cornish's guardian spirit ("daimon") Maimas and the Angel of Biography, the Lesser Zadkiel.

Early influences on Francis Cornish include his grandfather, Senator James Ignatius McRory, his grandmother Mary-Louise, his great aunt Mary Ben, and his aunt Mary-Tess. His mother, Mary-Jim, and his father, Major Francis Cornish, are largely absent from his early life. His parents married for convenience: Mary-Jim became pregnant as the result of a brief, drunken encounter and thus needed a husband, and Major Cornish wished to attach himself to the affluent McRory family. In a Dickensian plot twist, their first child is born retarded and not expected to live; it is reported that he has died, and a funeral is held, but instead he is confined to the family mansion, raised by Victoria Cameron, a kind but outspoken cook.

Young Francis is subjected to a broad range of religious influences. His nanny, Bella-Mae, is a member of the Salvation Army. Later, his aunt raises him in the Catholic faith, but secretly, because of his father's opposition to Catholicism. At school, he is an outsider, the victim of bullies (later, as the heir to his family's fortune, he finds himself bullied by an unfaithful wife and others who make demands on his wealth). At home, he relishes time spent with his grandfather, Victoria Cameron, and Zadok Hoyle, who prepares the village dead for burial. Zadok, it is revealed late in the novel, is the father of Francis's elder brother.

Art plays an important role in the novel. Francis learns to draw by studying the cadavers with which his friend Zadok works. Later, at boarding school, his aptitude for art as a painter and as a connoisseur gains him some attention. In England, he is recruited by British intelligence, and later, in the days before World War II, he serves an artistic apprenticeship in Germany, restoring old paintings, and becomes involved in a shady art-dealing ring aimed at defrauding the Nazis.

The artistic principles Francis learns under the tutelage of the "Meister" Tancred Saraceni are very significant. He learns that he will never be a modern artist in his own right, but he eventually manages, in a way, to become a Renaissance painter, producing two undetectable fake paintings. He experiences a brief victory when his painting is deemed genuine, but toward the end of his life, he sacrifices happiness by refusing to give his only friend Aylwin Ross the painting, sparing Ross the embarrassment of displaying a fake painting in the national museum. As a result, Ross commits suicide, and Cornish lives out the remainder of his life in miserly seclusion.

SUMMARY

One of Canada's most important novelists and playwrights, Robertson Davies is best remembered for his three trilogies of novels. Davies' novels explore provincial Canadian life, the interaction of the gifted, artistic individual with the world at large, and the role of the arts in everyday life. Davies' novels celebrate and explore the human need for connections with the supernatural, the mysterious, the unknown, and the unknowable.

James S. Brown

DISCUSSION TOPICS

- What role does Jungian theory play in Robertson Davies' novels, particularly the concept of archetypes (ideas or patterns of thought derived from the collective experience of the human species and inherited by the individual)?

- Davies began his writing career as a journalist. To what degree can a journalistic sensibility be discerned in his novels?

- Davies had a lifelong interest in the supernatural and even wrote a book of ghost stories. Where, in his mainstream fiction, does this interest in the supernatural manifest itself, and to what effect?

- Davies is one of Canada's best-known novelists. What about his novels is particularly Canadian, and what attitude toward Canada is presented in his novels?

- Many of the characters in Davies' novels are interested in arts other than fiction. How do such artistic endeavors as painting, drama, stage magic, and opera function in Davies' novels as metaphors for fiction writing and for life itself?

BIBLIOGRAPHY

By the Author

LONG FICTION:
Tempest-Tost, 1951 (with *Leaven of Malice* and *A Mixture of Frailties* known as the Salterton Trilogy)
Leaven of Malice, 1954
A Mixture of Frailties, 1958
Fifth Business, 1970 (with *The Manticore* and *World of Wonders* known as the Deptford Trilogy)
The Manticore, 1972
World of Wonders, 1975
The Rebel Angels, 1981 (with *What's Bred in the Bone* and *The Lyre of Orpheus* known as the Cornish Trilogy)
What's Bred in the Bone, 1985
The Lyre of Orpheus, 1988
Murther and Walking Spirits, 1991
The Cunning Man, 1994

DRAMA:
Overlaid, pr. 1947, pb. 1949 (one act)
At the Gates of the Righteous, pr. 1948, pb. 1949
Eros at Breakfast, pr. 1948, pb. 1949
Fortune, My Foe, pr. 1948, pb. 1949
Hope Deferred, pr. 1948, pb. 1949

The Voice of the People, pr. 1948, pb. 1949

Eros at Breakfast, and Other Plays, pb. 1949 (includes *Hope Deferred, Overlaid, At the Gates of the Righteous, The Voice of the People*)

At My Heart's Core, pr., pb. 1950

King Phoenix, pr. 1950, pb. 1972

A Masque of Aesop, pr., pb. 1952

A Jig for the Gypsy, pr. 1954 (broadcast and staged), pb. 1954

Hunting Stuart, pr. 1955, pb. 1972

Love and Libel: Or, The Ogre of the Provincial World, pr., pb. 1960 (adaptation of his novel *Leaven of Malice*)

A Masque of Mr. Punch, pr. 1962, pb. 1963

Hunting Stuart, and Other Plays, pb. 1972 (includes *King Phoenix* and *General Confession*)

Question Time, pr., pb. 1975

SHORT FICTION:

High Spirits, 1982

TELEPLAY:

Fortune, My Foe, 1953 (adaptation of his play)

NONFICTION:

Shakespeare's Boy Actors, 1939

Shakespeare for Younger Players: A Junior Course, 1942

The Diary of Samuel Marchbanks, 1947

The Table Talk of Samuel Marchbanks, 1949

Renown at Stratford: A Record of the Shakespeare Festival in Canada, 1953, 1953 (with Tyrone Guthrie)

Twice Have the Trumpets Sounded: A Record of the Stratford Shakespearean Festival in Canada, 1954, 1954 (with Guthrie)

Thrice the Brinded Cat Hath Mew'd: A Record of the Stratford Shakespearean Festival in Canada, 1955, 1955 (with Guthrie)

A Voice from the Attic, 1960

The Personal Art: Reading to Good Purpose, 1961

Marchbanks' Almanack, 1967

Stephen Leacock: Feast of Stephen, 1970

One Half of Robertson Davies, 1977

The Enthusiasms of Robertson Davies, 1979

The Well-Tempered Critic, 1981

Reading and Writing, 1993

The Merry Heart: Reflections on Reading, Writing, and the World of Books, 1997

"For Your Eyes Alone": Letters, 1976-1995, 1999

About the Author

Grant, Judith Skelton. *Robertson Davies: Man of Myth*. Toronto: Viking, 1994.

La Bossière, Camille R., and Linda M. Morra, eds. *Robertson Davies: A Mingling of Contrarieties*. Ottawa: University of Ottawa Press, 2001.

Lawrence, Robert G., and Samuel L. Macey. *Studies in Robertson Davies' Deptford Trilogy*. Victoria, British Columbia: University of Victoria, 1980.

Little, Dave. *Catching the Wind in a Net: The Religious Vision of Robertson Davies*. Toronto: ECW, 1996.

Stone-Blackburn, Susan. *Robertson Davies, Playwright: A Search for the Self on the Canadian Stage*. Vancouver: University of British Columbia Press, 1985.

SAMUEL R. DELANY

Born: New York, New York
April 1, 1942

One of the earliest and most influential black authors of science fiction, Delany has expanded the limits of the genre by blending it with stories drawn from myths and with modern interpretations of philosophical thought.

BIOGRAPHY

Samuel Ray Delany, Jr., was born into an upper-middle-class family in the Harlem district of New York City on April 1, 1942. His father had come to New York from North Carolina and, in the period before Delany's birth, had established a successful career as a funeral director. Delany's mother, the former Margaret Carey Boyd, was a library clerk with a long-standing interest in literature. In the late 1920's, she had been a friend of several authors in the literary movement known as the Harlem Renaissance.

The prosperity of Delany's family allowed the young Samuel to attend a number of prestigious schools. Having graduated from the private Dalton School, Delany enrolled at the Bronx High School of Science. There, a reading disorder which had troubled Delany throughout his early schooling was diagnosed as dyslexia. Despite his handicap, Delany was already making progress toward a literary career. While he was still in his early teens, he wrote several novels (none of them published) and served as coeditor of the *Dynamo*, his high school's literary review. Delany's early work won for him several local awards, and he was encouraged to continue with his literary pursuits.

Delany accepted his homosexuality. Nevertheless, on August 24, 1961, he married his former coeditor on the *Dynamo*, Marilyn Hacker. During that same year, he began taking courses at the City College of New York and became poetry editor of the college's literary journal, the *Promethean*. Hacker, meanwhile, left school and began work as a science-fiction editor for Ace Books. Because of Hacker's encouragement and his own conviction that he could write more interesting science fiction than that being published at the time, Delany completed his first successful science-fiction novel, *The Jewels of Aptor* (1962), when he was only nineteen. *The Jewels of Aptor*, like each of Delany's first eight novels, was published by Ace Books. At first, the novel appeared only in a heavily edited version, bound into the same volume as fellow science-fiction author James White's *Second Ending*. A revised edition of *The Jewels of Aptor* was issued by Ace in 1968, and the full text of the novel finally appeared in an edition published by Gregg Press in 1976.

Delany dropped out of college in 1963 and embarked upon an intense period of writing. While supporting himself as a musician, Delany published *Captives of the Flame* (1963), *The Towers of Toron* (1964), *City of a Thousand Suns* (1965), and *The Ballad of Beta-2* (1965). In each of those novels, he united the traditional narrative of the quest with a detailed account of imaginary civilizations. That same combination was to appear in much of his later fiction.

In 1965, Delany left the United States to begin a quest of his own. On an extended journey throughout Europe and Asia, he completed *The Einstein Intersection* (1967), publishing it upon his return to the United States. He then resumed work as a musician in New York City and continued to write novels and short stories. In 1966, with the publication of *Babel-17*, Delany reached a turning point in his career. *Babel-17* received a Nebula Award from the Science Fiction Writers of America and was the author's first novel to be read widely by the general public. Delany won a second Nebula Award for *The Einstein Intersection;* he would receive the award again for a short story, "Aye, and Gomorrah . . ." (1967), and a novella, "Time Considered as a Helix of Semiprecious Stones" (1969).

For a brief period during the late 1960's, Delany lived in San Francisco. Upon returning to New York City, he completed *Nova* (1968), a novel that proved to be another breakthrough for him. *Nova* was the author's first work to be published by a press other than Ace Books (it was issued by Doubleday) and his first novel to be printed in a hardbound edition.

In the early 1970's, Delany began experimenting with new media and avant-garde literary forms. He wrote, directed, and edited two short films, *Tiresias* (1970) and *The Orchid* (1971); developed plots for the comic-book series *Wonder Woman* (1972); and edited four volumes of *Quark* (1970-1971), a quarterly anthology devoted to experimental techniques of writing and analyzing science fiction. His coeditor of *Quark* was once again Hacker. By this time, she had become an award-winning poet in her own right. Hacker and Delany would continue to collaborate on various projects until their divorce in 1980.

Delany also began work on his most ambitious project to date, a long and difficult novel that was to be known as *Dhalgren* (1975). When *Dhalgren* was finally published, it met with mixed reaction. The novel sold exceedingly well—more than half a million copies were eventually printed—but critical reviews were largely negative. Many critics were puzzled by the ambiguity of the novel's plot—its central character is an amnesiac whose uncertainty about his own past clouds the narrative at many points—and by Delany's radical departure from the accepted conventions of science fiction. Rather than taking place in an imaginary future locale, for example, *Dhalgren* is set in a strangely distorted version of the 1970's. The setting proves to be an extended metaphor for modern life, with many of the problems of contemporary society taken to their logical—or perhaps illogical—conclusions.

While *Dhalgren* was still in press, Delany completed another novel, *The Tides of Lust* (1973). This work represented another radical departure from his earlier fiction. *The Tides of Lust* includes explicitly pornographic passages, a factor that seemed to alienate many readers. The book quickly went out of print. Nevertheless, Delany returned to the theme of sexuality in his next major novel, *Triton* (1976), which depicts a utopian society in which all restrictions on personal and sexual relationships have been removed.

In 1975, Delany was named Butler Professor of English at the State University of New York, Buffalo. While at Buffalo, Delany began devoting more of his energies to literary criticism and analysis than to fiction. He became a senior fellow at the center for Twentieth Century Studies at the University of Wisconsin, Milwaukee, in 1977 and at Cornell University's Society for the Humanities in 1987.

A few more fictional works were published by Delany during this period, including *Distant Stars* (1981) and the graphic novel *Empire: A Visual Novel* (1978). Nevertheless, Delany's most important work throughout the 1970's and 1980's remained in the field of literary criticism. After writing two volumes that he called "notes on the language of science fiction," *The Jewel-Hinged Jaw* (1977) and *Starboard Wine* (1984), Delany served in 1988 as professor of comparative literature at the University of Massachusetts at Amherst. In 1995, he served as a Distinguished Visiting Writer at the University of Idaho and in 1997 as a Master Artist-in-Residence at the Atlantic Center for the Arts. In 1999, he joined the faculty at the University at Buffalo. He continues to be active in the field of science fiction, attending conventions and teaching at the Clarion Science Fiction Writers' Workshop multiple times, and has achieved numerous awards in that field, including a multitude of Hugo, Lambda, and Nebula Awards. He teaches comparative literature at Temple University as of 2001.

ANALYSIS

It is not surprising that so much of Delany's work in the late 1970's and the 1980's was in the field of literary criticism; even his early fiction reveals an extensive knowledge of literary theory and of mainstream literary traditions. For example, in *The Jewels of Aptor*, the quest for telepathic jewels places Geo, the hero of the novel, in the same tradition as numerous other protagonists of epic quests, including Gilgamesh, Jason, and Percival. Delany even makes an explicit association between Geo and Jason, the leader of the Argonauts, by adopting the name "Argo" for one of the central deities in the novel.

In traditional epics, heroes of quests begin their journeys because of a desire to seek adventure or a wish to recover some physical object. Delany's characters, however, are motivated more by a desire to seek knowledge than by any hope of material gain. Thus Rydra Wong, the heroine of *Babel-17*, begins her voyage hoping to obtain the information that she needs to decipher a strange alien dialect. Joneny, the protagonist of *The Ballad of Beta-2*, sets out to learn about the Star Folk. In traditional quest stories, physical journeys usually serve as a metaphor for the protagonist's inner journeys of self-discovery. Delany, aware of this tradition, has merely exposed the metaphor, making knowledge both the symbolic and the actual goal of the quest.

Delany's familiarity with modern philosophy and with anthropology has had a major impact upon his novels. The goddess Argo in *The Jewels of Aptor* was inspired by Delany's reading of *The White Goddess* (1947), an examination of religion and folklore by the poet and novelist Robert Graves. *The White Goddess* dealt extensively with the origins and influence of the pre-Greek goddess Cybele. Graves's exploration of Cybele's connection with the earth and fertility may be seen in Geo, *The Jewels of Aptor*'s protagonist, whose name is derived from the Greek word for "earth." Moreover, in such novels as *Triton* and *Tales of Nevèrÿon* (1979), Delany used the techniques of modern anthropology to analyze the fictional societies which he himself had created.

The stories set in Nevèrÿon provide a space in which Delany can explore the form of "sword and sorcery" fiction while simultaneously critiquing it. At the same time, the world of Nevèrÿon provides a setting where Delany has explored the inadequacy of language, perceptions of gender roles, the psychology of bondage and domination, the shaping of society by economic pressures, alternate sexualities, slavery, semiotics, and the control of history.

BABEL-17

First published: 1966
Type of work: Novel

An intergalactic poet attempts to foil saboteurs by breaking their code and learning their language.

Babel-17, Delany's first novel to receive a Nebula Award, was also the first to address issues found in many of his later works. Part novel and part philosophical inquiry, *Babel-17* explores the degree to which language shapes the perception of reality. Babel-17, the artificial language from which the novel receives its name, is described by Delany as lacking both first- and second-person pronouns. As a result, Delany suggests, speakers of this language would not have any ability to be "self-critical" to separate reality from what the language has "programmed" them to see as reality. On the other hand, Babel-17's analytical superiority over other languages is said to ensure that its speakers develop technical mastery over most situations.

One of the questions raised by the novel, therefore, is how much one's language dictates the way in which one perceives the world. In Babel-17, the word for a member of the Alliance would mean something roughly translatable as "one-who-has-invaded"; this, Delany suggests, causes those who think in the Babel-17 language instinctively to view the Alliance as a hostile force that must be destroyed. As one reads the novel, one wonders how much one's own linguistic structures—including, for example, such expressions as "upper class," "Far East," and "New World"—not only reflect, but also actually determine, a system of values.

With a poet as its protagonist, *Babel-17* is also a work that explores the nature and power of literature. In the poetry of Rydra Wong, the novel's main character—as well as in the quotations taken from the poetry of Marilyn Hacker, Delany's wife, which serve as epigraphs for major sections of the novel—one finds poetry continually represented as an effective medium of communication. Rydra Wong's success throughout the galaxy is proof that words can unite individuals regardless of their backgrounds, cultures, or even the planets on which they live.

On yet another level, *Babel-17* functions as a sociological novel, exploring the ways in which people wrongly assume that social conventions reflect a universal law. In the intricately detailed world that Delany has created, many contemporary customs are presented in an exaggerated fashion so that the reader might view them from a new perspective. For example, a reader may be repulsed initially by the novel's description of "cosmeti-surgery," a procedure by which lights, flowers, and mechanical devices are implanted into one's body as decorations.

Yet, in the characters' discussions of this practice, it quickly becomes apparent that surgical alteration of the body for purposes of beauty or hygiene has parallels to the familiar customs of circumcision, ear-piercing, and creating tattoos. In a similar way, the discomfort that some of the novel's characters experience when encountering a "triple" (a form of marriage among three people) is intended to reflect the discomfort of Delany's readers' society when dealing with those whose sexual lives deviate from accepted norms.

THE EINSTEIN INTERSECTION

First published: 1967
Type of work: Novel

In the distant future, a musician attempts to defeat a mysterious figure who is murdering those who are "different."

The Einstein Intersection expands upon the theme of cultural diversity Delany had first explored in *Babel-17*. The alien race inhabiting the earth thirty thousand years in the future attempts to develop its "humanity" by imitating the traditions of the extinct human race. In the end, one of the lessons that the aliens learn is that they must accept their own unique natures and develop traditions appropriate to themselves.

Frequent mutations cause differences to emerge among the aliens. The protagonist of the novel is one of those "different" beings—as is, ironically, the figure who has been destroying the mutants. Thus, failure to accept one's own fundamental difference from others leads, in the novel, to hostility and ultimately to violence.

The narrator of the story, Lobey, is a musician. In the course of the novel, he sets out to regain his lost love, Friza, who is later taken from him again. Delany calls Lobey's opponent in the novel Kid Death. All these elements have been inspired by the Greek legend of Orpheus, Eurydice, and Hades, but the myth of Orpheus is only one of the mythic allusions central to *The Einstein Intersection*.

Like many of Delany's novels, the general structure of *The Einstein Intersection* is that of the quest. (Indeed, tying the plot of the story to his own artis-

tic quest, Delany includes among the chapter epigraphs a number of passages taken from the journals that he kept during his travels throughout the Mediterranean in 1965.) Moreover, the novel's frequent reference to mutations, both among the aliens themselves and in nature, was influenced by Ovid's *Metamorphoses* (first century B.C.E.), a Roman epic in which the transformations of mythical characters was a unifying theme. The *Metamorphoses*, too, had retold the legend of Orpheus.

The Einstein Intersection explores those myths in much the same way that *Babel-17* had explored language. The novel treats mythology as a phenomenon capable of determining the way in which reality is perceived. By the end of the novel, Lobey must free himself from the mythic patterns that he has inherited. He must permit his own "different" nature to emerge. This, Delany suggests, will prove to be the redemption of Lobey himself and of his entire culture.

DHALGREN

First published: 1975
Type of work: Novel

A schizophrenic and amnesiac narrator lacking a left shoe wanders through Bellona, a city cut off from the rest of the world by an unnamed catastrophe.

As *Dhalgren* begins, the narrator wanders through Bellona, which has been cut off from the rest of the country, in scenes which may convey either his impaired judgment or the city's hallucinatory nature: an extra moon, landmarks and street signs shifting without warning, and time's change, slowing and speeding at irregular intervals. In Bellona, distance and direction change without warning and other phenomena demonstrate the chaotic nature of this world: fires break out at random, the dense fog almost never dissipates, and buildings twist and collapse.

Even in this world of randomness, the inhabitants attempt to normalize their existence: a psychiatrist keeps office hours, people hold dinner parties, and a daily newspaper is produced. However, the world has broken down to the point where the only medium of exchange is gossip, not just about each other, but the world in which they live.

The narrator of *Dhalgren*, a drifter named various permutations of the word "Kid," wanders the city, witnessing the struggle of its inhabitants with the necessity of survival, the forces of boredom, and even each other. Over the course of the book, he is acclaimed as a poet, labeled a sexual magnet, and proclaimed the leader of a gang, but continues drifting, saved from the burden of expectation by his amnesia. Beyond the many modernist strategies employed by Delany, the book represents a radical shift from the conventions of science fiction, taking place in an altered version of modern-day life, and representing the kaleidoscopic nature of reality and perception. The book begins with a passage, "to wound the autumnal city," and then loops back to that passage at the end of the book, giving it a circularity that reflects on the nature of history.

Dhalgren has met with both praise and dislike from critics. The book's lack of a linear plot, combined with its circular nature and use of stream of consciousness, gives it at times a Joycean quality reminiscent of *Finnegan's Wake* (1939) at its most infuriating. Theodore Sturgeon said *Dhalgren* was "The very best ever to come out of the science fiction field . . . a literary landmark." Other critics, such as Philip K. Dick and Harlan Ellison, hated the book, and Ellison went so far as to say that when he was assigned the book to review, he got through two hundred pages, then threw it against the wall. Cyberpunk novelist William Gibson called *Dhalgren* "A riddle that was never meant to be solved." The book continues to be considered by many Delany's best and one of the most influential science-fiction novels of the twentieth century. It inspired its own online game, Dhalgren MOO, in 1994.

TRITON

First published: 1976
Type of work: Novel

In a future utopia, a judgmental young man struggles to find his place in society.

The role that language played in *Babel-17* and that mythic patterns played in *The Einstein Intersection* is assigned to traditional sexual identities in *Triton*. In this novel, Delany explores the way in which one's relationships, especially those dictated by the norms of society, determine one's self-image. *Triton* depicts a sexual utopia existing in the year 2112 C.E., a society in which all forms of personal relationships are permitted.

Without any restrictions placed upon them, the inhabitants of this society are free to invent or develop whatever social and sexual identities they choose. Sex-change operations are common, as are "refixations," procedures through which a person's sexual orientation may be altered. The reader expects, at first, that this degree of personal freedom will be liberating, and it is liberating for most of the characters in *Triton*. For Bron, however, the novel's central character, the unlimited choices available in his society create only a profound sense of discontent.

Bron is Delany's first antihero. Self-centered, intolerant, and opinionated, he makes an unusual protagonist; Delany wants his reader not to identify with Bron. Like Kid Death in *The Einstein Intersection*, Bron cannot endure what is different, even in himself. While Kid Death's hostility was directed outward, Bron's intolerance has its greatest effects upon himself, providing the source of his unhappiness and alienation. Despite Bron's best efforts (including, in the end, a sex-change operation and refixation), he is never able to overcome his limitations, and the novel ends with Bron still unhappy and disillusioned.

Triton thus contains Delany's most complete commentary on the social effects of intolerance.

Bron goes to extreme lengths to force himself and others into the sexual roles that he regards as right; however, Delany suggests that these sexual labels (and, by implication, any sorts of labels) can never bring one closer to understanding oneself or the identities of others.

ATLANTIS: THREE TALES

First published: 1995
Type of work: Novellas

Three novellas tell the stories of three young African American men in the twentieth century, one looking for his family, another musing on art and education, and a sailor who is raped.

Semiautobiographical in nature, the work begins with *Atlantis: Model 1924*, in which a young man, Sam, travels from North Carolina to New York in order to find his family. In the six months after his arrival, he has an encounter with a poetic stranger, in a complex and allusive narrative, as well as encountering historical figures such as Paul Robeson, Hart Crane, and Jean Toomer, and finally rejoins his older siblings.

In *Erik, Gwen, and D. H. Lawrence's Esthetic of Unrectified Feeling*, a second Sam, an artistic young boy in the 1950's, is taught both by his formalist art teacher and by a farmhand and gradually is awakened to his feelings about art as well as his own burgeoning sexuality. Sam muses on what art really is, how its definition has changed over the history, and its importance to both himself and the world.

In the final *Citre et Trans*, the third of the Sams, a twenty-something bisexual American writer in Greece in the 1960's, confronts the impact of rape after his roommate brings home a pair of Greek sailors. The darkest of the three stories, including both a homosexual rape and a dog's owner being forced to kill it, the story is still told with the finesse Delany brings to the entirety of his work.

All three of the novellas contained in *Atlantis: Three Tales* focus less on external action than on changes in the main character's consciousness. The work itself is highly experimental, playing with typography, splitting the work into columns to convey concurrent narration, marginal notes, surreal-

DISCUSSION TOPICS

- In many of his works, Samuel R. Delany explores the way in which preconceptions affect perceptions. How do the heroes come to realize that their perceptions may be at fault? Why might Delany consider this an important moment?

- Delany's work often uses a quest structure, in which a physically or psychically damaged protagonist attempts to find a way to reverse that damage. How does that structure work—for or against the story—in *Dhalgren*?

- Why does Delany use a genre form, the fantasy story, in his Nevèrÿon series? What phenomena does using it allow him to explore? What assumptions are automatically made in a fantasy story that Delany uses in the books?

- In *Atlantis: Three Tales*, why are all three protagonists named Sam? What similarities do they possess, and how do those similarities help them reach their final conclusions?

- Why, in *Triton*, does Delany deliberately use an antihero? What characteristics of Bron does he not want the reader to identify with? How would a traditional hero have acted differently?

ism, and stream of consciousness, in order to juxtapose time, memory, and fact. While they trace the interdepency of memory, experience, and the self, the book met with mixed reviews, many critics feeling that the experimental nature of the text made it overly difficult to extract the story.

SUMMARY

Delany's central characters are usually individuals whose quests for knowledge leads them to greater self-discovery. Frequently, this insight involves a realization that the very means that one uses to achieve understanding (for example, language and folklore) may actually be limiting in terms of what one is able to understand.

Samuel R. Delany

On the level of sociology, Delany's novels display a compassionate understanding for individuals who deviate from the norm. By presenting worlds that are exaggerations or distortions of the world known to Delany and his readers, he illustrates how illusory or arbitrary most societal norms really are and suggests that, if seen from a slightly altered perspective, each individual is "different" in some way.

Delany is constantly aware of the conventions and structures of both science fiction and fantasy and constantly questions and distorts them in an attempt to make them evident to the reader. His broad-ranging academic interests manage to inform his work without becoming obtrusive or ever talking down to his reader.

Jeffrey L. Buller; updated by Catherine Rambo

BIBLIOGRAPHY

By the Author

LONG FICTION:
The Jewels of Aptor, 1962
Captives of the Flame, 1963, revised 1968 (as *Out of the Dead City*)
The Towers of Toron, 1964
City of a Thousand Suns, 1965
The Ballad of Beta-2, 1965
Empire Star, 1966
Babel-17, 1966
The Einstein Intersection, 1967
Nova, 1968
The Fall of the Towers, 1970 (includes revised versions of *Out of the Dead City, The Towers of Toron,* and *City of a Thousand Suns*)
The Tides of Lust, 1973 (also known as *Equinox*)
Dhalgren, 1975
Triton, 1976 (also known as *Trouble on Triton*)
Empire, 1978
Tales of Nevèrÿon, 1979
Nevèrÿona: Or, The Tale of Signs and Cities, 1983
Stars in My Pocket Like Grains of Sand, 1984
Flight from Nevèrÿon, 1985
The Bridge of Lost Desire, 1987 (also known as *Return to Nevèrÿon*)
Hogg, 1993
They Fly at Çiron, 1993
The Mad Man, 1994
Phallos, 2004

SHORT FICTION:
Driftglass: Ten Tales of Speculative Fiction, 1971, revised and expanded 2003 (as *Aye and Gomorrah*)
Distant Stars, 1981
Atlantis: Three Tales, 1995

NONFICTION:
The Jewel-Hinged Jaw: Notes on the Language of Science Fiction, 1977
The American Shore: Meditations on a Tale of Science Fiction by Thomas M. Disch, 1978
Heavenly Breakfast: An Essay on the Winter of Love, 1979
Starboard Wine: More Notes on the Language of Science Fiction, 1984
The Straits of Messina, 1987

The Motion of Light in Water: Sex and Science-Fiction Writing in the East Village, 1957-1965, 1988 (memoir)
The Straits of Messina, 1989
Silent Interviews, 1994
Longer Views, 1996
Bread and Wine: An Erotic Tale of New York City, an Autobiographical Account, 1998
Shorter Views: Queer Thoughts and the Politics of the Paraliterary, 1999
Times Square Red, Times Square Blue, 1999
Nineteen Eighty-Four: Selected Letters, 2000

EDITED TEXT:
Quark: A Quarterly of Speculative Fiction, 1970-1971 (with Marilyn Hacker)

About the Author

Barbour, Douglas. "Cultural Invention and Metaphor in the Novels of Samuel R. Delany." *Foundation* 7/8 (March, 1975): 105-121.

Broderick, Damien. *Reading by Starlight: Postmodern Science Fiction*. New York: Routledge, 1995.

Dornemann, Rudi, and Eric Lorberer. "A Silent Interview with Samuel R. Delany." *Rain Taxi Review of Books* 5, no. 4 (2000).

Fox, Robert Elliot. *Conscientious Sorcerers: The Black Postmodernist Fiction of Leroi Jones, Amiri Baraka, Ishmael Reed, and Samuel R. Delany*. New York: Greenwood Press, 1987.

Sallis, James. *Ash of Stars: On the Writing of Samuel R. Delany*. Jackson: University Press of Mississippi, 1996.

Tucker, Jeffrey Allen. *A Sense of Wonder: Samuel R. Delany, Race, Identity, and Difference*. Middletown, Conn.: Wesleyan University Press, 2004.

_____. "Studying the Works of Samuel R. Delany." *Ohio University College of Arts and Sciences Forum* 15 (Spring, 1998).

DON DELILLO

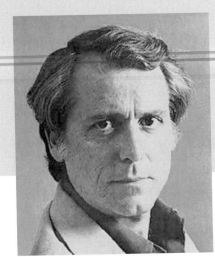

Thomas Victor

Born: New York, New York
November 20, 1936

DeLillo's novels, with their surrealistic and paranoid elements, eccentric characters, and comic set pieces, are an important contribution to post-World War II American fiction.

BIOGRAPHY

Don DeLillo was born in New York City on November 20, 1936. The son of Italian immigrants, he was raised as a Roman Catholic and grew up in Pennsylvania and in New York City's South Bronx. He graduated from Fordham University in 1958 with a degree in communication arts. He worked for several years in advertising before quitting to devote himself to writing. Earning a Guggenheim Fellowship, he lived for a while in Greece, which served as the setting for *The Names* (1982).

Among DeLillo's major works are the novels *Americana* (1971), *End Zone* (1972), *Great Jones Street* (1973), *Ratner's Star* (1976), *Players* (1977), *Running Dog* (1978), *The Names*, *White Noise* (1985), *Libra* (1989), and *Underworld* (1997). His books were always favorably reviewed, but he did not see a major breakthrough until the publication of *White Noise*, which caught many readers' attention with its depiction of a dangerous chemical leak and was honored in 1986 with the American Book Award. When DeLillo published the controversial *Libra*, a fictionalized version of President John F. Kennedy's assassination, he became firmly established in the canon of writers who are both successful in the marketplace, critically analyzed, and regularly included on syllabi. Besides his novels, DeLillo has published short stories as well as the experimental plays *The Engineer of Moonlight* (1979), *The Day Room* (1986), and *Valparaiso* (1999). Under the pseudonym of Cleo Birdwell, he collaborated on a wickedly funny sports novel titled *Amazons* (1980), ostensibly the story of the first woman to play professional hockey. His rise to critical prominence in the 1980's was capped in 1990 by "Fiction of Don DeLillo," a special issue of *South Atlantic Quarterly* devoted to his work, as well as a special issue of *Modern Fiction Studies* in 1999.

DeLillo has never been especially forthcoming about his private life, preferring his novels to speak for themselves. He has responded openly to interviews, however, thereby yielding a sense of how he feels about his work. As his career has progressed, DeLillo has learned to process his experience in the crucible of his imagination. With the success of *Libra* and after more than thirty years as something of a writer's writer, DeLillo began to emerge into the national cultural spotlight. To promote *Libra*, DeLillo agreed to undertake his first book tour, during which he encountered the realities of media attention at first hand. Perhaps reflecting that experience, 1991's *Mao II* uses the character of a J. D. Salinger-like reclusive writer to explore the implications of celebrity. The work secured DeLillo the PEN/Faulkner Award. His satiric play *Valparaiso*—about a systems analyst who tries to fly to Chicago and inadvertently becomes a talk-show celebrity when airline ineptness causes him to end up in Chile—is a brutal analysis of the media and fame. That interest in American culture is reflected in the novel that is largely recognized as DeLillo's defining achievement, 1997's *Underworld*, an ambitious look at American cultural history during the second half of the twentieth century. It was a best seller and received the 2000 William Dean Howells Medal, presented every five years by the American

Academy of Arts and Letters for the outstanding work of American fiction. In 1999, DeLillo became the first American to be awarded the prestigious Jerusalem Prize, which has been awarded every two years since 1963 to an international writer whose body of work best expresses the dignity of the individual.

ANALYSIS

DeLillo's first novel is titled *Americana*, and the title would serve well for his whole body of fiction. *Americana* is an account of a generally aimless trip around much of the United States—New York City, Maine, the Midwest, and Texas—and its first-person narrator, David Bell, calls it a "mysterious and sacramental journey." The novel has two features that have distinguished all of DeLillo's work: a true gift for the evocative and lyrical power of language and a talent for creating eccentric characters who are less believable characters and more satiric cartoon figures. These features have enabled DeLillo, a master satirist, to evoke American life effectively while downplaying the traditional reader expectations of plot and suspense. The characters in his novels are often dispossessed, alienated, and paranoid, and they dwell in an America as surreal as DeLillo's fictional universe.

The topics in these early works included rock music, football, mathematics, an "airborne toxic event," and scenarios of nuclear devastation. In treating such topics, implied criticism of the irrationality of much of American life is inevitable, but DeLillo's treatment of his characters is generally even-tempered rather than corrosive. He has even said of the unappealing Pammy and Lyle in *Players* that "I can't talk about them as people I love or hate. They're people I recognize."

One aspect of DeLillo's ongoing praise of folly is his extraordinary comic sense. The originality of his conceptions stands out immediately, but most of the discussions of this work try to keep this a secret. Examples include a man in *White Noise* who wants to hire a prostitute on whom to perform the Heimlich maneuver, a woman in *Ratner's Star* who is described as having no lap, and Esther and Vera Chalk, the two sisters in *End Zone* who host picnics with "meatless and breadless organic sandwiches." The novels are peopled through and through with these likable oddities; *Ratner's Star* in particular is a virtual megalopolis of such types, many of whom

seemed to have walked straight out of the pages of the third book of Jonathan Swift's satiric *Gulliver's Travels* (1726).

Of all of the United States' manic preoccupations during the 1960's, none was more intense or better publicized than rock and roll and recreational hallucinogenic drugs. These two subjects are often intimately identified in the popular imagination, and they become the twin plot strands of *Great Jones Street*. This novel's rock-and-roll hero, Bucky Wunderlick, sings tunes of America's heartland such as "VC Sweetheart," "Cold War Lover," "Protestant Work Ethic Blues," and his signature song, "Pee-Pee-Maw-Maw." Bucky suddenly abandons his rock group in Houston and goes into hiding in a "small crooked room, cold as a penny," on Great Jones Street in New York City. He is soon entangled in a bewildering plot to retrieve a package of a new, untried dope, and he is forced into illicit commerce with such figures as Epiphany Powell (a black woman bodyguard), Azarian (a band member), and Bucky's manager, Globki. Prominent in the swirling plot is Opel Hampton, educated—at least for a year—at Missouri State Women's College in Delaware, Texas. The plot of *Great Jones Street* is trivial, and the characters are comic-strip jokes, but the language is always strong, and the hallucinatory world of rock music and psychedelic obsessions is turned into an effective piece of Americana. Bucky Wunderlick will appear again in various incarnations as the man who goes to earth to hide out from the madness of life, a favorite DeLillo character.

Great Jones Street, then, is a minor novel but is typical DeLillo work in several ways. It was followed by *Ratner's Star*, and it and other early novels *Americana* and *End Zone* were mostly genial in mood. They featured protagonists who were vulnerable, human, and sympathetic. The next two novels, *Players* and *Running Dog*, introduced a more cynical tone. *Players* is a decided change of pace after the long, boisterous *Ratner's Star*. Its two "players"— Lyle and Pammy, husband and wife—are, respectively, a Wall Street broker and a writer for the Grief Management Council. Their life together disintegrates when a terrorist murders a broker on the floor of the stock exchange and when, soon after that, Pammy learns of Lyle's affair with an office secretary. Pammy flees from their marital nightmare by accompanying two homosexual friends to Maine, but one of these men commits suicide, and Pammy is left to face chaos again. Meanwhile, Lyle meets (through his mistress) the members of the terrorist cell and gets involved as a double agent working for the Federal Bureau of Investigation.

The theme of betrayal and intrigue introduced in *Great Jones Street* and developed in *Players* becomes more intense in *Running Dog*, which offers DeLillo's most elaborate plot to that point. The likable looneys of the early novels are here replaced by pornography merchants, mobsters, and hired killers. The aging smut peddler Lightborne seeks "the century's ultimate piece of decadence," an amateur film supposedly depicting the last days in Adolf Hitler's bunker. Other characters include the Central Intelligence Agency (CIA)-trained Glen Selvy, a regular customer of Lightborne who buys not for himself but for Senator Lloyd Percival. The sordid cast includes a mysterious figure known as Lomax, to whom Selvy sells information about Percival, who is investigating an intelligence unit called PAC/ORD. This group has a secret arm—Radial Matrix—that has prospered in its cover as a straight business firm under its chief, Earl Mudger, who is Lomax's boss.

Selvy acquires two women consorts, first Moll Robbins, a journalist from the magazine *Running Dog*, and later Nadine Rademacher, an Arkansas girl who has been scraping through life in a Times Square sleaze joint telling dirty stories while almost nude. Selvy has to flee New York with Nadine when Mudger suspects him of dealing independently for the film and sends two Vietnamese hit men to kill him.

His life in danger amid shadowy plots and subplots, Selvy does what DeLillo characters always do—he heads for cover where he can hold off the outside world. For Selvy, this hideout is the Marathon Mines, a bleak piece of Texas where the CIA once trained its agents. He faces his pursuers with only a bob knife; when he is killed, his head is packed in a bag for delivery for Mudger.

The whole story ends rather flatly for all its main characters when Lightborne gets the film and shows it to a Texas pornography king named Odell Armbrister, only to discover it is but a dull parade of women and children in innocuous pursuits, enlivened only by Hitler prancing around in the role of Charlie Chaplin playing Hitler. As the screening

ends, a hoodlum named Augie the Mouse shows up and claims the film for Mudger.

Running Dog is significant for its preview of *Libra*; DeLillo has a sure feel for the riffraff that populate the darker corners of American life, and he sniffs out their ties to the powerful and respectable. The paranoia of his characters is mitigated by the fact that someone is after them and sinister forces are indeed at work to disrupt their lives. A century ago, Bucky Wunderlick and Glen Selvy would have sought the anonymity available in the frontier, but in the 1970's they have to hunker down in uncongenial refuges in the outlands of Texas and New York City and wait out their tormentors. Pammy hopes for emotional relief in rural Maine, but she finds only more pain in the company of the two homosexual men, who are damaged in their own ways.

These early novels develop several distinct character types. There are the entertaining eccentrics, often oddly named, such as Epiphany Powell, the Chalk sisters, and the astonishing cast in *Ratner's Star*. They sometimes bear scars of psychic struggle, but they are more often comic constructions with no human interest. Then there are the central figures who retreat from defeat and humiliation, waiting for the end with a resignation born of their grim vision of the madness and meaninglessness of the world. In the more sour novels there are the pornography dealers, the hit men, and other vicious examples of human slag. The bleakness of DeLillo's universe derives more from metaphysical sources than political ones. That is, his anatomies of America and Americana expose the seven deadly sins as endemic throughout the body politic, but their etiology traces to human nature rather than to political figures such as Lyndon B. Johnson or Richard Nixon.

The language in DeLillo's work always appeals strongly, and it is the product of much conscious attention. He explains his concern with language in an interview with Tom LeClair:

> What writing means to me is trying to make interesting, clear, beautiful language. Working at sentences and rhythms is probably the most satisfying thing I do as a writer. I think after a while a writer can begin to know himself through his language. He sees someone or something reflected back at him from these constructions.

DeLillo believes that the power of fiction goes deep enough that, over time, a writer might be able to "shape himself as a human being" through the language he uses to "remake himself." In DeLillo's later novels, he expands that interest in language as a vehicle for self-expression to investigate how a culture shapes itself and its identity using language. In *Libra, Mao II*, and *Underworld*, DeLillo in turn explores the implications of American history itself and the responsibility of those who engage raw event and attempt to shape it into historic record. Recognized during the 1990's as an engaging and often satiric cultural anatomist, DeLillo explored a wide range of issues that have defined America since the end of World War II, including the paranoia of the Cold War era, the impact of the burgeoning media technology, the pressures of celebrity and the cult of charismatic figures, and the American fascination with violence and mayhem.

Following the publication of the massive *Underworld*, however, DeLillo surprised (and alienated) many of his longtime readers by retreating from large-scale sociocultural narratives to offer more intimate character studies in slender works that reveal, as he approached the age of seventy, his deep roots in Catholicism and his long interest in the spiritual definition of the human creature (he studied theology and philosophy at Fordham). *The Body Artist* (2001) uses the character of a successful thirty-something performance artist whose film-director husband inexplicably commits suicide to explore the complex problem of contemporary spiritual enervation and the importance of appreciating the stunning wonder of the everyday. Attempting to recover from the trauma of her husband's death, Lauren Hartke retreats to an isolated ocean cottage and there encounters a nameless stranger apparently living in the third floor of the cottage. Unsure of who the man is (initially she thinks he may be a mentally challenged drifter but comes to see him as a paranormal presence, even a guardian angel), Lauren uses the fragmented and eccentric conversations she conducts with him as a way to protect herself from accepting the painful reality of her husband's death and the role that her absorption in her art may have played in his growing sense of alienation and loneliness. It is only when she frees herself of the stranger's presence and accepts her responsibility that she opens herself up to the complicated beauty of being alive.

In the follow-up work, the spare *Cosmopolis* (2003), DeLillo tells a Dostoevskian parable of the financial ruin of a fabulously wealthy Wall Street asset manager telescoped into a single day, indeed a single drive across midtown Manhattan. As he inches through Manhattan traffic, Eric Packer—gambling on a longshot financial play and, in the process, losing his considerable fortune—is shadowed by a disgruntled former employee who believes that the Internet he manned in connection with his brief employment in Packer's conglomerate has sucked his soul from him. In a shattering denouement in an empty tenement in Hell's Kitchen, the man shoots Packer to death to teach him the value of humility. At the very moment that Packer, now helpless and penniless, registers the sound of the gunshot, he momentarily feels an inexplicable identity that catapults him beyond the tight confines of the flesh and blood. The reader, perhaps resisting the implications of such an ending, must wrestle with the possibility that Packer reclaims his soul in this richly ambiguous ending that extends the promise of redemption to a contemporary materialistic age.

END ZONE

First published: 1972
Type of work: Novel

A young man copes with college football and fears of nuclear war.

Gary Harkness is a talented young halfback with a troubled mind and soul, and Logos College in West Texas is a last chance for him. Gary's troubles begin with his father's saying about life: "Suck in that gut and go harder." His father had played football at Michigan State University, and his life creed is an amalgam of clichés from Teddy Roosevelt as adapted by Knute Rockne: "(1) A team sport. (2) The need to sacrifice. (3) Preparation for the future. (4) Microcosm of life." This parody of the work ethic and the American Dream sticks in Gary's throat, making him a constant disappointment to his pharmaceutical salesman father.

His father, who had spent most of his time on the bench, makes a real football player out of Gary, who becomes all-state and receives twenty-eight scholarship offers. He goes first to Syracuse University, where he meets a young woman who is hiding from the world and goes to ground with her—fortified by two boxes of Oreos and an economics text full of "incoherent doctrines." At Penn State the next fall, Gary succumbs to angst and retreats, this time to an Adirondack winter at home. Gary's next sojourn is at Miami, where all goes well until he becomes obsessed with the horrifying accounts of nuclear war that he finds in a textbook. Depression sends him home again, waiting out the year before moving on to Michigan State as an "aging recruit." When he and two other players hit an Indiana safety man so hard that he dies the next day, Gary gives up once more and stays in his room for seven weeks, shuffling a deck of cards.

Therefore, Logos College is Gary's final chance. At Logos, he finds himself playing for Coach Emmett Creed, who says of football, "It's only a game, but it's the only game." Gary's teammates are a colorful lot, notably Taft Robinson and Anatole Bloomberg. Taft is a transfer student from Columbia University, the first black student at Logos. He is brilliant in the classroom as well as on the football field, but he eventually gives up on football. Taft reads books about the Holocaust and ponders his claim that Rembrandt van Rijn and Johann Sebastian Bach had Masai blood in their veins. Taft is another DeLillo loner in retreat from the madness of the world.

Taft's roommate is Anatole Bloomberg, left tackle on offense. Anatole is also "a voluntary exile of the philosophic type." Anatole is overweight and suffers from enuresis. He is a northerner who is, he says, "unjewing" himself in West Texas:

> You go to a place where there aren't any Jews. After that you revise your way of speaking. You take out the urbanisms. The question marks. All that folk wisdom. The melodies in your speech. The inverted sentences. You use a completely different set of words and phrases. Then you transform your mind into a ruthless instrument. You teach yourself to reject certain categories of thought.

By these means he will relieve his "enormous nagging historical guilt."

Gary spends most of his time away from the football field with either Myna Corbett, a classmate in Mexican geography, or Major Staley, a Reserve Officers' Training Corps professor. Myna claims that she keeps her weight at 165 pounds to free herself from "the responsibility of being beautiful." Her Texas boots are studded with blue stars, and her mind is stuffed with the fantastic plots of science-fiction novels. She is especially fond of the trilogy written by Tudev Nemkhu, a Mongolian with an epic imagination. Gary and Myna spend time on picnics with Esther and Vera, the Chalk sisters, who specialize in breadless and meatless sandwiches.

Whereas Gary's closest friends all seem burdened by some great spiritual wound, Major Staley is brisk and competent. Gary finds in Major Staley an agreeable accomplice for conjuring up awful visions of a nuclear future. He cannot get the subject off his mind because he believes that "[s]omebody has to get it before the public regardless of language. It has to be aired in public debate, clinically, the whole thing, no punches pulled, no matter how terrible the subject is and regardless of language. It has to be discussed."

A second instructor to whom Gary is close is Alan Zapalac, who teaches exobiology. Zapalac voices the paranoia that many of DeLillo's characters feel: "I'm afraid of the United States of America. Take the Pentagon. If anybody kills us on a grand scale, it'll be the Pentagon. On a small scale, watch out for your local police."

With friends such as Taft, Anatole, and Myna, and professors of woe such as Major Staley and Zapalac, Gary's alienation gets worse and worse. At story's end he is confined to the college infirmary, being fed through plastic tubes.

End Zone is structured as a triptych, with the big football game between Logos and West Centrex Biotechnical Institute as its centerpiece. DeLillo's account of the game is a marvelous set piece. The ambience of college sports is evoked vividly. The dialogue rings true, and the game is convincing and entertaining—a narrative by someone who knows what happens in football. *End Zone* is, then, a sports story that gratifies with its knowledgeable game talk, an evocation of the terrible shadow of nuclear war as it was felt in the 1960's, and a picture of several unusual but ingratiating young people coping with an insane universe.

RATNER'S STAR

First published: 1976
Type of work: Novel

A boy genius tries to decode a mysterious signal from outer space.

Ratner's Star is a fantastic narrative in two parts built around an enticing plot idea. In part 1, "Adventures: Field Experiment Number One," Billy Twillig is summoned to a Connecticut think tank, the School of Mathematics of the Center for the Refinement of Ideational Structures. Billy is a boy genius, a fourteen-year-old winner of the first Nobel Prize in Mathematics who has done brilliant work with the "zorg," a kind of number but a "useless" one. The center occupies a huge cycloid—architecturally imaginative but impossible to visualize. Billy is summoned to the center to decode a mysterious radio signal that scientists believe is coming from a planet orbiting Ratner's star. The signal is fourteen pulses, gap, twenty-eight pulses, gap, fifty-seven pulses.

The signal has already been pondered at length by many of the great gurus of mathematics. The great mathematician Endor, for example, spent weeks on the pattern but ended up by going to live in a hole in the ground—a typical DeLillo loser who literally goes to earth. When Billy finds him in his burrow, Endor is subsisting on plants and worms. The other scholars who study the strange pulses are given some of the looniest of all DeLillo's loony characterizations: Peregrine Fitzroy-Tapps is one of the more amusing examples, hailing as he does from Crutchly-on-Podge, pronounced Croaking-on-Pidgett, a hamlet near Muttons Cobb, spelled Maternity St. Colbert.

Another absurd pedant is Gerald Pence, a student of myths who dresses in "old khaki shorts, bark sandals, and a string headband ornamented with eucalyptus nuts." Pence blathers on about the occult in a rambling lecture that features a white-haired aborigine hidden beneath a white canvas on a miniature flatcar. The mystery beneath the canvas is not disclosed even when the canvas-shrouded creature moans and whirls, finally turning inside out before subsiding into a quiet heap.

Other incredibly named characters include a fa-

mous obstetrician, Hoy Hing Toy, who once delivered a baby and ate the placenta in "five huge gulps." Elux Truxl identifies his name as a mere "nom de nom," "the sound identity I have assigned to my nom." Elux is a con man from Honduras who heads a cartel that wants to control the "money curve" of the world. His sidekick is Grbk, a very short person, "mal y bizarro," who is obsessed with exposing his nipples. Grbk is "a tragic person, very sadiensis." None of DeLillo's oddities, however, suffers a deformity more original, a physical deficiency more demanding of radical prosthesis, than does the young woman named Thorkild, a specialist in "decollation control." Billy chances upon her in her bath one day, but she will not allow him to view her naked because she has no lap.

Ratner's Star soon reduces to a parade of such original noncharacters. Orang Mohole, a star of "alternate physics" who has twice won the Cheops Feeley Medal, glazes his audience's eyes with talk of the "value-dark dimension" and the "mohole totality." Orang conceives of the universe as a "stellated twilligon" and predicts its "eventual collapse in a sort of n-bottomed hole or terminal mohole." His feeding habits feature regular trips to a vomitorium. He takes Billy to a party where the atmosphere is enlivened by unusual fragrances from aerosol cans, such as "heaped garments" and "nude female body (moist)—sense of urgency arises." The Cheops Feeley whom the medal honors suffers an uncommon spiritual malady; Cheops is, he says, a lapsed gypsy.

Making his way through this incredible throng, Billy gets to see the wizened Shazar Lazarus Ratner during a torchlight ceremony underneath the cycloid. Ratner lives on only thanks to the silicone injections he gets from his physician, a Dr. Bonwit, who keeps a yacht named the *Transurethral Prostatectomy*.

When he is not marveling at the doings of his coworkers, Billy is figuring out that the pulses derive from a "positional notation system based on the number sixty" and that they represent the number 52,137. His triumph is flat, however, because Billy is soon told by the chief mathematician, Dr. Softly, that work on Ratner's star is no longer needed and that he is to work on "a logistic cosmic language based on mathematical principles." Part 1 ends with the announcement of this assignment.

Part 2 is titled "Reflections. Logicon Project

Minus-One." DeLillo has explained that the two parts—"Adventures" and "Reflections"—refer to Lewis Carroll's *Alice's Adventures in Wonderland* (1865) and *Through the Looking-Glass* (1871). The parallels are structural, however, not thematic. DeLillo's lengthy commentary on *Ratner's Star* identifies numerous structural contrasts between parts 1 and 2 and notes that Pythagoras is the "guiding spirit" behind the work.

Billy learns in part 2 that "in the untold past on this planet a group of humans transmitted a radio message into space." This knowledge clears up the puzzle of the pulses: They came from Earth millions of years ago. Billy then deduces that the sixty-base notation suggests that 52,137 is a number of seconds and that the pulse sequence fourteen, twenty-eight, fifty-seven refers to twenty-eight minutes and fifty-seven seconds after two o'clock in the afternoon on the unspecified day. At the same time, Billy notices that the clock on the wall gives exactly that time; as the significance of the time sinks in, he hears a radio announcement of an unpredicted eclipse of the sun that is about to occur. Billy and Dr. Softly realize that the end is imminent, and both depart for Endor's hole, two more DeLillo characters digging in to wait for the end.

WHITE NOISE

First published: 1985
Type of work: Novel

A history professor copes with a deadly chemical spill and his wife's fear of death.

White Noise probably succeeded mostly for its dramatization of a topical issue: the danger to the environment—and to humankind—represented by the many substances continually issuing from chemistry laboratories. While death from chemical poisoning is a major theme of the novel, however, it is only subsidiary to the grim awareness of inevitable death and annihilation that seizes everyone's consciousness in the book. White noise fills up all frequencies, creating a steady hiss. In DeLillo's imagination, it becomes a sobering metaphor for that low, monotonous, but steady small whisper of human mortality constantly filling up the otherwise unused frequencies of an individual's mental processes.

White Noise has all the best features of a DeLillo novel: crazy characters presented with wit and imagination, language that carries its conceptions gracefully, several wonderfully conceived set pieces, and a major character who at the end braces himself against the world's madness. It also has the failure of plot that is not unexpected in a DeLillo novel.

White Noise is divided into three parts. Part 1, "Waves and Radiation," develops the comic characterizations and dwells on the ubiquitous noises that make up the background to everyday life; the "dull and unbeatable roar" of the supermarket, the "great echoing din" of the hardware store, and, most disturbing of all, a seven-hour spell of loud crying that inexplicably overtakes the protagonist's young son. Jack Gladney, the first-person narrator, chairs the department of Hitler studies at College-on-the-Hill.

Jack suffers much unease over his inability either to read German or to speak it, a scholarly failure that leads to a comic interlude when Jack hosts a conference on Hitler studies but hides from all the German participants. His welcoming speech includes all the words he can find that are the same in both German and English, and it features many allusions to Hitler's dog, Wolf, whose name is the same in both languages.

Jack's two closest colleagues are Howard Dunlop, a self-taught meteorologist, and Murray Jay Siskind, a researcher in popular culture. Howard's correspondence school degree in meteorology authorizes him to teach that subject "in buildings with a legal occupancy of less than one hundred." Even this eccentricity traces to a preoccupation with death, as Howard came to the subject when he found in patterns of weather data a structure that helped him cope with the trauma of his mother's death. Murray Jay Siskind's comic obsessions—reading the advertisements in *Ufologist Today* and performing the Heimlich maneuver on a prostitute, for example—are rooted in his overwhelming loneliness. He seeks to present a "vulnerability that women will find attractive" but manages only a "half sneaky look, sheepish and wheedling." These three wounded academics are complemented by a friend of Jack's son, the teenage Orest Mercator. Orest's desperation appears in his obsession with spending sixty-seven days in a cage of poisonous snakes.

Part 2 is "The Airborne Toxic Event," a sterile euphemism for the cloud of Nyodene derivative that drives everyone from the college town of Blacksmith for nine days. DeLillo invests the event with an appropriate menace and paranoia, and Jack Gladney's exposure to the toxic gas fills the back of his mind with a white noise exactly like the hum of nuclear warfare that settles into Gary Harkness's consciousness in *End Zone*. The deadly cloud forces everyone to face up to their thoughts of death, and it leads to the terrible human problem that Jack has to fight in the last section of the book.

Part 3, "Dylarama," reveals that Jack's wife, Babette, is overwhelmed by her fear of death. Jack learns of Babette's terror when he finds out that she is furtively taking an experimental drug, Dylar, that is supposed to neutralize the area of the brain in which fear of death arises. To pay for the Dylar, Babette sleeps with the distributor.

Jack's discovery of Babette's plight coincides with his realization that, given his medical history, he is doomed by his exposure to Nyodene. Suffering himself, he confronts Babette and persuades her to tell him her own nightmares about death and to tell of her sexual betrayal. They can only comfort each other.

At this point, the plot of *White Noise* disintegrates in a bizarre, surreal denouement prompted by a lecture on death that Murray gives to Jack. In Murray's interpretation of human nature, everyone must repress the fear of death to survive. Those who cope best are the killers, as opposed to the "diers." The killers feed on the lives of the diers and gain strength from "a fund, a pool, a reservoir of potential violence in the male psyche."

Swayed by Murray's vision of the weak and the strong, Jack distinguishes himself from those DeLillo protagonists who seek cover under stress. Jack takes a pistol left him by his father-in-law, steals his neighbor's car, and shows up at the hotel room of Willie Mink, the man who has sold Babette the Dylar and cuckolded Jack. The shootout that ensues is absurd: Jack shoots Mink twice, but Mink gets the gun and shoots Jack in the wrist. Jack drives them both to the emergency room and then returns his neighbor's bloodstained car, giving up on his destiny as a killer. The novel ends as it must, with

no resolution to the constant haunting awareness of the death that everyone faces.

Much of *White Noise* is rendered poetically through DeLillo's careful attention to language. The comic creations, both funny and poignant, are among his best; the set pieces on the crying child, the Hitler conference, and the toxic event are excellent. The good people deserve the reader's concern, and the bad person, Willie Mink, is straight from DeLillo's special gallery of unsavory human predators. Most significant, perhaps, is the sense of the menacing white noise that lingers on in the reader's consciousness.

LIBRA

First published: 1988
Type of work: Novel

A fictional re-creation of the Kennedy assassination.

In *Libra*, a novel that creates a plausible reading of the Kennedy assassination, the narrative center inevitably belongs to Lee Harvey Oswald, the alienated Nobody fed on tough-guy fantasies that he ingests without care from television and film and who, at age twenty-four, is determined to become part of history. In *Libra*, DeLillo meticulously recreates a believable Oswald, carefully balancing the conflicting extremes of the historic Oswald, specifically, his commitments to both the Left and the Right, his allegiance to the Soviet Union (he was a Soviet defector), and his allegiance to the United States (he was a Marine). Oswald's astronomical sign, Libra, serves as DeLillo's metaphor. Unlike others who have tackled the events in Dallas since the Warren Commission, DeLillo is not interested in solving the shooting of the president so much as examining the process of solution itself, how history becomes convincing narrative, how facts produce fictions.

In DeLillo's scenario, the assassination begins as a charade assassination, a designed near-miss on the president's motorcade that would convince the country to reconsider the threat from Cuba. That designed near-miss escalates in the hands of disgruntled Central Intelligence Agency (CIA) agents from the Bay of Pigs debacle into the actual assassination in Dallas. Oswald is a perfect dupe for the emerging plotters, the credible lone gunman necessary for the complex intrigue.

Although the play between the conspirators and the unsuspecting Oswald is mesmerizing and quite believable (indeed, some critics blasted DeLillo for irresponsibly confecting history), DeLillo is more interested in the tenuous nature of fact itself—no matter how much Dallas is investigated, no one will ever know for certain what happened. In addition to the conspirators who carefully fashion a "usable" Oswald by manufacturing phony documents and doctored photographs, Oswald himself keeps changing his identity (he maintains dozens of fake identities and goes by several names), uncertain over who he is politically and whether he wants to settle for being ordinary. DeLillo then adds the story of Nicholas Branch, a fictional retired CIA agent given the responsibility fifteen years after Dallas to piece together a "final" reading of the shooting using the formidable accumulation of evidence, a task he ultimately decides is impossible. Moreover, there is ultimately a fourth narrative voice—DeLillo himself—who argues finally that history itself is a delicate work of fiction, a necessarily contradictory reading of events into plausible-enough truths. Ambiguity, DeLillo argues, is the ultimate reward of awareness.

What DeLillo creates then is not a sympathetic portrait of one of American history's most notorious figures (although initial critical reaction accused DeLillo of trying to generate sympathy for Oswald by showing his economic struggles and his profound alienation). Oswald is never allowed to be simply one thing or another.

The elaborate replay of the Dallas shooting gives DeLillo the opportunity to explore not merely the creativity involved in supposedly factual history but also the vast reach and impact of contemporary media. DeLillo sees the Kennedy shooting as the birth of the media age, specifically of television news and the rush to broadcast catastrophe into American living rooms. Shortly before he is himself gunned down in police custody, Oswald imagines himself processed into a media figure, a three-name commodity, finally achieving what he had dreamed of since his troubled childhood: joining his puny and vulnerable self to the grand forces of history.

Mao II

First published: 1991
Type of work: Novel

A reclusive novelist dies attempting to help a Swiss poet kidnapped by Middle Eastern terrorists.

When *Mao II* opens, novelist Bill Gray has elected to withdraw from public scrutiny for more than twenty-five years. The author of two books that, in the 1950's, had found a cultlike following, Gray decided that such celebrity status made him a commodity and retired to a bunkerlike compound outside Manhattan. In that time, he has worked endlessly revising a novel-in-progress that rests in dozens of boxes and binders in his compound. Gray knows the book is a waste but cannot bring himself to acknowledge that. With curmudgeon eccentricity, Gray sees himself as the last fragile vestige of the written word, the last individual voice in an era of electronic media wherein the individual vanishes. DeLillo uses religious cults, communism, terrorism, and the media to suggest the cultural addiction to conformity.

The novel is set in 1989. Gray has reasoned that his withdrawal has, in fact, simply made him more of a celebrity. He decides to re-engage the world. He first agrees to sit for a photo shoot and then, far more dramatically (and disastrously), to assist in an international campaign to free a Swiss diplomat and minor poet who has been taken hostage in Beirut. However, when he participates in a public reading in London, he realizes that the consciousness-raising event is merely a publicity event that his publishers are using to promote the release of Gray's long-awaited new novel. Determined to help the kidnapped poet, Gray recklessly (or perhaps heroically) decides to go to Beirut in person to offer himself in a trade for the poet. As he travels to

Lebanon, Gray finds his imagination deeply moved to empathize with the Swiss poet and feels himself for the first time in a long time ready to write with renewed energy. Ironically, he is swiped by a careening taxicab in Athens and dies days later from unsuspected internal injuries on a ferry bound for Beirut. He dies ingloriously and anonymously—his identity papers are filched even as he collapses on the boat's deck.

With unsettling directness, DeLillo cautions against the hope of artists and writers campaigning successfully against the contemporary forces of violence and fanaticism, suggested here by the shadowy figure of the terrorist. Although Gray fails to save the poet (after Gray's death, the poet simply disappears into the forbidding underground world of the Middle East), Gray does, briefly, reclaim his imaginative energy—and that, DeLillo surmises, may be all for which the writer in the troubling contemporary era can hope—a theme holding considerable resonance in the post-September 11 world. Amid the special pressures of the late-century, media-driven world, DeLillo questions the value of the writer's long-established privilege to withdraw from society to create art in a sort of protective isolation. Without offering easy answers, DeLillo sees only the impossibility of the contemporary writer ever having the impact and clout of writers before the media age. What DeLillo fears is the marginalization of writers, the determination by the culture to simply disregard writers and their novels as central to the culture. It is a most unsettling anatomy of the contemporary writer.

UNDERWORLD

First published: 1997
Type of work: Novel

A cultural history of America's Cold War era using the life of a waste management executive.

At more than eight hundred pages, *Underworld* represents DeLillo's most complete and complex critique of postwar American culture. It is an audacious, massive text crossed by dozens of related plot lines and hundreds of characters, many drawn from history, that covers nearly five decades. An

ambitious cultural biography, it offers a wide-lens look at the nuclear age from the apocalyptic anxieties of the early Eisenhower years to the improbable collapse of the Soviet empire in the early 1990's. The narrative organizes its reading of this half-century by tracking the intricate (and entirely invented) movements of the home run ball Bobby Thomson launched on October 3, 1951, to give the New York Giants an improbable National League pennant, an artifact historically never recovered.

DeLillo positions that wide-ranging, global narrative against a more conventional story line, that of Nick Shay, a successful Arizona waste management executive in his fifties who comes to buy the fabled baseball (or at least what he thinks is the real ball). Well past mid-life, Nick has decided to make his peace with his own troubled history, specifically a difficult adolescence in the Bronx, including a father who abandoned the family, Nick's brief affair with a teacher's wife, and his accidental shooting of a neighborhood heroin addict. In the sections devoted to Nick's adolescence, DeLillo reveals—for the first time in his fiction—some of his own childhood recollections from the same New York environs.

Within those two narrative lines, DeLillo folds in a number of fascinating, tangentially related plots, including the story of Texas serial killer interested in television notoriety, an elderly nun who undergoes a religious experience when she sees the image of dead girl on a billboard, and a junk artist intent on converting dozens of decommissioned bombers into a massive desert art piece. The construction of the novel is itself unconventional and daunting. While sections devoted to Nick Shay move backward from the 1990's, chapters on the trek of the baseball move forward from the 1950's. The two complementary narrative movements create a fluid and elegant sense of history as something that is constantly happening. Along the way, DeLillo reinvestigates many of his long-defining themes: the penchant for violence in the American character, the pressure from the media and the im-

---

age industry, the emptiness of material success, the quiet discontent in suburbia, the uneasy sense in the post-Hiroshima culture of living within hailing distance of the apocalypse, the oppressive paranoia that defined so much Cold War thought, and ultimately, the difficult struggle to affirm a spiritual dimension in the late twentieth century in the face of so much death on such an unimaginable scale.

These are weighty ideas. However, DeLillo maintains an intimacy and a generous sympathy by drawing out the psychological implications of Shay's late-coming confrontation with his own life and inevitably with his approaching mortality. *Underworld* is a grand, imposing narrative, crowded with engaging side narratives (including the opening set piece that re-creates the late afternoon in the Polo Grounds when Thomson blasted his historic home run) whose deft architecture and tight control confirmed DeLillo's status among the major novelists of postwar American literature.

SUMMARY

In more than forty years of fiction, in a remarkable body of inventive work that crosses many genres, DeLillo has maintained a consistent interest in defining and defending the self in a late-century materialist and media culture that appears to militate against any assertion of the dignity and worth of the individual. As the son of immigrants, DeLillo brought to the post-World War II American novel the acute sensibility of the outsider, one who is both deeply aware of its culture and frankly critical of it. A gifted satirist who uses eccentric characters and often labyrinthine plots a vehicle to explore ideas and critique contemporary culture, DeLillo most often uses narrative to indict, yet he never relinquishes his faith in language itself to address these issues and, as a profoundly religious writer, ultimately in the dignity and grace of the individual to be greater, finer, than the surrounding culture.

Frank Day; updated by Joseph Dewey

BIBLIOGRAPHY

By the Author

LONG FICTION:
Americana, 1971
End Zone, 1972
Great Jones Street, 1973
Ratner's Star, 1976
Players, 1977
Running Dog, 1978
Amazons, 1980 (as Cleo Birdwell)
The Names, 1982
White Noise, 1985
Libra, 1988
Mao II, 1991
Underworld, 1997
The Body Artist, 2001
Cosmopolis, 2003

SHORT FICTION:
"Pafko at the Wall," 1992

DRAMA:
The Engineer of Moonlight, pb. 1979
The Day Room, pr. 1986
The Rapture of the Athlete Assumed into Heaven, pb. 1990
Valparaiso: A Play in Two Acts, pb. 1999

About the Author

Bilton, Alan. "Don DeLillo." In *An Introduction to Contemporary American Fiction*. New York: New York University Press, 2002.

Cowart, David. *The Physics of Language*. Athens: University of Georgia Press, 2002.

DeLillo, Don. Interview by Tom LeClair. In *Anything Can Happen: Interviews with Contemporary American Novelists*, edited by Tom LeClair and Larry McCaffery. Urbana: University of Illinois Press, 1983.

Keesey, Douglas. *Don DeLillo*. Twayne's United States Authors Series. New York: Twayne, 1993.

LeClair, Tom. *In the Loop: Don DeLillo and the Systems Novel*. Urbana: University of Illinois Press, 1987.

Lentricchia, Frank. *Introducing Don DeLillo*. Durham: Duke University Press, 1991.

Modern Fiction Studies 45, no. 3 (1999). Don DeLillo special issue.

Osteen, Mark. *American Magic and Dread: Don DeLillo's Dialogue with Culture*. Philadelphia: University of Pennsylvania Press, 2000.

Ruppersburg, Hugh, and Tim Engles, eds. *Critical Essays on Don DeLillo*. New York: G. K. Hall, 2000.

DISCUSSION TOPICS

- Don DeLillo acknowledges the influence on film in his novels. How is this interest in the cinema reflected in DeLillo's handling of character and plot?

- DeLillo has been called a gifted satirist. In what ways can his work be considered satiric?

- DeLillo worked for a time in commercial advertising and has written at length about the power of electronic media. How does DeLillo see the relationship between literature and the visual media?

- How do the lessons of the Kennedy assassination, which DeLillo cites as responsible for turning him into a novelist, figure in DeLillo's writing?

- DeLillo's novels are often called "novels of ideas," rather than novels of character and plot. What is the difference, and how does this affect the reader's role in approaching DeLillo?

- What evidence is there in DeLillo's writing of his interest in religion?

- As a cultural anatomist, DeLillo has long argued the central place of violence in American culture. What does he see as the causes of violence in late twentieth century America?

- How does DeLillo experiment with how a story is told, making the process of narrative itself the subject of interest rather than the story?

PHILIP K. DICK

Born: Chicago, Illinois
December 16, 1928
Died: Santa Ana, California
March 2, 1982

Widely recognized as one of the leading science-fiction writers of his time, Dick contributed to the growing recognition of science fiction outside the boundaries of fandom.

BIOGRAPHY

Philip Kindred Dick was born in Chicago on December 16, 1928, the son of Edgar and Dorothy Kindred Dick. He and his fraternal twin sister, Jane, were six weeks premature; Jane, the smaller and more frail of the two, died on January 26, 1929. When Dick was still a small boy, his mother told him about his sister's death. As a surviving twin, he felt a mixture of guilt and anger; in later years, he sometimes attributed Jane's death to his mother's negligence, probably unfairly so.

Some months after Jane's death, the Dick family moved to Berkeley, California, and Edgar took a job in the United States Department of Agriculture's San Francisco office. In 1933, when Edgar was transferred to Reno, Nevada, Dorothy refused to go. A strongly independent woman (she was a feminist and a pacifist at a time when those convictions placed her in a distinct minority), she chose to remain in Berkeley with Philip. A custody battle ensued, as a result of which, in 1935, Dorothy and Philip moved to Washington, D.C., where she wrote pamphlets on child care for the Federal Children's Bureau. In 1938, they returned to Berkeley, where Philip attended high school and, very briefly, the University of California. Except for a period of a few weeks in 1972 spent in Vancouver, British Columbia, he lived in California for the rest of his life.

In Dick's own account, he began his career as a writer at the age of twelve. That was when he learned to type—a skill at which he had to become extremely proficient in order to keep up with the pell-mell flow of his imagination. It was at age twelve that he discovered his first science-fiction magazine, inaugurating a lifelong attachment. By that time, too, he suffered from a variety of phobias and other emotional problems, connected, in part at least, to childhood traumas. As an adult, he seemed to move from one emotional crisis to another—he was married five times, attempted suicide several times, and experienced several breakdowns—but through it all he remained an immensely productive writer.

Anthony Boucher (the pen name of William Anthony Parker White), critic and writer of mysteries and science fiction and cofounding editor (1949) of *The Magazine of Fantasy and Science Fiction*, played an important role in the development of Dick's career. Though unimpressed by Dick's attempts at mainstream fiction, Boucher saw great promise in the young writer's more speculative fiction and encouraged him to develop his talent in that direction. In October, 1951, Boucher accepted Dick's story "Roog" for *The Magazine of Fantasy and Science Fiction*; it was Dick's first sale. In 1952, Dick sold four more stories. Soon he had established himself as one of the most prolific writers in the genre; in 1953 and 1954 he sold more than fifty stories.

In the early 1950's, there were many outlets for science-fiction short stories, as new magazines were appearing in abundance. By the mid-1950's, however, the boom was over; only a few magazines in the science-fiction field survived. At this time, Dick began to shift primarily to writing novels, though he continued to produce stories throughout his career. Commercial considerations aside, the novel form offered much greater scope. *Solar Lottery*, Dick's first science-fiction novel, was published in 1955. By the end of the decade, he had published five more. During the 1950's, Dick also completed a dozen mainstream novels, but publishers were not interested in his mainstream work. One of these novels, *Confessions of a Crap Artist*, written in 1959, was published in 1975, and several others were published posthumously.

Dick continued to write at a feverish pace through the 1960's. His novel *The Man in the High Castle*, published in 1962, received the Hugo Award, science fiction's most prestigious accolade. In the following two years, he wrote eleven novels, all of them readable, several outstanding. He was acknowledged as one of the leading figures in science fiction. Most of his books, however, earned only small advances and minimal royalties. Dick's sustained productivity came at a high cost. By the early 1960's, he had become a heavy user of amphetamines and a whole pharmacopoeia of medications; his dependence on amphetamines increased as the decade passed. While Dick also experimented occasionally with other drugs, he was never the LSD-inspired writer of legend. Later, he would describe the destructive impact of drugs on many of his friends and on his own life.

By the end of the 1960's, Dick was in poor health both physically and mentally, and his output of fiction decreased considerably. In February and March, 1974, he had a series of mystical experiences that preoccupied him for the remainder of his life. He devoted some two million words to a running commentary which he called "An Exegesis," a philosophical and autobiographical journal in which he reflected on his life and works, on problems such as the nature of good and evil, and particularly on his firsthand encounter with the divine (which, according to his mood, he was inclined to interpret in various, often contradictory, ways, sometimes debunking it altogether). He also published several novels influenced by the experiences of 1974, including *Valis* (1981), *The Divine Invasion* (1981), and the posthumous *Radio Free Albemuth* (1985).

Only in his last years did Dick begin to enjoy financial security. An impulsively generous man, he gave without ostentation to charitable organizations and to individuals in need. Foreign rights—his books were particularly popular in France, Great Britain, and Japan—and reprints brought significant income, as did the 1982 film *Blade Runner*, an adaptation of his novel *Do Androids Dream of Electric Sheep?* (1968). The film also attracted new readers to his work, but Dick did not live to see its premiere; he died in Santa Ana, California, on March 2, 1982, after a series of strokes.

While perhaps best known today to wide audiences through film adaptations of his work—including *Total Recall* (1990, from "We Can Remember It for You Wholesale"), *Paycheck* (2003), and *Minority Report* (2002)—Dick's contribution to the literary form of science fiction is officially commemorated by The Philip K. Dick Award. The PKD Award is given every year for original paperback science fiction and was inaugurated after his death by fellow science-fiction novelist Thomas Disch.

ANALYSIS

In his essay "How to Build a Universe That Doesn't Fall Apart Two Days Later" (written in 1978 but not published until 1985, as an introduction to the story collection *I Hope I Shall Arrive Soon*), Philip K. Dick outlined the principal themes of his fiction:

> The two basic topics which fascinate me are "What is reality?" and "What constitutes the authentic human being?" Over the twenty-seven years in which I have published novels and stories I have investigated these two interrelated topics over and over again.

Philosophers, it is sometimes said, are people who sit around asking "Is this table real?" The point of the caricature is to suggest that philosophy is too esoteric, divorced from the problems of everyday life. After all, except for the mentally ill, everyone knows what reality is, so why ask?

Dick was a writer of fiction, however, not a philosopher, and his concern with the nature of reality was anything but abstract. His stories and novels explore collisions between multiple realities. Dick was particularly interested in the interplay between subjective and objective reality. As he noted in a letter written in 1970,

I have been very much influenced by the thinking of the European existential psychologists, who posit this: for each person there are two worlds, the *idios kosmos*, which is a *unique* private world, and the *koinos kosmos*, which literally means *shared* world (just as *idios* means private).

To function as an "authentic human being," one must have these two worlds in balance, according to Dick. When the shared vision of the *koinos kosmos* ruthlessly dominates the private vision of the *idios kosmos*, the result is loss of identity, mindless conformity—a popular fear when Dick began publishing in the 1950's, the decade that produced Sloan Wilson's novel *The Man in the Gray Flannel Suit* (1955) and Vance Packard's early study of the coercive power of advertising, *The Hidden Persuaders* (1957). On the other hand, when one's private vision is not tempered by a "strong empathetic rapport with other people" (a fundamental value in Dick's worldview) and by an awareness of a reality that is greater than any individual, the result is delusion, even madness, destructive to oneself and often to others as well.

Science fiction allowed Dick to explore themes of multiple realities and cognitive dissonance more freely and thoroughly than he could in mainstream fiction. Many of his novels feature situations in which one character invades and distorts the perceptions of others, altering the way in which they experience reality. In *Eye in the Sky* (1957), for example, the premise is an accident at a particle accelerator. While the victims of the accident—a very diverse lot—lie unconscious, their inner worlds merge in some unexplained fashion; in this dreamlike state, the whole group experiences the world as it is seen by each of the group's members, one by one. Dick uses a similar plot device to good effect in *Ubik* (1969) and *A Maze of Death* (1970), and especially powerfully in *The Three Stigmata of Palmer Eldritch* (1964). Such science-fictional scenarios reflect real-life circumstances; one way to describe the Nazi era is to say that a single man, Adolf Hitler, with the complicity of many others, was able to impose his insane *idios kosmos* on an entire nation.

It would be very misleading, though, to suggest that Dick wrote stories and novels merely to explore certain recurring themes (no matter how important those themes might be). As a writer he was a consummate showman: funny, wildly inventive, with a sheer exuberance that could not be accommodated within the conventions of mainstream fiction. Even his best books are marked by inconsistencies, implausibilities, and stylistic rough edges aplenty. Yet these flaws go hand in hand with the qualities that make even his weakest books worth reading: the mind-twisting plots, the heady mixture of incongruous elements.

A typical Dick novel contains enough story ideas for four or five ordinary books. *Clans of the Alphane Moon* (1964), for example, takes its title from the inmates of a mental hospital on a distant moon, out of contact with Earth for twenty-five years as a result of a galactic war between humans and aliens. Left on their own, the inmates have divided into groups according to type of illness, the paranoids living in a state of constant suspicion, the depressives barely able to function, and so on. For their mutual benefit, the various groups maintain an uneasy coalition, threatened when a delegation from Earth arrives with plans to reinstitutionalize them.

At the same time, the novel is about marital discord and reconciliation. Dick's depiction of the conflict between protagonist Chuck Rittersdorf and his brilliant wife, Mary, rings painfully true, with enough blackly comic exaggeration to make it funny. The novel also has a political angle (the war against the aliens has not ended the Cold War, and Chuck's job is to program simulacra—that is, humanoid robots—which are used to infiltrate Communist territories, where they will disseminate pro-American propaganda). Also, like many of Dick's works, it contains an oblique self-portrait of the author. Stir in characters such as the telepathic Ganymedean slime mold Lord Running Clam (one of Dick's finest creations) and the themes discussed above, and the result is a uniquely Dickian concoction—imaginable only in science fiction.

Indeed, Dick employed the full panoply of the genre's props: aliens and androids, telepathy and precognition, parallel time tracks—his novel *Now Wait for Last Year* (1966) makes dazzling use of the latter—and all the rest. Yet along with these staples of science fiction, many of his books feature sharply rendered settings drawn from contemporary life, sometimes given a little twist to fit a futuristic scenario. *Time Out of Joint* (1959) depicts late-1950's suburbia; *Dr. Bloodmoney: Or, How We Got Along After the Bomb* (1965) is set in San Francisco and laid-back Marin County; *A Scanner Darkly*

(1977) evokes the drug culture of the 1960's; *Radio Free Albemuth* (1985) ranges from Berkeley in the 1950's to Southern California in the 1970's.

Wherever they are set, most of Dick's novels are grounded in the clutter and trivia, the mundane cares and joys, of everyday life. Most of his protagonists, too, are ordinary people, such as repairman Jack Bohlen of *Martian Time-Slip* (1964). Dick had a hard time ending his books—he could not settle the metaphysical questions that fueled them—and so, typically, he concluded not with a cosmic resolution but with a modest affirmation of simple human virtues. The last lines of *Martian Time-Slip* are representative:

> In the darkness of the Martian night her husband and father-in-law searched for Erna Steiner; their light flashed here and there, and their voices could be heard, business-like and competent and patient.

The rise of the cyberpunk movement after Dick's death emphasized the changing nature of identity and community in an increasingly online world, and science fiction's imagined futures were often matched by the realities of modern technology and its culture in the new millennium. While cyberpunk authors such as William Gibson and Neal Stephenson gained greater critical attention and acceptance for science fiction, the significance of Dick's work as a thematic and literary progenitor of the subgenre has been observed. Indeed, one of the first winners of the Philip K. Dick Award was Gibson's *Neuromancer* in 1984, popularly considered the first major cyberpunk novel.

crets. Instead of the money promised at the end of his contract, however, Jennings discovers his pre-erasure self asked to be paid with a collection of odd items: a code key, a ticket stub, a parcel receipt, a length of wire, half a poker chip, a green cloth, and a bus token.

As Jennings tries to unravel why his earlier self would request such items, he uncovers the truth of Rethrick Construction—also known as The Company—and the secret project Jennings worked on, a time travel device. Each pay item proves useful in this quest, as Jennings realizes his earlier self was able to see into the future, predict what his questing self would need, and provided accordingly. Jennings also discovers the scope of The Company's work and suspects its intention to mold the world's future.

Jennings uses Kelly, a receptionist at Rethrick Construction, to hide the evidence that he uncovers. However, Kelly is the daughter of Rethrick, which she reveals when Jennings tries to blackmail his former employer. Jennings demands that Rethrick let him become The Company's next leader but is refused by Kelly, who holds the parcel receipt that will lead to the evidence. A hand descends to grab the ticket from Kelly, a nod to the literary motif of the deus ex machina—the god out of the machine, who changes the course of a drama in an omnipotent fashion. If anything, "Paycheck" and its time travel puzzle is the story of how one person takes control of his life in an unexpected fashion and becomes his own deus ex machina, forced to trust his own judgment even when that judgment is obscure.

"PAYCHECK"

First published: 1953 (collected in *Selected Stories of Philip K. Dick*, 2002)
Type of work: Short story

An engineer whose past two years of work have been erased from memory unravels the mystery of what he did and why.

Jennings is an engineer who agreed to work for two years for Rethrick Construction and have his memory erased afterward to protect company se-

"THE MINORITY REPORT"

First published: 1956 (collected in *Selected Stories of Philip K. Dick*, 2002)
Type of work: Short story

The head of an organization that uses precognition to prevent crimes must find out the reasons behind a murder he's supposed to commit.

John Anderton is the founder and head of Pre-crime, which stops future crimes from occurring

by gathering data from three precogs—humans gifted with precognition, now reduced to caged idiot savants as their babble is recorded and collated. The day that a new assistant, Ed Witwer, joins, Anderton receives a report that he will commit a murder of an army general he does not know, Leopold Kaplan. Anderton confronts Kaplan, who harbors doubts about Precrime, and goes on the run with Kaplan's help. Anderton is chased by Precrime agents and tries to escape with Lisa, also an agent.

Anderton knows two precogs confirm a precrime before it is pursued, but there is often a dissenting minority report from the third precog. However, the prediction of Anderton's murder is supposed to change when Anderton discovers the news, changing the significance of the minority report. Kaplan has manipulated events so that Precrime will fall to a restrengthened Army headed by Kaplan. Discovering this, Anderton decides to actually murder Kaplan, thus saving Precrime; with Lisa, he accepts his punishment and goes into exile.

The story's premise is based on paradoxes raised by predicting the future: If one knows what will happen, can one change the outcome? If so, what does that say about the ability to predict the future in the first place? Precrime satirizes how law enforcement can overreach its mandate; in the modern world, racial profiling could be considered a kind of precrime. Anderton commits his predicted murder to reinforce the validity of his flawed system but in doing so, proves its correctness.

SOLAR LOTTERY

First published: 1955
Type of work: Novel

In the corrupt, feudalistic world of the twenty-third century, a troubled idealist refuses to conform.

Solar Lottery, Dick's first published science-fiction novel, was his best-selling book prior to *Do Androids Dream of Electric Sheep?* That fact says much about the audience for science fiction, for of all Dick's novels *Solar Lottery* most resembles the stereotypi-

cal and ephemeral products of the genre. Even in this early work, however, some of Dick's recurring preoccupations and distinctive gifts are apparent.

Most of Dick's novels are set in the near future (indeed, in certain instances, Dick's future has already become the reader's past). *Solar Lottery*, in contrast, takes place in the distant future, in the year 2203. In many science-fiction stories (especially those written in the period from the 1930's through the 1950's), the futuristic setting is never coherently or convincingly established. Rather than undertaking the difficult task of imagining a future society, the writer relies on the power of suggestion (simply to say "2203" is to conjure vague but exciting images), supplemented by a bit of technological extrapolation. Such is the case in *Solar Lottery*.

The world of 2203 is one in which space travel has long been a reality, yet in other respects humanity seems to have regressed. This future society is feudalistic. Skilled individuals must swear fealty to corporations or powerful figures. Loyalty is the highest virtue—but in practice, "loyalty" means blind obedience. Common people (unclassified, or "unks") are given a largely illusory measure of hope by an elaborate mechanism known as the Quiz; at the random twitch of a bottle, the single most powerful figure in the society, the Quizmaster, may be deposed, to be replaced by someone utterly obscure.

In this scenario one can detect familiar themes and issues of the 1950's, combined by Dick in a strange and whimsical amalgam: the growing influence of corporations in American life and the stultifying conformity they encouraged; the loyalty hearings conducted by Senator Joseph McCarthy; the appeal of television quiz shows, which were wildly popular at the time Dick was writing *Solar Lottery*; even the role of John von Neumann and Oskar Morgenstern's game theory in America's postwar nuclear strategy (the novel includes a mini-dissertation on game theory). Restless and dissatisfied in this static and unjust society, protagonist Ted Benteley ultimately rejects the system's overemphasis on loyalty and its complacent materialism. His inarticulate idealism is paralleled in a subplot involving the Prestonites, a sect inspired by the writing of maverick astronomer and linguist John Preston to search for a tenth planet in the solar system.

Solar Lottery concludes with a recorded message from the long-dead Preston, extolling "the highest goal of man—the need to grow and advance . . . to find new things . . . to expand." This platitudinous conclusion, unthinkable in Dick's later novels, actually has little connection with the conflicts that animate *Solar Lottery*—in particular the tension between Benteley and deposed Quizmaster Reese Varrick, the prototype for such ambivalently portrayed larger-than-life figures as Gino Molinari in *Now Wait for Last Year*, Glen Runciter in *Ubik*, and the Glimmung in *Galactic Pot Healer* (1969).

THE MAN IN THE HIGH CASTLE

First published: 1962
Type of work: Novel

In the alternate world imagined in this novel, Germany and Japan were victorious in World War II.

The Man in the High Castle belongs to the subgenre of science fiction known as alternate history. Most science-fiction novels postulate future developments (ranging from intergalactic travel to all manner of bionic devices) which have brought about a world much different from that of the reader. In contrast, alternate-history novels look into the past, imagining how subsequent history might have developed if the outcome of some key events or series of events had been different. Ward Moore's novel *Bring the Jubilee* (1953), for example, is based on the premise that the South won the Civil War. Kingsley Amis's *The Alteration* (1976) imagines a Europe in which the Reformation never took place. On a larger scale, Orson Scott Card in *Seventh Son* (1987) and its sequels has created an alternate history of America in the nineteenth century.

The Man in the High Castle imagines a world in which Germany and Japan, rather than the United States and the Soviet Union, are the two superpowers. In Dick's alternate history, President Franklin Delano Roosevelt was assassinated during his first term; the lack of his strong leadership was one factor that contributed to the Allies' defeat. World War II ended in 1947; the action of the novel takes place fifteen years later, in 1962 (the year in which *The Man in the High Castle* was published).

The setting is a conquered America, divided into several distinct zones. The Pacific States constitute one such zone, under the relatively benign administration of the Japanese. The Rocky Mountain States form a buffer of sorts, controlled neither by the Japanese nor by the Germans but lacking any real power. From the Rockies to the Atlantic Ocean are the United States, under brutal German control.

There are several intersecting plot lines in *The Man in the High Castle*. In no other novel does Dick develop such a variety of characters so fully. Moreover, he shifts point of view rapidly from character to character, allowing the reader to view the world of the novel from many different perspectives; even deeply flawed characters are presented with a measure of sympathy. Robert Childan owns a shop in San Francisco, specializing in Americana (the Japanese are passionate collectors). He is an obsequious racist, a classic "little man," full of envy and bitterness. Juliana Frink is a judo instructor in Colorado; her estranged husband, Frank, makes jewelry in San Francisco and hopes to keep his Jewishness a secret. Rudolf Wegener is a captain in the German navy who is morally opposed to his Nazi superiors; he comes to San Francisco under a false identity to meet with a Japanese official, Nobusuke Tagomi, and warn him of a secret German plan to stage a border incident in America that will serve as a pretext for an all-out nuclear attack on Japan.

Indeed, all of the characters are forced in some way to confront the horrors of Nazism. In the world of the novel, that includes not only the Holocaust but also a genocidal "experiment" in Africa that has resulted in the virtual depopulation of the continent. Yet *The Man in the High Castle* is not primarily concerned with the peculiar nature of the Nazi phenomenon. Rather, Nazism functions in the novel as an especially potent embodiment of primal evil.

Countless science-fiction novels depict an archetypal conflict between the forces of good and evil. Dick's treatment of this theme, however, is highly distinctive. Here, as Mr. Tagomi perceives in a moment of insight, evil is not simply a concept: "There is evil! It's actual like cement." Yet this palpable evil, Mr. Tagomi realizes, is not confined to the Nazis and their ilk: "It's an ingredient in us. In the world. Poured over us, filtering into our bodies, minds, hearts, into the pavement itself."

Such a recognition can be shattering; in a scene that is repeated with variations in many of Dick's novels, Mr. Tagomi finds that for a short time, reality itself appears to be dissolving before his eyes. What saves him from moral paralysis is a counter-recognition or intuition that, however muddled human attempts to do good and fight evil may be, they are in harmony with the order of things that underlies the world of appearances.

That such an order, though imperfectly perceived, really exists—that it is not merely a product of wishful thinking—is suggested in the novel in two ways. First, there is the role in the narrative of the *I Ching*, the ancient Chinese book of divination. To use this oracle, one tosses coins or yarrow stalks and then consults the text according to the patterns in which they fall. In the course of the novel, several of the characters repeatedly have recourse to the *I Ching*. The fact that its guidance generally proves to be reliable suggests metaphorically that beneath the seeming chaos of human experience there lies a meaningful order. At the same time, the fact that the oracle is frequently enigmatic, requiring considerable interpretation and never easily verifiable, suggests that human access to this immutable order will remain incomplete, always subject to distortion.

Second, there is the intriguing novel-within-a-novel, Hawthorne Abendsen's "The Grasshopper Lies Heavy," which is read or alluded to by many of the characters in *The Man in the High Castle* and from which several passages are quoted. Abendsen's novel, banned in German-controlled territories (where it nevertheless enjoys clandestine circulation) and very popular in the Pacific States, describes an alternate history in which Germany and Japan were defeated in World War II. The world of Abendsen's novel, while it closely resembles the real world outside the frame of *The Man in the High Castle*, is not identical to it. For example, Rexford Tugwell, not Franklin Roosevelt, is president of the United States during the war. (In Abendsen's version, Roosevelt is president through 1940 and is thus able to prepare the country for war.)

The climax of *The Man in the High Castle* occurs when Juliana Frink, having killed a Nazi assassin who was on his way to kill Abendsen, seeks the novelist out in his home in Cheyenne, Wyoming. Abendsen, who is rumored to be entrenched in a fortress (the "High Castle" of the title), is in fact living with his family in an ordinary stucco house on a residential street. There, with Abendsen looking on, Juliana consults the *I Ching* about "The Grasshopper Lies Heavy." (She has guessed, correctly, that the novelist himself used the *I Ching* when writing his book.) The oracle's verdict is at once clear and mysterious: the hexagram for Inner Truth. Abendsen's book is true.

Much of the fascination of alternate-history novels derives from the fact that, like allegories, they have two levels of meaning. On one level there is the imagined world of the story. At the same time, the reader is implicitly led to compare this fictional world with the actual historical world. In *The Man in the High Castle*, however, there is an added level of complexity, for in Dick's novel the characters themselves (some of them, at least) become aware of an alternate reality beneath or parallel to the surface reality of their world. This link between the situation of the characters and the situation of the reader is one of the features that makes *The Man in the High Castle* not only an exceptional example of the alternate-history novel but also one of the enduring classics of science fiction.

"WE CAN REMEMBER IT FOR YOU WHOLESALE"

First published: 1966 (collected in *Selected Stories of Philip K. Dick*, 2002)
Type of work: Short story

A man who wishes to visit Mars has false memories implanted of such a trip, only to discover that he is already living with false memories.

Douglas Quail dreams of visiting Mars, still in the midst of colonization, but is unable to do so. He contracts Rekal, Incorporated to have false memories implanted fulfilling his fantasy. He further adds a twist of adventure, as these memories will make him an undercover agent of Interplan. McClane, the head of Rekal, promises that the memories will be sharper and more vivid than real memories, which blur and fade over time. This highlights how modern technology is able to be more "real" than reality itself, providing sensory stimuli well beyond what normal human interaction gives.

Before the implants take place, however, technicians discover Quail already had an implant that erased his memories of actually visiting Mars as an undercover agent, blowing a government secret. Now aware of his true past and scared for his life, Quail tries to run; however, he is contacted by Interplan agents who convince him to surrender. Interplan agrees to give Quail a new set of memory implants to replace the real Mars memories; in these new implants, Quail foiled an alien invasion as a child and only his continued survival prevents the invasion from resuming. Unfortunately, McClane discovers this may be the truth as well, as a drug-induced Quail moans that this secret was never to be revealed—again, right before the implants take place.

The addition of false memories is less troubling than the uncovering of true memories suppressed for a reason. It becomes difficult to verify what is "real" and what is "false" since what one has to rely on are the altered memories of a damaged man.

DO ANDROIDS DREAM OF ELECTRIC SHEEP?

First published: 1968
Type of work: Novel

Androids of the latest model are harder than ever to distinguish from the humans whom they are so cunningly designed to mimic, but they still have one telltale flaw.

Thanks to the film *Blade Runner, Do Androids Dream of Electric Sheep?* is Dick's best-known novel. (A tie-in edition was issued in paperback under the title of the film, with Dick's original title given in small print.) That is ironic because, as is often the case, the screenwriters omitted significant elements of the novel, changed others, and added material of their own.

Do Androids Dream of Electric Sheep? is a postnuclear holocaust novel. This subgenre is one of the most crowded in science fiction, including masterpieces such as *A Canticle for Leibowitz* (1959), by William M. Miller, Jr., as well as countless forgotten books. Writers from outside science fiction have often contributed to this subgenre too; one notable example is Russell Hoban's *Riddley Walker* (1982).

Dick's novel, written in the mid-1960's and published in 1968, is set in 1992. World War Terminus and the resultant fallout have rendered much of Earth uninhabitable and much of the population sterile. Many of the survivors have emigrated to the barren landscape of Mars. Others, despite the hazards (there is a whole class of people damaged by radiation, known as "specials" or, more popularly, "chickenheads"), have chosen to remain on Earth.

This scenario is familiar enough, but Dick's way of developing it is characteristically fresh. Postnuclear holocaust tales tend to veer toward cynicism or sentimentalism; *Do Androids Dream of Electric Sheep?* avoids both of these extremes. In the world Dick imagines, animals of all kinds have a special value. Some species are extinct, while others are greatly diminished. To own an animal is a mark of status; it is also to enjoy a living link with the preholocaust world. There is a marvelous humor in this—animals are graded in the manner of collectible coins or stamps, with regular catalogs issued, and neighbors keep close track of one another's acquisitions—mixed with deep poignancy. For those who cannot afford a real animal, there are substitutes, such as the electric sheep owned by protagonist Rick Deckard.

Deckard is a bounty hunter. His quarry are rogue androids (called "replicants" in *Blade Runner*), so sophisticated in design that they are almost impossible to distinguish from genuine humans. Almost, but not quite—for androids lack one vital human quality: the ability to empathize, to put oneself in another's place. Here, as in many of his novels, Dick uses the device of the android (the simulacrum) to raise disturbing questions about people's identities as human beings. Such questions are highlighted by Deckard's attraction to the beautiful android Rachel Rosen and by the kindness and wisdom of the hapless chickenhead John Isidore.

The theme of empathy is developed in an important strand of the novel entirely omitted from the film. Like many members of their society, Deckard and Isidore participate in a quasi-religious movement known as Mercerism. Gripping the handles of a "Mercer box," the communicant experiences "fusion" with the thousands of others who are performing the rite at that moment; together they all experience identification with the archetypal figure of Wilbur Mercer, a white-haired old man ascending a steep hill, tormented by rock-throwing antagonists yet pressing on. To be fair to the filmmakers, it should be noted that perhaps they omitted this strand of the novel because Dick's development of it is self-contradictory. Late in the novel, the androids expose Mercer as a fake. After this startling reversal, Dick pulls a counter-reversal; yes, Mercer is a fake, but somehow, and in a more important sense, he is also real. Here the conflict between Dick's persistent skepticism and his equally strong yearning to believe is revealed in its naked form.

A SCANNER DARKLY

First published: 1977
Type of work: Novel

An undercover narcotics officer finds himself in conflict with his drug-using alter ego.

Fred is an undercover narcotics agent who poses as drug user Bob Arctor. Bob shares his house with two other users, Barris and Luckman, and has a girlfriend, Donna, who is a small-time dealer. Bob is addicted to Substance D—the "D" standing primarily for Death—and is ostensibly using Donna to find the source of this drug. To prevent corruption, the government uses scramble suits to protect the identity of agents; not even supervisors know who they are underneath. Fred is assigned to monitor the group at Bob's house, but by necessity, that means he must monitor himself as Bob or blow his cover.

When surveillance of Bob's house intensifies because of suspicious behavior, so do acts of sabotage occurring against Bob. On the same day that the government installs monitoring equipment in his house, Bob and his housemates almost die from somebody tinkering with his car. As Fred, he finds himself reviewing the recordings of Bob and his friends, finding himself in knotty discussions with his supervisor and fellow agents about the results. Fred also finds himself disassociated from Bob, reaching a point where the two are unable to guess each other's actions. The title of the novel refers to the surveillance tool and the consequences when Bob/Fred cannot comprehend what he sees.

Government agents conduct tests on Fred and discover Substance D has damaged his brain, splitting his personae. At the same time, Barris comes to the police and offers information that will get Bob busted as a major drug dealer-conspirator. Fred's cover is blown, and he is placed in the detoxification program of New-Path, where he takes on the name Bruce, his mental functions severely deteriorated.

Donna turns out to be a government narcotics agent, now using her former boyfriend to trace the source of Substance D, New-Path. The novel closes with Bruce pocketing Substance D, unwilling to give up his junkie habits as Bob or perhaps fulfilling his previous role as Fred, keeping evidence for Donna's bust.

The novel is loosely plotted, often going on tangents that help reinforce a sense of the drug community's frame of mind. Along that line, the paranoia that Bob/Fred suffers is never confirmed. Was Barris the one sabotaging Bob's belongings? Dick refers time and again to the capricious behavior of people on drugs and how one betraying whim does not necessarily link to others. Indeed, the odd behavior Bob must engage in to protect his Fred persona may have been the impetus for Barris's deal. Further, why is New-Path growing Substance D— outright greed and opportunism, or perhaps a means of gaining control of people who otherwise would resist being told what to do?

This is as much a story about a community of

drug users as about the split personality of one man. The first chapter focuses on a friend of Bob who must cope with hallucinatory aphids, mirroring Bob's own descent at the end. In an author's note, Dick dedicated the book to friends from his own drug-using community, not condemning their choice but fully cognizant of the consequences suffered.

SUMMARY

Ezra Pound suggested that artists are "the antennae of the race." Dick's novels would seem to bear out that judgment. As technological developments increasingly blur the distinction between the human and the artificial, the real event and the simulated happening, the prescience of Dick's vision becomes increasingly clear.

No one book by Dick stands out as a near-flawless expression of that vision. Taken together, though, his ten or twelve best books constitute a powerfully achieved and unmistakably individual body of work. Metaphysical probing, deliberately overloaded plots, quirky humor, and a fascination with the "junk" of popular culture as well as with esoteric lore are a few of the salient features of the unique cosmos of Philip K. Dick.

John Wilson; updated by Ray Mescallado

BIBLIOGRAPHY

By the Author

SHORT FICTION:
A Handful of Darkness, 1955
The Variable Man, and Other Stories, 1957
The Preserving Machine, and Other Stories, 1969
The Book of Philip K. Dick, 1973 (pb. in England as
    The Turning Wheel, and Other Stories, 1977)
The Best of Philip K. Dick, 1977
The Golden Man, 1980
I Hope I Shall Arrive Soon, 1985
*Robots, Androids, and Mechanical Oddities: The Science
    Fiction of Philip K. Dick,* 1985
The Collected Stories of Philip K. Dick, 1987 (5 volumes)
Selected Stories of Philip K. Dick, 2002 (Jonathan
    Lethem, editor)

LONG FICTION:
Solar Lottery, 1955 (pb. in England as *World of Chance,* 1956)
The World Jones Made, 1956

DISCUSSION TOPICS

- Science fiction often uses technology as a metaphor for broader philosophical and social concerns. Look at specific technological leaps in Philip K. Dick's work and consider the broader issues implicit in these imagined developments.

- Using specific works, how is Dick's writing a historical document of the times in which he lived and not just a projection of the future?

- Dick often mixes the fantastic elements of science fiction with more mundane aspects of life. What is achieved in this combination, and how does that influence our understanding of the science-fiction genre?

- What are Dick's targets of satire, and why does he choose to critique them? Keeping this in mind, explore Dick's sense of the absurd—that is, how he utilizes it and what it reveals.

- Name specific ways in which countercultures or underground cultures function in Dick's work. Are they always opposed to the mainstream, or do they provide valid alternatives? What does this reveal about Dick's views on society?

- Explore the logical puzzles that Dick's plots often create to call into question basic questions, such as "What is reality?" and "What defines identity?" Citing specific works, explain what he does to provide concrete answers for readers, and what he does to deny the same.

- Consider mysticism and religion in Dick's work. How do they relate to technology? When are they positive forces, and when do they work against characters?

Philip K. Dick

The Man Who Japed, 1956
Eye in the Sky, 1957
Time Out of Joint, 1959
Dr. Futurity, 1960
Vulcan's Hammer, 1960
The Man in the High Castle, 1962
The Game-Players of Titan, 1963
Clans of the Alphane Moon, 1964
Martian Time-Slip, 1964
The Penultimate Truth, 1964
The Simulacra, 1964
The Three Stigmata of Palmer Eldritch, 1964
Dr. Bloodmoney: Or, How We Got Along After the Bomb, 1965
The Crack in Space (Cantata 140), 1966
Now Wait for Last Year, 1966
The Unteleported Man, 1966 (pb. in England as *Lies, Inc.*, 1984)
Counter-Clock World, 1967
The Zap Gun, 1967
The Ganymede Takeover, 1967 (with Ray Nelson)
Do Androids Dream of Electric Sheep?, 1968 (reissued as *Blade Runner*, 1982)
Ubik, 1969
Galactic Pot-Healer, 1969
The Philip K. Dick Omnibus, 1970
A Maze of Death, 1970
Our Friends from Frolix 8, 1970
We Can Build You, 1972
Flow My Tears, the Policeman Said, 1974
Confessions of a Crap Artist, 1975
Deus Irae, 1976 (with Roger Zelazny)
A Scanner Darkly, 1977
The Divine Invasion, 1981
Valis, 1981
The Transmigration of Timothy Archer, 1982
The Man Whose Teeth Were All Exactly Alike, 1984
Radio Free Albemuth, 1985
In Milton Lumky Territory, 1985
Puttering About in a Small Land, 1985
Humpty Dumpty in Oakland, 1986
Mary and the Giant, 1987
The Broken Bubble, 1988

NONFICTION:
In Pursuit of Valis: Selections from the Exegesis, 1991 (Lawrence Sutin, editor)
The Selected Letters of Philip K. Dick, 1991-1993 (Don Herron, editor)
The Shifting Realities of Philip K. Dick: Selected Literary and Philosophical Writings, 1995 (Sutin, editor)
What If Our World Is Their Heaven: The Final Conversations of Philip K. Dick, 2000 (Gwen Lee and Elaine Sauter, editors)

MISCELLANEOUS:
The Dark Haired Girl, 1988

About the Author

Apel, D. Scott, ed. *Philip K. Dick: The Dream Connection.* San Diego: Permanent Press, 1987.

Carrere, Emmanuel. *I Am Alive and You Are Dead: The Strange Life and Times of Philip K. Dick.* Translated by Timothy Bent. New York: Metropolitan Books, 2003.

Lem, Stanislaw. *Microworlds: Writings on Science Fiction and Fantasy.* San Diego: Harcourt Brace Jovanovich, 1984.

Mackey, Douglas A. *Philip K. Dick.* Boston: Twayne, 1988.

Mason, Daryl. *The Biography of Philip K. Dick.* London: Gollancz, 2006.

Olander, Joseph, and Martin Harry Greenberg, eds. *Philip K. Dick.* New York: Taplinger, 1983.

Palmer, Christopher. *Philip K. Dick: Exhilaration and Terror of the Postmodern.* Liverpool, England: Liverpool University Press, 2003.

Sutin, Lawrence. *Divine Invasion: A Life of Philip K. Dick.* New York: Harmony Books, 1987.

Umland, Samuel J., ed. *Philip K. Dick Contemporary Critical Interpretations (Contributions to the Study of Science Fantasy).* Westport, Conn.: Greenwood Press, 1995.

Warrick, Patricia. *Mind in Motion: The Fiction of Philip K. Dick.* Carbondale: Southern Illinois University Press, 1987.

Williams, Paul. *Only Apparently Real: The World of Philip K. Dick.* New York: Arbor House, 1986.

JAMES DICKEY

Born: Atlanta, Georgia
February 2, 1923
Died: Columbia, South Carolina
January 19, 1997

A renowned post-World War II American poet, Dickey is also the author of the best-selling novel Deliverance.

Courtesy, *The Augusta Chronicle*

BIOGRAPHY

James Lafayette Dickey was born on February 2, 1923, in Atlanta, son of Eugene Dickey, a lawyer, and Maibelle Swift Dickey. The Dickeys' firstborn son, Eugene, died four years before James was born. Eugene's death from spinal meningitis at the age of six is the subject of Dickey's poem "The String," in which the poet's guilt feelings appear in the refrain "Dead before I was born."

Dickey was an excellent athlete who played football at North Fulton High School, from which he graduated in 1942. He then enrolled at Clemson Agricultural College in South Carolina, where he played football before quitting school after one semester to join the Army Air Force. Dickey spent four years, 1942-1946, in military service, flying about a hundred missions for the 418th Night Fighters in the South Pacific. The poem "The Fire-bombing" and many of the other poems in *Helmets* (1964) and *Buckdancer's Choice* (1965) raise questions prompted by his participation as a pilot in the devastation of Japanese cities. Dickey has remarked that he first began reading poetry while in the Air Force. He frequented the library stacks, he says, while waiting for the librarian he was dating to finish work.

In 1946, his military service completed, Dickey transferred from Clemson to Vanderbilt Univer-

sity. He also gave up football for track and set the Tennessee state record for the 120-yard high hurdles. Dickey enrolled at Vanderbilt in the wake of three significant literary movements at that university: the fugitive period of the 1920's, the agrarianism of the 1930's, and the blossoming of the New Criticism in the 1940's. Although he sympathized with the Vanderbilt writers in their skepticism about industrialization, he kept literary movements at arm's length throughout his career and is not identified with any school.

Dickey married Maxine Syerson in 1948, and they had two sons: Christopher Swift, born in 1951, and Kevin Webster, in 1958. Maxine died in 1976, and later that year Dickey married Deborah Dodson. Their daughter, Bronwen, was born in 1981. Dickey received his A.B. degree from Vanderbilt in 1949 and the next year was awarded an M.A. after writing a thesis on Herman Melville's poems. He was able to complete the fall semester as an instructor at the Rice Institute in Houston, Texas, before being called back into the Air Force to serve in the Korean War. Following his discharge from military service in 1952, Dickey returned to Rice for two more years and began writing poetry. A *Sewanee Review* fellowship in 1954 helped him support his family for a year in Europe, after which he returned in 1955 to teach at the University of Florida. His academic career proved a disappointment when he found himself loaded down with composition classes, and the final blow came when his reading of "The Father's Body" to a Gainesville audience led to demands for an apology. Rather than apologize, Dickey resigned from the university.

Dickey continued to write—and publish—poetry, but he did it while living in New York City, where he took a job writing advertising copy for the McCann-Erickson agency. In 1958, still with McCann-Erickson, Dickey returned to Atlanta; he soon switched to Liller Neal, a smaller firm, and then to Burke Dowling Adams, where he was creative director and vice president.

His poetry accumulated during these years, and he published two collections, *Into the Stone, and Other Poems* (1960) and *Drowning with Others* (1962). He was awarded the Union League Civic and Arts Foundation Prize (1958), the Vachel Lindsay Prize, and the Longview Foundation Award (both in 1959), followed in 1961 by a Guggenheim Fellowship. Dickey at this time left the advertising business to become a full-time poet and took his family to Italy, where he traveled and wrote for a year before taking up poet-in-residence appointments at Reed College (1963-1964) and San Fernando Valley State College (1964-1965).

Dickey's reputation as one of the United States' ranking poets was solidified by the publication of *Helmets* and *Buckdancer's Choice. Buckdancer's Choice* won the National Book Award for poetry, the Melville Cane Award from the Poetry Society of America, and the National Institute of Arts and Letters Award. With these honors in 1966 came a brief stint as poet-in-residence at the University of Wisconsin, Madison, and an appointment as consultant in poetry for the Library of Congress (1966-1968). In 1969, Dickey became Carolina Professor of English and writer-in-residence at the University of South Carolina in Columbia, where he remained until his death.

Although he continued to publish poetry in the 1970's and 1980's, some of which was well received, it was Dickey's early work in *Helmets* and *Buckdancer's Choice* that critics valued most highly. His first novel, *Deliverance* (1970), was both a popular and a critical success, and it was made into a successful film starring Jon Voight and Burt Reynolds, with Dickey himself writing the script and playing the sheriff. His second novel, *Alnilam* (1987), on which he worked for more than a decade, was not so well received.

Besides fiction and poetry, Dickey has written some notable criticism, especially in *Babel to Byzantium: Poets and Poetry Now* (1968). An outspoken critic, he gave poor grades to such major figures as

Robert Frost and William Carlos Williams and judged Allen Ginsberg an absolute failure. Among the poets he prized are Theodore Roethke, Rainer Maria Rilke, and D. H. Lawrence.

In 1974, Dickey published *Jericho: The South Beheld*, a sumptuous coffee-table volume in which his prose poems were accompanied by illustrations by Hubert Shuptrine. It was a commercial success, but it seemed to his critics to be a diversion from a serious literary career. The children's book *Tucky the Hunter* (1978) and another volume of poems, *The Strength of Fields* (1979), rounded out another decade of diverse and generally well-received accomplishment. The 1980's were most conspicuously marked by the second novel, *Alnilam,* and *Puella* (1982), a collection of poems about a young girl's maturing. Dickey published two poetry collections and a novel in the early 1990's. He died in 1997.

ANALYSIS

Dickey's essay "The Enemy from Eden" is a meditation on the metaphysics of snake hunting with a blowgun. The blowgun-wielding hunter—"the One," as Dickey identifies him—fashions his weapon from a length of aluminum pipe and arms it with sharpened lengths of coat-hanger wire guided by improvised vanes of typing paper scraps. With this weapon the snake hunter seeks his foe, alert not to walk "right into the fangs, the jungle hypodermic." When the "Universal Evil," the "Enemy from Eden," succumbs to the coat-hanger needle in the brain, his skin will become "something to have a drink with, at all times of day and night." After the kill, "For some reason, the One is well, full of himself and out of himself."

This brief essay contains much essential Dickey, an avid deer and snake hunter as he prided on portraying himself. Striding into the natural world, armed with the minimum of hand-fashioned weapons, and doing battle with the allegorical monster is an irresistible theme. It also relates directly to Dickey's concern in both his fiction and his poetry for the magic and mystery of nature and the dangers and satisfactions available to the man who will face up to the challenges. The attitudes expressed therein are typical of his main theme in literature and, likely, life: survival. Witness to harrowing scenes while serving in the Air Force during World War II, he confessed in one of his 1970 self-interviews to viewing existence from the standpoint of a survivor. Having been called "James Dickey, the Grateful Survivor," in a critical article from that period, the writer gratefully identified with it.

The major Dickey themes are all exemplified in *Poems, 1957-1967* (1967), a compilation from *Into the Stone, Drowning with Others, Helmets, Buckdancer's Choice*, and *Falling* (not previously published in book form). Several of the poems treat the death of Dickey's brother, Eugene, and the poet's ensuing guilt. Dickey's mother suffered from angina, and he became convinced that she would not have put herself through the exertion of bearing him if Eugene had not died. This view of his conception and birth troubled Dickey. "The Underground Stream" voices the poet's frequently stated urge to merge his identity with natural elements—in this instance, with the underground stream he perceives as he lives on the edge of a flowing well—and is infused with the poet's memory of his "one true brother,/ the tall cadaver, who/ Either grew or did not grow." Another early poem, "The String," recalls the story of his brother's having performed string tricks, "Incredible feats of construction," as "he lay/ In his death-bed singing with fever." The direct personal feeling of "The String" is strengthened by the elegiac refrain "Dead before I was born."

The same sense of the dead brother's haunting presence emerges in "Armor" and "In the Tree House at Night." The fantasy about armor conjures up a brother "whose features I knew/ By the feel of their strength on my face/ And whose limbs by the shining of mine." In the poem's moving resolution, the brother is armored in gold and the poet has:

let the still sun
Down into the stare of the eyepiece
And raised its bird's beak to confront
What man is within to live with me
When I begin living forever.

In the tree-house poem, it is the "dead brother's huge, freckled hand" that steadies the nails in the tree-house ladder; and it is his spirit that draws the speaker into the tree house at night, where he enjoys a mystical experience: "My green, graceful bones fill the air/ With sleeping birds. Alone, alone/ And with them I move gently./ I move at the heart of the world."

Of the numerous recollections of war in *Poems, 1957-1967*, "The Performance" is perhaps the most stunning. It is one of the most powerful elegies inspired by World War II. "The Performance" honors Donald Armstrong, master of the "back somersault, the kip-up," as the poet imagines the downed flier's execution. Doomed to dig his own grave before the enemy's "two-handed sword" falls on his neck, Armstrong does all his "lean tricks. . . . As the sun poured up from the sea/ And the headsman broke down/ In a blaze of tears," but at the end Armstrong "knelt down in himself/ Beside his hacked, glittering grave, having done/ All things in this life that he could."

"Awaiting the Swimmer" is one of Dickey's love poems. The speaker of the poem stands by a river, holding a white towel and waiting for a woman to reach him on the bank. He wraps her in the towel and leads her to the house, where he is overcome with feeling: "What can I perform, to come near her?/ How hope to bear up, when she gives me/ The fear-killing moves of her body?" Three other early love poems—"On the Hill Below the Lighthouse," "Near Darien," and "Into the Stone"—develop similar statements of awe at the power of love and sexual feeling. In each poem, the natural setting is important, with moonlight bathing the lovers in all three poems as the speaker works out his feelings in figures of light and shade, stone and water.

The early love poems contrast with some later ones in different moods, such as "Adultery," with its "Gigantic forepleasure," "wrist watch by the bed," and "grim techniques." This poem ends in a recital of illicit lovers' banalities and the speaker's lighthearted summing up: "We have done it again we are/ Still living. Sit up and smile,/ God bless you. Guilt is magical." In "Cherrylog Road," the speaker waits in a junked Pierce-Arrow for the archetypal farmer's daughter, here named Doris Holbrook. In the still heat of the junkyard, the hulks "smothered in kudzu," the young speaker and his consort "clung, glued together,/ With the hooks of the seat springs/ Working through to catch us red-handed." The wild ride over, they leave "by separate doors," and the speaker roars off on his motorcycle, "Wringing the handlebar for speed,/ Wild to be wreckage forever." Many of Dickey's best poems express a natural relationship between the world of man, as personified in the speaker, and the larger world of leaf and stone. These poems often evoke a natural creation trembling with transcendent spirit.

"THE OWL KING"

First published: 1962 (collected in *Drowning with Others,* 1962)
Type of work: Poem

A father calls to his blind son, lost in the woods but bonded by natural sympathies to the owl king.

The eight-page poem "The Owl King" is arranged in three parts. Part 1, "The Call," is the father's hopeful search for his blind son. This one-page section is characteristic of much of Dickey's poetry in several ways. It is written in eight-line stanzas, for example, with the first line recurring at the end as a refrain in italics. Many of Dickey's poems, especially the earlier ones, are told in stanzas of five to eight lines, and the refrain is fairly commonly used (examples include "Dover: Believing in Kings," "The String," and "On the Hill Below the Lighthouse"). The stanzas are linked by enjambment, although this poem has rather less of that device than usual in Dickey. The unrhymed lines are mostly of eight syllables, with Dickey's typically heavy anapestic stress heard everywhere. The metrical pattern found most frequently in a Dickey line is an iamb followed by two anapests, and "The Call" offers perfect examples, as in "It whispers like straw in my ear,/ And shakes like a stone under water./ My bones stand on tiptoe inside it. Which part of the sound did I utter?" The alliteration in these lines is not unexpected in a Dickey poem, and the word "stone" is perhaps the commonest word in Dickey's vocabulary.

The father's call is answered by the owl king's song, and the second part of the poem, two pages, is the owl's story; it is told in one long stanza. The owl king's vision allows him to see "dark burn/ Greater than sunlight or moonlight,/ For it burn[s] from deep within [him]." He hears, then sees, the blind boy with "His blue eyes shining like mine." They are immediately companionable, so that the father's call becomes a "perfect, irrelevant

music," and they sit each night on the owl's oak bough. The blind boy achieves something of the owl's vision, with the boy's eyes "inch by inch going forward/ Through stone dark, burning and picking/ The creatures out one by one."

In the five-page third part, "The Blind Child's Story," the boy describes, in short lines, his journey into the forest and the relationship he achieves with the owl. Perched on the oak bough, the boy "learn[s] from the master of sight! What to do when the sun is dead,/ How to make the great darkness work/ As it wants of itself to work." The owl weeps when the boy takes him in his arms in the glow of a heavenly light. The boy then walks through "the soul of the wood," for he can now "see as the owl king sees." The hints of religious allegory grow thicker at the end as the boy concludes, "Father, I touch! Your face. I have not seen/ My own, but it is yours./ I come, I advance,/ I believe everything, I am here."

"THE SHEEP CHILD"

First published: 1967 (collected in *Poems, 1957-1967,* 1967)
Type of work: Poem

The myth of the sheep child—half human, half sheep—inspires a lyric celebration of the will to life embodied in sexual desire.

"The Sheep Child" is in two parts. In the first section, the poet revives the old legends of anomalous deformed births resulting from humans copulating with animals. Among these is the much-whispered-about story of the "woolly baby/ pickled in alcohol" somewhere in an obscure corner of an unnamed museum in Atlanta. Even though "The boys have taken/ Their own true wives in the city" and the sheep are now safe in the pasture, the story persists in the "terrible dust of museums." Thus the poet imagines the sheep child saying, with his eyes, the story of his begetting, birth, and death. The sheep child's narrative, printed in italics, is a beautiful lyric of desire.

Speaking from his "father's house," the sheep child recounts his sheep mother's interlude in the west pasture, "where she stood like moonlight/ Listening for foxes." It was then that "something like love/ From another world . . . seized her/ From behind," and she responded to "that great need." From this event ensued the sheep child:

> I woke, dying,
>
> In the summer sun of the hillside, with my eyes
> Far more than human. I saw for a blazing moment
> The great grassy world from both sides,
> Man and beast in the round of their need,
> And the hill wind stirred in my wool,
> My hoof and my hand clasped each other,
> I ate my one meal
> Of milk, and died
> Staring.

From his birth in the pasture, the sheep child goes directly to his incarceration in the museum and his "closet of glass." He becomes a reminder of the taboo surrounding unnatural sex, driving the farm boys "like wolves from the hound bitch and calf/ And from the chaste ewe in the wind." The force celebrated in this poem is a terrible one and must be regulated. So, says the sheep child, "Dreaming of me,/ They groan they wait they suffer! Themselves, they marry, they raise their kind."

DELIVERANCE

First published: 1970
Type of work: Novel

Four city dwellers take a canoe trip that leads to violence and death amid struggle for survival.

Deliverance, Dickey's first novel, is a survivalist adventure story which quickly became a best seller, then a popular film directed by John Boorman and starring Burt Reynolds and Jon Voight. Dickey turned his interest in hunting and the outdoors into a suspenseful narrative that pits the four main characters not only against a wild river in north Georgia but also against several savage mountain men who prowl the wilderness along the river banks.

The novel's two epigraphs are much to the point of the events that follow. The first, from the modern French writer Georges Bataille, translates as

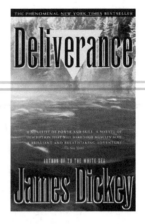

"there exists at the base of human life a principle of insufficiency." The second is from the Old Testament prophet Obadiah: "The pride of thine heart hath deceived thee,/ thou that dwellest in the clefts of the rock,/ whose habitation is high; that saith in his heart,/ Who shall bring me down to the ground?"

Bataille's observation explains well the urge that sends these comfortable professional men from Atlanta off on an arduous challenge to their bodies and their spirits. The ringleader is Lewis Medlock, a fitness guru and devotee of outdoor sports, whose mantra is being ever-ready to match himself against some grueling physical challenge. Professing his uncompromising ethic of survival, Lewis puts his philosophy to the test by cajoling others to join him on the trip. The narrator is his friend, Ed Gentry, an advertising agency executive who begins the trip as more or less Lewis's second in command. Lewis and Ed are accompanied by Drew Ballinger, a sales manager for a soft drink distributor, and Bobby Trippe, a mutual funds salesman.

The trip these four men take down the treacherous Cahulawassee River has the features of an archetypal journey fraught with hazards of nature and human evil, and it is a modern masterpiece of this genre. The novel also inverts the genre, however, in the sense that these men do not have to make such a perilous journey. Their adventure is a typical suburbanite vision of a weekend expedition to shore up their sense of virility, which instead turns into a nightmare. Looking for a deliverance from the ennui of modern city life, ironically the four men drive away from home in modern automobiles and then set themselves the task of getting home using the most difficult way possible. When it is all over, the decent Drew is dead, his body submerged under tons of water. Bobby, the least equipped of the four for the strains of the mythical outdoors, has been sodomized and permanently embittered. Lewis begins by playing the role he was born for, saving Bobby and Ed's lives from sexual predators with an arrow straight into the heart of one of the assailants. Lewis relishes the tense existential drama for which he has prepared himself through such a long novitiate but, in another ironic turn, suffers a crippling fracture in a canoe crash on the same rapids where Drew loses his life. It is then that Ed—the narrator, the skeptic, the apprentice—takes on Lewis's responsibilities and—killing a man who hunts for them—accomplishes his initiation triumphantly. Yet the question remains: From what has Ed been delivered?

Deliverance is tightly plotted and structured in three main sections of roughly equal length. A brief "Before" section introduces the characters and the dominant theme of survivalist ethos cultivated in the midst of modern civilization. The first day of the journey is narrated in "September 14th," and it takes the men by car to the little village of Oree, where they begin their journey to the camp where they will tent the first night. "September 15th" begins mildly but soon reaches a narrative peak in a confrontation on shore with two backwoods yahoos who assault the travelers and rape Bobby before Lewis unhesitatingly kills one with an arrow. The surviving backwoodsman escapes, and the four continue their trip in a grim frame of mind after taking a vote and deciding to bury the dead man instead of reporting the incident to the police. Their trip takes them through vicious rapids; at this juncture, Drew ends up overboard and upsets the lead canoe in which he is riding with Ed. Lewis's leg is badly mangled, and leadership devolves upon Ed, whom Lewis charges with tracking the woodsman and killing him. Convinced that the surviving mountaineer has laid for them in ambush and shot Drew in cold blood, Ed scales a high cliff in a test of physical endurance of which he would not believe himself capable a few days earlier and waits for their tormentor as the second day ends.

"September 16th" finds Ed in the tree waiting for their pursuer, who indeed appears armed with a rifle. In a tense shootout, in which Ed must divest himself of his placid, reflective nature and look inside for a survivalist and a killer, the mountain man dies. His body is consigned to the waiting river, and the three survivors continue on to the town of Aintry after burying Drew's body and agreeing on a cover-up story of his accidental death. This denouement of the classic plot pattern is completed by an "After" section in which their rickety story is

questioned by the local law but soon becomes part of the river's annals as the whole area is flooded, ensuring the eternal concealment of the three bodies.

Wherein does the deliverance lie in this story of violence and death? For the innocent four voyagers it beckoned them away from the ennui and death-in-life of suburban existence. Although for Drew there is no consolation, only oblivion, as a group the travelers are delivered from unprovoked assault, mortal peril, and raging forces of nature. Even as Bobby is brutally assaulted, he is delivered from an even greater peril by Lewis's unwavering arrow. For Lewis there is deliverance from the compulsions that drove him to rigorous physical disciplines, and a better understanding of his strength as well as its limitations. As Ed observes of Lewis at the last, "He can die now; he knows that dying is better than immortality." Ed himself has been delivered from a great hope, the aspiration to compensate for the insufficiency of life by heroic accomplishment. After Drew's death, when Lewis and Ed realize the predicament in which they are caught, Lewis observes that "here we are, at the heart of the Lewis Medlock country." Ed exults in the challenge he faces in Lewis's role: "My heart expanded with joy at the thought of where I was and what I was doing."

Ed's exaltation on the river has been partly prepared by a sequence in the opening exposition. In the flurry of preparations for their trip, Ed's male attention is caught by the gaze of a model at his agency, a woman with a "gold-glowing mote" in her eye; she represents for Ed the call to overcome the insufficiency of civilized man's quotidian rounds. The promise of the "gold-glowing mote" is fulfilled in the joy Ed experiences on the riverbank, a genuine deliverance from civilization's restraints. The culminating deliverance will come only later, in the journey's aftermath, when passions are stilled and peace is regnant. Then Ed reports that "the gold-halved eye had lost its fascination. Its place was in the night river, in the land of impossibility." Ed sees the woman now and again around the studio: "She is a pleasant part of the world, but minor. She is imaginary."

This, then, is the deliverance: the humiliation foreseen in Obadiah that beats out of recalcitrant, Faustian man the urge to surmount the sense that life is not enough. *Deliverance* is thus a moral tale of self-discovery that comes from a broader perspective on life and its trials. Manhood is but one aspect of it, and the ability to rise to the threat—whether posed by nature or by human assailant—is an inherent part of it. However, maturity transcends physical prowess and even personal valor and ironically may mean acceptance of things that would be perceived as usurping that manhood before. At the conclusion, Ed sits with his wife, Martha, in marital companionability: "In summer we sit by a lake where we have an A-frame cottage—it is not Lake Cahula, it is over on the other side of the lake—and look out over the water, maybe drinking a beer in the evening." It is a life of muted pleasures, true, but it is a true deliverance from the exhausting pursuit of the promise in the "gold-glowing mote."

ALNILAM

First published: 1987
Type of work: Novel

A blind man struggles to discover how his son died when his plane crashed at a North Carolina training base during World War II.

Alnilam is completely different from *Deliverance*. Whereas *Deliverance* unfolds swiftly around a tightly structured plot, *Alnilam*—much longer at 682 pages—rambles along, often faltering under the burden of its sometimes awkward split point of view. The main character, Frank Cahill, is an amusement park owner in Atlanta who learns that his son Joel has died in a mysterious training plane crash at the North Carolina Air Corps base where he is stationed during World War II. Joel's body cannot be found, and Cahill, recently victimized by blindness brought on by diabetes, travels by bus to the training base with his German shepherd seeing-eye dog, Zack. He hopes to learn exactly what happened to Joel.

Cahill is received well by the camp authorities, and he meets Joel's officers and friends. He trudges over the site of the fatal accident. He even sleeps with one of the local women well known to the airmen. He never discovers, however, exactly how Joel died. What he does discover is that Joel was the moving spirit of a mysterious cult named

for the star Alnilam deep in Orion, the hunter constellation. Their goal is a transcendence of the earthly and physical through the experience of flight, an experience that to them becomes virtually mystical.

Many pages of *Alnilam* are printed in double columns. A column on the left in boldface print renders the thoughts and sensations of the blind Cahill, groping around the base in both literal and figurative darkness. A column on the right in normal print maintains the usual flow of omniscient third-person narration. The device sometimes intrudes on the reader's consciousness, forcing a continuous re-evaluation of the events and of the narrator's role in fashioning them for the reader. When the double column arrangement goes on for several pages, for example, should the reader go all the way with the left column and then backtrack to the right column or try to keep up with both at once? At times, the tonal differences may not seem pronounced enough to warrant the double point of view, but as an overall strategy it is a bold move for a writer whose prose is not known for technical experimentation.

Dickey was always courageous about taking chances, however, and even if the split narration is not always successful, he does succeed in giving a moving impression of the blind Cahill's quest. This quest echoes the fertility myth of the Fisher King, which, through Ernest Hemingway's *The Sun Also Rises* (1926), came to embody Gertrude Stein's elegy for the "lost generation" of the other Great War. Strip the symbolic layer, and some of the scenes are memorable in their own right. The training plane fight, for example, is a gripping re-creation of a blind man's sensations at the controls of a PT-17 aircraft; and Cahill's night bundled up with the woman very effectively captures a different kind of experience.

Cahill's ordeal takes place in the dead of winter, and the cold contributes to the tactile imagery so necessary in recounting a blind person's movements around unfamiliar terrain. Cahill's adjustment to the sterile landscape of the base; his closeness to Zack, his dog (in whose fur he frequently fumbles for reassurance); and the slow revelation of what his son had been up to—all help give the story sufficient life for the reader often to forget the narrative contrivance.

To the White Sea

First published: 1993
Type of work: Novel

Shot down over Tokyo, an American World War II airman pushes northward to Hokkaido amid a survivalist rampage of killing and violence.

Parts of *To the White Sea* are good and original. Unfortunately, what is original can hardly count as the best of Dickey's prose, and what is good is not that original, leaning heavily on *Deliverance* and its survivalist ethos. In the opening section, Dickey reaches back into his own experience as an airman who took part in the 1945 firebombing of Japan. Later on he will smoothly segue into imagined, mystical passages of immersion in animal world and nature, scenes of hunting, stalking, and killing. Halfway through the novel, during the long train ride episode, his language will become even more poetic and associa-

tive. Overall, it is not inaccurate to describe the novel as a sustained internal monologue interlaced with curt, matter-of-fact, explosive sequences of action and violence. The mixture of these disparate styles may jar readers, but it is entirely deliberate. As a 1988 letter to Gore Vidal reveals, Dickey made no real distinction between fact, fiction, history, reminiscence, and fantasy because, as he put it, imagination inhabits them all.

Color imagery dominates the protagonist's progression from Tokyo to the northern tip of the island of Honshu and across the strait to Hokkaido. The dominant hue changes from the fire red during the bombing raid, to the whiteness of the polar landscape at the end. In between, the author strives to emphasize the imagistic play of other hues and shades, but the overall effect is often contrived and detracting from the protagonist's progress—and,

in some way, regress. Dickey's favorite structural device is to strip the plot and his characters to the barest essentials and then intimate emotionally laden questions about this cubist tableau. In *To the White Sea*, these questions seem to be aimed at the survivalist ethic in the days of human-made holocaust. Yet filtered through the mind of the American airman, Muldrow, whom the author himself characterized as a sociopath and a conscienceless murder much like the infamous serial killer Ted Bundy, they seem shallow at best, self-justifying the senseless killing.

Preaching and living the mantra of being ever-ready for the veneer of civilization to fall away, leaving everyone at the mercy of their survival skills, Muldrow instinctively—but also with full deliberation—seeks to leave the war behind and get to the wastelands of northern Japan. His separate peace has little to do, however, with the rituals of valor and respect. Its only trace is when the killer honors the fallen Japanese sword-master. For most of the journey, Muldrow is not so much apart from the human society as a part of a force of nature, almost amoral in his basic survivalist drives. His ultimate death at the hands of the Japanese is not an act of victory by the superior enemy but an act of supreme indifference to death from a man who has finally found his place in the nature-driven scheme of things—one that transcends human warfare, loyalty, and perhaps civilization as a whole.

Summary

The importance of nature and the inherent struggle for survival in a hostile, or just indifferent, world runs all through Dickey's work; the need for physical communion with the substantial world outside the all-consuming ego appears everywhere. *Deliverance*'s Ed Gentry scaling a two-hundred-foot cliff, embracing the solid earth of north Georgia, is emblematic of this longing for merging in Dickey's sensibility. With this spiritual yearning goes an acceptance of the violence that is built into natural selection and is a given fact of existence that is better acknowledged than suppressed. Dickey was a writer of considerable breadth of learning, although his work is never literary and allusive in diction and symbol.

Frank Day; updated by Peter Swirski

James Dickey

BIBLIOGRAPHY

By the Author

POETRY:

Into the Stone, and Other Poems, 1960
Drowning with Others, 1962
Helmets, 1964
Two Poems of the Air, 1964
Buckdancer's Choice, 1965
Poems, 1957-1967, 1967
The Eye-Beaters, Blood, Victory, Madness, Buckhead, and Mercy, 1970
The Zodiac, 1976
The Strength of Fields, 1977
Head-Deep in Strange Sounds: Free-Flight Improvisations from the UnEnglish, 1979
The Early Motion, 1981
Falling, May Day Sermon, and Other Poems, 1981
Puella, 1982
The Central Motion: Poems, 1968-1979, 1983
The Eagle's Mile, 1990
The Whole Motion: Collected Poems, 1945-1992, 1992

LONG FICTION:
Deliverance, 1970
Alnilam, 1987
To the White Sea, 1993

SCREENPLAY:
Deliverance, 1972 (adaptation of his novel)

TELEPLAY:
The Call of the Wild, 1976 (adaptation of Jack London's novel)

NONFICTION:
The Suspect in Poetry, 1964
A Private Brinkmanship, 1965 (address)
Spinning the Crystal Ball, 1967
Babel to Byzantium: Poets and Poetry Now, 1968
Metaphor as Pure Adventure, 1968
Self-Interviews, 1970 (Barbara Reiss and James Reiss, editors)
Sorties, 1971
Jericho: The South Beheld, 1974 (with Hubert Shuptrine)
The Enemy from Eden, 1978
In Pursuit of the Grey Soul, 1978
The Starry Place Between the Antlers: Why I Live in South Carolina, 1981
The Poet Turns on Himself, 1982
The Voiced Connections of James Dickey, 1989
Striking In: the Early Notebooks of James Dickey, 1996 (Gordon Van Ness, editor)
Crux: The Letters of James Dickey, 1999

DISCUSSION TOPICS

- Can you trace the poet in James Dickey's prose and the prosaist in his poetry?

- Why is the struggle for survival so central to Dickey's work? Is there any room for such a struggle in the modern civilized world?

- Why would the writer identify with being called a grateful survivor? Can you trace this gratitude to any dominant experiences in his life?

- Color imagery dominates Dickey's later work, including *To the White Sea.* What role does it play, and is this role as prominent in the two earlier novels?

- Dickey's poetry is heavily and intimately influenced by his World War II experience, yet he has always been negative about confessional poetry. Can you explain how his verse is different?

- The four men in *Deliverance* undergo assault, death, injury, pain, and trauma, as well as suspicion and investigation by the authorities. In what sense are they "delivered," then, and from what?

- Dickey is famous for commenting widely and intimately on his own works. What do these statements reveal about the writer and his art?

CHILDREN'S LITERATURE:
Tucky the Hunter, 1978

MISCELLANEOUS:
Night Hurdling: Poems, Essays, Conversations, Commencements, and Afterwords, 1983
The James Dickey Reader, 1999

About the Author

Bruccoli, Matthew J., and Judith S. Baughman, eds. *Crux: The Letters of James Dickey.* New York: Knopf, 1999.

Calhoun, Richard J., ed. *James Dickey: The Expansive Imagination.* Deland, Fla.: Everett/Edwards, 1973.

Calhoun, Richard J., and Robert W. Hill. *James Dickey.* Boston: Twayne, 1983.

Dickey, James. *Classes on Modern Poets and the Art of Poetry.* Edited by Donald J. Greiner. Columbia: University of South Carolina Press, 2004.

Dickey, James, Barbara Reiss, and James Reiss. *Self-Interviews.* Baton Rouge: Louisiana State University Press, 1970.

Heyen, William. "A Conversation with James Dickey." *Southern Review* 9 (1973): 135-156.

Kirschten, Robert. *James Dickey and the Gentle Ecstasy of Earth.* Baton Rouge: Louisiana State University Press, 1988.

_____, ed. *Critical Essays on James Dickey.* New York: G. K. Hall, 1994.

Lieberman, Laurence. *The Achievement of James Dickey: A Comprehensive Selection of His Poems with a Critical Introduction.* Glenview, Ill.: Scott, Foresman, 1968.

Van Ness, Gordon. *Outbelieving Existence: The Measured Motion of James Dickey.* Columbia, S.C.: Camden House, 1992.

EMILY DICKINSON

Born: Amherst, Massachusetts
December 10, 1830
Died: Amherst, Massachusetts
May 15, 1886

Dickinson's poems, in marked contrast to writings in the senti-mental, domestic style of her time, offer original ways of seeing the everyday through verse formulations that are distinctive, lyr-ical, and timeless.

BIOGRAPHY

Emily Elizabeth Dickinson was born in Amherst, Massachusetts, on December 10, 1830, the elder daughter of lawyer Edward Dickinson and Emily Norcross Dickinson. Dickinson was the second of three children, a year younger than her brother, William, and three years older than her sister, Lavinia. She was born in a large house built by her grandfather, Samuel Fowler Dickinson; except for absences of about a year for her schooling and seven months in Boston, she lived in it all of her life and died there at precisely 6:00 P.M. on May 15, 1886.

It is paradoxical that a woman who led such a cir-cumscribed and apparently uneventful life man-aged to acquire the rich perceptions that enabled her to write 1,775 poems unlike any others in the English language. Every one is recognizably her own, and many are masterpieces. The circum-stances of her life, therefore, hold a special fascina-tion for readers of her verse.

Dickinson's sharp perceptions and brilliant in-ner life arise primarily from her background. Her paternal grandfather, whom she never knew, re-mained an unseen presence in her family. A Trini-tarian deacon educated at Dartmouth College, he became moderately prosperous through his legal practice, investments, and a number of appointive

and elective government positions; he was also a vi-sionary. His religious zeal led him to use his entire fortune to found two Trinitarian educational insti-tutions: Amherst Academy (1814) and Amherst College (1821). It was he who built "the home-stead" in 1813, the great brick house that defined the daily life of his poet granddaughter.

Having spent thousands of dollars in the cause of education, he had become insolvent by early 1833. On May 22, 1833, he was even forced to sell the homestead. He moved to Cincinnati, Ohio, where he did church-related work, then Hudson, Ohio, where he died of pneumonia on April 22, 1838.

His son Edward, the poet's father, succeeded where the elder Dickinson had failed. Edward con-tinued in his father's position as trustee of the Amherst institutions. By the end of his term in 1873, Amherst College had assets of more than a million dollars. By March, 1855, he had repur-chased the house his father had built and lost. Educated at Yale University, he managed to com-bine religious zeal with practical business ability. His daughter would remember his long absences— as representative to the Massachusetts state legisla-ture, as chief financial officer of Amherst College, as land speculator with holdings in northern New England—but she clearly loved him in a way she never did her mother.

Edward was an undemonstrative man; he had struggled through Yale University with only the barest financial support of a father who ironically had directed all of his resources to the support of

Amherst College. The elder Dickinson believed, in characteristic Puritan spirit, that he owed the most support to the greatest number, even though this meant stinting a member of his own family.

Edward was, consequently, a man who had needed to stifle external emotions so many times that he had trouble expressing them at all. Many of the courtship letters he wrote to Emily Norcross Dickinson (the poet's mother) survive, but even during the emotionally charged period before marriage Dickinson found it possible to describe, entirely impersonally, what he considered the characteristics of an ideal wife. Edward also had found it disconcerting that he had to sacrifice an independent career, in effect, to redeem his father's good name. Despite his withdrawn nature and his long absences from home, he remained a primary figure in his daughter's life and poetry.

Dickinson did not have the same close relationship with her mother. Emily Norcross was not intellectual by nature—she barely understood much of her daughter's poetry—and was at least as undemonstrative as Edward. Many stories about the strange relationship of withdrawn mother and poet daughter are embellishments of the apparently cruel comments the younger Emily made in letters. Others follow from stories told by the relatively small number of persons admitted to the Dickinson circle. Most likely, the antagonism between mother and daughter arose from their different temperaments: the mother lonely and nonliterary, the daughter keenly intellectual and entrusted by her father with many of the household responsibilities that properly should have been her mother's.

Still, it would be wrong to assume that Dickinson's relations with her mother were filled with petty arguments. After her father's sudden death in 1874, during his first term in the Massachusetts House of Representatives, Dickinson and her mother grew closer. She nursed her mother faithfully, from 1875 to 1882, through the paralysis which ultimately took her life.

Dickinson's early relations with her only brother were competitive. In many ways they were alike; both were intellectual and ambitious. Though Dickinson's education was excellent for a woman of the mid-nineteenth century—coeducational training at Amherst Academy, from 1840 to 1845, and slightly more than a year at Mount Holyoke Female Seminary, in 1847 and 1848—it is likely that

she envied her brother's ability to circulate in the larger world. They were always friendly rivals.

Dickinson's sister had a personality much like that of her mother, though there is no indication of antagonism between Emily and Lavinia. Indeed, were it not for her sister's efforts after Dickinson's death it is likely that a first collection of her poems would never have appeared. With Thomas Wentworth Higginson and Mabel Loomis Todd, Lavinia sorted out the nearly eighteen hundred poems, some of which were written on billheads, envelopes, and odd scraps of paper. They deciphered Dickinson's cramped handwriting and "corrected" and standardized her punctuation.

Variations of this first edition, which first appeared in 1890, four years after the poet's death from kidney disease, remained substantially the only printed texts of Dickinson's verse until Thomas H. Johnson numbered and restored their original readings in his 1955 major edition. Dickinson had only eleven poems published during her lifetime.

The poet's surviving family members share some of the responsibility for creating the image of "the white nun of Amherst." This epithet refers to her habit of dressing exclusively in white after 1861. That she did this out of despair from some impossible love, either for young Ben Newton (her father's law clerk) or for Charles Wadsworth, a married Philadelphia minister with a family, is unlikely.

It is possible, as has been suggested, that Wadsworth's acceptance of a pastorate in San Francisco was an attempt to avoid temptation, but contemporary critics generally argue against the image of a Dickinson desolate because of a lost love. Johnson assigns most of Dickinson's bridal poems to the 1860's, based on this unhappy romance, but one can easily question the Johnson chronology. If correct, it would mean that Dickinson composed two-thirds of her entire output of verse in eight years and an astonishing number (681) in the years from 1862 to 1864.

Dickinson family members recalled, destroyed, and sometimes severely edited much of the poet's personal correspondence. "The belle" or "queen recluse" personae they created by default were infinitely preferable at the close of the nineteenth century to the rebellious, unconventional, but thwarted genius that she actually was. Dickinson had close relationships with several men her own age, particularly with Samuel Bowles, editor of the Springfield, Massachusetts, *Daily Republican*. Newton, a clerk in her father's law office, was a friendly critic of her verse. It is difficult, and mostly unnecessary, to speculate about whether these were romantic attachments.

Contrary to the widely accepted myth, Dickinson's literary friendships actually broadened during the last ten years of her life. Higginson reintroduced her to a girlhood acquaintance, Helen Hunt Jackson, an acclaimed writer and crusader for the rights of American Indians (Jackson's 1884 novel *Ramona* is her work most familiar to modern readers).

Another area of Dickinson's life obscured in the nineteenth and early twentieth century accounts is the poet's views on religion, and this directly affects the interpretation of many of her poems. Dickinson was raised in the conservative Trinitarian tradition of Jonathan Edwards. This contrasts her background with that of the liberal Unitarians, whose most famous minister was, at the time, Ralph Waldo Emerson. Dickinson remained, however, the only member of her family never to undergo a conversion experience. This was something of a disgrace given the heady zeal of Amherst, but Dickinson never compromised, though it meant being anathematized while in attendance at Mount Holyoke.

Some of her poems suggest science and empiricism as alternatives to unexamined belief; many others portray the particulars of church services against the need for reason. It is an indication of their tolerance that Dickinson's family never pressed her in these matters. Indeed, Dickinson's father provided his daughter with the kind of training that encouraged such inquiry. She was well read, particularly in the physical sciences, and she had ready access to her father's and the Amherst College libraries. The men of the family had read many of the same works as Dickinson, but such readings had merely strengthened their religious convictions. Dickinson always maintained her belief in a supreme deity, but she doubted that human institutions provided a necessary link.

Except for the vision problem that plagued her periodically as early as 1862, Dickinson's life was free of any medical incident until the uremic poisoning which ultimately took her life, swiftly and without pain, on May 15, 1886. Dickinson sought treatment for her severely blurred vision in Boston

in 1864. Her stay there of seven months was the only period, aside from her year at Mount Holyoke, that she remained away from home, and her letters emphasize her desire to return home. The vision problem seems to have abated of its own accord in Dickinson's later years, though it appears in her handwriting throughout the 1860's.

The Dickinson that remains, once one disregards myth and apocrypha, is an immensely gifted woman born a century and a quarter too soon. Rebellious in matters of family and religion, she nevertheless remained dutiful to those who needed her. Far from being an active feminist (for this was nearly impossible during the Civil War period in conservative Amherst), she accepted the enclosed life of a well-born but unmarried New England woman. Had she lived more extensively in the larger world, her verse would probably not have resembled the legacy she left.

ANALYSIS

Critics of Dickinson's verse generally note that the poems incorporate one or more of the following themes: death, love, religion, nature, eternity. This observation, of itself, does not take into account the amazing thematic combinations she managed or the extraordinary variety of poetic voices she employed. These range from the almost embarrassing cuteness of poems such as 61 ("Papa above!") or 288 ("I'm Nobody! Who are you?") to the skepticism of 338 ("I know that He exists.") and the passion, with intended or accidental double meaning, of 249 ("Wild Nights—Wild Nights!").

Some of her poems are high serious meditations, such as 258 ("There's a certain Slant of light"); others amount to waspish commentary, such as 401 ("What Soft—Cherubic Creatures—"). That she could see herself as a nobody, a seething volcano, a mouse, or a loaded gun all within the compass of several hundred poems is an indication of the variety of unconventional metaphor she used.

Even more astonishing is the fact that her style undergoes no linear development. Many of the early poems are as excellent as the later ones; bathetic and coy elements also appear throughout the collection. Absence of end-line punctuation creates enjambments that run for full stanzas, while dashes often create a hiatus at mid-line or end.

Early critics ascribed these eccentricities to

Dickinson's inability or unwillingness to punctuate (a characteristic her correspondence shares). Others see Dickinson's unconventional style as a flouting of convention, particularly as most nineteenth century verse written by women was conservative in both form and theme. Still others, noting the lyric configuration of the dashes, compare her poems to the lyric measures of nursery rhymes or to the hymnal melodies then sung in Trinitarian churches. These interpretations do not necessarily exclude one another. What is important is that the irregular rhythms these dashes create almost always improve the poetry.

Dickinson neither titled nor dated her poems, and this is one problem that Johnson faced when preparing the 1955 major edition. The result is that he assigned the poems numbers, arranging them in what appeared a likely chronological order. Sometimes he arrived at relatively secure dating, as when a poem appears in dated letters, on dated billheads, or on postmarked envelopes. Unfortunately, this precludes neither prior nor subsequent composition. Furthermore, because the poems show no radical shifts in style, the task of firm dating remains even more daunting.

A related curiosity of Dickinson's poems is their nearly complete exclusion of reference to external specifics. Number 61 ("Papa above!") might appear to imply her father's death, yet the Johnson chronology posits 1859 as its year of composition. Because Dickinson's father died in 1874, accepting the Johnson dating means having to limit application of the first line to the poet's divine father alone. The poem becomes merely a coy parody of The Lord's Prayer rather than a simultaneous hope that the poet's own father might remember his little mouse.

The complete run of Dickinson's poems is so marked by genius that one tends to forget the occasional lapses of obviously unsuccessful works. These seem to occur most often when she reaches beyond the microcosm of her immediate world. A good example of this is poem 196 ("We don t cry—Tim and I,"). Dickinson here attempts to parallel the pathetic condition of the poet's persona and that of Tiny Tim, the patient crippled child of Charles Dickens's *A Christmas Carol* (1843). Unfortunately, the effect is so cloying and sentimental that the poem descends to the bathetic, almost becoming parody.

Similarly, poem 127 ("'Houses'—so the wise Men tell me—"), though it begins with a biblical simplicity akin to that of William Blake's child songs, strains to such an extent to evoke sympathy that the verse becomes flaccid. What began as the Lord's promise of a mansion for his children quickly descends to sentimentality for its own sake: "Mansions cannot let the tears in,/ Mansions must exclude the storm!"

The mid-nineteenth century figures of Dickens's Tiny Tim and Little Nell thus continue to afflict Dickinson's verse at irregular intervals. In all fairness, so much maudlin sentiment pervaded the popular poetry of the time that it is a wonder Dickinson's style remained as distinct and uniformly superior as it did. Her poetry is generally on its weakest ground when her dry wit or high serious reflection aims merely to imitate popular trends of the day.

Amherst, in Dickinson's time, was an enlightened, relatively well-educated community, surrounded even in the nineteenth century by institutions of learning, many of them associated in one way or another with the Trinitarian or Unitarian churches. From Dickinson's perspective, however, its people were all too comfortable in religious outlooks she rejected.

Infant death was a common fact of life in the nineteenth century United States. Regular influenza epidemics claimed the lives of adults as well as children every winter. Tuberculosis, then called consumption, claimed still more, and all those deaths appeared listed on the front page of the Springfield *Daily Republican*, the newspaper Dickinson read every day. The room in which Dickinson wrote overlooked the Protestant cemetery. At one period, the funerals of Amherst friends and acquaintances became so common that Dickinson felt she had to move her writing desk to the center of the room to spare herself. In short, Dickinson and her contemporaries lived with death in a way most present-day Americans can hardly comprehend.

Added to this is the fact that Dickinson steadfastly resisted the doctrine of "election," the view that some people were marked from birth for salvation, while others were damned. Proof of such justification lay in what Trinitarians called a "conversion experience." This generally took the form of some personal religious insight experienced at a critical stage in life. Dickinson's grandfather, father, and brother had all undergone such an experience during or just after their college years. Even at Mount Holyoke, however, Dickinson was among "the unredeemed." She was one of only three students so categorized. To be included among "the saved" she needed only to profess some religious experience, yet she refused to make this claim merely for social acceptance.

By her late teenage years she had abandoned church attendance; for a New England woman raised in the tradition of nineteenth century Trinitarianism, this was anathema. It is little wonder, then, that particulars of the Congregationalist funeral service appear as they do in poem 280 ("I felt a Funeral, in my Brain"). Their droning monotony first causes the narrator's mind to go numb. Feet scrape the wooden floors of the frame church until the narrator feels "That Sense was breaking through—." The coffin seems to "creak across my Soul," and she is "Wrecked, solitary." Finally, "a Plank in Reason, broke," and the narrator "Finished knowing—then—." Literally, the poet describes her own death, a familiar starting point for many of her poems.

The particulars of the service are equally familiar, but her alterations are striking and reflect her nonconformist views, To the congregation, she is "wrecked" and "solitary." Reason breaks, and sense breaks through. She plunges downward into nothingness and finishes knowing, because at death she has certainty. There is no mention here of Heaven or Hell. The "World" she hits "at every plunge" is that of her inner self.

Dickinson here reverses the "plank of faith" metaphor familiar to most New England Protestants in the nineteenth century. This plank, firmly grounded on each side, bridges an abyss. One negotiates it while holding firmly to the Bible. One who looks to either side must surely plunge into the depths. Dickinson's family, as did most others of their station, owned William Holmes and John W. Barber's *Religious Allegories* (1848), which presents the metaphor accompanied by a woodcut showing one of the faithful attempting to cross the gap. Dickinson's plank is Reason, not Faith, however, and Sense does not break, it breaks through.

To modern readers such nonconformity may not seem particularly striking, but one must imagine the effect it had on Dickinson's family and churchgoing acquaintances. This poem, then, synthesizes the death and religion one finds so often separately treated in Dickinson's verse; more important, it gives some impression of the extent to which the poet felt obliged to argue her convictions. She did not take her theological position merely for the sensation it (no doubt) created, and her religious views were certainly more heterodox than many critics indicate.

Critics who analyze Dickinson's work must storm the verbal fortress of commentary written by her family and friends who, with all good intentions of making Dickinson the stereotype of a nineteenth century spinster who happened to write poetry, came close to neutralizing the double meanings of many of her best poems.

Higginson, whose advice Dickinson regularly sought on literary matters, is particularly blameworthy in this regard. During her lifetime, he repeatedly urged her not to publish, largely on the practical grounds that her verse was unsalable, though wider circulation of her poems would undoubtedly have brought her into correspondence with important writers of the day. One could also argue that this might have changed her style, made her less violently expressive, or rendered a life in Amherst impossible, but these are moot arguments.

Even after her death, Higginson was intent on perpetuating the Dickinson image he had helped to create. Typical is his famous disclaimer inevitably attached to commentaries on poem 249 ("Wild Nights—Wild Nights!"). The poem turns on the image of a storm; lovers can cast away both compass and chart and row in the safe harbor of their love. Higginson's scruples concerned the erotic implication of the poem's final lines: "Might I but moor— Tonight—/ In Thee!" Higginson feared to publish the poem, "lest the malignant read into it more than that virgin recluse ever dreamed of putting there."

One wonders, however, whether Higginson even noticed the much more perverse implications of a stormy Eden whose fallen lovers dispose of the compass and chart which would have kept them on the prescribed course—presumably, apart. Though one could argue that the erotic image of the moored lovers was unintended, it is much more difficult to reject the lovers' obvious abandonment of their set course. The reckless emotion of their love justifies the erotic implication of the final lines.

Comparable eroticism, in this case consummation of love, appears in poem 190 ("He was weak, and I was strong—then—"). Here the lovers alternate in conditions of strength and weakness. When the narrator becomes weak, her lover leads her "Home." The night is quiet, the lover says nothing. When "Day knocked" they had to part, neither the stronger: "He strove—and I strove—too—/ We didn't do it—tho'!" This final line refers to the lovers' refusal to part, but it also can imply their decision not to abandon the traditional rules of courtship. This naughtiness is an important element of Dickinson's verse. To deny it merely to create the image of a sainted recluse plays false with the facts and cripples the impact of her poetry.

Men much more than women were important to Dickinson the poet. She relied upon the literary judgments of Newton, a clerk in her father's office, and editors and Higginson, and she appears never to have questioned their separately expressed views that she should not attempt to circulate her poems more widely. They, no doubt as much as she, were affected by the stereotypes of domestic verse, the only kind considered suitable for a nineteenth century woman to publish.

If one examines the poems Dickinson did place during her lifetime, it becomes obvious that they suit requirements of prevailing taste. Were they the sole criterion by which to judge her as poet, she would have been considerably less important than critics agree she is. Of the 1,775 poems in Johnson's edition, only eleven appeared in Dickinson's lifetime, and six of those eleven were printed in the Springfield *Daily Republican*. Those six are poem 3 ("Sic transit gloria mundi," which appeared bearing a title "A Valentine"), poem 35 ("Nobody knows this little Rose"), and more substantive verse such as poem 214 ("I taste a liquor never brewed—," which was given the title "The May-Wine"), poem 216 ("Safe in their Alabaster Chambers—, called "The Sleeping"), poem 228 ("Blazing in Gold and quenching in Purple," titled "Sunset"), and poem 986 ("A narrow Fellow in the Grass," which appeared as "The Snake").

This small list allows one to see how editors consistently attempted to render Dickinson's verse immediately intelligible, both by means of clarifying titles and standardizing punctuation. Though

one could consider none of these poems inferior, they nevertheless fit within the parameters of what passed as "women's verse" in a way other of her works did not. It is easy to see how they are consonant with works published by Dickinson's female contemporaries: Charlotte Brontë's *Jane Eyre* (1847), Harriet Beecher Stowe's *Uncle Tom's Cabin* (1852), Elizabeth Barrett Browning's *Aurora Leigh* (1857), and George Eliot's *Middlemarch* (1872). By the time Eliot had published *Middlemarch*, Dickinson had written but not published—and had little hope of publishing—more than twelve hundred poems.

"POEM 160 (JUST LOST, WHEN I WAS SAVED!)"

First published: 1891 (as "Called Back")
Type of work: Poem

In this poem is one of Dickinson's anticipatory views of eternity.

Dickinson wrote this poem between 1860 and 1862, if one accepts the Johnson chronology. Her sister included it among the small selection of poems published after the poet's death. It appears that the title "Called Back" was appended based on a note the poet had written to her cousins on the day before her death. Perhaps she was inspired by the sudden conviction she was recovering that affects many terminally ill people, or (equally likely) she did not want her cousins to worry. In any event, she wrote, "Little cousins,—Called Back. Emily."

Dickinson's poems often focus on a proleptic view of the death experience; that is, they anticipate death yet present a living narrator to interpret the nearly experienced event. Not surprisingly, they are usually devoid of any overt Christian imagery; yet, there does appear, in this instance, the image of the "Reporter" who has stood before the apocalyptic "Seal." The narrator's wish to remain next time, to see "the things . . . By Ear unheard,/ Unscrutinized by Eye—" corresponds to Saint Paul's words in 1 Corinthians 2.9. The speaker, however, is far more like Samuel Taylor Coleridge's Ancient Mariner or Herman Melville's Ishmael, the narrator of *Moby Dick* (1851). All three have looked upon death and lived.

It is impossible not to sense the enlightened, humanistic tone of the poem's first two lines: "Just lost, when I was saved! / Just felt the world go by!" The third line, which repeats the initial word of the first two and adds "girt," implies that meeting "Eternity" is akin to a struggle or a hero's encounter with an opponent. Eternity is predatory, and the paratactic arrangement of lines 1-3 emphasizes its insistent claim on the speaker. Even so, the "breath" of line 4 allows her to overcome its influence and to "feel," so that she can "tell" what she has seen. Poetry, whose words one feels as much as hears, thus provides the strength for the poet to return. The desire to be a "pale Reporter"—that is, to be a poet interpreting universal experience in an insightful way—is too great for her to succumb to death, at least this time.

Nevertheless, Hercules' cry of *Plus ultra* (still further), shouted when he had erected Gibraltar and Ceuta at the edge of the world, has meaning for the poet, too. She desires to take language further than it has ever been, even though she faces the likelihood of destruction, or a poem without transcendent meaning. The death and rebirth which the poem describe thus resemble a fixed part of a mythic hero's experience, even as they correspond to the humanist insight of a poet who has gone beyond merely dabbling in verse and become a true poet.

this through alternating dactyls and trochees. The woman's "—low feet staggered" so many times that "Only the soldered mouth can tell—." Sealed coffin and mute corpse challenge anyone who desires to understand the hardship under which she labored to "Try" to "stir the awful rivet" and "lift the hasps of steel!" The corpse's forehead is "cool" because in death it is free of labor. Dickinson repeatedly shifts the housewife's burden to the reader through the imperatives "Try" (used twice) and "Lift." Ironically, the domestic burden of the housewife's duties becomes the weight of the coffin and the dead weight of handling the corpse itself: "the listless hair" and the "adamantine fingers," stiffened in death. Their steel-like unyieldingness can no longer wear a tin thimble.

Predatory flies, a death and disease symbol which regularly appears in Dickinson's poems, batter and speckle the woman's once-clean chamber window. Both they and the sun are "Brave"; both sun and ceiling cobweb are "Fearless." Even so, despite this oppressive imagery, the housewife has finally become "Indolent," lain in a field of daisies. The poem thus resolves itself in a single line through the double implication of "indolent": lazy, but also free from suffering. There is no contradiction at all in the two views of death Dickinson takes in her poetry. Seen from the aspect of the poet or of a woman whom household burdens do not confine, death becomes an awe-filled adventure contemplated with heroic anticipation. The moment the perspective becomes that of a housewife or a woman bound by domestic duties, death becomes a blessed release from labor.

"POEM 187 (HOW MANY TIMES THESE LOW FEET STAGGERED—)"

First published: 1890 (as "Requiescat"; also called "Troubled about many things")
Type of work: Poem

This work's burdened, domestic tone is characteristic of many Dickinson poems which have domestic settings.

"POEM 214 (I TASTE A LIQUOR NEVER BREWED—)"

First published: 1861 (as "The May-Wine")
Type of work: Poem

This poem describes the intoxicating feeling that poetry inspires.

Though this poem was written during the same period as poem 160, the appearance of the housewife figure in poem 187 required an altogether more plodding, heavy tone. Dickinson achieves

For the ancient Greeks, Dionysus, the god of the wine grape, was also the deity associated with dramatic poetry. Writing verse, and reading it, removed one from ordinary sense experience. Dickinson, though never invoking the god's name, makes all she can of the association between intoxication and ecstasy in poem 214. The rhythm of a reel (a whirling dance) supports this imagery. Significantly, this poem privileges the reading of verse to the writing of it. The speaker "tastes" the never-brewed liquor, which is held in pearl tankards, the mother-of-pearl covered verse anthologies of Dickinson's time. The "Frankfurt Berries," the hops used to produce fine beer, could never yield as rich a brew as can the well-distilled language of great poetry.

Those who consume the insubstantial metaphors of verse become drunk, debauched on air and dew; they reel through summers that never end from inns under eternally blue skies. The speaker is unrepentant for her drunkenness. She will stop consuming verse only when the "Landlords" of nature turn "the drunken Bee" from gathering pollen from flowers or when butterflies no longer gather their "drains"—in other words, when nature no longer furnishes precedents for the speaker's behavior. When she dies, the seraphim, highest order among the angels, will toss their halos, their "snowy Hats," in greeting, the saints come to their windows to see her, the "little Tippler" from the world of humans—as well as from the wine-grape district of Spain, which she calls "Manzanilla."

This poem furnishes a good example of how early editors often diminished the strength of Dickinson's verse through alterations they believed would make the poetry more consonant with prevailing taste. After Dickinson's death, Higginson and Mabel Loomis Todd changed the last lines from "To see the little Tippler/ From Manzanilla come!" to "To see the little Tippler/ Leaning against the sun." Their change rendered even more vapid the innocuous 1861 alteration made by the Springfield *Daily Republican*: "Come staggering toward the sun."

"POEM 216 (SAFE IN THEIR ALABASTER CHAMBERS—)"

First published: 1862 (as "The Sleeping")
Type of work: Poem

This poem, written in several sections, describes the justified dead awaiting resurrection.

Dickinson wrote several versions of this poem, sending them quite literally across the backyard hedge for the opinion of her sister-in-law. Unable to make a final decision, she sent two versions to Higginson, who printed the completely different final stanza of the second version together with the two stanzas of the first version, thereby creating a single poem one-third longer than Dickinson had intended.

There are curious implications in this poem that critics often overlook. Read straightforwardly, it states that the meek sleep safely in their satin-raftered, stone-roofed graves and confidently await their resurrection to ratify the salvation they already know is theirs. Breezes laugh in the castle above them; bees buzz "in a stolid Ear," and birds sing ignorantly in cadence. The poem concludes with a lament on the wisdom lost with the dead. In the second stanza of the 1861 version, the ages wheel by, crowns drop, and doges (Italian dukes) lose their power silently.

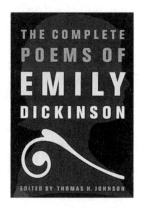

The cynical implication of the 1859 version's second stanza is that the breeze laughs at them as they wait, the bee gossips about them in the unyielding ear of creation, and the birds sing their meaningless songs in rhythm even as no resurrection occurs. In the 1861 version, years pass through the firmament, crowns drop, and power passes; it all happens silently, but the justified merely wait, safe in the comfort of their ignorance.

Emily Dickinson

"POEM 258 (THERE'S A CERTAIN SLANT OF LIGHT)"

First published: 1890
Type of work: Poem

The afternoon winter light is compared here with the despair one encounters in a search for transcendent meaning.

This poem begins by noting the oppressive sound of church bells heard in the bleak atmosphere of a winter afternoon. They give "Heavenly Hurt," though they leave no external scar. Within six lines, Dickinson synthesizes a description of depression in terms of three senses: hearing, sight, and feeling.

This depression is, however, more than ordinary sadness. It comes from Heaven, and it bears the biblical "Seal Despair." It hurts the entire landscape, its nonhuman as well as its human constituents, which listens, holds its breath for some revelation, yet perceives only the look of death. Significantly, the poet nowhere implies that no meaning exists; indeed, in other poems she is certain that a divine being exists and that there is a plan. Even so, the implications of what she writes are almost as devastating, for the apocalyptic seal of revelation holds fast, yielding no enlightenment to those below but the weak afternoon sun of a New England winter.

Read straightforwardly, the only means to combat this despair is, logically, faith, but in Dickinson's landscape one senses only its external sign: the weighty tunes of a cathedral carillon. The "internal difference," the scars of discouragement and despair remain within all, though visible to none.

"POEM 303 (THE SOUL SELECTS HER OWN SOCIETY—)"

First published: 1890 (as "Exclusion")
Type of work: Poem

The poem explicitly notes that individuals choose the particulars of their own environments but also implies renunciation of traditional beliefs.

Critics note that poem 303 was written in 1862, the year Dickinson made her decision to withdraw from the larger world. The poem, read in this simple way, simply states the need to live by one's own choice. This reading, perfectly acceptable in itself, overlooks several important phrases which have larger implications.

The first of these curious choices of language is "divine Majority," in line 3. "The Soul" of line 1, not merely "a soul" or a person, shuts her door not only to people at large but also to the majority, even those who bear the stamp of divine sanction. Read this way, the poem also indicates the poet's decision not to join the society of the Elect, this even though "an emperor be kneeling" on her doormat. The conduit of grace, an analogy favored in the sermons of Jonathan Edwards, becomes "the Valves" of the soul's discrimination.

Though she remains "unmoved," the soul is neither nihilistic nor solipsistic. Even as the capitalized letter implies zero, the soul chooses "One" then becomes deaf to all entreaties "Like Stone." To insist that this necessarily indicates preference for a Unitarian rather than a Trinitarian view carries the interpretation to a theological level that the poem's language will not sustain. Nevertheless, selectivity in all matters, including religion, is something the poet clearly favors.

On a complementary level, one notices the carefully crafted description of the woman not at home to any callers, except one or at most a few. Read this way, which merely supplements the other possible alternatives, the poem states the preference to live in a way unlike that of most nineteenth century women, spurning the conventions of social obligation and what society expects, even though an emperor might attempt to persuade her to join the larger group.

"POEM 328 (A BIRD CAME DOWN THE WALK—)"

First published: 1891
Type of work: Poem

Unexpected cruelty, distrust, ingratitude, and fear are described, all within an apparently placid, idyllic setting.

This is the finest example of Dickinson's nature verse, for it perfectly juxtaposes elements of superficial gentility against the inner barbarity that characterizes the workings of the world. The narrator chances to see a bird walking along a pathway, but just as the scene appears perfect, the bird seizes upon a worm, bites it in two, and devours it. The bird drinks some dew on nearby grass (note the alternate for a drinking "glass"), then graciously steps aside, right to a wall, to allow a beetle to pass. The bird, like one fearful of being caught in an unacceptable action, glances around quickly with darting eyes.

"Cautious" describes both the demeanor of the bird and that of the observing narrator. Both feel threatened, the bird of the possible consequences of its savagery, the narrator because she is next on the bird's path. She "offered him a Crumb," not because she admires the bird but out of fear and expediency. The bird, sensing that it has escaped any potentially harmful consequences for what it has done, struts a bit as "he unrolled his feathers" and "rowed him softer home—." Ironically, its walk is too casual, softer than oars dividing a seamless ocean or butterflies leaping into noon's banks, all without a splash. Behind its soft, charming, and genteel facade, nature is menacing, and its hypocritical attempts to conceal its barbarism make it more frightening.

"POEM 465 (I HEARD A FLY BUZZ—WHEN I DIED—)"

First published: 1896 (as "Dying")
Type of work: Poem

This is the most famous of the Dickinson poems that look ahead to death, set at the instant that lies between life and death.

This poem relies upon the poetic devices known technically as synesthesia (use of one sense to describe the workings of another) and paronomasia (wordplay). The predatory fly, functioning as in poem 187, waits to claim a corpse. The room is still, but this stillness resembles the interval between the heavings of a storm. Eyes had cried all they could; the patient, who is speaking, is beyond willing life,

though she has willed her "Keepsakes." The language is both theological and legal: "when the King/ Be witnessed—/ in the Room—." Then, hesitantly but unmistakably, the fly interposes itself between the dying speaker and the light. Its buzz is "Blue—uncertain stumbling." The windows fail, and the speaker cannot "see to see—."

Characteristically, there is no enlightenment at the moment of death, merely a failing of the human objects designed to admit light. Thus, human sight does not allow human understanding. Dickinson once wrote to Higginson, using her distinctive capitalizations, that, "The Ear is the last Face We hear after we see." Clearly, she identifies the "eye" with the "I." The King is present to witness the death, but it remains a legal transaction. Neither he nor the speaker have the will to alter things, beyond ensuring that the material objects willed fall to the wills of their new owners.

"POEM 640 (I CANNOT LIVE WITH YOU—)"

First published: 1890 (as "In Vain")
Type of work: Poem

This most famous of the love poems is often misread to argue for the poet's love relationship with Charles Wadsworth.

This poem's coherence results from the opposition of tensions that arise from Dickinson's dual understanding of life. To live with the beloved is impossible, for "it would be life." Life is, on the other hand, something eternal, the key to which resides with the church sexton, who keeps the key to the Lord's tabernacle. The cups of human life, however, hold no sacramental wine; the housewife discards them when they break or crack and replaces them with newer ware.

The speaker cannot die with the beloved, for the gaze of "the Other" intrudes; it can be shut neither out nor down. This apparent rival that spies on any possible pact is the metaphysical divine other that has first rights in matters of death as well as life. Similarly, it is impossible for the speaker to "stand by/ And see you—freeze"; the single death of the beloved denies death to the devoted speaker.

Even a joint resurrection of the lovers is impossible; this would anger Jesus and obscure the face of the redeemer. To this dual understanding of life the poet thus adds the stages of the Christian experience: life, death, judgment, and resurrection. When the beloved looked upon the "homesick Eye," grace would "Glow plain," but it would be "foreign" to him who sought a higher grace. Furthermore, "They d judge Us," saying that he sought to serve Heaven even though she could not.

The speaker could then no longer have her eyes on paradise; both would suffer damnation, but she would fall the lower, and they would still be apart. The effect would be the same even if the beloved were forgiven. The only alternative, "Despair," becomes their connection; their only conversation is their joint prayer, which allows them to link the immanent and the transcendent

"POEM 712 (BECAUSE I COULD NOT STOP FOR DEATH—)"

First published: 1890
Type of work: Poem

In the most famous of her eternity poems, Dickinson personifies death as a gentleman caller.

Death appears personified in this poem as a courtly beau who gently insists that the speaker put aside both "labor" and "leisure." He arrives in his carriage, having stopped for her because she could not have stopped for him, and he even submits to a chaperone, "Immortality," for the length of their outing together.

This death holds no terrors. Their drive is slow, and they pass the familiar sights of the town: fields of grain which gaze at them, the local school and its playground. Even so, the speaker realizes that this is no ordinary outing with an ordinary gentleman caller when they pass the setting sun, "Or rather— He passed Us—." She realizes that it has grown cold, that she wears only a gossamer gown and a tulle lace cap.

Death takes the speaker to her new home, "A Swelling of the Ground," whose roof is "scarcely visible." Though centuries have passed since the event, the entire episode, including the speaker's

awareness of her death, seems less than a day in length. The poem fuses elements of the secular seduction motif, with elements of the medieval bride-of-Christ tradition, arguable through inclusion of details such as the tippet of a nun's habit.

"POEM 754 (MY LIFE HAD STOOD—A LOADED GUN—)"

First published: 1929
Type of work: Poem

The most famous of the paradox poems deals with the Christian and secular understandings of life and death.

This poem is written as a riddle that challenges the reader to identify the speaker. On the literal level the speaker is a gun, loaded to do its owner's bidding. Its "smile" is like a Vesuvian eruption, laying low its master's enemies. None survive "On whom I lay a Yellow Eye—/ Or an emphatic Thumb—." Though the master must live longer than the gun, the gun may also live longer than its master.

Critics have given this poem every variety of interpretation, almost none of them totally satisfactory. Most common (and least satisfying) is the argument that the poet is herself the loaded gun, waiting to be called by her master, the Lord, ready to fight her Lord's battles, willing to make his enemies hers. Yet how can one reconcile this with the possibility of the gun's outliving her master, except by admitting the possibility of a mortal deity?

Though Dickinson doubts and even despairs in some of her poems concerning matters of election and redemption, she never denies that a deity exists. In fact, poem 338 explicitly records her certainty that there is a divine presence. Similarly, it does no good to see this poem merely as an emblem of the poet's personal, creative, or sexual frustration, as some critics have done.

Were one to have asked residents of Dickinson's Amherst the solution to the final riddle stanza, however, it is likely that they would have answered that the master was Christ and the gun was death. Christ has authority over life and death as Son of the Father; even so, Christ died before death disappeared from the world of the living, and in this sense death outlived him.

Another interpretation embraces a more classical alternative. Myth traditionally pictures deities dealing out death with weapons: Zeus uses thunderbolts, Apollo and Artemis bows and arrows, Wotan a spear fashioned from the great ash tree which underpins creation. Seen in this way, death is both master and means. It uses whatever tool stands at the ready and creates opponents even as it destroys creation. The single consolation to universal creation, which will one day encounter death, is that neither death nor the tools it uses has eternal life.

"POEM 986 (A NARROW FELLOW IN THE GRASS)"

First published: 1866 (as "The Snake")
Type of work: Poem

The archetypal snake in the grass is presented as a symbol of cunning.

One of the best-known Dickinson nature poems, poem 986 is more remarkable for its execution and technique than its content. The narrator unexpectedly encounters a snake in tall marsh grass. Far from tempting the narrator, as the serpent tempted Eve, it induces fear, panting, and a sudden chill. The first eleven lines describe the snake in a personified, almost amiable way. He sometimes "rides" through the grass, parting it like a comb does hair. Yet, when plain sight threatens to betray its exact location, the grass "closes at your feet/ And opens further on—."

The narrator of this poem is male, perhaps because boys rather than girls would be more likely to walk through marshes; however, the narrator's sex also underscores the phallic implications of this symbol. If one prefers to see this sexual imagery, it is possible to cite the sexual association of such words and phrases as "Whip lash," "tighter breathing," and "Zero at the Bone." In any event, reading the poem as a commentary on human cunning is entirely consistent with any further level of meaning. The narrator feels cordial toward "Several of Nature's People" but has only fear for the snake. In this, as in many Dickinson's poems, one must

beware of mixing biographical folklore with the poem and forcing the reading offered by structuralist critics that the poem is Dickinson's confession of sexual fear.

Reading the poem's first line aloud causes the tongue to flicker, like that of a snake; sibilants abound in increasing number as the lines describe the snake's approach. These elements are certainly intentional. Poem 1670 ("In Winter in my Room") presents a similar encounter, though with a worm-turned-snake. Relating the events as a dream sequence, this narrator flees whole towns from the creature before she dares set the experience down.

"POEM 1624 (APPARENTLY WITH NO SURPRISE)"

First published: 1890
Type of work: Poem

Nature is presented as the victim of the elements and an approving God.

The situation described in this short poem is simple. Frost "beheads" a "happy Flower" even as it plays back and forth in a breeze. The flower is not surprised that it has died in this way, even if the frost's power was "accidental." The wordplay on axe, beheading, and accidental is clear. What is a surprise is that the real assassin is "blonde." It is clearly the sun, which withheld its warmth and allowed the frost to do its dirty job. The sun "proceeds unmoved," the oxymoron emphasizing that the sun simply observes the workings of nature from its high vantage point. It metes out a day, and God, higher still, approves it all as director of the conspiracy.

SUMMARY

One can fully appreciate Dickinson's originality only by placing her verse against that of her poet contemporaries. She is certainly more mystical—and is a better poet—than Ralph Waldo Emerson or Henry David Thoreau. Her poetic works have greater substance than those of Edgar Allan Poe. She writes poems far richer in content than the school poets: James Russell Lowell, John Greenleaf Whittier, and Henry Wadsworth Longfellow. The only American poet of her century with whom she is comparable is Walt Whitman.

In the nineteenth century, women generally wrote only domestic verse-material suitable for ladies' magazines—or wrote under male pseudonyms. Higginson's advice that Dickinson avoid publication makes most modern readers of Dickinson angry, as do the alterations made by Dickinson's early editors. One can be grateful that Dickinson's creative energy remained undiminished.

Robert J. Forman

BIBLIOGRAPHY

By the Author

POETRY:
Poems, 1890
Poems: Second Series, 1891
Poems: Third Series, 1896
The Single Hound, 1914
Further Poems, 1929
Unpublished Poems, 1936
Bolts of Melody, 1945
The Poems of Emily Dickinson, 1955 (3 volumes; Thomas H. Johnson, editor)
The Complete Poems of Emily Dickinson, 1960 (Johnson, editor)

NONFICTION:
Letters, 1894 (2 volumes)
The Letters of Emily Dickinson, 1958 (3 volumes; Thomas H. Johnson and Theodora Ward, editors)

About the Author

Boruch, Marianne. "Dickinson Descending." *The Georgia Review* 40 (1986): 863-877.

Brantley, Richard E. *Experience and Faith: The Late-Romantic Imagination of Emily Dickinson*. New York: Palgrave Macmillan, 2004.

Carruth, Hayden. "Emily Dickinson's Unexpectedness." *Ironwood* 14 (1986): 51-57.

Eberwein, Jane Donahue. *An Emily Dickinson Encyclopedia*. Westport, Conn.: Greenwood Press, 1998.

Ferlazzo, Paul, ed. *Critical Essays on Emily Dickinson*. Boston: G. K. Hall, 1984.

Grabher, Gudrun, Roland Hagenbüchle, and Cristanne Miller, ed. *The Emily Dickinson Handbook*. Amherst: University of Massachusetts Press, 1998.

Juhasz, Suzanne, ed. *Feminist Critics Read Emily Dickinson*. Bloomington: Indiana University Press, 1983.

Kirk, Connie Ann. *Emily Dickinson: A Biography*. Westport, Conn.: Greenwood Press, 2004.

Lundin, Roger. *Emily Dickinson and the Art of Belief*. Grand Rapids, Mich.: William B. Eerdmans, 2004.

MacNeil, Helen. *Emily Dickinson*. New York: Pantheon Books, 1986.

Pollack, Vivian R. *A Historical Guide to Emily Dickinson*. New York: Oxford University Press, 2004.

Vendler, Helen Hennessey. *Poets Thinking: Pope, Whitman, Dickinson, Yeats*. Cambridge, Mass.: Harvard University Press, 2004.

DISCUSSION TOPICS

- Emily Dickinson lived a life constrained in many respects. What liberating experiences of her life—including self-created ones—contributed materially to her poetry?

- How have editors of Dickinson's poetry both obscured and clarified what she actually wrote?

- Examine three or four Dickinson poems with a theme of love. What particular effects of imagery and tone distinguish these poems?

- Repeat the above process with respect to poems on the theme of death.

- What factors account for the inclusion of weakly sentimental poems in her canon? Would the publication history of her poems be one of these factors?

- Dickinson's favorite stanza is basically that of many familiar hymns of her time. What differences in rhythm and phrasing do you note between the hymns and her poems?

- Compare the different versions of "Safe in Their Alabaster Chambers." Is it possible to determine the direction her revisions took or in fact which versions are revisions?

JOAN DIDION

Born: Sacramento, California
December 5, 1934

As an essayist and novelist, Didion has used a reporter's precise prose to reveal such widespread American flaws as dishonesty and lack of self-reliance.

Quintana Roo Dunne

BIOGRAPHY

Compensating for her own physical frailty and fears persisting from childhood, Joan Didion has long identified with the resilience of her great-great-great-grandmother, who in 1846 left the Donner wagon train and followed a northern pass through the Sierras just before a Nevada blizzard isolated the main party and drove some of them eventually to cannibalism. That frontier example sustained Didion as her father, Frank Didion, an Army Air Corps officer, moved the family from base to base during World War II. She and her brother entertained themselves by watching films, and her mother advised her to keep busy by writing stories. Her sense of insecurity diminished only after their return to Sacramento, where the family land went back five generations. What remained, however, was her sense of the theatrical. Stories of her pioneer ancestors always included near disasters, life on the edge. Her early fears, therefore, of rattlesnakes, collapsing bridges, and atomic bombs came only in part from reality. They came also from an imagination stirred to excitement but not wholly believing in actual tragedy. Added to her imagination is a curiosity which, while she was an eighth-grader, led her, notepad in hand, to walk calmly into the Pacific Ocean: It was a life wish, not a death wish. A wave dumped her back onto shore.

During Didion's senior year at the University of California at Berkeley, in 1956, she won first prize in *Vogue*'s nonfiction contest, along with an apprenticeship that, eight years later, had turned into an associate feature editorship. In New York City she never refused an invitation to a party, though she usually remained a silent observer. Meanwhile, in 1963, she published a first novel, *Run River*, a tale of a Sacramento valley dynasty, involving murder, suicide, and near-incest. The next year she married John Gregory Dunne, a writer for *Time*, who was as talkative as she was reticent. They moved from New York to California and in 1966 adopted a baby girl whom they named Quintana Roo (after a state in Mexico's Yucatán peninsula).

Although dismayed by escalating violence on the West Coast and desirous of making her separate peace, Didion forced herself to examine her times and, in 1968, published her essays on disorder in California and other places as *Slouching Towards Bethlehem*.

The effort caused her a serious breakdown. Although her second novel, *Play It as It Lays* (1970), was a best seller, critics who admired its cinematic style overlooked her compassion for Maria, the distraught narrator, and her admiration for the young mother's perseverance.

During a visit to Colombia in 1973, Didion contracted nearly fatal paratyphoid fever. The experience helped her write her third novel, *A Book of Common Prayer* (1977), which contrasts the irresponsible "flash polities" of South American men with two North American "marginal women" whose spirit maintains the core of civilization.

In 1982, despite health problems, Didion had the courage to travel to war-torn El Salvador. The result was *Salvador* (1983), a long report on the murder common in that country's ongoing revolution and the naïveté of American foreign policy. Without any political solutions to offer, Didion has to be satisfied with providing an honest record of the facts, the lies, the contradictions. History, she implies, is simply remembered events. Whether or not it contains heroic deeds, simply remembering accurately is heroism enough—especially for Americans, who, she claims, too often consider themselves exempt from history.

Didion's novel *Democracy*, published in 1984, presents both a rich American woman unhappily married to a morally questionable presidential candidate and a covert agent whose insight into the real world of insurrections and secret deals contrasts with the thinking of the candidate and his campaign manager.

Like *Salvador*, Didion's extended essay *Miami* (1987) is more intensely political than *Democracy* and goes beyond the status of Cubans in Florida to the hidden federal policy on Fidel Castro's regime.

Working as a team, Didion and Dunne wrote a number of screenplays together during the 1970's, because the pay freed them later to write their novels, but they resented letting a film director make decisions of pace and texture that they thought should be the writers' choices. Such an attitude is understandable because, for her own publications, Didion is an exacting taskmaster, requiring sometimes several years of revisions before her compressed short novels are released.

After she and Dunne divided their time between metropolitan Los Angeles and New York City in the mid-1980's, they moved to the latter in 1988. There her writing continued, as she turned out books, essays for magazines (especially the *New York Review of Books*), and, again with her husband, teleplays and the screenplay for *Up Close and Personal* (1996). In her book *After Henry*, appearing in 1992, she collects previously published essays about Americans and American events, including crime and politics. Her novel *The Last Thing He Wanted*, published in 1996, resembles *Democracy* in its use of covert operations in its plot and a maritally troubled, rich woman as the protagonist.

Her subsequent books have been nonfiction, starting with the collection of essays titled *Political Fictions* (2001), in which she presents herself as cutting through to the political facts behind the fic-

tions of the title and in which she describes herself as someone who grew up "among conservative California Republicans" who favored "low taxes, a balanced budget, and a limited government" that did not interfere in "the private or cultural life of its citizens." She happily voted for Barry Goldwater, the conservative Republican candidate for president in 1964, but, in part because of Ronald Reagan, eventually changed her registration to Democratic without, according to her, "taking a markedly different view on any issue." In *Political Fictions*, Didion attacks persons usually considered on the left, as well as persons usually considered on the right in American politics, but notably shows her disdain for prominent Republicans, presenting Reagan as primarily an actor, even as president. Although she calls President Bill Clinton a sexual predator, she also deplores the investigation Kenneth Starr led into Clinton's relationship with Monica Lewinsky, claiming that a public official's sexual conduct is no matter of public concern and that Starr and those supporting him were subverting American democracy.

Her next book, *Fixed Ideas: America Since 9.11* (2003), is a reprint of an essay first published in the *New York Review of Books* on January 16, 2003, with the addition of a preface by Frank Rich of *The New York Times*. After Rich's verbal attack on President George W. Bush in his preface, Didion claims that America invaded Afghanistan because of the fixed ideas found in New York City and Washington, D.C., and foresees (before Operation Iraqi Freedom) that America will also invade Iraq, again because of fixed ideas. She also claims that fixed ideas have also hurt the United States in its restriction on using embryonic stem cells in medical research and its inclusion of the words "under God" in the Pledge of Allegiance. America, says Didion, should rid itself of its harmful fixed ideas and study history to understand why jihadists attacked it. In this very short book, as in *Political Fictions*, Didion's intent apparently is to point out faults in politicians' thoughts and actions, rather than to explain with any detail what she would do were she in charge.

Where I Was From (2003), with the significant past tense in its title, marks a movement by Didion to a more personal story than in her previous two books, although even this book contains clear social and political commentary about the United States in general and California in particular. Didion studies her home state as a whole, the place to which her ancestors traveled in the mid-nineteenth century, breaking family bonds and gambling on success after perilous journeys across much of North America. She considers the changes in her own ideas, using passages in *Run River,* her 1963 novel, and she further develops her discussion by citing works from Californians of the late nineteenth and early twentieth centuries: the philosopher Josiah Royce, the journalist Lincoln Steffens, and the novelists Jack London and Frank Norris. She has come to see, she claims, that the idea that California was once a place of self-reliant people is a historical illusion that obscures the reliance the state has long had on the railroads and then the federal government. In the next-to-last chapter, Didion tells of a moment of revelation in the summer of 1971 or 1972 while she is walking through the supposedly re-created "Old Sacramento" with her daughter and her mother: Didion then realizes that what she is walking through is "no more than a theme, a decorative effect," and begins to sense the remoteness of her long family history and of "the dream of America, the entire enchantment" in which she has lived.

Beginning late in 2003, Didion endured hard personal times. Shortly before Christmas, her recently married daughter, Quintana Dunne Michael, fell ill, seemingly with influenza, but her condition so worsened that she suffered septic shock and was placed in a medically induced coma at Beth Israel North Hospital in New York City. After visiting her on December 30, Didion and her husband returned to their apartment on the upper East Side of Manhattan, where, as she was about to serve supper, he collapsed at the dining table from a heart attack. Despite the efforts of the emergency medical technicians who arrived at the apartment to treat him, Dunne was pronounced dead that night at New York-Presbyterian Hospital. Didion's strong, professionally productive marriage of almost forty years ended suddenly, and her daughter was unable to learn the news until January 15, 2004. In *The Year of Magical Thinking,* published in late 2005, Didion recounts her efforts, despite both her rejection of Christian hope and her ordinarily powerful sense of reality, to make her husband come back through what she calls "magical thinking." She recounts too her daughter's critical illness, apparent recovery, eventual collapse in Los

Angeles International Airport, and subsequent brain surgery. Didion finished the book before her daughter died in New York City on August 26, 2005, of pancreatitis. *The Year of Magical Thinking* won for its author a National Book Award in November, 2005.

ANALYSIS

As her essays and fiction demonstrate, Didion's perspective on life is that of the witness who is both part of and apart from what she so critically observes. She is a loner, resistant to identification with any movement or label—despite her many contributions to *The New York Review of Books,* often considered a leftist publication. She is a moralist, although one who does not offer herself as a model for others, in thought or behavior. Yet even in the absence of high expectations for either herself or society, she does make great demands on both. While acknowledging the extent of disasters in ordinary lives, she requires a willed effort to probe constantly for whatever degree of self-control and self-affirmation is possible. This is what "living on the edge" means to her, and therefore to her characters: the edge as impending cliff or as opening frontier.

As Didion fought to overcome her shyness, she also risked visits beyond the continental United States—typically to southern places: Hawaii, Latin America, Indonesia. Her reportage has always been incisive and therefore useful as a portrait not only of political temperaments in tropical places but also of the peculiarities of the United States' foreign policy. Too often, she implies, American alliances have been made with anticommunists who show no love of democracy. Such is the inference one draws from her novel *A Book of Common Prayer* and her nonfiction works *Salvador* and *Miami.* Didion does not pretend to be a social or political expert with an agenda of her own. She proceeds only from a carefully controlled mixture of detachment and compassionate interest in the possibilities of humane control of events. Her principal complaint is that American naïveté and arrogance have conditioned people to think that they are immune from reality and the forces of history.

The harshness of so much of reality, particularly for women such as the narrators or central characters in several of Didion's novels, might suggest a natural affinity between Didion and feminism;

however, she astonished radical feminists by her critical comments in her 1972 essay "The Women's Movement" (reprinted in *The White Album*, 1979). There she asserted that women unaware of the Marxist roots of American feminism misunderstood how "networking" was being manipulated to substitute mass identity for the ideal of individual selfhood. Feminists, in turn, argued that Didion was one of them, so often did she picture women as helpless victims. Yet Didion has never blamed her personal problems on a patriarchal society, as some feminists have done.

Furthermore, although some of Didion's male characters consider Maria, Charlotte, Grace, and Inez marginal, it is not their whims and weaknesses that Didion memorializes but their courage and persistence despite their seeming powerlessness. Such women find centers in themselves in the midst of crises and are not interested in controlling anyone else. Only Marin in *A Book of Common Prayer*, perhaps, is an exception, and she is the young revolutionary, the terrorist without a grasp of reality or a genuine cause.

For Didion, the impulse to write comes less from ideology than from curiosity. She writes not so much to persuade or incite to action or promote any movement as, according to her, to find out what she is thinking. In part, this reliance on herself as her own most accessible reader originated in the insignificance still attributed to women writers at the middle of the twentieth century. Consequently, she was free to write for herself and to find forms appropriate to her own perception of character and circumstance. Early in life she studied the techniques used by Ernest Hemingway to avoid abstraction and to particularize events. Her editor in chief at *Vogue* reinforced this hard focus, requiring exact language. Didion's essay "On Keeping a Notebook" (reprinted in *Slouching Towards Bethlehem*) explains that the accuracy of a factual record has never been quite as important to her as ambience, the associations resurgent in her mind as she rediscovers what otherwise passing moments have meant to her. Details are important, most of all, as clues to insights.

Didion's novels have particularly acknowledged the limitations of her narrators, the tenuousness of their hold on others' reality, and the often-interrupted continuity of their lives. Nevertheless, it is just such limited but sensitive narrators whom she respects and even admires. Although her novels are compact, they convey an intensity often lacking in longer novels by her contemporaries. The inner lives of her female characters are troubled, sometimes by their very "innocence." The greater menace, however, in Didion's eyes, lies in the complacent, self-congratulatory outer worlds in which moral ambiguities go largely unrecognized. She prefers outsiders who—like herself—struggle to survive society's losses of memory and of meaning.

SLOUCHING TOWARDS BETHLEHEM

First published: 1968
Type of work: Essays

The anarchy of the 1960's in the United States must be recognized and confronted, although perhaps it cannot be fully survived.

Didion rejected, but found that she could not ignore, the negative aspects of the drug culture associated with the anti-Establishment movements that grew out of the Beat Generation. Because it was threatening California's frontier traditions of responsible self-reliance, she decided to put aside her preference for privacy and describe the disorder. She discovered that in many ways the so-called counterculture mirrored the shallowness of the Establishment against which it purported to take its stand. The dropouts shared the same self-centeredness, indifference, and casual relationships that marked large corporations.

Many of Didion's articles from this period (including those on the hippies of the Haight-Ashbury district in San Francisco) first appeared in *The Saturday Evening Post*. She believed she was describing the nature of love and death in a "golden land," as revealed in sensational murder cases, or the limited realities of splinter groups of communists, drug addicts, such pacifists as singer Joan Baez and her disciples in Carmel Valley, or the Diggers, who tried to feed society's dropouts. Didion's descriptions are so accurate in their particulars that they seem impersonal; her anxiety over the slow erosion of solid citizenship can only be inferred from behind a mask of gentle representation. She had so successfully learned to distance herself through concreteness and compression—practiced by imitating Hemingway and that earlier journalist and writer of fiction, Katherine Anne Porter—that individually the first essays hardly seem to warrant the warning implicit in her choosing William Butler Yeats's foreboding poem "The Second Coming" as an epigraph to her book. Yet they are crucial to her indictment of a decaying society.

The later sections, subtitled "Personals" and "Seven Places of the Mind," proceed with equally quiet portraits, which tend to provide the positive values that she is remembering and, through memory, defending. "On Keeping a Notebook," for example, makes clear her invisible but close involvement in all that she describes—indeed, how each fragment is more essentially a clue to her feelings about herself than about the person or circumstance being reported. "On Self Respect" speaks of

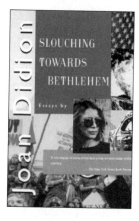

having the same courage to admit one's mistakes as one's disciplined ancestors had. "Notes from a Native Daughter" explains what it was about California in her childhood that brought her back to it from New York (whose own portrait is provided in "Goodbye to All That"). The code of conduct, an ethic of conscience that she associates with her California, is rendered somewhat abstractly in the essay "On Morality," but its basis in family closeness is explicitly dramatized in "On Going Home." Without such positive affirmations, Didion's critique of her contemporaries' negative outlook would have made her seem supercilious: a mere rebel against rebels without a cause.

The two aspects of American culture—the destructively artificial and the compassionately profound—are brought together in "Letter from Paradise, 21 19′ N., 157 52′ W.," a study of Hawaii. Those islands can be a state of mind, a place for tourists to enjoy their fantasies, or, as it was for Didion, visiting the sunken *Arizona* with all of its memorialized dead still submerged, a place of profound meditation on infamous betrayals and the death of innocence.

PLAY IT AS IT LAYS

First published: 1970
Type of work: Novel

Maria is more authentic and more substantial than Hollywood people, including her director husband and her "best friend," can ever realize.

The eighty-three brief scenes in this short novel at first appear to symbolize protagonist Maria Wyeth's anxious sense of being a displaced, discontinuous person. However, their interrupted continuity also comes to represent the failure of the film industry to comprehend her complexity and her needs. Maria's husband, Carter, never gets beyond his first image of her as an East Coast model; it is this superficial image that he prefers in the films which he makes of her. He is equally narrow in his attitude toward their daughter, Kate, born disabled. Carter has her institutionalized and attempts to prevent Maria from visiting her.

The fact that Maria's own mother died horribly, alone in the desert and attacked by coyotes, has reinforced her maternal feelings. She identifies with her rejected child; both are marginal, considered outside the "in group" of the "beautiful people." Starved for simple assurances that she is really alive and lovable, Maria has an affair with scriptwriter Les Goodwin. When she becomes pregnant, Carter declares that she must either have an abortion or never again see Kate. The fact that Les is already married drastically limits Maria's options. Forced to choose between her two children, both wholly helpless, Maria agrees to the abortion; as a result of her guilt, however, she suffers recurring nightmares, including those of children being led to gas chambers.

Helene, who has always played the part of her closest friend, can provide neither understanding nor consolation. Instead she offers a partnership in a sadomasochistic ménage à trois with her producer husband, BZ. Eventually, however, even BZ realizes the emptiness of his lifestyle and invites Maria to join him in a final overdose of drugs. She resists, still loyal instinctively to finding a purpose for herself and for Kate through a relationship whose pathetic aspects are offset by the desperation of her love, an obsessive need to be needed.

629

Didion takes enormous risks of misguiding the reader with several techniques. She allows Carter and Helene to pass judgment on Maria before turning the novel over exclusively to her key character. Then Maria's experience is narrated largely in a nonrational, often disconnected, seeming disorder. The author's faith lies with the reader's ability to contrast the strong feelings of attachment and resilience in Maria, despite all of her hardships, with the overripe and rotten opportunists for whom the American Dream (and its counterpart, the Western Dream) has reduced an imaginative vision to an imaginary delusion. Carter and Helene are captives, and BZ is a victim of the void concealed behind the spectacular pageantry of motion pictures. *Play It as It Lays* enacts much of the wisdom inherited by Didion from her idea of old California's high regard for commitment and courage.

Hollywood comes to stand for negative aspects in American society at large as it becomes less and less productive in a postindustrial age and more and more directed toward services and entertainment designed to fill increasing leisure hours with stimulation. Didion sees in a self-satisfied, developed nation such dangerous attributes as impermanence of human relationships and spiritual values; she sees either a lack of comprehension of, or an indifference to, the consequences of irresponsible behavior. It is a society out of control.

Maria thinks that she is a born loser, but it is the culture around her, not Maria herself, that is mindless and insensitive. The distinctions between her immediate world and her inner self are so subtle that many critics complained about the novel's nihilistic theme. Even though Didion and Dunne wrote the screenplay for this novel, the 1972 film version could not convey all the necessary nuances. Nevertheless, *Play It as It Lays* records the struggle of one woman for meaning in a society which, far from commending her, can only hold her in contempt for not adapting to its capricious ways.

A BOOK OF COMMON PRAYER

First published: 1977
Type of work: Novel

Biochemist Grace Strasser-Mendana recovers an interest in intimate human affairs through symbolic sisterhood with fellow expatriate and agonizing mother Charlotte Douglas.

Concerned that readers had difficulty perceiving the admirable qualities of Maria in *Play It as It Lays*, Didion, in *A Book of Common Prayer*, creates Charlotte Douglas, Maria's equivalent, observed and analyzed by an older, scientifically trained American woman. Grace Strasser-Mendana, orphaned at a young age in the United States, is the widow of a Latin American president who was probably killed by his brother in a struggle for power. What principally keeps Grace overseas, in fictional Boca Grande, is her desire to be close to her son, Gerardo, though he too is toying with political violence. At first she is merely distracted by the antics of Charlotte Douglas, a newcomer, until she perceives parallels between their values and their lives as "outsiders" in a world trained for irresponsibility—and therefore for destruction.

Charlotte, having been raised in an overprotected, middle-class environment, cannot cope with either Warren Bogart, her first husband, who tries to compensate for his inadequacies through physically abusing others; or with Leonard Douglas, her current husband, who pretends to be a liberal lawyer but is covertly a gunrunner. She turns all of her frustrated affection on her daughter, Marin, who has become a mindless revolutionary involved in bombing buildings. Charlotte believes that Marin may surface in Boca Grande. On part of her journey south, Charlotte brings with her a premature newborn who dies of complications. Leonard, the baby's father who cannot accept imperfection, wanted to let it die in a clinic. Charlotte, in

contrast, writes on her visa application "Occupation: mother."

Gradually Grace comes to understand Charlotte's innocence and goodwill, to empathize with this woman in shock, and to recover her own capacity for the compassion that helps define human purpose. The two women become, in effect, a substitute family. When Grace's brothers-in-law engage once again in coup and counter-coup, and refugees flee, Charlotte remains behind to tend the sick and wounded. She is slain. Dying, she cries out not for herself but for Marin. Grace is also dying, of cancer, yet is the only person other than Charlotte devoted to life. Therefore, as principal narrator of *A Book of Common Prayer*, she memorializes this other woman who, though considered comic by society, struggled so heroically to rise above circumstances. It is Charlotte's resilience, not her victimization, that Grace is celebrating.

Didion, a lapsed Episcopalian, still retains respect for rituals from her childhood, and she considers this novel the equivalent of Grace's prayer for the essential goodness in Charlotte. If Boca Grande symbolizes the danger of failing to come to terms with history (that is, the consequences of human actions) and therefore of being doomed to repeat its mistakes, the novel's reliance on psalms and litanies implies a divinely orchestrated design to life, epitomized by the connection between Grace and Charlotte. The novel also functions as Grace's prayer of thanksgiving for Charlotte's inadvertent restoration of Grace to a faith in humankind, in spite of all its errors and horrors.

That appeal to something eternal is paralleled by the time structure in this novel. The chronicle of events is only rarely linear. Instead, distant past, present, and near future tend to be looped together. At first this seeming disorder of cause and effect, as well as of chronology, conveys both the instability of Latin politics and the disconnectedness between Charlotte and reality. Eventually, however, what is conveyed is a kind of continuous present, with history the sum of all coexistent times. The loops become a sequence of knots, implying an eternal realization of what temporarily seems confused. The technique is moralist Didion's way of warning Americans that no one is immune from human events, from effects that he or she partially has caused.

THE WHITE ALBUM

First published: 1979
Type of work: Essays

This five-part book comprises twenty essays on topics ranging from motorcycle films to Georgia O'Keeffe's paintings and from Charles Manson's murders to Didion's own migraines.

With a title echoing the unofficial title of an album that the Beatles recorded in 1968, *The White Album* comprises mainly essays previously published in some form in various magazines, with each essay showing Didion's insight, precise diction, and ability to create powerful images.

The first part of *The White Album* is also called "The White Album" and includes only one essay, again called "The White Album" (1968-1978). That long essay is Didion's fifteen-section, associational consideration of why she could not tell herself the stories she needed to survive, why she could not find a "narrative" to connect the images confronting her when she lived in Hollywood and pondered such events as the Manson gang's murders, a recording session by the Doors, visits to Huey Newton and Eldridge Cleaver, and a student strike at San Francisco State.

The second part, "California Republic," consists of seven shorter essays. The first of them, "James Pike, American" (1976), presents the late Episcopal bishop of California as a man of "mindless fervor" whose idea of reinventing the world was typical of the 1960's in the United States. "Holy Water" (1977), the second of the essays, is Didion's account of her fascination with the mass movement of water, especially in California. Among the other essays in this part, particularly notable is "Many Mansions" (1977), contrasting the new, sprawling, unoccupied governor's mansion, which Didion regards as blandly conformist, with the previous one, which she regards as delightfully individual.

In the third part, "Women," Didion praises Georgia O'Keeffe but attacks Doris Lessing for her "torrent of fiction that increasingly seems conceived in a stubborn rage against the very idea of fiction." In "The Women's Movement" (1972), Didion takes on a bigger target by claiming that American feminism is essentially a kind of Marxism mixed oddly with New England transcendentalism, that feminist criticism fails because fiction is "in most ways hostile to ideology," and that many feminists seem averse to "adult sexual life itself" and would prefer "to stay forever children."

Of the seven essays in the fourth part, titled "Sojourns," the longest is "In the Islands" (1969-1977), in which, among other places in Hawaii, Didion presents Punchbowl, the military cemetery where the reports of the number of Americans killed weekly in Vietnam become real as she watches the graveside service for one of them. A much shorter but also memorable essay in this part is "At the Dam" (1970), in which Didion ponders why the image of Hoover Dam has haunted her.

The last part, "On the Morning After the Sixties," comprises an essay with that title and a second essay, "Quiet Days in Malibu" (1976-1978), in which Didion gives a favorable account of the famous suburb where she lived for seven years. She closes that essay and the book, however, with scenes of ruin and a sense of being dispossessed.

DEMOCRACY

First published: 1984
Type of work: Novel

Democracy, which can hardly exist without a well-informed citizenry, has to take its primary example from open communication within the family.

While *Democracy* was still a work in progress, Didion referred to it as "Angel Visits," a Victorian term meaning brief encounters. Closely attached to her own ancestry and her immediate family, she might have been expected to offer the Christian family as a shining example for others; instead, the opposite is true. Paul Christian, the father, represents the overbearing baronial class that ruled his native Hawaii's agribusinesses. Worse, he has the same imperious relationship with his own wife and daughters. Although he is free to wander across the world, the other Christians are expected to remain in place, anticipating his unregulated return.

Paul's wife, Carol, who expected a fuller life and greater stability through marriage, never is allowed any degree of self-worth. Finally, after their daughter Janet's wedding, Carol disappears on a cruise, never to return. Janet's husband, Dick Ziegler, invests the modest fortune which he made in Hong Kong housing in Oahu's windward real estate. Janet, however, conspires with her uncle, Dwight Christian, to circumvent Dick's plans. She is shot to death at her home, along with Congressman Wendell Omura, by her father late in March, 1975.

By that time, her sister Inez, the novel's central character, is forty years old, apparently well-married but still exceedingly unhappy and unfulfilled. Her husband, Harry Victor, has a political career that seems to be endlessly rising. From a liberal lawyer once assigned to the Justice Department, in 1969 he rose to appointive senator, replacing an incumbent who had died. In 1972, however, he failed to win his party's nomination for president. As his dream of a possible presidency wavers, his greater loss is to his sense of self. Making politics his career has required that Victor adopt so many positions on issues dear to lobbyists or constituents that his true identity is shredded. Inez, suffering from the same self-alienation, tells a reporter that loss of memory is the price of public life. Her twin children are also adrift: Adlai, a lazy student and an opponent of the Vietnam War, and Jessie, a drug addict out of touch with reality.

Consequently, Inez turns on occasion to Jack Lovett. Although he is a freelance covert agent, dealing with war and multinational businesses, and is no more readily available than members of her family, romantically she assumes that this mysterious, competent figure has a secret self that he knows and nurtures. When Jack rescues Jessie from Saigon just before it falls, Inez offers him her gratitude and love.

In her own way, Inez is as much a defective narrator as Charlotte in *A Book of Common Prayer.* Both, at best, can supply certain necessary facts but never an understanding of their implications. In *Democracy,* Didion offers herself as the sensitive equivalent of Grace Strasser-Mendana. The character "Joan Didion" knew Inez briefly when they both worked at *Vogue.* Later in California, she read of the double slaying of Janet and Omura, and as acquaintance and as professional reporter, she came when summoned by Inez, who needed someone with whom to communicate her pain and confusion. Eventually Inez and Jack flee to Jakarta, Indonesia, where he suddenly dies at the end of a long swim in the pool at the Hotel Borobudur. The only identity left Inez is that of displaced person, and she decides to work in Malaysia at the Kuala Lumpur refugee camp.

Didion, like Grace in the previous novel, recognizes that she is not the perfect witness to Inez's life. The novel's scenes are even more disjointed than those in *Play It as It Lays*. Though Didion withholds judgment of Inez, by implication she has indicted American politics, with its secret deals and obsession with appearances.

THE LAST THING HE WANTED

First published: 1996
Type of work: Novel

Becoming entangled in intrigue upon taking her father's place on a secret mission, Elena McMahon finds companionship with Treat Morrison, but her life ends violently.

The Last Thing He Wanted demands its readers' attention, starting with its ambiguous title and continuing through its complexly zigzagging plot, narrated by someone who does not give her name but reveals enough about herself to suggest she is a fictionalized version of Didion, with an ear for jargon that lets her suggest the truth behind the pretense.

The time of the main events is the summer of 1984, a year that suggests a dystopian society comparable to but not identical with the one in George Orwell's 1949 novel *Nineteen Eighty-Four*. The narrator, a journalist writing a story on the American diplomat Treat Morrison, eventually finds that this story involves her Los Angeles acquaintance Elena McMahon Janklow, whose daughter once attended a private school with the narrator's daughter. Elena, upon leaving her rich husband and dropping his surname, moves to the East Coast, enrolls Catherine in a private school in Rhode Island, and takes a job reporting for *The Washington Post*. She is covering the California primary for the newspaper when she walks off her job, flies to Miami, and, finding her seventy-four-year-old father so confused that he cannot remember that Elena's mother has died, substitutes for him in accompanying a clan-

destine planeload of land mines from south Florida to an airstrip in Costa Rica. This mission, the one Dick McMahon expects to bring the financial success that has eluded him, turns out to be a trap intended to lure the old man to a West Indian island where he will be tricked into appearing to assassinate the American ambassador stationed there and then be killed. The plot provides a pretext for a massive, open deployment of American forces on the island to deter communism in Caribbean and Latin American nations.

Awaiting the million dollars that never comes and submitting by near necessity to the manipulations of plotters who have stolen her passport and replaced it with one bearing the name "Elise Meyer," Elena finds herself stranded on the island, where she learns from an old newspaper of her father's death and, after hearing an offhand remark that a Salvadoran makes at an American embassy party, realizes her father was murdered and she herself is in danger, as even her daughter may be. The plot against her, however, does not work out as it was intended, because she does not go to the island airport as she was supposed to. Instead, she goes to a hotel, where she encounters Morrison, who has just arrived on the island and who is, according to the narrator, "the same person" that she is: "equally remote." They begin a romance that ends violently, because he is now the American official to be assassinated, while Elena is still the person to be labeled the assassin. In fact, according to the narrator, the island police fatally wound Elena, but Morrison recovers from his gunshot wounds and lives another five years.

Apparently influenced by such events of the 1980's as the politically motivated murders in El Salvador, the Iran-Contra affair, and the American invasion of Grenada, Didion presents in her novel a picture of a self-deluding man who finds brief happiness with a woman caught among sleazy operatives working for a government that, Didion implies, stoops to low means to reach its ends.

SUMMARY

What sustains Didion in her writing is her faith in the possibility of a better life than what people allow one another to live. That faith rises from her experience of history. All persons, of whatever gender, suffer from natural limitations, reinforced by their own refusals to admit to those imperfections.

Among Didion's exceptions are those women able to maintain their integrity, moral courage, and vision of a more mutually considerate society, under the most trying circumstances. Their resilience, rather than their unremitting agony, is only gradually perceived because it is only slowly earned, with much difficulty.

Leonard Casper; updated by Victor Lindsey

BIBLIOGRAPHY

By the Author

LONG FICTION:
Run River, 1963
Play It as It Lays, 1970
A Book of Common Prayer, 1977
Democracy, 1984
The Last Thing He Wanted, 1996

SCREENPLAYS:
The Panic in Needle Park, 1971 (with John Gregory Dunne)
Play It as It Lays, 1972 (with Dunne)
A Star Is Born, 1976 (with Dunne and Frank Pierson)
True Confessions, 1981 (with Dunne)
Up Close and Personal, 1996 (with Dunne)

TELEPLAYS:
Hills Like White Elephants, 1990 (with John Gregory Dunne)
Broken Trust, 1995 (with Dunne)

NONFICTION:
Slouching Towards Bethlehem, 1968
The White Album, 1979
Salvador, 1983
Joan Didion: Essays and Conversations, 1984 (Ellen G. Friedman, editor)
Miami, 1987
After Henry, 1992 (also known as *Sentimental Journeys*, 1993)
Political Fictions, 2001
Fixed Ideas: America Since 9.11, 2003
Where I Was From, 2003
Vintage Didion, 2004
The Year of Magical Thinking, 2005

About the Author
Eggers, Dave. "Dave Eggers Talks with *Joan Didion*." In *The Believer Book of Writers Talking to Writers*, edited by Vendela Vida. San Francisco: Believer, 2005.

DISCUSSION TOPICS

- How would you describe Joan Didion's style as a writer? Cite passages and give your opinion of the style in each, keeping in mind her remark in the essay "On Morality," from *Slouching Towards Bethlehem*, that her "mind veers inflexibly toward the particular."

- What evidence in Didion's works suggests her lifestyle? Does your knowledge of how she lives affect how you judge her stated or implied opinions?

- In the preface to *Slouching Towards Bethlehem*, Didion says that, because of her appearance and her manner, people fail to understand the harm she can do them and that her readers should remember that "writers are always selling somebody out." What evidence, if any, do you see in her writings that she sells people out?

- In the essay "On Keeping a Notebook," from *Slouching Towards Bethlehem*, Didion writes that she tells "what some would call lies" and adds the comment, "not only have I always had trouble distinguishing between what happened and what merely might have happened, but I remain unconvinced that the distinction, for my purposes, matters." Do you believe those ideas apply not only to her novels but also to her essays?

- In *Political Fictions*, Didion says that the "genuflection toward 'fairness' is a familiar newsroom piety, in practice the excuse for a good deal of autopilot reporting and lazy thinking but in theory a benign ideal." How do you think Didion, a reporter herself, would define reportorial fairness as it applies to her? How do her remarks about fairness affect your opinion of her nonfiction or her fiction?

- Do you think many people outside academic life in the twenty-second century will read Didion's books? Why or why not?

Felton, Sharon, ed. *The Critical Response to Joan Didion.* Westport, Conn.: Greenwood, 1994.

Friedman, Ellen G., ed. *Joan Didion: Essays and Conversations.* Princeton, N.J.: Ontario Review Press, 1984.

Gagné, Laurie Brands. "The Child and the Mother: Joan Didion, Mary Gordon, Virginia Woolf." In *The Uses of Darkness: Women's Underworld Journeys, Ancient and Modern.* Notre Dame, Ind.: University of Notre Dame Press, 2000.

Henderson, Katherine Usher. *Joan Didion.* New York: Frederick Ungar, 1981.

Kuehl, Linda. "Joan Didion." In *Writers at Work.* 5th series, edited by George Plimpton. New York: Viking Press, 1981.

Smith, Louise Z. "Homeless in the Golden Land: Joan Didion's Regionalism." In *Rethinking American Literature,* edited by Lil Brannon and Brenda M. Greene. Urbana, Ill.: National Council of Teachers of English, 1997.

Stout, Janis P. "Joan Didion and the Presence of Absence." In *Strategies of Reticence: Silence and Meaning in the Works of Jane Austen, Willa Cather, Katherine Anne Porter, and Joan Didion.* Charlottesville: University Press of Virginia, 1990.

Van Meter, Jonathan. "When Everything Changes: Joan Didion on John, Quintana, Her Devastating Memoir, and Her Persistent Critics." *New York Magazine* 10 (October, 2005).

Winchell, Mark Royden. *Joan Didion.* Rev. ed. Boston: Twayne, 1989.

ANNIE DILLARD

Born: Pittsburgh, Pennsylvania
April 30, 1945

Dillard, a twentieth century Transcendentalist, explores the place of humankind in the natural world.

Courtesy, Harper & Row

BIOGRAPHY

Annie Dillard, born Meta Ann Doak to Frank and Pam (Lambert) Doak on April 30, 1945, in Pittsburgh, Pennsylvania, grew up as a member of the comfortable upper class. At the private schools she attended, she was rebellious and dissatisfied, a bright, precocious young woman who felt that she did not fit in with her surroundings. Frequently in trouble at school—she went joyriding and was suspended once for smoking—Dillard wanted to escape the lifestyle that in her family, school, and class was most young women's destiny: marriage and the Junior League.

After graduating from high school, Dillard entered Hollins College, where she was inducted into Phi Beta Kappa, earning her B.A. (1967) and M.A. (1968), both in English. In 1965, when she was a sophomore at Hollins, she married her creative writing professor, R. H. W. Dillard, a poet and novelist. When she finished her graduate degree, Annie Dillard began painting, concentrating on developing a talent she believed that God had given her. At this time she also began reading voraciously in natural history, literature and criticism, classics, and poetry. She also began keeping track of her reading and experiences in extensive journals, a practice she would continue to follow.

In 1971, after a serious case of pneumonia, Dillard turned her energies outward to exploring

the natural world. Her experiences inspired and informed her first book of prose, *Pilgrim at Tinker Creek*, which was published in 1974, the same year as her book of poetry *Tickets for a Prayer Wheel*. Both works deal with finding meaning in a universe that, on the surface at least, appears meaningless and devoid of God. In her twenties, Dillard embraced Christianity, a practice she still adheres to; she claims Catholicism as her denomination, preferring it, she says, to Protestantism. However, as has been observed by many of Dillard's readers, her work is infused with threads drawn from many other belief systems as well.

After the publication of *Pilgrim at Tinker Creek*, Dillard became a contributing editor for *Harper's Magazine* and traveled to the Galápagos Islands. The resulting essay, "Innocence in the Galápagos," received the New York Presswomen's Award for Excellence in 1975. Dillard's fame brought problems for a woman who valued her privacy; she was besieged with offers of public appearances, readings, and film scripts. Her popularity troubled her because she felt it took her away too often from her writing. Dillard, a writer who values her privacy and guards her energies, left Virginia in 1975 to take a position as a scholar-in-residence at Western Washington State University in Bellingham, Washington. In that same year, she also divorced R. H. W. Dillard.

During the following years, Dillard contributed columns to *Living Wilderness*, the journal of the Wilderness Society, and began work on *Holy the Firm*, which was published in 1977. In 1976, while teaching at Western Washington State University, Dillard met anthropology professor Gary Clevidence, who taught at Fairhaven College. They moved to Middletown, Connecticut, where Dillard began teaching as a distinguished visiting professor at Wesleyan University in 1979; she is now professor emerita from there. Dillard and Clevidence married in 1980, and their daughter, Cody Rose, was born in 1984. They separated in 1987 and later divorced. In 1988, Dillard married writer Robert D. Richardson, Jr., whom she met after writing him what she describes as a fan letter about his book *Henry David Thoreau: A Life of the Mind* (1986).

Although reviewers and critics persist in describing Dillard's books as collections of essays, she insists that *Teaching a Stone to Talk: Expeditions and Encounters* (1982) is the only volume that truly fits that description. Dillard has also published *Encounters with Chinese Writers* (1984), an account of her 1982 trip to China as a member of a United States cultural delegation; *Living by Fiction* (1982), a book about modern writers; *An American Childhood* (1987), her memoir; *The Writing Life* (1989); and *For the Time Being* (1999), which chronicles her travels in China and Israel. She has also edited *Best American Essays, 1988*.

Dillard is a member of the usage panel of the *American Heritage Dictionary* and has been a jury member for the Bollingen Prize, the nonfiction Pulitzer Prize, and the PEN/Martha Albrand Award. Besides being awarded the Pulitzer Prize for *Pilgrim at Tinker Creek*, Dillard has been named a New York Public Library Literary Lion and has received the Washington State Governor's Award for Literature (1978), the Appalachian Gold Medallion from the University of Charleston (1989), and Boston's St. Botolph's Club Foundation Award (1989). *An American Childhood* was nominated for the 1987 National Book Critics' Circle Award. Dillard received the Campion Award in 1994, was elected to the Connecticut Women's Hall of Fame in 1997, and served as a Fellow at Yale's Calhoun College from 1997 to 1999. In 1998, Dillard received the Academy Award in Literature from the American Academy of Arts and Letters, and in 1999, she was named a fellow to the Academy of Arts and Letters. *For the Time Being* received the PEN Diamond-Vogelstein Award for a book of essays in 1999, despite Dillard's assertion that it is not a collection of essays.

ANALYSIS

Dillard is much more than the voice of her most popular book, *Pilgrim at Tinker Creek*. In fact, those readers and critics who view her as an untutored Appalachian local who both rhapsodizes about and is horrified by the natural world of rural Virginia greatly misjudge their subject. That Dillard can make her readers share in such small and private activities as seeking out praying mantis egg cases or sitting quietly trying not to scare a muskrat attests to both her powers of observation and her skill at descriptive narration. All of Dillard's writing displays this almost photographic evocation of place, a skill that has prompted critics to label her a naturalist. Dillard does not agree; for her, the natural world provides the only avenue by which to contemplate the ultimate, the absolute, the divine. Nature provides metaphors that describe human agonies and activities; nature, for Dillard, is the only place where she can catch glimpses of an otherwise silent and invisible God.

Surprisingly to some people, Dillard does not think of herself as an environmentalist or as a champion of wilderness preservation; rather, she sees herself as someone for whom the world is her greatest subject because it allows her to consider those questions she sees as being most vital. Because she believes that it is a writer's goal to bring enlightenment, give clarification, search out answers, and provide inspiration, her writing probes the nature of being and the meaning of meaning. She looks to nature—to the concrete world—for examples of courage and inspiration, and sometimes her search is a painful one, for wherever she turns she confronts the hard realities of living in an eat-or-be-eaten world, a place where things are born only to die and where destruction seems to be waiting around the next corner.

The mystery that infuses the natural world does not provide Dillard with easy answers to a core question such as "Why am I here?" In *Pilgrim at Tinker Creek*, for example, she looks at the prolific activity of the insect world and comes away frightened by the ravenous and destructive appetites that even seem to compel females laying eggs to devour their offspring. What should be one of the most powerful images of hope—birth and the perpetuation of life—becomes an image of destruction. The explanation she offers suggests that what Dillard hopes for is not affirmation through explicit religious salvation but acceptance of the great dance of birth, death, and renewal that surrounds and includes every living being on earth.

From that acknowledgment comes tranquillity, for Dillard can see herself as a part of, rather than apart from, the teeming activity that surrounds her at Tinker Creek.

The search for the answers, the quest to bring meaning to day-to-day events underpins all that Dillard writes. In *Holy the Firm* (1977) she again looks at pain, suffering, death, and chaos. She wants to find a reason for human suffering, and again her answer is to affirm that there does, indeed, exist a tie between living beings and God, but a tie that is not always immediately obvious in the daily round of accident, pain, and irrationality. In both *Pilgrim at Tinker Creek* and *Holy the Firm*, Dillard perhaps raises more questions than she answers, or at least so it seems to those critics who want her to tie up all the loose ends satisfactorily. However, loose ends are precisely what interest Dillard; the world as she sees it offers even the most practiced observer more loose ends than easy answers.

In *Teaching a Stone to Talk*, although Dillard ranges further afield than her immediate "backyard" and presents essays not only about the goings-on near Tinker Creek but also about the creatures of the Galápagos Islands and the Arctic Circle, her intention remains the same: witnessing nature. For Dillard, this witnessing is a religious act; in everything she sees and experiences, she seeks answers to primal questions. In this sense, one could say that Dillard's work reveals the nature of the writer intensely, yet she insists that she never writes about herself, that she works painstakingly to keep her personality out of what she has to show her readers.

Dillard brings her precision and sense of detail to *An American Childhood*, a book that explores her growing up in Pittsburgh. In her earlier work, the person of Dillard remained behind the scenes; the reader saw what she saw, heard what she heard, and reacted. The personality of the narrator was somehow distanced, muted. In contrast, in *An American Childhood*, although Dillard insists that she is not revealed, this book offers a much more intimate view of Annie Dillard than any of her previous volumes. Most important, *An American Childhood* allows readers insight into the careful observer and deep thinker that is the "voice" of all that Dillard writes.

One important side of her personality that surfaces in *An American Childhood* is something that was also apparent in her earlier work: a voracious intellectual curiosity. Concrete knowledge serves as her catalyst, allowing her to spring from mere facts to a consideration of their metaphysical implications.

In *Holy the Firm*, for example, she describes a plane accident in which a young girl is horribly disfigured, and the girl's burns then serve as the vehicle by which Dillard explores the meaning of pain and, by extension, the nature of a divinity that could allow such horrors to occur.

In *The Writing Life* (1989), Dillard examines the profession of writing: how one writes, what it means to write, why one writes. With her usual intimacy—but typical lack of concrete personal details—she discusses the solitary struggle that writing is. As in all of her earlier work, Dillard concerns herself with knowing, meaning, and interconnectedness. For her, the world is both the palette and the canvas: She draws her materials from her surroundings, and she colors her surroundings with the philosophical considerations that are her preoccupation. Like Henry David Thoreau, whose heir Dillard has been called, she travels far and rarely leaves home. Her universe starts in her study or at her back door and extends from there to the farthest corner of the universe . . . and beyond.

PILGRIM AT TINKER CREEK

First published: 1974
Type of work: Essays

The beauties and horrors of the natural world offer the careful observer access to the divine.

In *Pilgrim at Tinker Creek* Dillard touches on all the important themes that would continue to inform her writing. At first glance, this book might appear to be a collection of occasional essays that track the changing seasons through one calendar year. In fact, that is how some critics have viewed this work: as essays on the perplexities of nature. While the book does take up this theme again and again, it is not for the simple pleasure of holding up a quirk of nature for its thrill value.

Dillard carefully built this volume after months of painstaking observation of and research about both metaphysics and the natural world. The rhythms of the book are tightly controlled and depend on recurrent images and themes that surface over and over, allowing Dillard to focus on the key issues at the heart of the narrator's personal journey. As much as anything, this book is about seeing and about gaining the ability to see within oneself, into the surrounding world, and beyond to the divinity that informs the world.

The book opens with a startling image of violence, creation, and death in a description of the bloody paw prints left on the narrator by her returning tomcat. The world Dillard sees as she looks out from her cabin beside Tinker Creek in Virginia is one in which little seems to make obvious sense. Wherever Dillard turns, she sees the raw, brutal power of nature to reproduce itself, and she finds the sheer exuberance of the natural world startling, overwhelming, and stupefying. She cannot look at an insect laying its eggs, for example, without being reminded of all the instances in the insect kingdom where the mother devours its mate, its eggs, or its young—or is food for them in return for giving them life.

What is the point, Dillard asks, in bothering to replicate oneself only to serve as grist for the mill, food for the soon-to-be-born? In *Pilgrim at Tinker Creek*, Dillard questions a god that would set such a horror show in motion, and she wonders how one can go on in the face of such depressing statistics: No matter what, everyone must die.

Yet Dillard wants to find an answer that will allow her to celebrate rather than be repulsed by what she sees. Rather than being only a collection of essays about her observations of the natural world, *Pilgrim at Tinker Creek* traces the author's abundance and vitality. By looking carefully at the world around her confined neighborhood of Tinker Creek, Dillard discovers a pattern and gains some conviction that there is something more going on than a mad dance of death. She learns to see beyond the particular individual, past the moment, to a larger picture.

While some readers will find her answers depressing, others will discover that Dillard achieves an acceptance of what she sees around her. Unlike many others, who look on the violence of nature and see no possibility for a divine plan, Dillard comes to believe that the endless cycle—birth, death, and transformation into atoms of other

beings—is in itself a way of gaining transcendence over death and achieving immortality.

Certain central natural images, such as her cat's bloody paw prints, surface again and again after Dillard has once told their story. For example, she stands transfixed beside the creek, at first seeing the water and a frog that appears to collapse into itself as she looks on. Then her eyes shift focus, and she sees the giant waterbug that has just finished draining its captured frog. This picture of the malign side of nature hovering immediately below an apparently tranquil and innocent surface is one which Dillard will revisit time and time again. Dillard sees the death's head behind the living form many times; she confronts nature's seeming blind preference for the species over the individual. She sees things up close and notices the ragged wings, the frayed leaves, the living things being ground to dust. A more timid person would have given up and perhaps turned suicidal. Dillard, however, continued to look for answers, realizing that there is more to nature than the surface turmoil and violence.

In one chapter, Dillard recounts the story of a young woman who was born without sight. When surgery allows the woman to see for the first time as a young adult, she at first cannot see anything, then she begins to see but cannot comprehend or distinguish one image from another, then she sees in distorted fashion because she has yet to gain the experience by which to interpret what her eyes show her. Thus, when the young woman is asked to describe the tree outside her hospital room that so fascinates her, she talks about a tree with lights in it. To her untutored, inexperienced eyes, the focal point is the spaces between the tree's leaves backlit by the sun. The young woman sees the world from a fresh perspective, one denied most of us who have been "taught" how to "see"—to focus on what is deemed "important." This story serves as a central parable in *Pilgrim at Tinker Creek* and is an image to which Dillard returns many times in the book, serving as her metaphor for that which she seeks in her journey through the natural world. She is looking for the divine power behind the everyday; its discovery is something that she comes to realize happens infrequently at best, but it does happen. When Dillard least expects it, the force behind the universe shines out and nearly blinds her.

In a sense, Dillard had to suffer through the

deep, pessimistic despair she describes in many chapters of *Pilgrim at Tinker Creek* so that she could emerge with the understanding she attains by the book's final chapter, "The Waters of Separation." Like many mystics before her, Dillard had to despair of ever finding God before she could apprehend the presence of the divine. By showing her readers the power, might, and violence of the world of Tinker Creek, she takes them along with her on her quest to make sense of a seemingly senseless world. She gains freedom or salvation by recognizing that she is a part of the great dance of birth and death that she has so carefully recorded.

HOLY THE FIRM

First published: 1977
Type of work: Nonfiction

This work suggests that pain is a necessary part of living and does not negate the existence of the divine.

In *Holy the Firm* Dillard explores the metaphysical and religious concerns that inform her first two books, *Tickets for a Prayer Wheel* and *Pilgrim at Tinker Creek*. In this book, Dillard looks more closely at the problem of pain: How can one reconcile the existence of pain, suffering, and death with a belief in a benevolent God? Set near Puget Sound, Washington, where Dillard lived while writing it, the book is short, spanning only three days. In the first of its three sections, "Newborn and Salted," Dillard describes a moth being attracted to the flame of a candle and burned to death. The moth's death is an image to which she often returns in her discussion of the nature of the divinity.

The second section, "God's Tooth," is concerned with Julie Norwich, a seven-year-old child who, with her father, survives the crash of his small plane. Unlike her father, however, the child is horribly burned, and her face is destroyed. Asking if God were responsible for this tragedy, Dillard concludes that God cannot be present in a world where an innocent child is mutilated for no reason. "Holy the Firm," the book's third and final section, attempts to find a place for a merciful God in a violent world. The solution Dillard achieves is that

God owes humankind no explanations. Because God created humans and not vice versa, God is not required to answer to them. Dillard also concludes that the control that people cherish so dearly is only an illusion, that humans are only passengers on earth, along for the ride rather than behind the steering wheel, and on a journey whose destination they cannot know.

For Dillard, accepting or affirming that God is the foundation for all things allows her to believe again in the unity of all things, even when some things—such as the disfigurement of a child—seem unjust. Acceptance of the ineffable nature of God enables Dillard to reaffirm her desire to proclaim the mysteries of the universe through her art and her life, thereby reaffirming the essentially divine nature of creation.

Many people see *Holy the Firm* as a powerful visionary statement, a testament to the triumph of faith in a seemingly irrational universe. Dillard does not find the role of prophet a comfortable one and denies that her intention was anything other than to describe her personal visionary experience. As in *Pilgrim at Tinker Creek* and *Teaching a Stone to Talk*, Dillard again struggles to work through her dark night of the soul, her bleakest despair. Like other mystics, she must find a way to come to terms with those things that challenge her belief in a divine purpose for the world.

In *Holy the Firm*, Dillard reaches an understanding of God's relationship to her world and the natural world that she observes around her. She seems able to resolve the contradictions by something that esoteric Christianity calls "Holy the Firm," a universal substance that keeps the human world in touch with God—a god who remains present but invisible and unknowable. This is enough to allow Dillard to believe that God exists and for her to worship him.

TEACHING A STONE TO TALK

First published: 1982
Type of work: Essays

By observing nature, both close to home and in remote places, one can discover the presence of the divine.

Teaching a Stone to Talk: Expeditions and Encounters resembles both *Pilgrim at Tinker Creek* and *Holy the Firm* in that Dillard is still seeking answers to what she considers to be key questions: What is the universe about? What is the god like who created such a place as this? How is it possible to make sense of a universe that contains so much destructive energy and violence? In this book she again hunts for the silent god who created the natural world that Dillard often finds disturbingly violent and indifferent. This time, rather than center her investigations around one locale, as she did in *Pilgrim at Tinker Creek*, she ranges far afield. Dillard is adamant that her other books are not, as some critics and reviewers have asserted, collections of essays; as far as she is concerned, only *Teaching a Stone to Talk* fits that description.

A trip to the Galápagos Islands provides her with the opportunity to examine evolutionary theory in her essay "Life on the Rocks: The Galápagos." In "The Deer of Providencia," she describes a small deer caught and suffering in a hunter's snare, unable to do anything but injure itself more severely as it struggles. "Total Eclipse" recounts her experiences in Yakima, Washington, during a total eclipse of the sun when she felt overwhelmed by the power of nature as the moon's shadow slammed across the earth. She shared the primal fear that the sun's light would be extinguished forever. "Living Like Weasels" discusses the fierce competitive energy of these hunters, and Dillard wonders if, freed from the constraints of society, she could fight as viciously for her survival as they do every day.

As in *Pilgrim at Tinker Creek*, Dillard uses the things that surround her as starting points in her search for meaning in a violent, indifferent universe. Unlike in the earlier book, however, she occasionally interacts with other people. Here she tries to fit in, to feel comfortable in a world that seems to threaten from all sides and at all times. Sometimes the world looks like home, while at others it appears completely unfamiliar and aloof.

In "An Expedition to the Pole" she interweaves a description of the Catholic church that she attends (after having given up her family's Presbyterianism when a teenager), an account of the ill-fated Franklin expedition to find the Northwest Passage, and her own trip to the Arctic Circle. In all three instances she finds herself in alien territory, yet at the essay's conclusion she joins in the song, frantically:

What choice does she have but to become a part of the only congregation, the community of humankind?

Although Dillard says that *Teaching a Stone to Talk* is a true book of essays rather than a tightly knit series of pieces, the pieces in this book wrestle with what for Dillard are central issues. The title essay, "Teaching a Stone to Talk," clearly makes this point, recounting the story of a man who kept a stone and each day tried to get it to utter a word. Absurd as this sounds at first, it is precisely what Dillard tries to do in almost everything she writes: get an answer back from the universe. She listens and listens to nature, hoping to hear the voice of the creator; sometimes, as in "An Expedition to the Pole," "Lenses," "A Field of Silence," and "Life on the Rocks: The Galápagos," she seems to detect a faint whisper in response to her questions, "Are You out there?"

AN AMERICAN CHILDHOOD

First published: 1987
Type of work: Autobiography

Childhood experiences shape and prepare a person to be and to see as an adult.

In *An American Childhood* Dillard uses herself and her experiences growing up in Pittsburgh to examine the nature of American life. She claims that the book is not an autobiography but is rather a capturing of what it means for a child to come of age in the United States. Dillard seems to be uncomfortable with revealing information about herself; despite the fact that *An American Childhood* is intensely autobiographical, she denies that her purpose was to compose a memoir. Nevertheless, it is her account of her inward intellectual journey, offering incidents in her life through her mid-teenage years, the time Dillard says that the consciousness that directs her perceptions of the world as an adult was formed. She believes that it is as a child that one is truly alive, can feel most deeply, and is affected most strongly by experiences.

Perhaps Dillard feels compelled to attempt to escape the merely personal because she intends, as she says, to make a commentary on the univer-

sal nature of her experiences. Perhaps she also so strongly asserts the separation between her personal life and the life that she presents in this book because she is a genuinely private person. It is rare that Dillard gives interviews, does readings or lectures, or provides information about herself. She repeatedly insists that the personality of the writer is not what is important; rather, it is the ideas an individual conveys about the meaning of life, nature, and meaning that count and are what both readers and writers should pursue. She does not like the limelight because it takes away from the time she needs to read, reflect, and write. *An American Childhood*, then, offers readers a rare glimpse of the private side of Annie Dillard.

Her intention was to use herself as an example so that she could examine the way in which a child comes to consciousness—that is, arrives at the perceptions and attitudes that will guide her as an adult. She is by no means the first writer, American or otherwise, to attempt such an undertaking: Marcel Proust's *À la recherché du temps perdu* (1913-1927; *Remembrance of Things Past*, 1922-1931), James Joyce's *A Portrait of the Artist as a Young Man* (1916), and William Wordsworth's *The Prelude: Or, The Growth of a Poet's Mind* (1850) are three oft-cited examples of this mode. *An American Childhood* is particularly reminiscent of Wordsworth's famous spiritual epic. Like Wordsworth, who is regarded as one of the most important poets of nature, Dillard provides her readers with accounts of those childhood events that caused her to have such a passionate regard for and interest in the natural world. Also like Wordsworth is Dillard's intense focus on the spiritual, mystical, and violent aspects of the natural world and her need to fit herself and, by extension, all of life into a meaningful pattern that makes sense of the seemingly senseless aspects of the natural realm.

Like Wordsworth, Dillard was a youthful rebel, always out of place in her upper-class environment. In *An American Childhood*, she explores the values that she could not adopt, the goals that she did not share, and the manners that she would not practice in order to examine the alternatives she ultimately chose.

Wordsworth was a child who needed solace; nature in all of its terrible majesty gave him the comfort that he could not find in other people. Dillard, too, needed an escape from her fears; for her, knowledge—in particular, knowledge about the natural world—gave her the power to triumph over her fears.

An American Childhood also provides readers with glimpses of Dillard's family that tell more about Dillard than about her parents and siblings. It is not so important that these events be true as it is that she thinks that her interpretations of them are accurate. We see a loving family that does not quite know what to do with a daughter who rejects their Presbyterian religion, craves and seeks out solitude, is wild and unruly at school. The reader sees the psychic place in which Dillard grew up, and that view, no matter what she says to the contrary, offers readers a closer look at her as a person than did her earlier works. Even so, the book still maintains a distance between the reader and the person of Dillard.

THE LIVING

First published: 1992
Type of work: Novel

The difficult early years of the Pacific Northwest town of Bellingham are chronicled in the account of the various people who were drawn to settle there.

In *The Living*—a book that took her three years to research and write—Dillard creates a tapestry of the American Frontier but set in an area not generally portrayed in novels: the Pacific Northwest. In her only novel to date, Dillard chronicles the lives of the people who settled at Whatcom on Bellingham Bay and built the town of Bellingham in what would later become the state of Washington. The book's setting is one with which Dillard became personally acquainted while artist-in-residence at Western Washington State University in Bellingham.

The people in this novel are pioneers of the first order who struggle against so many difficulties that it seems unlikely that they should succeed. However, these people persist, even in the face of great odds. Moreover, because Dillard wished to create a novel in the spirit of nineteenth century novels, *The Living* is a "big" book, full of violence and murder, offering many plot threads and spanning several generations in its telling.

Besides being a departure from her usual forms in that it is a novel, *The Living* also marks a change in Dillard's focus, from one sighted mostly on a solitary person to that which takes in multitudes. She accomplishes this breadth of perspective by creating four interconnected groups which each include various types of people: white, Chinese, and Lummi and Skagit Native Americans; rich and poor; hardworking and conniving; good and evil. In this manner the perspective of Dillard's writing vision expands outward in a way different from her previous work; yet the result is the same: to explore people's place in a vast and oftentimes unwelcoming or at least seemingly indifferent universe. In fact, Dillard makes a point of noting that she chose to make this shift to include others, to get away from the self-absorption of her earlier writing and concentrate on many people rather selecting just one person as her main focus. In that regard, *The Living* provided Dillard with a large and complicated cast of characters to move among. Dillard said that in writing this book she "wanted to write about little-bitty people in a great big landscape." For the same reason, characters "come and go" throughout the novel, appearing and disappearing from the story as individuals would in real life. To achieve the verisimilitude she sought, Dillard immersed herself in research, reading extensively in the literature of the period so that she could replicate the language and spirit of the time.

The Living opens in 1855 when the young married couple Ada and Rooney Fishburn move West by covered wagon, embodying the struggle facing pioneers leaving home seeking a "better" life. This novel accurately and brutally portrays what the people making this journey experienced on the way and found once they arrived at their destination, thousands of miles from home and family. The times are never easy for the people of Bellingham; it is a cruel world in which there can seem

to be no rational reason for the bad things that happen, as in the case of the actions of the dark, twisted Beal Obenchain or the violent Thompson family: they just "are"—as so many "evil" things in the world just "are," as Dillard has so carefully described in earlier works such as *Pilgrim at Tinker Creek.* Many other characters exemplify persistence, sometimes even courage: Minta Honer, a former socialite, or the stalwart pioneer, Clare Fishburn. At the same time that these "settlers" are learning to survive and sometimes thrive, the Native Americans such as the Lummis watch as their culture is superseded by one built on the lust for gold and land and carried into their country by the newly arrived railroad.

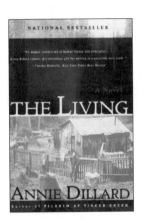

This novel is not meant to focus on one character, or even on one generation, but it is meant to tell the story of the birth and growth of a place, Bellingham. The novel concludes with the grandchildren of Ada and Rooney at the time of the 1897 stock market crash; in the forty-two years between the time Ada and Rooney left the East and the 1897 economic disaster, Dillard brought a large number of characters momentarily to the forefront and then moved on to new arrivals; although this large cast of characters prevents maintaining a focus on any one family or person's individual story, it captures the period's turbulence and energy, a time when so many easterners and Europeans were coming west to start anew.

SUMMARY

Dillard stalks the infinite by tracking the finite in the world of nature. A mystic who looks for a divine force behind the natural world, she is a deeply spiritual person who sometimes can only console her readers with the assurance that they are all participants in the great dance of the universe. That contradictions exist, that danger, tenor, and destruction are part of the world she observes are all facts of life. Her interests revolve almost exclusively around making sense of the events that she observes in the natural world in order to gain entrée to the world of the divine. Dillard's prose is powerful, evocative and lyrical, and the subjects she examines are of universal interest.

Melissa E. Barth

BIBLIOGRAPHY

By the Author

NONFICTION:
Pilgrim at Tinker Creek, 1974 (nature)
Holy the Firm, 1977 (theology)
Living by Fiction, 1982 (criticism)
Teaching a Stone to Talk: Expeditions and Encounters, 1982 (essays)
Encounters with Chinese Writers, 1984 (essays)
An American Childhood, 1987 (autobiography)
The Writing Life, 1989
For the Time Being, 1999

LONG FICTION:
The Living, 1992

POETRY:
Tickets for a Prayer Wheel, 1974
Mornings Like This: Found Poems, 1995

EDITED TEXT:
The Best American Essays, 1988, 1988 (with Robert Atwan)

MISCELLANEOUS:
The Annie Dillard Reader, 1994

About the Author

Bischoff, Joan. "Fellow Rebels: Annie Dillard and Maxine Hong Kingston." *English Journal* 78 (December, 1989): 62-67.
Davidson, Jenny Emery. "Stalking a Prayer: Crossing of the Hunter and the Shaman in *Pilgrim at Tinker Creek.*" In *Such News of the Land: U.S. Women Nature Writers,* edited by Thomas S. Edwards and Elizabeth A. De Wolfe. Hanover, N.H.: University Press of New England, 2001.
Dillard, Annie. "PW Interviews Annie D." Interview by Katharine Weber. *Publishers Weekly* 236 (September 1, 1989): 67-68.
_____. Web site. http://anniedillard.com.
Gary, McIlroy. "*Pilgrim at Tinker Creek* and the Social Legacy of *Walden.*" *South Atlantic Quarterly* 845, no. 2 (Spring, 1986): 111-122.

DISCUSSION TOPICS

- Annie Dillard is someone for whom nature holds special significance. In what ways does nature have an impact on her thinking and on her beliefs?

- If Dillard is a philosopher of life, someone who searches for meaning in a seemingly meaningless universe, then what answers does she find in nature? What contradictions?

- *Pilgrim at Tinker Creek* explores the violence and isolation inherent in the living world and universe. What specific examples illustrate this perspective? How does Dillard use such vignettes to make a larger point?

- Dillard asserts that she is a Christian. In what ways do her writings such as *Holy the Firm* support this worldview, and in what ways do they depart from a purely Christian perspective?

- Memoir is a particular form of narrative writing that involves the purely personal. In what ways are *An American Childhood* and *Pilgrim at Tinker Creek* examples of this form? Why would someone choose to write in this way? In what ways do these books go beyond the individual to make larger statements?

- *The Living* focuses on the settling of the American West. What is it about the West that symbolizes the spirit of America? How are these aspects of the American Dream evoked in this novel?

- Dillard is often described as a writer who focuses on what it means to be a writer. What specific kinds of instruction about being and becoming a writer can you find in such books as *Pilgrim at Tinker Creek, Teaching a Stone to Talk,* and *An American Childhood*?

Papa, James A., Jr. "Water-Signs: Place and Metaphor in Dillard and Thoreau." In *Thoreau's Sense of Place: Essays in American Environmental Writing*, edited by Richard J. Schneider. Iowa City: University of Iowa Press, 2000.

Parrish, Nancy C. *Lee Smith, Annie Dillard, and the Hollins Group: A Genesis of Writers*. Baton Rouge: Louisiana State University Press, 1998.

Radford, Dawn Evans. "Annie Dillard: A Bibliographical Survey." *Bulletin of Bibliography* 51, no. 2 (June, 1994): 181-194.

Ross-Bryant, Lynn. "The Self in Nature: Four American Autobiographies." *Soundings: An Interdisciplinary Journal* 80, no. 1 (Spring, 1997): 83-104.

Smith, Pamela A. "The Ecotheology of Annie Dillard: A Study in Ambivalence." *Cross Currents: The Journal of the Association for Religion and Intellectual Life* 45, no. 3 (Fall, 1995): 341-358.

E. L. DOCTOROW

© Barbara Walz

Born: New York, New York
January 6, 1931

Doctorow is one of the most significant and controversial novel-ists of his generation, an award-winning innovator in the realm of historical and political fiction.

BIOGRAPHY

Born in the Bronx in 1931, Edgar Lawrence Doctorow has written fiction set in almost every major historical era since the Civil War, but he has returned again and again to urban themes, to the life of New York City at the beginning of the twenti-eth century and in the 1920's and 1930's. Greatly influenced by the radical politics of the Depression and by the work of John Dos Passos, Doctorow has chosen to write an updated version of proletarian fiction, reflecting his concern with the domination of the means of production by government and in-dustry. Doctorow sides with the masses—the immi-grants, the minorities, and all the downtrodden, underdog characters who populate his novels. Un-like the proletarian fiction of the 1930's, however, Doctorow's work is rarely sentimental. Rather, it is distinguished by an elegance and irony that per-haps are attributable to his formal education and to his early conventional and middle-class pursuit of a career. Writing a generation after the Palmer raids that rounded up and imprisoned radicals in the 1920's and the great industrial strikes of the Depression, he has had the opportunity and the in-centive to meditate on both the persecution of American radicals and the failure of the Left to mount a credible alternative to the capitalistic power structure.

Doctorow graduated from Kenyon College with a major in philosophy. Known for its prestigious lit-erary review and the presence of important writers such as the poet John Crowe Ransom, Kenyon pro-vided Doctorow with examples of literary careers he could emulate, for he was educated in a college generation that had exposure to writers who were, for the first time, being placed in significant num-bers in faculty positions. Writers continued to be critics of society while being employed by society's influential institutions. This dual and ambiguous role has had an impact on the marginalized con-sciousness of writers such as Doctorow who earn a living from the society they criticize, and it may ex-plain his repeated use of journalists, or other de-tached observers, to narrate his fiction. Writers in this context are both inside and outside the sys-tem and are subject to the social and antisocial at-titudes, the bifurcated points of view of the rich and the poor, that mark so much of Doctorow's fiction.

After serving in the Army, Doctorow worked for publishers in New York City, editing the work of im-portant writers, such as Norman Mailer, who came out of World War II with their hostility toward the status quo intact. Mailer, Doctorow has observed, was part of a wartime generation that believed that a writer had to fight for and win a reputation in a so-ciety more or less hostile toward writers. Doctorow, on the other hand, has eschewed Mailer's military metaphors and his sense of embattlement for a vi-sion of the writer as ironic commentator—an elu-sive fictional narrator who is implicated in and yet aloof from the action he describes.

Doctorow's cool stance may also reflect his philosophical training. In his novels, he tries to infuse serious ideas into popular genres such as the Western in *Welcome to Hard Times* (1960), science fiction in *Big as Life* (1966), and detective fiction in *The Waterworks* (1994). Identifying with the disadvantaged and with the dissenters, he has fashioned fiction with a leftist orientation, and on occasion he has joined his voice to public protests against government censorship and other forms of tyranny.

Ragtime (1975), a popular and critical success, catapulted Doctorow into prominence as one of the finest and most exciting novelists of his generation. With *Welcome to Hard Times* and *The Book of Daniel* (1971), he had already established a solid reputation, but the rave reviews of *Ragtime* and the subsequent film adaptation of the novel secured his place in popular culture. *World's Fair* (1985) won the American Book Award in 1986, and *Billy Bathgate* (1989)—nearly as successful as *Ragtime*—shows that Doctorow continues to explore the astute blending of fact and fiction and of history and literature that has distinguished his most important novels. *City of God* (2000) suggests a renewed interest in philosophical studies, and *The March* (2005) establishes Doctorow as a master at portraying historical events, while at the same time demonstrating their effect on the lives of everyday citizens.

With residences in New York City and New Rochelle, New York, he has divided his time between the city and the suburbs; he has taught at Sarah Lawrence College and New York University. Since 2004, he has occupied the Gluckman Chair in American Letters at New York University.

ANALYSIS

E. L. Doctorow is a political novelist concerned with those stories, myths, public figures, and literary and historical forms that have shaped public consciousness. Even when his subject is not overtly political—as in his first novel, *Welcome to Hard Times*—he chose the genre of the Western to comment upon the American sense of crime and justice. Knowing that the Western has often been the vehicle for the celebration of American individualism and morality, Doctorow purposely writes a fable like novel in which he questions the American faith in fairness and democracy. At the same time, he writes from within the genre by maintaining the customary strong opposition between good and evil, between the bad guys and the good guys, and a simple but compelling plot.

The struggle in *Welcome to Hard Times* is between the Man from Bodie, who in a fit of rage destroys a town in a single day, and Blue, the tragic old man who almost single-handedly tries to rebuild it. The plot and characters echo classic Western films such as *High Noon* (1952), with their solitary heroes who oppose villains tyrannizing a community. Doctorow's vision, however, is much bleaker than the traditional Western and cannot be encompassed by the usual shoot-out or confrontation between the sheriff and the outlaw. In fact, Doctorow's novel implies, the West was chaotic and demoniac, and order was not usually restored in the fashion of a Hollywood motion picture. The reality of American history has been much grimmer than its literature or its popular entertainment has acknowledged. Indeed, Doctorow's fiction shows again and again a United States whose myths do not square with its history.

It is a paradoxical aspect of Doctorow's success that his parodies of popular genres are themselves usually best sellers. Perhaps the reason for this is that alongside his ironic use of popular genres is a deep affection for the literary forms he burlesques. The title of his first novel, for example, is a kind of genial invitation to have some fun with the pieties and clichés of the Western. Doctorow is deadly serious about the "hard times" and grave flaws in American culture, but he usually finds a way to present his criticism in a comic vein.

There is not much humor, however, in *The Book of Daniel*—a major political novel about the Cold War period of the 1950's, centered on a couple bearing a striking resemblance to Ethel and Julius Rosenberg, who were executed for espionage in 1954 after they were accused and convicted of stealing the "secret" of the atomic bomb for the Soviet Union. Doctorow has one of their children, Daniel, narrate the novel and investigate what happened to his parents while trying to come to terms with his own sense of radicalism. Concerned less with whether the couple are actually guilty of spying, Doctorow has Daniel search for his own identity by tracking down and interviewing those closest to his parents.

Through this personal story, Doctorow also conducts an analysis of the failure of American radicalism, of one generation to speak to another. By and large, the novel shows that 1960's radicals do not know much about the history of the Left and that the traditional Left has done little to pass on its history, so that young men such as Daniel feel isolated, bereft, and angry about their lack of connection to a heritage of social protest.

Like *The Book of Daniel*, *Ragtime* is anchored in the story of a family—this time of a little boy who grows up at the turn of the twentieth century during events such as the development of motion pictures, polar exploration, and political upheavals led by radicals such as Emma Goldman. From his naïve viewpoint, the boy observes the explosive changes and the stresses of a society that does not know how to handle its own dissenting elements. Coalhouse Walker, for example, a proud black man who is insulted by a group of white firemen and who (more in the style of the 1960's) resorts to violence and hostage taking, demands that society recognize his human rights.

Ragtime is similar to *Welcome to Hard Times* in that it has a fairy-tale quality. The prose is quite simple, descriptive and declarative, so that Doctorow could almost begin with the phrase "once upon a time." It is clear, however, that his point is to link the past and the present, to show that the craving for mass entertainment at the beginning of the twentieth century naturally had its outlet in the invention of motion pictures, just as the urge of Arctic explorer Robert Peary and other explorers to roam the world had its industrial and societal counterpart in the mass production of the automobile. Repeatedly, Doctorow links the innovations in domestic life with great public adventures and events, fusing public and private affairs in an almost magical, uncanny manner.

The class distinctions that play an important role in *Ragtime* become the focal element of *Loon Lake* (1980), which, like *The Book of Daniel*, contains a double narrative perspective, shifting between the experience of a poet on a rich man's isolated estate and a poor man's picaresque adventures across 1930's America. The power of the materialist, the millionaire capitalist, is meant to be balanced by the imagination of the poet, but the novel fails to measure up to *Ragtime*'s astonishing feat of fusing the realms of fiction and history. The poetic interludes in *Loon Lake* are reminiscent of the introverted, stream-of-consciousness "Camera Eye" sections of novelist John Dos Passos's *U.S.A.* (1937),

but they seem excessively obscure and introverted and disruptive of the novel's narrative pace.

Nevertheless, *Loon Lake* has a haunting, ineffable quality, evoking a metaphorical but almost tangible sense of history which is akin to the novel's image of the lake: a dazzling surface of ever-shifting and widening perspectives above glinting depths that are only suggested. History as mirror—refracting, distorting, highlighting, and obscuring human actions—is a palpable presence in *Loon Lake*. A great social novelist, Doctorow manages to describe every level and grouping of society in the soup kitchens, monasteries, mansions, and assembly lines of the United States between the two world wars.

In much of Doctorow's work there is a tension between a naïve, childlike point of view, with fresh perceptions, and an older, ironic, detached perspective. Sometimes this split is expressed in terms of dual first-person and third-person narration, as in *The Book of Daniel*. In *Ragtime*, the narrator seems simultaneously to be the little boy and his older self, both witnessing and remembering the past. Likewise, throughout most of *The Waterworks*, McIlvaine appears to be describing events as they occur, but near the end of the novel he reveals that he has reflected upon this story for many years before finally telling it. Similarly, in *City of God*, Sarah's father speaks in the voice of an adult describing childhood experiences in the ghetto, but at times the voice of the young messenger breaks through. *World's Fair* and *Billy Bathgate* also seem more conventional than the earlier novels, for they are told from the standpoint of two narrators, both mature men reviewing their youth. Yet both novels unfold with such immediacy that they appear to be taking place as their narrators reminisce.

In *The Waterworks*, Doctorow again begins with a traditional genre: this time, the detective story. McIlvaine's search for Martin Pemberton soon becomes a quest for truth beneath the veneer of Gilded Age society. The conflict between ethics and selfishness is once more played out within a family—the Pembertons. Most of the conflicts involve ethical decisions, and the most sympathetic characters are those whose integrity will not allow them to succumb to the corruption of the era. The most ambiguous character—and apparently the one most fascinating to Doctorow—is Dr. Wrede Sartorius, a German doctor who served as a Union Army surgeon during the Civil War. In *The Water-*

works, he is portrayed as an obsessed scientist who has allowed his pursuit of medical knowledge to destroy his humanity. When Doctorow returns to Sartorius, in *The March*, the doctor's compassion can be seen more clearly, though his experiences as an Army surgeon eventually result in a detachment that seems to anticipate his later isolation from humanity. Perhaps McIlvaine's interest in Sartorius's ideas implies a similar isolation on his part, as the roles of both journalist and doctor require them to be primarily observers of human life.

Similar quests for truth and knowledge are significant elements in *City of God*. The novel begins with a discussion of the Big Bang theory, and references to science, particularly astronomy, recur throughout the novel, apparently suggesting a universe in which humans may be left to devise their own moral and ethical standards without the guidance of religious doctrine. One likely result is seen in the scenario devised by Everett, the writer and would-be filmmaker: A man begins an affair with a married woman, through plastic surgery remakes himself until he literally (as well as figuratively) usurps her husband's life, and is killed by the displaced husband, who finally is convicted of killing himself in the person of the impostor. In this supposed film script, Everett deals symbolically with one's position in the postmodern world where scientific possibility has replaced religion as the governing force in human interactions.

On an individual level, however, Thomas Pemberton (Pem) doubts the religious tenets his father taught, and his eventual rejection of the church may in part be a break with his father similar to Martin Pemberton's renunciation of his patrimony in *The Waterworks*. Though no explicit link appears, Doctorow may want the reader to see Pam as both a literal and a symbolic heir of Martin. Pem's quest leads him to explore the meaning of human suffering and perhaps even of human history. As Everett, the narrator and observer of his actions, comes to realize, humankind's satisfaction cannot be achieved through science, violence, revenge, intolerance, or analysis of the culture; like medieval theologians, Doctorow suggests that the search for God is more significant than the conclusions one reaches.

While *City of God* is more overtly philosophical than most of Doctorow's fiction, it uses some of the familiar devices. The lives of well-known historical figures, such as Albert Einstein, often parallel the lives of the major characters, usually unknown people who are searching for their own identities, often within a meaningful family relationship. Doctorow's most innovative strategy for thematic development, though, is the interspersed performances by the Midrash Jazz Quartet. Their commentaries on the so-called standards, ranging from "Me and My Shadow" to "The Song Is You," serve as a commentary on the characters' thoughts and actions. When Pem hears the young nun singing these songs to McIlvaine in the charity hospital, he decides that secular songs can affect him in the same way as hymns.

In contrast, the short stories collected in *Sweet Land Stories* (2004) reflect their magazine roots; plots are highly compressed, with the primary focus on characters, many of whom are duplicitous. Nevertheless, these stories develop several familiar Doctorow themes: Within families, intergenerational conflicts develop, involving ethical questions; generally poor characters are relatively powerless in dealing with wealthy Establishment types; and social issues frequently are seen both in the wider context of society and in the narrower context of the family, and conventional ties can be badly strained as a result. Nevertheless, these stories have not received the critical acclaim usually accorded to Doctorow's novels. The difference may be that the short-story format does not allow Doctorow to create his customary detailed historical backgrounds or to develop representative characters that evoke reader empathy. Thus "A House in the Plains" can be described as an unduly macabre comment on American public taste, and "Child, Dead, in the Rose Garden" can be characterized as another indictment of governmental and corporate indifference to the effects of environmental pollution. Perhaps Doctorow has recognized this problem because in *The March*, he returned to the novel format, emphasizing representative characters as they deal with situation and issues of historical importance.

THE BOOK OF DANIEL

First published: 1971
Type of work: Novel

In the turbulent 1960's, in the midst of social protest and calls for revolution, Daniel searches for the significance of his parents' execution for espionage.

The Book of Daniel is in many ways a political mystery story. As young children, Daniel and his sister lose their parents. Condemned as spies and betrayed by members of their own family, Daniel's parents are martyrs in the view of the Left, which is sure they are innocent. As far as Daniel is concerned, however, his parents abandoned him, and he is doubtful that they understood the implications of their actions or how much their behavior actually played into the hands of the government that executed them.

Daniel finds it both fascinating and frustrating to try to piece together the past. When he finally tracks down the relative who informed on his parents, for example, Daniel finds that he is senile. So many years have passed that it is difficult either to re-create the feelings of another age or to determine the truth of the charges against his parents. Without a heritage he can share with others, Daniel feels isolated and without an identity. He wonders on what basis he can live his own life when he has such fundamental and apparently unanswerable questions about his own parents.

As a student of history, however, Daniel is capable of seeing things in terms larger than his own personal obsessions. The chapters of the novel alternate between first-person and third-person narration as Daniel himself swings from subjectivity to objectivity. His plight, he gradually realizes, is not so different from that of his country, which tends either to obliterate the past or to sentimentalize it. Daniel's images of his parents lack a certain substance, as they have become figures in Cold War ideological battles, and the truth often eludes Americans who are fed a steady diet of entertaining, pacific, and nostalgic pictures of the past.

Near the end of *The Book of Daniel*, there is a brilliant set-piece description of Disneyland, which comes to stand for the forces in American life that threaten a complex sense of history. At Disneyland, which resembles a film set, are arranged the figures and artifacts of American history, the symbols and the tokens of the national heritage, wrenched from their social and historical context, abstracted into a series of entertainments for customers who do not have to analyze what is presented to them. This spectacle of history substitutes for the real thing, demeaning the past and replacing it with a comfortable and convenient product that need only be enjoyed and consumed.

What fuels Daniel's anger is the way his parents allowed themselves to become symbols in the ideologies of the Left and the Right. Their willingness to sacrifice themselves, no matter what the cost to their family, appalls him. The human element, the complexity of loyalties to family and friends and country, is what distinguishes Doctorow's novel, taking it out of the realm of the merely political while at the same time asking the most fundamental questions about the relationship between ideology and individualism. Until Daniel comes to terms with the humanity of his parents, he finds it impossible to get on with his own life and to care for his wife and child. Only by reclaiming his mother and father in terms that are far more complex than those of their public immolation can Daniel function as a husband and father.

RAGTIME

First published: 1975
Type of work: Novel

At the beginning of the twentieth century, on the eve of world war and tremendous cultural changes, a proud black man defends his dignity by force.

Ragtime begins with a description of a comfortable American household in New Rochelle, New York, at the turn of the twentieth century. At the dinner table, Father, Mother, the little boy, and Mother's Younger Brother are interrupted by the visit of a young black man, Coalhouse Walker. Eventually, it is discovered that Walker is the father of the child who had been abandoned by a young black woman who, along with the child, has been given refuge in the household. The appearance of Walker changes everything in the family's life and eventually links the New Rochelle household directly to the fate of the United States. By not giving the family names, Doctorow emphasizes their role as representatives of white, middle-class life, gradually and inexorably drawn into the changing times of radicals, immigrants, and African Americans.

Doctorow uses Walker as the agent of change. This proud black man is offended when his motorcar is stopped by a group of unruly volunteer firemen who then block his way and (when he goes for assistance) deface his prized possession. Unable to obtain satisfaction from the law (he finds it impossible to file charges or to be taken seriously by the authorities), Walker takes justice into his own hands, recruiting a group of black comrades who devise an ingenious plan to occupy the J. P. Morgan Library in New York City and demand the return of Walker's car in pristine condition—or the precious building will be detonated with explosives.

While no such incident occurred in the years *Ragtime* covers, and it is unlikely that such an incident could have taken place, Doctorow is less concerned with realism than with the implications of historical change. His novel is a compression of history, a fable making the point that the Establishment in the twentieth century will eventually find it more and more difficult to ignore the new immigrants and blacks and to give them the runaround that Walker experiences. Thus the participation of Younger Brother—the only white man in Walker's gang—is again symbolic of what is about to happen in history: the joining together of white dissenters, radicals, and (in some cases) communists with disaffected minorities who will demand their rights. Younger Brother, after all, chafes under the paternalistic, authoritarian household of his brother-in-law and sees in Walker the chance to overturn—or at least challenge—the status quo.

Indeed, *Ragtime* is studded with historical characters who, through their politics, their inventions, or their imaginations, disrupt the status quo. Emma Goldman, a communist, Jacob Riis, a photographer of the slums, and Harry Houdini, the great escape artist, all figure in the novel, because each of them speaks to the public's dream of overcoming or breaking out of the status quo. Younger Brother, for example, is attracted not only to political activity but also to Evelyn Nesbit, the nubile

model who excited public attention when her husband shot and murdered famous architect Stanford White because of White's alleged defilement of her. In turn, Doctorow has Nesbit form an infatuation with both Emma Goldman and with Tateh, the immigrant silhouette maker and (later) filmmaker, because each of them, in different ways, embodies romantic visions of America—of America as an equal and just society, as a land of dreams fulfilled.

The novel's intricate layering of historical and invented figures tends to dissolve the barriers between public and private life and between the wealthy and the poor. Doctorow is not concerned with whether such characters could, in fact, meet; rather, he is intent on demonstrating that in terms of the way people have experienced the United States there is a kind of imagination of the country that pervades every level of life. Evelyn Nesbit's dream of success, in other words, is much the same as the immigrant's, and so she eventually stars in one of Tateh's films. In the deepest sense of the word, Doctorow is a democratic novelist who shows that class divisions dissolve in the light of the commonality of American behavior, that the very things that split Americans apart are also the things that unite them.

Walker's concern for his car is itself a very American concern—attaching his sense of dignity to a piece of machinery and making it an extension of himself. There is much humor and irony in Doctorow's treatment of America, but it is also the sly criticism of an insider, of a writer who revels in the country's contradictions and who shows that the myth of America, seen in its broadest terms, can encompass all groups, classes, and races of people.

WORLD'S FAIR

First published: 1985
Type of work: Novel

A remembrance of New York City in the 1930's, from the perspective of a boy writing about "The Typical American Boy" for an essay contest.

In comparison to Doctorow's earlier novels, *World's Fair* seems remarkably straightforward. It resembles a work of conventional nonfiction, and like a memoir, it is largely bound by a chronological structure. Much of the action is seen through the consciousness of a young boy, Edgar, growing up in the Bronx during the 1939-1940 World's Fair. Given the character's name and background, it is difficult not to conclude that Doctorow has himself and his family in mind. He had used his New Rochelle house as a model for the house in *Ragtime* and the mind of a young boy as the intuitive medium through

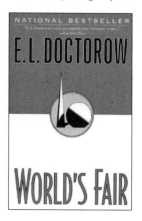

which many of the domestic, private events of the novel were filtered. Doctorow's interest in the way the fictional and factual impinge upon each other would naturally lead to this exercise in quasi-autobiography, in which the materials from his own background underpin the plot. The World's Fair becomes a metaphor for the boy's growing up and for the United States' maturation.

Unlike many American novelists, Doctorow does not merely criticize American materialism, seeing in the emphasis on things a soul-deadening culture which is antithetical to the artist's imagination. On the contrary, he enjoys playing with and observing the materiality of the United States—decrying, to be sure, the way in which the culture turns its important figures and events into toys and commercials for capitalism but also capturing the American delight in inventiveness and machinery and honoring it. In *World's Fair,* he triumphantly combines the personal and the familiar aspects of life with the way a society celebrates itself. In doing so, he recovers the synthesis of history and literature that made *Ragtime* such a resounding success.

Compared with the characters in his other fiction, Edgar is unusual. He is a well-behaved boy with none of the rebelliousness that characterizes Younger Brother or Billy Bathgate. Society impinges just as significantly in *World's Fair* as it does in the other novels, with Edgar getting roughed up in his neighborhood for being a "Jewboy" and shaken up by the portentous crash of the German

dirigible *Hindenburg*, which shows him how the apparent calm of his life and other American lives can be abruptly shattered by disaster.

As are Doctorow's other novels, *World's Fair* is full of fascinating period detail and places—the arrival of a water wagon, the Good Humor man, and a New York Giants game at the Polo Grounds. There is less plot, however, than in other Doctorow works to hold this novel together. Essentially, the narrative turns on Edgar's anticipation of the fair, on his preparations for it, on his anxieties about whether his rather undependable father will take him, and on his chances of winning the essay contest.

World's Fair is structured as a series of vignettes, the logic of which depends upon Edgar's sensibility rather than on the events themselves. In this respect, Doctorow reverses the pattern of *Ragtime*, in which human character is so definitely at one with the pattern of history. Called nostalgic and charming by many reviewers, *World's Fair* is somewhat surprising in that Doctorow does not analyze the ideological basis of the World's Fair, dissecting what it means for a modern technological society. The author in this work is much more concerned with the actual "feel" of experience, with a man remembering his youth, than with using it as a pretext for a political lesson.

BILLY BATHGATE

First published: 1989
Type of work: Novel

A Bronx boy grows up infatuated with Dutch Schultz and his gang, learning to survive and prosper even as the gangsters of his youth die out.

The first long sentence of *Billy Bathgate* launches right into the excitement of a scene in which Dutch Schultz is disposing of a disloyal associate, Bo Weinberg. The setting is described by fifteen-year-old Billy Bathgate, the novel's narrator, who is impressed with the smooth running of the Dutchman's criminal enterprise. A car drives up to a dark dock; without using any light or making a sound, Schultz's crew gets on a boat with Bo and his girlfriend, Drew Preston. Schultz's control over the situation is awesome and inspiring for the young boy, who has been given the honor of running errands and performing other chores for the famous gang. He becomes their mascot and good luck charm.

Schultz has a way of utterly changing the face of things, and for a long time, working for him has a fairy-tale quality to it. Billy is enchanted by the sheer magic of the way Schultz gets things done. No sooner is Bo Weinberg overboard with his cement overshoes than Schultz is making love to Drew Preston—a socialite who is fascinated, for a while, by his presence and energy. She even accompanies Schultz to Onondaga in upstate New York, where he takes over a town, plying the locals with gifts and setting up a cozy atmosphere in preparation for what he rightly expects will be a favorable jury verdict in the case the government has brought against him for tax evasion.

Schultz's great strength, however, is also his great weakness. By making all of his business revolve around him, he fails to see how crime is becoming organized and corporate. His way of doing business is almost feudal—depending almost entirely on violence and on the loyalty of subordinates—and he has no grasp of how to put together an organization that can compete with the combinations of power being amassed by the government and by his rival, Lucky Luciano. Schultz wants to personalize everything so that it all evolves out of his own ego. That ego is unstable, however; on an impulse, he kills an uncooperative colleague in an Onondaga hotel. This is only one of many instances when he goes berserk and literally pounds his opponent into the floor.

Members of Schultz's gang—particularly his accountant, Abbadabba Berman—sense that the old ways of doing things are nearly finished. Weinberg's defection is only the beginning of events which put Schultz on the defensive and which culminate in his gangland murder near the end of the novel. Berman tries to convince Schultz to do business in the new way, to recognize that he is part of a larger crime network, but Schultz can think only in terms of his own ambitions. He calls off plans to amalgamate with Lucky Luciano and other gangsters. In compensation, perhaps, for Schultz's inability to adapt to new times, Berman turns to Billy, making him an apprentice and lavishing attention

on the boy. Berman plies Billy with advice and gives him assignments that build his confidence and extend his knowledge of the business.

Through Berman and Preston, Billy gains perspective on Schultz. Preston, Billy finds, has her own sort of power and sense of ease. When she tires of Schultz, she simply leaves him, conveying to Billy the impression that Schultz's charisma has its limits. Billy never dares to think of actually leaving the gang, but he keeps his own counsel and is prepared to take care of himself when Schultz is murdered. At the death scene, in which Schultz, Berman, Lulu, and Irving have been shot, Billy learns from Berman the combination of the safe in which Schultz

has stashed much of his loot. Evasive about his subsequent career, Billy intimates at the end of the novel that he has indeed amassed the Dutchman's fortune, but he does not vouchsafe what he will do with it.

In this fast-paced adventure novel, which takes quick tours of the Bronx, upstate New York, Saratoga, and the docks of Manhattan, Doctorow supplies the color and the texture of the 1930's. As Billy prospers in the service of gangster Dutch Schultz and gets to know these different worlds, he finds it impossible to return as he was to his old neighborhood. When he does return, he is immediately perceived as a different person. He dresses differently, carries himself differently, and has a consciousness of a world that extends far beyond the Bathgate Avenue from which he derives his assumed name. Billy becomes, in other words, a self-invented figure, transcending his origins not only in the actions he narrates but also in his very language, which is at once colloquial and formal, a blend of popular and sophisticated vocabulary that precisely captures the boy and the man who has become the narrator of this novel. In this quintessential American story, Doctorow has managed yet another stunning version of the hero's quest for identity and success.

THE WATERWORKS

First published: 1994
Type of work: Novel

Class exploitation is exemplified in both political corruption and scientific experiments by which wealthy men are kept alive at the expense of poor children.

The Waterworks, set in New York City in 1871, poses the lives of Doctorow's characters against the background of significant social and political change. Civil War idealism has deteriorated into selfishness at all levels: "A conspicuously self-satisfied class of new wealth and weak intellect was all aglitter in a setting of mass misery."

Robber barons control the city's financial life, and the newspapers refuse to print anything negative about them, even when several die and leave their families as paupers. Graft and corruption dominate the city's political life; no business or civic projects can exist without payoffs to Boss Tweed's notorious political machine. Most judges, prosecutors, and police officers take bribes.

Millennial religious groups are challenging traditional religious authority and actively opposing scientific inquiry. Scientists suggest public acceptance of scientific inquiry has progressed little beyond the antidissection riots of one hundred years earlier. The enthusiasm for technological advances, celebrated by Walt Whitman, no longer exists.

These elements are significant in *The Waterworks*'s plot as McIlvaine, editor of *The Telegram*, searches for his lost reporter, Martin, the self-disinherited son of recently deceased tycoon Augustus Pemberton. Immediately before his disappearance, Martin told family and friends that he had begun to doubt his own sanity because twice he had seen his father riding in a city stage. Reverend Charles Grimshaw of St. James Church suggests that this vision could be a hallucination caused by Martin's guilt about his estrangement from his father, but he cannot explain why Augustus, a long-time communicant of St. James, chose to be buried elsewhere.

McIlvaine interviews Martin's fiancé, his stepmother, and his closest friend, but progress begins when he consults Captain Edmund Donne, one of the city's few honest police officers. From one of Donne's informants, they learn that poor children supposedly are being taken to the Home for Little Wanderers, an institution no one seems able to locate geographically. Initially McIlvaine believes they have located another instance of Boss Tweed's graft, but eventually "the Home" is identified as an elaborate laboratory located under the municipal waterworks. There they find Martin, barely alive.

In several weeks as a captive in this laboratory, Martin has learned that Augustus and several other wealthy but dying men have surrendered all their possessions to finance the experiments of Dr. Wrede Sartorius, a skilled surgeon who now is experimenting with ways to extend the lives of dying patients by using blood and glands from young children. Though they violate society's laws and religious tenets, his secret experiments have been allowed to continue because bribes have been paid to politicians and policemen. Meanwhile, the laboratory's business manager has been stealing the money that the dying robber barons have in effect stolen from their own families.

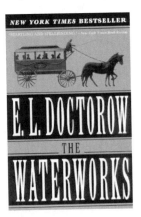

After Dr. Sartorius is committed to a mental institution, McIlvaine interviews him, trying to determine if the doctor is a dedicated scientist (as he claims) or a monster without human feelings. McIlvaine insists that he wants to tell the doctor's story in his newspaper. The reader learns, however, that this search happened years ago, but McIlvaine has never written his exclusive story, though he is still a newspaper editor. Doctorow seems to suggest that McIlvaine, like Martin initially, remains fascinated by the personalities and ethical problems raised by some of the actors in this drama, especially Dr. Sartorius. The novel seems to question the point at which experiments on human subjects cease to be justified as advancing scientific knowledge.

CITY OF GOD

First published: 2000
Type of work: Novel

Inspired by St. Augustine's treatise, this novel analyzes the factors behind the decline of Christianity in the twentieth century.

In *City of God*, Doctorow's underlying theme is humanity's quest for meaning. Everett, the writer-narrator, is compiling a nonfiction account of the way his friend Pem (Thomas Pemberton) is dealing with loss of religious conviction. The son of a clergyman, Pem has repeatedly been disillusioned by his own ethical failures, especially his failure to discover a rational basis for Christian faith. He is considering a complete break with the church—a literal rejection of Christianity and a symbolic rejection of his father.

Then, a seemingly random street crime brings Pem into contact with Joshua Green, his wife Sarah Blumenthal, and their Synagogue of Evolutionary Judaism. A large brass cross stolen from the wall of St. Timothy's is found on the synagogue's roof. The cross seems symbolic of Pem's diminished religious conviction: Beneath its brass veneer, it is steel, and it can easily be dismantled because it consists of two parts held together with screws. Pem never discovers the identity or motives of the thieves, but he sees the theft as a sign leading him to Joshua and Sarah, rabbis whose search for the City of God parallels his own. Complicating their quest, though, are stories of the Holocaust told by Sarah's father, who is sinking into dementia. For Joshua especially, modern society seems overwhelmed by what St. Augustine called "the City of the World," and he is martyred as he tries to reveal the ghetto horrors, thus ending humanity's apparent indifference to the Holocaust.

Everett too becomes obsessed with the ghetto stories, which become the new focus of his book. Recording those stories brings him into closer contact with his own heritage, as he explores his father's World War I exploits and those of his brother in World War II.

First Joshua and later Pem search for the long-lost ghetto records. In effect, Pem avenges his friend's death by locating the trunk of records written by ghetto leaders, smuggled out by Sarah's father and preserved by an anti-Nazi Roman Catholic priest. Sarah gives the originals to the government to be used as evidence against war criminals, and Everett uses her photocopies to complete his book.

Near the end of the novel is another symbolic film scenario. Obsessed with a war criminal living in the United States, a writer stalks the old man, considering ways to execute him, then accidentally kills him in a bike accident. Although the writer escapes capture, newspaper accounts portray him as the villain, and the old man is honored instead of dishonored. In contrast, even though the ghetto accounts are located too late to prosecute the local commandant, using contemporary accounts to authenticate his atrocities proves a more effective revenge.

As the novel ends, Pem converts to Judaism and, with Sarah, continues his quest to establish meaningful religious traditions. Soon they are married—a symbolic union of Jewish and Christian traditions prefigured early in the novel when Everett observes a great blue heron and a snowy white egret perched back to back, sharing a New York City pier. Near the novel's end, another ecumenical symbol appears as Everett describes the City of Birds, near Madrid, where many species of birds peaceably pick over a huge garbage dump.

"A HOUSE IN THE PLAINS"

First published: 2001 (collected in *Sweet Land Stories*, 2004)
Type of work: Short story

In this macabre story set at the turn of the twentieth century, Doctorow demonstrates that predatory behavior is not a modern or urban phenomenon.

In "A House in the Plains," Earle, the eighteen-year-old narrator, describes the machinations of Mama, who insists that he call her Aunt Dora, following their hasty departure from Chicago when Dora's latest husband dies. Earle regrets leaving city attractions, especially Winifred, an older woman who is his longtime sexual partner.

Dora and Earle move to a farm outside LaVille, Illinois, where Dora establishes herself as a wealthy widow who takes in three foster children from the New York slums. She also brings in a cook-house-keeper who speaks no English. The only local she employs is Bent (the handyman), with whom she begins a sexual relationship.

Once Dora establishes her positive image, her character as a black widow emerges. Taking advantage of Nordic immigrants with enough money to buy land but no real understanding of American culture, she offers them a partnership in the farm, which she has heavily mortgaged at the local bank. Bent is jealous of these men, but none seem to remain. Meanwhile, Dora's bank account mysteriously grows.

Two incidents lead to a climactic resolution. Henry Lundgren, a Swedish immigrant, shows up, demanding to know what happened to his brother Per, who disappeared after meeting with Dora; and Winifred writes Earle that the husband's remains were exhumed and the police are looking for Dora.

A few days later, the farmhouse burns, and two headless bodies are found inside, along with the bodies of the three children. Bent has been very thoroughly framed for the crime. The site of this tragedy draws gawkers from as far away as Chicago and Indianapolis—arguably Doctorow's comment on Americans' fascination with the macabre. Winifred arrives to see where Earle died, but as he reveals that he is alive, he also tells her that she is now an accessory after the fact and insists she accompany him and Dora to California.

"CHILD, DEAD, IN THE ROSE GARDEN"

First published: 2004 (collected in *Sweet Land Stories*, 2004)
Type of work: Short story

Contemporary concerns with environmental pollution and government cover-ups are seen as justified as this story reflects their destructive effects—physical and ethical.

The narrator of "Child, Dead, in the Rose Garden" is Federal Bureau of Investigation (FBI) special agent Brian W. Molloy. The morning after a White House concert, a sixty-year-old groundskeeper discovers the shrouded body of a young boy. Hysteria in the post-September 11 world leads to his detention as a terrorist, until his daughter (a lawyer at the Treasury Department) files a missing person report. Probably no further investigation would have been conducted, but the Washington, D.C., police and the *Post* receive letters informing them about the boy.

As Molloy investigates, he quickly encounters officials who want the case ignored. Using his own time and money, Molloy follows a lead to Utilicon, a Southwestern power company headquartered in Beauregard, Texas. There he learns that the boy, Roberto Guzman, died of an incurable disease caused by environmental pollution from Utilicon. Roberto's father, a gardener at Utilicon, has been detained by the Immigration and Naturalization Service (INS) and is scheduled for deportation.

Clearly someone wants to draw public attention to the dangerous pollution, and Molloy quickly discovers that Christina Stevens (daughter of Utilicon's chairman) and her boyfriend, a Marine assigned to the White House, are responsible for placing Roberto's body in the Rose Garden. As a result, Christina has been confined to a private mental hospital and fed a diet of tranquilizers.

Realizing that he is essentially powerless, Molloy nonetheless calls the government official and quietly informs him that unless the Guzmans are allowed to return to their home, the story will quickly be distributed to the media. This action marks the end of his career; so, as the story ends, Molloy has just written his letter of resignation.

SUMMARY

E. L. Doctorow has shown himself to be a master stylist, an adept delineator of characters, a lyric portrayer of places and eras, and a shrewd commentator on popular genres and political themes who also maintains a strong sense of narrative and storytelling. Indeed, his work is a major evocation and critique of the American mythos and a brilliant creation of new American fables. His experiments with point of view and with the relationship between history and fiction have marked him as a major innovator.

Carl Rollyson; updated by Charmaine Allmon Mosby

BIBLIOGRAPHY

By the Author

LONG FICTION:
Welcome to Hard Times, 1960
Big as Life, 1966
The Book of Daniel, 1971
Ragtime, 1975
Loon Lake, 1980
World's Fair, 1985
Billy Bathgate, 1989
The Waterworks, 1994
City of God, 2000
The March, 2005

SHORT FICTION:
Lives of the Poets, 1984
Sweet Land Stories, 2004

DRAMA:
Drinks Before Dinner, pr. 1978

SCREENPLAYS:
Three Screenplays, 2003

NONFICTION:
Jack London, Hemingway, and the Constitution: Selected Essays, 1977-1992, 1993
Poets and Presidents, 1993
Conversations with E. L. Doctorow, 1999
Lamentation 9/11, 2002
Reporting the Universe, 2003

EDITED TEXT:
The Best American Short Stories, 2000, 2000

About the Author

Bloom, Harold, ed. *E. L. Doctorow.* New York: Chelsea House, 2001.

Fowler, Douglas. *Understanding E. L. Doctorow.* Columbia: University of South Carolina Press, 1992.

Kakutani, Michiko. "Do Facts and Fiction Mix?" *The New York Times Book Review,* January 27, 1980, pp. 2-3, 28-29.

Levine, Paul. *E. L. Doctorow.* London: Methuen, 1985.

Morris, Christopher D. *Conversations with E. L. Doctorow.* Jackson: University Press of Mississippi, 1999.

Strout, Cushing. "Historizing Fiction and Fictionalizing History: The Case of E. L. Doctorow." *Prospects,* 1980, 423-437.

Trenner, Richard. *E. L. Doctorow: Essays and Conversations.* Princeton, N.J.: Ontario Review Press, 1983.

Weber, Richard. "E. L. Doctorow: Myth Maker." *The New York Times Magazine,* October 20, 1985, 25-26, 42-43, 74-77.

DISCUSSION TOPICS

- In what ways is the effect of E. L. Doctorow's novels enhanced by his practice of creating representative characters who interact with historical figures?

- Doctorow is usually classified as an urban writer. Which novels seem to justify that description? Which ones contradict it?

- Few of Doctorow's characters are heroic in the traditional sense, but several of them are admirable because they pursue self-knowledge as well as literal truth. Which characters of this type do you find most admirable?

- Doctorow has sometimes been criticized for writing fiction that is too "political." Which of his political positions are actually controversial? Why?

- Doctorow has been compared to Theodore Dreiser, a major figure in American literary naturalism, because both have written sympathetically but unsentimentally about the seamiest side of American life. Dreiser's view of society was extremely negative, and he seemed pessimistic about the human potential for creating or even appreciating pure beauty. What elements in Doctorow's writing seem to focus on the dark side of human nature? Are there redeeming positive qualities in some or all of his unlikable characters? Which ones?

- Sometimes praised for the lyrical quality of his prose, Doctorow has maintained that his writing has been as much influenced by his parents' emphasis upon music as by his own voracious childhood reading. In which books can you detect the underlying influence of music? Is that influence more prevalent in his nonfiction than in his fiction?

JOHN DOS PASSOS

Born: Chicago, Illinois
January 14, 1896
Died: Baltimore, Maryland
September 28, 1970

A pioneer in experimenting with forms of fiction, Dos Passos was one of the most important novelists of the modernist period in the 1920's and 1930's.

National Portrait Gallery, Smithsonian Institution

BIOGRAPHY

Born in Chicago, the illegitimate son of a wealthy lawyer of Portuguese descent and a mother whose family lived in Maryland and Virginia, John Roderigo Dos Passos grew up in the Washington, D.C., area. He attended private schools in England, The Choate School, and later Harvard University. He graduated from Harvard in 1916 and planned to study to be an architect, but when the United States entered World War I he joined a medical corps in France and later enlisted in the United States Army. After World War I he spent a number of years as a freelance newspaper reporter.

Soon after the war, Dos Passos wrote his first novel, *One Man's Initiation—1917* (1920), based on his experiences as an ambulance driver; his second, *Three Soldiers* (1921), appeared soon after. Both these early works are bitter condemnations of the war and what it did to young Americans who happened to be caught in the violence. The central character in the first novel and all three of the soldiers depicted in the second are destroyed, physically or spiritually, by their experiences. In these novels, Dos Passos was already presenting a radical critique of the official view of the United States as the selfless defender of freedom for everyone.

Dos Passos would extend his criticism in his major work, beginning with his first genuinely experi-

mental novel, *Manhattan Transfer* (1925), and continuing with new and unusual techniques in the three novels which formed his first trilogy: *The 42nd Parallel* (1930), *1919* (1932), and *The Big Money* (1936); they were collected as *U.S.A.* in 1937. During the 1920's, Dos Passos became more and more deeply involved in radical protests against what he saw as the degradation of American ideals. He served on the board of the communist magazine *The New Masses* and contributed time and effort to a number of communist causes, although he never joined the Communist Party.

He was most disturbed by the Sacco-Vanzetti affair, a celebrated case in the 1920's in which two immigrant anarchists were accused of murder during a robbery and sentenced to death. Many people at the time believed that their trial had been unfair, that evidence against them had been faked, and that they had been condemned because of their politics. Dos Passos was among the protesters, and he was jailed for picketing in 1927 prior to their execution.

Dos Passos eventually became disillusioned with left-wing politics, giving up his communist activities in 1934. Toward the end of the 1930's, he became increasingly alienated from his former causes. He traveled as a correspondent to Spain, where the Spanish Civil War had broken out in 1936. His sympathies were on the side of the Loyalist government, which was trying to suppress a rebellion by a group of insurgents led by army officers with the support of the Catholic Church. The insurgents received military aid from Adolf Hitler's Germany and Benito Mussolini's Italy; the Loyalists were aided by the Soviet Union. Dos Passos found that the Loyalist government was dominated by Soviet agents and that the Communists were ruthlessly suppressing their opponents on the Loyalist side. He also was convinced that he had been lied to by the American novelist Ernest Hemingway about the fate of a mutual Spanish friend who, Dos Passos discovered, had been executed for opposing Communist domination.

Dos Passos was also dismayed by what he perceived as the betrayal of the labor movement in the United States. In *U.S.A.*, he had presented sympathetic portraits of union organizers and leaders who selflessly worked for the betterment of workers as well as scathing depictions of men who betrayed the workers. However, he later became convinced that as unions gained power they became corrupt organizations which deprived their members and others of freedoms. He expressed his disillusionment in a second trilogy, *District of Columbia* (1952), which consisted of *Adventures of a Young Man* (1939), *Number One* (1943), and *The Grand Design* (1949). These works dealt respectively with Spain, with the notorious corruption in governor Huey Long's Louisiana, and with the worse corruption in Washington, D.C. His most bitter portrayal of unions and their evils came in his last long novel, *Midcentury* (1961).

After World War II, Dos Passos lived in the area around Washington and Baltimore and devoted much of his attention to historical writings. He expressed his profound admiration for one of the United States' founding fathers in *The Head and Heart of Thomas Jefferson* (1954) and wrote a more general history of the American Revolution in *The Men Who Made the Nation* (1957). He also wrote a number of autobiographical works, including *The Theme Is Freedom* (1956) and *Occasions and Protests* (1964). In the 1950's and 1960's he wrote regularly for *The National Review*, the conservative journal edited by William F. Buckley, Jr.

When liberal friends such as Edmund Wilson, a longtime summer neighbor on Cape Cod, teased him about his new friends and commitments, Dos Passos replied that his overriding interest had always been, and remained, the freedom of the individual. He would support whatever movement or party seemed to him to share that dedication.

Dos Passos first married Katharine (Kay) Smith in 1929; she was killed in an automobile crash in

1947, while they were driving from Cape Cod to Virginia. In 1949 he married Elizabeth Hamlin Holdridge, with whom he had a daughter.

ANALYSIS

Dos Passos was the most experimental of the major novelists of what critics now refer to as the period of "high modernism," which lasted roughly from 1910 until 1940. His great contemporaries in the American novel, Ernest Hemingway, F. Scott Fitzgerald, and William Faulkner, all concentrated on writing about specific areas or groups. Hemingway, during the 1920's, wrote mostly about expatriate Americans living in Europe and about such upper-class sports as big-game hunting and bullfighting. Fitzgerald, too, wrote about expatriates but also about bored flappers and socialites, upper-class young people with too much money and too little to do. Faulkner, while using such experimental techniques as stream of consciousness, focused all of his attention on the Deep South, especially his native corner of northern Mississippi.

Dos Passos was looking for techniques that would enable him to portray the wide range of characters and economic situations to be found in American society. He was also looking for a style that would reflect the fast pace of modern life and the actual speech of its people. Even as early as *Three Soldiers* he was engaged in this pursuit, choosing as his principal characters a farm boy from Indiana, an aesthete from the East Coast, and an Italian working-class man from San Francisco and making no attempt to combine their stories, except to make clear that all were destroyed by the machinelike nature of the modern Army.

Dos Passos's experimentation took a major step forward in *Manhattan Transfer*, which also brought him wide public attention. He attempted to create a cross-section of urban life in the United States by introducing a wide range of characters. While much of the book's attention is devoted to a young newspaper reporter and a young woman who becomes an actress, depictions are also given of a young man from a farm who cannot find work, who becomes homeless and eventually dies, either accidentally or by suicide; a French immigrant who makes himself something of a success by marrying a widow who owns a delicatessen; a man who had once been a rich Wall Street investor but whose luck went bad and who sinks to the lowest levels of society; a war veteran who turns to crime; and a milkman who is injured in an accident and uses the settlement as a springboard to a successful political career.

Each chapter in *Manhattan Transfer* is introduced by a brief section of impressionistic prose about some aspect of New York City and its life, which will appear in that chapter. For example, where a couple of the characters are to find their way to the waterfront and others are to arrive by ship in New York harbor, the opening segment depicts the shoreline and the dirty waters of New York Bay. In each chapter, as it proceeds, episodes in the lives of several of the characters are described, with occasional brief references to individuals who are mentioned only a single time. The intention is to produce a kaleidoscopic effect, a novel that will give the reader a vivid impression of what it is to live in a city as bustling and energetic and squalid as New York.

Dos Passos's most radical experiments are the techniques used in *U.S.A.* The prose style makes frequent use of a device he used sparingly in *Manhattan Transfer*, that of run-together words. The narrative segments move rapidly, with little attention to extended depictions of characters; the "Camera Eye" segments are more relaxed, and the "Newsreel" collages are jagged and sometimes almost incoherent as they skip from subject to subject.

In the novels that compose this trilogy, Dos Passos interweaves the stories of eleven major figures from various parts of the United States and various economic and social levels. Along with these narratives, three very different devices are employed. One is the "Newsreel," a collage of headlines from newspapers, brief stories of violence or betrayal, snatches of popular songs of the time, and quotations from public officials and from government reports. The second is the "Camera Eye," impressionistic pictures in vivid prose from the perspective of a single individual responding to the events of the times. The third consists of portraits of important historical figures of the time, from the industrialist Henry Ford and the financier J. Pierpont Morgan to the Socialist leader Eugene V. Debs and the economist Thorstein Veblen. Dos Passos's views about politics and economics are most clearly suggested in these portraits.

MANHATTAN TRANSFER

First published: 1925
Type of work: Novel

Characters from all walks of life struggle with the tensions and pressures of life in New York City.

Dos Passos, in *Manhattan Transfer*, tried to show what life was like between the last years of the nineteenth century and the early 1920's for a wide variety of people living in the largest of American cities, New York. At the center of the action are two characters, Ellen Thatcher, whose birth occurs in the novel's opening pages, and Jimmy Herf, who is first seen as a young boy. Ellen's background is lower middle class; her father is an unsuccessful accountant, her mother an invalid who dies while Ellen is still a child. Jimmy's background is more wealthy, but his father is dead and his mother dies after a series of strokes. Instead of Yale or Harvard, he goes to Columbia University.

In the course of the novel, Ellen becomes a minor star in the theater and marries an actor who, it is revealed, is homosexual. She divorces him, and after a frustrating affair with a rich young alcoholic, she goes abroad with the Red Cross during World War I and meets Jimmy, whom she had known in New York. He has been a newspaper reporter. The two marry and have a son, but eventually they become bored with each other. Ellen has abandoned the theater and becomes a successful magazine editor. When she and Jimmy divorce, she reluctantly agrees to marry a longtime suitor, George Baldwin. Jimmy becomes increasingly restive as a reporter, and at the end he quits his job and sets out to see the rest of America.

This thin plot is only a means for holding the novel together while Dos Passos provides glimpses of a number of very different lives. A few of these are from upper levels of society. Jimmy's aunt and

her husband live well, and their son, James Merivale, becomes an officer in the war and then a stuffed-shirt banker. Phineas T. Blackhead and his partner, Densch, run an export-import business which seems very successful until the end of the novel, when it goes bankrupt.

A few characters represent the lower depths of society. Bud Korpenning is a young farm boy who comes to the city after stealing his father's savings. He never finds a permanent job, drifting from handout to handout and eventually becoming a Bowery bum before falling, perhaps deliberately, from the Brooklyn Bridge. Anna Cohen, a poor Jewish girl, makes a meager living as a seamstress until she joins a strike against intolerable conditions and loses her job. She takes a job in a dress store and, dreaming of something better, is horribly burned in a fire. Dutch Robertson, a war veteran, and his girlfriend, Francie, are barely surviving until he begins robbing stores. She joins him and is romanticized by the press as a "flapper bandit." They are caught when she gives birth to their baby.

Most of the characters, however, belong at some level of the middle class; a few of them rise. Gus McNiel is a milkman who negligently allows his cart to be hit by a train and is injured. An ambulance-chasing lawyer named George Baldwin sues, seduces McNiel's wife, Nellie, and wins a large settlement for McNiel. The money is the springboard that launches McNiel on a successful political career. It also helps Baldwin to become a successful lawyer and eventually to be named district attorney. Another success, at least financially, is Congo Jake, a French sailor who becomes a bootlegger after retiring from the sea. Prohibition gives Congo Jake the opportunity for wealth; he marries a showgirl and offers to help Jimmy financially after Jimmy has quit his job.

Others drop down or out in society. Jimmy's cousin, Joe Harland, was once one of the most successful gamblers on Wall Street, but his luck changed, and he sinks lower and lower, unable finally even to hold onto a job as a night watchman. Ruth Prynne, one of Jimmy's girlfriends, who at one time lived in the same boardinghouse as Ellen, has a brief success as a singer but then loses her voice, resorting to dangerous treatments in doomed attempts to restore her career.

The picture given of New York life is sordid, whether it is depicted in the poetic tones of the introductions to each of the chapters in *Manhattan Transfer* or in the flat style of the narrative sections. Dos Passos's city is noisy, dirty, and dangerous. Characters such as Ellen find their lives unrewarding; others find them crushing. Somewhat confusingly, characters appear and disappear, sometimes without being given names, to emphasize the anonymity of city life for most people. The city is also pulsing with life, however; even as the author undercuts the glamour of show business and scoffs at the stodgy businessmen, the picture presented is gaudy, exciting, and challenging. Jimmy feels a sense of relief when he cuts his ties to the city and heads west across the river, but what he leaves behind is, on balance, far more interesting than the unknown he is entering.

Manhattan Transfer contains less harsh social criticism than Dos Passos's other early novels, and far less than *U.S.A.* There is political corruption; Anna Cohen's boyfriend talks to her about the revolution and the need for solidarity among workers; society has no place for the Bud Korpennings and the Dutch Robertsons. Yet these are minor matters in this novel. What stands out is the vibrancy, the clatter, the feverish activity of the city.

U.S.A.

First published: *The 42nd Parallel,* 1930; *1919,* 1932; *The Big Money,* 1936 (as *U.S.A.,* 1937)

Type of work: Novel

Life in the United States from the 1890's to the Great Depression of the 1930's is depicted in an encyclopedic novel.

The three volumes that make up *U.S.A.* were originally published separately; the trilogy was published as a single novel in 1937. The themes introduced in the first volume run throughout the others: the corrupting influence of wealth and the desire for money, the humiliation and penury inflicted by American society on those who occupy the lower levels of that society, the pretentious fakery of most of those who profess to have artistic talent or inclinations, and the heroism of a few dedicated souls whose lives are ground down in the effort to serve others.

The techniques employed by Dos Passos in *U.S.A.* develop and expand upon those he used in *Manhattan Transfer*. A dozen different characters from various parts of the United States and different levels of society are given one or more episodes during the course of the novel, and numerous other characters appear and disappear at various stages of the action. Frequently the paths of different characters intersect and run together. The narrative segments occupy less space than they do in *Manhattan Transfer*, as three other methods are given great significance.

In *The 42nd Parallel* there are nineteen sections of the "Newsreel," in which Dos Passos skillfully blends together newspaper headlines, snippets of popular songs, brief quotations from political speeches, and other material from the years between 1900 and 1917, when the novel ends. The "Newsreel" sections provide the authenticity of historical background. There are also, in this first volume, twenty-seven segments of "The Camera Eye," in which individuals experiences are presented in a stream-of-consciousness technique, representing one perspective on the events of the passing years.

Finally, there are in this first volume nine brief portraits of prominent individuals from the same period of time: Eugene V. Debs, Socialist leader and frequent presidential candidate who was later imprisoned for opposing American participation in World War I; Luther Burbank, "The Plant Wizard" who hybridized numerous vegetables and trees to the benefit of American agriculture; "Big Bill" Haywood, a radical labor organizer who moved from the Western Federation of Miners to the International Workers of the World (the IWW, or "Wobblies"); William Jennings Bryan, "the boy orator of the Platte," famous for what was called his "cross of gold" speech, leader of the Populist movement in the late nineteenth and early twentieth centuries; and several others prominent in one field or another.

Dos Passos's sympathies in these portraits are clearly with the rebels and the innovators. He is much more ironic and dismissive in calling the section on steel magnate Andrew Carnegie "Prince of Peace." He is also somewhat scornful of the idealistic inventor Charles Steinmetz, who allowed him-

self and his inventions to be exploited by General Electric.

The same devices are used throughout *U.S.A.*, but there is a subtle shift in tone between *1919* and *The Big Money*, noticeable in all four of the devices used by Dos Passos. The subject of the narrative sections changes from "Mac," a journeyman printer and part-time rebel, who disappears at the end of *The 42nd Parallel*, to Charley Anderson, a midwesterner with skills as a mechanic who flies in World War I, rises with the system in *The Big Money*, and is eventually crushed by it. The sleazy public relations expert, I. Ward Moorehouse, becomes more important, as do the women who are involved with him, the neurotic decorators Eleanor Stoddard and Eveline Hutchins.

There is a parallel shift in the subjects chosen for the brief biographical sketches. In *The 42nd Parallel* and *1919* these are, for the most part, devoted to individuals who are presented as worthy of the reader's admiration: Debs, Haywood, and Burbank. In *1919* there are favorable depictions of many. These include John Reed, the left-wing American journalist who went to Russia to report on the Russian Revolution and stayed on, dying in Moscow and being buried in the Kremlin wall; other journalists such as Randolph Bourne and Paxton Hibben, also radicals in their ways; and the IWW organizer and writer of labor songs Joe Hill, who was framed for murder and executed in Utah after trying to organize miners.

There are scathing portraits of President Woodrow Wilson and the financier J. P. Morgan, but Dos Passos saves for last two figures who share his admiration and his sympathy. The first is Wesley Everest, a logger and organizer of a strike for the IWW in the Pacific Northwest, who was brutally lynched after a violent episode in Centralia, Washington. The other is John Doe, the "Unknown Soldier," an ordinary American who was killed in World War I and made into a hero in a patriotic burial ceremony which Dos Passos portrays as a kind of ultimate exercise in hypocrisy.

In *The Big Money*, however, the emphasis has changed. There are fewer portraits, and those that there are emphasize the corruption of the American Dream rather than the heroics of those who, in the author's view, try to keep the dream alive. The only sympathetic figures in the final volume are the pioneers in aviation, the Wright Brothers; bitter social critic Thorstein Veblen; and the innovative architect Frank Lloyd Wright. The dancer Isadora Duncan and the film actor Rudolph Valentino are not so much admired as pitied. The subjects of the other depictions are scathingly portrayed as dehumanizers and exploiters and as defenders of a cruel and unfair economic system: the manufacturer Henry Ford, the efficiency expert Frederick W. Taylor, the newspaper tycoon William Randolph Hearst, and the stock market manipulator Samuel Insult.

The tone of the narrative sections becomes darker as well. The central figure in the first half of *The 42nd Parallel* is Fenian McCreary, known as "Mac" once he leaves Chicago and begins his travels. Mac becomes a symbol of the entire novel. At one time or another he lives in every section of the United States except the Deep South; he is balanced between his commitment to the kind of men who shared his life on the road and become involved in the IWW, and his middle-class aspirations: He wants a home and a "good life" for his wife and children. Eventually he moves to Mexico, where he sees a real revolution but does not take part in it. In the earlier years of the twentieth century, someone such as Mac can survive without making a definite commitment.

In later years, however, especially those which include the "roaring twenties," this kind of survival becomes less and less possible. Charley Anderson abandons his roots, has some success as a manufacturer, is drawn into the circle that includes Eveline Hutchins and Eleanor Stoddard, and eventually winds up with Margo Dowling, another major character who has been in the entertainment business and has become a gold digger.

Charley's business goes downhill as he drinks more and more, and eventually he dies as the result of an automobile crash. Eveline Hutchins commits suicide. Richard Ellsworth Savage, who grew from a pleasant young boy to a career-minded toady in *1919*, becomes part of Moorehouse's enterprise and eventually gives in to what had been his suppressed homosexual inclinations. The young woman from Texas known as "Daughter" is tangentially involved in radical activities without being a radical herself; she goes abroad to do relief work after World War I, becomes involved with Savage, becomes pregnant by him, and is killed in an airplane crash.

The bitterness of the final volume is presented most directly in a "Camera Eye" segment toward the close of *The Big Money* dealing with the end of the Sacco-Vanzetti affair: "They have clubbed us off the street they are stronger they are rich they hire and fire the politicians the newspapereditors the old judges the small men with reputations the collegepresidents the ward heelers." Later in the same section the narrative voice says, "all right we are two nations," and at the end, "we stand defeated America." By this time, Dos Passos sees no hope in radical political movements. They have, in his view, self-destructed, and the society as a whole is headed for a disaster of which the 1929 stock market crash is only the first stage.

The final section of *The Big Money*, "Vag," presents a contrast between the two Americas as Dos Passos saw them at the time. On the ground is an anonymous young man, out of work, half-starved, beaten by police, walking and hitchhiking across the United States. In the air is an airplane carrying the rich, including a man who thinks only of wealth and power, who vomits up his dinner but does not mind—he is wealthy, so a single meal does not matter to him. The "Vag" is aware of the airplane, but the man in the plane is totally ignorant of the man on the ground. The two men and their circumstances represent the vast gulf that separates the two parts of the country.

SUMMARY

John Dos Passos's reputation rests solidly on the novels he published between 1925 and 1939. In *Manhattan Transfer* and the three long novels that make up *U.S.A.*, he showed himself to be a daring and imaginative experimenter with prose style and a vivid depicter of the American scene. He does not present deep or penetrating analyses of his characters, but in part this results from the fact that he wishes to show that American society has a leveling influence that diminishes the differences between people's characters even as it exaggerates the economic and social differences between them. The picture Dos Passos provided of life in the United States in the first thirty years of the twentieth century remains lively and immediate. That picture, and the new directions he provided for prose style, secure for him a place among American novelists of modern times.

John M. Muste

John Dos Passos

BIBLIOGRAPHY

By the Author

LONG FICTION:
One Man's Initiation—1917, 1920
Three Soldiers, 1921
Streets of Night, 1923
Manhattan Transfer, 1925
The 42nd Parallel, 1930
1919, 1932
The Big Money, 1936
U.S.A., 1937 (includes previous 3 novels)
Adventures of a Young Man, 1939
Number One, 1943
The Grand Design, 1949
Chosen Country, 1951
District of Columbia, 1952 (includes *Adventures of a Young Man, Number One,* and *The Grand Design*)
Most Likely to Succeed, 1954
The Great Days, 1958
Midcentury, 1961
World in a Glass, 1966
Century's Ebb: The Thirteenth Chronicle, 1975 (posthumous)

DRAMA:
The Garbage Man, pr., pb. 1926 (pr. as *The Moon Is a Gong,* pr. 1925)
Three Plays, pb. 1934

POETRY:
A Pushcart at the Curb, 1922

NONFICTION:
Rosinante to the Road Again, 1922
Orient Express, 1927
In All Countries, 1934
Journeys Between Wars, 1938
The Ground We Stand On: Some Examples from the History of a Political Creed, 1941
State of the Nation, 1944
Tour of Duty, 1946
The General, 1949
The Prospect Before Us, 1950
The Head and Heart of Thomas Jefferson, 1954
The Theme Is Freedom, 1956
The Men Who Made the Nation, 1957
Prospects of a Golden Age, 1959
Mr. Wilson's War, 1962
Brazil on the Move, 1963
Occasions and Protests, 1964
Lincoln and the Gettysburg Address, 1964
Thomas Jefferson: The Making of a President, 1964

DISCUSSION TOPICS

- What two communications media influenced John Dos Passos's technique in his novels? How successful do you consider these innovations?

- Who or what functions as the protagonist of *Manhattan Transfer*?

- Is it possible to justify Dos Passos's relative inattention to character development in his fiction?

- How does Dos Passos unify the multifarious contents of *U.S.A.*?

- Dos Passos's allegiances and activities over the years suggest great shifts in his political and social attitudes. What underlying consistencies persist in his works over the decades?

The Shackles of Power: Three Jeffersonian Decades, 1966
The Best Times: An Informal Memoir, 1966
The Portugal Story, 1969
Easter Island: Island of Enigmas, 1971
The Fourteenth Chronicle, 1973

About the Author

Carr, Virginia Spencer. *Dos Passos: A Life.* Garden City, N.Y.: Doubleday, 1984.

Casey, Janet Galligani. *Dos Passos and the Ideology of the Feminine.* New York: Cambridge University Press, 1998.

Colley, Lain. *Dos Passos and the Fiction of Despair.* Totowa, N.J.: Rowman & Littlefield, 1978.

Koch, Stephen. *The Breaking Point: Hemingway, Dos Passos, and the Murder of José Robles.* New York: Counterpoint, 2005.

Ludington, Townsend. *John Dos Passos: A Twentieth Century Odyssey.* Rev. ed. New York: Carroll & Graf, 1998.

McGlamery, Tom. *Protest and the Body in Melville, Dos Passos, and Hurston.* New York: Routledge, 2004.

Maine, Barry, ed. *Dos Passos: The Critical Heritage.* London: Routledge, 1988.

Nanney, Lisa. *John Dos Passos.* New York: Twayne, 1998.

Sanders, David. *John Dos Passos: A Comprehensive Bibliography.* New York: Garland, 1987.

Strychacz, Thomas. *Modernism, Mass Culture, and Professionalism.* New York: Cambridge University Press, 1993.

FREDERICK DOUGLASS

Library of Congress

Born: Tuckahoe, Talbot County, Maryland
February, 1817
Died: Washington, D.C.
February 20, 1895

Douglass, as one of the progenitors of African American prose, wrote three autobiographies, which helped establish the genre of African American autobiography; authored the first African American novella; and founded as well as edited two African American newspapers.

BIOGRAPHY

Frederick Douglass, renowned abolitionist, orator, journalist, editor, autobiographer, and statesman, was born Frederick Augustus Washington Bailey in February, 1817, at Holme Hill Farm, near Tuckahoe Creek, in Talbot County, Maryland. Douglass was the son of Harriet Bailey, a slave, and a white man. Douglass was the fourth of at least sixth children born to Bailey. At birth, Douglass and his siblings were designated slaves because the law was that a slave mother's status was transferred to her progeny.

From 1818 to 1823, Douglass was raised on Holme Hill Farm by Betsey Bailey, his grandmother. In 1824, Bailey took her grandson to Colonel Edward Lloyd's plantation, where he resided until he moved to Baltimore in 1826. Douglass lived with Hugh and Sophia Auld and was ordered to take care of their two-year-old son. Sophia Auld gave Douglass his first reading lessons. In 1829, Douglass learned to write while working at a shipyard. In 1831, Douglass purchased a used copy of *The Columbia Orator* and was inspired by its speeches on liberty.

In 1834, Douglass was hired out to Edward Covey, a Talbot County farmer who was known for his ability to physically and mentally break slaves. Douglass received frequent beatings from Covey until they fought in August, 1834, and Douglass was never beaten by Covey again. After an unsuccessful escape attempt in 1836, Douglass was jailed before he returned to the Auld residence in Baltimore and learned the caulking trade.

In 1838, Douglass became engaged to Anna Murray, a free African American who worked as a domestic. He was required to give most of his shipyard wages to Hugh Auld, yet he managed to save money for his escape. With additional money from Murray and the seaman's protection papers of a retired sailor, Douglass, dressed as a sailor, boarded a train to Wilmington on September 3, then a steamer to Philadelphia, and finally a train to New York. He arrived in New York on September 4 and used Johnson as his surname. Douglass slept on wharves to avoid detection by slave catchers until he met David Ruggles, who assisted fugitive slaves. Douglass stayed at Ruggles's house and was reunited with Murray; they were married on September 15. The couple moved to New Bedford, Massachusetts. They changed their surname to Douglass, and he worked as a general laborer while Anna took in washing and did domestic work. The Douglasses had five children.

At the 1841 convention of the Massachusetts Anti-Slavery Society, Douglass recounted his life as a slave. The audience was so impressed with his remarks that Douglass became a full-time lecturer for the society. He held the position for four years. In 1845, Douglass's first autobiography, *Narrative of the Life of Frederick Douglass, an American Slave, Written by Himself,* was published. The initial edition of five thousand copies was sold in four months, and more than thirty thousand copies were sold from 1845 to 1850. After the book's publication, Douglass's status as a fugitive slave was in danger; in order to avoid slave catchers, he lectured in England and Ireland for two years. Douglass's freedom was purchased by his British friends in 1846, and in 1847, he returned to the United States.

Douglass and his family moved to Rochester, New York, and with funds from British donors, he founded *North Star*, a weekly newspaper; it was renamed *Frederick Douglass' Paper* when it merged with the *Liberty Party Paper* in 1851. Douglass's newspaper contained editorials that denounced slavery and reported incidents such as the Harpers Ferry raid. In July, 1848, Douglass was the only man who was featured prominently at the Seneca Falls, New York, convention that advocated equal rights for women; this meeting marked the formal start of the women's rights movement in the United States. On July 5, 1852, Douglass delivered his most memorable speech, *What to the Slave Is the Fourth of July?* In March, 1853, Douglass's novella, *The Heroic Slave*, based on a mutiny aboard the slave ship *Creole* and considered the first work of long fiction in African American literature, was published in Julia Griffiths's edited collection of antislavery works, *Autographs for Freedom*. Douglass's second autobiography, *My Bondage and My Freedom*, was published in 1855. In 1858, he established *Douglass' Monthly*. *Frederick Douglass' Paper* was published until 1860, and *Douglass' Monthly* was published until 1863. Douglass's Rochester printing shop was a stop on the Underground Railroad, and he helped more than four hundred slaves escape to Canada.

On June 2, 1852, fire destroyed Douglass's home and the only complete archive of his newspapers, and the Douglass family relocated to Washington, D.C. While residing in the nation's capital, Douglass began a new career as a statesman as he was appointed assistant secretary of the Commission on the Annexation of Santo Domingo by President Ulysses Grant in 1871, District of Columbia marshall by President Rutherford Hayes in 1877, recorder of deeds of the District of Columbia by President James Garfield in 1881, and consul general to Haiti by President Benjamin Harrison in 1889. Douglass's additional honors included being nominated in 1872 for the vice presidency on the Equal Rights Party's ticket; however, he supported Grant's reelection, and in 1874, Douglass was named president of the Freedman's Savings and Trust Company. His third autobiography, *Life and Times of Frederick Douglass, Written by Himself,* was published in 1881, and one year later, an expanded edition was printed. Also in 1882, Anna Douglass died in August after suffering a stroke in July. In 1884, Douglass married Helen Pints, a white woman who was his former clerk at the Office of Record of Deeds and was active in the women's rights movement. Two years later, they traveled to Great Britain, France, Italy, Greece, and Egypt.

Douglass, who fled from slavery and became one of the nineteenth century's most influential leaders, died at his Washington residence after a heart attack on February 20, 1895. Only hours earlier, he delivered a speech at the National Convention of Women. Thus, to the very end of his life, Douglass was a crusader for freedom.

ANALYSIS

Narrative of the Life of Frederick Douglass, an American Slave, Written by Himself, My Bondage and My Freedom, and *Life and Times of Frederick Douglass, Written by Himself* are landmark publications, yet they are not the earliest African American autobiographies. African American prose and more specifically, African American autobiography begin with *A Narrative of the Uncommon Sufferings and Surprizing Deliverance of Briton Hammond, a Negro Man* (1760). Hammond's fourteen-page memoir is the first published slave narrative, and other slave narratives that predate Douglass's three autobiographies include *A Narrative of the Most Remarkable Particulars in the Life of James Albert Ukawsaw Gronniosaw, an African Prince, as Related by Himself* (1772) and *The Interesting Narrative of the Life of Olaudah Equiano, or Gustavus Vassa, the African, Written by Himself* (1789). Frances Smith Foster, in *Witnessing Slavery: The Development of Ante-bellum Slave Narratives* (1979), states that the total number of slave narratives written or dictated in formats ranging from interviews of a single page to books is at least six thousand. However, *Narrative of the Life of Frederick Douglass* is considered the preeminent slave narrative and a classic in American literature. Douglass's two additional autobiographies are expansions of *Narrative of the Life of Frederick Douglass.*

Douglass's autobiographical trilogy documents his journey from slavery to freedom. *Narrative of the Life of Frederick Douglass* recounts his life from birth to his arrival in New Bedford in 1838 as a fugitive slave and a married man. *My Bondage and My Freedom*, published eight years after Douglass's British friends purchased his freedom, reveals more details about his escape from Maryland and his activities as an abolitionist; Douglass, who also discusses his twenty-one-month stay in Great Britain, ends his second autobiography with his return to the United States and his founding of *North Star*. *Life and Times of Frederick Douglass* covers the same information contained in the first two autobiographies and highlights Douglass's activities leading up to the Civil War, during the war, and after the war. *Narrative of the Life of Frederick Douglass*, as Douglass states in chapter 10, shows how as a boy, he becomes a slave and how as a seventeen-year-old slave, he becomes a man. In *My Bondage and My Freedom*, Douglass becomes an abolitionist, and in *Life and Times of Frederick Douglass*, he becomes a statesman. Thus, in each autobiography, Douglass expands his persona. Douglass, as well as other slave narrators, were the first African American authors who seized the opportunities to write extended accounts of African American life. Prior to the slave narrators, most published prose images of African Americans were created by non-African Americans who usually portrayed African Americans in a false and unflattering manner. Douglass and his contemporaries were the first to offer self-definitions of the African American experience.

Douglass's first-person narratives offer his accounts of slave life, yet the three autobiographies are more than his story; the subtitle of his first autobiography identifies him as an American slave. Thus, he writes for the multitude of enslaved men and women who were unable to write or tell their own stories. The subtitle is also Douglass's audacious indictment: How could America, the land of the free, permit slavery to exist and thrive on its very shores? Each of Douglass's autobiographies contains incidents of slaves who endured greater examples of "man's inhumanity to man" than that which Douglass suffered.

The first chapter of each of Douglass's autobiographies begins with a number of negative statements. He does not know his exact birth date. He does not know the identity of his father. He does not have many memories of his mother. He does not have any contact with his grandmother after 1824. Although each autobiography begins in un-

certainty, Douglass ends each one on a triumphant note. He enjoys conditional freedom at the end of *Narrative of the Life of Frederick Douglass*, he rejoices after his manumission at the end of *My Bondage and My Freedom*, and he takes pride in his life's work at the end of *Life and Times of Frederick Douglass*.

Throughout each work, Douglass employs objectivity. While he is quick to document the many injustices to slaves, Douglass also criticizes them. For example, they are victims of discrimination, yet some feel superior to their fellow slaves simply because their masters are wealthier and own more slaves. In addition to documenting slavery's harmful effects on African Americans, Douglass describes how slavery hurts slave owners as well. The most memorable example is Sophia Auld, whose gentle disposition disappears after the arrival of Douglass, her first slave.

Although each autobiography's emphasis on slavery is obvious, *My Bondage and My Freedom* as well as *Life and Times of Frederick Douglass* provide additional insight into nineteenth century African American life: They offer glimpses into black middle-class life, since the Douglasses resided in New Bedford, Rochester, and Washington, D.C.

Douglass wrote his first autobiography to document slavery's horrors; critics have asserted that he wrote his third autobiography so people would not forget slavery's injustices.

LIFE AND TIMES OF FREDERICK DOUGLASS, WRITTEN BY HIMSELF

First published: 1881
Type of work: Autobiography

Douglass, born into slavery, gains his freedom and becomes one of America's most dedicated abolitionists as well as the nineteenth century's preeminent African American leader.

Life and Times of Frederick Douglass, Written by Himself documents the author's life in the 1800's, a century that includes Douglass's birth in its second decade and his ascension to governmental appointments during the 1870's and 1880's. Douglass's third autobiography is divided into three sections. Part 1, in the same manner as Douglass's earlier autobiographies, focuses on the first twenty years of Douglass's life as a slave in Maryland. *Life and Times of Frederick Douglass* is an autobiographical *Bildungsroman* that is more than Douglass's coming-of-age story; it is also an eloquent narrative of Douglass's choosing to live his life as a free man instead of living his life as a slave owner's chattel. Among the most memorable scenes in part 1 are five incidents prior to Douglass's tenth birthday: his mother, whenever she could, walks twelve miles to visit the son separated from her by slavery and walks twelve miles back to the neighboring plantation before sunrise; his aunt Esther's beating by her master because she had visited her beau; Demby, a slave who is frequently beaten by the overseer, is again whipped by him, yet Demby manages to break away, runs into the creek, refuses to come out of the water, and is shot to death; a slave girl who sleeps while her mistress's baby cries is murdered by the irate mistress; and Douglass realizes education is the pathway from slavery to freedom after his master becomes enraged when he discovers his wife teaching young Douglass to read. The most significant incident in part 1 is Douglass's self-empowerment after a two-hour battle with Covey, the infamous slave breaker; Douglass boldly announces that while society views him as a slave, he no longer considers himself one. Consequently, he plans his escape, and when it is unsuccessful, he remains obdurate as he plans another escape. Part 1 ends with Douglass fleeing slavery on September 3, 1838.

Part 2 begins with Douglass's journey to freedom. As with Douglass's years spent as a slave, *Life and Times of Frederick Douglass* divulges more details about Douglass's career as an abolitionist than do *Narrative of the Life of Frederick Douglass* and *My Bondage and My Freedom*. Part 2 of *Life and Times of Frederick Douglass* highlights Douglass's antislavery activities before and after his freedom is purchased. Among Douglass's endeavors as an abolitionist recounted in the third autobiography are his oratories at antislavery rallies and conventions, a two-year lecture tour in England and Ireland, founding of *North Star* and *Douglass' Monthly*, his association with other well-known African American and white abolitionists, and using his Rochester, New York, printing shop as a haven for fugitive slaves. Part 2 also reveals Douglass's activities during the Civil

War, including his recruitment of African American soldiers for the Fifty-fourth and Fifty-fifth Colored Regiments as well as Douglass's meeting with President Abraham Lincoln at the White House on behalf of the African American troops. In part 2, Douglass mentions that his house was destroyed by fire, but arguably the most interesting event in this section is Douglass's encounter with his former master's granddaughter, who had read Douglass's *Narrative of the Life of Frederick Douglass* and freed all of her slaves when they became

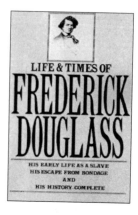

of age. Parts 2 and 3 highlight Douglass's presidential appointments. Part 3 also details Douglass's European tour. The final paragraph of *Life and Times of Frederick Douglass* finds Douglass summarizing his life, expressing his gratitude, believing that he did not accomplish great things, and stating that his life was not in vain.

Summary

Frederick Douglass remains an icon in American history. His three published autobiographies span the years 1818 to 1891 (four years prior to his death). Thus, *Narrative of the Life of Frederick Douglass, an American Slave*; *My Bondage and My Freedom*; and *Life and Times of Frederick Douglass* are a rare legacy. Douglass's autobiographies are also valuable as landmark publications in African American prose literature. Douglass and his fellow slave autobiographers influenced the early African American novelists such as William Wells Brown, a slave autobiographer and author of *Clotel* (1853); Frank J. Webb, author of *The Garies and Their Friends* (1857); and Frances E. W. Harper, author of *Iola Leroy* (1892). Douglass and his contemporaries have also influenced the works of twentieth and twenty-first century novelists such as Arna Bontemps, Octavia Butler, Barbara Chase-Riboud, Margaret Walker Alexander, Ernest J. Gaines, Alex Haley, Charles Johnson, Edward P. Jones, Toni Morrison, Lalita Tademy, and Sherley Anne Williams, all of whom evoke images of slavery in their writing. Douglass's additional contributions include speeches such as his 1852 oration, *What to the Slave Is the Fourth of July?* and his periodicals, *North Star,* which was renamed *Frederick Douglass' Papers,* and *Douglass' Monthly.* Thus, Douglass remains an important historical and literary figure for future generations.

Linda M. Carter

BIBLIOGRAPHY

By the Author

NONFICTION:
Narrative of the Life of Frederick Douglass, an American Slave, Written by Himself, 1845
What to the Slave Is the Fourth of July?, 1852
The Claims of the Negro Ethnologically Considered, 1854
The Anti-Slavery Movement: A Lecture, 1855
My Bondage and My Freedom, 1855
Two Speeches by Frederick Douglass, 1857
The Constitution of the United States: Is It Pro-Slavery or Anti-Slavery? A Speech, 1860
Life and Times of Frederick Douglass, Written by Himself, 1881, revised 1892
The Lessons of the Hour, 1894
Frederick Douglass: Selected Speeches and Writings, 1999 (Philip S. Foner, editor)

LONG FICTION:
The Heroic Slave, 1853

EDITED TEXTS:
North Star, 1847-1851
Frederick Douglass' Paper, 1851-1860
Douglass' Monthly, 1859-1863
New National Era, 1870-1874

MISCELLANEOUS:
The Frederick Douglass Papers, 1979-1992 (5 volumes)
The Oxford Frederick Douglass Reader, 1996 (William L. Andrews, editor)

About the Author
Andrews, William L., ed. *Critical Essays on Frederick Douglass.* Boston: G. K. Hall, 1991.
Chander, Harish. "Frederick Douglass." In *African American Autobiographers: A Sourcebook,* edited by Emmanuel S. Nelson. Westport, Conn.: Greenwood Press, 2002.
Gass, T. Anthony. "Frederick Douglass." In *Notable Black American Men,* edited by Jessie Carney Smith. Detroit: Gale, 1999.
Huggins, Nathan I. *Slave and Citizen: The Life of Frederick Douglass.* Boston: Little, Brown, 1980.
McFeely, William S. *Frederick Douglass.* New York: W. W. Norton, 1991.
Preston, Dickson J. *Young Frederick Douglass: The Maryland Years.* Baltimore: Johns Hopkins University Press, 1980.
Quarles, Benjamin. *Frederick Douglass.* Englewood Cliffs, N.J.: Prentice-Hall, 1968.

DISCUSSION TOPICS

- It is obvious that not all slaves reacted to their bondage in the same manner. Provide examples from Frederick Douglass's writing of the various ways slaves reacted to being the legal property of another.

- Provide examples from *Life and Times of Frederick Douglass, Written by Himself* that show an individual's resiliency.

- What ironic incidents are found in *Life and Times of Frederick Douglass, Written by Himself?*

- Describe life in nineteenth century United States as Douglass knew it.

- Provide examples that prove Douglass was a courageous man.

- Are the literary aspects of Douglass's autobiographies overshadowed by the historical aspects?

- After Douglass obtained his freedom, he could have lived a private life, a life where his only concerns would be related to earning a living and taking care of his family. Why did he not live his life in this manner?

- Why should twenty-first century individuals read slave narratives?

RITA DOVE

Born: Akron, Ohio
August 28, 1952

Although she has published fiction, Dove is known primarily for her Pulitzer Prize-winning poetry.

Fred Viebahn

BIOGRAPHY

Rita Dove was born in the highly industrialized city of Akron, Ohio, on August 28, 1952. On her mother's side, her family had well-established roots in this northern urban center, and they had achieved a certain level of comfort and prosperity. Her father's side of the family had moved to the North during the great migration of African Americans that took place in the years after World War I. Brought up in a strict but loving environment, Rita Dove became a precocious and highly inquisitive young student. Her first attempt at writing was a childhood story titled "The Rabbit with a Droopy Ear." The young author solved the rabbit's problem and straightened his ear by having him hang upside down from a tree.

The city of Akron left a deep and lasting impression on Dove's mind. The parks and hilly streets, the Goodyear rubber and tire factories, and the Quaker Oats oatmeal plant all became graphic images that she employed in the poetry and fiction of her mature life. In a real sense, Dove never left Akron.

After completing high school in Akron, Dove moved to the college town of Oxford, Ohio, to continue her education at Miami University. The surrounding countryside, with its barns and silos and its abundant corn and bean fields, also left her with vivid memories that she would later use in her writing. After her graduation from Miami University,

Dove moved to Germany to continue her studies at the Universität Tübingen. While in Germany, she met her husband, the novelist Fred Viebahn, with whom she had a daughter, Aviva. She returned to the United States to study at the prestigious Iowa Writers' Workshop at the University of Iowa. In 1977, she received an M.F.A. in creative writing from Iowa and joined the ranks of the school's famous graduates, many of whom were regular contributors to literary publications such as *The American Poetry Review, Georgia Review,* and *Poetry.*

With this rich and complicated background, Dove began to publish widely in little magazines. Her first book of poems, *The Yellow House on the Corner* (1980), appeared when she was twenty-eight, and it was soon followed by a second book of poems, *Museum* (1983). Both of these books bear the strong influence of the Iowa Writers' Workshop: They contain many surrealistic poems and literary imitations in a style made famous by that university program. The poems are still undeniable literary accomplishments, but Dove had not yet come entirely into her own.

That situation was to change dramatically with the publication of Dove's first book of prose, a collection of short stories titled *Fifth Sunday* (1985), and a masterful volume of narrative poems titled *Thomas and Beulah* (1986). Dove was clearly speaking in her own unique voice and following the inspiration of her own poetic muse, a fact recognized by a national literary audience; in 1987, she was awarded the Pulitzer Prize for poetry. In a short time, she published *Grace Notes* (1989), a singularly beautiful book of lyric poems, and *Through the Ivory Gate* (1992), a highly poetic novel that makes extensive use of autobiographical details. The years from 1980 to 1992 represented a period of remarkable literary growth and achievement for Dove; in the space of twelve short years, she produced six important volumes. In 1995, she published *Mother Love*, a poetry collection which was then followed by *On the Bus with Rosa Parks* (1999) and *American Smooth* (2004).

All this literary output was rewarded with many literary honors besides the Pulitzer Prize. Dove won a grant from the National Endowment for the Arts and a Guggenheim Foundation Fellowship, and she received the General Electric Foundation Award and the Ohio Governor's Award. In addition, she was presented with honorary doctorates from Miami University and Knox College. She has taught creative writing at Arizona State University and the University of Virginia and served briefly as a Fellow at the National Humanities Center in North Carolina. In 1993, Dove became the first black author to serve as poet laureate of the United States, an honor that also made her the poetry consultant to the Library of Congress. She was poet laureate from 1993 to 1995, and in 2002 was named a member of the Council of Scholars of the Library of Congress. She is Commonwealth Professor of English at the University of Virginia in Charlottesville.

ANALYSIS

The title of Dove's *Grace Notes* might well serve as a metaphor for her basic strategy as a writer, for everything she writes is, to some extent, a "grace note," a subtle embellishment or addition to the basic "melody" of experience. Dove's attention as a poet is always on the overtones, the implications, the echoes, and reverberations of meaning that somehow surround even the simplest of plain facts. "Silos," the poem that opens the first section of *Grace Notes*, is a telling example of this powerful tendency in her writing.

At first glance, a group of silos may not seem like a very promising subject. Silos are merely humble receptacles for storing grain. They are the plain, generic landmarks of the Midwest, largely ignored and unconsciously accepted by nearly everyone who sees them—except, that is, the poet. For Dove, the white silos represent a marvelous string of metaphorical possibilities, even if they are "too white and/ suddenly there." She rejects the obvious similarities, refusing to see the silos as "swans," "fingers," "xylophones," or "Pan's pipes." Instead, she

sides with the children who recognize them as a huge "packet of chalk." She ends with her own favorite comparisons, suggesting erotic, surreal, and anatomical possibilities for looking at silos: "They were masculine toys. They were tall wishes. They/ were the ribs of the modern world." The point is that if Dove can make such an artistic production from the simplicity of silos, then anything becomes a possible—and fruitful—subject matter for her art.

Grace Notes as a title and silos as a subject are also ways of talking about the two poles that define the boundaries of Dove's writing—the aesthetic and the autobiographical. The concept of "grace notes" is eminently aesthetic, the product of a mind that is steeped in music. Indeed, musical references abound in Dove's work. The heroine of *Through the Ivory Gate* is a cellist. *Fifth Sunday*, Dove's short-story collection, contains a piece titled "The Vibraphone" that concerns a classical pianist who turns to jazz and "new age" music. Thomas of *Thomas and Beulah* also happens to be a musician, a gifted mandolin player.

Musical cues are not the only aesthetic concerns voiced in Dove's work. The cellist-heroine of *Through the Ivory Gate* is also a talented actress and puppeteer. *Grace Notes* even contains a poem titled "Ars Poetica" (the art of poetry), as if to signal the reader that these poems are not only about things but also about the nature of art itself. In fact, Dove, although she wears her learning lightly, is a profoundly cultured woman who often makes delicate and appropriate references to the great composers and artists of the Western world. Each section of *Grace Notes*, for example, opens with an epigraph or quotation from such writers as Toni Morrison, David McFadden, Hélène Cixous, and Claude McKay.

The mention of African American writers such as Morrison and McKay brings the reader to the other pole of Dove's literary world—the realm of autobiography and the self. Dove is clearly not a "black" writer in the manner of such poets as Maya Angelou or Gwendolyn Brooks, nor is she overtly concerned with African American history in the manner of novelists Alex Haley and Richard Wright. Because Dove's mature work began in the late 1970's, she did not feel the need to repeat the highly charged political or social themes of earlier African American writers. Dove, then, could best be described as an African American author who is most concerned about representing art and autobiography in her work—not in putting forth a political agenda, no matter how valid or urgent, and for whom the woman's life is at the center of her work.

Dove's work, however, never omits her African American heritage, nor does it sidestep the issues of racism or bigotry. Her focus, in her poetry and in her fiction, is on the personhood of the voices and characters she evokes. One does not encounter African American stereotypes in Dove's work. Her characters and the voices one hears in her poetry speak wisely and with profound conviction; in fact, one might even argue that Dove has helped to redefine the image of African Americans in American literature.

Dove thus draws upon the totality of her own experience as well as on the history and traditions of her own family, including a musician grandfather, an overbearing mother, and a proudly intellectual father. She recalls, in minute detail, the particulars of specific streets and houses in Akron, the noise and smells of industries, and the various shades of gray taken on by a sky filled with smoke, smog, snow, and the ever-present mists of the Great Lakes. In this connection, the silos from *Grace Notes* become one more talisman, allowing the poet to call up the past.

In like manner, Dove uses her memories of Phoenix and the Arizona desert landscape to great advantage in the flashbacks of *Through the Ivory Gate*, a novel in which the heroine lives in Akron before her family moves to Phoenix. Dove uses memories of Germany in "Poem in Which I Refuse Contemplation" from *Grace Notes*, a poem in which she receives a letter from her African American mother while she is living with her German mother-in-law. The result is a realistic transcription, with quotations from the actual letter, and also an artistic transformation in which autobiographical fact becomes artistic truth. This interplay between art and autobiography is the hallmark of Dove's work, creating everything that is beautiful, memorable, and most human in her writing.

THOMAS AND BEULAH

First published: 1986
Type of work: Poetry

Thomas, an African American man, leaves the South for Ohio, marries Beulah, and raises a large family.

Thomas and Beulah is a tour de force, a virtuoso performance by a major poet operating at the height of her powers. *Thomas and Beulah* takes the form of a two-part book of narrative poems that collectively tell the stories of Thomas (in "Mandolin," the book's first part) and his wife, Beulah (in "Canary in Bloom," the second part). The parts are meant to be read sequentially and offer the male and female perspectives on some seventy years of private history. The two parts are followed by a "Chronology" that provides an imagined framework of the critical years in the married life of Thomas, a mandolin player and talented tenor, and Beulah, his proud and sometimes unforgiving spouse. The poems are a mixture of lush imagery involving food, musical instruments, cars, and weather, as well as quotations from songs and specimens of actual "Negro" speech. Although the poems form interlocking units, many of them (such as "The Zeppelin Factory" and "Pomade") are self-sufficient and freestanding works of art that could be read individually, without reference to the book as a whole.

The story is a fairly simple one, even if the reader must fill in some gaps. Thomas takes a riverboat and leaves Tennessee. After two years of rambling and playing his mandolin, he settles in Akron, where there are many good jobs, and where Beulah's family has already established itself after leaving Georgia. Thomas cuts a dashing figure, with his mandolin and fancy clothes, and becomes a womanizer. Beulah is naturally suspicious of him, but they eventually marry, and his dalliances with various women ("canaries") cease as he becomes a respectable family man, a member of the church choir, and, finally, a grandfather. Beulah takes up dressmaking. Thomas dies in 1963, the year of the March on Washington, and Beulah dies six years later.

Thomas is captured in poems such as "Jiving" (about his mandolin playing), "The Zeppelin Factory," and "Aircraft" (about his work at the Goodyear plant). "Roast Possum," though, epitomizes the man and his unique speech, as he talks to his granddaughters in language that is both colloquial and literary. He uses similes and metaphors to dramatize the possum's ferocity ("teeth bared like a shark's" and "torpedo snout"), ending his description with a folksy twist as he notes that even the possum was no match "for old-time know-how."

Beulah comes to life in such poems as "Dusting," in which she dusts every item in the house while trying to recall the name of a long-forgotten boyfriend—Maurice, the final word of the poem. "Weathering Out" shows her wobbling around the house during the awkward months of pregnancy. "Pomade" is perhaps the finest of the "Beulah" poems; in it, Beulah is revealed as a poetess who reminisces about a backwoods recipe for making pomade. She experiences a flashback that is triggered by Thomas's coming home with a catfish and tracking mud on her kitchen floor. At the end of the poem, while the catfish "grins/ like an oriental gentleman," she has an epiphany, a moment of pure spirituality, in which she momentarily feels herself "rolling down the sides of the earth."

GRACE NOTES

First published: 1989
Type of work: Poetry

This work shows that everyday events and unnoticed objects can be turned into art if looked at properly.

On the surface, *Grace Notes* might almost seem to be a kind of poetic autobiography. As a book, it is neatly divided into five discrete sections, and this five-part format corresponds, in a general way, to phases in Dove's life. The first section deals with childhood memories, the second with her thirtieth

birthday, and the third with her daughter, Aviva. The last sections, however, do not seem to follow this pattern of personal evolutionary growth, at least not on first reading. Sections 4 and 5 contain poems with such titles as "Ars Poetica," "Medusa," "Genie's Prayer Under the Kitchen Sink," "Obbligato," and "Lint." Yet these poems also represent part of the artistic evolution of the poet, because the most sophisticated growth occurs on the spiritual and artistic planes. The final poems thus reveal general truths about art discovered by personal meditation on items as ordinary and ubiquitous as lint.

Grace Notes is such a remarkable example of poetic craftsmanship that it might almost serve as a textbook for literary devices. Similes and metaphors abound in this little masterpiece. In the poem titled "Hully Gully," the moon is "riding the sky/ like a drop of oil on water." In "Horse and Tree," the entire poem becomes a complex metaphor linking horses and trees; the rider of a beautiful tree-horse experiences the magical sensation of "hair blown to froth."

Many of the poems in *Grace Notes*, however, deal with entirely personal matters—the poet as a ten-year-old child responding to flash cards, the poet's mother, and especially her daughter, Aviva. One of the most moving and tender poems in this group is the mother-daughter poem with the improbably long title of "After Reading Mickey in the Night Kitchen for the Third Time Before Bed." The poem describes the mother's responses to her three-year-old daughter's questions about sex and the mysteries of menstruation and genitals. "She demands," the poet explains,

> to see mine and momentarily
> we're a lopsided star
> among the spilled toys,
> my prodigious scallops
> exposed to her neat cameo.

If "scallops" and "cameo" can serve as metaphors for the most intimate parts of the female body, then a nasty cut on the arm can become an emblem for an opening in the poet's identity. She may be a proud African American person, but she nevertheless dwells on the puzzle of skin color. In "Stitches," after falling and receiving a gash on her arm, she immediately focuses on one thought: "So I am white underneath." But even this bloody moment of self-recognition is transformed immediately into "grace notes," as the ministering physician's teeth are seen as "beavery, yellow." He sews up her wound, and the "skin's tugged up by his thread/ like a trout." In fact, the poet chides herself for being so clever in a moment of pain: "You just can't stop being witty, can you?" Yet the wittiness extends even to the punning title; her elaborate poetic "jokes" have, in effect, kept her and her audience in "stitches." Once again, Dove and her readers have been sustained by the exquisite grace notes that resonate powerfully, and unforgettably, in all of her poems.

THROUGH THE IVORY GATE

First published: 1992
Type of work: Novel

Virginia King, a recent college graduate, returns to her hometown to teach children about puppetry.

Although Rita Dove is known primarily as a poet, *Through the Ivory Gate* offers eloquent proof that she is a talented storyteller capable of spinning a highly readable yarn. Virginia King, the sensitive and highly introspective young heroine of the novel, has just graduated from college with an acting degree as well as a strong commitment to playing the cello. Unable to do either one professionally, she takes a brief job with a troupe of puppeteers. She lands a job in her hometown of Akron spending a month as an artist-in-residence at a local elementary school, where she instructs the children in the art of puppetry.

One of the little girls idolizes Virginia and becomes strongly attached to her, as does Terence, the father of one of her young puppeteers. There

are no startling, dramatic moments in the book; the month in Akron is largely an opportunity for Virginia to rediscover her childhood roots and relive (through flashbacks) the most important moments in her life. The point of the book seems to be the way that Virginia defines her life internally; she lives, as it were, in the confines of her powerful imagination and memory. Although she becomes romantically attached to Terence, she leaves Akron at the end of the month with her future still unclear. This interlude, though, has allowed her to take an inventory of her life, thereby defining herself as an artist. At last, she has found the courage to make this supreme commitment, and the book ends at the precise moment her new life begins.

The title of the novel refers to a passage in which the Greek poet Homer describes all human dreams and fantasies as the process of passing through one of two gates, the gate of horn (for dreams that become reality) and the gate of ivory (for dreams that remain pure fantasy and illusion). Virginia's journey to self-discovery includes scenes of racial confusion: She throws away a new black doll in favor of a white one; later, she is rejected by a white friend with the stinging epithet "Nigger!" Virginia's quest also includes many false starts in which she tries on other artistic hats, first as a baton twirler, then as an actress, and finally as a cellist. The novel is filled with discussions of art and technique (baton twirling, cello suites, and Javanese shadow puppets).

As Virginia unravels these clues to her own psyche, she is simultaneously visiting her relatives and unlocking family mysteries—including the mystery of an incestuous affair between her father and her aunt Carrie (a scene based verbatim on the story "Aunt Carrie" from her earlier collection of short stories *Fifth Sunday*). One's true identity is always difficult to discover; as this novel beautifully demonstrates, however, the most elusive of all identities is that of the artist.

MOTHER LOVE

First published: 1995
Type of work: Poetry

This collection shows the joys and pains of mother love through a variety of real and mythical figures.

Published during Rita Dove's tenure as poet laureate, *Mother Love* shows her grace and skill as a poet. The title announces the subject clearly, but the poems have a range of emotion and observation that surprises the reader continually. The figures behind the poems are Persephone and Demeter, a daughter and mother who learn to be together and apart. Real places and other mothers and daughters blend with the mythic. Stylistically, the poems have a range, but most of them are sonnets—not traditional sonnets, but sonnets nevertheless—and the concluding section is a crown of sonnets associating Demeter and Persephone with a woman's relationship with the earth that mirrors her, and with the whole mother-daughter cycle of love and loss. The poet herself slips into the cycle too, as another face of woman. Dove comments in her introduction that "The Demeter/Persephone cycle of betrayal and regeneration is ideally suited for this [sonnet] form since all three—mother-goddess, daughter-consort, and poet—are struggling to sing in their chains."

The first poem, "Heroes," although not a sonnet, is a nightmarish representation of a woman's mixed feelings of desperation, responsibility, and guilt. It reads, in fact, like a bad dream—the person addressed as "you" picks a poppy in the field and asks at a nearby house for a jar of water to preserve it, but the woman of the house "starts/ screaming: you've picked the last poppy/ in her miserable garden . . ." The main character addressed as "you" starts apologizing, then hits the woman, who falls and strikes her head. The thief has to flee, terrified and ashamed, with the stolen flower. "Oh why/ did you pick that idiot flower?" The poem concludes. "Because it was the last one/ and you knew/ it was going to die."

The subjects of the book converge in this dreamlike parable: Persephone is picking flowers when abducted, the poet is in some ways a thief, and a woman's life of mothering and being mothered is fraught with the kind of anxiety that this poem evokes—terror of harming instead of nurturing, of being blamed for destruction when the intent was to preserve. The poem suggests that a woman cannot avoid her fate as a woman, which is to be nurturer and destroyer.

The power in these poems is in the blend of reality and myth; the sonnet "Missing" is a prime example. The speaker is a daughter who is missing and has various identities: Persephone and any missing daughter (and broadly, any daughter) who at some point in her life is "missing" to her mother. She comments that "nothing marked my 'last/ known whereabouts,' not a single glistening petal." She is "returned" and watches her mother's reception of her explanations: It seems almost as though the speaker is mother and daughter at once, the missing and the one who misses. The poem pulls subtle strings in its analysis of the mother-daughter relationship.

"Persephone Abducted" is also a sonnet, this time describing the abduction of the daughter from an ambiguous point of view, the "we" who may represent the point of view of those left. The poem explores the grief of the mother who cannot fathom her loss. The standard answers for grief do not apply in real cases: "Some say there's nourishment for pain,/ and call it Philosophy." However, that is "for the birds," who are, in fact, the birds of prey—hawk and vulture. There is no answer to loss except endurance and acceptance of fate.

The loss of Persephone and Demeter's rage and grief blur with other stories of mothers and daughters, evoking all daughters' departures, whether voluntary or involuntary, temporary or permanent. Reading the collection is painful because mother-love is so intermingled with mother-loss—whether it is the child or the mother who is removed—that its brief patches of sunlight and joy seem few. "Statistic: The Witness" seems to blend Persephone's story with that of a young woman abducted. The speaker begins "No matter where I turn, she is there/ screaming." The speaker tries various means of forgetting, but cannot—the tiniest details of the abduction obsess her and will not pass from her mind. The speaker cannot forget, and so she turns to the earth—the ultimate mother whose "green oblivion" will finally obliterate what she has seen. As in other poems, the contemporary is superimposed on the mythic—mother and Mother Earth, the abducted child with Persephone—in order to provide an emotional impression of the terrible fragility of motherhood.

The combination of mythic and ordinary is clearest perhaps in "The Bistro Styx," a clever poem in five eccentrically rhyming sonnets which details a luncheon meeting between a mother, the speaker, and her "blighted child," who has given up her own life to be a muse to her lover, an artist. The daughter gives details of her life in what her mother sees as Hades and misses her mother's intimate question about her happiness because she is biting into "the starry rose of a fig"—her version of the fatal pomegranate that Persephone tasted, binding her to Pluto for the winter months. This daughter has clearly made her choice; all her mother can do is resign herself. The poem is highly specific and evocative in its description of restaurant and conversation—it takes the title to remind the reader of the mythic grounding.

Dove's poems in this collection are more open and allusive than in some others and sometimes defy explication, but they communicate with extraordinary clarity to the intuition. The use of the sonnet form is both appropriate and teasing. The poems foreground Dove's lifelong theme of woman's experience as mother and daughter. Some of the poems by their evocative detail reflect her commitment to African American issues, but for the most part the themes of *Mother Love* are universal.

SUMMARY

The character of Virginia King of *Through the Ivory Gate* offers an important clue to the understanding of Dove's work. As Virginia cradles the cello to her body, she experiences the pure physical reality of the instrument—its contours, its weight, and its musical reverberations—but she is also transported by the purely intellectual pleasure of the music she is making. In like manner, she is deeply attracted to the physical beauty of Terence (as she was to Clayton, her first, ill-fated lover). With each man, though, the physical intimacy is merely a prelude to emotional transcendence: "When he touched her again their bodies merged into one long, yearning curve, and the sea rose up to meet them." Like her creator, Virginia is living proof that art and life are not at distant removes from each other. What Dove has shown, again and again, is that art is the most passionate and enduring expression of life itself. And the creation of art, often represented as music, merges in her later work with her notion of motherhood, that kind of nurturance that is creativity itself.

Daniel L. Guillory; updated by Janet McCann

BIBLIOGRAPHY

By the Author

POETRY:
The Yellow House on the Corner, 1980
Museum, 1983
Thomas and Beulah, 1986
Grace Notes, 1989
Selected Poems, 1993
Mother Love, 1995
On the Bus with Rosa Parks, 1999
American Smooth, 2004

LONG FICTION:
Through the Ivory Gate, 1992

SHORT FICTION:
Fifth Sunday, 1985

DISCUSSION TOPICS

- How does Rita Dove represent the lives of African American women?
- What defines motherhood for Dove?
- The role of the artist is a frequent theme in Dove's work. What does she find this role to be? What different kinds of art appear in her works?
- How does Dove use form in her poetry? What does she do with sonnet form that is original and unusual?
- How does Dove use myth in her work?

Rita Dove

DRAMA:
The Darker Face of the Earth, pb. 1994, revised pb. 2000

NONFICTION:
The Poet's World, 1995

EDITED TEXT:
The Best American Poetry, 2000, 2000

About the Author

Bellafante, Ginia. "Poetry in Motion." *Time*, May 31, 1993, 73.

Carlisle, Theodora. "Reading the Scars: Rita Dove's *The Darker Face of the Earth*." *African American Review* 34, no. 1 (Spring, 2000): 135-150.

Conde, Maryse, and Rita Dove. Interview by Mohamed B. Taleb-Khyar. *Callaloo* 14, no. 2 (Spring, 1991): 347.

Dove, Rita, "A Poet's Topics: Jet Lag, Laundry, and Making Her Art Commonplace." Interview by Felicity Barringer. *The New York Times*, June 20, 1993, p. E7.

Ingersoll, Earl G., ed. *Conversations with Rita Dove*. Jackson: University Press of Mississippi, 2003.

Lofgren, Lotta. "Partial Horror: Fragmentation and Healing in Rita Dove's *Mother Love*." *Callaloo* 19, no. 1 (1996): 135-142.

Pereira, Malin. *Rita Dove's Cosmopolitanism*. Urbana: University of Illinois Press, 2003.

Righelato, Pat. "Geometry and Music: Rita Dove's *Fifth Sunday*." *Yearbook of English Studies* 31 (2001): 62-73.

Vendler, Helen. "A Dissonant Triad (Henri Cole, Rita Dove, August Kleinzahler)." *Parnassus* 16, no. 2 (1990): 391.

THEODORE DREISER

Library of Congress

Born: Terre Haute, Indiana
August 27, 1871
Died: Hollywood, California
December 28, 1945

Although known as a naturalistic writer, Dreiser adapted the deterministic philosophy of naturalism by creating characters capable of weighing moral issues and making conscious decisions.

BIOGRAPHY

Theodore Herman Albert Dreiser was the twelfth of thirteen children born to John Paul Dreiser and Sarah Schnepp Dreiser. John Paul Dreiser, a weaver, had come from Mayhen, Germany, in the mid-1840's, settling in New England. After several years, he moved to a German community in Indiana, where he met Sarah, the daughter of a Mennonite farmer. Because Dreiser was unable to find work in this community, he and Sarah eloped to Dayton, Ohio, but returned to Fort Wayne, Indiana, before their first child was born.

At first, the elder Dreiser tried to build a secure life for his family, establishing his own woolen mill at Sullivan, Indiana, in 1867. Unfortunately, the mill burned to the ground just when it was starting to prosper. While Dreiser was supervising the building of a new mill, a ceiling beam slipped from the hands of a workman, striking Dreiser on the head. Following this accident, which resulted in what is now known as minimal brain dysfunction, he lost interest in his mill, as well as his ambition and his ability to hold a steady job. He became fanatical in the practice of his Catholic faith and extremely strict in the discipline of his children.

Sarah Dreiser has often been called the family's financial and emotional mainstay, keeping things together by taking in boarders and laundry. Biographers who understand the family well, however, report that she was inept in handling money, overly lenient with the children (perhaps in compensation for her husband's strictness), and given to fancy and superstition. Although Sarah could be a strong and supportive mother (as she demonstrated when her daughter Maine became pregnant), she could also be "lovingly cruel." When the children were naughty, for example, she threatened to abandon them, once even packing her bag and hiding in a cornfield while the younger ones cried hysterically.

Because Theodore was rather puny as a toddler, Sarah singled him out for special attention, often inviting him to sit at her feet while she sewed. This tender tableau also had a sinister side, however, for she would call the child's attention to her broken shoes, asking him if he did not pity his mother in her poverty. Perhaps because of this repeated experience, Theodore became very aware of women's clothing, especially the condition of their shoes—a detail frequently mentioned in his writing.

Thus, Theodore grew up in an atmosphere of financial instability and emotional conflict. The family moved frequently, which meant that the children's education suffered. Nevertheless, Theodore was an avid reader and educated himself. Although he had completed only one year of high school, he was admitted to Indiana University in 1889 as a special student. Not being academically inclined, however, he dropped out after one year.

During the 1890's, Dreiser worked as a feature reporter for a number of newspapers, among them the Chicago *Globe*, the St. Louis *Globe-Democrat* and

Republic, the Pittsburgh *Dispatch,* and the New York *World.* In addition, he edited *Ev'ry Month,* a musical magazine, and contributed essays, poems, and stories to magazines such as *Harper's, Cosmopolitan, Munsey's,* and *Metropolitan.* While he strove for realism in his magazine stories, Dreiser always tinged them with a subtle sense of optimism.

Dreiser's friend Arthur Henry had been urging him to write a novel but had no idea for a topic. Finally, while Dreiser was visiting at Henry's home, he took a piece of yellow paper and scribbled the title "Sister Carrie," evidently thinking of his sister Emma, whose real life experiences were similar to those of Carrie. From the title to the point when Carrie meets Hurstwood, the novel "wrote itself"; after the Hurstwood incident, however, it moved in a series of spurts and halts. Henry urged Dreiser on, occasionally writing bits of *Sister Carrie* himself to keep the novel going.

Sister Carrie was published by Doubleday in 1900, but its sales were suppressed for seven years on the grounds that it showed a despairing, animalistic view of humanity. The suppression of *Sister Carrie* discouraged Dreiser from trying another novel for nearly a decade, when he began work on *Jennie Gerhardt,* published in 1911. In the meantime, he continued to write short stories and became editor of *Smith's Magazine* and the *Butterick* trio, consisting of *Delineator, Designer,* and *New Ideas for Women.* Through the efforts of a literary agent named Flora Holly, *Sister Carrie* was republished in 1912; this time it was hailed as a work of genius.

Although Dreiser is best known for his novels *Sister Carrie, Jennie Gerhardt, An American Tragedy* (1925), and the Cowperwood trilogy—*The Financier* (1912), *The Titan* (1914), and *The Stoic* (1947)—he also published collections of poems, stories, and essays as well as several plays, a biography, and book-length treatises. Two of his novels, *The Bulwark* (1946) and *The Stoic,* were published posthumously.

In 1927, Dreiser visited the Soviet Union at the Russians' expense. Not entirely enchanted with this nation (he was appalled by the crowded and unsanitary housing), he nevertheless admired the Soviets' efforts to educate the workers and make their places of employment safe and clean. Dreiser's exposure to Soviet Communism "hit home" during the Great Depression. Throughout these bleak years, he traveled around the United States, writing and lecturing for reform in such areas as prison codes, birth control, and employment laws. Moreover, in 1931, the Department of International Labor Defense asked him to investigate labor conditions in the mines of Bell and Harlan Counties, Kentucky. These activities on behalf of workers may have induced Dreiser to join the Communist Party in 1945.

He married twice. His first wife was Sarah Osborne White, nicknamed "Jug." Unfortunately, Dreiser so idealized his wife that marital relations were difficult. They separated in 1910, and Dreiser took as his mistress Helen Patges, a young divorcée, whom he married after Jug's death in 1941. Dreiser died of a heart attack on December 28, 1945.

ANALYSIS

Dreiser is best known as a leading American naturalist writer. Naturalism, a literary trend which began in France and reached the United States in the 1880's, depicted life realistically, often concentrating on the lower classes of society. Naturalism held that the lives of human beings were determined by circumstances and inborn traits, or drives. Thus, people acted purely on instinct, had no free will, and were unable to change. This philosophy of human life consequently gave naturalistic writing a depressing and pessimistic tone.

The name most frequently associated with French naturalism is Émile Zola, but when Dreiser wrote *Sister Carrie,* he had not read any of Zola's work. Neither had he read *McTeague* (1899), the recently published novel of American naturalist Frank Norris, who acclaimed *Sister Carrie* as wonderful. Although Dreiser had read the works of such writers as Honoré de Balzac, Charles Darwin, the philosopher Herbert Spencer, and the British novelist Thomas Hardy, it is doubtful that his view of human nature derived as much from the theories of others as from his own observations of his family and the people he interviewed as a feature reporter.

Events of fate, such as the mill fire and the brain injury that had wiped out his father's early ambition, had probably made it clear to Dreiser that people's lives are not entirely under their own control. As three of his sisters had become mistresses or given birth to illegitimate children, he may have also reached the conclusion that human libido was a stronger force than any moral precepts established by church or society.

Nevertheless, Dreiser's works do not follow the theory of naturalism to the letter. Although his characters' lives and actions are strongly influenced by their youthful environments and their own innate personalities, he does not present them simply as animals or robots at the mercy of nature or outside forces; Dreiser's characters are real. They make thoughtful and conscious decisions—proving the existence of free will—even though these decisions are often guided by outside events, and some characters show the potential for positive change. Moreover, while Dreiser's works are somber, they are not totally pessimistic. Although the conclusions to *Sister Carrie, Jennie Gerhardt,* and *An American Tragedy* are far from happy, each contains a subtle hint of hope for the characters, provided the reader chooses to interpret them in that way.

Despite his deviations from theoretical naturalism, however, Dreiser still believed that most people are in the firm clutches of money and sex, which he considered the strongest and most basic of human drives. The drive toward money is obvious in all of Dreiser's major novels. Sex is equally powerful, but Dreiser presents it as more than a simple physical instinct. To the male characters, sexual conquests imply possession and confidence. After Jennie Gerhardt has yielded to her first lover, for example, he tells her that she belongs to him. Clyde, in *An American Tragedy,* assures himself that as one young woman has given herself to him freely, there must be others willing to do the same.

Among Dreiser's female characters (with the possible exception of Roberta Alden, in *An American Tragedy,* who appears to regard it as a genuine physical pleasure as well as an expression of deep love), sex is viewed either as the means to an end or as an instrument of control. Sex as the gateway to a higher standard of living is a major theme in both *Sister Carrie* and *Jennie Gerhardt,* but its controlling aspect comes forth more obviously in *An American Tragedy,* wherein Clyde becomes attracted to Roberta, a shop girl whose meager salary cannot afford an expensive fur coat she ardently desires. Not really caring for Clyde, but sensing his pliability regarding her wishes, she bribes him into buying the coat on the installment plan by promising sex once the coveted garment is in her possession.

Sondra Finchley uses sexual control in a more subtle form. She keeps Clyde at bay by insinuating that in the mores of her society—to which Clyde aspires to belong—sex does not occur before the wedding. While Dreiser had abandoned the practice of Catholicism quite early and no longer had faith in a personal God, his belief in the driving power of money and sex alienated him from all forms of organized religion. He believed that their moral teachings tried to change people from what nature intended them to be: sexual and material beings, enjoying the good, sensual things of life. Dreiser usually portrayed churches in a negative manner.

Many critics have objected that Dreiser's writing is cumbersome and overly descriptive. His descriptions, however, can often be enlightening. His detailed portrayals of street scenes in *Sister Carrie,* for example, give realistic pictures of Chicago and New York in the 1890's; his digression into the steps involved in shirt manufacturing in *An American Tragedy* provides information about that industry in the early twentieth century. Moreover, Dreiser's minute descriptions of certain characters, from their broken shoes to their frayed cuffs, help the reader to feel compassion for these people in the unfortunate circumstances which are probably beyond their control.

At times, Dreiser does tend to tell about his characters instead of "showing" them through their own words and actions. Furthermore, he frequently interrupts his narrative to philosophize on human nature in general. While it may be annoying to some readers, this habit serves a purpose. Not only does it arouse empathy for fictional characters, but it also reminds the reader that the problems of these characters are those of the entire human race. Dreiser compensates for any heaviness in his style by producing tightly knit plots that move chronologically. Furthermore, while his novels contain a few symbols, he does not overload his writing with them. In some ways, therefore, his works are easier to read than modern novels. They continue to have value, for they treat human dramas that have always existed and will always exist.

SISTER CARRIE

First published: 1900
Type of work: Novel

A young woman uses her relationships with men as stepping-stones in her quest for material beauty.

Although Carrie Meeber, the protagonist of *Sister Carrie*, may seem somewhat shallow in her preoccupation with clothing and popular entertainment, she has been called a seeker of beauty. Carrie has grown up in an impoverished rural district, probably knowing only the essentials of life. To her, luxuries such as fashionable clothes, theaters, and elegant restaurants are beautiful things.

At first, Carrie plans to acquire material beauty through her own efforts, working in Chicago. She soon learns, however, that her lack of training and experience qualifies her only for factory work,

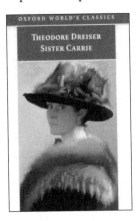

which does not pay well. Following a bout of flu, Carrie loses her job in a shoe factory (sick leave did not exist in 1889) and cannot find another position. During one of her futile job searches, she chances to encounter Charles Drouet, a traveling salesman whom she had met on the train to Chicago. As Carrie is rather passive and pliable by nature, Charles easily persuades her to postpone her job search, have dinner with him, and let him buy her some nice clothes. Before long, Carrie has moved into this man's cozy apartment, enjoying material comforts she has never known, without having to scrabble for work.

When Carrie meets George Hurstwood, the manager of a prosperous saloon, however, she realizes that this man is superior to her present lover. Not only is Hurstwood more intelligent, but also his clothes are finer in quality—a clear indication that he can provide her with a higher form of material beauty. Attracted to Carrie, Hurstwood plans an elopement to New York. In order to execute this plan, he needs a supply of ready cash—something he lacks because most of his money is in investments. This situation leads to a scene that exhibits Dreiser's belief in one's ability to weigh moral issues rather than only acting on impulse.

Closing the saloon one night, Hurstwood notices that the lock on the safe is not fastened. Tempted, he reaches in, takes out ten thousand dollars in bills, puts them back, then takes them out again. Aware that theft is intrinsically wrong as well as tremendously damaging to one's reputation, he knows that he should replace the cash. Yet he hesitates, fondling the green paper that represents accessible spending power. Then an act of fate occurs that ends his conflict: The safe suddenly snaps shut, and he does not know the combination. Hurstwood decides to take the money but to send back most of it, retaining only enough to settle himself and Carrie in their new environment.

Once in New York, however, Hurstwood's luck changes, as he cannot find steady employment. Carrie becomes a chorus girl, eventually acquiring speaking parts in comedy shows. While her salary is modest, it is sufficient to cover essentials, such as rent, coal, and groceries. Resenting what she interprets as Hurstwood's laziness, however, and still on her search for material beauty, she spends all of her earnings on her wardrobe, so that the couple rapidly falls into debt. Eventually, Carrie and Hurstwood separate, and the latter, now homeless, commits suicide by gas inhalation.

In *Sister Carrie*, Dreiser shows his faith in the ability to change, as opposed to remaining in the "trap" of one's origin or inborn personality. Although Hurstwood's life ends tragically, he had exhibited progress in his youth. Starting as a bartender with little money, he worked his way into increasingly better positions, finally becoming the well-paid manager of a fashionable saloon. Carrie also changes—she loses her emotional dependence on men. When she happens to meet Charles Drouet in New York, he asks her to dinner. In former days, Carrie would have followed along, flattered by his enduring interest in her. This time, however, she declines, using a theater engagement as an excuse. Subsequent invitations from Drouet are also refused.

Robert Ames, a friend of Carrie, sees in her even greater potential for change. Robert points out that there is more to life than the acquisition of material luxuries. Having seen Carrie in comedy shows, he believes that she is capable of acting in more serious drama—a form of beauty that can transform people's lives and might bring true happiness to the actress. This gives Carrie something to think about, but whether she will act on Robert's advice is questionable, for Carrie is more a dreamer than a doer. Her tendency to dream is symbolized by the rocking chair—a frequent image throughout the novel. It is Carrie's wont to rock for hours, singing and dreaming of a rosy future. Hurstwood also uses the rocker, but to dream of his past.

While the rocking chair is the novel's primary symbol, Dreiser uses another, which reflects his awareness of the gulf between economic classes. Each evening, a homeless man called the Captain stands on a corner in the wealthy theater district. Surrounded by other homeless men, he begs for money so that each man might rent a bed for the night. The Captain's station emphasizes the great divergence between classes within the same vicinity.

Sister Carrie ends with an image of Carrie in her rocker, "dreaming of such happiness as [she] may never feel." The word "may" suggests ambiguity as to Carrie's future. She may remain a perpetual dreamer, or she may take Robert's advice and seek a form of beauty that could bring her lasting satisfaction.

JENNIE GERHARDT

First published: 1911
Type of work: Novel

Jennie, an unwed mother, becomes the mistress of an affluent man, who eventually leaves her to marry a wealthy widow.

Dreiser's second novel, *Jennie Gerhardt*, is often considered his most popular, having sold more than five thousand copies in its first six months. Not only does the author show his characters through their own dialogue (rather than relying on description and narration), he also injects a bit of realistic humor in the "baby talk" conversations between a toddler and her grandfather. Moreover, he presents a heroine whose sexual liaisons stem not from a long-

ing for possessions but from a sense of family responsibility.

Because Jennie's father is an unemployed glassblower with six children, Jennie helps out by doing the laundry of George Brander, a senator who resides at a fashionable hotel. Having taken a fancy to Jennie, Brander tells her that if ever she or her family are in need, he will help. Thus, when Jennie's brother gets into trouble with the law, Brander gives Jennie the ten dollars bail that her parents cannot afford. In her relief and gratitude, Jennie yields herself to him completely.

Shortly afterward, Brander dies of heart failure, and Jennie learns that she is pregnant. Although she is mortified by her condition, Jennie's maternal instinct comes through. Her strength during the pregnancy comes largely from the supportiveness of her mother, Mrs. Gerhardt, whose behavior Dreiser probably modeled on that of his own mother throughout the pregnancy of his sister Maine.

When her daughter, Vesta, is six months old, Jennie meets Lester Kane, heir to his father's flourishing carriage business. Lester is quickly attracted to Jennie and asks her to become his mistress, promising financial support to her family. This proposal throws Jennie into a conflict. Although the attraction is mutual, she has determined not to "fall" again—yet her family is always short of money. Finally, fate intervenes, helping her to make a decision. Gerhardt, who has since found work, seriously burns his hands in a factory accident, to the extent that he will no longer be able to use them in the glassblowing trade. Thus, the major portion of the family's meager income is gone; knowing their need, Jennie accepts Lester's offer, lying to her parents that they have been secretly married.

In *Jennie Gerhardt*, Dreiser broaches two topics that he did not discuss in *Sister Carrie*. One is the issue of birth control: Dreading the idea of bearing another illegitimate child, Jennie tells Lester at the outset that she does not want a baby. Lester, who does not particularly want children himself, promises to protect her from this unwanted event. Dreiser also explores the compatibility of mates and the ability of partners to satisfy each other's needs. Unquestionably, Jennie provides Lester with a comfortable home: For his part, Lester comes to care for Vesta, taking a genuine interest in this child of another man.

In time, however, fate disrupts their simple yet contented life. While traveling abroad with Jennie, Lester happens to encounter Letty Pace, a former girlfriend, now a rich widow. In his reunion with Letty, who comes from his own privileged background, Lester realizes how much he has missed high society, with its cultural interests and intellectual repartee. As his father has already threatened to cut him from his will if he continues living with Jennie (promising only a pittance if he marries her), Lester begins thinking. Letty can obviously provide more social and intellectual stimulation than Jennie. Therefore, it might be financially and socially advantageous to leave his mistress and marry a woman of his own kind.

Lester's supposedly ideal marriage, however, does not bring him complete happiness, for despite her intelligence and social grace, Letty cannot offer Jennie's warm companionship—a situation suggesting that no one can entirely fulfill the needs of another. Ironically, it is Jennie who comes to Lester at the time of his sudden death, Letty being on a cruise and arriving home only in time for the funeral.

As in *Sister Carrie*, Dreiser's closing passage is somewhat ambiguous. After Vesta's death from typhoid, Jennie has adopted two orphans who "would marry and leave after a while, and then what? Days and days in endless reiteration, and then—?" Depending on the view of the reader, this conclusion can imply endless futility for Jennie, or, in time, the advent of a whole new life—something, perhaps, of which she has not yet dreamed.

AN AMERICAN TRAGEDY

First published: 1925
Type of work: Novel

Infatuated with a wealthy young woman, Clyde Griffiths drowns his working-class lover, the mother of his unborn child, a crime which results in his execution.

An American Tragedy, Dreiser's longest novel, has often been hailed as his masterpiece. It is divided into three books, the first of which foreshadows the events of the second, while the third describes

Clyde's trial. The protagonist is Clyde Griffiths, the son of street preachers who live in dire poverty. Thus, Clyde grows up longing for material things he can never attain except through his own efforts.

After a series of dead-end jobs, Clyde ventures to Lycurgus, New York, hoping for a place in his uncle's prosperous shirt factory. Before long, he becomes supervisor of the stamping room, where he meets Roberta Alden, a hardworking, pretty, vivacious young woman whose attraction to him matches his interest in her. After a few months of casual dating, the two become lovers and Roberta gets pregnant. In the meantime, however, Clyde has met Sondra Finchley, a girl of wealth and social prestige, whose way of life represents everything of which he has ever dreamed. Infatuated with Sondra, but being pressured toward marriage by Roberta (who cannot obtain an abortion), Clyde feels himself in a trap. As in Dreiser's previous novels, however, two incidents of fate influence his actions.

The first is a news report of a drowning, in which the woman's body was found but not the man's. Shortly after reading this, Clyde discovers a chain of isolated lakes north of the resort where the Finchleys have their summer home. It occurs to him that as Roberta cannot swim, an "accidental" drowning might be the way out of his predicament. Telling Roberta he will marry her, he plans a pre-wedding jaunt on one of these lonely lakes, choosing a boat that will easily overturn, When Roberta tries to draw closer to Clyde in the boat, he pushes her back, causing her to lose her balance and fall into the water. At this moment, Clyde experiences a fleeting change of heart. Reaching over to rescue Roberta, however, he upsets the boat, which hits her on the head, knocking her unconscious. Although Clyde might still have pulled Roberta from the water, a "voice" inside him says that fate has acted in his favor. Therefore, he lets her sink and heads back to Sondra.

When compared with *Sister Carrie* and *Jennie Gerhardt*, *An American Tragedy* seems closest to the spirit of naturalism, for Clyde appears to have no conscience. Dreiser foreshadows Clyde's indifference to murder in book 1. Clyde and some other youths are involved in an automobile crash which kills a child. No one, including Clyde, seems to care about the child. Their only concern is to get the car out of sight and then hide from the police, like hunted animals.

Dreiser also refers several times to Clyde's "thin, sensitive hands," a symbolic reminder of his innate weakness that makes him run from a crisis. Finally, the author foreshadows Clyde's tendency to place his own needs over those of others. When his unwed sister Esta becomes pregnant, Mrs. Griffiths asks him for some money toward the "confinement." Although Clyde has fifty dollars in his pocket, he contributes a mere five, keeping the rest to buy his girlfriend a coat in return for her sexual favors.

In *An American Tragedy*, Dreiser strongly implies his own attitude toward religion. Before she can sleep with Clyde, Roberta must overcome the scruples of her church, which say that she will be a "bad girl" if she yields. Through Roberta's moral struggle, Dreiser suggests that the ethical teachings of organized religion are not in accord with the drives of human nature. Furthermore, he implies that religion is ineffective in bringing about desired results. In prison, some of the men condemned to die chant the prayers of their faiths, hoping for a favor from God; they still end up in the electric chair. Clyde's mother, who prays for her son's acquittal and tries to raise money for a second trial, fails in her efforts, and Clyde dies, doubtful of God's existence and peace in the hereafter.

Nevertheless, Dreiser suggests that for some, religion is a source of strength. Clyde's mother is an example, as is the Reverend Mr. McMillan, who visits Clyde in prison. Although Clyde cannot fully believe what McMillan tells him about making peace with God, he is drawn to the man's personal magnetism. McMillan's magnetism may derive, in part, from his deep religious faith.

The title of the novel is significant. Besides the youthful deaths of Roberta and Clyde, it is a tragedy that no one can really understand the yearnings of another's heart. Clyde confesses to McMillan the true motive behind his crime: the material deprivation that drove him to an obsession with Sondra and her glittering world. McMillan, who has never experienced such strong longing for wealth, cannot understand, and he is unable to offer the court this evidence in Clyde's favor. Clyde's obsession with wealth also leads him to forfeit his chance for a warm and companionable marriage with Roberta. His matrimonial tragedy is particularly "American," for during the 1920's, the United States was still recovering economically from World War I, and many saw wealth as their highest goal, sacrificing other joys.

The conclusion to this novel, like those of the others, is open to interpretation. *An American Tragedy* ends the way it begins, with the Griffiths preaching on a street corner. Now, however, they are accompanied by Esta's son, Russell, and two converts. In one sense, it looks as if everything is hopelessly the same. On the other hand, there is a glimmer of hope in Mrs. Griffiths's reflections concerning Russell. Before returning to the mission, Russell asks for money to buy an ice-cream cone. As he runs to the vendor, Mrs. Griffiths tells herself, "she must be kind to him, more liberal with him, not restrain him too much, as maybe, maybe, she had. . . . 'For *his* sake.'" It is possible, then, that she has learned something from her son's ordeal and that Russell's fate will not be a repetition of his Uncle Clyde's.

SUMMARY

In all of his works, Dreiser portrayed society realistically. His observations of life taught him that human destiny is often affected by accidents of fate and by deep human yearnings or drives—particularly the drives toward money and sex. Yet Dreiser never felt that people are totally at the mercy of these forces, with no will of their own, even though individuals who are emotionally strong by nature seem more successful in coping with fate and drives than those who are passive or weak. Dreiser treated all of his characters with sympathy, however, proving himself to be a man of compassion.

Rebecca Stingley Hinton

BIBLIOGRAPHY

By the Author

SHORT FICTION:
Free, and Other Stories, 1918
Chains: Lesser Novels and Stories, 1927
Fine Furniture, 1930
The Best Stories of Theodore Dreiser, 1947 (Howard Fast, editor)
Best Short Stories, 1956 (James T. Farrell, editor)

LONG FICTION:
Sister Carrie, 1900
Jennie Gerhardt, 1911
The Financier, 1912, 1927
The Titan, 1914
The "Genius," 1915
An American Tragedy, 1925
The Bulwark, 1946
The Stoic, 1947

DRAMA:
Plays of the Natural and Supernatural, pb. 1916
The Girl in the Coffin, pr. 1917
The Hand of the Potter: A Tragedy in Four Acts, pb. 1919
The Collected Plays of Theodore Dreiser, pb. 2000

POETRY:
Moods: Cadenced and Declaimed, 1926, 1928
The Aspirant, 1929
Epitaph: A Poem, 1929

NONFICTION:
A Traveler at Forty, 1913
A Hoosier Holiday, 1916
Twelve Men, 1919
Hey, Rub-a-Dub-Dub!, 1920
A Book About Myself, 1922 (revised as *Newspaper Days*, 1931)
The Color of a Great City, 1923
Dreiser Looks at Russia, 1928
My City, 1929
Dawn, 1931 (autobiography)
Tragic America, 1931
America Is Worth Saving, 1941
Letters of Theodore Dreiser, 1959
Letters to Louise, 1959
Notes on Life, 1974 (Marguerite Tjader and John J. McAleer, editors)
American Diaries, 1902-1926, 1982
An Amateur Laborer, 1983
Selected Magazine Articles of Theodore Dreiser, 1985
Dreiser's Russian Diary, 1996 (Thomas P. Riggio and James L. W. West, editors)

DISCUSSION TOPICS

- Americans have long been inclined to apply the adjective "American" freely to all sorts of universals. Is the tragedy of Theodore Dreiser's *American Tragedy* a uniquely or distinctively American tragedy?

- Does Carrie Meeber's persistent inclination to dream keep her from developing into a mature adult in *Sister Carrie*?

- What aspects of Dreiser's characterization seem least adequately explained by his commitment to literary naturalism?

- Is money the root of all evil in Dreiser's fiction?

- What can be said in defense of Dreiser's communist sympathies?

- Do Dreiser's novels provide evidence of his having been an optimistic man?

Theodore Dreiser's "Ev'ry Month," 1996 (magazine articles; Nancy Warner Barrineau, editor)
Art, Music, and Literature, 1897-1902, 2001 (Yoshinobu Hakutani, editor)
Theodore Dreiser's Uncollected Magazine Articles, 1897-1902, 2003 (Hakutani, editor)
Theodore Dreiser: Interviews, 2004 (Frederic E. Rusch and Donald Pizer, editors)

About the Author

Dreiser, Vera. *My Uncle Theodore.* New York: Nash, 1976.

Gerber, Philip. *Theodore Dreiser Revisited.* New York: Twayne, 1992.

Gogol, Miriam, ed. *Theodore Dreiser: Beyond Naturalism.* New York: New York University Press, 1995.

Lingeman, Richard. *Theodore Dreiser: At the Gates of the City, 1871-1907.* New York: Putnam's, 1986.

_____. *Theodore Dreiser: An American Journey, 1908-1945.* New York: Putnam's, 1990.

Loving, Jerome. *The Last Titan: A Life of Theodore Dreiser.* Berkeley: University of California Press, 2005.

Lydon, Michael. "Justice to Theodore Dreiser." *The Atlantic* 272 (August, 1993): 98-101.

Pizer, Donald. *The Novels of Theodore Dreiser: A Critical Study.* Minneapolis: University of Minnesota Press, 1976.

Riggio, Thomas P. "Following Dreiser, Seventy Years Later." *The American Scholar* 65 (Autumn, 1996): 569-577.

Zayani, Mohamed. *Reading the Symptom: Frank Norris, Theodore Dreiser, and the Dynamics of Capitalism.* New York: Peter Lang, 1999.

PAUL LAURENCE DUNBAR

Library of Congress

Born: Dayton, Ohio
June 27, 1872
Died: Dayton, Ohio
February 9, 1906

At one time one of America's best-loved poets, Dunbar was the first African American poet to gain a national and international reputation.

BIOGRAPHY

Paul Laurence Dunbar was born in Dayton, Ohio, on June 27, 1872, the son of Joshua and Matilda Glass Burton Murphy Dunbar, former slaves from Kentucky. Matilda Dunbar had two sons, William and Robert Murphy, by a previous marriage to R. Weeks Murphy prior to the emancipation; Paul Laurence Dunbar, born shortly after Matilda's marriage to Joshua Dunbar, was the only child that Joshua and Matilda had together.

Dunbar's parents were divorced when he was still a small boy, and his father died when Dunbar was twelve. After her two older sons left home, Matilda Dunbar focused all of her attention on young Paul. Not only did she teach him to read, but she also exposed him to a number of literary works. More important, both mother and father passed on a number of stories from slavery days. These stories triggered a strong interest and imagination in Dunbar and became the basis for his most popular and enduring works.

Dunbar's interest in writing dated back to his high school days at Dayton's Central High School. Although he was the only black student in his class, he was immensely popular. Dunbar's first published poem appeared when he was about sixteen years old, and as he continued publishing, he also became class president, editor of the high school newspaper, class poet, and president of the literary

society. In addition, Dunbar founded the short-lived *Dayton Tattler*, a newspaper which reported news of Dayton's black community.

Because of a lack of funds, Dunbar was not able to attend college upon his graduation from high school in 1891; instead, he accepted a job as an elevator operator in the Callahan Building in downtown Dayton. This was one of very few reasonably respectable jobs open to African Americans at the time. For his services, Dunbar earned only four dollars per week, but the job gave him plenty of time to read and write poetry and to write articles which he published in various newspapers. In addition, Dunbar wrote several short stories during this period.

Shortly before Dunbar's twentieth birthday, he got the break that brought him to the attention of the literary establishment and launched his career as the United States' foremost black poet. At the invitation of Helen Truesdale, Dunbar's former English teacher, he gave the welcoming address for the Western Association of Writers, then meeting in Dayton. The members were so impressed by Dunbar's eloquence and talent that he was asked to become a member of the association and was much praised by writers James Newton Matthews and James Whitcomb Riley.

Later in 1892, Dunbar's friend and high school classmate Orville Wright encouraged him to publish a collection of his poems. *Oak and Ivy*, a collection of more than fifty poems, appeared early in 1893, published by Dayton's United Brethren Publishing House. The volume contained Dunbar's early dialect poems and sold reasonably well. To further his career and widen his audience, Dunbar began giving poetry readings throughout Ohio and later moved to Chicago, where he met a number of other important African Americans, including Frederick Douglass, who had gathered for the occasion of the 1893 World's Columbian Exposition.

Upon returning to Dayton, Dunbar resumed his job as elevator operator and continued writing poems, a number of which appeared in his second volume, *Majors and Minors*, in 1895, along with several previously published poems. *Majors and Minors* received a glowing review from the novelist and influential critic William Dean Howells, which guaranteed Dunbar's acceptance among the literary establishment of the United States. Later that year, he signed a contract with Dodd, Mead to publish *Lyrics of Lowly Life* (1896), a collection of more than a hundred poems, most of which had appeared in *Oak and Ivy* and *Majors and Minors*, with an introduction by William Dean Howells. This became Dunbar's most successful book.

In 1897, Dunbar toured England, where he gave a number of successful readings. Upon his return to the United States, he began a clerkship at the Library of Congress in Washington, D.C., which lasted for a year and a half. During this time, he did a considerable amount of writing, publishing—among other things—two short-story collections and a partly autobiographical novel, *The Uncalled* (1898).

In 1898, Dunbar married Alice Ruth Moore, a New Orleans poet and short-story writer, with whom he had corresponded since 1895. The marriage was ill-fated because Moore's family was opposed to Dunbar's dark skin; after a frequently stormy marriage, the couple separated in 1902.

Beginning in 1898, Dunbar's health began to deteriorate rapidly. By 1899, he was suffering from tuberculosis and pneumonia and was near death. On the advice of doctors, he moved to Colorado, where he regained some of his strength and resumed his writing career. In 1900, Dunbar returned to Washington and continued to write short stories and novels in rapid succession: *The Love of Landry* (1900), *The Fanatics* (1901), and the best of his novels, *The Sport of the Gods* (1902).

Becoming increasingly ill and suffering from bouts of alcoholism and depression, Dunbar left Washington for New York in 1902. From New York he traveled to Chicago, where, failing to achieve a reunion with his wife, he suffered a nervous breakdown. This was Dunbar's final period of decline, yet he continued to write and publish. In 1903, he returned to Dayton, where he saw the publication of two more volumes of short fiction and one book of poetry. His health continued to worsen, and he died at his home on February 9, 1906.

ANALYSIS

Dunbar's poetry can be divided into two distinct classes: those poems written in Negro dialect and those written in standard English. The former, Dunbar wrote to gain an audience because of their popular appeal; in the latter, he expressed himself more as he believed a poet should. It is clear that Dunbar preferred the poems in standard English to the dialect poems, as seen in "The Poet" (1903): "But ah, the world, it turned to praise / A jingle in a broken tongue." The praise for the dialect poems, often at the expense of those written in standard English, caused him considerable concern throughout his career.

In the dialect poems, Dunbar presents scenes from plantation life, mostly in the light, humorous, and lively manner of the plantation tradition popularized by white writers Joel Chandler Harris and Thomas Nelson Page. Dunbar's characters are simple, good-natured, big-hearted folk who always speak in a dialect that Dunbar created. There is little overt protest in these poems, but often protest is subtly masked with the dialect.

Dunbar transforms the technique of masking into the theme of the mask in certain of his standard English poems, of which "We Wear the Mask" is the most obvious example. In addition, Dunbar eloquently addresses a variety of subjects, from love and death to nature and religion. The poems written in standard English are often lyrical and reflect a keen sensitivity on the part of the poet. Furthermore, these poems represent experiments with a number of different poetic forms as well as a mastery of rhyme and meter.

Similarly, Dunbar's short stories can be divided into two distinct types. First, there are the simple, lighthearted tales told in the plantation tradition—stories of a simple folk and their pleasures, pains, and sorrows. Then there are those stories written in a weak vein of protest but designed, nevertheless, to uphold the humanity of the black man. Regardless of type, however, the stories are structurally weak, and the characterization rarely transcends stereotype.

Dunbar's novels were largely unsuccessful. Three of them concern white characters: *The Uncalled*, *The Love of Landry*, and *The Fanatics*. The last novel, *The Sport of the Gods*, has black characters who are central to the story, but the plot is overly contrived and, while the characters are somewhat more complex, they are still largely stereotypes and thus fall short of creditable portrayals.

Regardless of genre, the one characteristic that stands out in all of Dunbar's writing is his sincerity, his deep regard for subject and craft. This, coupled with often delightful poems and stories, helped Dunbar achieve a high degree of popular success.

"WHEN MALINDY SINGS"

First published: 1895 (collected in *Majors and Minors*, 1895)
Type of work: Poem

In old plantation days one slave praises the singing talents of another slave, Malindy.

"When Malindy Sings" appeared in Dunbar's second collection of poems, *Majors and Minors*. Because it is a dialect piece, Dunbar placed it in the latter half of the collection, subtitled "Minors." Ironically, "When Malindy Sings" quickly became one of Dunbar's most popular poems and has since become perhaps his most anthologized dialect poem.

"When Malindy Sings" was inspired by Dunbar's mother's constant singing of hymns and Negro spirituals. In particular, Dunbar attributes the powerful melody and unmatchable phrasings to particular natural gifts of black singers.

The narrator, himself apparently a house servant, admonishes all to keep quiet as Malindy, probably a field slave, sings various songs of religious import. Miss Lucy, perhaps the plantation mistress, is told that her trained singing from a written score is no competition for Malindy's natural talent; indeed, the birds, though they sing sweetly, hush of their own accord when Malindy sings her superior melodies. Whenever Malindy sings, the narrator observes, it is a singular spiritual experience, one that should be taken advantage of every time.

In this early poem, Dunbar's gifts as a poet are evident: the meter and rhyme are regular, as are the quatrains that make up the poem. Furthermore, Dunbar is quite adept at creating images and imparting feeling through his use of sensory detail, talents he would continue to employ and capitalize upon in succeeding works.

"WE WEAR THE MASK"

First published: 1896 (collected in *Lyrics of Lowly Life*, 1896)
Type of work: Poem

Dunbar emphasizes the necessity for a black person to mask pain and suffering with a happy face.

"We Wear the Mask" is an often-anthologized poem that shows Dunbar at his best in his standard English poems. In this fifteen-line poem, he points specifically to the immense suffering of black people and the necessity of painting on a happy face as a survival tactic. In so doing, Dunbar challenges the plantation tradition, of which he had become a well-known participant. In short, he emphasizes that slaves, while they may have appeared happy and docile, were in reality paradigms of suffering and strength. This could have applied as well to the suffering that Dunbar no doubt observed during his own lifetime, certainly one of the harshest periods in history for African Americans in the United States.

Technically, the poem shows Dunbar as a mature and expert craftsman. It is written for the most part in strict iambic tetrameter lines with a repetitive rhyme pattern, but Dunbar interrupts this regular rhythm in the last lines of the second and third stanzas to deliver the jolting sobering statement, "We wear the mask." "We Wear the Mask" is perhaps the finest example of Dunbar's employment of masking as a theme. He would continue to use masking as both theme and technique throughout his writing career.

"THE LYNCHING OF JUBE BENSON"

First published: 1904 (collected in *The Heart of Happy Hollow*, 1904)
Type of work: Short story

Dr. Melville, a white doctor, expresses remorse over participating in the lynching of his black friend Jube Benson, wrongly accused of raping Melville's fiancé.

"The Lynching of Jube Benson" appeared in one of Dunbar's last collections of short stories, *The Heart of Happy Hollow* (1904). The story, like many of his others, is set in the post-emancipation South and is written to uphold the humanity of the black race. As such, "The Lynching of Jube Benson" is perhaps his strongest piece of protest fiction.

In the library of a southern gentleman named Gordon Fairfax, Dr. Melville, a relatively young medical doctor, and Handon Gay, a young newspaper reporter, are discussing various issues of the day, one of which is lynching. Gay expresses the desire to see one; Fairfax does not necessarily want to see one but would not avoid one if such an opportunity arose; Dr. Melville adamantly insists that he would avoid one, because, he relates to his companions, he had seen and taken part in one some seven years earlier, the lynching of Jube Benson.

At the time of the lynching, Dr. Melville was recently out of medical college and had moved to Brandon to open a medical practice among the white and black residents. Soon after his arrival, he began to fix his attentions on the young, pretty Annie Daly, daughter of a prosperous townsman from whom he rented office space. During this time, Dr. Melville also met Jube Benson, the black man who worked for the Dalys and who was fiercely devoted to young Annie.

Jube Benson became Dr. Melville's ally in his quest for the attentions of Annie Daly, to the point that he discouraged all other suitors. Also, during an outbreak of typhoid fever, which Dr. Melville contracted after treating most of the townspeople, Jube Benson served as devoted nursemaid to the doctor.

One afternoon of the following summer, Dr. Melville returned to his house from a visit in a neighboring village to find Annie Daly beaten, raped, and near death. Dr. Melville fought to save her, but she died, but not before identifying her attacker as "That black—." As Jube Benson was nowhere to be found, it was immediately assumed that he was the perpetrator of this vicious crime. A lynch mob formed immediately to find and punish Jube Benson.

Jube, who in reality had been to visit his own girlfriend, Lucy, was soon found, confronted with Annie's corpse, and immediately hanged despite his excuses and earnest pleas. Dr. Melville was the first to pull the rope.

No sooner had Jube's body swung from the tree limb than his brother, Ben Benson, arrived, dragging with him the real culprit, Tom Skinner, "The worst white ruffian in town," who had blackened his face with soot. Dr. Melville's efforts to revive Jube Benson were unsuccessful, and he felt all the more guilty when he reexamined Annie Daly and found the skin of a white man beneath her fingernails. He thus feels the burden of guilt because he helped murder an innocent man and a faithful friend. Seven years later, he still suffers from the guilt as he tells his companions, "Gentlemen, that was my last lynching."

The story is fast-paced and is written with sharp, crisp prose which emphasizes the action. While Dunbar's characters fail to rise beyond stereotypes, in this story they are successful in communicating Dunbar's purpose, that of articulating his abhorrence of lynching.

SUMMARY

Dunbar strived to address real concerns about the lives of black people throughout his relatively short career. In his poetry, short stories, novels, and song lyrics, he was often caught between becoming an artistic or a popular success, yet Dunbar rarely compromised his sincerity in treating his subject matter or his craft. This fact has earned for him an enduring place in American literature.

Warren J. Carson

Paul Laurence Dunbar

BIBLIOGRAPHY

By the Author

POETRY:
Oak and Ivy, 1893
Majors and Minors, 1895
Lyrics of Lowly Life, 1896
Lyrics of the Hearthside, 1899
Lyrics of Love and Laughter, 1903
Lyrics of Sunshine and Shadow, 1905
Complete Poems, 1913

LONG FICTION:
The Uncalled, 1898
The Love of Landry, 1900
The Fanatics, 1901
The Sport of the Gods, 1902

SHORT FICTION:
Folks from Dixie, 1898
The Strength of Gideon, and Other Stories, 1900
In Old Plantation Days, 1903
The Heart of Happy Hollow, 1904
The Best Stories of Paul Laurence Dunbar, 1938

MISCELLANEOUS:
In His Own Voice: The Dramatic and Other Uncollected Works of Paul Laurence Dunbar, 2002 (Herbert Woodward Martin and Ronald Primeau, editors)

DISCUSSION TOPICS

- What circumstances led Paul Laurence Dunbar to discount the value of his dialect poems? Were he writing today, what circumstances might encourage him to value dialect poems more?

- To what extent do Dunbar's poems in standard English reflect his African American identity?

- How does the mask function generally in Dunbar's poetry and specifically in the poem "We Wear the Mask"?

- Many modern-day poets and readers regard adherence to meter as a limitation on the poet's freedom. Explain how its use, including its irregularities, contribute to the effect of Dunbar's poems.

- What lessons can a young black person accustomed to, and comfortable with, black English but resistant to, or unsuccessful in, standard English learn from Dunbar?

About the Author

Alexander, Eleanor. *Lyrics of Sunshine and Shadow: The Tragic Courtship and Marriage of Paul Laurence Dunbar and Alice Ruth Moore.* Albany: New York University Press, 2001.

Best, Felton O. *Crossing the Color Line: A Biography of Paul Laurence Dunbar.* Dubuque, Iowa: Kendall/Hunt, 1996.

Bone, Robert. *Down Home: Origins of the Afro-American Short Story.* New York: Columbia University Press, 1988.

Hudson, Gossie Harold. *A Biography of Paul Laurence Dunbar.* Baltimore: Gateway Press, 1999.

Revell, Peter. *Paul Laurence Dunbar.* Boston: Twayne, 1979.

Turner, Darwin T. "Paul Laurence Dunbar: The Rejected Symbol." *Journal of Negro History,* January, 1967, 1-13.

Wagner, Jean. "Paul Laurence Dunbar." In *Black Poets of the United States from Paul Laurence Dunbar to Langston Hughes,* translated by Kenneth Douglas. Urbana: University of Illinois Press, 1973.

ROBERT DUNCAN

Born: Oakland, California
January 7, 1919
Died: San Francisco, California
February 3, 1988

Duncan is widely recognized as one of the most original voices of the twentieth century, and no modern American poet took his poetic office as seriously or made greater claims for the imagination's ability to create reality through language.

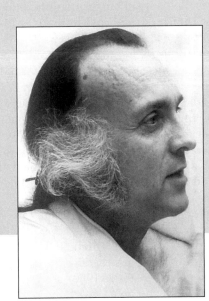

Matthew Foley/Courtesy, New
Directions Publishing

BIOGRAPHY

Robert Duncan was born in Oakland, California, on January 7, 1919, to Marguerite Wesley and Edward Howard Duncan. His mother died immediately following his birth as a result of an influenza epidemic. His father, a day laborer, was unable to support and care for the child. Therefore, as an infant, Robert was put up for adoption and subsequently adopted by a family named Symmes. Mr. Symmes was a prominent architect who had offices in both Alameda and Bakersfield, California, where Robert spent his early childhood and adolescence.

The Symmes family was deeply involved in various forms of theosophy (a religious movement influenced by Buddhism). Robert's adoptive mother's sister would frequently interpret children's stories, fairy tales, and myths with Gnostic and esoteric explanations to show young Robert the secret, deeper meanings of these seemingly harmless narratives. Duncan's grandmother had been an elder in a hermetic religious order similar to Irish poet William Butler Yeats's Order of the Golden Dawn.

Duncan's early childhood experiences remained with him throughout his life and caused him to interpret practically all seemingly normal daily events as allegories corresponding to larger cosmic orders. Gnostic, hermetic, and alchemical lore continuously informed his imagination and be-

came the groundwork for all of his major poetry. As Yeats's imagination found its sustenance in Celtic folklore and mythology, Duncan's spiritual core also found its center in his early apprehensions of his life as a spiritual enactment of mysterious powers he could only dimly perceive.

A sympathetic high school English teacher, Miss Edna Keough, spotted his obvious sensitivity to the beauty and seriousness of poetry; she helped him to envision it, as Duncan explained, "not as a cultural commodity or an exercise to improve sensibility, but as a vital process of the spirit." She also introduced him to the dramatic monologues of Robert Browning, such as "My Last Duchess" and "The Bishop Orders His Tomb at St. Praxed's." Many of Duncan's early poems resemble in both form and tone those sophisticated works of Browning, poems that historians of English literature have called the first modern poems in the language.

Ezra Pound, another spiritual mentor of Duncan during his college years, had also been heavily influenced by Browning's ability to entertain multiple voices in his dramatic monologues, poetic devices that both he and Duncan practiced throughout their careers. Miss Keough also introduced the young Duncan to the work of a woman whose poetry became as vital to his own as that of Pound— Hilda Doolittle, or "H. D."

By the time Duncan graduated from Bakersfield High School, he had accepted his vocation as a poet and conducted himself accordingly as he began his college career at the University of California at Berkeley. He spent the years 1936 to 1938

693

there, where he published his first poems in a literary journal called *Occident*. He also lived an openly homosexual lifestyle and left California to follow his first lover to New York.

In Manhattan he became involved with a group of young writers which included Anaïs Nin, Henry Miller, Kenneth Patchen, and George Barker, all of whom were considered avant-garde outsiders of modern literature at the time. He also helped edit and publish the famous *Experimental Review* with Sanders Russell in Woodstock, New York. His marriage to Marjorie McKee lasted only a short time. He and his fellow writers were influenced by the quirky genius of both the French artist, poet, and filmmaker Jean Cocteau and the English poet Edith Sitwell.

In 1944, Duncan published an essay in Dwight Macdonald's journal, *Politics*, titled "The Homosexual in Society," an essay that was simultaneously an admission of his own homosexual orientation and an argument for more humane treatment of homosexuals in general. After a storm of protests over such sexual honesty, Duncan returned to Berkeley in 1945 to resume his studies.

At Berkeley, he met and became part of a group of writers associated with the poet Kenneth Rexroth, who was highly critical of the literary establishment of the universities. At about the same time, Duncan also came under the intellectual tutelage of the great medieval and Renaissance historian Ernst Kantorowicz, an association so profound that much of Duncan's work from the Berkeley years onward reverberated with medieval and Renaissance themes and allusions.

One of his first publications was called *Medieval Scenes* (1950), which attempted to evoke spiritually, via the creative process, "the eternal ones of the poem" in re-creating a specifically medieval mode or scene. Kantorowicz's brilliant lectures turned Duncan's attentions to medieval and Renaissance alchemy, which added considerable historical and philosophical depth to his earlier interests in Gnosticism and hermeticism.

It was also at this time that Duncan met and fell in love with a young art student named Jess Collins, with whom he spent the remainder of his life. Much of Duncan's later poetry frequently alludes to the joyfully fulfilling domestic scenes of the household that he and Jess created for themselves over a thirty-seven-year period.

Having gained a small but distinguished poetic reputation, Duncan was invited to teach at Black Mountain College in North Carolina in 1956 by its rector, Charles Olson, himself a burgeoning poet and literary theorist. He subsequently returned to San Francisco and participated in the literary ferment that Allen Ginsberg and Jack Kerouac were creating as spokesmen for the Beat movement. Duncan became, over the years, the only writer whose concerns were broad enough for him to be considered a part of the Beat poets, the Black Mountain poets, and the poets of the San Francisco Renaissance.

Duncan published more than twenty-six volumes of poetry and numerous limited publications from small presses during his lifetime. His literary reputation with the larger reading public began with *The Opening of the Field* (1960), an especially auspicious first major work, as it contained a number of poems that are included in virtually all important anthologies of American literature. Duncan began a series of open-ended prose-poem commentaries on poetics called "The Structure of Rime" that he weaves throughout the other poetic texts in *The Opening of the Field*. This series continued without closure until his death in 1988.

His next critically acclaimed volume of poetry was *Roots and Branches* (1964), which added not only eight more installments of "The Structure of Rime" but also several notable long poems, including "Apprehensions" and "The Continent," and a closet drama on theosophical themes called "Adam's Way." Both these earlier volumes show Duncan's poetic technique and range to be spectacularly accomplished and absolutely individual. *Bending the Bow* (1968) demonstrated Duncan's ability to articulate his rage against the Vietnam War while at the same time deepening and delineating the multiple themes of "The Structure of Rime."

He also initiated a new open-ended series of poems called "Passages." After a self-imposed rule to publish no major volume for fifteen years, he produced the great works of his later years, *Ground Work: Before the War* (1984) and *Ground Work II: In the Dark* (1987).

There is little doubt that Duncan has taken his place as one of the major poets of modern American literature and that his complex but spiritually sustaining poetry will continue to inspire and nourish readers who view poetry as a serious spiritual enterprise rather than as the highly polished artifacts that fill up most poetry journals.

ANALYSIS

The key to understanding the complex poetry and poetics of Duncan can be found in his attitude toward his role as a poet, which for him was identical with his humanity. The primary task of both the poet and the man can be seen most clearly in Duncan's definition of the word "responsibility." Instead of giving the reader the standard dictionary definition of the word, he breaks it down etymologically—that is, into its most original and, therefore, obvious parts: "response-ability; or, keeping the ability to respond."

His role or function is to respond to any and all movement or activity of the spirit: emotions, feelings (however small they may appear), hunches, impulses, daydreams, memories, echoes, verbal puns, and linguistic reverberations and resonances. Duncan's consciousness includes experiences of any kind because everything is eventual grist for his comprehensively Romantic imagination. He is, in short, open to all influences, and it is no accident that his first major volume of poetry was titled *The Opening of the Field*.

No other American poet of the twentieth century took his or her vocation as a poet as seriously as did Duncan. He viewed it as a literal "calling" to serve the imagination, much in the mode of the medieval knight pledging his love and obedience to his lady. For Duncan, "the Lady," the feminine creative element in a Jungian sense, the White Goddess as creator and destroyer that poet Robert Graves studied for years, is one of many embodiments of the imagination that Duncan located himself within and spoke from each time he wrote.

The principal vehicle through which he activates his participation in this archetypal source is language itself. Language is the key in two ways. He speaks it, and it speaks through him as poet; it is the order within which he experiences consciousness, both individual and universal, and also the agency through which he makes contact with his own and the collective unconscious. All of his major books of poetry can be understood as attempts to deepen and refine his commitment to his poetic office as embodied in language.

Because Duncan was raised in a family that be-

lieved in the basic fundamentals of theosophy—that spiritual worlds do exist and influence everyone's lives—he sees his poetic office as thaumaturgic or magic. A thaumaturge is a wonder worker, a caster of spells, a word with which Duncan frequently puns, reminding his reader that the present limited use of "spell"—as a correct or incorrect spelling of a word—is a far cry from its older and much more important meaning as creating a condition of magic. As a verbal magician, he wishes to transport readers to spiritual orders or realms of which they are not conscious, even though they are available if one possesses the right vision.

Duncan's whole poetic project is to exhort his audience to attend to the source of reality as it is embodied in language, to pay attention to the dynamics of the linguistic structures in which everyone is involved on a daily basis. His spiritual orientations would suggest, for example, that Christianity drastically limited the scope of spiritual enquiry when it proposed Jesus Christ as the one and only designation for "the Word." Duncan would urge one, rather, to see that "the Word" is obviously about "words" and the unique structures they generate, known as language.

One of Duncan's spiritual sources over many years was his persistent study of certain Hebrew mystical texts such as the Kabbala and the *Zohar*. One of his important early works, *Letters: Poems MCMLIII-MCMLVI* (1958) came out of a deep examination of the *Zohar*, a work in which ancient scholars searched the letters of the alphabet for their secret revelations. So Duncan's poems in *Letters* refer not to correspondence but rather to meditations and exercises on the letters of the alphabet, the most basic elements of language itself, possessing their own creative powers that, with time and devoted concentration, can reveal mysteries of the cosmos.

Because he trusted in the ability of language to reveal mystery, he went back to language's source, its individual letters, and examined how they are arranged and rearranged to "spell" out meaning. He found that the method used in the *Zohar* gave him "a new picture of language in which the letters of the Logos dance"; he quite consciously used the same method in *Letters*.

In 1966, Duncan published a group of poems actually written between 1939 and 1946, calling it *The Years as Catches: First Poems, 1939-1946* (1966), and wrote an introduction in which he explained their influences and origins. He openly confessed that his etymological studies of words contribute heavily to the content of his poetry. The word "catch" contains various levels of interpretation, such as viewing his art as a "net of catches," fishing around hoping to "catch" something, and what "catches" him at work or "catches" his ear.

His influences in the early poems are fairly obvious: John Milton, Ezra Pound, E. E. Cummings, Wallace Stevens, Gerard Manley Hopkins, and Laura Riding. More notable, however, is evidence that his imagination was, and remained throughout his life, very process-oriented. The process of poem-making becomes a part of the subject matter of most of his major poems from these early works onward. The interplay generated between and among the various voices in the poem creates the tension that energizes the poem's movement, but instead of moving toward an orderly resolution or poetic product, the poems expand into multiple perspectives much in the manner of the *Cantos* of Ezra Pound (1917-1970).

The first volume of Duncan's poetry that drew national attention and critical acclaim was *The Opening of the Field*, a book which many critics believe to be Duncan's finest single collection. It contains three poems that have been frequently anthologized and are viewed as typical Duncan poems: "Often I Am Permitted to Return to a Meadow," "The Dance," and "A Poem Beginning with a Line by Pindar." He also initiated, in the volume, a series of open-ended prose poems which constitute an ongoing discussion of the procedures of the poetic imagination and their relationship with the evolution of Duncan's interconnecting theories of rhyme and measure. The first thirteen of an eventual twenty-nine sections appear in this volume. The major themes that will he developed in all of his subsequent work are present here.

The title of the work, *The Opening of the Field*, encapsulates the direction and scope of the collection. The individual poems are all interconnected by the possibilities of the activity of language when it is permitted to operate in an open field. The title and the organization of the work are direct responses to the kind of collection of individual poems that most poets had been producing during the post-World War II era. These poems were highly crafted, closed systems, which the poet-

critics involved in the so-called New Criticism were producing.

Just as Allen Ginsberg's *Howl* (1956) opened up the possibility of an American poetry recalling and rekindling the open-form tradition of Walt Whitman, so Duncan's first major work exhorted American writers not to limit themselves to imitating conservative British models but to permit expansion into American and continental European literary, artistic, and musical expressions. He also revealed his sources as coming out of a wisdom tradition of Gnosticism, hermetic and alchemical texts, and theosophical lore.

Indeed, the first poem in the collection, "Often I Am Permitted to Return to a Meadow," presents virtually all the motifs that Duncan would develop during the remainder of his poetic career: origins, permission, fields and meadows, the Lady, dreams (the genesis of this poem was in a dream), boundaries, architecture, the Beloved, the Dance, and—most important—the poetic process itself.

Another project that *The Opening of the Field* initiates in its open organization is the possibility of an intertextual reading of many of its poems. One can read "A Poem Slow Beginning" as a gloss or comment on the first poem in the book, but "A Poem Slow Beginning" can also be read as a single poem with its own inner structure and thematic development. Both readings are valid; however, as this poem rests between the first two crucial "The Structure of Rime" sections and the next five, one can also view it as an example of what Duncan has been theorizing about in the first two and as a logical preparation of what he is about to discuss in the next five.

The next major volume that refines Duncan's highly complex poetic project of embodying the theme of process by enacting the dynamics of process itself is the highly romantic *Roots and Branches*, an obvious outgrowth of the poetic field of his previous book. Duncan concentrates on his poetic origins and inspirations, envisioning them as the "roots and branches" of the tree of language. Many of these branches go back to "branches" of study that helped formulate his mythopoeic imagination as a child, such as songs, fairy tales, myths, and the "old lore" that his spiritualist parents avidly studied.

The language of this book is highly charged, almost baroque in its testings of the boundaries of expression. The long poem "Apprehensions" is not only one of his greatest poems but is also another example of how the poem's title simultaneously comments on and enacts the process of "apprehending" the cosmic event in the individual event.

Roots and Branches also includes, in keeping with Duncan's continuous return to origins, a number of blatant poetic imitations of his acknowledged literary masters. He writes sonnets based on Dante, poems imitating Percy Bysshe Shelley and the Latin poet Ovid, ballads that were obviously influenced by one of his contemporaries, Helen Adam, and a theosophical drama called "Adam's Way." In short, he wants to show his literary "roots" and their multiple "branchings" throughout his poetic career.

Duncan's next major collection is called *Bending the Bow.* The title continues the organic metaphor from the "field" in the first book to the "roots and branches" of his second to the "bow" carved from the wood of the tree of language into an instrument of war or into a bow across which stretch the strings of the lyre or harp that the ancient bards strummed as they declaimed their poetry. Duncan's attention moves from his preoccupation with origins to his rage over the American involvement in the Vietnam War. Much of the poetry of this volume consists of five additions to the series "The Structure of Rime" and of the beginning of what would eventually become his major poetic sequence, the "Passages" poems. The first thirty appear in *Bending the Bow* and interweave with both "The Structure of Rime" sequence and the other poems in the book.

Included in *Bending the Bow* is an introduction in which Duncan defines his idiosyncratic uses of some key terms such as "rime" and "measure" and explains his peculiar blending of political ideas and their relationship with his highly individual poetics. He defines what poetry is for him:

The poem is not a stream of consciousness, but an area of composition in which I work with whatever comes into it. . . . So there is not only a melody of sounds but of images. Rimes, the reiterations of formations in the design, even puns, lead into complexities of the field. But now the poet works with a sense of parts fitting in relation to a design that is larger than the poems.

He then uses a scientific term, "polysemous" (marked by a multiplicity of meaning), to explain further his unique understanding of form, while suggesting that Dante was the first consciously structuralist poet: "The artist, after Dante's poetics, works with all parts of the poem as *polysemous*, taking each thing of the composition as generative of meaning, a response to and a contribution to the building of form."

Duncan's two late works, *Ground Work: Before the War* and *Ground Work II: In the Dark*, constitute a full flowering of all his poetic projects from his earliest work. In keeping with his relentless search for origins, he returns to the literal, organic source of the body and spirit, the ground of his being—earth. The work has come full circle from the "field" through the "roots and branches" to the leaves of his expression in the "bow" of his poetic lyre back to the earth.

Walt Whitman's *Leaves of Grass* (1855) can always be read as a subtext in Duncan's work as both a metaphor for poetry and a reaffirmation of their mutual Romantic inheritance. Certain long poems, such as "The Santa Cruz Propositions," "The Dante Etudes," and the great hymn to homoerotic passion, "Circulations of the Song" from *Ground Work: Before the War*, will undoubtedly become examples of how the late work of this great poet, though as dense as anything he ever produced, will reveal itself to those who view poetry as a vital activity of the spirit. The poetic sequence "The Regulators," in *Ground Work II: In the Dark*, is as sublime an attempt to synthesize the powers of nature and the imagination as its nineteenth century counterpart, Shelley's *Alastor: Or, The Spirit of Solitude* (1815).

"THE STRUCTURE OF RIME"

First published: 1960-1987
Type of work: Poetry

"The Structure of Rime" is interwoven throughout all the major poetic collections of Duncan's poems as a continuous discussion of his ever-changing poetic theory.

"The Structure of Rime" sections of Duncan's books were never gathered together in one specific volume, and their author never wished them to be. Indeed, Duncan wrote them as a series of ongoing prose-poem discussions of his poetics. The initial thirteen were interspersed throughout his first major collection, *The Opening of the Field*, the next

seven were included in *Roots and Branches*, while five appeared in *Bending the Bow*. Three appeared in *Ground Work*, with one final section in *Ground Work II*.

These highly complex open-form prose poems demonstrate Duncan's adherence to the poetry of open forms—that is, the more open the field of possibilities, the more inclusive it becomes. He also firmly believed in poet Robert Creeley's brilliantly comprehensive definition of both "form and content" when Creeley expanded upon poet Charles Olson's statement that "form is never more than an extension of content," a proposition that arguably closed the pedantic discussions over such obvious matters.

These multiphasic works, along with many essays and the new formalistic ground broken with his "Passages" poems, both define and demonstrate Duncan's original ideas on what constitutes a long poem. Most major American poets from Whitman to the present had come to terms with the demands of the long poem: Ezra Pound in the *Cantos*, Robinson Jeffers in *The Women at Point Sur* (1927), Olson in *The Maximus Poems* (1960), Hart Crane in *The Bridge* (1930), and many others. Duncan, however, produced not one but two major poetic sequences, which he interweaves throughout all of his work in a DNA-like configuration. On several occasions, they actually become part of each other's process.

To further complicate the situation, Duncan has stated that neither "The Structure of Rime" nor "Passages" can be called "long poems": They are "large" poems. He questions the whole definition of what "long" means in regard to poetic form, explaining quite lucidly that his two works are "serial" works involved in the process of poem making. They are not a chronology or journey; their activity participates in neither a linear, circular, nor cyclic progression. They constitute exactly what Duncan proposed in his first book: a field, a large canvas or configuration that gathers meaning as it accumulates items. With the addition of each section, the area begins to radiate a kind of energy field, a field of memory which resonates correspondences which grow exponentially, as additions accumulate. The field expands and enlarges as new combinations of patterns or motifs appear, and these, in turn, begin to interconnect multiphasically.

In the first "The Structure of Rime," Duncan locates his primary task as a poet, "which is first a search in obedience" to language, a pledge that will, if he is steadfast, enable him to create himself out of words: "In the feet that measure the dance of my pages I hear cosmic intoxications of the man I will be."

He further creates, in the next several sections, a mythological figure he calls the "Master of Rime," who engages him in a discussion of the nature of poetry and of time as destroyer, finally defining for Duncan the "Structure of Rime": "An absolute scale of resemblance and disresemblance establishes measures that are music in the actual world . . . the actual stars are music in the real world. This is the meaning of the music of the spheres." Duncan employs the first principle of alchemy throughout much of his poetry: "As above, so below," an orientation that enables him to view physical reality as an allegory of invisible worlds which only those possessing a spiritual vision can apprehend.

Throughout "The Structure of Rime" series in *The Opening of the Field*, he mythopoeically creates a world of his own and peoples it with figures from world mythology and theosophic lore: Adam and Eve; the garden with the cosmic ash tree, Yggdrasil, bleeding language from its branches; and the dance of the Heraclitean Fire whose "tongues" also speak. Duncan then catalogs other figures, transforming their traditional roles into linguistic tasks; he transforms Chiron, the guide to Hades, into a syntactical grammarian.

The natural cyclic movement of water from river to clouds to rain becomes a metaphor for the process of the activity of language. The poetic impulse becomes a fish in the sea of language, then a gopher and a snail struggling to create for themselves homes in the chaos of nature, as archetypal memories erupt from beneath the earth and break the rocky surface. All these events remind the world of its origin, the sun, which subsequently became the source of people's first religions and humanity's attempt to use language to express that ineffable relationship.

As everything is perceived, named, and measured in language, it is evident that Duncan's use of the term "rime" refers to much more than similar sounds at the end of lines of poetry. Rather, "rime" designates any and all reiterations or repetitions that appear in these works and form a structure or pattern of some kind which, in short, humanizes the vast, unnameable void with language. Duncan can only experience his world if he can imagine it in terms of linguistic or musical orders, scales, or measures. His poetry contains its own measures, which are divided into rime and rhythm—both measurable and, therefore, knowable.

The remaining sections of "The Structure of Rime" further delineate their basic motifs throughout the rest of Duncan's work. "The Structure of Rime XIV" in *Roots and Branches*, however, appears as section 5 in a long poem called "Apprehensions," functioning as an active unit of both the single poem and a section of the series "The Structure of Rime." The combination works well because "Apprehensions" concerns itself with memories of Duncan's childhood, especially the spiritualist influences of his parents. He also delves into the history of his grandfather's family and their migrations from the east to the northwest to the west, and how those patterns become a cave of remembrances and, therefore, a "cave of rimes!"

Mythological figures from German folklore appear by way of composer Richard Wagner's *Parsifal* (1882) and its Grail quest as it moves through the poetry of French poet Paul Verlaine, resurfacing eventually in T. S. Eliot's *The Waste Land* (1922). True to Duncan's obsession with origins, he finds himself in the company of the originators of "sexual wound literature," Isis and Osiris. All the wounded figures in these legends could be cured if a questing hero, usually an innocent fool, speaks the loving and, therefore, "healing" words. The words must take the form of a question, and Duncan again locates the hidden and healing word "quest" within "question." The answer is in the "question" itself, because reality is always a matter of language continuously probing its sources for meaning.

"PASSAGES"

First published: 1968-1987
Type of work: Poetry

The "Passages" poems are interwoven throughout Duncan's poetry after 1968 as interconnecting responses, but they can also be read within their own unique structure.

As in the case of "The Structure of Rime" series, Duncan would not permit these poems to be collected into one volume. Indeed, he was so vehement about their nonsequential structure that he stopped numbering them after "Passages 37" so that readers would not be tempted to see any kind of evolving progressive structure. They share certain common functions with "The Structure of Rime" sections but are almost purely poetry, and they can be viewed as a poetic counterpart enacting the poetic process that "The Structure of Rime" sections probe and discuss.

Looking at their mutual relationship also reveals a counterpoint, in a musical sense, which intermittently creates common measures and scales that Duncan would also consider a kind of "rime." One of the reasons for the expanding canvas of "Passages" is that Duncan no longer speaks through fictive voices and masks. It is his own highly musical, bardic voice speaking throughout; he has broken away from the kind of mythological personae that Pound and Olson used throughout their long poems.

The first thirty "Passages" poems appeared in *Bending the Bow* in 1968 and immediately established Duncan as a master of long formal structures. The next ten were published in *Ground Work: Before the War*, while the concluding thirteen are in *Ground Work II: In the Dark*. In all, fifty-three "Passages" poems appeared over a twenty-year period.

Part of the function of the first crucial "Passages" was a demonstration of Duncan's consistent habit within these works of talking about a topic while simultaneously activating that subject's archetypal reverberations and illustrating how a poem comes into being. "Passages 1" is titled "Tribal Memories" and becomes, in effect, an invocation to the muse of memory, Mnemosyne, and a depiction of how she enters Duncan's afternoon nap with dreams of his individual poems, participating in the eternally recurring act of creation.

In "Passages 2: At the Loom," Duncan further defines the poetic process in its relationship to his mind: "my mind a shuttle among/ set strings of the music/ lets a weft of dream grow in the day time,/ an increment of associations,/ luminous soft threads,/ the thrown glamor crossing and recrossing,/ the twisted sinews underlying the work." Not only has he continued the proposal of the preceding "Passages," but he has also instructed the reader how to read his poems by comparing his imagination to the activity of a loom.

"Passages 3" interweaves Christ with his prototype, Osiris, archetypal twins that Duncan uses throughout the collection. In the first thirty "Passages," old topics are reintroduced, such as the Grail, alchemy, magic and puns on "spell," language, and homosexual dedication and passion, while new French masters, such as Victor Hugo and Jean Genet, appear. Throughout "Passages" 13-30, Duncan rails against the American involvement in the Vietnam War. In "Passages 21: The Multiversity," he bitterly condemns the military-industrial-university complex, identifying the chancellor of the University of California, Clark Kerr, with William Blake's destructive "old Nobodaddy."

Many of these poems are vehemently concerned with the political abuse of power by the rich and privileged, and Duncan explores in a deeply Freudian mode the connections between the etymological origins of "phallic" aggressiveness and the impulse toward "fascism" that the United States, to him, seemed to be demonstrating during those years in the 1960's. He boldly compares President Lyndon Johnson with both German chancellor Adolf Hitler and Soviet premier Joseph Stalin.

In the later "Passages" that appeared in both *Ground Work* volumes, he moves away from the concerns of war and back to his search for origins. He moves comfortably from music and its source in utterance, vision, and dance, as subjects for the great "Tribunals Passages" to the more mundane concerns of "Passages 34: The Feast," which is obviously a recipe for cooking lamb. By changing the spelling of the word "EWE," he finds beneath it the name "EVE," transforming a seemingly casual dinner into a re-enactment of the Fall into consciousness and knowledge.

The late "Passages" become extended meditations delving even more deeply into the "language beyond speech" and its ability to enter the pantheon of the spirits and the archetypal sea of words. Grief and ecstasy enter the work more intensely as his language brings him closer to the terror of the cosmological void in "Passages: Empedoklean Reveries": "There is a field of random energies from which we come." In the concluding "Passages" in *Ground Work II*, he finds himself a participant in the drama of wound literature in "In Blood's Domaine"; in his case, the wound is invisible. Indeed, because of complications from high blood pressure, Duncan died after several years of serious illness, ironically a "victim" of his own blood.

One of Duncan's last and most appropriate metaphors for his life was that of "a theme and variations," an early musical form from which all subsequent musical forms, such as the sonata and the symphony, emerged. In the final dark "Passages," he realizes that language does not come into the mind to be used by the poet. Rather, "Mind comes into this language as if into an Abyss." His two valedictory "Passages" are homages to vital sources of his imaginal and physical life: "The Muses" and his own circulatory system, with his heart at the center.

His last "Passages" poem envisions the fluctuating dynamics of his entire creative mechanism, which he had earlier called the scales "of resemblance and disresemblance, and sees them still operating, but now with the "inflatus/deflatus" or the "blood/air pump" of his own weakening heart as it nourishes the "ex-change artist." He had found in the title of one of psychologist James Hillman's books a perfect amalgamation of all his late themes as he embodied them and they embodied him: *The Thought of the Heart*.

SUMMARY

There is little doubt that Duncan's contributions to American poetry are unique; no other writer approaches the poetic office as an activity of the spirit with the intensity of Duncan's devotion. For him, poetry was as valid a way of exploring and knowing reality as chemistry or physics. His one consistent rule was that, though calling himself a traditionalist, he permitted the voices of his spiritual influences and ancestors to register their presences as long as he kept his poetic procedures open and trusted the changing structures of his primary source, language itself. He is unquestionably one of the major American Romantic poets.

Patrick Meanor

BIBLIOGRAPHY

By the Author

POETRY:
Heavenly City, Earthly City, 1947
Poems, 1948-1949, 1950
Medieval Scenes, 1950 (reprinted as *Medieval Scenes 1950 and 1959*)
Fragments of a Disordered Devotion, 1952
Caesar's Gate: Poems, 1948-1950, 1956
Letters: Poems, MCMLIII-MCMLVI, 1958
Selected Poems, 1959
The Opening of the Field, 1960
Writing, Writing: A Composition Book for Madison 1953, Stein Imitations, 1964
Roots and Branches, 1964
Passages 22-27 of the War, 1966
The Years as Catches: First Poems, 1939-1946, 1966
Six Prose Pieces, 1966
A Book of Resemblances: Poems, 1950-1953, 1966
Epilogos, 1967
Names of People, 1968
Bending the Bow, 1968
The First Decade: Selected Poems, 1940-1950, 1969
Derivations: Selected Poems, 1950-1956, 1969
Achilles' Song, 1969
Play Time: Pseudo Stein, 1969
Poetic Disturbances, 1970
Tribunals: Passages 31-35, 1970
Ground Work: Before the War, 1971
Poems from the Margins of Thom Gunn's "Moly," 1972
A Seventeenth Century Suite in Homage to the Metaphysical Genius in English Poetry, 1590/1690, 1973
An Ode to Arcadia, 1974 (with Jack Spicer)
Dante, 1974
The Venice Poem, 1975
Veil, Turbine, Cord, and Bird, 1979
The Five Songs, 1981
Ground Work: Before the War, 1984
A Paris Visit, 1985
Ground Work II: In the Dark, 1987

DRAMA:
Faust Foutu: An Entertainment in Four Parts, pb. 1959
Medea at Kolchis: The Maidenhead, pb. 1965

DISCUSSION TOPICS

- Is the caption "The Structure of Rime," applied to Robert Duncan's collective writings on the art of poetry, misleading in its scope?

- Examine the unusual (that is, unexpected in their context) words in the poem "Often I Am Permitted to Return to a Meadow," beginning with the word "permitted." What do such words contribute to the poem—especially to the tone?

- Considering Duncan's interpretation of responsibility as "the ability to respond," what evidence do his poems furnish of his capacity to respond to a variety of subjects and influences?

- What is Duncan's concept of spirituality? What religious and philosophical traditions contribute to it?

- How can careful attention to the diction of Duncan's poems contribute to a person's understanding of the subject of etymology?

- By what techniques does Duncan overcome his reader's possible reluctance to commit to and enjoy a long poem?

NONFICTION:
As Testimony: The Poem and the Scene, 1964
The Sweetness and Greatness of Dante's "Divine Comedy," 1965
The Cat and the Blackbird, 1967
The Truth and Life of Myth: An Essay in Essential Autobiography, 1968
A Selection of Sixty-five Drawings from One Drawing-Book, 1952-1956, 1970
Fictive Certainties, 1985
The Last Letters, 2000
The Letters of Robert Duncan and Denise Levertov, 2004 (Robert J. Bertholf and Albert Gelpi, editors)

About the Author

Bertholf, Robert J. *Robert Duncan: A Descriptive Bibliography.* Santa Rosa, Calif.: Black Sparrow Press, 1986.

Bertholf, Robert J., and Ian W. Reid, eds. *Robert Duncan: Scales of the Marvelous.* New York: New Directions, 1979.

Duncan, Robert. Interview. In *Towards a New American Poetics: Essays and Interviews,* edited by Ekbert Faas. Santa Barbara, Calif.: Black Sparrow Press, 1978.

Faas, Ekbert. *Young Robert Duncan: Portrait of the Poet as Homosexual in Society.* Santa Barbara, Calif.: Black Sparrow Press, 1983.

Johnson, Mark. *Robert Duncan.* Boston: Twayne, 1988.

O'Leary, Peter. *Gnostic Contagion: Robert Duncan and the Poetry of Illness.* Middletown, Conn.: Wesleyan University Press, 2002.

Sagetrieb 4 (Fall/Winter, 1985).

T. S. ELIOT

Born: St. Louis, Missouri
September 26, 1888
Died: London, England
January 4, 1965

Critic, dramatist, and Nobel laureate, Eliot was one of the foremost poets of the twentieth century; his startling originality heralded modernism, and his poetic complexity continues to challenge readers.

E. O. Hoppe

BIOGRAPHY

Thomas Stearns Eliot was born in St. Louis, Missouri, on September 26, 1888, the son of Henry and Charlotte (Stearns) Eliot, whose ancestors were among the early settlers of seventeenth century Massachusetts. Eliot's grandfather, the Reverend William Greenleaf Eliot, left New England in 1834 to evangelize an outpost of civilization at St. Louis. There he founded the (first) Unitarian Church of the Messiah and Eliot Seminary which, under his leadership as chancellor (1870-1887), became Washington University.

Eliot's early schooling at Smith Academy and his summers at coastal Rockport and Gloucester, Massachusetts, would inform the imagined landscapes of his subsequent poetry, as would visits to his ancestral home in East Coker, Somerset, England. Eliot studied for a year at Milton Academy (Massachusetts) and then entered Harvard College, where he received the B.A. degree in 1909 and pursued a doctoral degree program from 1909 to 1914, in which he completed but did not defend a dissertation on F. H. Bradley's philosophy.

In 1910-1911, Eliot visited Germany and France and studied at the Sorbonne in Paris. In addition to his philosophical studies at Harvard, he explored several subjects, the Pali and Sanskrit languages among them. World War I halted his plans to study at Marburg, Germany, where he had received a fellowship stipend in 1914. Instead, he transferred to the University of Oxford's Merton College. Two highly significant events followed: On September 22, 1914, he met the expatriate American poet Ezra Pound; on June 26, 1915, Eliot married Vivien Haigh-Wood.

Pound, who observed that Eliot had already "trained himself *and* modernized himself *on his own*," was to become Eliot's lifelong friend and sometime editor, "the better craftsman" to whom Eliot dedicated *The Waste Land* (1922). Eliot's unhappy marriage was to last until Vivien's death in 1947, although Eliot wrote to her from the United States in 1933 announcing their official separation.

With his added fiscal responsibilities, Eliot left Oxford and embarked on a short-lived teaching career at High Wycombe Grammar School and Highgate School and as an extension lecturer for Oxford between 1915 and 1917. In March, 1917, he joined Lloyd's of London bank as a clerk in its Colonial and Foreign Department and, except for three months of sick leave in fall, 1921, remained there until 1925, when he became an editor with the publishing house of Faber and Gwynn (later, Faber and Faber). It has been suggested that his early career as a poet of somber things was directly influenced by his marriage, financial circumstances, and unchallenging work.

The period from 1916 to 1922 was marked by Eliot's extraordinary literary productivity. He regularly contributed essays and reviews to the *Athenaeum*, *The Dial*, *The Egoist*, *The Times Literary Supplement*, and other journals. Thanks to Pound's

703

influence, his early poems, published in *Prufrock and Other Observations* (1917), *Poems* (1919), *Ara Vos Prec* (1920), and *The Waste Land* (1922), were published in British and American journals. This last poem reshaped the post-World War I literary world, made Eliot the obvious choice to be editor of the new journal *The Criterion* (1922-1939), and gained for him a lasting place among twentieth century poets.

A year after joining Faber and Gwynn, Eliot was Clark Lecturer at Trinity College, University of Cambridge, and a year later he underwent profound changes: In June, 1927, he joined the Church of England and within five months became a British subject. In his book *For Lancelot Andrewes* (1928), he explained himself: "The general point of view may be described as classicist in literature, royalist in politics, and Anglo-Catholic in religion." Like most authorial statements, this may reflect more desire than achievement and may be less than accurate. It does, nevertheless, help account for an evolution in Eliot's poetic thought and concerns from "The Hollow Men" (1925) through *Four Quartets* (1943).

Eliot returned to the United States in 1932 and to his alma mater as Charles Eliot Norton Professor of Poetry at Harvard (1932-1933). While in America, he obtained a legal separation from his wife. Before returning to England, he lectured at the University of Virginia on Christian apologetics, a topic that had already begun to suffuse his poetry and that was to inform much more of it, as well as his dramas. His work in the 1930's was largely given to spiritual topics such as those in the verse pageant plays *The Rock: A Pageant Play* (1934) and *Murder in the Cathedral* (1935) and in the poems *Ash Wednesday* (1930) and the first of his *Four Quartets*, "Burnt Norton" (1939).

With "Burnt Norton" as a beginning, Eliot continued work on his *Four Quartets*, producing "East Coker" (1940), "The Dry Salvages" (1941), and "Little Gidding" (1942), and publishing them together in one volume in 1943. This was to be the last of his major poetic efforts; thereafter, he turned principally to prose and to writing verse dramas. The restoration of poetic drama to the stage was a project to which he had committed himself, as had Irish poet William Butler Yeats, in a conscious reaction to the vogue and influence of the realistic plays of Henrik Ibsen. In 1948, Eliot was

awarded both the British Order of Merit and the Nobel Prize in Literature.

More honors and distinctions were to follow in the 1950's and 1960's. He won the Hanseatic Goethe Prize (1954), the Dante Gold Medal (Florence, 1959), the Emerson-Thoreau Medal (American Academy of Arts and Sciences, 1959) and the U.S. Medal of Freedom (1964). He received honorary degrees from American, British, and other European colleges and universities.

Another important change came to Eliot when he married Valerie Fletcher on January 10, 1957, a change decidedly for the better—theirs was a happy marriage. While he continued to write plays and essays, he wrote little poetry in the 1950's, *The Cultivation of Christmas Trees* (1954) standing as the sole volume of new poetry in this period.

Eliot died on January 4, 1965, survived by his wife, Valerie. A memorial to Eliot is in Poets' Corner, Westminster Abbey; his ashes are interred in the parish church of East Coker, Somerset, the church of his ancestors.

ANALYSIS

Dante, Eliot once observed of the great Italian poet, his favorite writer, is "a poet to whom one grows up over a lifetime." So, too, is Eliot himself. Indeed, although he was a formidable, forceful, and original critic, a tireless advocate of Elizabethan and Jacobean drama, and a dramatist whose work endures, the one title he preferred was "poet." This is not to slight his other work but to emphasize the principal orientation and habit of mind from which his prose and drama sprang. He assessed his own critical work in "To Criticize the Critic," a lecture he presented at Leeds University in 1961, by distinguishing several categories of critics and placing himself among those whose criticism is a by-product of their creative activity.

Eliot's far-ranging critical work, like his poetry, dealt with artists and styles, writers and literature, that appealed to him and contained elements he would mine for his own poetic work. From the English religious and devotional work of the seventeenth century to the work of his contemporary, the classical scholar Gilbert Murray, from the French Symbolist poets of the nineteenth century to William Shakespeare, Eliot interpreted literary production in ways that seemed original and fresh. His most notable critical concepts were the necessities of tradition, of impersonality in art, of the poet's mind as a catalyst, as expressed in "Tradition and the Individual Talent" (1919), and of an objective correlative between ideas or emotions and the precise words to express them, which he discussed in "Hamlet" (1919).

Schooled in classical drama, a critic of Shakespeare (and of such dramatists as John Dryden as well as the Elizabethans and Jacobeans), and a poet who incorporated dramatic speech and situations into his poetry, Eliot came to write poetic drama only in the 1930's. His work includes the religious pageant plays *The Rock* and *Murder in the Cathedral*. The former is more static than dramatic, a chronic piece that owes much to classical Greek drama. The latter is somewhat more dramatic, but it relies heavily on choric elements, a sermon, and a trial scene following the murder of the archbishop of Canterbury.

The sparsity of Eliot's stage directions allows for considerable latitude in handling elements of costume, set design, lighting, and stage "business" to heighten the drama of the play. While his later efforts, *The Family Reunion* (1939), *The Cocktail Party* (1949), *The Confidential Clerk* (1953), and *The Elder Statesman* (1958) enjoyed a brief vogue and are occasionally revived, *Murder in the Cathedral* remains his most popular play.

Eliot's poetry may be generally divided into three periods, the first beginning with his earliest efforts, the most famous of which is "The Love Song of J. Alfred Prufrock" (1915). "Gerontion" (1919) marks the inception of the second period, with *The Waste Land* as its apex and "The Hollow Men" as its terminus; it is also the terminus of what has been called his poetry of secular humanism. "Ash Wednesday" opens the final phase of his poetic practice, which may be characterized as one of Christian humanism. As with any attempt at poetic classification, this is a descriptive one which must be applied flexibly.

Eliot's early poetry, although steeped in tradition, was startlingly new and individual; his later poetry, similarly heavily informed by tradition, continued his own tradition of innovation. In a literary career that spanned more than half a century, he became the premier poet of his age, remembered especially for his three masterworks, "The Love Song of J. Alfred Prufrock," *The Waste Land,* and *Four Quartets*. From his earliest until his last poetry, he dealt with the essentially modernist themes of anxiety, depersonalization, the quest for identity and meaning, and the search for meaning through language, as well as with the timeless theme of love, both erotic and divine, and the physical and spiritual dualities of human existence.

Among the many influences on Eliot's poetry were the organizing structures used by the French Symbolists, particularly Jules Laforgue, and the synaesthetic practice of musical poetry. Influences on his finely honed expression included Ezra Pound, the French novelist Gustave Flaubert, and the English critic Walter Pater (whose influence Eliot was eager to disavow). The works he criticized and, in part, helped to revive were grist for his poetic mill; his poetry is filled with echoes of Shakespeare and seventeenth century dramatists, of the Metaphysical poets, of Dante, and of the poets of antiquity.

Biblical and liturgical echoes also chime through in his poetry. Eliot's use of "the dead poets," as he called them, arose not so much from erudite pedantry as from a desire to belong to and alter the tradition in which he wrote. If his references and allusions at first appear obscure and arcane, a careful study of their place in his poems usually reveals that the one text complements or adjusts the meaning of the other.

Eliot also has a lighter side, which surfaces in his appreciative essay of Marie Lloyd, the British music-hall star, in his "five-finger exercises" of the 1930's, and, most popularly, in his *Old Possum's Book of Practical Cats* (1939), the foundation for Andrew Lloyd Webber's popular 1980's musical play *Cats*. In a later, amused reassessment of his own critical work he could point to lapses that he said surfaced as "the occasional note of arrogance, of vehemence, of cocksureness or rudeness, the braggadocio of a mild-mannered man safely entrenched behind his typewriter." The humorous side of Eliot's work helps inform the ironic and sardonic elements of his more serious endeavors.

A consummate wordsmith and creator of memorable phrases, Eliot imbued his poetry with locutions that range from the gemlike to highly wrought goldsmith's work as he sought the phrase and sentence that is right, "where every word is at home." He consistently strove, as he wrote in "Little Gidding," to find "The common word, exact without vulgarity/ The formal word, precise but not pedantic/ The complete consort dancing together." His many poetic achievements have led him to be hailed as a poet's poet.

"THE LOVE SONG OF J. ALFRED PRUFROCK"

First published: 1915 (collected in *Collected Poems, 1909-1962*)
Type of work: Poem

Prufrock invites the reader on an inward journey through the dreamscape of his mind.

The masterpiece of his poetic apprenticeship, "The Love Song of J. Alfred Prufrock" remains one of Eliot's most intriguing and challenging poems; it may be usefully examined by listening to the voices it embodies. Like much of the poetry of Robert Browning, it is a dramatic monologue. Like the poetry of Jules Laforgue, it is a Symbolist poem that explores the narrator's stream of consciousness as he relates, in fragmented fashion, his seemingly random thoughts that are unified by the structure of the poem.

One key to this song of misprized, reluctant, hesitant love is in the epigraph from Dante's *Inferno* (XXVII) in which the speaker, Guido, reluctantly reveals the reason he is in Hell. While Prufrock finds it difficult to say what he means, he relates his thought as Guido had to Dante, without fear that his secret will be revealed to the living. The Dantean clue places the reader among the dead: This is one of the several suggestive possibilities for reading the poem and viewing its world as one of the circles that hold dead souls. The reader immediately enters what the critic Hugh Kenner has called a "zone of consciousness," not a realistic setting, and listens to a story that is not sequential: One is invited to share a dream with disturbing overtones.

The often perplexed reader needs to make numerous decisions about the teller and the tale. Is Prufrock actually addressing the reader, as Guido did Dante, or is he talking to himself? Is he any or all of the self-caricatures he contemplates—ragged claws, John the Baptist, Lazarus, Polonius? Is he bound on an erotic mission, a visit of social obliga-

tion, or merely an imaginary prowl through half-deserted streets; does he move at all from the spot where he begins his narrative, or is all animation suspended and all action only contemplated or remembered? Readers must negotiate these and similar questions, open to a variety of answers, to determine the speaker's identity and judge the situation in which they find themselves with Prufrock.

Similarly important are the sensory images that the voice projects, from the etherized patient to the ragged claws to the mermaids and one's own death by drowning, which involves all the senses until consciousness is extinguished. As the voices—Prufrock's, the women's, the woman's, the mermaids', Lazarus's, John's—must be heard, so the images must be seen, the yellow fog and the seawater smelled and tasted, the motion of walking and the pressure of reclining felt along the nerves. Like many of Eliot's dramatic poems, this drama calls for total sensory involvement as the reader observes with the mind's eye the many scenes to which Prufrock refers.

Apart from its intrinsic significance, this poem foreshadows many of the concerns and techniques Eliot would explore and use in the remainder of his poetry. It stands, then, as a prelude to other work and, as Eliot would have it, is modified by that work.

"GERONTION"

First published: 1920 (collected in *Collected Poems, 1909-1962*)
Type of work: Poem

Gerontion speaks the thoughts of a "dry brain in a dry season."

Like Eliot's earlier "Portraits of a Lady" (1917) and "The Love Song of J. Alfred Prufrock," the poem "Gerontion" is a dramatic but interior monologue in which the voice of the narrator is distinctly realized, and his words reveal his character and the dramatic situation or scene in which he acts. A difficult poem, it may be approached as a collage, entered as one would a stream, in this case the stream of consciousness of the narrator, who is, literally, a "little old man."

The narrator weaves personal history with more universal themes to form a meditative reverie of remembrance interspersed with remembered fragments from the Bible and from the Elizabethan and Jacobean dramatic poets William Shakespeare, Ben Jonson, George Chapman, Cyril Tourner, and Thomas Middleton. Other *dramatis personae* are the Jew, Christ, Mr. Silvero, Hakagawa, Mme de Tomquist, Fraulein von Kulp, De Bailhache, Fresca, and Mrs. Cainmel, as well as the anonymous boy who reads to the narrator.

Like the Fisher King of *The Waste Land* whom he prefigures, Gerontion is an old man waiting for rain, for rebirth in a period of aridity. Yet since the juvenescence of the year brings Christ the tiger who is eaten and who devours, there is some ambiguity and possibly some ambivalence about a rebirth that leads to death in a recurring cycle. There is also the equally large concern about action, phrased by one who denies that he has acted: He was not at the Battle of Thermopylae (the hot gates), nor did he fight knee-deep in the salt marsh (possibly before the gates of windy Troy). He has, instead, been acted upon, driven by the trade winds to a sleepy corner.

The space-time continuum figures prominently in the poem. Eliot's use of space varies from the inner space of a dry brain to the house to the location of the house to the Jew who has wandered from Antwerp to Brussels to London to the ethnic origins of Hakagawa and company to the celestial Ursa Major. Some of the characters, in a trope reminiscent of the poems of seventeenth century poet George Herbert, are gone into a world of light, whirled beyond the Bear's circuit in fractured atoms. Similarly, time is confused and variable as past, past remembered in the past and present, the present, and the future coalesce in the mind of the narrator. Similarly, the meditation on history and its gifts shuttles across time and raises ethical issues such as concerns over how and whether to act.

Above all, the poem represents an authorial attempt to present a speaker's attempt to order his experience, to make sense of the present in the light of the past, to think, and, in the act of thinking, to create meaning. What Gerontion does is essentially what the principal narrator of *The Waste Land* will do; he is shoring up fragments of language and of meaning against the ruins of a life.

THE WASTE LAND

First published: 1922
Type of work: Poem

The Waste Land *explores human history and experience in a quest for regenerative wholeness.*

The most celebrated poem of the twentieth century, *The Waste Land* epitomizes modernism—its anxious usurpation of previous texts in the literary tradition, its self-conscious desire to be new, its bleak analysis of the present as a post-lapsarian moment between a crumbling past and an uncertain future. Composed of five separate poems, the overarching poem is, in poetic range and effect, greater than the sum of these parts. Eliot combines many of the themes and techniques he had examined in his earlier work, themes such as aridity, sexuality, and living death, and techniques such as stream-of-consciousness; narration; historical, literary, and mythic allusions; and the dramatic monologue. As in his earlier works, he is intent upon voice and vision, but not to the exclusion of the other senses.

When he republished the poem in book form, also in 1922, he added more than fifty notes to it, some of which direct the reader to such sources as Jessie L. Weston's *From Ritual to Romance* (1920) and Sir James Frazer's *The Golden Bough* (1890-1915), the former for its handling of the Grail Quest and the waste land motifs, the latter for its expositions of vegetation myths and rituals.

Eliot's note to line 218 helps explain the overall unity of the work and offers a useful starting place for a serious and necessary rereading of the poem by newcomers to the poem and to Eliot. "Tiresias," he wrote, "although a mere spectator and not indeed a 'character,' is yet the most important personage in the poem, uniting all the rest." All the male characters become one, all the women, one woman, and the two sexes meet in Tiresias. What Tiresias *sees*, in fact, is the substance of the poem.

The poem's title, derived from the medieval Grail Quest, holds a clue: The questing reader must ask the right question of the Fisher King (who merges into Tiresias, the blind prophet of Thebes, and, indeed, into the poet). The Greek and Latin epigraph concerns the Cumaean Sibyl who, asked by a boy what she wishes, states that she wishes to die—an impossibility, since she had asked of Apollo and been granted as many years as he had grains of sand in his hand. Unfortunately, she had not made the right first request: for eternal youth. One must, then, ask carefully. The Dantean dedication, to Ezra Pound, "the better craftsman," fuses ancient, medieval, and modern at the outset of the poem, while acknowledging Pound's role in shaping the work.

"The Burial of the Dead," part 1, contains a number of speakers, ranging from Marie to Madame Sosostris to Stetson, whose fragments of conversation in English, French, and German wind

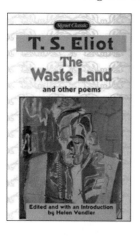

around ritual reenactments of burial and rebirth. From the Dantean vision of the dead walking over London Bridge to the dangerous business of doing a simple errand to the buttonholing last line from the French poet Charles Baudelaire, in which the reader is addressed directly as hypocrite and brother, the atmosphere is menacing. Structurally, the poem contains varieties of motion to organize it: motion in time across days, months, seasons, years, and centuries, motion in change from youth to age, action to stillness, and death to rebirth, as Bernard Bergonzi has observed.

Part 2, "A Game of Chess," elaborates the themes of aridity and rebirth in the story of Lil's barren sexuality and Philomel's mythic reincarnation after sexual abuse, thus blending the mythic and the prosaic to reveal a relatively mindless luxury devoid of satisfying significance. Whether in the ornate boudoir which opens the sequence or the working-class pub which closes it, the pleasures of the world seem unsatisfying. In a memorable phrase that has rung through every English pub since their Victorian regulation, the barman's call for closing becomes, in the poet's hands, an advent call for change or a hastening of some final, eschatological closure: *"HURRY UP PLEASE ITS TIME."*

In part 3, "The Fire Sermon," the poet deals with the refining fire of purgation, unites Western and Eastern mystical theology in Saint Augustine and

the Buddha, and combines ancient and medieval literary tradition in Tiresias and the Fisher King. These higher quests are played off against the more sordid ones of Sweeney and Mrs. Porter, the typist and the carbuncular young man, and Mr. Eugenides ("well-born" but decadent), as Tiresias begins to tie elements of the poem together.

The brief, ten-line "Death by Water," part 4, presents water as destroyer, cleanser, and paradoxical life-giver in the case of Phlebas, the Phoenician sailor who passes, two weeks dead, backward through the stages of his age and youth and enters the whirlpool. This, too, Tiresias sees and possibly relates.

"What the Thunder Said," part 5, brings rain and its promise of rebirth. The thunder reverberates with the words of the Upanishads (Hindu philosophic writings) for "give, sympathize, control," keys to unlocking the prisons in which each individual is kept a solitary prisoner. The resolution offered to those journeying to Emmaus, to the Chapel Perilous, through "the present decay of eastern Europe," depends upon the trinity of commands or counsels from the thunder and becomes "the peace which passeth understanding" ("shantih," quoted from the Upanishads) repeated at the close of the poem.

Eliot's achievement in this highly sophisticated poem is the blending of the disparate elements of varied traditions into a unity that may itself be both an object lesson in and a plea for the necessity of artistic wholeness. This is one possible reading of the piece as a metapoetical work that points as much to itself as it does to the traditions in which it exists and which it, in turn, alters.

"THE HOLLOW MEN"

First published: 1925 (collected in *Collected Poems, 1909-1962*)
Type of work: Poem

Eliot explores spiritual emptiness in this masquelike work.

This poem of emptiness, "The Hollow Men," opens with a double epigraph, one from the novelist Joseph Conrad's *Heart of Darkness* (1902) and one from the traditional children's request for a penny on Guy Fawkes Day, November 5. The former seems intended to draw the reader to Conrad's short masterpiece and to the announcement of the death of Mr. Kurtz—perhaps the ultimate hollow man—to Charlie Marlow, the first narrator of that work. (Marlow had observed of London that it, too, was once one of the dark places of the world.) The latter epigraph also involves light and darkness, as it recalls the 1605 Gunpowder Plot, an alleged Roman Catholic attempt to blow up the English monarch and the houses of Parliament. The "guy" is a stuffed effigy of Guy Fawkes; the pennies collected by children are to purchase materials and fireworks to celebrate the ritual evening burning of the effigy. Both epigraphs allude to an emptiness, one spiritual and one physical.

Divided into five parts, the poem begins in a choric proclamation of emptiness, as if a chorus of stuffed men were appearing before the reader in a frozen *tableau vivant* that will quicken to a dance round in part 5, followed by an antiphonal and concluding with another dance round.

The playfulness of some of the motion implied in the poem is in sharp contrast to the words of the hollow men. The poem's first part also introduces the notion of a double kingdom of death, one in this world and one in the next.

The second part explores death's dream kingdom, sleep, and the hope that the speaker, one of the hollow men in soliloquy, would not meet eyes he would wish to avoid, eyes that he would prefer remain distant. Part 3 sets the reader in a dead land, a desert place of isolation that thwarts, like death's other kingdom, the ability to kiss, to express emotion. Part 4, filled with negation, describes a hollow valley, a broken jaw of lost kingdoms, where the hollow men gather silently on the beach of a tumid river and await the only hope of empty men, death.

The fifth part, the most complex and challenging, opens and closes with variants of children's game-songs. The first substitutes the prickly pear for the traditional mulberry bush; the last is a version of "London Bridge Is Falling Down." Both, if sung and danced by the effigies, produce even more incongruity between the song and the words, the action and the statement. Framed by these songs are the shadow verses of one chorus played off against another chorus repeating phrases and

variants from the Anglican conclusion to the Lord's Prayer.

In his highly suggestive language and the characters' elliptical speech, Eliot exposes an incompleteness that for these hollow men will be consummated not with the blaze and explosions customary on November 5 but with the inarticulate whimper that concludes the masque.

"ASH WEDNESDAY"

First published: 1930 (collected in *Collected Poems, 1909-1962*)
Type of work: Poem

In a poem of intercession, the speaker reluctantly seeks conversion.

"Ash Wednesday" contains many traces of Eliot's newly found Anglo-Catholic orientation; he had officially joined the church in 1927. The poem's title comes from the Christian movable feast day celebrating the onset of Lent, forty days before Easter: It is a day of mortification of the flesh and of turning toward the spiritual. The poem exemplifies the tensions between the flesh and the spirit, borrowing much from Dante's medieval mysticism, as the story of conversion is told in a Symbolist dream, a favorite technique of Eliot. As in *The Waste Land*, characters merge; the Lady merges with other ladies, such as Ecclesia (church), Theologia (theology), and Beatrice (the blessed one, from Dante), possibly to represent the anima, or feminine principle.

The first portion of this six-part poem opens with a despairing lack of hope for conversion, followed by a prayer for mercy, a famous request for a holy indifference: "Teach us to care and not to care/ Teach us to sit still." It concludes with a refrain from the last sentence of the Ave Maria, "Holy Mary, Mother of God, pray for us sinners now and at the hour of our death." Eliot thus endows the poem with fragments of prayer (along with Shakespearean allusions), varied renunciations, and some recognition of the need for rejoicing. The negative assertion of hope's lack at the outset is modified by prayers which indicate a realization of the need for spiritual help.

Biblical references crowd part 2, forming a litany; the response to many of its phrases is the unvoiced but expected "Pray for us." In part 3, the speaker ascends a spiral staircase, past a devil and past a vision of an earthly paradise; this portion ends with the liturgical prayer before Communion from the Mass of the Faithful, echoing phrases from one of the miracle stories about Jesus. Part 4 blends the biblical Mary with other female figures, asks for a redemption of time, and concludes with a phrase from the prayer *Salve, Regina,* which asks that Mary show the fruit of her womb, Jesus, "after this our exile."

Part 5 is a meditation on the Word of God, the *Logos* from the Gospel according to John, that Eliot would amplify in *Four Quartets.* This is accompanied by the refrain from the *Improperia* of the Good Friday service, "O my people." The poem's final segment returns to the original state of mind of the narrator as the poet recapitulates the themes and images of the entire poem and ends with a phrase addressed to the Lord in the *Indulgentiam* of the Mass of the Catechumens, the early dialogue between priest and laity which asks God to forgive sins, show mercy, hear prayers, "and let my cry come unto Thee."

In many respects, Eliot's *Ash Wednesday* is a poetic public demonstration of a change of heart, an assertion of Christian desire balanced by a recognition of frailty, that ends with a striving, itself a conversion from the poem's opening posture.

FOUR QUARTETS

First published: 1943
Type of work: Poetry

This sequence represents Eliot's most mature poetic statement on spiritual and artistic health.

Simpler, more direct in style than much of his early work, *Four Quartets* stands as the masterpiece of Eliot's poetic maturity and as an index of the extent to which his poetic concerns had changed and his spiritual concerns had deepened. Each poem of the group, as C. K. Stead has ably documented, is in five movements in quartet or sonata form. The first part of each concerns the movement of time, in which fleeting moments of eternity flicker. Dissatisfaction with worldly experience is the keynote of each of the second parts. Part 3 is a spiritual quest for purgation and divestiture of worldly things. The lyric fourth part comments upon the need for spiritual intercession, while the concluding part probes the issue of artistic wholeness, an issue allied to the achievement of spiritual health.

Formed from lines originally written for *Murder in the Cathedral,* "Burnt Norton" (1939), the first of the sequence, is thematically linked to the play but goes beyond it, as Eliot probes more deeply the motivation for action and the role of the poet as a participant in the *Logos* (Word). His epigraphs from the Greek philosopher Heraclitus concern the neglect of the law of reason (Logos) and cite the paradoxical phrase, "The way upward and downward are one and the same." A problematic proposition, "If all time is eternally present/ All time is unredeemable," is part of the poem's meditative opening, which also reiterates Thomas à Becket's line from the play, "human kind/ Cannot bear very much reality." The ascendent spirit and descendent body are the Heraclitean oppositions of part 2, in a continuing meditation on the limits of time and its eternity and the desire to purge the human condition of its limitations.

In "a place of disaffection," the narrator seeks to approach the condition of fire with a "dry soul" (part 3); part 4 celebrates the dark night of the soul, "at the still point of the turning world." The final segment treats words and music moving in time, artistic wholeness and spiritual health involving words as part of the Divine Logos, and love as a timeless present.

"East Coker" (1940) recalls Eliot's ancestral home in Somerset (which is also his burial place). Pursuing the poet's beginning in his end (1) and his role as craftsman of words (5), the poem contains a rueful look backward at "years largely wasted, years of *l entre deux guerres*" essaying to learn to use words. In this poem, the focus is on the earth from which the poet springs; it has relevance to

God the Son in some readings (as in the first of the poems, air is the dominant element), and some see direct relevance to God the Father. In this interpretation, the next poem, "The Dry Salvages" (1941), has as its motifs Mary, the Mother of God, and the element of water, and "Little Gidding" (1942), the element of fire and the Holy Ghost. These remain suggestive possibilities for interpretation, but they are supported by the texts.

"The Dry Salvages," a group of rocks off the Cape Ann coast, reflects the poet's early life in the United States, as does "the strong brown god," the Mississippi River at St. Louis. Much more explicitly religious in statement than the first two quartets, the poem has direct references to God and the Annunciation made to Mary (part 1), the tenets of Krishna (part 3), and the Queen of Heaven, *figlia del tuo figlio*, the "daughter of your son" (part 4). The occupation for the saint in part 5, "The point of intersection of the timeless/ With time," is also the poet's occupation, as Eliot continues to play out variations upon his themes.

His most famous poem in the sequence, "Little Gidding," is also his last major poetic statement. This place name is meant to evoke its seventeenth century associations as a center of spiritual life and its contemporary symbolism for the poet as the place of "the intersection of the timeless moment" (part 1). Encountering "the shade of some dead master," the speaker finds in the spirit's disillusionment yet another cause to reassess the poet's task: "To purify the language of the tribe" (part 2). The burden of the third part, that prayers and intercession are needful in the face of sin's inevitability, reinforces each of the prior third parts of the sequence.

In the final segment, all birds coalesce to become one bird, as the Heraclitean fire of the epigraph is subsumed into the descent of the Holy Spirit at Pentecost. The final and often-quoted and anthologized hymn to poetic practice as a means of achieving unity and spiritual health concludes the poem and the sequence in a complete affirmation unprecedented in Eliot's poetry.

Taken together in the light of their ending, the poems of *Four Quartets* rank among the most highly accomplished works of devotional poetry and treatments of a poet's vision of poetry itself. With this sequence, Eliot capped his career as a poet.

MURDER IN THE CATHEDRAL

First produced: 1935; first published, 1935
Type of work: Play

Eliot dramatizes the killing of Thomas à Becket, archbishop of Canterbury.

Eliot's best-known and most performed play, *Murder in the Cathedral* dramatizes the assassination of Thomas à Becket, archbishop of Canterbury, in 1170 at the hands of four knights and at the bidding of King Henry II. In this play, written for production at the Canterbury Festival, June, 1935, Eliot put into practice his long-held desire to reestablish verse drama as a viable form of theater, a wish shared by the Irish poet and playwright William Butler Yeats, whose work preceded Eliot's. Both sought to return poetry to the stage for historical and aesthetic reasons, as they viewed the popular realistic plays of the nineteenth and twentieth centuries as less desirable than poetic drama. Both writers have secured lasting places in the history of modern drama.

Modeled upon the chorus of ancient Greek tragedy, the chorus that opens the play introduces the place and the time—the return from a seven-year exile of the archbishop, at odds with the king for whom he had served as chancellor. Three priests, a messenger, Thomas, and four tempters of some demoniac reasonableness fill out the players of the first act. These last, for echoic effect, should be read/played by the same actors who play the four knights in the third act: This was Eliot's original design, and it is one reason he altered the lines of the knights in the play's second edition (1937), the text now current.

The chorus of the women of Canterbury comments on the action and presents its own sense of foreboding, fear, and, at the play's end, desolation. The priests, who may be seen as chorus leaders, voice their own concerns and trepidations. They seek to act according to conventional wisdom, counsel Thomas to flee back to France, seek to protect him from martyrdom, and finally look to the martyr for spiritual help in a time of personal need for comfort.

Of greater dramatic interest is the interplay between Thomas and the tempters, who offer him fleshly delights and good times, earthly political power by regaining the chancellorship he had resigned upon becoming archbishop, temporal sovereignty by joining a coup against the king, and glorious triumph over the king by seeking martyrdom. Once the murder is committed—onstage (a break with classical and neoclassical traditions but quite Jacobean)—the knights offer the audience-turned-jury their defense of disinterestedness in carrying out the king's will; finally, they claim that Thomas has sought martyrdom and seek a verdict of "suicide while of Unsound Mind."

Throughout the play, Eliot's language echoes scriptural injunctions, parables, and situations. In his stage directions and dialogue, Eliot uses liturgical hymns and portions of the Anglo-Catholic Mass. The interlude between the two acts is a Christmas sermon stylistically reminiscent of those of the seventeenth century ministers John Donne and Lancelot Andrews.

"Tradition and the Individual Talent"

First published: 1919 (collected in *Selected Essays*, 1932, 1950)
Type of work: Essay

Eliot places the poet in a literary tradition and argues for the impersonality of art.

"Tradition and the Individual Talent," one of Eliot's early essays, typifies his critical stance and concerns; it has been called his most influential single essay. Divided into three parts, appearing in *The Egoist* in September and December, 1919, the essay insists upon taking tradition into account when formulating criticism—"aesthetic, not merely historical criticism."

Eliot opens the essay by revivifying the word "tradition" and arguing that criticism, for which the French were then noted more than the English, in his view "is as inevitable as breathing." The first principle of criticism that he asserts is to focus not solely upon what is unique in a poet but upon what he shares with "the dead poets, his ancestors." This sharing, when it is not the mere and unquestioning following of established poetic practice, involves the historical sense, a sense that the whole of literary Europe and of one's own country "has a simultaneous existence and composes a simultaneous order."

A correlative principle is that no poet or artist has his or her complete meaning in isolation but must be judged, for contrast and comparison, among the dead. As Eliot sees it, the order of art is complete before a new work of art is created, but with that new creation all the prior works forming an ideal order are modified, and the order itself is altered.

One of the essay's memorable and enduring phrases concerns the objection that the living know so much more than the dead writers could have: Eliot counters by asserting, "Precisely, and they are that which we know." In gaining that knowledge, the artist engages in a "continual surrender" to tradition, and his or her progress "is a continual self-sacrifice, a continual extinction of personality." The definition of depersonalization that Eliot offers forms another of the essay's enduring phrases: As the novelist Gustave Flaubert and the English critic Walter Pater had written before him, Eliot seeks a scientific base for his works and likens the poet's mind to "a bit of finely filiated platinum . . . introduced into a chamber containing oxygen and sulphur dioxide."

The poet's mind, then, is a catalyst, as Eliot explains it in the essay's second part. His point is that the poet's transforming mind stores up feelings, phrases, and images until all the particles that can form a new work of art come together to do so. The poet has not so much a personality to express as a medium for the expression of complex emotion that is separable from the poet's own emotions. Poetry, Eliot emphasizes, is not a turning loose of personal emotion but a consciously deliberate escape from it. The emotion of art, he reminds his readers in the essay's final section, is impersonal.

Summary

Eliot's multiyear quest "to purify the language of the tribe" found its reward in his reception of the Nobel Prize in Literature in 1948—"for the entire corpus," he supposed. A poet in the forefront of modernism whose later work sought to give life to a vigorous union of the poetic and the spiritual, Eliot's poetry, drama, and criticism remain cultural forces to which successive generations have had recourse in probing the same issues—sometimes disquieting issues—that Eliot had examined before them.

John J. Conlon

BIBLIOGRAPHY

By the Author

POETRY:

"The Love Song of J. Alfred Prufrock," 1915
Prufrock and Other Observations, 1917
Poems, 1919
Ara Vos Prec, 1920
The Waste Land, 1922
Poems, 1909-1925, 1925
Ash Wednesday, 1930
Triumphal March, 1931
Sweeney Agonistes, 1932
Words for Music, 1934
Collected Poems, 1909-1935, 1936
Old Possum's Book of Practical Cats, 1939
Four Quartets, 1943
The Cultivation of Christmas Trees, 1954
Collected Poems, 1909-1962, 1963
Poems Written in Early Youth, 1967
The Complete Poems and Plays, 1969

DRAMA:

Sweeney Agonistes, pb. 1932, pr. 1933 (fragment)
The Rock: A Pageant Play, pb., pr. 1934
Murder in the Cathedral, pb., pr. 1935
The Family Reunion, pb., pr. 1939
The Cocktail Party, pr. 1949, pb. 1950
The Confidential Clerk, pr. 1953, pb. 1954
The Elder Statesman, pr. 1958, pb. 1959
Collected Plays, pb. 1962

NONFICTION:

Ezra Pound: His Metric and Poetry, 1917
The Sacred Wood, 1920
Homage to John Dryden, 1924
Shakespeare and the Stoicism of Seneca, 1927
For Lancelot Andrewes, 1928
Dante, 1929
Thoughts After Lambeth, 1931
Charles Whibley: A Memoir, 1931
John Dryden: The Poet, the Dramatist, the Critic, 1932
Selected Essays, 1932, 1950

DISCUSSION TOPICS

- How does T. S. Eliot alter the poetic traditions to which he contributes? For instance, what is new and distinctive about the protagonist and the "love song" in "The Love Song of J. Alfred Prufrock?

- Which images in J. Alfred Prufrock's interior monologue best convey his insecurity and the reasons for it?

- Choose one theme of *The Waste Land* and trace its development over the five parts of the poem.

- What musical conventions does Eliot employ in his poetry?

- Given Eliot's theory of the impersonality of poetry, is it possible to read his poetry from first to last as a spiritual autobiography?

- What does the assertion that *Murder in the Cathedral* is "more choric than dramatic" mean?

- Contrast Eliot's and William Faulkner's use of Christian symbols and allusions. In particular, how do their attitudes toward these Christian elements differ?

713

T. S. Eliot

The Use of Poetry and the Use of Criticism, 1933
After Strange Gods, 1934
Elizabethan Essays, 1934
Essays Ancient and Modern, 1936
The Idea of a Christian Society, 1939
The Music of Poetry, 1942
The Classics and the Man of Letters, 1942
Notes Toward the Definition of Culture, 1948
Poetry and Drama, 1951
The Three Voices of Poetry, 1953
Religious Drama: Medieval and Modern, 1954
The Literature of Politics, 1955
The Frontiers of Criticism, 1956
On Poetry and Poets, 1957
Knowledge and Experience in the Philosophy of F. H. Bradley, 1964
To Criticize the Critic, 1965
The Letters of T. S. Eliot: Volume I, 1898-1922, 1988

About the Author

Ackroyd, Peter. *T. S. Eliot: A Life*. New York: Simon & Schuster, 1984.

Browne, Elliott Martin. *The Making of T. S. Eliot's Plays*. London: Cambridge University Press, 1969.

Donoghue, Denis. *Words Alone: The Poet, T. S. Eliot*. New Haven, Conn.: Yale University Press, 2000.

Eliot, Valerie, ed. *The Letters of T. S. Eliot, 1898-1922*. Vol. 1. New York: Harcourt Brace Jovanovich, 1988.

Gordon, Lyndall. *Eliot's Early Years*. New York: Oxford University Press, 1977.

_____. *Eliot's New Life*. New York: Farrar, Straus and Giroux, 1988.

_____. *T. S. Eliot: An Imperfect Life*. New York: Norton, 1999.

Litz, A. Walton, ed. *Eliot in His Time: Essays on the Occasion of the Fiftieth Anniversary of "The Waste Land."* Princeton, N.J.: Princeton University Press, 1973.

Schuchard, Ronald. *Eliot's Dark Angel: Intersections of Life and Art*. New York: Oxford University Press, 1999.

Courtesy, Washington University Libraries

STANLEY ELKIN

Born: Brooklyn, New York
May 11, 1930
Died: St. Louis, Missouri
May 31, 1995

Elkin was as concerned with the verbal texture of his finely crafted prose as he was with the tragicomic nature of his characters' lives.

BIOGRAPHY

Born in New York City on May 11, 1930, Stanley Elkin was raised in Chicago. His father, Philip, a highly successful traveling salesman for a costume-jewelry concern and an equally accomplished raconteur, had a pronounced influence on Elkin's writing, in terms of both style and subject. Just as important were the elder Elkin's fear of being thought less than he was and the four heart attacks that would cut short his career and then his life.

For all the rhetorical as well as geographical expansiveness of his fiction, Elkin stayed close to home, first by choice, later by medical necessity. He attended the University of Illinois at Urbana, where he earned a B.A. in 1952, an M.A. in 1953, and, following a stint in the Army, a Ph.D. in 1961. It was during his military service that Elkin became interested in radio broadcasting, which figures so prominently in his third novel, *The Dick Gibson Show* (1971). In 1960, he joined the English faculty at Washington University in St. Louis, where he taught creative writing. Elkin began writing fiction while still a graduate student. His first published story, "A Sound of Distant Thunder," appeared in *Epoch* in 1957, and his first mass-market publication, "I Look Out for Ed Wolfe," appeared in *Esquire* five years later.

Also in 1962, Elkin, with financial assistance from his mother, went to Europe to write his first novel, *Boswell: A Modern Comedy* (1964). Although

the collection *Criers and Kibitzers, Kibitzers and Criers* (1965) has proven his most enduring work (it has remained in print almost continuously, and many of its stories are frequently anthologized), Elkin subsequently concentrated on novellas and especially novels. He also wrote a screenplay, *The Six-Year-Old Man* (1968), a radio drama, *The Coffee Room*, a monologue for the Mid-America Dance Company, and a collection of essays, *Pieces of Soap* (1992).

The same year that his second novel, *A Bad Man*, appeared (1967), Elkin suffered his first heart attack. He was diagnosed as having multiple sclerosis (MS) while in England five years later. As his maladies both worsened and multiplied (he underwent quintuple and quadruple bypass surgery in the 1980's, was several times hospitalized for a collapsed lung, and was forced to use first a walker and then a wheelchair), the former hypochondriac managed to deal with his various ills in a manner that his longtime friend and colleague, the writer William Gass, called "heroic."

Elkin may have been unable to button his shirts, but he was still able to teach and write, producing *Searches and Seizures* (novellas, 1973), *The Franchiser* (1976), *The Living End* (interrelated novellas, 1979), *Stanley Elkin's Greatest Hits* (retrospective, 1980), *George Mills* (1982), *Early Elkin* (stories, 1985), *The Magic Kingdom* (1985), *The Rabbi of Lud* (1987), *The MacGuffin* (1991), and *Van Gogh's Room at Arles: Three Novellas* (1993). This last appeared following a drug-induced "bout of temporary insanity" in April, 1991, an episode that left Elkin feeling not only humiliated (his other illnesses had already done that) but also, for the first time, embarrassed. Although he received numerous honors, including a National Book Critics Award for *George Mills*, Elkin never achieved the kind of popular and commercial success that a writer so attentive to his craft, so steeped in the popular culture, and so sympathetic to the plight of his tragicomic characters deserves.

ANALYSIS

Elkin is a difficult writer to place within the scheme of existing literary categories. He is not, other than by birth and upbringing, a typically Jewish American writer in the tradition that stretches from Abraham Cahan to Saul Bellow. The rich verbal texture of his work notwithstanding, he is not an experimental writer (a term he especially disliked); nor, despite the bleakness and grotesquerie of his fiction, did he think of himself as a black humorist. Moreover, for all the density of social detail in his stories and novels, Elkin did not see his fiction as being in any way sociological or his role as writer as involving any social obligations other than that of writing well. Despite, or perhaps because of, these many disclaimers, Elkin is an important if idiosyncratic writer whom Robert Coover has rightly called "one of America's great tragicomic geniuses."

At the heart of Elkin's fiction lies his sense of character and the ways in which character manifests itself. Elkin's style draws on and extends the American tradition of vernacular writing begun by Mark Twain and continued by such writers as Ring Lardner and Saul Bellow. Elkin, however, does not so much employ the vernacular perspective as exploit it, pushing it beyond the merely colloquial into the realm of what he called "heroic extravagance." This "rhetorical intensity," as Coover terms it, is one that Elkin shares with his characters, whose compulsive, even crazed "arias" serve "to introduce significance into what otherwise may be untouched by significance."

In Elkin's fiction, even in his essays, speech is character and character is speech. The typical Elkin hero is obsessive, isolated (frequently an orphan and therefore free to follow his obsession), powerless yet egocentric, and resentful yet oddly, even perversely sympathetic, most sympathetic in his (less often, her) need to speak, to tell his tale. He is at once envious and insecure, humbled and vindic-tive, in a word, "driven," not by anything in particular but by need itself in a world of the "never enough." Not likable in any conventional sense, he nevertheless earns the reader's respect insofar as he embodies, in Elkin's words, "the egocentric will pitted against something stronger than itself." At his best, at his most verbally egocentric, he becomes both "crier" and "kibitzer," hapless whiner and hopeful joker.

Elkin's characters often have good, albeit grotesquely funny, reasons to complain. In a way, they are all like the title character in "I Look Out for Ed Wolfe," who tries to determine his exact worth by converting everything he owns into cash, only to learn that it is not much, certainly not enough. Bobbo Druff, in *The MacGuffin*, finds himself "on the downhill side of destiny" despite his position as commissioner of streets. With his degree from an "offshore yeshiva," Jerry Goldkorn is the rabbi of Lud, a cemetery complex in northern New Jersey. Marshall Preminger, in "The Condominium," finds himself similarly "left out." Boswell, the hero of Elkin's first novel, makes the mistake of taking literally the advice offered by the world-famous Dr. Herlitz and so becomes "a strong man" (a professional wrestler) in the first of his several attempts to achieve immortality.

In *A Bad Man*, Feldman, the felled man, caters to the desires of others, legal and illegal, permissible and perverse, until a computer error sends him to prison. There, rather than throw himself on the warden's mercy, he rejects the warden's advice to adjust to the world as it is. Feldman insists upon his innocence. The protagonist of *The Dick Gibson Show* discovers quite by accident that not one person has been listening to his radio broadcasts, not even the station's owners or technicians. Later, as host of a late-night radio call-in show, he will enjoy a success that proves no less problematic, as his callers' obsessions begin to overwhelm him.

Control is also the key for Alexander Main in "The Bailbondsman." Against all that he can neither understand nor control in his own life, Main asserts his power as bailbondsman to choose who will go (temporarily) free and who will not. Unlike the ostensibly bad men who predominate in Elkin's fiction, Ellerbee in *The Living End* is saintly, excessively so. Killed by a robber, he is permitted a glimpse of heaven (which looks "like a theme park") before being unfairly sent to hell, "the ultimate inner city." Discovering there "the grand vocabulary" of pain, he learns to speak with the same intensity and extravagance as many of Elkin's other heroes, all of them suffering the bad luck that comes of just being alive. In this, they are indeed made in their makers' images: Elkin, with his bad heart and multiple sclerosis, as well as the God of *The Living End*. This is a God who has created heaven and hell, affliction and, finally, apocalypse, "because it makes a better story."

Elkin's jokey fiction is suffused with intimations of mortality. In *The Magic Kingdom*, Simon Bale organizes a trip to Disney World for a group of English children suffering from various terminal diseases. The children's fate is cruel, and the novel itself is painfully, unsparingly funny, but the pain, here and elsewhere in Elkin's fiction, is to a degree offset by the characters'—and the author's—affirmation of life and spirit of defiance.

This is not to say that Elkin's fiction resolves itself in any conventional way. Beginning with nothing more than a situation (and in the case of at least one story, nothing more than the word "bailbondsman"), Elkin does not develop his stories and novels in terms of plot and the Enlightenment ethos it implies. Instead, following the rule of whim and the muse of serendipity, he proceeds on the basis of opposition, of "action and respite, tension and release," obsession and resistance, of "what the character wants to happen and what he does not want to happen." Elkin's protagonists move through their worlds comically repeating themselves, "the stammer of personality" asserting itself over and over.

"A Poetics for Bullies"

First published: 1965 (collected in *Criers and Kibitzers, Kibitzers and Criers*, 1965)
Type of work: Short story

Against the logic of submission and adaptation, the young protagonist defines himself in terms of his own perverse desires and supercharged rhetoric.

Of the nine stories in *Criers and Kibitzers, Kibitzers and Criers*, "A Poetics for Bullies" was the last to be written and the one Elkin liked best. The story marks Elkin's breakthrough from his earlier, more realistic, and generally more sedate style to the approach that characterizes his later work. The story's young protagonist-narrator is the unlovable but irrepressible Push the Bully. Push imposes his perverse will and vision on others, all of them, like Push, grotesques: Eugene, with his overactive salivary glands, fat Frank, Mim the dummy, Slud the cripple, Clob the ugly. A trickster as much by compulsion as by choice, Push claims that were magic real, he would use it to change the world, but because it is not real, he spends his time asserting himself and disillusioning others. Although this "prophet of the deaf" seems in many ways a younger version of one of Saul Bellow's "reality instructors," he also resembles the typical Bellow hero, Eugene Henderson, for example, in *Henderson the Rain King* (1959), whose clamorous "I want, I want" is Push's own. "Alone in my envy, awash in my lust," Push feels forever the outsider, though not in any clearly existential sense; he is more the perennial new kid on the block than the absurdist antihero of Jean-Paul Sartre and Albert Camus.

As if to prove Push right, an actual new kid, John Williams, immediately gains the acceptance that Push both desires and despises. Tall, blond, and handsome, the well-traveled and well-dressed Williams cuts a princely figure. A version of the main character in the slightly earlier "On a Field Rampant," Williams is a "paragon" of virtue and Christlike lover of all, including those defectives whom Push loves to hate. He puts Frank on a diet and Slud in the gym, and he even tries to befriend Push, who has always tried to live his life so that he "could keep the lamb from the door."

Push decides to fight Williams, "not to preserve honor but its opposite." Willing to risk the pain he has always avoided, he is determined that his nemesis will not turn the other cheek. In this, Push claims, he is only following natural law: "Push pushed pushes." Push succeeds; Williams strikes back, only to then extend his hand in friendship. "Hurrah!" cry the others, like the chorus of children at the end of Fyodor Dostoevski's *Bratya Karamazovy* (1879-1880; *The Brothers Karamazov*, 1912). After a moment's hesitation, however, Push rejects all offers and pleadings; he chooses instead to follow his own inexorable self rather than adapt and submit: "Logic is nothing. Desire is stronger." Bully in no ordinary sense, Push is the "incarnation of envy and jealousy and need," ready to "die wanting," possessing nothing more and nothing less than "the cabala of my hate, my irreconcilableness."

THE FRANCHISER

First published: 1976
Type of work: Novel

The apotheosis of self-effacement, Ben Flesh tries to live without desire and therefore without personality.

If *Push the Bully* represents one extreme of character in Elkin's fiction, then Ben Flesh, protagonist and narrator of *The Franchiser,* represents the other. "A Poetics for Bullies" and *The Franchiser* are also representative of two other aspects of Elkin's writing. One is generic; there is the story's depiction of "acute character" manifesting itself in a crisis situation versus the novel's presentation of "chronic character" manifesting itself over a serendipitously (or whimsically) developed series of episodes. The other difference is autobiographical. "A Poetics for Bullies" and the other stories in *Criers and Kibitzers, Kibitzers and Criers* were all written before "anything bad" had ever befallen Elkin; *The Franchiser* was written after the author had suffered heart attacks, temporary blindness, and multiple sclerosis.

"Deprived of all the warrants of personality," Ben is a man "without goals, without obsession, without drive" but in possession of a substantial inheritance from his wealthy godfather. That inheritance enables Ben, who has "no good thing of his own . . . to place himself in the service of those who had." For Ben, this means buying franchises (buying names), in effect becoming Evelyn Wood (speed reading), Fred Astaire (dance studio), Mr. Softee (ice cream), Colonel Sanders (chicken dinners), America's Innkeeper (Holiday Inn), and the like.

Ben's efforts to define himself in terms of others prove as unsatisfying as his attempts to control his various, mainly outdated or poorly located businesses, the inflation-prone economy, the weather, even his own body. The prime rate rises, the temperature soars, energy suddenly becomes scarce,

and Ben learns that he has multiple sclerosis. His illness is diagnosed in, of all places, the tropical fever ward of a hospital in South Dakota, where a fellow patient offers him this stiff-upper-lip advice: "Be *hard,* Mr. Softee." Ironically, even perversely, that is precisely what Ben is doing, as the disease hardens patches on his brain.

His own health deteriorating and his eighteen nearly identical godcousins dying of bizarre maladies, Ben finally takes leave of his anonymity long enough to stake nearly all of his other franchises on a Travel Inn located in the town of Ringgold, Georgia. The inn, of course, fails, but not before Ben, putting his ear to the doors of the few occupied rooms, discovers that romance, even in its most perverse forms, is "as real as heartburn." He is amazed and delighted, but his "ecstasy attack," while clearly an affirmation of life, is also a chemically induced symptom of his worsening multiple sclerosis. "Nope," Ben says to himself in the novel's closing pages, "he couldn't complain." Would that he could, for (the novel suggests) he should. Lacking Push the Bully's rage and resentment, however, Ben can only sigh, tragicomically resigned, perversely contented.

HER SENSE OF TIMING

First published: 1993 (in *Van Gogh's Room at Arles*)
Type of work: Novella

Confined to a wheelchair, a political geographer finds himself in the land of farce, where he discovers the actual extent of his helplessness.

Best known as a novelist and frequently anthologized as a writer of short stories, Elkin also produced a significant body of work in a form, the novella, that most contemporary American writers have, perhaps for commercial reasons, avoided. That Elkin found the novella form so appealing is understandable, for it allowed him to combine the emphasis on situation and acute character that typifies his short stories with the spatial freedom of the novel so necessary to the development of his poetics of resentment and obsession.

What especially distinguishes *Her Sense of Timing* is how painfully close Elkin—never an autobiographical writer but always willing to draw on personal material—is working to the autobiographical bone. He takes his own increasing state of helplessness and dependency (on the drugs used in the treatment of his heart disease and multiple sclerosis, on his wheelchair and stair-glide, and, above all, on his wife, Joan) and asks a simple question: What would happen if a character who is not the author but who is like him in terms of age, personality, academic affiliation, and medical history suddenly found himself home alone, abandoned by a wife who, after thirty-six years of marriage and a decade or so spent caring for her disabled husband, decided that she had had enough?

Although he can understand Claire's leaving, political geographer Jack Schiff greatly resents her going and resents most her leaving on the very eve of his annual party for the graduate students whom he, in fact, does not particularly like. With Claire gone, Schiff must, quite literally, fall back on his own limited resources and abilities (including his ability to exploit others). Forced to "shift" for himself, he will come to understand better than ever before not only his humiliating helplessness but also the farcical nature of his situation. He takes pratfalls despite the presence of an expensive medical alert system, which he has installed the day Claire leaves and which the cunning, conniving Schiff will abuse, claiming a medical emergency when, in fact, he wants only someone to empty his urine container and close the front door.

Schiff is adept at beating the system, at taking revenge by taking advantage. Elkin makes Schiff's situation at once convincing, comical, and emotionally affecting. "'I'd like,' said Schiff, sorry as soon as he permitted the words to escape, 'for my life to go into remission.'" Failing that, the coward will once again turn bully, playing his handicap as if it were a trump card. In doing so, he seeks not just to assert himself but also to avenge himself, though invariably in petty ways. In Elkin's fiction of obsession and resentment, the ways are always petty. The pettiness serves as further proof of the powerlessness that his characters feel so acutely and struggle against so mightily.

MRS. TED BLISS

First published: 1995
Type of work: Novel

An elderly widow copes as best she can with present concerns while, like Lot's wife, she casts a backward glance over her life.

Mrs. Ted Bliss is the last novel Elkin published before he died. Elkin was always attuned to the wantings and wasting of the body and its connections to the body politic within and against which his characters measured their successes and, more usually, their failings. In his earlier novel, *The Franchiser,* Elkin focuses on a man stricken in his prime with MS (after inheriting a fortune from his godfather) and sets Ben Flesh's cross-country travels against the backdrop of Ben's own unraveling myelin and the nation's energy crisis. *Mrs. Ted Bliss* is, as the title character's name indicates, no less ironically allegorical but far more retrospective, even elegiac. Published in the middle of the roaring 1990's with its soaring stock market, *Mrs. Ted Bliss* offers a sobering and highly affecting memento mori, made all the vivid by Elkin's characteristically pyrotechnic prose.

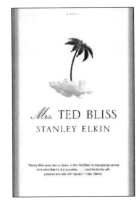

This time the pyrotechnics are more subdued, as befits the novel's aging main character, carefully doled out like a widow's savings. Not that Mrs. Ted Bliss is financially strapped; she is merely at a loss following the death of the husband—a butcher, a dealer in flesh, sold by the pound—who, like many men of his generation, had done everything for their wives except, naturally, prepare them for widowhood. Dorothy's story is a bit of Americana, a Jewish urbanized version of American Gothic, a rags-to-riches tale that takes her from Russia to Chicago and finally to Miami Beach where, at novel's end, she awaits the coming of Hurricane Andrew and, likely, death. The hurricane is no tornado that will set this modern-day Dorothy down in wondrous, full-color Oz. Rather, she finds herself in the real-life version of the hell that Elkin conjured in *The Living End*, where God is a stand-up comedian playing to a literally captive audience of the unjustly damned. In *Mrs. Ted Bliss*, the fears are more mundane even if the punishment meted out to this female Job no less unjust, as Dorothy's worries make her retreat from scam artists and encroaching urban blight into the relative safety of her aptly named but decaying condominium block, the Towers. Like Elkin's other protagonists, this Sleeping Beauty/Rapunzel is presented, warts and all, and with a sympathy that Elkin had previously often tried hard to hide.

Like Elkin's earlier fiction, *Mrs. Ted Bliss* is not concerned with developing plot or character conventionally. Just as the plot of *The Franchiser* parodies that of Jack Kerouac's *On the Road* (1957), the plot of *Mrs. Ted Bliss* is little more than a peg on which Elkin hangs his prose as he traces Dorothy's adventures, or rather pratfalls, including selling her late husband's 1978 Buick LeSabre to a drug kingpin, who really just wants the parking place. When he is caught, Dorothy, more schlemiel than naïf, becomes a suspect in the investigation, having been paid five thousand dollars over book value. "Shorn of her decibels," her beauty, her son Marvin, her husband Ted, and her freedom, she becomes increasingly ridiculous and fearful. As powerless as Elkin's other, younger protagonists and no less angry with a God whose creation, seemingly so full of promise, turns out to be "fatally flawed," the most she can hope for is the scaled back revenge of "being quits" with those who have done her wrong. Mrs. Ted Bliss is part Dorothy from *The Wizard of Oz* and part King Lear maddened and raging on the hearth. Less like the one with her three companions than like the other comforted by Edgar, Dorothy Bliss is last seen, terrified but not alone, in her darkened apartment as the storm approaches, huddling together with a security guard, a biblical Rachel in reverse, who, searching for her own mother, found Dorothy instead.

SUMMARY

The Book of Job, Elkin claimed, "is the only book . . . because all books are the *Book of Job*," and the best proofs of this assertion are the books Elkin himself has written. Thematically, they make the case for the position taken by one of William Faulkner's characters, that "between grief and nothing, I will take grief." Stylistically, Elkin's books make a virtue and an art of excess, of obsession, of the extraordinariness of the ordinary, and above all of naked human need. It is an art that is at once defensive and self-assertive, a way of out-grotesquing life's grotesquerie and all of its bad jokes, including the painful MS that Elkin painstakingly transforms into MS, or malady into manuscript.

Robert A. Morace

BIBLIOGRAPHY

By the Author

LONG FICTION:
Boswell: A Modern Comedy, 1964
A Bad Man, 1967
The Dick Gibson Show, 1971
The Franchiser, 1976
George Mills, 1982
Stanley Elkin's the Magic Kingdom, 1985 (also known as *The Magic Kingdom*)
The Rabbi of Lud, 1987
The MacGuffin, 1991
Mrs. Ted Bliss, 1995

SHORT FICTION:
Criers and Kibitzers, Kibitzers and Criers, 1965
The Making of Ashenden, 1972

Searches and Seizures, 1973
The Living End, 1979
Stanley Elkin's Greatest Hits, 1980
Early Elkin, 1985
Van Gogh's Room at Arles: Three Novellas, 1993
Mrs. Ted Bliss, 1995

SCREENPLAY:
The Six-Year-Old Man, 1968

NONFICTION:
Why I Live Where I Live, 1983
Pieces of Soap: Essays, 1992

About the Author

Bailey, Peter J. *Reading Stanley Elkin.* Urbana: University of Illinois Press, 1985.
Bargen, Doris G. *The Fiction of Stanley Elkin.* Frankfurt, West Germany: Lang, 1979.
Dougherty, David C. *Stanley Elkin.* Boston: Twayne, 1990.
Gass, William. Afterword to *The Franchiser,* by Stanley Elkin. Boston: David Godine, 1980.
MacCaffery, Larry. "Stanley Elkin's Recovery of the Ordinary." *Critique: Studies in Modern Fiction* 21, no. 2 (1978): 39-51.
Pughe, Thomas. *Comic Sense: Reading Robert Coover, Stanley Elkin, Philip Roth.* Boston: Birkhäuser Verlag, 1994.
Salzman, Arthur, ed. *Review of Contemporary Fiction* 15, no. 2 (1995). Special Stanley Elkin issue.

DISCUSSION TOPICS

- What makes Stanley Elkin's style so distinctive? How is a typical Elkin sentence or paragraph structured?

- Elkin's plots tend to accrete rather than develop. Locate places in his work where plot is most clearly subordinated to Elkin's interest in language and jazzlike riffs.

- Elkin's fiction depends on his characters' occupations: the language, rhythms, and activities of their jobs, whether franchiser or widow. How does this interest in occupation manifest itself? How does it demonstrate the author's command of different kinds of work?

- How and how well does Elkin draw his characters? How well can readers "see" them? Are they more seen or heard?

- Voice—that of author and character—is especially important in Elkin's work. What does this voice sound like? Is the voice that of Elkin, or does he modify his narrative style to fit a particular character?

- Elkin's characters have been described as obsessed. What exactly are they obsessed about? Find passages in which their obsessions and obsessiveness are especially apparent.

- Elkin said on more than one occasion that "The Book of Job is the only book." In what ways do his characters suffer? What justification is there for their suffering? What reward?

- Rage and the desire for revenge often fuel Elkin's characters. Over what do they rage? At whom do they direct their revenge?

RALPH ELLISON

National Archives

Born: Oklahoma City, Oklahoma
March 1, 1914
Died: New York, New York
April 16, 1994

Ellison's 1952 novel Invisible Man *is recognized as one of the finest achievements in modern American fiction as well as one of the most complete statements of the African American experience.*

BIOGRAPHY

Ralph Waldo Ellison was born in Oklahoma City, Oklahoma, on March 1, 1914. His father, Lewis, named him after Ralph Waldo Emerson, the famous American poet. Lewis was an adventurous and accomplished man who served overseas in the military and started his own ice and coal business in Oklahoma City. Ellison's mother, Ida, was affectionately known as "Brownie." She was a political activist who campaigned for the Socialist party and against the segregationist policies of Oklahoma's governor, "Alfalfa Bill" Murray. After her husband's death, Ida supported Ralph and his younger brother, Herbert, by working at a variety of domestic jobs.

Ellison benefited from the advantages of the Oklahoma public schools but took odd jobs to pay for supplemental education. His particular interest was music. Influenced by his good friends Jimmy Rushing, a blues singer, and trumpeter Hot Lips Page, Ellison played the trumpet throughout high school. In return for yard work, Ellison received lessons from Ludwig Hehestreit, the conductor of the Oklahoma City Orchestra. At nineteen, with the dream of becoming a composer, he accepted a state scholarship and used it to attend Tuskegee Institute in Macon County, Alabama (1933-1936).

Unlike the protagonist of *Invisible Man*, Ellison was not expelled from Tuskegee, but like the character he later created, Ellison did not graduate. Instead, he traveled to New York City in 1936 to study sculpture during the summer between his junior and senior years, intending to return to Tuskegee in the fall. Soon after his arrival in New York, however, Ellison met Alain Locke and Langston Hughes, major literary figures of the Harlem Renaissance. Through his acquaintance with Hughes, Ellison was introduced to Richard Wright, who encouraged Ellison to write and published Ellison's first review in *New Challenge*, a journal that Wright edited.

Ellison supported himself with a variety of jobs during his first years in Harlem. In 1938, he joined the Federal Writers' Project, for which he and others employed by the Living Lore Unit gathered urban folklore materials. This experience introduced Ellison to the richness of black urban culture and provided him with a wealth of folklore materials that he incorporated into *Invisible Man*.

In the early 1940's, Ellison published several essays, reviews, and short stories for various periodicals, including *New Masses*, and he worked as the editor for *Negro Quarterly*. During World War II, he served from 1943 to 1945 as a cook on a merchant marine ship. Upon the war's end, he traveled to New Hampshire to rest, and there he wrote the first lines of *Invisible Man*. With the financial assistance of a Rosenwald Foundation grant, Ellison worked on the novel for seven years, publishing it in 1952.

Invisible Man was controversial and attacked by

militants as reactionary and banned from schools because of its explicit descriptions of black lifestyles. Critics, however, generally agreed on the book's significance. In 1965, a poll of literary critics named it the most outstanding book written by an American in the previous twenty years, placing it ahead of works by William Faulkner, Ernest Hemingway, and Saul Bellow. For his literary achievements and academic service, Ellison earned several awards, including the National Book Award (1953), the Russwurm Award (1953), a fellowship to the National Academy of Arts and Letters in (1955-1957), the Medal of Freedom (1969), Chevalier of the Order of Arts and Letters (1970), and the National Medal of Arts (1985). He was elected vice president of American PEN in 1964.

In 1958, Ellison accepted a teaching position at Bard College. In subsequent years, he taught at Rutgers University, the University of Chicago, and New York University, where he was the Albert Schweitzer professor in the humanities and from which he retired in 1979. He accepted numerous honorary doctorates and published two collections of essays. The essays in *Shadow and Act* (1964) focus on three topics: African American literature and folklore, African American music, and the interrelation of African American culture and the broader culture of the United States. *Going to the Territory* (1986) collected sixteen reviews, essays, and speeches that Ellison published previously.

Following the 1960's, Ellison worked on a second novel, *Juneteenth,* that he planned to publish as a trilogy. His work on the novel was disrupted in 1967 when approximately 350 pages of its one-thousand-page manuscript were destroyed in a house fire. Unfortunately, after a long bout with pancreatic cancer, the novel was left unfinished upon Ellison's death on April 16, 1994. However, the two thousand pages of manuscript were later edited by John Callahan, and *Juneteenth* was published posthumously in 1999.

ANALYSIS

The central theme of Ellison's writing is the search for identity, a search he sees as central to American literature and the American experience. He once said that "the nature of our society is such that we are prevented from knowing who we are," and this struggle toward self-definition is applied in *Invisible Man* within a social context. The partic-

ular genius in Ellison's novels is his ability to interweave these individual, communal, and national quests into a single, complex vision.

On the level of the individual, *Invisible Man* is, in Ellison's words, a clash of "innocence and human error, a struggle through illusion to reality." In this sense, the book is part of the literary tradition of initiation tales; stories of young men or women who confront the larger world beyond the security of home and attempt to define themselves in these new terms. Through the misadventures of his naïve protagonist, Ellison stresses the individual's need to free himself from the powerful influence of societal stereotypes and demonstrates the multiple levels of deception that must be overcome before an individual can achieve self-awareness. Ellison describes the major flaw of his protagonist as an "unquestioning willingness to do what is required of him by others as a way to success." Although Ellison's hero is repeatedly manipulated, betrayed, and deceived, Ellison shows that an individual is not trapped by geography, time, or place. He optimistically asserts that human beings can overcome these obstacles to independence if they are willing to accept the responsibility to judge existence independently.

The communal effort of African Americans to define their cultural identity permeates both of Ellison's novels. *Invisible Man* surveys the history of African American experience and alludes directly or indirectly to historical figures who serve as contradictory models for Ellison's protagonist. Some of the novel's effect is surely lost on readers who do not recognize the parallels drawn between Booker T. Washington and the Founder, between Marcus Garvey and Ras the Destroyer, or between Frederick Douglass and the narrator's grandfather. W. E. B.Du Bois's description of the doubleness of the African American experience fits the *Invisible Man*'s narrator, and Du Bois's assertion that the central fact of an African American's experience is the longing to attain self-conscious manhood, to merge his double self into a better and truer self, stands as a summary of the novel's overriding action.

Ellison does not restrict himself to the concerns of African Americans, however, because he believes that African American culture is an inextricable part of American culture. Thus, *Invisible Man* shows how the struggles of the narrator as an individual and as a representative of an ethnic minority are paralleled by the struggle of the United States to define and redefine itself. This theme permeates Ellison's second novel, *Juneteenth*, as well. In it, the superficiality of race as a color rather than as a culture is told through the cyclical nature of Bliss's notions of identity. Ellison's frequently expressed opinion that African American culture's assimilation by the dominant culture of the United States is inevitable and salutary has led some African American critics to attack him as reactionary. The suspicion that he "sold out" was also fed by his broad popularity among white readers and his acceptance of teaching positions at predominantly white universities.

The breadth and diversity of Ellison's novels make it possible to fit them into several American literary traditions. As part of the vernacular tradition, exemplified by Mark Twain and Ernest Hemingway, Ellison skillfully reproduces the various speech patterns and rich folklore of rural and urban African Americans. As part of the Symbolist tradition, exemplified by Herman Melville and T. S. Eliot, Ellison builds his novel around a full set of provocative and multifaceted symbols. As part of the tradition of African American literature, Ellison echoes the theme of Du Bois's *The Souls of Black Folk* (1903), reproduces the northward flight to freedom in Douglass's *Narrative of the Life of Frederick Douglass* (1845), explores the ambiguity of identity as James Weldon Johnson did in *The Autobiography of an Ex-Coloured Man* (1912), and appropriates the striking underground metaphor of Richard Wright's "The Man Who Lived Underground" (1944).

In *Invisible Man*, Ellison employs a "jazz" style in which an improvisation of rhetorical forms is played against his central theme. Letters, speeches, sermons, songs, nursery rhymes, and dreams are used throughout the novel, and the novel's style adjusts to match the changing consciousness and circumstances of the protagonist. In the early chapters, Ellison employs a direct, didactic style similar to that of the social-realist protest novels of the 1930's and 1940's. In the middle portions of the novel, after the narrator moves to New York City, Ellison's prose becomes more expressionistic, reflecting the narrator's introspection. In the last section of the novel, as the story moves toward the climactic race riot in Harlem, the prose becomes surreal, emphasizing the darkly comic absurdities of American existence.

In *Juneteenth*, Ellison also draws from his musical background to stylistically frame the story. In his National Book Award acceptance speech, Ellison noted his dream of creating a novel that incorporated "the rich babel of idiomatic expression around me, a language full of imagery and rhetorical canniness." He implements sermons, folk tales, the blues, and the rapidity of jazz music to reveal the flawed notions that the protagonist has about his identity.

In all sections, *Invisible Man* is enriched by Ellison's versatile use of symbols that focus attention on his major themes while underscoring the ambiguous nature of the human condition. Structurally, the book is episodic and cyclic, presenting the reader with versions of a basic pattern of disillusionment enacted in increasingly complex social environments. In each cycle, the narrator eagerly accepts an identity provided by a deceitful mentor and eventually experiences a revelation that shatters the illusory identity he has adopted. This repeated pattern demonstrates the pervasiveness of racism and self-interest and convinces the narrator that he must find his individual answers and stop looking to others.

Although *Invisible Man* addresses some of the most serious concerns of American society, it is also a comic novel in which Ellison relies on both the traditional picaresque humor of initiation and the rough-edged and often disguised humor of urban African Americans. Its dark comedy, sophisticated play of rhetorical forms, complex use of symbolism, and original examination of difficult social issues distinguish the book as a masterpiece of modern fiction.

INVISIBLE MAN

First published: 1952
Type of work: Novel

An ambitious but naïve black youth journeys through American society in search of his identity.

Ellison's *Invisible Man* is framed by a prologue and an epilogue that are set at a time after the completion of the novel's central action. The novel's pica-

resque story of a young black man's misadventures is presented as a memoir written by an older, more experienced embodiment of the protagonist. The narrator of the prologue and epilogue has withdrawn into a state he calls "hibernation" after surviving the multiple deceptions and betrayals that he recounts in his memoir. As he says, "the end is the beginning and lies far ahead."

The prologue foreshadows the novel's action. It prepares the reader for the narrator's final condition; focuses the reader's attention on the major themes of truth, responsibility, and freedom; and introduces the reader to the double consciousness that operates in the book. Throughout the novel, the naïve assumptions of the youthful protagonist are counterbalanced by the cynical judgments of his more mature self, creating an ironic double perspective.

The broken narrator to whom the reader is introduced in the prologue is hiding in an underground room, stealing power from the Monopolated Power Company to light the thousands of bulbs he has strung up. An angry and damaged man, he explains his frustration at his "invisibility," a quality that prevents others from seeing anything but "surroundings, themselves, or figments of their imagination." The narrator experiences a desperate need to convince himself that he does "exist in the real world." As he listens to Louis Armstrong's recording of "What Did I Do to Be So Black and Blue?" he dreams and then recounts his experiences.

The first episode, which goes back to his graduation from a black high school in the South, is a representative anecdote, a story that sets the pattern and themes of subsequent misadventures. Throughout *Invisible Man*, the young hero builds illusory expectations based on the deceitful promises of people who set themselves up as his mentors. In each cycle, he is eventually disillusioned by a dramatic revelation of deceit and sent spiraling toward his final confrontation with himself.

In the initial episode, he is invited to repeat his valedictory speech before the white leaders of the town. These men, however, humiliate him and some other black youths by forcing them to engage in a "battle royal," a blindfolded fistfight in which the last standing participant is victorious. They also tempt the black youths to fight for counterfeit coins tossed on an electrified rug, and they rudely disregard the protagonist's remarks when he is finally allowed to speak.

The episode demonstrates how racist leaders disempower African Americans by encouraging them to direct their anger at one another while rewarding the more acceptable submissive behavior, such as the protagonist's speech about "social responsibility." Although the corrupt and even bestial nature of these men is clear to the reader, the protagonist is blinded by his eagerness to succeed, and he gratefully accepts the briefcase he is given after his speech.

Ellison develops the ocular symbols of blindness/sight, darkness/light in this episode that are used in the novel to describe the protagonist's invisibility and his stumbling quest for truth. It also introduces the briefcase, a symbol of his naïve effort to accept prescribed identities. The briefcase stays with him until the end of the novel, accumulating objects and documents to represent the false identities he assumes. These two symbols are united at the end of the novel when he burns the contents of his briefcase in order to see in his underground hideout.

At the black college that the protagonist attends, he is introduced to the misuse of black power. Dr. Bledsoe, the ruthless college president (whose name implies his deracinated disregard for other African Americans), is blindly idolized by the protagonist, for whom the college is a paradise of reason and culture. The protagonist says that "within the quiet greenness I possessed the only identity I had ever known."

When he mishandles a visiting white trustee named Norton, however, by allowing him to hear Jim Trueblood's shocking tale of incest and taking him to a brothel where they are beset by a group of World War I veterans, Dr. Bledsoe banishes the protagonist from the collegiate Eden. It is only later, after fruitless efforts to find employment in New York City, that the protagonist discovers that Bledsoe's supposed letters of recommendation have betrayed him.

The revelation of Dr. Bledsoe's perfidy destroys the narrator's dream of returning to college. Determined to make his own way, he accepts a job with Liberty Paints. The factory, which is a microcosm of capitalist America, produces Optic White, "the purest white that can be found." Optic White will "cover just about anything" and is purchased in large amounts by the government, but the secret ingredient is a small amount of black base that is produced in a boiler room by an aging African American named Lucius Brockaway. The protagonist is assigned to Brockaway, but the veteran employee's paranoid suspicion that his new helper is a company spy and the protagonist's resentment at being assigned to an African American supervisor results in a fight. As the two quarrel, pressure builds until the boilers explode.

The protagonist awakes in the factory's infirmary, where masked doctors discuss ways to make him pliable. Half-conscious, the narrator is dimly aware of the doctors' efforts at behavior modification, but their bizarre treatment only succeeds at stripping away layers of superficial personality and revealing a changed man who looks at the world with "wild infant's eyes." In this reborn state, the dazed hero is adopted by Mary Rambo, the maternal owner of a boardinghouse in Harlem. Mary's nurturing restores the protagonist and awakens his sensitivity to injustice. When he comes across an elderly couple being evicted from their apartment, he speaks up on their behalf, stirring a gathering crowd to resist the eviction.

The protagonist's effective oratory is overheard by Jack, a leader of the Brotherhood, an organization that closely resembles the Communist Party. Jack recruits the protagonist and makes him the party's new spokesman in Harlem. Armed with a new name supplied by the Brotherhood, the protagonist eagerly takes on his organizational duties, dreaming that he will become a modern Frederick Douglass. He successfully builds Brotherhood membership in Harlem and effectively competes with rival organizations such as that led by Ras the Destroyer, an African American nationalist who is reminiscent of the historical Marcus Garvey. Instead of being rewarded, the protagonist is suddenly reassigned to a downtown position. The protagonist's protests result in a climactic showdown where Jack plucks out his glass eye, demonstrating at once the organization's demand of personal sacrifice and his own blindness.

Eventually, the protagonist realizes that he is being used by Jack, that the Brotherhood is willing to sacrifice the progress made in Harlem for the larger ends of the party, and that his dream of becoming another Frederick Douglass is a sham. With another prescribed identity deflated, he suddenly finds that he is being mistaken for the protean character Rinehart, a mysterious con man who is at once a minister and a pimp, a man whose name suggests the ambiguous relation of inner and outer realities. The protagonist considers adopting the cynicism of Rinehart, a decision that would end the search for a true identity, but he concludes that he cannot abandon his own conscience.

As the book nears its conclusion, the protagonist runs through a race riot that the Brotherhood has encouraged. Pursued by armed men, he finds sanctuary underground, where he is forced to burn the symbolic contents of his briefcase in order to see. He thus destroys the prescribed identities that others have supplied for him in order to prepare for the "hibernation" during which he hopes to discover himself.

Invisible Man's epilogue completes the frame begun in the novel's prologue, returning the reader to the subterranean narrator of the memoir, who says that although the world outside is as deceitful and dangerous as ever, the process of telling his story has made him "better understand my relation to it and it to me." He has come to accept the responsibility of determining his own identity and rejects formulaic responses to injustice. He advises his reader that "too much of your life will be lost, its meaning lost unless you approach it as much through love as through hate," and he now sees his own life as "one of infinite possibilities." Thus, at the novel's conclusion, the narrator is preparing to reenter the world. As Ellison put it, his narrator "comes up from underground because the act of writing and thinking necessitated it."

JUNETEENTH

First published: 1999
Type of work: Novel

A racist senator and his black reverend father figure find themselves wading through buried memories, which illuminate a context of understanding selfhood, kinship, and race.

Ellison began work on his second novel in 1954, but a house fire in November, 1967, destroyed much of his manuscript. It was an event about which he was particularly tight-lipped until 1994, when he publicly discussed the loss of his manuscript with David Remnick: "There was, of course, a traumatic event involved with the book. We lost a summer house and, with it, a good part of the novel. It wasn't the entire manuscript, but it was over three hundred and sixty pages. There was no copy." Ellison spent thirty years re-creating and polishing his manuscript, unable to finalize it before his death in April, 1994. Although the book was originally intended to be published as a trilogy, John Callahan, Ellison's literary executor, sifted through Ellison's papers to find the one self-contained narrative that stood alone best. He edited it into *Juneteenth.*

In the book, Adam Sunraider, a U.S. senator in the 1950's who claims the only black person he knows "is the boy who shines shoes at his golf club," was once called Bliss and raised by a southern black minister. As a boy he is a preaching prodigy in the Reverend Hickman's traveling ministry, but he runs away in search of his identity. While Hickman keeps in touch with Bliss's life during the years of separation, the senator successfully suppresses his childhood memories of his southern black community. Bliss brings scandal to the Senate floor when, upon receiving a near-fatal shot by a young black man, calls for the Reverend Hickman.

With Hickman at his side, Bliss is suddenly uncomfortable with his outburst. Ellison writes, "time, conflicts of value, the desire of one to remember nothing and the tendency of the other to remember too much, have rendered communication between them difficult." Hickman's determination to revisit the memories of Bliss's life prevail, and the senator realizes his flight from Hickman and the black community was not an attempt to find his genetic identity, but rather a further displacement from his true American self. In his last moments before death, the senator reaches for consolation from Hickman and "that vanished tribe into which I was born," to whom the book is dedicated.

The novel's title is taken from the African American celebration of emancipation from slavery: "Words of Emancipation didn't arrive until the middle of June so they called it Juneteenth." Mimicking a theme that he started in *Invisible Man* that African American culture is an inextricable part of American culture, Ellison uses the two protagonists of *Juneteenth* to detail the indivisibility of the American experience and American language. This is a stunning example of Ellison's ability to weave voice, racial, and cultural awareness into the least likely of characters. The senator symbolizes all readers, to some extent, who do not answer Ellison's call to embrace, rather than evade, one's identity. Bliss comes to understand that being "true American" also means "also somehow black," a fact that Ellison believed is true for everyone.

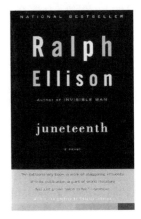

SUMMARY

Although Ellison modestly claimed that *Invisible Man* is "not an important novel," the book has demonstrated its ability to speak to a variety of readers for more than five decades. Its author continues to be ranked among America's greatest fiction writers, and his second novel, *Juneteenth*, does not disappoint. In it, he continues his plea for collective racial, cultural, and individual consciousness.

Invisible Man earned for Ellison a special place in African American literature because the novel goes beyond the thematic and rhetorical limitations of the protest novel, extending the story of the African American experience to all Americans. The novel's concluding question, "Who knows but that, on the lower frequencies, I speak for you?" underscores this universality.

Carl Brucker; updated by Amanda B. Wray

BIBLIOGRAPHY

By the Author

LONG FICTION:
Invisible Man, 1952
Juneteenth, 1999 (John F. Callahan, editor)

SHORT FICTION:
Flying Home, and Other Stories, 1996

NONFICTION:
Shadow and Act, 1964
The Writer's Experience, 1964 (with Karl Shapiro)
Going to the Territory, 1986
The Collected Essays of Ralph Ellison, 1995 (John F. Callahan, editor)
Conversations with Ralph Ellison, 1995 (Maryemma Graham and Amritjit Singh, editors)
Trading Twelves: The Selected Letters of Ralph Ellison and Albert Murray, 2000
Living with Music: Ralph Ellison's Jazz Writings, 2001 (Robert O'Meally, editor)

About the Author

De Santis, Christopher C. "'Some Cord of Kinship Stronger and Deeper than Blood': An Interview with John F. Callahan, Editor of Ralph Ellison's *Juneteenth*." *African American Review* 34, no. 4 (2000): 601-621.

Hersey, John. *Ralph Ellison: A Collection of Critical Essays.* Englewood Cliffs, N.J.: Prentice-Hall, 1974.

Hobson, Christopher Z. "Ralph Ellison, *Juneteenth*, and African American Prophecy." *MFS: Modern Fiction Studies* 51, no. 3 (2005): 617-647.

Jackson, Lawrence. *Ralph Ellison: Emergence of Genius.* New York: John Wiley & Sons, 2002.

McSweeney, Kerry. *"Invisible Man": Race and Identity.* Boston: G. K. Hall, 1988.

Nadel, Alan. "Ralph Ellison and the American Canon." *American Literary History* 13, no. 2 (2001): 393-404.

Porter, Horace A. *Jazz Country: Ralph Ellison in America.* Iowa City: University of Iowa Press, 2001.

Warren, Kenneth. *So Black and Blue: Ralph Ellison and the Occasion of Criticism.* Chicago: University of Chicago Press, 2003.

Watts, Jerry Gafio. *Heroism and the Black Intellectual: Ralph Ellison, Politics, and Afro-American Intellectual Life.* Chapel Hill: University of North Carolina Press, 1994.

Yuins, E. "Artful Juxtaposition on the Page: Memory Perception and Cubist Technique in Ralph Ellison's *Juneteenth*." *PMLA: Publications of the Modern Language Association* 119, no. 5 (October, 2004): 1247.

DISCUSSION TOPICS

- Consider the role of racial stereotypes in Ralph Ellison's *Invisible Man*. How does the border between the narrator's self-perception and how others view him relate to the theme of blindness and invisibility within the text?

- What does the narrator's briefcase in *Invisible Man* symbolize within the text?

- Some critics argue that *Juneteenth* can be viewed as a continuation of the themes outlined in *Invisible Man*. Where do you see the two novels merging and diverging in how one searches and views his or her identity?

- What is the relationship between individual and community identity? How do the two conflict in *Juneteenth* and merge in *Invisible Man*?

- Ellison was born and raised in Oklahoma. What is the role of this space, this community, in telling the stories of Senator Bliss and the Reverend Hickman in *Juneteenth*? How might the moments of the character's stories that take place in Oklahoma relate to Ellison's childhood and adulthood?

- Why is it significant that the senator in *Juneteenth* calls out for the Reverend Hickman when he is on his deathbed? What sort of literary devices is Ellison utilizing within this scene in the Senate meeting?

RALPH WALDO EMERSON

Library of Congress

Born: Boston, Massachusetts
May 25, 1803
Died: Concord, Massachusetts
April 27, 1882

One of the most influential figures in American literary history, Emerson used essentially everyday language to articulate his thought, thereby consummating the art of prosaic discourse.

BIOGRAPHY

Ralph Waldo Emerson was born in Boston, Massachusetts, on May 25, 1803, the third son of the Reverend William Emerson and Ruth Haskins Emerson. Stern and disciplined, his parents normally refrained from displaying intense affection in the family, as so many Bostonians did at the beginning of the nineteenth century. Partly because of this upbringing, coldness, as Emerson himself noted throughout his life, became a distinct feature of his character, later, perhaps unconsciously, making him search in his writing for a spiritual life rich in sentiment.

Characteristic of his time, Emerson was enrolled in a dame school at age two and in the Boston Public Latin school at nine. While in the Latin school, he displayed unusual talent in declamation, a gift that eventually paved his way to becoming a great speaker. His aunt Mary Moody Emerson, who lived intermittently with his family for a considerable length of time during his childhood, greatly influenced Emerson in encouraging him to set high goals and do things which he might otherwise be afraid to do. The early death of his father in 1811 left the family in poverty, to the extent that he had to share an overcoat with his younger brother. This impoverishment, however, disciplined him all the more.

In 1817 Emerson, then fourteen, entered Har-vard College. In his third year at Harvard, he began keeping a journal, an endeavor which would last for more than fifty years, often serving as the source of ideas for his literary writing. In his last year, he distinguished himself by being chosen as class poet and winning second prize in the Boylston competition for delivering a dissertation on ethical philosophy. After graduating in 1821, Emerson taught at his elder brother's school for young ladies for three years, earning enough money for him to return to Harvard in 1825 to pursue studies in theology.

His reading of Michel de Montaigne, a French Renaissance writer, at the beginning of 1825 made him believe that good essays can be written in plain language. In 1826, Emerson preached with approbation his first sermon from his uncle's pulpit, an episode that marked the beginning of his long career as a speaker. Shortly after this sermon, bad health forced him to travel to the South for better climate and a quick recovery. Not until 1829, when Emerson became somewhat sure of his health, was he ordained as a junior pastor to the Unitarian ministry and began to preach regularly.

In 1827, he met Ellen Tucker and, after a short courtship, married her in 1829 regardless of her rapidly deteriorating health caused by tuberculosis (a disease that plagued their era). As expected, this marriage soon ended with Ellen's death in 1831. The bereaved Emerson was thus able, as the beneficiary of his wife's will, to receive a sufficient amount of money for him to live without having to hold a regular job—an event that enabled him to concentrate on his literary creativity.

729

Ralph Waldo Emerson

The following year witnessed a turning point in Emerson's thought. Unsatisfied with the conventional Christian form of worship and now somewhat assured of his future livelihood, he resigned his pastorate at the Second Church in Boston, stating that he could no longer administer Communion as a ritual. Apart from the emotional turmoil Emerson experienced from the loss of his beloved wife and the resignation of his pastorate, his own health was failing him in 1832; he eventually embarked upon a journey of recovery to Europe at the end of this year. While in Europe, he visited some of the important literary figures of his time, such as the renowned English poets William Wordsworth and Samuel Taylor Coleridge and the Scottish essayist Thomas Carlyle, with whom Emerson was to correspond for the rest of his life.

Shortly after returning from Europe, Emerson began his career as a lecturer and settled at Concord, Massachusetts, where he lived until his death. In 1835, after specifying his conditions—to remain a poet and to live in the countryside—he married Lydia Jackson of Plymouth, who had to compete with the memory of his first wife for Emerson's respect and affection.

The following years, between 1836 and 1842, witnessed one of the most creative periods in Emerson's life. The publication of his first book, *Nature*, in 1836, though it was short, established him as a prose writer. The series of lectures he gave in the following two years, such as "The Philosophy of History," "The American Scholar," "Divinity School Address," and "Literary Ethics," helped him to gain recognition. Because of his unorthodox stance toward Christianity, expressed in the "Divinity School Address" delivered at Harvard in 1838, Emerson received ruthless criticisms from some conservative believers and was barred from giving any lectures at his alma mater until almost thirty years later.

The publication of his *Essays: First Series* in 1841 further established him as a major figure in American literature. As a result of his growing fame, Emerson gradually became the literary leader of his time, though he preferred to lead people to themselves rather than to himself. Compared with his prose, his poetry gained recognition much more slowly. Not until the end of 1847, when his first collection of poems was published, did his poetry receive some serious attention. Although Emerson regarded himself mainly as a poet, his poetry never gained as much prestige as did his essays.

From October, 1847, to July, 1848, Emerson, already internationally known, made his second trip to Europe, visiting friends and giving lectures while in England. Many of his impressions on this trip eventually found expression in his *English Traits* (1856). Later works, often of inferior quality, continued to appear during his remaining years. A few years after the end of the Civil War, a war characterized by unprecedented casualties in American history which certainly disturbed him, the aging Emerson began to lose his memory. The burning of his house in Concord in 1872 accentuated the decline of his health. His last decade brought about the continuous growth of Emerson's reputation, along with the failure of his faculties. He died in 1882 at the age of seventy-eight.

ANALYSIS

Throughout his literary career, Emerson consistently advocated the idea of self-reliance, of making self the ultimate judge of things in this world. The self he celebrates, however, is not the same as the individual self, which threatens to become selfishness, but an autonomous spirit which wills to act according to universal moral laws. This spirit, which is located in all objects, may grow as a result of communion with nature.

Like many Romantics, who give nature an essential role in their intrinsic lives by treating it either as an equal partner with, or as a substitute for, God, Emerson often expresses a passion for nature, as can be seen in his famous work *Nature* (1836). His love for nature appears to he the expression of his heart based on nature's utilitarian value; however, his reason tells him otherwise. In his analytical reasoning, he follows the argument of traditional idealism in conceiving nature as an ephemeral phenomenon without independent existence. As a result of the conflict between his intellect and his emotion, Emerson remains essentially indecisive as to the ontological being of nature.

From his early work *Nature* to the publication of *Letters and Social Aims* (1875), he consistently uses the image of shadows to illustrate the essence of nature. What is emphasized in an equally consistent manner throughout Emerson's life is the utilitarian value, both spiritual and physical, of nature to humankind. Because of the extremely important role that it enjoys in a person's daily life, Emerson cannot afford to part with nature, which is emotionally close to him, nor can he follow the traditional doctrine of idealism without misgivings.

His love for nature often makes him doubt the statement of idealism, and these emotions force him to endow nature with life—hence the persistent tension between emotion and intellect in Emerson. When his reason gains ascendancy, he will deny that nature has a soul. Once his emotion becomes dominant, however, he will not hesitate to attribute a spirit or apply the metaphorical expression of transcendence to nature.

In "The Over-Soul" (1842), Emerson works out the framework for his idea of oneness, a metaphysical basis for the celebration of ego. The Over-Soul is the embodiment of wisdom, virtue, power, and beauty, among which virtue is supreme. To be the partner of the Creator—or to be a creator—one's duty lies only in assuring the unceasing circular flow between one's own soul and the Over-Soul. It follows that when Emerson says in his "Divinity School Address" that the man who renounces himself comes to himself, he means only the renunciation of the willful interference with the free flowing of the universal spirit, not biblical self-denial.

To obey the soul, according to Emerson, one's acts would naturally arrange themselves by irresistible magnetism in a straight line. Because of the constant communication with and participation of the divine essence of the universe, each individual becomes part of the essence and is, thus, self-sufficient in every moment of his or her existence. As the divinity of the Over-Soul is inherent in the soul of each individual, one fulfills this divinity by being true to the transcendental spirit in oneself and by keeping it free from the harmful interpositions of one's own artificial will. Virtue is not, as is made clear in "Spiritual Laws" (1841), the product of conscious calculation and should not be interfered with by will.

Applied to history, the idea of the Over-Soul leads to a subjective view of the past. History, according to Emerson, is only a record of the universal mind, and its task is to find the expression of one's soul. Under this notion, what is called history is actually biography. A similarly moralistic view characterizes his theory of art. Although Emerson's theory of the Over-Soul lays the groundwork for Walt Whitman's "Song of Myself" (1855), his

view of art focuses more on a poet's character than on the work of art.

What characterizes a poet, according to Emerson, is the power to perceive the unity of nature and the ability to impart one's impression of it through imagination. As every person is susceptible to the work of the Over-Soul and possesses imagination, every person is thus potentially a poet. In cultivating one's power and exercising one's imagination, the poet should communicate with nature. Because of the ability to see the essence of this world and the power to employ signs to express it, the poet animates and illuminates other people and thus becomes a spiritual emancipator. The prestige that the poet enjoys, however, is not exclusive:

> It is equally shared by the hero and the sage. These three sovereigns—the namer, the doer, and the knower—are simply different names for the highest progeny of the Over-Soul.

A change has been noted in Emerson's thought in his later period, when fate and limitation are emphasized. Emerson speaks of fate with awe; nevertheless, his tone remains defiant. Apart from, or in spite of, the emphasis on fate, assertions of thought and will are frequently made in his later works, as is demonstrated by the posthumous book *Natural History of Intellect* (1893), which primarily concerns the soul rather than the exterior world. Even in the essays "Fate" and "Allusions" (1860), where limitation is a major concern, the fundamental views expressed are still those that characterize his early period. As a counterbalance to the idea of illusion, sincerity is invoked by Emerson in his later works. With the recognition of this limitation as well as the corresponding stress on will and thought, Emerson's doctrines thus become more profound.

It has been noted that every work of Emerson appears to contain all of his major ideas. His works are, indeed, often a highly crystallized form of writing resulting from the long process of modifications based on his audiences' different responses. Because of the complexity of ideas, his essays often convey the impression of great diversity without clear logical connections. The central statements—usually simple, short, and concise—tend to be the most powerful expressions, calling for no lengthy modifier, yet yielding great insight. Emerson's masterly command of everyday language continues to be a wonder in American literature.

NATURE

First published: 1836
Type of work: Essay

Through communion with nature, one is able to transcend oneself and this world and achieve union with the divine essence of the universe.

Composed of an introduction and eight chapters, *Nature*, Emerson's first book, contains all the fundamental ideas that were to be developed at length later in his life. The dominant theme of this work—the harmony between humans and nature—also became the theoretical basis of many literary works composed after it in the nineteenth century United States.

The treatise begins with a criticism of reliance on the past and a suggestion to depend on oneself to explore this world. In explaining the justification for self-trust, Emerson espouses a dualistic view of the universe, which, according to him, is divided into two parts: one, the self which represents the soul, the other, the exterior world, which he terms nature, the latter being subordinated to the former. Perfect correspondence, in his view, exists between these two parts, a link which makes one's communication with the outside world possible. To him, nature is all benevolence; community, by contrast, often signifies waywardness.

In communicating with nature, he believes, one is able to purge oneself of all cares and eventually achieve a mystical union with the universe. Apart from spiritual nourishment, nature provides an individual's material needs. At higher levels, it further fulfills one's aesthetic sentiment, serves as the vehicle of thought, and disciplines one's mind. Under the heading "Beauty," which constitutes the third chapter, a theory of aesthetics is advanced. Emerson distinguishes three kinds of beauty in nature: the beauty of exterior forms, which is the lowest kind; spiritual beauty, with virtue as its essence; and the intellectual beauty characterized by a search for the absolute order of things.

Characteristic of Emerson, unity can be found among these three kinds of beauty, which, at the ultimate level, are but different expressions of the same essence: "God is the all-fair. Truth, and goodness, and beauty, are but different faces of the same All." The equation of beauty, truth, and virtue is typical of Romantic aesthetics.

In discussing the use of nature as the vehicle of thought, Emerson further illustrates the correspondence between nature and soul, and matter and mind, using this link as the basis for his theory of language. According to him, language originally came from and should remain in close contact with natural images or facts. A language characterized by, or a discourse drawing heavily upon, vivid images is thus most desirable.

Because of the identification of beauty, truth, and virtue as different expressions of the Creator, the corruption of a person's character is necessarily followed by that person's corrupted use of language. Viewed in this light, people with strong minds who lead simple lives in the countryside cannot but have an advantage in the use of powerful language over people residing in the city, who are prone to be distracted by the material world.

After language, discipline—another use of nature at a still higher level—occurs. Following Coleridge and some of the nineteenth century German idealists, Emerson distinguishes two kinds of cognitive faculties: one, reason, which perceives the analogy that unites matter and mind, the other, understanding, which discerns the characteristics of things. Apart from the reiteration of the tremendous healing power of nature, which is esteemed as a religious preacher, the idea of unity is presented.

It is Emerson's belief that what unites nature and soul, matter and mind, is a moral sentiment, sometimes called the Creator, the Universal Spirit, or the Supreme Being, which both pervades and transcends the two different parts of the universe. The ultimate discipline that one receives from nature, he maintains, should be the recognition and acceptance of this Universal Spirit underlying both the world and the self.

The tremendous importance that nature commands in his thought prompts Emerson to discuss its metaphysical status in the sixth chapter, titled "Idealism." Before exploring this issue, he makes it clear that whether nature substantially exists or is simply a reflection of one's mind is not exactly settled and makes little difference to him in terms of his love for nature. He then proceeds, however, to maintain that senses or understanding based on senses tends to make one believe in the absolute existence of nature, whereas reason, the better cognitive faculty, modifies this belief. The further distinction between a sensual person, who is confined by the material world, and a poet, who frees himself or herself with imagination from the domination of the material world, shows that Emerson favors the view that nature does not have absolute existence.

The discussion of the issue eventually ends with the reiteration of the superiority of the soul and trust in God, whose creation of nature is to be regarded for humankind's emancipation. Having emphatically asserted the superiority of the soul, Emerson gives the following chapter the title "Spirit" to indicate that the essential function of nature is to lead one back to the Universal Spirit. In order to do so, one needs to employ a creative imagination rather than a mechanical analysis to achieve communion with nature: "a guess is often more fruitful than an indisputable affirmation, and . . . a dream may let us deeper into the secret of nature than a hundred concerted experiments." The problem with this world, according to him, can only be a problem with self. In concluding *Nature*, Emerson therefore exhorts one to achieve unity with nature, to trust in oneself, and eventually to create one's own world.

"THE AMERICAN SCHOLAR"

First published: 1837 (as *An Oration Delivered Before the Phi Beta Kappa Society*)
Type of work: Lecture

The American scholar should avoid being enslaved to the past or foreign influences; people should rely upon the self as the ever-dependable source of inspiration.

In 1837, Emerson was invited to deliver the address "The American Scholar," one of the most influential American speeches made at his time, to the Harvard chapter of Phi Beta Kappa; the same topic of the address had been prescribed year after year since his boyhood.

When Emerson urged American scholars at the beginning of his address to create an original literature free from European influence, he was to some extent reiterating a conventional theme. The creation of an original literature, Emerson maintained, however, would have to be based on an inner spirit of self-reliance—the opening and concluding theme of *Nature*. The primary concern of this address is thus with an intellectual's spiritual cultivation—the eventual goal being "Man Thinking"—rather than the actual composition of literary works.

In the discussion of the scholar's education, three kinds of influence are mentioned: nature, books, and action. Of primary importance, permanent nature corresponds to one's mind, hence it should be studied for the enhancement of the understanding of the self. The close relationship between the soul and nature is explained here in terms of a seal and print. The second source of influence is the mind of the past, which can best be seen in books. Emerson criticizes those scholars who allow themselves to be dominated by the past great minds to the extent that they think for the historical figures rather than for themselves, thereby becoming bookworms instead of "Man Thinking."

As a result, creative reading is advocated for one's own inspiration. Because of his belief in the union of the self with the Universal Spirit, Emerson further urges scholars to communicate with it first, drawing upon its creative force to compose their own original books. Only when one encounters difficulty in communicating with this spirit or God directly, he insists, should one depend on books. Action is considered the third source of influence upon the scholar. In encouraging a scholar to act, Emerson not only emphasizes the importance of the actual experience for one's mental growth but also, and especially, attempts to identify a person of action with a contemplative mind, a hero with a poet.

After illustrating the three kinds of influence upon the scholar, Emerson describes the scholar's duty, which is to guide people to find the universal mind within themselves and to achieve unity with it. To be qualified for such a work, the scholar would naturally need to be confident and self-trusting: "In self-trust all the virtues are comprehended." When one looks within and becomes a master of oneself, Emerson states, one actually examines all minds and becomes a master of all people.

Because of the unceasing manifestation of the Universal Spirit in every object, the here and now is thus greatly emphasized. Instead of looking to great minds in the past and from afar, he prefers to embrace the lowly and common in the present—a common Romantic theme. To conclude, Emerson repeats the theme of self-reliance on the most grandiloquent level, assuring his audience that "if the single man plant himself indomitably on his instincts, and there abide, the huge world will come round to him."

"SELF-RELIANCE"

First published: 1841 (collected in *Essays: First Series*, 1841)
Type of work: Essay

Because of the inherent moral sentiment, which partakes of the divine spirit, the best principle for behavior is to trust one's own intuition.

In his book titled *Essays*, "Self-Reliance" follows "History" so that a balanced and self-contained unit can be created out of these two. Abounding with short aphorisms, the essay begins with an admonition to believe in the true self, which is considered in essence identical with the Universal Spirit: "Trust thyself: every heart vibrates to that iron string." Emerson then holds infancy, which is favorably contrasted with adulthood, as a model for one to follow in the cultivation of a spirit of independence or nonconformity. His metaphorical use of a babe as a model of nonconformity is a radical twist of Christ's elevation of it as an emblem of total dependence on God.

As does Wordsworth, Emerson regards a person's growth normally as a process of losing one's moral sentiment or spirit of nonconformity. Society is considered to have an adverse effect on the growth of each individual's independent spirit, whereas solitude may contribute to it. Senseless philanthropy, which encourages dependence on outside help, is thus also thought to be detrimen-

tal. When Emerson states that one should live by one's instinct, whether or not it be from the devil, he is attempting to use exaggeration to shock his audience; his idea is that the inherent moral sentiment, which makes one self-sufficient, cannot come from the devil. Total trust in one's emotions may well result in contradiction when one's emotions change, however; noting this, Emerson simply retorts that life itself is an organic process, inevitably involving contradiction. Acting in accordance with true feeling, he believes, will automatically bring about a sound life.

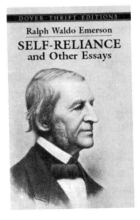

Viewed in light of self, history is thus the biography of a few unusually powerful figures. Having emphasized the importance of nonconformity, he begins to explore the philosophical basis for self-reliance. According to Emerson, there is an instinct or intuition in each individual drawing upon the Universal Spirit as the ever-dependable guiding principle. Because of the identification of intuition with the Universal Spirit, one is simply following its command when one acts in accordance with one's intuition. The presence of the self-sufficing and self-contained Universal Spirit in each individual thus justifies one's living in and for the present without having to refer either to the past or to the future.

Whereas Christ alone has traditionally been regarded as the Word made flesh, Emerson regards every human potentially as a reincarnation of the Word. Consequently, regret of the past and prayer for the future as a means to effect private ends are both diseases of human will and should be avoided. Traveling with the hope to see something greater than the self, in Emerson's view, would simply be senseless. As a result of this moralistic view, society, like nature, may change but never advance. Typical of his conclusions, the end of this essay, which repeats the theme of self-reliance and predicts the subjugation of Chance under human will based on self-reliance, sounds greatly optimistic.

"THE OVER-SOUL"

First published: 1841 (collected in *Essays: First Series*, 1841)
Type of work: Essay

"The Over-Soul" underlies the universe, giving birth to and justifying the existence of all objects.

Greatly influenced by a third century neoplatonist philosopher, Plotinus, "The Over-Soul" explicates one of Emerson's essential ideas, one on which his entire thought is based. Beginning with an approval of a life based on hope, Emerson posits the idea of unity or "Over-Soul" as the metaphysical basis for the existence of everything. According to him, the Over-Soul is a perfect self-sufficing universal force, the origin of which is unknown and the essence of which is characterized through wisdom, virtue, power, and beauty, giving sustenance to all objects. Maintained by this force, all objects are thus self-sufficient in every moment of their existence, having no need to concern themselves with the future. With no hearkening back to the past and no anticipation of the future, the meaning of one's ever-progressive life simply exists in the "here and now."

Because of the unifying power of the Over-Soul, differences between objects can be eradicated: "The act of seeing and the thing seen, the seer and the spectacle, the subject and the object, are one." In explaining the nature of this universal spirit, Emerson makes a distinction between the natural self—the body and its faculties—and the transcendental spirit residing in each individual and animating the natural self. This transcendental spirit, he emphasizes, cannot be defined by the intellect; it can be detected only with the intuition. A child, who acts according to instinct, is thus celebrated as the model for the reception of this spirit.

As the ultimate force in this universe, the Over-Soul ought to be obeyed as the absolute commander of the self, as it can guide one to lead a most sound life. The movement of the universe, in this sense, can be interpreted as the ceaseless communication between each individual soul and the Over-Soul. The more one communicates with the universal soul, the more powerful one may become. Jesus, who, according to Emerson, heeded the voice from the spirit within oneself, is held as a perfect example of such a communication between the individual soul and the Over-Soul. A genius is simply the person who lets the spirit flow into the intellect and then speaks from within. In order to communicate with this universal spirit, one needs only to be plain and true, as it normally descends upon the lowly and simple, the type of people who consistently received Emerson's attention after the composition of *Nature*.

Echoing a statement from the Hindu sacred text, the Upanishads, Emerson maintains that one may also partake of divinity from communicating with the divine force: "The simplest person who in his integrity worships God, becomes God." The presence of this universal spirit in each individual thus makes it imperative for one to look not without but within for the source of inspiration.

Viewed in this light, the greatness of renowned poets lies thus in their ability to remind people of the immense resource under their control and to instruct them to disregard all their achievements. All exterior authority, be what it may, Emerson states, should be disregarded; only the self guided by the Over-Soul is to be trusted. The orthodox faith based on exterior authority is interpreted at the end of the essay as a result of the withdrawal of the soul and the decline of religion. To be a master of the world around him, Emerson concludes, a person has to achieve unity with the divine soul and follow the dictate of his or her own heart.

"FATE"

First published: 1860 (collected in *The Conduct of Life*, 1860)
Type of work: Essay

Although fate is a horrendous force in this world, mind and will are equally powerful and can subjugate fate to a good use.

A great change occurred in Emerson's thought in his later life, as can be demonstrated in the essay "Fate." Whereas freedom and optimism were emphasized in his early life, fate and limitation eventually became his great concern. Having, in his later life, read much oriental literature, which greatly emphasizes the power of fate, Emerson felt it necessary to reckon with this subject and include it in his thought.

Unlike his earlier essays, which nearly always begin with an optimistic trust in the potentiality of the self, "Fate" begins with an emphasis on obstacles, which are described as immovable and which individuals would inevitably experience in their attempts to achieve goals. To avoid the misunderstanding that he has radically changed his view regarding the grand nature of humankind, which had been effectively advocated during most of his life, Emerson affirms the importance of liberty immediately after his opening statement on the significance of fate.

The ideal principle, according to him, is to strike a balance between liberty and fate, rather than overemphasize either of them. After setting forth this principle, Emerson turns his attention back to fate, citing Hinduism, Calvinism, and Greek tragedy as examples for their emphatic treatment of this grim aspect of life. Contrary to his earlier idea, Nature—equated with fate in this essay—is now perceived as potentially rough and dangerous. He describes various kinds of limitations—environment, race, physique, character, and sometimes thought.

In order to illustrate the importance of fate, Emerson even makes an overstatement that one is predetermined the moment one is born. A criticism is further made on the narrow focus of his own previous thought (the optimism emphasizing the power of the self) with the recognition that circumstance, the negative side which one cannot fully control, ought to be considered. According to Emerson, fate manifests itself in both matter and mind, the latter being affected in a much more subtle way.

Having elaborated the significance of fate, he begins to assert liberty again: "Intellect annuls Fate." To counteract fate, one is advised first to transform it intrinsically by regarding it as a positive force working for one's ultimate good rather than a negative force. Furthermore, one should draw upon the ever-resourceful universal force, the moral sentiment within oneself, to take oneself out of bondage into freedom. Only by so doing, Emerson maintains, can one expect to reconcile fate and freedom: "Person makes event, and event person."

After analyzing the way to reconcile the opposite forces of fate and freedom, he moves a step further in holding that one can subjugate fate to one's will because event is only the exteriorization of the soul—an idea that is in agreement with his early thought. In doing so, he applies the law of cause and effect to human life, regarding the soul as the cause and event as its effect. Nature, in his view, best serves those who concentrate on refining their moral sentiment. The essay concludes with an assertion of the balanced interplay of fate and freedom, giving the enduring impression that by trusting oneself, one is eventually able to become what one wants to be: "Let us build altars to the Blessed Unity which holds nature and souls in perfect solution."

"THE RHODORA"

First published: 1839 (collected in *Poems*, 1847)
Type of work: Poem

Beauty needs no rational justification for its self-sufficient existence.

Consisting of sixteen lines, "The Rhodora" is one of Emerson's most admired poems. The major theme in this poem, a work written two years before *Nature*, can be found in many of his later works as well as in the Romantic literature of his time. As indicated by the subtitle, "On Being Asked, Whence Is the Flower?" the poem has a philosophical import concerning the existence of the flower.

A spiritual communication between humankind and nature appears at the very beginning (represented by sea winds, a favorite theme in Emerson's works), when the speaker states that the sea winds in May "pierced our solitudes." A common image in Romantic poetry, the wind often connotes inspiration. In this regard, the opening statement may also imply that the poet was inspired by the muse through his communication with nature, thereby beginning his creative process—an act which corresponds with the growing season of May in the outside world, as is mentioned in the poem.

Freed from solitude by the sea winds, the speaker notices the Rhodora—a rather obscure flower—blooming in the woods in a somewhat private location ordinarily unlikely to catch one's attention. The presence of this flower, the spelling of which is capitalized throughout the poem to emphasize its significance as the symbol of beauty, is described as pleasing to both land and water. The service that the Rhodora offers to the world almost involves self-sacrifice, as is reflected in the description of the pleasure that its fallen petals were able to give to the pool: "The purple petals, fallen in the pool! Made the black water with their beauty gay."

After examining the objects on land and water, Emerson proceeds to note the creature in the sky, the "red-bird," courting the flower, thereby making his poem symbolically comprehensive of all the objects in this world. A radical transition occurs at the center of this poem; whereas the first half essentially describes various objects with the focus on the beauty of the Rhodora, the second half primarily concerns the metaphysical meaning of the flower.

Further division exists in the second half, which contains two sets of questions and answers, each set occurring every four lines. Corresponding to this structural pattern, the tenses also shift from the past in the first half to the present mixed with the past in the second. Furthermore, the rhyme scheme of *aabbcdcd*, which occurs twice in the poem, reinforces the theme of the dichotomy between nature and self (the description of the Rhodora and the inquiry about the metaphysical meaning of its existence) and the correspondence between them.

Emerson begins the second half with an apostrophe to the Rhodora, asking in the name of the sages why its beauty is wasted on earth and sky. The reason, central to this poem as well as to Emerson's thought, is that the flower is self-sufficient, existing for its own sake; "Tell them, dear, that if eyes were made for seeing,/ Then Beauty is its own excuse for being." By refusing to justify the being of the flower with analytical rationalization, activity that characterizes the sages, the poet implies that intuition or instinct rather than rationalization is necessary for leading a satisfactory life.

A similar question is posed in the last four lines, where the Rhodora is regarded as the rival of the rose, a favorite flower in Western tradition. The rivalry between the Rhodora and the rose possibly signifies a contrast between the lowly and plain and the high and flamboyant in stylistics, the former being the poet's choice. The concluding answer may

be given by the Rhodora as well as the speaker, or by the latter speaking for both: "But, in my simple ignorance, suppose/ The self-same Power that brought me there brought you."

The poet's affirmation of the quality of simple ignorance represented by the flower indicates his predilection to use the lowly and humble as the basis of his aesthetics, a theme presaged by the seclusive setting. The eventual naming of the Power, which unifies various objects in the universe, not only serves as a link between the poet and the flower—a spiritual rapport between humankind and nature already seen at the beginning—but also hearkens back to the subtitle of the poem, thereby giving the poem a highly structured unity.

"BRAHMA"

First published: 1857 (collected in *May-Day and Other Pieces*, 1867)
Type of work: Poem

The universal spirit Brahma is effable and transcends the dichotomy of a person's thinking.

Greatly influenced by a sacred text of Hinduism, Katha-Upanishad, "Brahma" is a philosophical explication of the universal spirit by that name. The poetic form of elegiac quatrain is used to represent the solemn nature of the subject. Throughout the poem, Brahma appears as the only speaker, sustaining the continuity of the work. That the spirit is the only speaker signifies not only its absolute nature but also its sustaining power, upon which the existence of the entire universe—metaphorically, the poem—is based.

The poem begins by examining the common-sensical view that the spirit ends with one's death. Even though the body may be destroyed, Brahma, which resides in each individual as the fountain of life, never ceases to exist: "If the red slayer think he slays,/ Or if the slain think he is slain,/ They know not well the subtle ways/ I keep." When the body is destroyed, the poet maintains, the spirit will appear again, likely in a different form. By employing the examples of both the slayer and the slain, the speaker is suggesting not only the prevalence of their view (that the spirit may not be eternal) but also the dichotomy that normally characterizes a person's perception.

The dichotomy recurs in the second stanza, in which opposite notions such as far and near, shadow and sunlight, vanishing and appearing, and shame and fame are juxtaposed. To the speaker, who unifies the universe, the seemingly unbridgeable differences between opposite concepts can be perfectly resolved; hence, the paradoxical statements. Brahma's great power is further described in the third stanza, where the spirit states that it comprehends yet transcends everything—both "the doubter and the doubt," the subject and object, and matter and mind. In addition, the rhyme scheme befittingly reinforces the spirit's interweaving power, yielding a sense of wonder based on unusual metrical symmetry.

Different from the otherworldly spirit in Hinduism, however, the transcendental spirit represented by Brahma in this poem leads the follower not to Heaven but to this world. By using the conjunction "but" in the last stanza, Emerson prepares his reader for his own interpretation of the universal spirit. The concluding statement that justifies self-sufficient existence in this world, "But thou, meek lover of the good!/ Find me, and turn thy back on heaven," makes this poem characteristically Emersonian.

SUMMARY

Emerson's thought is characterized by optimism and tremendous hope for humankind. Although some critics, represented by George Santayana, believe that Emerson failed to reckon with the force of evil, his advocacy of looking within and acting sincerely as the ultimate mode of behavior still appeals to the modern age.

Especially in a society dominated by technology,

DISCUSSION TOPICS

- Ralph Waldo Emerson often employs powerful imagery to support the ideas expressed in his prose. Cite particular examples of this trait in *Nature.*

- What, according to Emerson, are the uses of nature? Is "using" nature an unfortunate term? Would another expression convey his meaning better?

- Some students of Emerson's "The American Scholar" have seen this address as an attempt to define his own vocation. Why in 1837 would he have needed to do such a thing?

- How does the style of "Self-Reliance" enforce its theme?

- What is the point of Emerson's reformulation of religious concepts? For instance, what is the effect of his employment of a term such as "Over-Soul" or "Power" when he appears to be referring to God?

- What evidence can you find in Emerson's writing that he acknowledged the existence and force of evil?

Emerson's poetic vision of the transcendent mind offers an intriguing alternate way of life emphasizing the spirit. Furthermore, the dynamic style primarily based on powerful short sentences, insightful aphorisms, and natural transitions makes Emerson unequivocally one of the greatest essayists of all time.

Vincent Yang

BIBLIOGRAPHY

By the Author

NONFICTION:
Nature, 1836
An Oration Delivered Before the Phi Beta Kappa Society, Cambridge, 1837 (better known as "The American Scholar")
An Address Delivered Before the Senior Class in Divinity College, Cambridge . . . , 1838 (better known as "Divinity School Address")
Essays: First Series, 1841

Orations, Lectures and Addresses, 1844
Essays: Second Series, 1844
Addresses and Lectures, 1849
Representative Men: Seven Lectures, 1850
English Traits, 1856
The Conduct of Life, 1860
Representative of Life, 1860
Society and Solitude, 1870
Works and Days, 1870
Letters and Social Aims, 1875
Lectures and Biographical Sketches, 1884
Miscellanies, 1884
Natural History of Intellect, 1893
The Journals of Ralph Waldo Emerson, 1909-1914 (10 volumes; E. W. Emerson and W. E. Forbes, editors)
The Letters of Ralph Waldo Emerson, 1939 (6 volumes; Ralph L. Rusk, editor)
The Journals and Miscellaneous Notebooks, 1960-1982 (16 volumes)

POETRY:
Poems, 1847
May-Day and Other Pieces, 1867
Selected Poems, 1876

EDITED TEXT:
Parnassus, 1874

MISCELLANEOUS:
Uncollected Writings: Essays, Addresses, Poems, Reviews, and Letters, 1912

About the Author

Allen, Gay Wilson. *Waldo Emerson: A Biography.* New York: Viking Press, 1981.

Bosco, Ronald A., and Joel Myerson, eds. *Emerson in His Own Time: A Biographical Chronicle of His Life, Drawn from Recollections, Interviews, and Memoirs by Family, Friends, and Associates.* Iowa City: University of Iowa Press, 2003.

Buell, Lawrence. *Emerson.* Cambridge, Mass.: Belknap Press of Harvard University Press, 2003.

Goodman, Russell B. *American Philosophy and the Romantic Tradition.* New York: Cambridge University Press, 1990.

Jacobson, David. *Emerson's Pragmatic Vision: The Dance of the Eye.* University Park: Pennsylvania State University Press, 1993.

Lopez, Michael. *Emerson and Power: Creative Antagonism in the Nineteenth Century.* De Kalb: Northern Illinois University Press, 1996.

Myerson, Joel, ed. *A Historical Guide to Ralph Waldo Emerson.* New York: Oxford University Press, 2000.

Porte, Joel, and Saundra Morris, eds. *The Cambridge Companion to Ralph Waldo Emerson.* New York: Cambridge University Press, 1999.

Richardson, Robert D. *Emerson: The Mind on Fire.* Berkeley: University of California Press, 1995.

Robinson, David M. *Emerson and the Conduct of Life: Pragmatism and Ethical Purpose in the Later Work.* New York: Cambridge University Press, 1993.

Sacks, Kenneth S. *Understanding Emerson: "The American Scholar" and His Struggle for Self-Reliance.* Princeton, N.J.: Princeton University Press, 2003.

Yanella, Donald. *Ralph Waldo Emerson.* Boston: Twayne, 1982.

LOUISE ERDRICH

Born: Little Falls, Minnesota
June 7, 1954

Drawing on her Chippewa and German-immigrant heritage, Erdrich's novels and poetry have created a wide-ranging chronicle of American Indian and white experience in twentieth century North Dakota.

Michael Dorris

BIOGRAPHY

Although born in Minnesota, Louise Erdrich grew up in Wahpeton, a small town in southeastern North Dakota, just across the Red River from her native state. Her father, Ralph Erdrich, was a German immigrant who taught in the Wahpeton Bureau of Indian Affairs boarding school. Her mother, Rita Journeau Erdrich, a three-quarters Chippewa Indian, also worked at the school. Erdrich was the oldest of seven children. Her parents encouraged Louise's interest in writing by paying her a nickel for each of her stories and binding them in homemade book form.

Erdrich's mixed religious and cultural background provided a rich foundation for her poetry and fiction. Along with the Indian boarding school, there were two convents in Wahpeton, and Erdrich commented in 1985 and 1986 interviews that she had a "gothic-Catholic childhood," including a close relationship with her paternal grandmother, who embraced "a dark, very Catholic kind of mysticism." Erdrich also paid frequent visits to her Chippewa relatives on the Turtle Mountain Reservation in north-central North Dakota. Her maternal grandfather served as tribal chairman, and he participated in both traditional Chippewa religion and Roman Catholicism.

In 1972, Erdrich enrolled at Dartmouth College

in New Hampshire, arriving on the same day that Michael Dorris, her future husband, came to campus to teach anthropology. Nine years her senior, Dorris later became a tenured professor and head of the Native American Studies Program at Dartmouth. Erdrich majored in creative writing, and though she took a course from Dorris in her junior year, she has stated that she did not form a close relationship with him or take a strong interest in her Indian heritage until years later.

Encouraged at Dartmouth by prizes for poetry and fiction, Erdrich decided to pursue writing as her career. During and immediately after her college years, she worked at a variety of jobs in the Northeast and in North Dakota to support herself and broaden her experience. The jobs included waiting tables, working in a mental hospital, teaching poetry in prisons and schools, and editing an Indian newspaper. In 1978, Erdrich entered a creative writing program at Johns Hopkins University. After earning her M.A. in 1979, a return to Dartmouth to give a poetry reading sparked a closer friendship with Dorris. In 1981, the two were married.

Erdrich and Dorris devoted their lives to ambitious family, literary, and humanitarian goals. Like Erdrich, Dorris was three-eighths Indian, and years before his marriage to Erdrich, he adopted three Indian infants from midwestern reservations. Dorris and Erdrich had three more children.

Erdrich and her husband collaborated on virtually all the works that either one published—whether fiction, poetry, or nonfiction—until Dorris's death in 1997. They conceived of subjects, plots, and characters together; one did the writing, and the other helped in the editing stage, which might have involved as many as seven drafts. Their first major literary success came in 1982, when Erdrich's story "The World's Greatest Fishermen" won the five-thousand-dollar first prize in the Nelson Algren fiction competition. Set in 1981, this story involves members of two Chippewa families (the Kashpaws and the Morrisseys), and Erdrich and Dorris built on the success of the story by conceiving others that intertwined its characters with members of three other Chippewa and mixed-blood families in the years from 1934 to 1984. The stories appeared in magazines such as *The Atlantic Monthly* and the *Kenyon Review*, and two were selected for honorary anthologies: "Scales," for *Best American Short Stories, 1983* (1983), and "Saint Marie," for *Prize Stories 1985: The O. Henry Awards* (1985).

In 1984, Erdrich gave birth to her first child, became pregnant with her second, and published two books. *Jacklight*, a collection of forty poems and four folk tales, met with high critical praise. Erdrich collected fourteen of the Chippewa family stories and presented them as a novel, *Love Medicine*, which became a national best seller and won several prizes, including the 1984 National Book Critics Circle Award for fiction.

The success of *Love Medicine* encouraged Erdrich and Dorris to plan three more novels chronicling the interwoven lives of Chippewas and whites in twentieth century North Dakota. The second novel, *The Beet Queen* (1986), ranges over a slightly earlier period (1932 to 1972) than *Love Medicine* and focuses less on Native Americans than on whites and their small-town lives. The third novel in the trilogy, *Tracks* (1988), goes further back in time to 1912 to 1924, when members of the Chippewa and mixed-blood families of *Love Medicine* engage in a bitter struggle for survival. Although neither *The Beet Queen* nor *Tracks* was as monumental a success as *Love Medicine*, both merited high critical acclaim and became best sellers. In addition, two stories from *Tracks* were reprinted in honorary anthologies: "Fleur," in *Prize Stories 1987: The O. Henry Awards* (1987), and "Snares," in *Best American Short Stories, 1988* (1988).

Along with the North Dakota novels that have been the main source of Erdrich's fame, she and her husband participated in other literary and humanitarian projects. In 1987, Dorris published his first novel, *A Yellow Raft in Blue Water*, a story of three Indian women. The couple spent a year in Montana while Dorris conducted research on fetal alcohol syndrome (FAS), a group of physical and psychological symptoms that afflict many Indian children, including one of Dorris's adopted sons. In 1989, Dorris published a study of FAS, *The Broken Cord*, and he and Erdrich donated money and campaigned for legislation to combat this debilitating disease. Also in 1989, Erdrich published her second volume of poetry, *Baptism of Desire*. The book did not receive as much critical attention as her earlier works, though the poems and folk tales in it deal vividly with many of Erdrich's recurring themes: sexual and spiritual desire, birth, and parenting.

Erdrich and Dorris separated in 1996, and he committed suicide the following year. Erdrich continued to write, publishing several acclaimed novels.

ANALYSIS

In a 1985 essay titled "Where I Ought to Be: A Writer's Sense of Place," Erdrich wrote that the essence of her writing emerges from her attachment to a specific locale: North Dakota, the site of a Chippewa reservation and of the neighboring white communities founded by European immigrants. In this essay, Erdrich defines her mission as a writer by comparing it with the function of a traditional storyteller in tribal cultures like the Native American Ojibwe:

> In a tribal view of the world, where one place has been inhabited for generations, the landscape becomes enlivened by a sense of group and family history. Unlike most writers, a traditional storyteller fixes listeners in an unchanging landscape combined of myth and reality. People and place are inseparable.

Although three-eighths Chippewa, Erdrich has not aspired to become precisely this kind of traditional storyteller. She realizes only too keenly that the tribal view in its pure form is no longer tenable for American Indians because the "unchanging" relationship of Indian people and landscape, of myth and reality, has been destroyed by the massive dislocations and changes brought by European settlement and nineteenth, twentieth, and twenty-first century "progress." On the other hand, Erdrich's writing creates a neotribal view by dramatizing the intricate relatedness of people and place in her North Dakota locale. The central paradox of her work is that, though her characters often feel disconnected and isolated, the works themselves reveal how deeply interrelated these people are with their North Dakota homeland, the landscape and the spirits that inhabit it, as well as with other Native people, contemporaries and ancestors.

Erdrich reveals this relatedness by her precise use of setting. Virtually every poem and story gains effectiveness from the way details of location, season, time of day, and weather reflect the emotional state or social situation of her characters. The often extreme elements of the North Dakota environment—its flat plains and dense forests; its marshes and lakes; its scalding, dry summers and frigid, snowy winters; its rivers that vacillate between raging spring torrents and late summer trickles—all function dramatically in Erdrich's work.

Animals are another feature of North Dakota locale that Erdrich uses to dramatize relationships among humans and of humans with their environments. In traditional Indian myths and folk tales, animals and humans are often closely related—even interchangeable. Erdrich's poetry repeatedly draws on this aspect of Indian literary heritage in individual figures of speech and as the narrative basis for entire poems. For example, Erdrich sets the poem "A Love Medicine" on a night when the Red River reaches flood stage; she describes her sister Theresa, a young woman seeking sexual experience who is oblivious to possible disaster, in this way:

> Theresa goes out in green halter and chains
> that glitter at her throat.
> This dragonfly, my sister,
> she belongs more than I
> to this night of rising water.

Erdrich's presentation of animals and the supernatural in her fiction is more complex than in her poetry and is related to the unusual mixture of realism and exaggeration in her fiction. Rather than boldly asserting the metaphoric or mystical connections of animals and people, as she does in poetry, her stories and novels generally begin by establishing a realistic base of recognizably or-

dinary people, settings, and actions. As her tales develop, these people become involved in events and perceptions that appear to the reader quite extraordinary—exaggerated in ways that may seem deluded or mystical, grotesque or magical, comic or tragic, or some strange mixture of these.

The chapter (or story) titled "Love Medicine" in Erdrich's first novel richly illustrates this mixture of realism and exaggeration as well as other characteristic features of her fiction. In this story, the young man Lipsha Morrissey begins by reflecting on how mundane his life has been: "I never really done much with my life, I suppose. I never had a television." Under pressure from his grandmother, Marie Lazarre Kashpaw, who wants to rein in her husband's straying affections, Lipsha tries to concoct a love potion based on the hearts of Canadian geese—birds that mate for life. The story develops comically as Lipsha fails to shoot down the wild geese he thinks he needs and instead substitutes turkey hearts that he buys in a supermarket. The story takes a grotesque, tragicomic turn when Marie's suspicious and reluctant husband, Nector, chokes to death on a turkey heart that Marie nags him into eating.

The story leaves the reader wondering how to interpret Nector's death. Is it evidence of the power of traditional Indian spiritualism, an ironic punishment of Marie for trying to trick her husband into loving her, or mere monstrous bad luck? As so often in her fiction, Erdrich withholds authorial comment that would provide a direct or conclusive answer to the often supernatural mysteries she presents. Instead, she relies on a first-person or, occasionally, third-person limited point of view. She concentrates on dramatizing what the characters think and feel about the mysteries in their lives. In "Love Medicine," Lipsha and Marie share a sense of guilt over Nector's death until, in another surprising twist, his ghost returns to visit them. Lipsha's interpretation of this event is so moving and profound that it seems a more meaningful act of "love medicine" than the supernatural magic he had failed to perform earlier:

> Love medicine ain't what brings him back to you,
> Grandma. No, it's something else. He loved you
> over time and distance, but he went off so quick he
> never got the chance to tell you how he loves you,
> how he doesn't blame you, how he understands.

It's true feeling, not no magic. No supermarket heart could have brung him back.

One other element of Erdrich's fiction often praised by critics is her poetic, often lyrical style. Erdrich intensifies many moments through aptly chosen images or figures of speech, yet she is also a master at drawing such poetically heightened language from her characters' experience. For example, in "Love Medicine," after Lipsha has encountered the spirit of his dead grandfather, he compares life to a kind of clothing that he knows well:

> Your life feels different on you, once you greet death and understand your heart's position. You wear your life like a garment from the mission bundle sale ever after—lightly because you realize you never paid nothing for it, cherishing because you know you won't ever come by such a bargain again.

Erdrich often ends her stories with a lyrical flourish, a series of images that extends feelings and themes in vivid, though sometimes oblique and unexpected ways. At the conclusion of "Love Medicine," Lipsha decides to pick some dandelions as a way of reconnecting his life with the forces of nature. Rather than ending the story with clear narrative sentences that neatly tie up a conclusion, Erdrich ends with a curious series of sentence fragments, images of what Lipsha sees that invite interpretation like lines in a poem: "The spiked leaves full of bitter mother's milk. A buried root. A nuisance people dig up and throw in the sun to wither. A globe of frail seeds that's indestructible."

"JACKLIGHT"

First published: 1984 (collected in *Jacklight*, 1984)

Type of work: Poem

In the harsh glare of "jacklight," animals emerge from the woods and beckon hunters to follow them back into a realm of mystery.

"Jacklight," the opening and title poem in Erdrich's first book of verse, is a haunting dramatization of male-female and of white-Indian relations. The poem begins with an epigraph citing that "the same Chippewa word is used both for flirting and for hunting game," so that the encounter between hunters and animals enacted in the poem is also an allegory for sexual gamesmanship between men and women. The title refers to an artificial light, such as a flashlight, used in hunting or fishing at night. This detail, along with a number of others, suggests that the poem is also an allegory of an encounter between white and Indian cultures. Erdrich does not indicate whether the male hunters in the poem are white or Indian, but in either case their equipment and character traits clearly suggest aggressive and exploitative aspects of white culture.

The poem begins not with the hunters going into the woods, but with the animals coming out—perhaps because of their curiosity, flirtatiousness, or trusting openness:

> We have come to the edge of the woods,
> out of brown grass where we slept, unseen,
> out of knotted twigs, out of leaves creaked shut,
> out of hiding.

In these lines and throughout the poem, Erdrich's use of assonance and consonance (such as "Out of brown" and "knotted twigs") and of parallel syntax (such as the repetition of "out of") creates a charged atmosphere that suggests repeated, ritualistic behavior.

The harsh assaultiveness of males and of white culture is portrayed in the beams of the jacklights, which "clenched to a fist of light that pointed,/ searched out, divided us." The perverse power of this jacklight, in contrast with the powers of nature, is such that the animals (or females, or Indians) are compelled into separating from their group. Although the animals in the poem smell many repulsive aspects of the hunters ("the raw steel of their gun barrels," "their tongues of sour barley," "the itch underneath the caked guts on their clothes"), they do not retreat. Erdrich seems to be suggesting that women (if they want to have husbands) and Indians (if they want to avoid total destruction by the advancing white culture) have no choice but to deal with such brutishness.

In the last two stanzas, however, the animals declare that it is time for some concessions:

We have come here too long.

It is their turn now,
their turn to follow us. Listen,
they put down their equipment.
It is useless in the tall brush.
And now they take the first steps, not knowing
how deep the woods are and lightless.

For the male who is in search of a female, or the white in confrontation with an Indian, or the reader who may be white or male and about to enter the world of a female Indian poet, there must be a willingness to deal with complexities and mysteries for which their "equipment" or preconceptions are inadequate. Yet Erdrich's readers may also be assured that though "the woods" of her poetry may seem "deep" and at times "lightless," they always contain authentic rewards of feeling and experience.

LOVE MEDICINE

First published: 1984 (revised and expanded, 1993)
Type of work: Novel

In the years from 1934 to 1984, members of five Chippewa and mixed-blood families struggle to attain a sense of belonging through love, religion, home, and family.

Love Medicine is both the title and the main thematic thread that ties fourteen diverse short stories into a novel. Although it refers specifically to traditional Indian magic in one story, in a broader sense "love medicine" refers to the different kinds of spiritual power that enable Erdrich's Chippewa and mixed-blood characters to transcend—however momentarily—the grim circumstances of their lives. Trapped on their shrinking reservation by racism and poverty, plagued by alcoholism, disintegrating families, and violence, some of Erdrich's characters nevertheless discover forms of "love medicine" that can help to sustain them.

The opening story, "The World's Greatest Fishermen," begins with an episode of "love medicine" corrupted and thwarted. In 1981, June Kashpaw, once a woman of striking beauty and feisty spirit,

has sunk to the level of picking up men in an oil boomtown. At first she hopes a man she meets will be "different" from others who have used and discarded her, then tries to walk to the reservation through a snowstorm. June fails in those last attempts to attain love and home, two goals she and other characters will seek throughout the novel. Although she appears only briefly in this and in one other story, June Kashpaw is central to the novel because she embodies the potential power of spirit and love in ways that impress and haunt the other characters.

Part 2 of "The World's Greatest Fishermen" introduces many other major characters of *Love Medicine*, when June's relatives gather together several months after her death. Several characters seem sympathetic because of their closeness to June and their kind treatment of one another. Albertine Johnson, who narrates the story and remembers her Aunt June lovingly, has gone through a wild phase of her own and is now a nursing student. Eli Kashpaw, Albertine's great-uncle who was largely responsible for raising June, is a tough and sharp-minded old man who has maintained a traditional Chippewa existence as a hunter and fisherman. Lipsha Morrissey, who, though he seems not to know it, is June's illegitimate son, a sensitive, self-educated young man who acts warmly toward Albertine.

In contrast to these characters, others appear flawed or unsympathetic according to Albertine, who would like to feel her family pulling together after June's death. Zelda and Aurelia, Albertine's gossipy mother and aunt, host the family gathering but do little to make Albertine feel at home. Albertine admires "Grandpa," Zelda's father Nector Kashpaw, for having once been an effective tribal chairman, but Nector has become so senile that Albertine cannot communicate with him. Gordie Kashpaw, the husband whom June left, is a pleasant fellow but a hapless drunk. In marked opposition to Lipsha, June's legitimate son King is a volatile bully. Although King gains some sympathy when he voices his grief over his mother's death, his horrifying acts of violence—abusing his wife, Lynette, battering his new car, smashing the pies prepared for the family dinner—leave Albertine and readers with a dismayed sense of a family in shambles.

Love Medicine then moves back in time from 1981, and its stories proceed in chronological order from 1934 to 1984, presenting ten earlier episodes in the lives of the Kashpaws and related families and three later episodes that follow the events in "The World's Greatest Fishermen." "Saint Marie" concerns a poor white girl, Marie Lazarre, who in 1934 enters Sacred Heart Convent and a violent love-hate relationship with Sister Leopolda. In "Wild Geese," also set in 1934, Nector Kashpaw, infatuated with Lulu Nanapush, finds his affections swerving unexpectedly when he encounters Marie Lazarre on the road outside her convent. By 1948, the time of "The Beads," Marie has married Nector, had three children, and agreed to raise her niece June. Marie's difficulties multiply: Nector is drinking and philandering, and June, after almost committing suicide in a children's hanging game, leaves, to be brought up by Eli in the woods.

"Lulu's Boys," set in 1957, reveals that the amorous Lulu Lamartine (née Nanapush) had married Henry Lamartine but bore eight sons by different fathers; years later, she still has a mysterious sexual hold over Henry's brother Beverly. Meanwhile, in "The Plunge of the Brave," also set in 1957, Nector recalls the development of his five-year affair with Lulu and tries to leave his wife Marie for her. All ends badly when he accidentally burns Lulu's house to the ground.

The offspring of these Kashpaws and Lamartines also have their problems. In "The Bridge," set in 1973, Albertine Johnson runs away from home and becomes lovers with Henry Lamartine, Jr., one of Lulu's sons, who is a troubled Vietnam veteran. "The Red Convertible," set in 1974, also involves Henry, Jr., as Lyman Lamartine tries unsuccessfully to bring his brother out of the dark personality changes that service in the Vietnam War has wrought in him. On a lighter note, "Scales," set in 1980, is a hilarious account of the romance between Dot Adare, an obese white clerk at a truck-weighing station, and Gerry Nanapush, one of Lulu's sons who is a most unusual convict; enormously fat, amazingly expert at escaping from jail, but totally inept at avoiding capture. "A Crown of Thorns," which overlaps the time of "The World's Greatest Fishermen" in 1981, traces Gordie Kashpaw's harrowing and bizarre decline into alcoholism after June's death.

Although in *Love Medicine*'s early stories the positive powers of love and spirit are more often frustrated than fulfilled, in the last three stories several characters achieve breakthroughs that bring members of the different families together in moving and hopeful ways. In "Love Medicine," set in 1982, Lipsha Morrissey reaches out lovingly to his grandmother Marie and to the ghosts of Nector and June. In "The Good Tears," set in 1983, Lulu undergoes a serious eye operation and is cared for by Marie, who forgives her for being Nector's longtime extramarital lover. Finally, in "Crossing the Water," set in 1984, Lipsha Morrissey mentions that Lulu and Marie have joined forces in campaigning for Indian rights, and he helps his father, Gerry Nanapush, escape to Canada. As Lipsha heads home to the reservation, he comes to appreciate the rich heritage of love, spirit, and wiliness that he has inherited from his diverse patchwork of Chippewa relatives—especially from his grandmother Lulu, his aunt Marie, and his parents, June Kashpaw and Gerry Nanapush.

THE BEET QUEEN

First published: 1986
Type of work: Novel

In a North Dakota small town in the years 1932 to 1972, two orphaned children, along with their relatives and friends, struggle in attempts to sustain love and family.

In *The Beet Queen*, Erdrich shifts her main focus from the American Indian to the European immigrant side of her background, creating in impressive detail the fictional town of Argus, modeled on Wahpeton, where she grew up, but located closer to the Chippewa reservation. The novel captures both the flat surfaces of life in small-town North Dakota and the wild incidents and strange passions that seem all the more startling, comic, and heart-rending for their appearing in such a mundane environment.

As in *Love Medicine*, *The Beet Queen* features first-person and third-person-limited narration to present characters' diverse points of view. In this novel, however, Erdrich focuses more closely on a few main characters, four later expanded to six, and devotes more time to their childhoods. The novel conveys a richly detailed perspective on how the dynamics of family and friendship affect characters over time.

Like *Love Medicine, The Beet Queen* begins with a vividly symbolic episode, shifts back in time, and then proceeds chronologically through a series of decades. The opening scene, "The Branch," dramatizes two contrasting approaches to life that many characters will enact throughout the novel. On a cold spring day in 1932, two orphans, Mary and Karl Adare, arrive by freight train in Argus. As they seek the way to the butcher shop owned by their aunt and uncle, Mary "trudge[s] solidly forward," while Karl stops to embrace a tree that already has its spring blossoms. When they are attacked by a dog, Mary runs ahead, continuing her search for the butcher shop, while Karl runs back to hop the train once again. As the archetypal plodder of the novel, Mary continues to plod solidly forward throughout; she is careful, determined, and self-reliant in pursuit of her goals. Karl is the principal dreamer—impressionable, prone to escapist impulses, and dependent on others to catch him when he falls.

The Adare family history shows that Karl is following a pattern set by his mother, Adelaide, while Mary grows in reaction against this pattern. Karl, like Adelaide, is physically beautiful but self-indulgent and impulsive. Driven to desperation by her hard luck in the early years of the Depression, Adelaide startles a fairground crowd by abandoning her children, Mary, Karl, and an unnamed newborn son, to fly away with the Great Omar, an airplane stunt pilot.

In Argus, Mary tangles with another beautiful, self-centered dreamer: her cousin Sita Kozka, who resents the attention that her parents, Pete and Fritzie, and her best friend, Celestine James, pay to Mary. Yet Mary prevails and carves a solid niche for herself among Pete, Fritzie, and Celestine, who, like Mary, believe in a strong work ethic and lack Sita's pretentious airs.

Several episodes gratify the reader with triumphs for Mary and comeuppances for the less

sympathetic characters Karl, Adelaide, and Sita. Mary becomes famous for a miracle at her school. She falls and cracks the ice in the image of Jesus. She gains Celestine as a close friend and, in time, becomes manager of the Kozka butcher shop.

Karl becomes a drifter who finds only sordid, momentary pleasure in brief homosexual affairs, and twice recklessly injures himself. Meanwhile, Adelaide marries Omar and settles in Florida, but she becomes moody and subject to violent rages. Similarly, Sita fails in her vainglorious attempts to become a model and to establish a fashionable French restaurant. She escapes her first marriage through divorce and becomes insane and suicidal during her second.

As Erdrich charts the strange and sometimes grotesque downfalls of her flighty characters, she also develops her more sympathetic ones in ways that suggest that the opposite approach to life does not guarantee happiness either. Mary fails in her attempt to attract Russell Kashpaw, Celestine's Chippewa half brother, and she develops into an exotically dressed eccentric obsessed with predicting the future and controlling others.

Like Mary, Celestine James and Wallace Pfef are hardworking and successful in business, but their loneliness drives them to ill-advised affairs with Karl, and he causes each of them considerable grief. Celestine and Karl's affair results in the birth of Dot Adare, who grows up to be the obese lover of Gerry Nanapush in the story "Scales" in *Love Medicine*. Because Celestine, Mary, and Wallace all spoil the child, Dot turns out, in Wallace's words, to have "all of her family's worst qualities . . . Mary's stubborn, abrupt ways, Sita's vanity, Celestine's occasional cruelties, Karl's lack of responsibility." As a teenager, Dot comes to grief when she learns that Wallace has rigged the election for Queen of the Argus Beet Festival so that she, an unpopular and ludicrously unlikely candidate, will win.

In opposition to the defeats and disappointments that characters bear, Erdrich dramatizes the joy they derive from life. The compensations of family and friendship—ephemeral and vulnerable as these may be—turn out to be significant for all the characters at various times in the story, particularly at the end. The irrepressible vitality of these people, troublesome as they often are to one another, keeps the reader involved and entertained throughout the novel.

TRACKS

First published: 1988
Type of work: Novel

In the years between 1912 and 1924, Chippewa Indians struggle to maintain control of their lives and their lands despite the ravages of plagues, starvation, internecine feuding, and white encroachment.

Tracks is arguably Erdrich's most concentrated, intense, and mystical novel before the appearance of *The Antelope Wife* (1998). Her shortest novel, it covers the briefest period of time, twelve years. It alternates between only two first-person narrators compared with seven and six in the preceding novels. This compression serves the story well, for the human stakes are high. At first, and periodically throughout the novel, the Chippewa characters fear for their very survival, as smallpox, tuberculosis, severe winters, starvation, and feuds with mixed-blood families bring them close to extinction. Later in the novel, government taxes and political chicanery threaten the Chippewas' ownership of their family homesteads. In response, Erdrich's Chippewa characters use all the powers at their command, including the traditional mystical powers of the old ways, to try to survive and maintain their control over the land.

Nanapush, one of the novel's two narrators, is an old Chippewa whom Erdrich names after the trickster rabbit in tribal mythology that repeatedly delivers the Chippewas from threatening monsters. In *Tracks*, Erdrich's Nanapush often does credit to his mythological model by wielding the trickster rabbit's powers of deliverance, wiliness, and humor. First, he saves Fleur Pillager, a starving seventeen-year-old girl and the sole survivor of a Chippewa clan that others fear for their legendary dark magic. Then he twice delivers young Eli Kashpaw from the sufferings of love by advising him how to win Fleur's heart. Nanapush is also instrumental in saving the extended family that forms around Fleur, Eli, and himself. This family grows to five when Fleur gives birth to a daughter, Lulu, and Eli's mother, Margaret Kashpaw, becomes Nanapush's bedmate.

As these five come close to starvation in the winter of 1918, Nanapush sends Eli out to hunt an elk,

and in one of the most extraordinary passages of the novel, Nanapush summons a power vision of Eli hunting that the old man imagines is guiding Eli to the kill. Nanapush demonstrates the humor associated with his mythological model in his wry tone as a narrator, his sharp wit in conversation, and the tricks that he plays on his mixed-blood antagonists.

Foremost among these antagonists is the novel's other narrator, Pauline Pukwan. A "skinny big-nosed girl with staring eyes," Pauline circulates in Argus from the Kozkas' butcher shop to the Sacred Heart Convent, and on the reservation from the Nanapush-Pillager-Kashpaw group to the Morrissey and Lazarre clans. At first attracted to Fleur by the beauty and sexual power that she herself lacks, Pauline later takes an envious revenge by concocting a love potion that seems to drive Fleur's husband, Eli, and Sophie Morrissey to become lovers.

The word "seems" is appropriate because Pauline's account of her perceptions, actions, and powers is sometimes so distorted that she becomes an unreliable narrator. She is so torn between desires for inclusion and revenge, between the earthy sexual and spiritual powers of the Chippewas on one hand and the self-mortifying, otherworldly religion of the Catholic nuns on the other, that at times her character and narration go over the edge into gothic dementia. Ironically, Pauline gives birth out of wedlock to a girl named Marie. At the end of her narrative Pauline enters the convent to become Sister Leopolda—*Love Medicine*'s cruel nun who influences her own daughter, Marie Lazarre, to grow into a similarly warped personality, torn between fanatical Catholic piety and earthy sexuality.

Although Erdrich clearly feels passionately about the sufferings visited on her Chippewa characters in *Tracks*, she treats this politically charged material with her usual disciplined restraint. Her dispassionate, deadpan use of first-person narrators never suggests authorial commentary and matches the understated, stoic attitude that Nanapush adopts toward the numerous waves of hardship and betrayal that the Chippewas must endure. It is a measure of Erdrich's impressive lack of sentimentality that in the struggle over Chippewa family lands that in the last quarter of the novel, it is not merely the whites and their mixed-blood accomplices who rob the Indians. In a startling act of betrayal,

Margaret and Nector Kashpaw misappropriate the money that the Nanapush-Pillager-Kashpaw group had raised together. They use it to secure the Kashpaw lands while letting the hereditary Pillager lands fall prey to lumber interests.

Tracks seems to conclude with a feeling of fragmentation and defeat but strikes some notes of solidarity and survival, especially when considered in relation to *Love Medicine* and *The Beet Queen*. Fleur disappears, leaving her husband and daughter, but Nanapush's wiliness helps him to become tribal chairman and then to retrieve Lulu from a distant boarding school. In the end, the reader is reminded that Nanapush has addressed his entire narrative to Lulu: The old man hopes that his story will convince Lulu to embrace the memory of Fleur, "the one you will not call mother."

THE ANTELOPE WIFE

First published: 1998
Type of work: Novel

Part myth, part history, the novel begins with Scranton Roy's and Blue Prairie Woman's nineteenth century stories and follows the poignant, intertwined tales of their offspring.

Erdrich's novel *The Antelope Wife* makes a leap of style, incorporating deep history from a scene similar to nineteenth century Ojibwe clashes with the United States Army with a mythic child who is raised by a herd of antelope. Her narrative shifts from the physical world of the plains to the spiritual world of animals who can communicate with humans and lend them their traits. She also leaps several generations, bringing the mythic influence on Matilda Roy into the twentieth century where it shimmers in the actions and personalities of the antelope women Klaus Shawano shadows in the early chapters. When Klaus kidnaps the mother of the girls, he has taken on more than he can handle, and the results play themselves out several generations later.

Rozina Whiteheart Beads invites us in to the narrative as a modern voice in chapter 3. Mother of Cally and Deanna, the fourth set of twins in the Blue Prairie Woman line, she says at the close of her chapter: "I would go back if I could, unweave the

pattern of destruction. Take it all apart occurrence by slow event." She refers to early complications when soldier Scranton Roy follows, saves, and raises a female Indian child after he has been involved in slaughtering members of the child's band. The unassuaged grief of the girl's mother leads her toward madness until she is renamed and treks off to find her lost daughter, leaving the first set of twins to be raised by their grandmother. Years later, Rozina, one of the third set of twins in the Shawano line, picks up the story, which entwines offspring of the Roy and Shawano families in ways so complicated that readers must often keep a list to sort out who is related to whom.

Throughout the novel, characters try and decipher who they are. All seem to be seeking answers in love or history, family or tribe. Cally confronts her Grandma Zosie midway through the book.

What does my name mean? Where is my sister? What about my father? And Mama, will she ever stop avoiding Frank and make him her destiny? What does she want? . . . I look into her too-young brown eyes and get lost in all that I don't know.

Rozin makes the final journey to Frank's arms from loss and grief teetering between the real and spirit worlds. There are answers for Cally and a future for the characters who survive in Minneapolis, the city full of noise and danger for Ojibwes. Erdrich's novel ends with a catalog of questions. "Did these occurrences have a paradigm . . . [?] Who are you and who am I, the beader or the bit of colored glass sewn onto the fabric of this earth?" The answers reside in the nest of her words.

THE LAST REPORT ON THE MIRACLES AT LITTLE NO HORSE

First published: 2001
Type of work: Novel

Covering the years from 1910 to 1996, the history of Father Damien on the Ojibwe Little No Horse reservation unfolds, complete with an earth-shattering secret.

The Last Report on the Miracles at Little No Horse plunges readers into the lifetime saga of Father

Damien and his work among the Ojibwes on the Little No Horse reservation. A prologue, containing a 1996 a letter to the pope from Father Damien, begins the book's four-part narration by returning to 1910-1912. As in all Erdrich's work, landscape plays a major role. "Eighty-some years previous, through a town that was to flourish and past a farm that would disappear, the river slid—all that happened began with that flow of water." Novitiate Sister Cecelia, the former Agnes De Witt, is introduced as a young nun whose piano playing contains such emotion it disturbs her community and prompts her leaving. The arrangements she makes to live on a nearby farm catapult her into an adventure that will engulf her life. An accidental brush with petty criminals causes her common-law husband's death and sets the stage for the rest of the novel. Themes of passionate devotion, religious life, individual will, and survival in the face of overwhelming odds are set in motion in part 1, "The Transfiguration of Agnes." After a disastrous flood washes her out of her home, Agnes takes the role of Father Damien Modeste, a drowned priest whose body she finds. She walks onto Ojibwe land, and the novel's main conceit is in place.

Throughout part 2, "The Deadly Conversions," and part 3, "Memory and Suspicion," Erdrich continues the technique of interspersing chapters about the aged priest's daily routine and life in his parish with chapters about the past. In these sections Father Jude, an emissary from the Vatican, interacts with Father Damien and the parishioners that he has come to know and accept over the years. As Father Jude Miller investigates Sister Leopolda's life and the miracles reported at Little No Horse, the novel incorporates earlier episodes between Father Damien, Nanapush, and Fleur Pillager as well as revealing the history of the Payut clan and the tale of the Kapshaw wives, the drama of Mary Kapshaw in the convent kitchen and Lulu Pillager's struggle with her mother, Fleur. Lulu's hatred for Fleur takes root in these sections when she is sent to Indian Boarding School. To further complicate life, another priest arrives to help Father Damien, and this means sharing a living space—a huge difficulty for "Father" Damien. The two of them discover each other with a passion that cannot be contained.

Part 4, "The Passions," gives both report and prophecy concerning Lulu Pillager, returned as a woman to the reservation. It contains Sister Leopolda's final confession of a murder and her threat to unmask "Father" Damien to the authorities when they quarrel. Father Jude Miller begins his account of Leopolda's passion and finds himself spending equal time thinking about Father Damien's life as he writes. Father Damien, unwilling to be indefensible in death, plans his disappearance, and Mary Kapshaw helps him carry it out. Finally, it is the love that Father Damien shared with his Ojibwe flock that they and readers remember.

THE MASTER BUTCHERS SINGING CLUB

First published: 2003
Type of work: Novel

The novel details Fidelis Waldvogel's emigration from Germany to Argus, North Dakota, and his life as a butcher there intertwines with Delphine Watzka's life through work and family involvement.

The Master Butchers Singing Club adds another family saga to those of the residents of Argus, North Dakota, whom Erdrich's readers have been getting to know since the 1980's. Fidelis Waldvogel's return from World War I in 1918 and his emigration from Germany in 1922 begin a narrative that moves through the development of small-town culture in the upper Midwest at the twentieth century's beginning to the Great Depression; it culminates nine years after the end of World War II.

Erdrich's genius for metaphor is employed in her creation of chapter titles. For example, chapter three, "The Bones," begins with Argus's structure as a town; the framework of Fidelis's life shifts when Eva arrives with "their" son; Fidelis opens a butcher shop which schedules his life through work; Cyprian and Del-

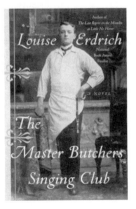

phine establish a fake marriage to mollify the townspeople; and Roy is found wallowing in filth and confusion. The chapter's events allude to bones' functions as support, and other chapter titles suggest metaphors for memory, time, and patterns of connection in human lives.

Early in the novel, Fidelis founds a singing club like the one he remembers in his German home, Ludwigsruhe, and the men begin weekly meetings to harmonize and socialize. Delphine struggles to negotiate the early childhood loss of her mother and the alcoholic incompetence of her father. Cyprian struggles with his homosexual desires. Confronting Cyprian after she discovers him in an encounter with a man, Delphine means to remind him of their one night of passion, but instead she asks, "How do you balance?" Delphine and Cyprian tour successfully with a vaudeville group and traveling circus until Delphine needs to return to Argus and quiet her worries about her father, Roy Watzka. Argus then becomes the backdrop for how the two couples struggle for equilibrium.

The couples' lives mingle when Delphine begins to help out in the butcher shop. She is drawn into Eva's kitchen for coffee the first day that she comes to the shop as a customer, and in that room, she senses the domestic tranquillity she had longed for. Eva becomes fatally stricken with cancer, and Delphine nurses her friend through a painful death. All the while she and Cyprian maintain the charade of marriage while they live nearly platon-ically. Erdrich introduces two eccentrics: Tante Maria Waldvogel, Fidelis's embittered spinster sister, and Step-and-a-Half, a wandering collector of junk. Gradually the plot becomes more about how the women manage to maintain order and live than how the men prosper.

Finally, Fidelis proposes to Delphine, and she is free to accept him. She has been a surrogate mother for his sons and has achieved a respected place in Argus through her economic ways, her efficient way of meeting her responsibilities, her steady presence, and her wide reading. The novel is weighted with the vision of what it means to survive and achieve balance in the world as one finds it, not as one wishes it.

SUMMARY

If Erdrich had been born two hundred years earlier, she might have been a traditional Chippewa storyteller whose tales reminded her listeners of their unchanging relationship to the land and to the mythic and legendary characters that inhabited it. Several generations removed from such a stable and undamaged culture, Erdrich creates a richly neotribal view of people and place. Erdrich's poetry and fiction show the profound interrelatedness of her characters—Indian and white—with contemporaries and ancestors, one another and their North Dakota homeland.

Terry L. Andrews; updated by Karen L. Arnold

BIBLIOGRAPHY

By the Author

SHORT FICTION:
"The Red Convertible," 1981
"Scales," 1982
"The World's Greatest Fisherman," 1982
"American Horse," 1983
"Destiny," 1985
"Saint Marie," 1985
"Fleur," 1987
"Snares," 1987
"Matchimanito," 1988

LONG FICTION:
Love Medicine, 1984 (revised and expanded, 1993)
The Beet Queen, 1986

Tracks, 1988
The Crown of Columbus, 1991 (with Michael Dorris)
The Bingo Palace, 1994
Tales of Burning Love, 1996
The Antelope Wife, 1998
The Last Report on the Miracles at Little No Horse, 2001
The Master Butchers Singing Club, 2003
Four Souls, 2004
The Painted Drum, 2005

POETRY:
Jacklight, 1984
Baptism of Desire, 1989
Original Fire: Selected and New Poems, 2003

NONFICTION:
The Blue Jay's Dance: A Birth Year, 1995
Books and Islands in Ojibwe Country, 2003

CHILDREN'S LITERATURE:
Grandmother's Pigeon, 1996 (illustrated by Jim La-Marche)
The Birchbark House, 1999
The Range Eternal, 2002
The Game of Silence, 2004

DISCUSSION TOPICS

- In each novel and most stories, Louise Erdrich links characters to the past as a way to offer solutions to present dilemmas. Choose a character, such as Father Damien in *The Last Report on the Miracles at Little No Horse,* and list three ways in which his past helped him cope with difficulties in his declining days. Choose an Indian character, such as Rozin in *The Antelope Wife,* and list three ways that the link to Indian history and myth help her face her contemporary life.

- Select a passage in which the landscape or wildlife takes on the role of a character in *The Antelope Wife.* What human characteristics does it exhibit?

- Discuss how Nanapush displays the characteristics of the Ojibwe trickster rabbit in *Tracks.*

About the Author

Bruchac, Joseph. "Whatever Is Really Yours: An Interview with Louise Erdrich." In *Survival This Way: Interviews with American Indian Poets.* Tucson: Sun Tracks and University of Arizona Press, 1987.

Coltelli, Laura. "Louise Erdrich and Michael Dorris." In *Winged Words: American Indian Writers Speak.* Lincoln: University of Nebraska Press, 1990.

Erdrich, Louise. "Where I Ought to Be: A Writer's Sense of Place." *The New York Times Book Review* 91 (July 28, 1985): 1, 23-24.

_____. "The Writing Life: How a Writer's Study Became a Thing with Feathers." *The Washington Post Book World,* February 15, 2004, 13.

Hafen, P. Jane. *Reading Louise Erdrich's "Love Medicine."* Boise, Idaho: Boise State University Press, 2003.

Meadows, Susannah. "North Dakota Rhapsody." *Newsweek* 141, no. 8 (2003): 54.

Rifkind, Donna. "Natural Woman." *The Washington Post Book World,* September 4, 2005, 5.

Sarris, Greg, et al., eds. *Approaches to Teaching the Works of Louise Erdrich.* New York: Modern Language Association of America, 2004.

Stookey, Loreena Laura. *Louise Erdrich: A Critical Companion.* Westport, Conn.: Greenwood Press, 1999.

JAMES T. FARRELL

Born: Chicago, Illinois
February 27, 1904
Died: New York, New York
August 22, 1979

The literary heir of Theodore Dreiser, Farrell wrote naturalistic fiction about Chicago's working class and the effect of the environment on his protagonists.

Library of Congress

BIOGRAPHY

James T. Farrell was born in Chicago on February 27, 1904, the son of James and Mary Daly Farrell. Although Farrell's father was a hardworking Chicago teamster and served as a symbol of the toil and troubles of the working classes in Farrell's fiction, he did not make enough money to support his large family. Of the Farrells' fifteen children, six lived to maturity. As a result of the financial pressure, James T. Farrell was moved to his maternal grandparents' house at the age of three. That move, from dire poverty to some affluence, provided him with material advantages but at the cost of a normal family life. Later in life, Farrell observed that he was both in the events he wrote about and outside them, a situation that produced the identity problems he treats in his young protagonists.

He was educated in Catholic parochial schools. In grammar school, he was active and accomplished in sports, particularly baseball and boxing, and thereby succeeded in partially overcoming his early loneliness. Farrell's other great early interest was religion, though his enthusiasm was primarily the product of his relationship with Sister Magdalen, the Sister Bertha of *Young Lonigan: A Boyhood in Chicago Streets* (1932), who encouraged him and prompted his academic interests. He attended the nearby St. Cyril High School, where he took the

four-year scholastic course, which focused on religion and the classics. While he early criticized the authoritarian rigidity of his "miseducation," he later noted that it had instilled moral values in him. At St. Cyril he was outstanding in athletics and writing (he wrote his first Danny O'Neill story there), but despite his achievements, he still did not receive the acceptance he sought—he was still, in part, the "misfit."

After graduation in 1923, he worked at an express company. In 1924 he also enrolled in night classes at De Paul University, where he first read the work of Theodore Dreiser, the single greatest influence on Farrell's work. In the following year, with funds saved from his job as a gasoline attendant, he entered the University of Chicago, an experience that radically changed his life. He became an avid reader, particularly in the social sciences: Sigmund Freud, Friedrich Nietzsche, Thorstein Veblen, and John Dewey transformed his devout Catholicism into a pragmatic naturalism, and novelists Dreiser, Ernest Hemingway, Sherwood Anderson, and James Joyce provided examples of literary naturalism and inspired his own literary ambitions. Farrell wrote book reviews and, in 1929, placed one of his stories in *Blues*, a little magazine, and commenced his work on *Studs Lonigan*.

After his story "Studs" appeared in *This Quarter*, a Paris journal, Farrell and his wife, Dorothy, whom he married in 1931, left for Paris, where, despite initial financial problems and personal calamities (their son Sean died only five days after birth), Farrell's writing career finally prospered. After moving to the suburb of Sceaux-Robinson, he revised *Young Lonigan*, wrote most of *Gas-House McGinty* (1933), and finished many short stories, which soon appeared in *The New Review, The American Mercury*, and *Story*, among other publications. During this fruitful period, Farrell also received the welcome encouragement of poet Ezra Pound.

After he returned to New York in 1932, Farrell experienced a meteoric rise in reputation; the 1930's became, despite a lifetime of literary productivity, his literary decade. His novels appeared with astonishing regularity: *Young Lonigan, Gas-House McGinty, The Young Manhood of Studs Lonigan* (1934), *Judgment Day* (1935), and the culminating *Studs Lonigan: A Trilogy* (1935). Farrell was awarded a Guggenheim Fellowship in 1936, and in 1937 he received a Book-of-the-Month Club Fellowship for *Studs Lonigan*. His second major series, the books concerned with Danny O'Neill, began with the publication of *A World I Never Made* (1936). The O'Neill novel was the target of censorship; although Farrell and Vanguard Press, Farrell's regular publisher, were cleared of the charges against them, the censorship issue continued to plague Farrell throughout his career.

As a writer with strong sociopolitical views, it was inevitable that Farrell would be embroiled in the political controversies of the times. He joined the League of American Writers, a communist-controlled organization, in 1935, and in 1936 supported the Socialist ticket; yet in spite of early left-wing praise for his "proletarian" writing, he was no doctrinaire communist. He opposed the communist literary critics, such as Granville Hicks, who equated left-wing propaganda with literary merit. His *A Note on Literary Criticism* (1936) espoused the dual function of literature: It should have both aesthetic and functional purposes. He retained his liberal views and spent the rest of his life working for various liberal causes and organizations. For example, he served as chairman of the Civil Rights Defense Committee (1941) and the Committee Against Jim Crow in Military Training (1950).

Although he peaked in popularity during the 1930's, Farrell continued his writing until his death of a heart attack in New York City on August 22, 1979. More than twenty-five novels, almost twenty collections of short stories, two volumes of poetry, and some ten volumes of prose, including literary criticism, personal essays, satirical prose under his Fogarty pseudonym, and a book about the Chicago

White Sox flowed from a man who wrote almost every day of his life. Because he was before the public eye as a practicing writer and a political activist, he continued to receive both critical recognition and honorary degrees from such institutions as the University of Oxford, Columbia University, and the University of Chicago—the last particularly appropriate in the light of his early years there.

ANALYSIS

The literary heir of Dreiser, Farrell is the epitome of the naturalistic writer whose protagonists' behavior is shaped by their social, psychological, political, and financial environment. In his essay "Some Observations on Naturalism, So Called, in Fiction" (1950), Farrell defines his concept of naturalism: "By naturalism I mean that whatever happens in this world must ultimately be explainable in terms of events in this world." The definition effectively distinguishes his fiction from that of those naturalistic novelists such as Frank Norris who frequently resort to the supernatural or mystical in shaping their plots. Moreover, Farrell documents his novels, piling up realistic details that circumscribe his characters choices, making them victims of their environment.

Farrell's world is, for the most part, Chicago's South Side, where he grew up. His Irish Catholic protagonists closely resemble their creator, particularly when the Danny O'Neills and Bernard Cams are intellectuals and writers confronting the role of the artist in an alien society. Even the Studs Lonigan figures, who are less articulate and more passive, are alienated (though they ironically belong to a gang) and isolated from their peers by their insecurity and their insistence on being stereotypical tough guys rather than individuals. The Farrell protagonist is often alone and typically alienated from self; consequently, he is a person divided into outer toughness and an inner tenderness, which must be consciously repressed. Despite his somewhat simplistic notion of personality, Farrell does succeed in creating unforgettable characters.

Although Farrell was praised by left-wing critics, some of them avowed communists, he viewed literature as distinct from propaganda. His novels do have a sociopolitical message and do indict society, but Farrell was not naïve about what literature could accomplish. His aim was to inform his readers, to lead them to discover truths about themselves and their society, rather than to change that society. His readers discover characters who are ill-equipped to control the rapidly changing world of the 1930's and 1940's and who cling stubbornly to ineffective but traditional beliefs in family, patriotism, capitalism, religion, and the American Dream.

His characters' inability to cope is tied directly to their stunted lives and minds, which have been destroyed not only by their physical environment but also by their spiritual and domestic environment. While Chicago is not a "character" in Farrell's novels, the city permeates the books and restricts the characters' world. The priests mouth platitudes about morality and Catholic education, and these clichés, repeated often enough, provide solace to their parishioners. There is material, spiritual, and mental poverty on the South Side, where the characters react to their problems with formulas, homilies, and conventional wisdom. Innovation and creativity are absent, and when the rote answers do not work, silence or physical force is the result. Unless the Farrell protagonist is a writer, there can be no inner life, no stream of consciousness, because the characters literally do not think.

Relationships between men and women consequently are shallow and superficial, with each sex responding to the other in terms of stereotypes. Farrell's males are sentimental but insensitive, violent but insecure; they tend to regard women as either spiritual creatures or tramps rather than as individuals. Women, on the other hand, mourn the loss of love and redirect their energies and ambitions to their children, whom they view with naïve idealism.

Characterization is Farrell's strength; plot and style are his weaknesses. At best, the plots are episodic, and often the subplots are only tangential to the story because they develop a political message or some social criticism. The main plot concerns the maturation and attendant alienation and debilitation of the "hero." The movement toward tragedy or pathos is inexorable; though the protagonist has free will, it is so circumscribed by environment that it is theoretical rather than actual. The style is only a bit less predictable; there is a decided lack of subtlety, much repetition, and dated slang, most of which is taken from the 1930's and 1940's. One of the most frequent criticisms of Farrell is that his novels never escaped from those decades.

For the most part, Farrell's novels focus on character, which he believed was of utmost importance in the novel, and most of his characters are provided with lengthy biographies. The plots proceed chronologically, but they are often juxtaposed with newspaper headlines and stories, as well as with anecdotes about characters who do not appear elsewhere in the novel. These techniques indicate the Dreiser influence on both Farrell's content (urban determinism) and style. An added Dreiser technique is the fragmentation of chapters, which become in some novels a series of snippets that work cumulatively to produce both an emotional effect and a commentary on the plot and the characters, themselves fragmented beings.

The newspaper stories, newsreels, and films that appear, often with elaborate plots that serve as counterpoint to his narrative, reflect Farrell's preoccupation with the impact of the media on American life. Characters are guided by newspaper stories, and they are shaped by Hollywood's version of the truth and provided with emotional escapes. Readers are also, through the ironic clash between a character's vision and the real world, made aware of a character's illusions and inevitable failure. For Farrell, to learn about others is to learn about oneself. In "The Function of the Novel," he writes, "One of the major functions of the novel is to help us in gaining this expanded image of ourselves."

YOUNG LONIGAN

First published: 1932
Type of work: Novel

In the 1910's in Chicago, a young man is torn between his tough-guy image and his "softer side" and struggles to find his true identity.

Young Lonigan: A Boyhood in Chicago Streets, the first volume of the *Studs Lonigan* trilogy, concerns Studs's development from his graduation from St. Patrick's Grammar School to the end of the year he was supposed to attend Loyola High School. Farrell is unsparing in his criticism of the platitudes mouthed by the Catholic priests (the influence of Irish novelist James Joyce is particularly evident in Father Gilhooley's graduation address) and repeated by parents who bask in "burgher comfort" as they naïvely contemplate their children's glowing futures. (In reality, Frank "Weary" Reilley becomes a sadistic rapist rather than a lawyer, and William "Studs" Lonigan hardly fulfills his mother's ambition to have him become a priest.)

Farrell is primarily concerned with Studs's struggle to create and maintain an identity, even if the tough-guy image he constructs is at odds with the "real" Studs. Sections 1 and 2 begin with Studs before a mirror contemplating his "image." Studs is relieved when he looks "like Studs Lonigan was supposed to look," the way he must appear to win peer acceptance. Here, as elsewhere, the ties between Studs and Farrell are quite evident. Although he later assures himself, "He was STUDS LONIGAN," he does have lingering doubts about his true self: "He wished he was somebody else."

For his peers, Studs is, despite being rather small, a tough guy whose reputation depends on his successful fights with Weary Reilley and Red Kelley.

Studs fears that he is a misfit, someone with a split personality, someone who has a "mushy," "queer," "soft" side that he must repress. This romantic, poetic (if poetry were not beyond the relatively inarticulate Studs) side is associated with "angelic" Lucy Scanlon, the epitome of the "purer" Catholic girls, the "higher creatures." Farrell writes, "But the tough outside part of Studs told the tender inside part of him that nobody really knew, that he had better forget all that bull." When he and Lucy go to the park, which Farrell describes in terms of escape, of flight from self, Studs allows his tender side the ascendancy, but this idyllic interlude is followed by Studs, the victim of peer pressure, coarsely rejecting Lucy. At the end of the novel, Studs unconsciously mourns the lost Lucy, while his father, whom Studs is beginning to resemble, procrastinates again about taking his wife for a night out—thus, Farrell prepares his readers for the further adventures of Studs Lonigan.

THE YOUNG MANHOOD OF STUDS LONIGAN

First published: 1934
Type of work: Novel

As a young man passes from adolescence to adulthood, his self-doubt and fears increase, leading him to self-destructive behavior.

In *The Young Manhood of Studs Lonigan*, the second novel of the trilogy, Farrell continues the saga. Though the title mentions Studs's "young manhood," Farrell depicts his protagonist as a boy in search of manhood. When he and some friends try to enlist in the Army, the recruiter advises them to "get your diapers pinned on," and when he attempts a holdup, his intended victim states, "Son, you better put that toy away." Even when Studs is in his twenties, Lucy tells him that he is "just like a little boy," an image at odds with his created persona.

The self-doubt, fear, and identity problems first mentioned in *Young Lonigan* are developed in greater detail in the second novel: "He was a hero in his own mind. He was miserable." As he ages, Studs seems more uncertain of his identity; he sees himself as Lonewolf Lonigan, Yukon Lonigan (an image inspired by a film), and K.O. Lonigan (a boxer), then as Pig Lonigan and Slob Lonigan as his self-pity increases. Studs seems to fear being "found out"; his tough-guy facade crumbles when he is outfought by young Morgan. Although Studs occasionally feels "mushy" when he dates Lucy, his coarse "outer" nature again destroys their relationship, and his contempt for his social-climbing sisters really marks his own sense of inferiority.

While he continues to focus on Studs, Farrell gives his second novel more sociopolitical context than he had included in *Young Lonigan*. Farrell depicts changing neighborhoods and the heightening of racial tensions, the blacklisting of unionists such as Mr. Le Gare, and the political persecution of "un-American" ideas such as communism. The Irish American community in Chicago, paranoid about race and communism, retreats, as Studs does, to patriotism, white supremacy, and the Church. Farrell suggests, however, through Father Shannon's morally edifying sermons, that the Church is ineffective—when the religious revival is over, the community's finest young Catholic men get drunk and look for women. There is little to believe in, as the plight of Danny O'Neill, the young University of Chicago intellectual, suggests: He rejects society's political and religious values but has nothing with which to replace them.

The novel concludes with a New Year's party at which Weary Reilley rapes Irene, and a drunken Studs lies in the gutter, leading to his getting pneumonia. This party is followed by an italicized chapter (this novel is more experimental in style, with its snippets of chapters and choruslike, italicized chapters) in which Stephen Lewis, a young black man, reenacts Studs's behavior in *Young Lonigan*. Times and characters change, but the behavior, values, and themes remain constant.

JUDGMENT DAY

First published: 1935
Type of work: Novel

A young man's self-inflicted physical problems and his incapacity for action lead to his early death in a hostile environment.

Judgment Day, which begins with a "devotion to be said at the beginning of the mass for the dead," is the third volume of the *Studs Lonigan* trilogy. It begins, appropriately, with Shrimp Haggerty's funeral and ends with Studs's death, but the novel also chronicles the death of the American Dream and the fall of the middle-class Irish Catholic community in Chicago. Farrell elaborates on the racism and political intolerance of the first two novels and adds anti-Semitism to the ills that afflict not only his characters but also American society.

In the course of *Judgment Day*, Studs declines physically, suffers a heart attack, cannot find work during the Depression, and finally dies—but not before impregnating his intended bride, Catherine. Although he still looks to his past exploits as the key to his identity, the self-doubt and fear increase until even his Walter Mitty dreams of being a champion golfer and a secret service agent falter: Even his imagination fails him. He cannot ignore the baseball game in which he fails miserably, thereby signaling the end of the athletic prowess that helped shape his identity. As in the second novel, he attends a film in which he empathizes with the hero; but this time the title of the film, *Doomed Victory,* and the hero's death ironically foreshadow Studs's life and death.

In *Judgment Day*, Studs seems to have lost his unrealized poetic nature and becomes almost inarticulate. Unable to communicate with Catherine, he enjoys "a vision of himself as a strong man whose words always meant something," yet his squabbles with her usually result from his silences. He also is unable to act and watches his stock plummet in value until he realizes that he is trapped financially, sexually, and vocationally. Standing before the mirror, a self-pitying Studs ironically tells his image, "You're the real stuff." Whatever Studs is, he is the product of his environment and is his father's son—a procrastinating, sentimental person who believes in the fraternity of the St. Christopher Society, the platitudes of the Church, and the American Dream (itself symbolized by a dance marathon). All fail him, as they have failed his father, and as they will fail his brother, who emulates Studs.

SUMMARY

In "On the Function of the Novel," Farrell writes, "Novels can enable us to gain a fuller sense of participation in the culture of our own time, and in the history of human thought and feeling." Like Dreiser, Farrell realistically documents a time, the 1930's, and a place, Chicago's South Side, in order to indict a society by chronicling events that produce alienated, fragmented human beings. He depicts the chronological maturation and the arrested emotional and spiritual development of his young protagonists, who cannot articulate their feelings, who cling precariously to stereotypical images of themselves, and who are ridden by self-doubt and fear.

Thomas L. Erskine

BIBLIOGRAPHY

By the Author

LONG FICTION:
Young Lonigan: A Boyhood in Chicago Streets, 1932
Gas-House McGinty, 1933
The Young Manhood of Studs Lonigan, 1934
Judgment Day, 1935
Studs Lonigan: A Trilogy, 1935 (collective title for *Young Lonigan, The Young Manhood of Studs Lonigan,* and *Judgment Day*)
A World I Never Made, 1936
No Star Is Lost, 1938
Tommy Gallagher's Crusade, 1939
Father and Son, 1940
Ellen Rogers, 1941
My Days of Anger, 1943
Bernard Clare, 1946
The Road Between, 1949
This Man and This Woman, 1951
Yet Other Waters, 1952
The Face of Time, 1953
Boarding House Blues, 1961
The Silence of History, 1963
What Time Collects, 1964
When Time Was Born, 1966
Lonely for the Future, 1966
New Year's Eve/1929, 1967
A Brand New Life, 1968
Judith, 1969
Invisible Swords, 1971
The Dunne Family, 1976
The Death of Nora Ryan, 1978

SHORT FICTION:
Calico Shoes, and Other Stories, 1934
Guillotine Party, and Other Stories, 1935
Can All This Grandeur Perish?, and Other Stories, 1937
Fellow Countrymen: Collected Stories, 1937
The Short Stories of James T. Farrell, 1937
$1,000 a Week, and Other Stories, 1942
Fifteen Selected Stories, 1943
To Whom It May Concern, and Other Stories, 1944
Twelve Great Stories, 1945
More Fellow Countrymen, 1946
More Stories, 1946
When Boyhood Dreams Come True, 1946
The Life Adventurous, and Other Stories, 1947
A Hell of a Good Time, 1948

DISCUSSION TOPICS

- How does James T. Farrell's most famous character, Studs Lonigan, change through the course of the trilogy? Do these changes constitute maturation and self-development?

- Can Farrell's concept of naturalism be distinguished from that of Theodore Dreiser?

- Do the second and third novels of the *Studs Lonigan* trilogy come to be more about the South Side of Chicago than about Studs?

- Is Farrell, as one critic has called him, a "revolutionary," or does his naturalistic outlook preclude a revolutionary attitude?

- Farrell was regarded as a major literary figure in the 1930's but not often thereafter. Review his fiction from the following four decades. What value would you assign to this later work?

James T. Farrell

An American Dream Girl, 1950
French Girls Are Vicious, and Other Stories, 1955
An Omnibus of Short Stories, 1956
A Dangerous Woman, and Other Stories, 1957
Saturday Night, and Other Stories, 1958
Side Street, and Other Stories, 1961
Sound of a City, 1962
Childhood Is Not Forever, 1969
Judith, and Other Stories, 1973
Olive and Mary Anne, 1977

DRAMA:
The Mowbray Family, pb. 1946 (with Hortense Alden Farrell)

POETRY:
The Collected Poems of James T. Farrell, 1965

NONFICTION:
A Note on Literary Criticism, 1936
The League of Frightened Philistines, and Other Papers, 1945
The Fate of Writing in America, 1946
Literature and Morality, 1947
The Name Is Fogarty: Private Papers on Public Matters, 1950
Reflections at Fifty, and Other Essays, 1954
My Baseball Diary, 1957
It Has Come to Pass, 1958
On Irish Themes, 1982

About the Author

Branch, Edgar M. *James T. Farrell.* Minneapolis: University of Minnesota Press, 1963.
_____. *James T. Farrell.* New York: Twayne, 1971.
_____. *Studs Lonigan's Neighborhood and the Making of James T. Farrell.* Newton, Mass.: Arts End Books, 1996.
Fanning, Charles. "Death and Revery in James T. Farrell's O'Neill-O'Flaherty Novels." In *The Incarnate Imagination: Essays in Theology, the Arts, and Social Sciences, in Honor of Andrew Greeley,* edited by Ingrid H. Shafer. Bowling Green, Ohio: Bowling Green State University Popular Press, 1988.
Fried, Lewis F. *Makers of the City.* Amherst: University of Massachusetts Press, 1990.
Landers, Robert K. *An Honest Writer: The Life and Times of James T. Farrell.* San Francisco: Encounter Books, 2004.
Pizer, Donald. "James T. Farrell and the 1930's." In *Literature at the Barricades: The American Writer in the 1930's,* edited by Ralph F. Bogardus and Fred Hobson. University: University of Alabama Press, 1982.
_____. *Twentieth-Century American Literary Naturalism: An Interpretation.* Carbondale: Southern Illinois University Press, 1982.
Smith, Gene. "The Lonigan Curse." *American Heritage* 46 (April, 1995): 150-151.
Twentieth Century Literature: A Scholarly and Critical Journal 22 (February, 1976).
Wald, Alan M. *James T. Farrell: The Revolutionary Socialist Years.* New York: New York University Press, 1978.

WILLIAM FAULKNER

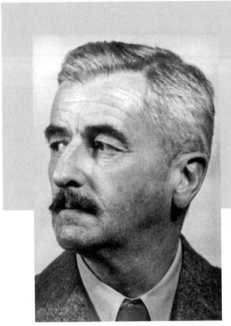

Born: New Albany, Mississippi
September 25, 1897
Died: Byhalia, Mississippi
July 6, 1962

Faulkner, internationally acclaimed as one of the foremost American novelists, is also noted for his short stories and novellas.

© The Nobel Foundation

BIOGRAPHY

William Faulkner was born William Cuthbert Falkner in New Albany, Mississippi, September 25, 1897, to Murry C. and Maud Butler Falkner. He was the oldest of four children, all boys. The family moved in 1898 to nearby Ripley and in 1902 to Oxford, Mississippi, the author's primary home throughout his life. His father's employment included being treasurer of a railroad, owner of businesses, and administrator of the University of Mississippi. Faulkner's early loves included trains, horses, hunting, and reading. After years of truancy and low performance, he quit high school in his senior year. Friendship with the future lawyer Phil Stone and frequenting the university campus were positive influences.

In 1918, Faulkner left Oxford to work in Connecticut at an arms factory. Rejected by the U.S. Army as too short and too small, he joined the Royal Canadian Air Force, training as a cadet in Toronto, Canada, until the end of World War I.

He traveled in the United States and abroad, worked as the university postmaster, attended the university as a special student, and began publishing poems in university and other periodicals. In New Orleans, he was befriended by writer Sherwood Anderson. Important works published early in Faulkner's career were a collection of poems,

The Marble Faun (1924), and two novels, *Soldiers' Pay* (1926) and *Mosquitoes* (1927). Three works in progress during 1927 treated the places and people of Faulkner's future work: Yoknapatawpha County, Mississippi, the Compsons, the Sartorises, and the Snopeses; Faulkner had taken Anderson's advice to return home and write about what he knew.

The years 1929 through 1937 mark the first major phase of Faulkner's writing career. *Flags in the Dust* (not published until 1973), his first "Yoknapatawpha" novel, had been rejected; it was shortened, revised, and published as *Sartoris* (1929). A few months later his greatest novel, *The Sound and the Fury* (1929), also appeared. In anger over its poor reception, Faulkner wrote *Sanctuary*, a violent, salacious novel. It was rejected as unfit for publication.

Also in 1929 he married the recently divorced Estelle Franklin, his childhood sweetheart. Following a honeymoon, they and her two children lived on the University of Mississippi campus. Working and writing in the boiler room, Faulkner published *As I Lay Dying* (1930). Starting with "A Rose for Emily" (1930), he began publishing short stories in national magazines. Forty-eight would appear in six years, including some of his best stories. Republishing of his works in England and translations elsewhere (the French versions of Maurice Coindreau, for example) added to Faulkner's international reputation; it would be some time before his own country recognized him. A severely revised *Sanctuary* was published in 1931, as was the first of many collections of stories, *These Thirteen*.

In 1932, Faulkner launched a second career, one that would compete for his time and presence

759

for the next thirteen years: He became a Hollywood scriptwriter. Also in 1932, *Light in August* was published, and Faulkner's father died, making Faulkner the head of the Falkner family. The next year, his daughter, Jill, was born. Faulkner took flying lessons; soon he would be a pilot, own a plane, help establish the local airport, and instruct would-be pilots.

He published another volume of poems, *A Green Bough* (1933), and a second collection, *Doctor Martino, and Other Stories* (1934). His works often served as the bases for films: In 1933, the story "Turn About" (1932) became *Today We Live*; *Sanctuary* (1931) became *The Story of Temple Drake*. In 1935, Faulkner's brother Dean died in a crash of Faulkner's plane. *Pylon* (1935) is a novel set in New Orleans (under another name) about flyers. Publication of *Absalom, Absalom!* (1936) marked the end of production of the earlier major novels.

During this time Faulkner supported a wife, three children, Dean's widow and daughter, and two black servants (Uncle Ned and Caroline Barr, known as Mammy Callie), primarily by selling short stories and writing film scripts. In 1929 he had purchased a large antebellum house, the Sheegog place, renaming it Rowan Oak (or Rowanoak); he restored the house and did the landscaping himself. In 1937, he purchased Bailey Woods and renamed it the Greenfield Farm.

The second major period of his writing career seems to have begun with the publishing of *The Unvanquished* (1938), a novel of the Civil War that uses six previously published stories and one written for this work. Faulkner became less private in his life and in his ideas than he had been previously. His works became more philosophical and at times even moralistic. *The Wild Palms* (1939) is actually two novellas with alternating chapters. The first of the Snopes trilogy, *The Hamlet*, appeared in 1940. It was followed by a novel incorporating stories about black people, *Go Down, Moses* (1942). In 1939, the first of many honors came with Faulkner's election to the National Institute of Letters.

During the following twenty years, Faulkner's final period, he became increasingly a public person, speaking out on racial segregation and representing the United States as an ambassador of goodwill in places as diverse as Japan, Venezuela, and Europe. In 1945 he was finally released from a contract to write scripts; in the meantime his contributions to magazines had become fewer. In 1947 he conducted classroom interviews at the University of Mississippi. Later he would become writer-in-residence, doing the same at the University of Virginia and buying a home in Charlottesville.

He received the Nobel Prize in Literature in 1950 and the Pulitzer Prize in 1955; the French bestowed membership in the Legion of Honor upon him. His daughter married Paul D. Summers, Jr., in 1954; she gave birth to Faulkner's three grandsons between 1956 and 1961. Faulkner died in Byhalia, Mississippi, July 6, 1962, while undergoing medical treatment following a fall from a horse.

His works published after 1942 include the novels *Intruder in the Dust* (1948), *Requiem for a Nun* (1951), *A Fable* (1954), *The Town* (1957), *The Mansion* (1959), and *The Reivers* (1962). Collections include *The Portable Faulkner* (1946), *Collected Short Stories of William Faulkner* (1950), and *Big Woods* (1955); also appearing after 1942 were occasional stories, letters to editors, and essays in periodicals. Numerous works, such as collections of interviews, letters, previously unpublished works, biographies, and new editions, have appeared since Faulkner's death.

ANALYSIS

Faulkner's works, like their creator, are highly complex. His style has caused much difficulty for readers, especially if *The Sound and the Fury*, *Light in August*, *As I Lay Dying*, or *Absalom, Absalom!* is the reader's introduction to Faulkner. These best of his earlier Yoknapatawpha novels vary in structure but are alike in one point—an obscurity that results from unusual, complicated organization and presentation. *The Sound and the Fury* has multiple narrators, extended streams of consciousness, and subtle time shifts. It is divided into four, at times seemingly disconnected, parts. *Light in August* has three narratives interwoven, with past and present intermixed. *As I Lay Dying* is a series of numerous brief chapters, each a stream of consciousness, usually but not always by a member of the Bundren family. *Absalom, Absalom!* is told using various levels of time and narrator viewpoint.

Faulkner himself and some of his major critics have recommended *The Unvanquished* as the best starting place. In spite of multiple narratives, real and metaphorical, there is one narrator: Bayard Sartoris, an old man recalling experiences of his early life during the American Civil War. Several viewpoints are presented, but all by him. Time is interrupted by an occasional flashback or digression, but generally the thrust is chronological, once the digressive nature of the entire narrative is recognized. Violence and hardship are moderated by generous doses of good-natured humor. The novel's focus is on two races, blacks and various classes of Mississippi whites. Because Bayard Sartoris is a rather normal adolescent through much of the plot, his viewpoint is not tedious. Another good entree into Faulkner is *Intruder in the Dust*, in which the traditional form of single narrator and chronological time are, with some lapses, followed.

Place is extremely important to Faulkner; in most of his better works his setting is the fictional Yoknapatawpha County (based in part on his own home county of Lafayette), with its town of Jefferson, largely Oxford renamed and without the state university (he moves Oxford and the university to another site). Faulkner uses local people, including members of his own family: His grandfather, J. W. T. Falkner, becomes old Bayard Sartoris; his great-grandfather, a mythic figure with a shady past and a record of violence, Civil War experience, and public leadership, becomes Colonel John Sartoris. V. K. Surratt, Faulkner's genial peddler/storyteller, is lifted from real life and temporarily given his real name. Various other characters are based on one or more real people. Similarly, the narratives are based on tales, often traditions handed down by his family or others.

In turn, he might borrow freely from history or classical mythology, from existentialism, psychology, the Bible, or any of the numerous books that he read. Next to the Bible, he most often mentioned Miguel de Cervantes, author of *El ingenioso hidalgo don Quixote de la Mancha*, 1605, 1615 (*Don Quixote de la Mancha*, 1612-1620). Other influences on Faulkner included Charles Dickens, Mark Twain, and Polish-British novelist Joseph Conrad.

Following the philosophy of Henri Bergson, the French thinker, Faulkner did not view time as chronological. Having watched a man write the Lord's Prayer on the head of a pin, Faulkner sought to write the history of the human soul in one sentence. Faulkner's style is often verbose, especially if a talkative narrator is speaking or a troubled individual is pouring out thoughts in a stream of consciousness. There may even be an occasional sentence that goes on for pages. The later novels, with obvious exceptions (the commissary section of "The Bear" in *Go Down, Moses*, for example), and the short stories are written in a style much more readable than some of the earlier novels.

Although Faulkner's writing is recognized as excellent by critics both in the United States and abroad, it should be noted that his work is uneven; this fact is especially obvious now that almost everything he wrote is now available, including apprenticeship poems and stories. Even his mature work, however, is somewhat uneven; critics regard his earlier Yoknapatawpha novels and a few later ones such as *The Hamlet* and *Go Down, Moses*, for example, to be of better literary quality than the apprenticeship novels (*Soldiers' Pay* and *Mosquitoes*) or *Pylon*.

Faulkner's philosophy has been difficult for many critics. He believed in God but did not pretend to be a Christian. He borrowed freely from the Bible, yet used as parallels to Christ uncouth characters such as Joe Christmas in *Light in August*. His attitude toward race, especially toward black and white relations, angered whites and blacks, integrationists and segregationists. He was in favor of moderate, gradual integration. In his works, he often treats the themes of incest and miscegenation; sometimes they are combined, as in *Absalom, Absalom!*

His attitude toward the American South combines regional pride with shame at offenses past and present. His complex treatment avoids the two extremes that one often finds in works about the South—squalid poverty on one hand, magnolias and hooped skirts on the other. His setting is more a particular region—northern Mississippi—than the entire South. A most successful regional writer, he nevertheless achieves universality by combining the local perspective with a broad treatment of the human condition. Both a Greek stoic and a Christian humanist, he believed in the worth of the individual, most especially his or her ability to endure and prevail; thus, in spite of much darkness in Faulkner's works, they possess an overriding optimism in an age of pessimistic trends in literature.

SARTORIS

First published: 1929
Type of work: Novel

A troubled World War I ace returns home to seek and eventually find a violent death.

Sartoris, Faulkner's first published mature novel, and the first to treat the people and places of his fictional county of Yoknapatawpha, is a fitting introduction to his settings and characters. The title is the name of one of his leading families. In one sense, young Bayard Sartoris is the protagonist; in another, it is the entire Sartoris family (at least the first, second, and fourth generations). Also introduced are two members of the Snopes clan—Flem and Byron, employees of old Bayard Sartoris's bank. Protagonists of an interwoven subplot are the Benbows—brother and sister Horace and Narcissa. Other characters include the MacCallums (spelled McCallum in later works).

The setting begins in Jefferson, the county seat of Yoknapatawpha, and moves to other parts of the region (and occasionally other parts of the United States) in the main narrative but shifts to the Civil War and World War I in digressions.

Colonel John Sartoris, the legendary ancestor of the two Bayards, was modeled after Faulkner's great-grandfather, Colonel William C. Falkner, a colorful adventurer of the periods before, during, and after the Civil War. Colonel Sartoris's twin brother, Bayard, was killed while engaged in a prank during the Civil War; Colonel John's presence still permeates the atmosphere three generations later. Old Bayard is passive and nonviolent. Young Bayard experiences guilt because he has seen his twin brother John's plane shot down; he is also driven by the Sartoris penchant for violent endings—partly fatalism, partly recklessness. He drives his car too fast, endangering himself and his passengers. Once he drives off a bridge and breaks his ribs; another time he drives over a cliff and back onto the road, only to learn he has caused his grandfather, old Bayard, to die of a heart attack.

The Benbow house is in Jefferson, as are the cemetery, the courthouse, the church, and other places of interest. Horace is a young lawyer recently returned from wartime experience as a YMCA worker in Italy; he is interested in poetry and art, bringing a glassblowing apparatus home with him. He becomes involved with another family, Harry and Belle Mitchell and their daughter, little Belle. Eventually Belle divorces Harry and marries Horace. Narcissa and Horace are very close, with strong emotional ties to each other. She is friends with old Bayard's aunt, Miss Jenny DuPre, whose common sense offers a contrast to the Sartoris attitudes and actions. Byron Snopes writes anonymous letters to Narcissa, eventually breaking into her house and stealing an undergarment. He, like his people, is low-bred, amoral, and grasping.

The Sartoris family is also treated at length in *The Unvanquished*; the Benbows are among the important characters of *Sanctuary*. The MacCallums (McCallums) are the protagonists of the short story "The Tall Men" (1941). In *Sartoris*, their hill farm home, more than fourteen miles north of Jefferson, becomes young Bayard's refuge after old Bayard's death. Here drinking and hunting (two of Faulkner's favorite avocations) take place. Another family, a nameless and poverty-stricken black family, share their hospitality on Christmas Day. They stand in contrast to others in the novel who are stereotypes of black characters in literature and drama of the time. Following the death of young Bayard, who has foolheartedly flight-tested an unsafe plane in Dayton, Ohio, the focus is on Benbow Sartoris, who represents a new generation of the family. Bayard's wife, Narcissa, has named the son Benbow in hopes that he will avoid the curse of the Sartoris men.

THE SOUND AND THE FURY

First published: 1929
Type of work: Novel

A once-distinguished family degenerates and eventually disintegrates.

The Sound and the Fury is about another family, the Compsons; like the Sartorises, they are of the aristocratic social level, the planter class. Unlike the Sartorises, who live north of Jefferson, the Compsons live in town. They consist of Mr. and Mrs. Compson and four children: Quentin, the oldest son, commits suicide while a student at Harvard University; he is attracted to his sister Caddy. Benjy, born Maury, is an idiot son. Jason, the youngest son, is grasping and amoral, without feeling for other people. The other important members of the household are Miss Quentin, Caddy's illegitimate daughter (named for her uncle), and the black servant Dilsey, modeled to a great extent after the Falkner family's Mammy Callie.

Faulkner's most esoteric novel, especially through the first two of the four parts, *The Sound and the Fury* is his most difficult to read, causing problems for both scholar and beginner. Obviously modeled after James Joyce's novel *Ulysses* (1922), it consists of three streams of consciousness, each by a male character, followed by a fourth section in omniscient viewpoint with strong partial focus on a female. Part 1 unfolds the thoughts and emotions of Benjy, who on his birthday (he is thirty-three), Sat-

urday, April 7, 1928, confuses the present with the past of 1910. His pasture, sold to pay for Caddy's wedding and Quentin's education at Harvard, is now a golf course; players' shouts to their caddies remind him of his sister and of his former dependence on her.

Quentin's section is set at the earlier time of Thursday, June 2, 1910. During the events before his death, he tears the hands off his watch, wanders through the town, becomes friends with a young girl, has a violent confrontation as he tries to find her people, and eventually dresses and brushes his teeth before killing himself. His death results from his inability to accept his sister's infidelity, an act foreshadowed by an experience on the day of their grandmother's wake: Climbing up to look in the window after having sat in the mud, she has revealed her soiled drawers.

Jason's section is less esoteric, more direct, because it pours out the thoughts of a crass, greedy, cruel man who is unimaginative. Remaining at home after the deaths of Quentin and his father, he works in a business. He extorts money from Caddy by insisting that she avoid contact with her daugh-

ter and by threatening to expose Miss Quentin's background. The money that Caddy sends her, Jason takes for his own. His section is set in the present: Friday, April 6, 1928, the day before Benjy's birthday and two days before Easter. Miss Quentin, now seventeen, runs off with a man from a carnival, stealing money from Jason, who ironically had previously stolen it from her.

Much of the section serves to characterize Jason, especially his contempt toward Quentin, Benjy, Caddy, Miss Quentin, Dilsey, women in general, and nearly everyone else. Throughout the sections, the parents and a relative, Uncle Maury, are also characterized: The father fails to assume authority, the mother is a whining, dependent hypochondriac, and the uncle is an immoral ne'er-do-well.

Jason's conflict with Dilsey, who tries vainly to keep the family from disintegrating, and his pursuit of Miss Quentin are depicted in both the third and fourth sections. The latter, sometimes called the Dilsey section in spite of its third-person narrator, reaches its grand climax in Dilsey's worship experience on Easter Sunday morning, April 8, 1928, the day after Benjy's birthday. She takes Benjy with her and walks to the Second Baptist Church, the black church, where a small, unattractive substitute minister preaches. In the course of the Reverend Sheegog's sermon, she reaches a state of ecstasy—one of the rare genuine religious experiences in all of Faulkner's work. The setting of the days of Easter week, though not in chronological order, parallel those in Dante's *La divina commedia* (c. 1320; *The Divine Comedy*, 1802). The year 1928 reflects a Faulkner custom often employed: to make the time of writing the present in a work in progress.

SANCTUARY

First published: 1931
Type of work: Novel

This novel's characters are the victims of murder, rape, lynching, and miscarriages of justice.

In 1929, while angered at the poor reception of his *The Sound and the Fury* (and possibly at the previous rejection of *Flags in the Dust*), Faulkner wrote a first version of *Sanctuary* as the most violent, most salacious novel possible, in order to make money. Later, Phil Stone, his lawyer friend and mentor, persuaded him that the work was unworthy of the author of *The Sound and the Fury* or of the short stories "A Rose for Emily" and "That Evening Sun Go Down" (1931). Faulkner did extensive revision, toning down the violence and sex (although much remains) and rewriting *Sanctuary* as a work of excellent literary quality. Whereas the earlier version had been rejected, the later was published.

Sanctuary's main characters include Horace Benbow and, to a lesser extent, his sister Narcissa, already seen in *Sartoris*. She is living in the family home with Aunt Sally (no blood kin); he is out in the country, a troubled soul separated from his wife, Belle, and her daughter Little Belle. Horace comes to some property closely guarded by a criminal element of people: Popeye is an amoral, almost inhuman, unfeeling psychotic killer, a petty gangster; Lee Goodwin is a bootlegger in business with Popeye; Ruby Lamar is his wife. Horace is sexually attracted to Ruby. Eventually, he is allowed to leave the premises.

Later, Gowan Stevens, a self-centered young Virginia man, gets drunk and causes Temple Drake, an eighteen-year-old college student who is the daughter of a judge, to forfeit a trip to a football game. Eventually they, too, find themselves at Goodwin's place, Gowan too drunk to cope and Temple, warned by Ruby of her danger and shocked by the men she observes, hysterical, running all around the place.

One of the men is murdered by Popeye, who attacks Temple and later holds her captive in a Memphis brothel. Lee Goodwin is imprisoned in Jefferson for the murder, and Horace agrees to defend him, presumably to be paid in services by Goodwin's wife if he is acquitted. Horace is not the proper attorney; not only is he not a criminal lawyer, but also he is personally involved. Narcissa betrays Horace's confidence to her, as does state senator Snopes, with the result that a politically ambitious prosecuting attorney gets Temple freed (from Popeye), and he, rather than Horace, uses her as a witness.

Temple's false testimony that Goodwin is the murderer, in the emotional climate created by her revelation that she has been raped with a corncob,

causes mass hysteria in the courtroom. Horace does not even cross-examine her. Goodwin is later taken from jail and, in Horace's presence, burned to death in the courthouse square. Popeye, who has escaped prosecution for this and other murders, is later arrested and convicted for one that he did not commit. His early life, in the manner of that of Joe Christmas in *Light in August*, is revealed as he awaits execution in Florida. His death is poetic justice.

Certainly, the plot is effective enough, especially for those who like mystery, crime, violence, and sex, but the question remains whether *Sanctuary* as published is more than a violent, salacious fiction. A literary novel is a proper balance of three elements, all fully effected: a structured plot, clearly realized (delineated) characters, and manners (the characterization of a society in a particular time and place). *Sanctuary* is highly effective in all three respects. The plot is structured effectively. The manners of both the criminal class and the respectable people are delineated. Ruby is the wife of a criminal and is herself a former prostitute, but she is a faithful wife to an unworthy husband who was untrue to her while in the armed forces; her prostitution was to earn money to free him from prison. She shows concern and a gruff type of kindness to intruders into her sordid world; she shows courage by telling Horace about Popeye and Temple. She is also willing to pay in the only way she can to free her husband.

The genteel class are also of mixed virtue. Both Horace and Gowan are immoral and given to drink. They are both weak men who bring violence to others by their weakness yet bear no responsibility for their actions. Temple, who could prevent her rape and a man's murder simply by walking away from Goodwin's place, succumbs to panic and fails to act. Once she is in court, her father is concerned that she testify no longer; he should know that testimony without privilege of cross-examination is a travesty. The presiding judge should certainly know that it is inadmissible as evidence. Horace puts his lust ahead of his client's life. Narcissa is willing to let an innocent man die so that her brother can return to her—or to his wife—rather than becoming involved with a fallen woman. The characters function within the plot as individuals and as members of a society.

LIGHT IN AUGUST

First published: 1932
Type of work: Novel

A man of uncertain origins and race turns to violence and is himself a victim of violence.

Light in August, Faulkner's fifth Yoknapatawpha novel, brings together, in and near Jefferson, characters with varying backgrounds and personalities but with one common bond—they all have deep-seated problems. Lena Grove arrives in town from Alabama, pregnant but unmarried and in search of Lucas Burch, the father of her child. She finds instead Byron Bunch, a good man who is timid and withdrawn. Burch, using the name Brown, has just burned Miss Joanna Burden's house to cover her murder by Joe Christmas, who killed Joanna after being her lover for three years. Joe had lived at her place while being partners with Brown in the bootleg whiskey business.

Gail Hightower, a defrocked minister who withdrew from society after its rejection and mistreatment of him, now has a different religion: ancestor worship of his grandfather, who fought in the Civil War. Hightower is friends with Bunch, who involves him with Lena (he delivers her baby) and with Joe (he lies when Joe takes refuge in his house, attempting to prevent the fugitive's murder at the hands of his pursuers). The leader of the three-man posse pursuing Joe is Percy Grimm, a deputized young man who has a storm-trooper mentality years before Adolf Hitler's rise to power. He shoots the armed Joe Christmas and mutilates his body.

Much of the novel is devoted to the events and people that have influenced Joe's character. The son of a Mexican (or black) carnival worker and Doe Hines's granddaughter, he is left at a Memphis orphanage on Christmas Day (thus his assumed name). His questionable parentage and his age (thirty-three when arriving in Jefferson), together with his name, suggest parallels to Jesus. The parallels were even more obvious in earlier versions, but Faulkner later toned them down. The use of biblical matter paralleling Jesus or some other biblical character or incident with an opposite type of person is a Faulknerian technique known as an inver-

sion. Doe Hines takes a job at the orphanage so that he can watch the boy. Hines is an extreme religious fanatic and a racist; he tells people that Joe is a Negro. Joe's foster parents, the MacEacherns, are strict Calvinists, Mr. MacEachern harshly so.

The belief in Joe's black blood, though it is never actually established in the novel, is the focus of much of the action. Doe Hines's attitude is primarily racist. Joe himself has ambivalent feelings: At times he calls himself a Negro, but he always functions as a white man in a white-dominated society. After killing Joanna, Joe disturbs worship at a Negro church, thinking to establish himself in their society but only terrifying them and doing violence to one of the worshippers.

The novel closes as it opened, quietly, with the focus on Lena Grove. The final chapter is told by a furniture maker and dealer who has given Lena, Byron Bunch, and the baby a ride from Mississippi to Jackson, Tennessee. Byron cannot get Lena to marry him, and he is unsuccessful in his attempt to rape her, but he continues to be her traveling companion.

ABSALOM, ABSALOM!

First published: 1936
Type of work: Novel

A man with dreams of affluence and family dynasty sees everything crumble around him.

Absalom, Absalom!, another Yoknapatawpha novel and another work with multiple structures, has different levels of narrator viewpoint; that of Quentin Compson and his Canadian roommate at Harvard University is the primary level. Shreve McCannon has asked Quentin to tell him about Mississippi; the result is a story told in true Faulkner fashion. It is far from chronological; sometimes Quentin speaks from his own observation, but most often he repeats a secondhand narrative as given him by Miss Rosa Coldfield, Jason Compson III, and others. Some gaps are filled in by the boys' speculative dialogue.

The story is about Thomas Sutpen, who as a young man left his western Virginia home and was severely rebuked by a black servant at a tidewater

Virginia mansion. Emotionally scarred, he traveled to the West Indies, where he married the daughter of a wealthy planter and became a man of wealth himself. Upon discovering that his wife was part black, he left her and traveled to Mississippi.

The novel opens with Miss Rosa's earliest childhood memory of Sutpen, who has taken her sister as his second wife. Sutpen's violent manner of driving his horses up to the front of the church outrages the townspeople; his cockfights and brutal boxing matches have left her with a sense of terror. He has fathered a daughter, Judith, and a son,

Henry, by this marriage, and he dreams of family, dynasty, and great wealth. A few miles out from Jefferson, he has built a mansion and established a large plantation; he owns many slaves. Problems arise when Charles Bon is brought into the family: He is Sutpen's son by his previous marriage. Charles's friendship with Henry and his budding relationship with Judith present the problems of incest and miscegenation.

Sutpen is generally regarded more highly throughout the novel than he is in the eyes of Miss Rosa, who despises him because he has offered to marry her on the condition that she will bear him a son. He is characterized as a worthy soldier, being elected commander of the battalion organized and led by Colonel John Sartoris. When, after the Civil War, he is threatened by a vigilante committee, he faces down the group. He cannot cope, however, with the disintegration of his family and his fortune.

The end of the novel is uncertain; Quentin describes having found the aged Henry, who has been hiding at the old Sutpen place after killing Charles Bon. A sequel to *Absalom, Absalom!* is the short story "Wash," which tells of the death of Sutpen at the hands of a "poor white" employee and drinking companion, Wash Jones, whose daughter Millie's child Sutpen has fathered and spurned. As is typical of Faulkner's chronology, the story was published in 1934, two years before the novel.

"THE BEAR"

First published: 1942 (in *Go Down, Moses*)
Type of work: Short story

A boy is initiated into manhood and participates in the killing of a great bear that symbolizes the wilderness.

"The Bear" is Faulkner's best-known and most highly regarded story; it takes its place among his wilderness narratives, such as *Old Man* (one of the two novellas that make up *The Wild Palms*), "Red Leaves" (1930), the best of Faulkner's Indian stories, and the escape of the black architect in *Absalom, Absalom!* Its genesis is typical of Faulkner's writing and publishing career: He used his material to the greatest degree. A short story titled "Lion" appeared in 1934; it was enlarged in 1941 and 1942 as "The Bear," to be a section of the novel *Go Down, Moses*.

A shortened form was published in a magazine in 1942; then, two days later, the novel appeared, with what is sometimes called "The Bear II" included. Because this contained section 4, which adds to the novel but detracts from the hunting story, the novel version without section 4 was anthologized in *Big Woods* in 1955; with section 4, it appeared in *Three Famous Short Novels* in 1961.

The work symbolizes the destruction of the wilderness. It is also concerned with the mythic initiation of a boy, young Isaac (Ike) McCaslin, into manhood. In the later versions, Quentin Compson as narrator is dropped in favor of omniscient narration, and "the boy" becomes Ike. The magazine and novel versions differ in that the bear is killed only in the latter.

Old Ben is a mythic two-toed bear who has eluded hunters for years; Lion is the huge dog, the appearance of whom foreshadows the end. Sam Fathers, Major De Spain, General Compson, McCaslin Edmunds, and Boon Hogganbeck are among those chasing but not killing Old Ben; the major's hunting camp is on what was once Thomas Sutpen's estate. McCaslin (Cass) is Ike's older cousin; Sam, an Indian of noble blood, is Ike's friend and wilderness mentor; Boon is a big man (partly of plebeian Indian blood) with the mind of a child.

The time of the opening and of the climactic killing of Ben is 1883, when Ike is sixteen. Through digressions, previous events are related: At ten, Ike had gone on his first hunt with the men; at eleven, he had seen Ben for the first time. At thirteen, he killed his first deer and underwent initiation when Sam marked his face with the blood. When Ike was fourteen, the special dog, Lion, was brought into camp; when he was fifteen, Lion attacked Ben, and Ben was wounded by a gun. Comic interludes have to do with Boon—his attitude toward Lion and his ineptitude with a gun.

Section 4, sometimes called "The Land," consists of one 1,600-word sentence unfolding a dialogue between Ike (now twenty-one) and Cass regarding ownership of the land: Ike will waive his right to his inheritance. The brief final section is two years after the last hunt on this land; Ike at nineteen revisits the site (two years before section 4) to find Boon under a lone tree full of squirrels: Having broken his gun, Boon is clubbing at the squirrels and shouting at would-be intruders. The high, serious tone of the novella gives way to the comic, seeming to contrast the awe and majesty of the now-departed wilderness with the civilization that has taken its place.

"SPOTTED HORSES"

First published: 1931 (collected in *Three Famous Short Novels*, 1958)
Type of work: Short story

People experience injury and loss when they are sold wild horses.

As did "The Bear," Faulkner's "Spotted Horses" evolved over a period of years. As early as 1927 and 1928, he was writing about the Snopeses in a work titled "Father Abraham" (it was never published as such). In *Flags in the Dust* and *Sartoris*, Flem and Byron Snopes appear as minor characters. The first-published fuller treatment of Flem was in the short story version of "Spotted Horses" in 1931; originally titled "Aria con Amore," it had been revised into this version for *Scribner's* magazine. It was also enlarged into a novella and was included as a key episode in the first Snopes novel, *The Hamlet*, in

1940. Five years later, parts were included in Malcolm Cowley's collection *The Portable Faulkner.*

"Spotted Horses," then, marks the beginning of the Snopes stories (others include "Barn Burning," 1939, and "Mule in the Yard," 1934) and (as part of *The Hamlet*) the Snopes novels. Flem's rise from obscurity to prominence and affluence is the subject of the Snopes trilogy (*The Hamlet*, *The Town*, and *The Mansion*); his first important stride is his gaining ascendancy over the Varners. By marrying the pregnant Eula, he gains not only a most desirable woman but also opportunities for advancement. "Spotted Horses" opens with Flem, Eula, and her baby returning from a honeymoon in Texas. They bring with them a stranger, the Texan Buck Hipps, and a string of wild pinto horses straight from the range.

In this work Faulkner uses some of the people and places of *As I Lay Dying*, including the farmers of Frenchman's Bend. In addition to the Snopeses and Varners are the Armstids, the Littlejohns, and others. V. K. Suratt is an outsider but no stranger; he has already appeared briefly in *Sartoris* (by *The Hamlet*, his name will be V. K. Ratliff). Here, he is driving a wagon pulled by a mixed team. Buck Hipps is a congenial but tough man; he carries a pistol in his pocket and continually eats ginger snaps.

The setting, Frenchman's Bend, is based on the region in and around Taylor, southeast of Oxford. One might consider the community the protagonist and Flem the antagonist. As elsewhere, Faulkner effectively blends violence with robust humor. The horse auction and the farmers' attempts to claim their purchases cause inconvenience, injury, and property damage. Faulkner based the story on a real-life incident that had happened in Ripley. As a boy, after outgrowing his pony, Faulkner himself had purchased and tamed one of these very horses; it became his first horse.

SUMMARY

Faulkner wrote more than nineteen novels and dozens of stories. His best have established him as one of the great novelists and storytellers. Each work is complete in itself, yet his works also inform and relate to one another. His variety is vast: Settings range from the Civil War to the twentieth century, from Mississippi to war-torn France. He used the people and places of his own region to write on universal themes, creating not only characters but also entire families and communities. His reputation grew steadily, first in Europe and Japan, later in the United States and the rest of the world.

George W. Van Devender

BIBLIOGRAPHY

By the Author

LONG FICTION:
Soldiers' Pay, 1926
Mosquitoes, 1927
Sartoris, 1929
The Sound and the Fury, 1929
As I Lay Dying, 1930
Sanctuary, 1931
Light in August, 1932
Pylon, 1935
Absalom, Absalom!, 1936
The Unvanquished, 1938
The Wild Palms, 1939
The Hamlet, 1940
Go Down, Moses, 1942
Intruder in the Dust, 1948
Requiem for a Nun, 1951
A Fable, 1954
The Town, 1957
The Mansion, 1959
The Reivers, 1962
The Wishing Tree, 1964 (fairy tale)
Flags in the Dust, 1973 (original version of *Sartoris*)
Mayday, 1976 (fable)

SHORT FICTION:
These Thirteen, 1931
Doctor Martino, and Other Stories, 1934
The Portable Faulkner, 1946, 1967
Knight's Gambit, 1949
Collected Short Stories of William Faulkner, 1950
Big Woods, 1955
Three Famous Short Novels, 1958
Uncollected Stories of William Faulkner, 1979

SCREENPLAYS:
Today We Live, 1933
To Have and Have Not, 1945
The Big Sleep, 1946
Faulkner's MGM Screenplays, 1982

DISCUSSION TOPICS

- Develop the following statement with reference to *The Sound and the Fury*: Some of the seemingly impenetrable difficulties in reading William Faulkner's prose disappear once his purpose is explained.

- Is it meaningful to regard the past as a "presence" in Faulkner's fiction?

- How seriously should we take the parallels between Joe Christmas and Jesus Christ in *Light in August*?

- What values does Faulkner affirm most stoutly as distinctly southern ones?

- At what point in Faulkner's literary career does his comic genius assert itself strongly? Does it appear to signal a fundamental change in his outlook?

- Discuss *Old Man* as a kind of tall tale or extended joke.

- Is Yoknapatawpha County merely a fictional equivalent of Lafayette County in Mississippi, where Faulkner lived, or does it have a larger significance? If so, what is it?

POETRY:

The Marble Faun, 1924
A Green Bough, 1933

NONFICTION:

New Orleans Sketches, 1958
Faulkner in the University, 1959
Faulkner at West Point, 1964
Essays, Speeches, and Public Letters, 1965
The Faulkner-Cowley File: Letters and Memories, 1944-1962, 1966 (Malcolm Cowley, editor)
Lion in the Garden, 1968
Selected Letters, 1977

MISCELLANEOUS:

The Faulkner Reader, 1954
William Faulkner: Early Prose and Poetry, 1962

About the Author

Blotner, Joseph. *Faulkner: A Biography.* 2 vols. New York: Random House, 1974.

Brooks, Cleanth. *William Faulkner: The Yoknapatawpha Country.* New Haven, Conn.: Yale University Press, 1963.

Gray, Richard. *The Life of William Faulkner: A Critical Biography.* Oxford, England: Blackwell, 1994.

Hoffman, Frederick, and Olga W. Vickery, eds. *William Faulkner: Three Decades of Criticism.* New York: Harcourt, Brace, 1960.

Inge, M. Thomas, ed. *Conversations with William Faulkner.* Jackson: University Press of Mississippi, 1999.

Labatt, Blair. *Faulkner the Storyteller.* Tuscaloosa: University of Alabama Press, 2005.

The Mississippi Quarterly 50 (Summer, 1997).

Parini, Jay. *One Matchless Time: A Life of William Faulkner.* New York: HarperCollins, 2004.

Peek, Charles A., and Robert W. Hamblin, eds. *A Companion to Faulkner Studies.* Westport, Conn.: Greenwood Press, 2004.

Rovit, Earl, and Arthur Waldhorn, eds. *Hemingway and Faulkner in Their Time.* New York: Continuum, 2005.

Singal, Daniel J. *William Faulkner: The Making of a Modernist.* Chapel Hill: University of North Carolina Press, 1997.

Vickery, Olga W. *The Novels of William Faulkner.* Baton Rouge: Louisiana State University Press, 1959.

Volpe, Edmond L. *A Reader's Guide to William Faulkner: The Novels.* Syracuse, N.Y.: Syracuse University Press, 2003.

_____. *A Reader's Guide to William Faulkner: The Short Stories.* Syracuse, N.Y.: Syracuse University Press, 2004.

Williamson, Joel. *William Faulkner and Southern History.* New York: Oxford University Press, 1993.

EDNA FERBER

Born: Kalamazoo, Michigan
August 15, 1885
Died: New York, New York
April 16, 1968

Although she wrote short stories and plays as well, Ferber's main achievement was in her novels, where she created forceful female characters and described complex family dynamics.

Library of Congress

BIOGRAPHY

Edna Ferber was born in Kalamazoo, Michigan, to the Hungarian Jewish immigrant Jacob Charles Ferber and his American-born Jewish wife, Julia Neumann. Jacob Ferber was a storekeeper whose business failures caused the family to move frequently. As a result, Ferber spent her childhood in various towns and in Chicago. She lived in Ottumwa, Iowa, from 1890 to 1897 and then for several years in Appleton, Wisconsin. In Ottumwa, Ferber was exposed to anti-Semitism, which may have helped produce the strong opposition to bigotry seen in her fiction. Also in this period, her father began to go blind, and her mother took over his business and became the power in the family.

Ferber's early ambition was to become an actress, and she performed in plays in high school. She would have liked to attend the Northwestern University School of Elocution, but her family did not have the money to send her there. She pursued a career in journalism instead, first working for the Appleton *Daily Crescent* and then for the *Milwaukee Journal*. An illness forced her to leave Milwaukee, her job, and journalism, and she turned to writing fiction, selling the short story "The Homely Heroine" to *Everybody's Magazine* in 1910. She sold a number of stories to magazines over the following

several years, including a popular series about an independent saleswoman named Emma McChesney. Three volumes of McChesney stories appeared in book form between 1913 and 1915.

Fearing that she was becoming repetitive and superficial in her McChesney stories, Ferber turned to novels, in 1917 producing *Fanny Herself*, her most autobiographical work, about a mother and a daughter in a Jewish family. She rarely wrote about Jewish characters in her later works (an exception is the storekeeper Sol Levy in the 1930 novel *Cimarron*), but her focus on outsiders and minorities can be seen as drawing on her Jewish background.

Ferber's first major success as a novelist came with *So Big* (1924), which won the 1925 Pulitzer Prize. She followed this with the even more successful *Show Boat* (1926), which was made into a Broadway musical by Jerome Kern and Oscar Hammerstein and then into a motion picture. During this period, Ferber moved to New York and became a regular at the Algonquin Hotel, where she was a member of the famous Round Table group of writers and theater people.

Ferber herself tried her hand at Broadway shows, usually in collaboration with other writers such as George S. Kaufman. That pair had success with such plays as *The Royal Family* (1927), *Dinner at Eight* (1932), and *Stage Door* (1936). She also continued to write short stories, but her main focus during the second half of her life was on novels, including such works as *Cimarron* and *Saratoga Trunk* (1941). Ferber's practice was to set each of her novels in a different region of the United States, sometimes with the result of offending residents of that region, who criticized her for caricaturing them. This was true to a certain extent with *Cimarron*, set in Oklahoma, and was even more true of *Giant* (1952), which was set in Texas. Her last novel, *Ice Palace* (1958), is sometimes criticized as being mere propaganda in favor of Alaskan statehood, but is also sometimes credited with helping bring Alaskan statehood about.

In her later years Ferber suffered from ill health, which limited her output. She died in New York City in 1968.

ANALYSIS

An interesting but seldom remarked upon aspect of Ferber's fiction is her supple way with chronology. Her stories effortlessly leap forward and backward in time, so that one moment the reader is following the young Sobig DeJong and the next is back twenty years reading about the childhood of Sobig's mother.

One of the few commentators to note this technique, Ellen Serlen Uffen in her article "Edna Ferber and the 'Theatricalization' of American Mythology," says it is a means of reassuring the reader. By leaping forward and letting the reader glimpse a character's future, as she often does, Ferber is letting her readers know that the character will survive. Surely, however, there is more to the technique than that. Although it is done effortlessly in novels like *So Big*, *Show Boat*, and *Cimarron*, the reader eventually notices the time lapses and begins to wonder what they signify. Perhaps they are connected to the idea of repetition also found in Ferber's novels, for instance in Kim Ravenal turning out to be so much like her grandmother in *Show Boat*. They could merely indicate the broad sweep of Ferber's canvas, covering several generations in every novel. They may also signify something about the nature of time in Ferber's universe, that past, present, and future are all happening simultaneously for her, or that destiny is something fixed for her characters. It is all very suggestive and yet tantalizingly uncertain.

Another prominent aspect of Ferber's fiction is her emphasis on strong, hardworking women. Selina DeJong in *So Big* and Sabra Cravat in *Cimarron* both work incredibly hard, Selina as a farmer, Sabra as a newspaper editor. Even Magnolia Ravenal in *Show Boat*, once she is free of her husband's influ-

ence, works diligently at becoming an actress. For that matter, her mother, Parthy, also works hard at running the show boat, especially after her husband dies.

It is noteworthy that all these women are best able to flourish after their husbands die or desert them. With Pervus DeJong dead, Selina can introduce the innovations that turn a failing farm into a prosperous one. With Yancey Cravat away on his adventures, Sabra can develop her powers and become a leading figure in her town. Ferber almost seems to be saying that women are better off without men or at least that if a woman wants to pursue a career, as the unmarried Ferber did, she must in some way get free of her husband. A negative example, an exception which proves this rule, is Leslie in *Giant*, who remains in a loving marriage close to her husband for the whole book—and never develops a career at all.

If her women are strong, Ferber's men tend to be weak—charming, romantic, idealistic, but weak and irresponsible. Gaylord Ravenal, the dashing *Show Boat* gambler, cannot reliably provide for his family and eventually deserts them. Yancey Cravat, though another dashing and romantic figure, is constantly deserting his wife and children. Pervus DeJong is weak in another way: too stubborn and unimaginative to see how to improve his farm. Captain Andy in *Show Boat* is the quintessential henpecked husband, bossed around by his wife, Parthy, though often contriving to get around her commands.

Captain Andy is an interesting case, raising another issue in Ferber's works: the conflict between responsibility and fun. Captain Andy is fun-loving and lighthearted, enjoying the life of producing shows on his show boat. In contrast, Parthy is such a great believer in order and responsibility that she often becomes a killjoy. It is easy for the reader to take Captain Andy's side against Parthy.

It is less easy to take sides against Sabra Cravat in *Cimarron*. Like Parthy, Sabra seems opposed to all things joyful, from saloons to gambling. She is also bigoted against Indians. At the same time, she commands the reader's respect because of her hard work in the wilderness of Oklahoma, while her adventure-loving husband is neglecting his family. Whereas in *Show Boat* Ferber's point seems to be to favor Captain Andy's lightheartedness over Parthy's Puritanism, in *Cimarron* Ferber seems to

771

Edna Ferber

prefer Sabra's seriousness, despite its killjoy aspects, to the irresponsible lightheartedness of her husband.

It is a fine line, in Ferber's fiction, between an admirable appreciation of the joyful side of life and an irresponsible abandonment of one's duty, and it is a rare character in Ferber who is able to combine joyfulness and duty as Selina does in *So Big*. More often in Ferber's fiction, dedication to duty comes, as it does with Parthy, Sabra, and also Pervus, with an inability to take joy in life. Even worse, these dutiful characters seem intent on denying joy to others and on controlling the other characters' lives.

Controlling others' lives is another recurrent theme in Ferber's works. Even the virtuous Selina is guilty of this, trying to turn her son into an artist when he is actually more interested in conventional forms of success and making money. The nature of true success is also an issue for Ferber; she seems clearly on the side of pursuing self-fulfillment rather than monetary gain, but this attitude ends up conflicting with her dislike of controlling others when the artistic Selina tries to force an artistic life on Sobig. People have to be allowed to pursue their own lives and make their own mistakes, more than one Ferber character says. This seems to be Ferber's view as well, but the result is a certain despair when people choose in favor of materialism instead of art.

So Big

First published: 1924
Type of work: Novel

A young woman struggles to survive and raise a son on an Illinois farm.

So Big, a sensitive portrayal of the struggles of Selina Peake (later Selina DeJong), is best in its first half, when its focus is on Selina; it loses some of its edge later when the focus shifts to Selina's son, Dirk (nicknamed So Big or Sobig).

The novel begins with the ten-year-old Sobig fighting other children who mock him for his nickname but, in a manner characteristic of Ferber, the story almost immediately jumps back in time to when Sobig was two and just receiving the nick-

name. Then it looks ahead to the successes of the adult Dirk, and then, still within the opening chapter, it leaps back to Selina's childhood.

Most of Selina's childhood is spent with her widower father, Simeon Peake, a gambler whose philosophy is that life is a big show in which the aim is to experience as much as possible. Selina is able to be both creative and responsible with her father and much prefers living with him to living with her prim and proper maiden aunts in New England. However, her father is killed when Selina is nineteen, and she is forced to take a job as a schoolteacher in the Illinois countryside, teaching the children of Dutch farmers.

Selina is quite frightened at first to be on her own and to be such a small figure in a large world. She feels very much like an outsider. When she admires the look of the countryside and says that cabbages are beautiful, the farmers laugh at her. Only Roelf, the sensitive twelve-year-old son of the farmer with whom she boards, understands her. He has artistic ability, which she encourages.

After a year of teaching, Selina catches the eye of Pervus DeJong, a widowed farmer. They marry, though Selina can hardly believe that she is becoming a farmer's wife. She fears giving up the finer things in life and becoming old before her time like the other farm wives she sees. Selina finds life on the farm very arduous, and she also begins to realize that her husband, though kind, is dull and resistant to change. She is full of ideas for improving the farm, at which he merely laughs. When she tries to inject some color and fun into their lives, he reproaches her for being a loose woman.

In this section of the novel, Ferber shows Selina fighting against the conventional limitations imposed on women. Selina insists on working in the fields with her husband, despite his protests, and after he dies unexpectedly of pneumonia, she ignores the objections of neighbors and delivers her farm produce to market herself instead of relying on her incompetent male field hand.

With her husband gone, Selina is free to introduce her new farming ideas, and the farm prospers as it never had before. Ferber seems to be suggesting that women can do good things if only they can free themselves from male control and the disapproval of society. There is a price to pay for Selina, however: she ends up looking prematurely old and worn out. Also, she does not succeed entirely on her own; she relies partly on the assistance of the rich father of an old school friend of hers.

Though her friend's father warns her that she cannot live someone else's life for them, Selina's goal at this point has become to arrange things so that her son can pursue a fulfilling profession. She has given up all hope of creating a life of culture and intellectual fulfillment for herself; instead, she sees herself as sacrificing so that her son can enjoy such a life.

The last half of the novel shows that her friend's father was right. Selina cannot force Dirk into the sort of career she wants. He trains to be an architect, something of which she approves, but he gives up architecture to be a bond salesman, sacrificing creative fulfillment for money and aiming for what Selina thinks is the wrong sort of success.

The last section of the novel shows Dirk rising in society, much to his mother's dismay. She is much more pleased with the artistic success of her old friend Roelf, who has become a sculptor in France. The book ends somewhat abruptly, with Dirk apparently in despair. There can be little doubt that Ferber wants the reader to think Dirk has chosen badly and that Roelf's life, and even Selina's, have been more fulfilling.

SHOW BOAT

First published: 1926
Type of work: Novel

A fun-loving husband and a Puritanical wife clash over the proper approach to life, while bringing up their young daughter on a Mississippi show boat.

Show Boat, an interesting portrayal of family dynamics and the conflict between romantic adventure and responsibility, begins with the birth of Kim Ravenal on the show boat known as the Cotton Blossom Floating Palace Theatre. As in *So Big*, the story quickly moves backward—in this case, all the way back to the courtship of Kim's grandparents, Parthenia Ann (known as Parthy) and Captain Andy Hawks.

In Parthy, Ferber describes a stern, domineering, Puritanical mother figure who nags her husband but also provides him with home cooking, order, and comfort. Captain Andy, in contrast, is a fun-loving, good-natured type. Their daughter, Magnolia, takes after her father, and the two seem constantly in a conspiracy against Parthy. The narrator notes that the balance created by the captain's lightheartedness and Parthy's strictness is good for Magnolia, as if life requires both responsibility and fun.

After four or five interesting chapters exploring this family dynamic, Ferber shifts the story into a description of a life on a show boat. She describes the actors who play in the shows, the audiences that come to see them, and the vagaries of the Mississippi River. This turns the book for a while into a sort of travelogue or guidebook.

During this part of the story, Ferber introduces one of her recurrent themes: the treatment of minorities. The young Magnolia likes to spend time with the African American kitchen staff on the boat, who teach her Negro spirituals. This appalls her mother, who has a rather bigoted attitude. It also turns out that one of the actresses on board, who has been passing as white, is actually black. Because she is married to a white man, in violation of southern laws at the time, there is trouble.

Over the objections of her mother, Magnolia begins acting in the plays on the show boat. Also over her mother's objections, Magnolia marries Gaylord Ravenal, a dashing gambler who takes up an acting career on the boat after he glimpses Magnolia. The charmingly irresponsible Gaylord is presented as an even greater contrast with Parthy than her husband was; it is as if Ferber is setting up two polar opposites, each with its flaws. Gaylord is fun and inspires passion but cannot be relied on. Parthy is reliable but a killjoy.

At this point, Ferber indulges in some of her characteristic time shifting: She makes the story jump forward to the adulthood of Magnolia's daughter Kim and has Kim remember her early years on the show boat, including the unfortunate death of her grandfather, Captain Andy. Though she often complained of the goings-on aboard the show boat, Parthy stays on it after the death of her husband. She puts herself in charge and eventually makes the boat more prosperous than ever, somewhat as Selina DeJong made her farm more prosperous after her husband died.

However, Magnolia and Gaylord cannot stand being on a boat run by Parthy and move to Chicago, where Gaylord returns to the precarious life of a professional gambler. Magnolia gets frustrated with this life, which causes them to move into cheap lodgings and pawn their jewelry every time Gaylord has bad luck. Magnolia is especially interested in finding a more stable source of income at this time because she needs to provide for her daughter's education. She thus decides to return to acting, which she had given up when she left the show boat.

Gaylord is unsympathetic to Magnolia's planned return to the stage, and she is able to carry it out only after he takes his leave of her, which he does soon afterward, abandoning his family, never to see them again. Ferber makes this out to be an irresponsible act of desertion and yet at the same time something that liberates Magnolia to pursue a career.

Kim, in the meantime, though she ends up following her mother into the acting profession, mostly takes after her stern grandmother. One curious result of this is that Magnolia remains the fun-loving child till the end, while her daughter takes on more and more of the responsible mother's role in relation to her own mother.

At the end of the book, Parthy, who has continued to run the show boat, dies, and Magnolia returns to the boat for the funeral. She then realizes that the show boat is where she belongs. There she can be on the wild Mississippi; she needs the wildness, unlike her daughter, whose life is one of order. Kim tries to persuade her mother to return home, but Magnolia is obstinate, and Ferber seems clearly to think that the show boat, with all its vitality, sordidness, and magnificence, is the better place to be.

GIANT

First published: 1952
Type of work: Novel

A Virginia woman tries to adjust to life as the wife of a Texas rancher.

Giant opens with a description of a party thrown by the Texan millionaire oilman Jett Rink, which is being attended by a host of other millionaires and their wives, most of them arriving by airplane and speaking in a folksy Texan dialect about inconsequential matters such as clothes.

At first it is difficult to tell which characters are meant to be central, but eventually the focus settles on Mrs. Jordan Benedict (the former Leslie Lynnton) and her regal-looking husband, who goes by the nickname Bick. Leslie makes critical remarks about Texas, saying that despite its size its views are not broad. As if to prove this, Ferber has a South American visitor barred from the party because he is mistaken for a Mexican.

At this point, using a favorite technique, Ferber sends the story twenty-five years into the past to describe how Leslie Lynnton of Virginia became the wife of millionaire rancher Bick Benedict. She describes Leslie's family upbringing, including her gentle doctor father and her bossy mother and sisters.

The family dynamic is similar to that in *Show Boat*, with a domineering mother and a creative but somewhat weak father. However, the family here does not come alive the way Parthy and Captain Andy do in *Show Boat*, and in describing the scenes in Virginia, and elsewhere in the novel, Ferber becomes very self-conscious about her own narration, frequently saying that the incidents in the story are melodramatic or out of a bad stage play.

Another problem with the story is that the characters spend most of their time talking instead of actually doing anything. Leslie is supposed to be a strong woman in the mode of Selina and Magnolia in Ferber's earlier works, but whereas Selina runs a farm and Magnolia becomes an actress, Leslie pursues no career and is content to be Mrs. Jordan Benedict.

Also in contrast to the earlier novels, Leslie's husband sticks by her, and the two frequently declare their love for each other. The result is to drain the tension from the book; almost all the conflict in the story is confined to verbal disagreements about issues not directly affecting the characters, notably the treatment of the Mexican minority in Texas.

The book ends with Jett Rink's oil interests transforming the state, depressing Bick, who prefers the old ranching ways to the "stink" of oil. Bick becomes gloomy, saying his whole family has been a failure, but Leslie is upbeat and says she is sure they will be a success.

SUMMARY

A best-selling author in her own time, Ferber never attracted much critical commentary, being seen as merely a popular writer. However, at her best, for instance in her portrayal of Selina DeJong

DISCUSSION TOPICS

- What is the significance of Edna Ferber's frequent use of flashbacks and other time-shifting devices in her fiction?

- Discuss Ferber's attitude toward the conflicting ideals of responsibility and creativity.

- Discuss Ferber's attitude toward mothers.

- Discuss Ferber's depiction of outsiders and minorities in her fiction.

- What is Ferber's attitude toward success in her fiction?

in *So Big* and in her description of the family dynamic in *Show Boat*, she creates forceful characters and touches on important issues concerning the proper way to live one's life.

Sheldon Goldfarb

BIBLIOGRAPHY

By the Author

DRAMA:
Our Mrs. McChesney, pr., pb. 1915 (with George V. Hobart)
$1200 a Year, pr., pb. 1920 (with Newman A. Levy)
Minick, pr., pb. 1924 (with George S. Kaufman)
The Royal Family, pr. 1927, pb. 1928 (with Kaufman)
Dinner at Eight, pr., pb. 1932 (with Kaufman)
Stage Door, pr., pb. 1936 (with Kaufman)
The Land Is Bright, pr., pb. 1941 (with Kaufman)
Bravo!, pr. 1948, pb. 1949 (with Kaufman)

LONG FICTION:
Dawn O'Hara: The Girl Who Laughed, 1911
Fanny Herself, 1917
The Girls, 1921
So Big, 1924
Show Boat, 1926
Cimarron, 1930
American Beauty, 1931
Come and Get It, 1935
Saratoga Trunk, 1941

Edna Ferber

Great Son, 1945
Giant, 1952
Ice Palace, 1958

SHORT FICTION:
Buttered Side Down, 1912
Roast Beef Medium, 1913
Personality Plus, 1914
Emma McChesney and Co., 1915
Cheerful—By Request, 1918
Half Portions, 1919
Mother Knows Best, 1927
They Brought Their Women, 1933
Nobody's in Town, 1938 (includes *Nobody's in Town* and *Trees Die at the Top*)
One Basket, 1947

NONFICTION:
A Peculiar Treasure, 1939, revised 1960 (with new introduction)
A Kind of Magic, 1963

About the Author

Ferber, Edna. *A Peculiar Treasure.* New York: Doubleday, 1939.

Gilbert, Julie Goldsmith. *Ferber: A Biography.* Garden City, N.Y.: Doubleday, 1978.

Kenaga, Heidi. "Edna Ferber's *Cimarron*, Cultural Authority, and 1920's Western Historical Narratives." In *Middlebrow Moderns: Popular American Writers of the 1920's,* edited by Lisa Botshon and Meredith Goldsmith. Boston: Northeastern University Press, 2003.

Lichtenstein, Diane. "American Jewish Women Themselves." In *Writing Their Nations: The Tradition of Nineteenth-Century American Jewish Women Writers.* Bloomington: Indiana University Press, 1992.

Shaughnessy, Mary Rose. *Women and Success in American Society in ` the Works of Edna Ferber.* New York: Gordon Press, 1977.

Uffen, Ellen Serlen. "Edna Ferber and the 'Theatricalization' of American Mythology." *Midwestern Miscellany* 8 (1980): 82-93.

F. SCOTT FITZGERALD

Library of Congress

Born: St. Paul, Minnesota
September 24, 1896
Died: Hollywood, California
December 21, 1940

An outstanding stylist and acute social observer, Fitzgerald captured the essence of American life between World War I and World War II.

BIOGRAPHY

Francis Scott Key Fitzgerald, one of the most talented of American writers, was born on September 24, 1896, in St. Paul, Minnesota. His father, Edward, was unsuccessful in a variety of enterprises, and the family moved numerous times until Fitzgerald's mother inherited sufficient money for them to settle in one of the more exclusive neighborhoods of St. Paul. Even as a young boy, Fitzgerald was acutely aware that his mother, rather than his father, provided the financial foundation of the family. It was a situation—a wife's inherited money—that was to recur frequently in his writing.

In 1911, Fitzgerald entered Newman School, a Catholic institution in Hackensack, New Jersey. It was there that he decided upon Princeton University as the ideal college, thus beginning one strand that would run throughout his writing, especially in his earlier works and his popular first novel, *This Side of Paradise* (1920), with its collegiate setting.

It was also at Newman that Fitzgerald met and was encouraged in his literary ambitions by Father Sigourney Fay, a priest who became one of the most important influences upon Fitzgerald's development. Father Fay strengthened the young Fitzgerald's sense of a noble character as an essential element in achieving high goals—and of the accom-

panying dangers of anything that would weaken that character, disrupt its resolve, or corrupt its nature: the lure of unearned wealth, sins of the flesh, moral weakness. These beliefs were woven deep into Fitzgerald's psyche and found repeated, perhaps obsessive, expression in his fiction.

After he entered Princeton in the fall of 1913, Fitzgerald was active in the literary and social activities of the college; he was a talented and frequent contributor to the shows of the Triangle Club and the literary magazines. Perhaps as a result, his grades were marginal at best, causing him to drop out for a semester during his junior year, returning to Princeton a year behind his classmates.

By then another goal had presented itself: With the entry of the United States into World War I, Fitzgerald had determined to join the Army. He was commissioned as a second lieutenant in October, 1917. He started the first draft of a novel provisionally titled "The Romantic Egotist," which, greatly reworked, would become *This Side of Paradise.* In June, 1918, Fitzgerald was transferred to Camp Sheridan near Montgomery, Alabama, where he met and fell in love with Zelda Sayre, a southern beauty. Fitzgerald received orders for Europe, but the war ended before he sailed for France.

His engagement with Zelda flickered on and off while Fitzgerald was discharged from the Army, worked briefly in advertising in New York, sold his first commercial short stories, and continued with his novel. In September, 1919, *This Side of Paradise* was accepted by Scribner's; the editor who made the decision, Maxwell Perkins, was one of the most discerning and influential figures in publishing during the period, and he was to have a close professional association with Fitzgerald for many years. Fitzgerald also began publishing short stories in *The Saturday Evening Post,* one of the most popular and highly paying magazines of the time. Now a success, Fitzgerald married Zelda in New York City on April 3, 1920.

Scribner's had published *This Side of Paradise* the month before, and the novel was an immediate success, making its twenty-three-year-old author a critical and commercial success. Later in 1920, Fitzgerald's first collection of short stories, *Flappers and Philosophers*, was also published. Young, wealthy, and in love, the Fitzgeralds lived well on their income during a period when the United States was shaking free the past and entering a period later to be known as the Jazz Age. F. Scott Fitzgerald was its chronicler: His second collection of stories, published in 1922, was titled *Tales of the Jazz Age.*

Residing in a succession of rented houses, traveling to Europe, living the good life, and beginning to drink perhaps more than he should, Fitzgerald still found time to write. His second novel, *The Beautiful and Damned,* came out in 1922, and he tried a play, *The Vegetable: Or, From President to Postman,* which was unsuccessful; it closed at its tryout in Atlantic City in November, 1923. Undeterred, he began work on his third, and probably most important, novel, *The Great Gatsby,* which was published in 1925, bringing its author the best critical reception he received during his lifetime.

The Fitzgeralds continued to travel, often living for months at a time in Europe, where they associated with literary figures such as Ernest Hemingway and James Joyce. Perhaps because of his drinking, perhaps because of his wife's deteriorating mental and emotional health, Fitzgerald practically abandoned the novel to concentrate on short stories. While among these were some masterpieces, there are many that were written quickly (although well) for money. In a sense, Fitzgerald was succumbing to the temptations against which Father Fay had warned him earlier in his life.

In April, 1930, Zelda Fitzgerald had her first serious mental breakdown. She was placed in a Swiss clinic, and it was not until September, 1931, that the couple returned to the United States. Zelda's condition did not improve; in early 1932, she went into a clinic of the Johns Hopkins Hospital in Baltimore. In the meantime, Fitzgerald had turned this stuff of personal tragedy into the material for art, and his fourth novel, *Tender Is the Night,* which concerned a mental patient and her doctor husband, was published in April, 1934. It met with a mixed reception, and Fitzgerald continued his slide into alcoholism, while Zelda was moved from clinic to clinic.

Although Fitzgerald had been successful as a novelist and was one of the most highly paid short-story writers of the time, the couple's expensive lifestyle and the costs of Zelda's care had plunged them deeply into debt. In the summer of 1937, Fitzgerald took a course that was often, if reluctantly, followed by serious authors of his time: He went to Hollywood as a screenwriter. He was not a success in that medium, but he did begin work on another novel, *The Last Tycoon* (1941), which used the motion-picture world, modern America's greatest example of the power of illusion, as its theme. He was working on the novel when he died on December 21, 1940, of a heart attack. Eight years later, after dying in a fire that destroyed the North Carolina clinic where she was staying, Zelda Fitzgerald was buried beside her husband.

ANALYSIS

In one of the most haunting passages of *The Great Gatsby*, the narrator, Nick Carraway, sees his mysterious neighbor perform a strange ritual:

> [H]e stretched out his arms toward the dark water in a curious way, and, far as I was from him, I could have sworn he was trembling. Involuntarily I glanced seaward—and distinguished nothing except a single green light, minute and far away, that might have been the end of a dock. When I looked once more for Gatsby he had vanished, and I was alone again in the unquiet darkness.

What Gatsby is trying to do in the novel, literally as well as symbolically, is reach out to recapture the past. For Gatsby, that past is embodied in Daisy Buchanan, the woman he loved as a young lieutenant while stationed in her hometown in the South. He loves her still and, as a rich man, hopes to regain her and in doing so recapture his youthful dreams and promise.

It is a scene and a dream that runs throughout Fitzgerald's fiction. All of his heroes carry that sense of the lost past, of misspent promise. They are outsiders in some form or other—usually because they come from the lower or middle class—and they are further set apart because of the high goals and exacting standards they have set for themselves. From Amory Blame, in Fitzgerald's first novel, through Monroe Stahr, in his last, left unfinished at the time of his death, Fitzgerald created protagonists who aspired to be larger than life but who were destroyed by the commonplace existence they sought to rise above.

In a sense, these fictional characters have many of the attributes of their author; in particular, they share with him a keen sense of morality and destiny that applies particularly to them. When they fail, betrayed by human lapses into drink or by the dark promise of sex, they find themselves on a downward spiral, often overindulging in the failings that distracted them initially. Their tragedies are largely self-made, as they become victims of their own romantic moralism.

This romantic moralism is especially painful in the relationships between men and women. A love which begins as strengthening, almost magical in its nature, turns out badly; the woman is frequently the agent of the hero's downfall. Anthony Patch, in *The Beautiful and Damned*, sinks into dissipation after his marriage to Gloria Gilbert. Dick Diver, the brilliant and promising young psychiatrist in *Tender Is the Night*, is undermined personally and professionally when he marries his patient, the heiress Nicole Warren. Most notably of all, Jay Gatsby is destroyed because of his love for Daisy: shot dead in his own swimming pool at the end of a series of sordid and entangling events that never would have occurred without Gatsby's obsessed pursuit of her.

The style in which these tragedies are told is one of the most famous in American literature: a brilliant, sensuous, lyrical prose that re-creates for the reader the sense of emotional ecstasy and despair felt by the Fitzgerald character. As he developed as a writer, Fitzgerald's style gained in strength and clarity, dropping much of its earlier, self-conscious rhetoric but retaining its beauty, until it became a powerful and supple instrument that captured both particular insights and wide-ranging social observations.

Perhaps because Fitzgerald felt so keenly his own role as an outsider, he had a sharp and most perceptive view of American social mores. A large part of the power—and a cause for the immediate success—of *This Side of Paradise* was its fresh, vivid portrayal of college life, presenting it in a more realistic fashion than had been done before. Whether etching the characters of heedless expatriates on the French Riviera, giving sharp, thumbnail portraits of New York gangsters, or presenting the excesses of the irresponsibly rich during the jazz age, Fitzgerald was a master of creating accurate, indelible images of American life—what they wore, drove, drank, and sang—during his time. His writings are a social history of the first rank.

These were the qualities which won for Fitzgerald success early in his career and which, for a while, made him the most popular and highly paid writer of his day. He was especially gifted in the short-story form, finding it particularly suited to his skills in crafting characters who have come to a point of crisis in their lives, a crisis that requires them to make a choice that will, almost inevitably, destroy their youthful dreams. The best of these stories, such as "The Rich Boy," "The Diamond as Big as the Ritz," or "Babylon Revisited," are recognized as authentic masterpieces.

All Fitzgerald's writings come, sooner or later, to the themes which he explored throughout his career: early promise betrayed, the romantic hero broken by the indifferent world, love lost, and the impossibility of recapturing the past. These are themes woven deep into the American mind as well, and in pursuing them Fitzgerald is perhaps the most "American" author in the literature of the United States.

In the end, that dual sense of promise and loss, innocence and fall, is Fitzgerald's characteristic tone. It sounds strongest in *The Great Gatsby:*

> I thought of Gatsby's wonder when he first picked out the green light at the end of Daisy's dock. He had come a long way to this blue lawn, and his dream must have seemed so close that he could hardly fail to grasp it. He did not know that it was already behind him, somewhere back in that vast obscurity beyond the city, where the dark fields of the republic rolled on under the night.

Gatsby, like Fitzgerald's other heroes, is ignorant of his loss until the realization of it destroys him. The message of F. Scott Fitzgerald is that knowledge is tragedy but that such tragedy summons forth true greatness.

THIS SIDE OF PARADISE

First published: 1920
Type of work: Novel

The intellectual and moral development of Amory Blame is described, from his pampered childhood to his early manhood.

This Side of Paradise, Fitzgerald's first novel, made him an enormously successful popular author when he was only twenty-three years old. The combination of romanticism and realism, mingled with a fresh and—for the time—sometimes startling depiction of college life, caught the attention of the reading public and made the novel representative of an entire generation.

This Side of Paradise is loose and episodic, a collection of vivid scenes which do not fuse into a well-structured novel. It is divided into two sections:

"The Romantic Egotist" (the title of the novel's first draft) and "The Education of a Personage."

The first takes Amory Blame from his childhood through his years at Princeton University and concerns his intellectual and moral development.

Convinced that he has a great, if obscure, destiny, Amory is greatly influenced by a Catholic priest, Father Darcy, who awakens him to the reality and power of evil. Darcy is based upon Father Sigourney Fay, who exerted a comparable influence on Fitzgerald. In the novel, this moral and spiritual education is dramatized by incidents that appear supernatural, as when Amory is pursued by a diabolic figure through the streets of New York. Perhaps a remnant of Father Fay's moralism, the sense of sin and the power of sex are mixed in Amory's mind in an inextricable, if often confusing fashion.

The second section is restricted to one year, 1919, and concentrates on Amory's character development, which it traces by following his adventures after service in World War I. As Fitzgerald had no experience of combat, he wisely omitted any actual description of Amory in the conflict. In book 2, Amory's courtship of Rosalind Connage is ended after the sudden loss of his family fortune. Having weathered this traumatic event, Amory undergoes another supernatural experience, involving the death of Father Darcy and again related to his confused feelings about sex, sin, and morality. Yet the death of Father Darcy frees Amory, in a sense, and at the end of the novel he gazes on the lights of Princeton and vows to begin his real search for his unknown but surely glorious destiny.

Readers responded to several different aspects of *This Side of Paradise*. It was one of the first novels to use the college setting in a realistic way—as opposed to the simplistic "Dink Stover at Yale" genre—and, although later generations were to see it as sentimental, even naïve, Fitzgerald's contemporaries were treated to a fresh and innovative point of view concerning the young. His scenes of college life, enticing to younger readers, were even thought shocking by some—including the president of Princeton, John Grier Hibben, who wrote Fitzgerald an aggrieved letter.

Hibben was troubled that *This Side of Paradise* seemed to emphasize the facile and superficial aspects of Princeton life. On the other hand, it should be noted that Fitzgerald's novel is highly concerned with the development of Amory Blame's intellect. A recurrent theme in *This Side of Paradise* is the importance of reading in forming character: One critic has counted sixty-four book titles and the names of ninety-eight authors in the novel. In this concern with its hero's intellectual growth, *This Side of Paradise* is very similar to another influential novel of the period, James Joyce's *A Portrait of the Artist as a Young Man* (1916). Both books startled many by their blend of the mental and physical desires of their protagonists, including what was, for the times, a frank approach to sexual awakening.

Also startling to many readers, long accustomed to conventional portraits of women, were the manners and actions of Fitzgerald's women characters. Such young women as Eleanor Savage, a heedless and self-indulgent romantic, for example, were far removed from conventional morality. Actually, this realistic aspect of the novel fit quite well with the highly moral, even religious, sentiments of Amory Blame concerning sex, by underscoring the dangerous power of physical desires.

The style of the novel, remarked upon by many critics, remains its most distinguishing feature. Although *This Side of Paradise* is in many passages highly rhetorical, even excessively so, it contains the essential qualities of Fitzgerald's writing: the precise social observation aptly rendered, the flowing, rhythmic passages, and the presentation of abstract ideals embodied in specific individuals. In his later books and stories, Fitzgerald refined and developed these attributes, but they are clearly present from the start of his career.

THE BEAUTIFUL AND DAMNED

First published: 1922
Type of work: Novel

The moral characters of a young couple disintegrate as they wait to inherit a vast fortune.

The Beautiful and Damned, Fitzgerald's second novel, follows the decline—fiscal, physical, and moral—of Anthony and Gloria Patch. Like so many of Fitzgerald's figures, the Patches are destroyed by great wealth; the irony in this novel is that they are undone not by the possession of money but merely by expecting it.

Anthony, the only heir of his wealthy grandfather, Adam Patch, is a young Harvard University graduate who lives on money left by his father and disdains work because he believes nothing is equal to his supposed abilities. He marries the beautiful Gloria Gilbert, and they sink into a pointless and destructive life, squandering their income in an endless round of parties and extravagant expenses. When Grandfather, an inflexible and intolerant reformer, walks in unexpectedly on one their gin-soaked parties, he writes Anthony out of his will. Following his death, the Patches must sue to claim the inheritance which lured them into destruction. At novel's end, they triumph, but the cost has been high: Gloria's beauty has been coarsened, and Anthony's mind snapped by worry and drink.

Anthony and Gloria are selfish, self-indulgent characters who begin the novel with some perverse appeal but quickly deteriorate under the influence of greed, excess, and alcohol. As they move through their pointless round of pleasures, they demand wilder and stronger stimulation, but this only contributes to their downward spiral. Rejected as officer material when the United States enters World War I, Anthony is later drafted and, while on training in the South, has an affair. In the meantime, Gloria fails to win the film role she covets, which had been offered to her by a former admirer. All in all, the aptly named Patches made shreds of their lives.

A strong sense of moralism runs though all Fitzgerald's works, and in *The Beautiful and Damned* it is married to the sophisticated, modern style of *This Side of Paradise*. The two elements are not cleanly fused, and this causes difficulties with the novel, chiefly with the view Fitzgerald takes of the main characters. The third-person narrator veers between bemused appreciation of Anthony and Gloria as unapologetic hedonists and hardly veiled disapproval of their waste of talent and lives. In the earlier portions of the book, Fitzgerald seems to have some sort of respect for the code the Patches have adopted for themselves, but as their lives and code cheapen, the tone of the book becomes harsher. It seems that even dissipation has its standards.

As with most of Fitzgerald's writings, *The Beautiful and Damned* has many autobiographical elements. Quite a few of the pleasure-seeking, carefree antics of Anthony and Gloria—at least in the earlier sections of the novel—are based on escapades of Fitzgerald and his wife. In the second portion of the novel, Anthony is stationed in the South and has a love affair with a local woman; this echoes Fitzgerald's history, but with significant exceptions. Fitzgerald was an officer, while Anthony Patch is an enlisted man; Dot, Anthony's lover, is a common sort of woman, quite unlike the aristocratic Zelda. Most notably, Anthony and Dot have a simple but sordid relationship, unlike the romantic passion of which Fitzgerald and Zelda believed themselves to be the central characters.

Although *The Beautiful and Damned* is a more structured and planned book than *This Side of Para-*

dise, it still shows Fitzgerald as a writer learning the difficult skills of crafting a novel. Too often uncertain and wavering in its tone and point of view, overwritten in many of its descriptive passages, the book is redeemed by the power of its depiction of the deterioration of the Patches, who emerge for the reader as flawed but vividly memorable characters.

THE GREAT GATSBY

First published: 1925
Type of work: Novel

Seeking to recapture his lost early love and all that she symbolizes, a man is destroyed.

The Great Gatsby is Fitzgerald's finest novel, an almost perfect artistic creation which is perhaps the single most American novel of its time. It should be seen as the ultimate vehicle for the themes that form the central concerns of Fitzgerald's career, and indeed of so much of the United States' national life: lost hope, the corruption of innocence by money, and the impossibility of recapturing the past. These elements are fused together by Fitzgerald's eloquent yet careful prose in a novel that transcends its period and has become a touchstone of American literature.

Nick Carraway, the first-person narrator of the novel, lives on Long Island, New York, next door to the enormous mansion of a mysterious man named Gatsby, who throws gaudy, glittering parties. Wild, improbable rumors circulate about Gatsby, but when Nick meets him, he finds himself charmed and intrigued. He learns that Gatsby is in love with Nick's cousin, Daisy Buchanan, whom Gatsby met while stationed in her hometown in the South during World War I. Gatsby seeks to rekindle that earlier love in Daisy, now married to a coarse, brutal husband, Tom. The effort fails, and Gatsby becomes entangled in the lives of the Buchanans and is killed, shot by the confused and grieving husband of Tom's mistress. Gatsby's glowing dream ends in sordid confusion.

In this novel Fitzgerald relies on a narrative technique that he clearly learned from the works of the English writer Joseph Conrad: He gradually unveils Gatsby's story as Nick pieces it together a bit at a time. Each chapter allows Nick, and the reader, more insight into Gatsby's past and his true character. The facts are sifted from rumors and speculation until Jay Gatsby (born Gatz) is revealed as a flawed, but still great, hero.

Like so many of Fitzgerald's heroes, Gatsby is a romantic, a man who began with a high, even exalted, vision of himself and his destiny. He aspires to greatness, which he associates with Daisy. If he can win her, then he will have somehow achieved his goal. Gatsby's wealth, his mansion, his parties, his possessions, even his heroism in battle are but means to achieve his ultimate end. Gatsby is mistaken, however, in his belief that money can buy happiness or that he can recapture his past. His story is clearly a version of the traditional American myth, poor boy makes good, but is it a distorted version or an accurate one? Fitzgerald leaves this ambiguity unresolved, which adds to the power of his novel.

As a romantic, Jay Gatsby does not understand how money actually works in American life. He believes that if he is rich, then Daisy can be his. This is displayed most powerfully and poignantly in the scene where Gatsby shows Daisy and Nick the shirts he has tailored for him in London: He hauls them out in a rainbow of color and fabric, almost filling the room with the tangible yet useless symbols of his wealth. The shirts cause Daisy to cry, but they do not win her; they cannot let Gatsby realize his dream.

Gatsby has amassed his money by dealings with gangsters, yet he remains an innocent figure—he is a romantic, in other words. Ironically, Daisy Buchanan, his great love, is a much more realistic, hard-headed character. She understands money and what it means in American society, because it is her nature; she was born into it. Gatsby intuitively recognizes this, although he cannot fully accept it, when he remarks to Nick that Daisy's voice "is full of money." Even so, Gatsby will not admit this essential fact because it would destroy his conception of Daisy. In the end, this willful blindness helps lead to his destruction.

Actually, both Gatsby and Daisy are incapable of seeing the whole of reality, as he is a romantic and she, a cynic. This conflict is found in the other characters of the novel as well and is a key to *The Great Gatsby*. Fitzgerald uses a variety of symbolic scenes and images to express the blindness that the characters impose upon themselves. Gatsby's ostentatious material possessions are aspects of illusion. So is the green light at the end of Daisy's dock, the light that Gatsby gazes upon but cannot reach.

Other symbolic touches illuminate the book: the ash heaps which litter the landscape between Long Island and New York, for example, or the eyes of Doctor Ecleberg, found on a billboard dominating the valley of the ash heaps. The ash heaps are a reference to the vanity of life (and a nod at T. S. Eliot's poem *The Waste Land*, published in 1922), and the eyes a comment on the blindness of the book's characters, who do not fully understand what they behold.

While such devices add to the depth of *The Great Gatsby*, its true power derives from it being a quintessentially American novel, full of American characters and American themes. Nick Carraway, the midwestern narrator, encounters the sophistication of the East: New York, gangsters, the promise and hollowness of wealth. Tom and Daisy Buchanan, insulated by their money, do what they want without consequence, showing no remorse for their actions and no concern for those they have harmed. Jay Gatsby, like the hero in a story by Horatio Alger, rises from being a penniless youth through ambition and good fortune, only to discover that his wealth cannot buy what he most desires—and is, in fact, the very agent of his destruction. They are all American characters in an American setting.

Fitzgerald's skill as a novelist was at its peak with *The Great Gatsby*, and this is shown best in his command of the book's structure. By using Nick Carraway as the first-person narrator, Fitzgerald establishes a central focus for the novel, a character who is partly involved with the plot but partly a commentator upon it. Nick is presented as an honest, reliable person, and his perceptions and judgments are accepted by the reader. Nick ties the novel together, and through him it makes sense. Most important, Nick's solid, midwestern common sense

validates Gatsby as a character despite Gatsby's outrageous background and fabulous adventures. In the end, if Nick Carraway accepts Gatsby and approves of him—and he does—so does the reader.

Nick's approval is what allows Gatsby to be called "great," but his greatness has a curious, puzzling quality to it, as it cannot be easily or completely defined. Gatsby certainly lacks many of the qualities and fails many of the tests normally associated with greatness, but he redeems this by his exalted conception of himself. It is to this romantic image of Gatsby that both Nick and the reader respond.

TENDER IS THE NIGHT

First published: 1934
Type of work: Novel

The career and character of a brilliant young psychiatrist are undermined by wealth and an irresponsible lifestyle.

Nine years elapsed between the publication of *The Great Gatsby* and *Tender Is the Night*, and during that time Fitzgerald worked on his fourth novel in several stages, completing the final version in about a year. It is an ambitious novel, a multilayered work which charts the moral and psychological decline of Dick Diver, a young and promising American psychiatrist, set against the background of American expatriates in Europe during the 1920's. In a sense, Fitzgerald is tracing two parallel cases of decay—an individual's and a generation's.

Tender Is the Night is divided into three books and covers the years 1925 through 1929. Dick and Nicole Diver are at the center of an amusing circle of friends, including the alcoholic composer Abe North, who has never fulfilled his early promise, and the sinister mercenary Tommy Barban, who is in love with Nicole. Through a flashback, Fitzgerald reveals that Nicole was originally Dick's patient, placed in his care after being traumatized by being raped by her father.

It is an essential part of Dick Diver's personality to feel loved and needed, and this causes him to marry Nicole. The dual pressures of being Nicole's husband and her doctor, combined with the lure of Nicole's inherited fortune, undermine Dick's dedication to his work. Using Nicole's money, Dick becomes partner in a psychiatric clinic in the Swiss Alps but is unable to concentrate on his duties. In the meantime, the master treatise that he has long planned goes unwritten, and he sinks deeper into pointless and frenzied activity, fueled by alcohol.

As his career sinks further into decline, Dick reaches bottom, symbolized by a drunken brawl and arrest in Rome. The Divers return to the Riviera, the scene of their earlier triumphs, but to no avail: Nicole leaves Dick for Tommy Barban, and Dick returns to the United States, losing himself in obscurity as an unsuccessful doctor, wandering from town to small town.

In *Tender Is the Night*, Fitzgerald returns to the technique he employed so successfully in *The Great Gatsby*, that of gradually revealing the full nature of his characters—in this case, by the use of flashbacks. This allows the reader to become almost a participant in creating the novel, building the characters while reading. The method does have one drawback, as some critics have noted, in that it makes the deterioration of Dick Diver difficult to understand and accept. It requires careful reading to discern that the flaw in Dick's character is his desire—almost a compulsion—to be loved and needed. It is this that draws him into his fatal relationship with Nicole.

Dick's decline occurs on two levels, personal and professional, and both are directly connected with his wife. Nicole had originally been his patient, a deeply disturbed young woman whose personality was fragile and whose grasp of reality was uncertain. As the novel progresses, Nicole grows stronger psychologically and more distant from Dick emotionally. As his wife comes to depend upon him less, Dick loses his purpose. He begins to drink more—and more irresponsibly. He has an affair with a young American actress, less out of physical desire than from the need to find someone who depends upon him and will admire him, as Nicole had done. His once-promising professional career also fades, and the important book that he had planned to write is never finished. The clinic, bought with Nicole's money, slips out of his control, and he must let it go. He ends up a failure, no longer respected (or even known) by his peers.

This trajectory follows a pattern familiar in Fitzgerald's works. A hero with a high conception of his potential is diverted from his original purpose and wastes his gifts. The growing realization that he is squandering his talents only hastens the process and causes the downward slide to accelerate. Alcohol and unearned money are essential elements in the collapse, and although they do not cause the hero's fall, they certainly speed it along.

This pattern shows Fitzgerald's romantic moralism, which flows through all of his novels. Women, in particular women with inherited money, are often agents of moral destruction, diverting the hero from his goals. Without Nicole's wealth, Dick Diver is an acute and resourceful psychiatrist, skillful and capable in exploring the human mind. When his wife's fortune takes hold, Dick loses his vision, literally becoming incapable of understanding the psychology of people, including himself. Once a diver into the mind, as his symbolic name indicates, he has gotten out of his depth.

An ambitious and sensitive novel, *Tender Is the Night* has a keen sense of character, especially for the two main figures. The structure of the book, which moves back and forth in time, and the way in which Fitzgerald gradually reveals important information, however, have been confusing to some readers. Some critics have believed that these are damaging flaws and that a more straightforward, chronological approach would have been better. Fitzgerald himself considered this possibility after the novel was published, even reworking it for reissue in a revised form. Still, given the complex theme and psychological aspects of the work, the original presentation is undoubtedly the more appropriate. *Tender Is the Night* is a complex novel because the human mind and heart are themselves complex, complicated, and mysterious.

"THE DIAMOND AS BIG AS THE RITZ"

First published: 1922 (collected in *The Short Stories of F. Scott Fitzgerald*, 1989)
Type of work: Short story

A young man falls in love with the daughter of the world's richest man and is nearly destroyed.

"The Diamond as Big as the Ritz" is Fitzgerald's most successful fantasy story, a genre in which he worked mainly during the early phase of his career. While it contains what might be read as a happy ending, the story carries many of the tragic elements inherent in Fitzgerald's most enduring theme: how a young man is destroyed by the wealth of the woman he loves.

The plot of "The Diamond as Big as the Ritz" is relatively simple. John T. Unger, a young man from the small midwestern town of Hades, is sent by his ambitious parents to the exclusive eastern school of St. Midas. There he makes friends with Percy Washington and is invited to spend the summer at the Washington estate in the far West. Unger learns that the Washingtons are literally the richest family in the world, because they own a flawless diamond that is as large as the Ritz-Carlton Hotel. There is also a darker side to this fortune: To protect it, the Washingtons have made their estate a fortress, completely isolated from the outside world, and intruders are held captive in a giant cage.

While in this strange combination of luxury and prison, Unger meets and falls in love with Kismine, Percy's sixteen-year-old sister. From Kismine, Unger learns that all invited visitors to the Washington estate are murdered before they can leave. As Unger and Kismine flee, the place is attacked by airplanes, led there by one of the prisoners who managed to escape. The fabulous estate is destroyed as Unger and Kismine discover they have fled with worthless rhinestones instead of diamonds; they are free but penniless.

"The Diamond as Big as the Ritz" is a story full of symbolic and allegorical touches, many of them dealing with the soul-destroying potential of wealth. The hero, named Unger, is avid for more than his hometown can offer, and he seems to find it in Kismine Washington: young, beautiful, and heiress to a great fortune. The Washington fortune has become a prison for the family, however: They are isolated from the world, guarded by blacks who have been tricked into believing that slavery still exists. There is an obvious parallel between the two kinds of bondage, a parallel ironically emphasized by the family name of Washington, so closely associated with American freedom.

Wealth is also destructive in a religious sense. The train that carries Unger and Percy stops at the town of Fish, which has a population of only twelve men, who await the arrival of the train as a mystical event directed by the "Great Brakeman." (The fish was an early Christian symbol for Jesus, who urged his followers to renounce wealth, often in extremely pointed terms.) Yet these twelve have no real belief: By mere proximity to the Washingtons, these counterparts to the twelve Apostles have been drained of all faith.

Even more emphatic are the baneful effects of incalculable wealth on the family. Their land is literally nowhere, as they have taken extraordinary measures to keep it off even official government maps. To protect their secret, the Washingtons are ready to perpetuate slavery, imprison the innocent, and even commit murder, including fratricide. When the estate is about to be overrun, Percy's father offers a bribe to God—an enormous gem, backed by promises of human sacrifice—and then destroys his estate himself, rather than submit.

These various elements, which do not quite fit together in a consistently coherent fashion, are united by Fitzgerald's use of both fantasy and realistic descriptions, which allow the reader to accept the fairy-tale premises of the story. In a sense, "The Diamond as Big as the Ritz" is a magical counterpart to the more realistic *The Great Gatsby*, and the two explore many of the same themes and concerns.

"THE LAST OF THE BELLES"

First published: 1929 (collected in *The Short Stories of F. Scott Fitzgerald*, 1989)
Type of work: Short story

A romantic young Army lieutenant and a southern belle learn that dreams are destroyed by time.

"The Last of the Belles" combines autobiographical elements of Fitzgerald's courtship of Zelda Sayre and his theme of the lost dreams of youthful promise. Beautiful, blond, and vivacious, Ailie Calhoun captivates all the young officers who meet her in the small Georgia town of Tarleton, where they are in training for World War I. Many pursue her, including the narrator, Andy, and one young man may even have killed himself in a plane crash because of her. Ailie is perversely attracted to—and at the same time repelled by—Earl Schoen, an uncouth Yankee who is alien to everything she has known. In the end, she rejects all her beaux but is herself rejected by time and the modern world, which leaves her as the last of the traditional southern belles, a memory of what was once youthful and applauded.

The tone of the story is wistful and elegiac. All the events are in the past, which heightens the sense of lost opportunity and gives added emphasis to the connections between Fitzgerald's own life and the fictional work. At the end of the story Andy returns to Tarleton and, with Ailie, revisits the now desolate site of the abandoned Army camp. Andy wanders there, "in the knee-deep underbrush, looking for my youth in a clapboard or a strip of roofing or a rusty tomato can," another of Fitzgerald's heroes wondering what became of his youthful dreams and promise.

"BABYLON REVISITED"

First published: 1931 (collected in *Babylon Revisited, and Other Stories*, 1960)
Type of work: Short story

A reformed alcoholic tries to regain his daughter and start life anew, but his efforts are undermined by his past.

Charlie Wales, the central character of "Babylon Revisited," is a man who lived high and wildly in Paris during the late 1920's and then lost everything with the Great Depression, including his wife and daughter. After the death of his wife—perhaps hastened when, in a drunken rage, he locked her out of their apartment during a snowstorm—Charlie had given guardianship of his daughter, Honoria, to his sister-in-law.

When the story opens, Charlie has returned to Paris to regain Honoria. Just when it seems he has convinced his suspicious relatives that he is indeed reformed, Charlie has his hopes dashed by the unexpected and disastrous arrival of two drinking companions from the bad old days. At the story's end Charlie maintains his sobriety, determined to continue in his attempts to regain his daughter.

Once again, Fitzgerald's theme is the waste of promise, fueled by the harmful effects of alcoholic

indulgence. In this story, the theme is made explicit as Charlie comes to realize the meaning of the word "dissipate": "to dissipate into thin air; to make nothing out of something." Paris, the place where this wasting has taken place, is for Charlie a Babylon, a city of wasting—not only materially but morally and spiritually as well. Wales has repaired some of the effects of that dissipation—he has partially restored his finances and is once again sober—but the story ends with both Charlie and the reader uncertain if the most tragic loss can be restored and father and daughter reunited.

The character of Charlie Wales is an important part of "Babylon Revisited," because he is believable and sympathetic, a fully rounded individual who is presented through suggestion and inference, dialogue and reference. As the story moves in and out of Charlie's present and past, the reader comes to understand more than is openly told, largely through Fitzgerald's selection of details.

Fitzgerald's style in "Babylon Revisited" is remarkable: In place of the lush, romantic prose of earlier stories such as "The Diamond as Big as the Ritz," he uses a spare, careful technique that conveys intense and often painful emotions through understatement and implication. The language is supple and powerful, so graceful that the reader is almost unaware of it, but a close and attentive study shows that Fitzgerald has achieved a masterpiece of the modern short story.

SUMMARY

Fitzgerald was an acute social observer and an incomparable stylist. His central concern was with the individual whose promise is destroyed by an uncaring or hostile world, a destruction made possible by some inherent flaw in an otherwise noble nature. Fitzgerald's writings all have this viewpoint, which can best be described as romantic moralism.

Immensely popular with his first novel, highly successful with his short stories, and critically acclaimed for his masterpiece, *The Great Gatsby*, Fitzgerald has come to be recognized as one of American literature's premier authors and the creator of some of its most memorable and individual characters. Although his work is clearly a product of and a reflection of its time, Fitzgerald's best efforts transcend that specific period to become universal.

Michael Witkoski

BIBLIOGRAPHY

By the Author

SHORT FICTION:
Flappers and Philosophers, 1920
Tales of the Jazz Age, 1922
All the Sad Young Men, 1926
Taps at Reveille, 1935
The Stories of F. Scott Fitzgerald, 1951
Babylon Revisited, and Other Stories, 1960
The Pat Hobby Stories, 1962
The Apprentice Fiction of F. Scott Fitzgerald, 1907-1917, 1965
The Basil and Josephine Stories, 1973
Bits of Paradise, 1974
The Price Was High: The Last Uncollected Stories of F. Scott Fitzgerald, 1979
The Short Stories of F. Scott Fitzgerald, 1989 (Matthew J. Bruccoli, editor)
Before Gatsby: The First Twenty-six Stories, 2001 (Bruccoli, editor)

LONG FICTION:
This Side of Paradise, 1920
The Beautiful and Damned, 1922
The Great Gatsby, 1925
Tender Is the Night, 1934
The Last Tycoon, 1941

DRAMA:
The Vegetable: Or, From President to Postman, pb. 1923

NONFICTION:
The Crack-Up, 1945
The Letters of F. Scott Fitzgerald, 1963
Letters to His Daughter, 1965
Thoughtbook of Francis Scott Fitzgerald, 1965
Dear Scott/Dear Max: The Fitzgerald-Perkins Correspondence, 1971
As Ever, Scott Fitzgerald, 1972
F. Scott Fitzgerald's Ledger, 1972
The Notebooks of F. Scott Fitzgerald, 1978
A Life in Letters, 1994 (Matthew J. Bruccoli, editor)
F. Scott Fitzgerald on Authorship, 1996
Dear Scott, Dearest Zelda: The Love Letters of F. Scott and Zelda Fitzgerald, 2002 (Jackson R. Bryer and Cathy W. Barks, editors)

MISCELLANEOUS:
Afternoon of an Author: A Selection of Uncollected Stories and Essays, 1958
F. Scott Fitzgerald: The Princeton Years, Selected Writings, 1914-1920, 1996 (Chip Deffaa, editor)
Conversations with F. Scott Fitzgerald, 2005 (Matthew J. Bruccoli and Judith S. Baughman, editors)

DISCUSSION TOPICS

- The style of *This Side of Paradise* is described as "highly rhetorical." What does this phrase mean? Is it a strength or a weakness?

- What is the significance of the "green light" in *The Great Gatsby*?

- Is F. Scott Fitzgerald's habit of depicting woman as the cause of man's downfall a sexist weakness?

- Consider Nick Carraway as an observer-narrator. How do his motives and relationship to the other characters differ from George Willard's in Sherwood Anderson's *Winesburg, Ohio* (1919)?

- The setting of *The Great Gatsby* seems quaint and remote by modern-day terms, yet the novel remains popular in the twenty-first century. How do you account for its capacity to outlive the era that it depicts?

- Fitzgerald ends "Babylon Revisited" without a clear-cut resolution of the situation. What are the potential denouements? Does Fitzgerald tip the balance in favor of one of them?

About the Author

Berman, Ronald. *Fitzgerald, Hemingway, and the Twenties.* Tuscaloosa: University of Alabama Press, 2001.

_____. *"The Great Gatsby" and Fitzgerald's World of Ideas.* Tuscaloosa: University of Alabama Press, 1997.

Bloom, Harold, ed. *Jay Gatsby.* Philadelphia: Chelsea House, 2004.

Bruccoli, Matthew J., ed. *New Essays on "The Great Gatsby."* Cambridge, England: Cambridge University Press, 1985.

_____. *Some Sort of Epic Grandeur.* New York: Harcourt Brace Jovanovich, 1981.

Curnutt, Kirk, ed. *A Historical Guide to F. Scott Fitzgerald.* New York: Oxford University Press, 2004.

Eble, Kenneth. *F. Scott Fitzgerald.* Rev. ed. Boston: Twayne, 1977.

Gale, Robert L. *An F. Scott Fitzgerald Encyclopedia.* Westport, Conn.: Greenwood Press, 1998.

Gross, Dalton, and MaryJean Gross. *Understanding "The Great Gatsby": A Student Casebook to Issues, Sources, and Historical Documents.* Westport, Conn.: Greenwood Press, 1998.

Kuehl, John. *F. Scott Fitzgerald: A Study of the Short Fiction.* Boston: Twayne, 1991.

Lee, A. Robert, ed. *Scott Fitzgerald: The Promises of Life.* New York: St. Martin's Press, 1989.

Meyers, Jeffrey. *Scott Fitzgerald: A Biography.* New York: HarperCollins, 1994.

Miller, James E., Jr. *F. Scott Fitzgerald: His Art and His Technique.* New York: New York University Press, 1964.

Stanley, Linda C. *The Foreign Critical Reputation of F. Scott Fitzgerald, 1980-2000: An Analysis and Annotated Bibliography.* Westport, Conn.: Praeger, 2004.

Tate, Mary Jo. *F. Scott Fitzgerald A to Z: The Essential Reference to His Life and Work.* New York: Facts On File, 1998.

Taylor, Kendall. *Sometimes Madness Is Wisdom: Zelda and Scott Fitzgerald, A Marriage.* New York: Ballantine, 2001.

RICHARD FORD

Born: Jackson, Mississippi
February 16, 1944

As a leading novelist and short-story writer, Ford has become a model in narrative style and structure for other American writers.

James Hamilton

BIOGRAPHY

Richard Ford was born February 16, 1944, in Jackson, Mississippi, shortly after his parents, Parker Carrol Ford and Edna Akin Ford, moved there from Arkansas. By the time Ford graduated from high school, his father had died suddenly of a heart attack, and his mother decided to return with her son to Arkansas. The conditions of his youth—growing up in the Deep South as an only child, living alone with his widowed mother—contributed much to the tone and content of the fiction he was to write in later years. His essay "My Mother, in Memory" (1987), reflects on the events of his early years and on the influence of his relationship with his parents.

After Ford received his B.A. in 1966 from Michigan State University, he worked for a year as a writer for a sports magazine, an occupation that was to influence his novel *The Sportswriter* (1986). It was two years after his graduation that he determined to abandon his intention to be a lawyer and to become a writer instead. The same year, he married Kristina Hensley, a fellow student at Michigan State who subsequently became a professor of urban affairs and political science as well as a planner for several American cities. In 1970, Ford earned an M.F.A. from the University of California, Irvine,

where he studied creative writing with novelists Oakley Hall and E. L. Doctorow. He taught for one year at the University of Michigan before the publication of *A Piece of My Heart* (1976), his first novel.

In 1979 and 1980, Ford held a position as a lecturer at Williams College, followed by two years as a lecturer and George Perkins Fellow in Humanities at Princeton University, where he completed *The Ultimate Good Luck* (1981). This second novel, set in Mexico, exemplifies his tendency to use a variety of locales and represents his turning away from the Southern environment of his childhood.

Though Ford began to direct serious attention to the short story only with "Going to the Dogs" (1979), he wrote his first short story, never published, when he was seventeen. From 1979 to 1986, he spent much of his time writing short works of fiction, although he was also at work on a third novel. *The Sportswriter* represents yet another departure in setting, in type of protagonist, and in some of its themes. This novel brought him wide recognition both in the United States and abroad as a major fiction writer. The next year, the stories he had written in the 1980's were published in the collection *Rock Springs* (1987). His fourth novel, *Wildlife* (1990), is his first with a teenage protagonist and thus shows the influence of his short stories, in many of which a young man is the central figure.

In addition to writing fiction, Ford has produced a number of essays that comment on the craft of writing, on other authors, on members of his family, on sports and hunting, and on a variety of other topics ranging from motorcycles to rock musicians to friendship. In the 1990's, the range of his mastery of genres was indicated by his publication of the short story "Jealous" (1992), his novella,

The Womanizer (1992; also published in *Women with Men*, 1997), and personal and critical essays in several periodicals.

Ford has lived with his wife in a variety of locales, including New York, New Jersey, Rhode Island, rural Mississippi, Montana, Louisiana, and Maine, and this geographical flexibility is reflected in his fiction.

ANALYSIS

Ford's theory of fiction arises from what the poet Wallace Stevens called the "rage for order." Ford sees life as essentially chaotic and the writing of fiction as the act of taking the often disordered material of experience and creating a new setting, atmosphere, and order for it. His discontent with the way life is, he states, leads him to attempt to find an alternative. Thus, he says, fiction has moral implications because it implies hope of a better future, a better existence. The moral element of his work involves his concern with the proper responses to certain situations, the good or evil of a character's deeds, and a concern for how those deeds will shape a character's future. His final test for good art concerns the idea of unification, a belief that somehow the novel or the story may restore order to an otherwise chaotic and destructive pattern of existence. Although he professes a distrust of ambiguity, the endings of his works, like those of Nathaniel Hawthorne and Henry James, may lead two equally sensitive readers to two contrasting interpretations of the actions and responses of the characters.

While Ford has denied any religious implications or unified view of the world in his works, more than one critic has insisted that such elements are to be found there. Certainly, people in his novels and stories ponder more than most fictional characters the ethical significance of their acts and the acts of others. In contrast to those contemporary authors who believe in no ideal existence beyond the immediate reality, Ford portrays people who, in the face of the slings and arrows of outrageous fortune, find hope for the future, a belief in love, and a recognition of the importance of human relationships.

In addition, certain recurrent themes, optimistic in their tone despite the stark environment and the often disturbing nature of the action, are to be read in Ford's work. There is a continuing concern with loyalty among people, with courage, and with the ability to accept whatever fate hands one, however hard it may be. In this respect, Ford's work seems similar to that of Ernest Hemingway, although it is finally more optimistic.

Ford has insisted that "drama arises from individuals attempting to accommodate to an environment or to a place where they want to be, need to be, or must be." This relationship of characters and setting is reflected in work after work of Ford's. His protagonists often are placed in some alien environment in which they attempt to find an identity as well as a sense of belonging. In *A Piece of My Heart*, for example, the two protagonists, Robard Hewes and Sam Newel, men from different backgrounds and with different personalities, find themselves for two quite different reasons living on an uncharted island in the Mississippi River. Out of the conflict between the two men and their new environment, both the drama of the story and the philosophical theme develop.

Despite the fact that only one of his novels and a few of his stories have southern settings, the influence of the region of his birth on Ford's work is apparent in several elements: a belief in the significance of place in life and fiction, a particular kind of moral vision, and the issues and themes he has chosen to employ. He has commented on more than one occasion that, despite the variety of his residences through the years, he still considers himself a Mississippian and likes southerners for a variety of reasons, a major one being that they often speak in a way that does not truly reflect their minds. The discrepancy between a character's words and his actions, a major concern of many twentieth century authors, is also evident in much of his fiction.

Ford's interest in character is as wide-ranging as his use of settings. In *A Piece of My Heart*, for example, Sam Newel is a law-school graduate who is trying to make sense of his life, while Robard Hewes is a laborer drawn to the new environment by his lust for a young woman. *The Sportswriter*'s protagonist, Frank Bascombe, on the other hand, is established in an occupation; despite the earlier death of a son and his subsequent divorce, he manages to enjoy life, though he senses that something is missing. In marked contrast, *The Ultimate Good Luck* has a protagonist who finds himself in an alien environment, Mexico, trying to effect the release of his brother-in-law, who has been imprisoned for drug dealing.

Ford's fascination with Sherwood Anderson's short stories, one of the major influences on his work, grew out of his love of two Anderson works, "I Want to Know Why" and "I'm a Fool." In both stories, young men endeavor to come to terms with growing up and discovering the many confusing facts of life. Most Ford stories and novels could be subtitled "I Want to Know Why," for his characters are always engaged in an attempt to find answers to many questions: What are human beings? What is their purpose? What is their place? What should they do? How can they find direction for their lives?

Much of the power of Ford's work lies in his remarkable control of style. In an era when many fiction writers seem unconcerned about the exact meaning of words, Ford's prose employs diction as exact as Hemingway's, a finely tuned use of language that often startles with its force. Ford has several times expressed in interviews and articles his desire to avoid irony, that is, never to speak indirectly but to attack his subject head-on, using concrete words to evoke images that are immediately identifiable and not subject to misinterpretation. The reader finishes a Ford novel with the sense of having been led deep into the consciousness of a character, sometimes quite different from the reader, and of knowing that character as intimately as a family member, a friend, or one's own self.

THE SPORTSWRITER

First published: 1986
Type of work: Novel

A decent, caring man moves through the confusing events of his life searching for the right action, the right attitude, the haven of rest.

The Sportswriter is one of Ford's most acclaimed novels, the one that firmly established him as a major American writer. Ford asserts that the novel was written in answer to his wife's question, "Why don't you write a book about someone happy?" His intention was to produce a protagonist without irony who always says what he believes. Frank Bascombe is a failed novelist turned sportswriter, which he

thinks of as not "a real profession but more of an agreeable frame of mind, a way of going about things rather than things you exactly do or know."

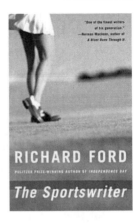

The "sport" of this novel is life itself, with the games grown-up boys play employed as metaphors for actions and ideas much more important than weekend pursuits in stadiums and gymnasiums. *The Sportswriter* bears some resemblance to Walker Percy's Christian existential fiction, although Ford denies any religious intention. Frank is an "anticipator" who dwells in the realm of possibilities, a typical trait of southerners, according to Percy. Frank is also a man who values life for its own sake, despite the despair that is part of it, and who puts a premium on mystery, that element of life one cannot explain. Though he is a decent man, his life would be judged by many standards to be a failure: His marriage ended in divorce, his current love affair is on the rocks, two previous careers have been unsuccessful, and his choice of sportswriting as a substitute is almost accidental.

Nevertheless, Frank has never lost the ability to hope: "I've always thought of myself as a type of human weak link, working against odds and fate," he says, "and I'm not about to give up on myself." The death of one of his three children has left him vulnerable but never pathetic. He is a modern antihero, so credible that it is easy to empathize with him and almost impossible not to sympathize with his plight.

This is a novel of character rather than action; there is a suicide and a humorous scene in which Frank is briefly trapped in an outdoor phone booth that is attacked by a young man in a car, but the action is generally subdued. Ford's portrayal of characters is grounded in a keen perception of human weaknesses and virtues. *The Sportswriter* is a philosophical novel that comments on life in general and modern American life in particular. The style is subtle, often poetic, filled with aphoristic statements, as when Frank states, "Writers—all writers—need to belong. Only for real writers, unfortunately, their club is a club with just one member."

ROCK SPRINGS

First published: 1987
Type of work: Short stories

The ten short stories in Rock Springs *portray protagonists attempting to understand themselves and their relationship to the often hostile environments in which they dwell.*

Rock Springs is a collection of stories Ford wrote during the 1980's. There are no heroes in the traditional sense in these short works, nor are there villains. Some readers might be inclined to label the characters "victims," for certainly the environment and the influence of other people determine the characters' actions, often for the worse. Yet Ford should not be confused with the naturalistic authors of the early 1900's who portrayed hapless human specimens under a microscope.

Though the situations in which characters find themselves seem, for the most part, not of their own making, rather than being dehumanized or victimized, they become more credible and sympathetic. Many are loners struggling to find some meaning in limited lives lived out against harsh environments. In the title story, Earl, the narrator, is a petty criminal fleeing bad-check charges in Montana with his girlfriend and his daughter. As his troubles mount—his car breaks down and his girlfriend decides to leave him—he experiences a self-revelation. He comes to see himself as a victim of happenstance, unable to take charge of his life: "There was always a gap between my plan and what happened, and I only responded to things as they came along and hoped I wouldn't get in trouble." Like many Ford stories, "Rock Springs" concludes as it begins, with a question that remains unanswered.

Like several protagonists in the stories, Les, the narrator of "Communist," is a teenager. On an illegal expedition to hunt migrating Siberian geese with his mother, Aileen, and her friend Glen, he acquires a painful truth about life and himself. When Glen decides to leave a wounded bird to die, Aileen rejects him, explaining her action by asserting, "We have to keep civilization alive somehow." Years later, remembering the incident, Les thinks, "A light can go out in the heart. All this happened

years ago, but I can still feel now how sad and remote the world was to me." With "Communist," Ford perfected the type of ending that is a hallmark of his stories: The protagonist analyzes past events because, like Sherwood Anderson's character, he wants to know why. Anderson's influence is clearly evident in *Rock Springs*, and Ford has often expressed admiration for Anderson's plain diction and his fondness for simple American people. All these elements permeate Ford's own fiction in his choice of characters and the style of his narration.

In *Rock Springs*, Ford reveals hopes and desires of characters whose limited lives belie their depth of feeling and capacity for love. Most of the endings are, to some degree, positive, for they involve hope on the part of characters that some understanding of reality is possible. No matter how insignificant their lives and acts appear on the surface, Ford makes readers observe, listen, and identify with these people. He believes that a short story should treat readers to language, make them forget their problems, and give "order to the previously unordered for the purpose of making beauty and clarity anew."

WILDLIFE

First published: 1990
Type of work: Novel

Sixteen-year-old Joe, the narrator, witnesses the breakup of his parents' marriage and attempts to understand them, himself, and the purpose of his existence.

The wide-open spaces, the mountains, and the forest fires in *Wildlife* serve not only as backdrops and symbols but also as catalysts for the action of the novel. The lives of four main characters—Joe Brinson, his parents, and the man with whom his mother has an affair—are shaped by their environment. The action occurs in 1961 in Great Falls, Montana, which for Joe is "a town that was not my home and never would be." This sense of disorientation and alienation is central to the message of Ford's novel.

Wildlife is a rite-of-passage novel in which Joe, remembering events that occurred when he was sixteen, confronts life, death, change, and truth. His father, who moved the family to Montana during an oil boom in hopes of bettering their lot, finds a job fighting fires in the mountains. During his absence, Joe's mother briefly takes a lover. In an important passage, Joe considers the average youth's ignorance of his parents, "which can save you from becoming an adult too early." On the other hand, he believes that shielding oneself is a mistake, "since what's lost is the truth of your parents' life and what you should think about it, and beyond that, how you should estimate the world you are about to live in."

Faced with his mother's infidelity and his father's rage, Joe must make choices that most young people are spared. The significance of decision making in this novel relates Ford's work to the existential belief that human beings create their identities through the choices they make. Without the aid of any authority, Joe alone must decide for himself, and his decision may be the wrong one, may even be fatal. His isolation is intensified by the mobility of his family and his consequent lack of longtime friends or other relatives in whom to confide. Alone, he faces unavoidable change, and with his new knowledge, he suffers the inevitable "fall" from the grace of childhood. Joe's strength derives from what his mother terms "inquiring intelligence." "Everything will always surprise you," she tells him, and when he has faced his dilemmas and acted, perhaps wisely, perhaps not, he seems well on the way to shaping a meaningful life for himself.

In *Wildlife*, Ford strongly evokes the troubled and puzzling teenage years of a boy on the border of maturity. With a spare, carefully shaped prose style that reflects the setting of the action and the quality of the problems and choices Joe faces, Ford creates a character and situations with which many young people can, no doubt, identify.

INDEPENDENCE DAY

First published: 1995
Type of work: Novel

As Frank Bascombe, who was also the protagonist of The Sportswriter, *moves toward the millenium, he is involved in the age-old search of reestablishing communication between himself and his son and thereby finding meaning in his life.*

Independence Day marks a new stage of the career of Richard Ford, winning, as it did, both the Pulitzer Prize and the PEN/Faulkner Award for Fiction. On the surface, *Independence Day* is deceptively simple: A divorced father takes his son on a trip to several sports halls of fame, the son suffers eye damage that may be permanent, and the father returns home to ponder his experiences. In reality, the novel is a re-creation of an age-old mythic quest. In this case, it is the establishment of communication between the father and son and an internal journey on the part of the protagonist to find himself, confront his demons, and move into a new phase of his life. Bascombe, the sportswriter of the book by that name, has become a real estate agent. Nearing fifty years of age, he has entered a period of life that he refers to as "the Existence Period," in which he measures every act, every meeting with another person, every idea in his mind as if life depended upon it. He is a good man, an affable man, although he might seem to many as a failure: He is divorced, his children live with his former wife, and he has moved from career to career without any marked sign of progress in his life.

Like Walker Percy's Binx Bolling in *The Moviegoer* (1961) and John Updike's Rabbit Angstrom, Frank is an existential protagonist, seeking to find meaning in his life in a world that seems meaningless. Yet unlike those characters, Frank is an agnostic, finding no solace in any religious belief. He ponders the fact that human beings are generally unhappy, without knowing why, and that free will is restricted to the degree that people "can live with the consequences" of their deeds. In the Existence phase of his life, Frank believes that everything is "limited or at least underwritten by" the simple fact of existence. Because all that human beings

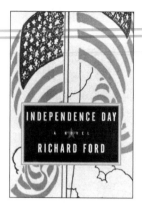

know is subject to change and finally destruction, he believes that human actions can be judged only by how practical they are and what their consequences may be. Whatever his situation, Frank believes, a man must persist, shedding from his life that which is nonessential, relying on "common sense, resilience, good cheer."

As a realistic real estate agent, Frank has jettisoned his earlier belief that places are endowed with metaphysical qualities; yet he adopts the optimism of Ralph Waldo Emerson in his relationship with people and endeavors to practice Emerson's beliefs in self-knowledge and self-reliance. Among other things, then, this book is about individual independence—what it means, what its value is, and what obligations come with it. The human is independent because he has no higher power on which to depend, and that is his tragedy; however, that loss has set him free to seek his true self and assert it in his actions, and that can be his triumph, limited though it may be.

The novel is constructed around numerous contrasts, both stylistic and thematic. In contrast to many of his contemporary novelists, Ford expresses, through his protagonist, deep emotions and sentiments, such as the meaning of the Fourth of July as "an observance of human possibility." Frank can embrace liberal causes with conviction, while at the same time pointing out the problems which he believes that liberalism has produced in the United States. Frank (one may assume, like his creator) is not constrained by the need to be "politically correct," but rather looks at the world clearly and rationally, reserving his pity for the tenuous position of humanity in general rather than expending it on the individual.

By the conclusion of *Independence Day*, Frank Bascombe is perhaps no nearer to establishing any degree of communication with his son Paul, who has been wounded in their quest for a meaningful relationship. On the other hand, as a result of the major crisis that marred their vacation, Frank has experienced a number of epiphanies that have forced him out of "the Existence Period" into what he terms "the Permanent Period," in which he perceives new meaning for the word "independence" and abandons many of those concepts by which he has lived. This new, more optimistic phase he views as "that long, stretching-out time when my dreams would have mystery like any ordinary person's" and something better than what is will become possible. He believes that he may marry again, that his son Paul may come to live with him—in short, that life will go on and even improve. In this period, which he views as the final one that will endure until death "hauls me off to oblivion," his identity will be established by his words and deeds, both for himself and for others.

This transformation, while not positing any belief in a Supreme Being or anything beyond this life, seems a step toward a more positive view of life, and the phases through which Frank has moved—as the "anticipator" in *The Sportswriter* to the inhabitant of the realm of existence, and finally to "the Permanent Period"—bears a marked resemblance to the movements of the protagonists of the novels of Percy and Updike. Ford is a realist, and therefore offers no pat solutions to the problems of his characters, but in Frank Bascombe's life and the changes in his attitudes, the reader can trace a pattern that seems to imply the possibility of a better life to come.

WOMEN WITH MEN: THREE STORIES

First published: 1997
Type of work: Two novellas and one long story

Three men, typical Ford protagonists, basically good and reliable but confused in the face of events they cannot control, learn lessons about life and love.

Although referred to in its subtitle as stories, *Women with Men* is in fact a collection of two novellas and one long story. That Ford refers to the works as stories is significant, for he has shown interest in the long story as a separate genre of literature.

The first novella in this volume, *The Womanizer,*

belongs in the long tradition of "Americans in Paris" literature produced by numerous fiction writers in the nineteenth century and the 1920's. It is ironically named, since the protagonist, Martin Austin, has been "temporarily distracted" by some women far from his home but seems for the most part unsuccessful in his relationships with the opposite sex. Although he loves his wife, Barbara, while in France he attempts to initiate a relationship with a Frenchwoman, Josephine Belliard, hoping to establish some connection that transcends sexuality. His attempts end in confusion and a minor scandal, and the trip he had looked forward to as "romantic," a chance to open himself to new possibilities, turns out to be the opposite. Like other Ford protagonists, he wants to do good but fails to do so during a crisis involving Leo, Josephine's young son.

Martin's wife, who is "systematically optimistic," exhibiting what he thinks of as the American attitude toward life, accuses him of being distant and unapproachable because "he took himself for granted." Determined to make the rest of his life "as eventful and important" as what had passed, Martin feels a strong sense of freedom, a belief that his life is entirely under his control, and he is convinced that, although one must live with one's mistakes, nevertheless "all is potential." His temporary loss of Josephine's son, left in his care, and the ensuing police probe leaves him feeling that he had lost "his newly found freedom" and the chance for something new.

The short story "Jealous" is narrated by Larry, who was nineteen at the time of the events he is recalling. Like Martin Austin in *The Womanizer*, he becomes involved in events over which he has no control, although his instinct is to do good whenever possible. On their way for a Thanksgiving visit with Larry's mother, who is estranged from his father, Larry and his Aunt Doris wait for their train in a bar in a small Montana town. There they witness the police killing of a local Indian suspected of murdering his wife. Ironically, Larry has thought of a bar as having "a sense of something expected that stayed alive inside them even if nothing ever happened there at all."

Like the protagonists in the other two works in this volume, Larry seems more acted upon than acting. He is keenly aware of what goes around him but seems unable to participate in it more than

as an observer; indeed, his only self-initiated action in the story is to buy his mother a watch as a gift. When his aunt embraces him in a way that might be considered potentially sexual, he simply acquiesces and listens without comment to her confession about a lesbian relationship in which she was involved. He seems to agree with Doris's statement that, "It's not what happens, it's what you do with what happens." As his aunt sleeps on the train, he thinks that, "Maybe for the first time in my life, I felt calm."

The second novella, *Occidentals*, again set in Paris, hinges on the various meanings of the word "translation." Charley Matthews, a professor with one unsuccessful novel to his credit, is in Paris with a former student in one of his adult education classes, Helen Carmichael, to meet the woman scheduled to translate his book into French, Madame Grenelle. Estranged from his wife, Penny, and his daughter, Leila, he feels that he has always been "the center of things," but now he wants to lose himself in whatever happens without being central to events, and Helen's illness—she is a cancer survivor—gives him that opportunity. His beliefs reflect the idea of the Danish philosopher Søren Kierkegaard that to achieve meaning in life, one must move from the aesthetic phase, where one is concerned only with himself, to the moral phase, where he cares for others. Charley professes to believe in things improving, and by the end of his experiences in Paris, he feels that his own life "is changing for the better."

The translation of his novel, *Predicament*, provides the major motif for this work. He ponders the importance of "having a translator," and Helen tells him, "You're hoping to translate yourself now," after he says that he is in search of "a new life." Later, however, he ponders the possibility that perhaps he may somehow become (or be translated into) what happens to him in Paris. Near the conclusion of the story, after Helen's suicide, Charley finally meets Madame Grenelle, who informs him that sometimes an author does not truly understand his book until it had been translated. Ultimately, he feels that he is moving into a new phase as a result of what he has experienced.

SUMMARY

Ford's philosophy of art involves his belief that the creative artist is driven to create order in a world that is essentially chaotic. The writing of fiction is, for him, an act of finding meaning in events that otherwise merely confound the participant and the observer.

Dealing with characters who are usually out of the mainstream of American life, writing in a language controlled and even subdued, Ford evokes sympathy from his readers, who must recognize, in the painful and persistent questionings of his protagonists, their own attempts to understand life. Ford's novels and stories, centered on events that are often depressing in nature, nevertheless celebrate the persistence of the human longing to be a part of the world and to find ultimate answers.

W. Kenneth Holditch

BIBLIOGRAPHY

By the Author

LONG FICTION:
A Piece of My Heart, 1976
The Ultimate Good Luck, 1981
The Sportswriter, 1986
Wildlife, 1990
Independence Day, 1995

SHORT FICTION:
Rock Springs, 1987
Women with Men: Three Stories, 1997
A Multitude of Sins, 2001
Vintage Ford, 2003

NONFICTION:
Good Raymond, 1998

EDITED TEXTS:
The Granta Book of the American Short Story, 1992
The Essential Tales of Chekhov, 1998
The Granta Book of the American Long Story, 1998

DISCUSSION TOPICS

- How do the settings of Richard Ford's fiction relate to the themes of his short stories and the novels?

- Comment on the multiple meanings of the title *Independence Day*.

- Consider the desire for order as exhibited in Ford's novels *The Sportswriter*, *Wildlife*, and *Independence Day*.

- Ford's narrators and/or protagonists fall generally into two categories, young men or middle-aged men. Compare his portrayal of the points of view between one character from each work; for example, compare the narrator of *Wildlife* to Frank Bascombe in *The Sportswriter* or *Independence Day*.

- Although Ford's stories and novels are considered by many critics to be pessimistic in their outlook, there are optimistic elements in the endings of some of these works. Comment on one or two that exhibit this view.

- Comment on the ambiguity in the ending of one or more of Ford's stories or novels.

- Ford acknowledges Sherwood Anderson as a major influence on his work and cites specifically "I'm a Fool" and "I Want to Know Why." Comment on how "I Want to Know Why" would be an appropriate title for several of Ford's works of fiction.

- Discuss self-analysis as a major element of various Ford characters.

About the Author

Ford, Richard. "What a Sea of Stories Tell Me." *The New York Times Book Review*, October 21, 1990, 1, 32-34.
Gray, Paul. "Trials of a Transient Household." *Time* 135 (June 4, 1990): 86.
Guagliardo, Huey, ed. *Conversations with Richard Ford*. Jackson: University Press of Mississippi, 2001.
_____. *Perspectives on Richard Ford*. Jackson: University Press of Mississippi, 2001.
Prescott, Peter. "I Dreamed Our House Caught Fire." *Newsweek* 115 (June 11, 1990): 64.
Seabrook, John, and Maude Schuyler Clay. "Of Bird Dogs and Tall Tales." *Interview* 19 (May, 1989): 104-107.
Weber, Bruce. "Richard Ford's Uncommon Characters." *The New York Times Magazine* 137 (April 10, 1988): 50-51, 59-65.

BENJAMIN FRANKLIN

Born: Boston, Massachusetts
January 17, 1706
Died: Philadelphia, Pennsylvania
April 17, 1790

Franklin's writings attest his intellect: He epitomizes the Age of Reason in his ability to take philosophical ideas and formulate them into prose regarding a practical, efficient, yet beneficent lifestyle.

Library of Congress

BIOGRAPHY

Benjamin Franklin was born in Boston, Massachusetts, on January 17, 1706, to Josiah and Abiah Folger Franklin. His father, a candle and soap maker, was a devout Puritan who had left England for the American colonies during the religious upheavals of the seventeenth century. Benjamin was the tenth son of a family of sixteen. (Josiah had seven children by his first wife, who died about 1700.) The elder Franklin encouraged Benjamin to pursue the ministry. Unfortunately, economic circumstances forced Josiah to abandon that idea; young Benjamin was not even able to attend grammar school. He asked his father for permission to go to sea.

Josiah compromised by allowing Benjamin to become an apprentice to his older brother James, a successful printer, who operated a thriving business as publisher of a newspaper, the *New England Courant.* Under James's tutelage, Benjamin acquired great skill in the trade and furthered his love of books and learning through a number of James's customers. Eventually, Franklin took up the pen himself, and in 1722, James published his sixteen-year-old brother's fourteen satirical "Do Good" essays, modeled, in part, on Joseph Addison and Richard Steele's London periodical *The Spectator.*

Franklin adopted a pseudonym, as was the custom of the day, of "Silence Do Good," a young widow, who offered "her" opinion on a variety of topics, including fashion, religion, temperance, and education. Most scholars point to these essays as the genesis of Franklin's literary career; in fact, many see the essays as the finest literature to be found in early eighteenth century New England.

In spite of this success, Franklin had a serious disagreement with his brother over the terms of his indenture and in 1723 left Boston for Philadelphia. After an unproductive stint as a journeyman printer, Franklin sailed for London and worked as a typesetter for one of London's finest printing houses. It was there that he developed his intellectual acumen and published numerous pamphlet essays, in his own name, on religious and philosophical controversies of the day.

Returning to Philadelphia in 1726, Franklin was immediately hired as a print shop manager. He also formed a literary and social club, called the Junto, in which members wrote essays to share with all members of the group. Franklin's organizational efforts became the impetus for America's first circulating library, which began operation as the Library Company of Philadelphia in 1731.

Franklin's business acumen, bolstered by a strong penchant for honesty, enabled him to buy out the newspaper of his first Philadelphia employer in 1729 and purchase his own business. His new paper, *The Pennsylvania Gazette,* frequently graced by Franklin's intuitive essays, such as "A Scolding Wife," became immensely popular. In 1732, after years of planning, Franklin launched his own almanac, *Poor Richard's Almanack,* loosely based on a version his brother James had begun in Boston a few years earlier. Not only did *Poor Richard's Almanack* offer calendars, weather forecasts, and astronomical figures, as all almanacs do, but it also included the wise and pithy sayings for which Franklin is known. This "extra" made *Poor Richard's Almanack* a success in Pennsylvania and throughout the colonies, assuring Franklin's financial success.

Poor Richard's Almanack became the forum for many of Franklin's greatest literary successes and afforded him the opportunity to explore other areas that interested him, specifically science and public service. He was appointed clerk of the Pennsylvania Assembly and Philadelphia postmaster. Franklin proposed a "Military Defense Association" to protect Philadelphia from French and Spanish privateers roaming near the mouth of the Delaware River, incurring the wrath of pacifist Quakers in the colony. By the late 1740's, Franklin was particularly interested in electricity and its uses, and he described his famous kite experiment in detail in *Experiments and Observations on Electricity* (1751).

In 1757, Franklin was appointed envoy to England by the assembly, with the express purpose of settling a tax dispute between Pennsylvania and England. It was during this mission that Franklin first began to consider the debilitating system under which England's colonies found themselves. For the next fifteen years, Franklin published numerous pamphlets on English-colonial policies, many of which drew praise from Edmund Burke, a British statesman sympathetic toward the American colonies.

In 1771, on one of Franklin's diplomatic missions to London, he began his autobiography, which he titled "Memoirs." It begins as an extended letter to his son William, later colonial governor of New Jersey. Franklin had two children, Francis Folger and Sarah, from his common-law marriage of forty-four years to Deborah Reed. William was Franklin's illegitimate son and not only later a governor but also an outspoken Tory, hotly opposed to the revolutionary fervor of his father.

The remainder of Franklin's life involved serving the rebellious colonies and, later, the new republic. He served as delegate to the Second Continental Congress and on the committee that drafted the Declaration of Independence. In 1776,

Franklin was appointed minister to France and secured crucial support for the revolution from King Louis XVI. When the Revolutionary War ended in 1781, Franklin negotiated and signed the Treaty of Paris, ensuring the United States' independence. Franklin's last public activity was as a delegate to the Constitutional Convention in 1785. When he died in 1790, twenty thousand people attended his funeral, indicating his status as perhaps the greatest American of the eighteenth century.

ANALYSIS

Franklin achieved his intellectual and literary prowess in an era known for its philosophical advances. The eighteenth century is frequently cited as the beginning of the so-called modern era in philosophy. The century is known as the Enlightenment, or the Age of Reason, an ideal also found in the literature of the period, whether colonial, British, or Continental.

Two factors—or, more specifically, two intellectuals—epitomize this era: Sir Isaac Newton (1642-1727) and John Locke (1632-1704). Newton, an English mathematician and astronomer, made revolutionary scientific discoveries concerning light and gravitation and formulated the basis of modern calculus. His genius changed humankind's view of itself and its capabilities, showing that individuals can practically, rationally, and reasonably order their world for the benefit of all human beings. English philosopher Locke formulated these attitudes into his *Essay Concerning Human Understanding* (1689). Locke's basic thesis asserts that humans are born devoid of any preformed ideas or perceptions; in essence, a person is a tabula rasa, or "blank slate." Through experience, as perceived through the senses, people develop knowledge.

This theory, revised and amended by numerous philosophers of the century, casts doubt upon the previously accepted role of a divine being in the lives of humans. With the Christian idea of predestination called into question, a new attitude toward the Creator was developed to coincide with these new philosophical concepts. This "religion," termed Deism, espoused a belief in a "clockwork universe," in which the Creator provided the spark to create the world but then took an inactive role in its operation. Thus, people, through reason (not through a reliance on revelation), had the responsibility to arrange their own affairs, both personally and socially. Many American colonists adhered to this philosophy, most notably Thomas Jefferson, the radical revolutionary Thomas Paine, and Franklin. Early in his autobiography, Franklin concludes, after much study, that he has become "a thorough Deist."

Franklin, however, took his Enlightenment ideas a step further than most of his scholarly contemporaries. While the philosophers of the era were content to argue among themselves about the nature of humankind, Franklin believed in bringing these new philosophical and scientific ideas to the common people. His wit, coupled with his intellect, had an immediate appeal to his readership. His maxims and aphorisms in *Poor Richard's Almanack* made the colonists laugh but also revealed some of their foibles. Franklin's *Memoirs de la vie privée ecrits par lui-même*, (1791; *The Private Life of the Late Benjamin Franklin*, 1793; *Memoirs of the Life*, 1818; best known as *Autobiography*) is essentially a story of the application of rationality, practicality, and wise frugality to everyday life. Also inherent in Franklin's writings is the belief in the innate liberty of common people and the right of people to pursue their own destinies.

Many twentieth century intellectuals have taken exception to what they see as Franklin's materialism. German sociologist Max Weber's Marxist interpretation takes issue with the aims of Franklin's philosophy: "It [the earning of money] is thought of purely as an end in itself . . . [I]t appears entirely transcendental and absolutely irrational. Man is dominated by the making of money, by acquisition as the ultimate purpose of his life."

Such criticism has evolved not as much from Franklin and his writings as from inferences by readers who believe Franklin's philosophy justifies abject materialism. In fact, the true character of Benjamin Franklin reveals a man concerned about society and its treatment of humankind. His concern for public education, public safety, and public health made Philadelphia the most modern city not only in the colonies but also in the entire Western world. Franklin also refused to apply for patents for many of his inventions, thus making them more accessible to the public. Thus, Franklin's philosophy not only defined the American ideal but also defined the entire concept of human progress.

AUTOBIOGRAPHY

First published: Part 1, 1791; complete, 1818
Type of work: Autobiography

Franklin's Autobiography, *begun in 1771, presents his thoughts on practicality, frugality, and Enlightenment ideals.*

Franklin's *Autobiography* is divided into three parts, with a short addendum added a few months before Franklin's death in 1790. Each has a distinct thematic purpose and thus serves, in part, to make the work an important philosophical and historical tract. Part 1 is, in essence, an extended letter to Franklin's son William, written in England in 1771. It recounts Franklin's ancestry, his early days in Boston and Philadelphia, and his first journey to London in 1724. In fact, *Autobiography* is by far the best source for information on Franklin's early life. Part 1 ends with Franklin's marriage to Deborah and the beginning of his subscription library in late 1730, when he was twenty-four years old. Franklin ends part 1 with this explanatory note:

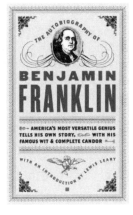

"Thus far was written with the Intention express'd in the Beginning and therefore contains several little family Anecdotes of no Importance to others. . . . The Affairs of the Revolution occasion'd the Interruption."

In spite of this rejoinder, there are important ideas developed in part 1. Franklin concludes that, after a youthful prank brought parental admonishment, that, "tho' I pleaded the Usefulness of the Work, mine convinc'd me that nothing was useful which was not honest." Part 1 also discusses Franklin's Deistic inclinations and his predilection for the art of disputation, which is similar to modern-day debate. Franklin thus believed in the mind's ability to use logic and reason over and above strong emotions. He comments:

Therefore I took a Delight in it [disputing], practic'd it continually and grew very artful and expert in drawing People of even superior Knowledge into Concessions the Consequences of which they did not foresee . . . and so obtaining Victories that neither myself nor my Cause always deserved.

One should not conclude that Franklin had a thoroughly optimistic view of human nature; too many whom Franklin called his friends took advantage of his good nature and left him with their debts or in embarrassing situations. Franklin, however, frequently blamed himself for allowing such developments—and others, such as his failure to pursue his courtship of Deborah actively after first meeting her. He terms such faults *errata*, a term that appears frequently in part 1.

Part 2 is less autobiographical and more philosophical than part 1 but no less revealing of Franklin's character. His Philadelphia friend Abel James encouraged Benjamin in 1782 to follow through on his idea of continuing the *Autobiography*, with the idea of depicting, in Franklin's words, "My Manner of acting to engage People in this and future Undertakings." The essence of part 2 can be found in Franklin's discussion of his attempts to achieve "moral perfection," "a bold and arduous project."

He devises a list of thirteen virtues, such as temperance, industry, moderation, and humility, and includes a precise definition for each. He then orders them in a vertical list, according to the theory that "the previous Acquisition of some might facilitate the Acquisition of certain others." A list of the days of the week composes the horizontal axis of the chart. Each of the virtues has its own separate chart, thus allowing Franklin to concentrate on a particular virtue for those seven days. Theoretically, at the end of thirteen weeks and after a religious maintenance of the charts, noting all transgressions at the appropriate points, moral perfection, an attribute attainable by "people in all religions," can be achieved.

This "Book of Virtues" is joined by Franklin's "Scheme of Order," an organizational plan to meet each workday, to complete his precise scheme of living. Was Franklin himself able to realize the edicts of moral perfection? He comments:

In Truth I found myself incorrigible with respect to Order; and now I am grown old, and my Mem-

ory bad, I feel very sensibly the want of it. But on the whole, tho' I never arrived at the Perfection I had been so ambitious of obtaining, but fell far short of it, yet I was by the Endeavour made a better and happier Man than I otherwise should have been, if I had not attempted it.

Part 3 does not have the literary value of the first two parts, but it is an intriguing recollection of Franklin's career as a public administrator. It particularly focuses on his efforts as Pennsylvania representative to British General William Braddock in a plan to lease civilian "waggons and baggage horses" to the British army in 1755. The plan nearly failed as a result of Braddock's arrogant contempt for the colonists. This incident had a profound effect on Franklin's future attitudes toward Great Britain.

POOR RICHARD'S ALMANACK

First published: 1732 for the year 1733; published in annual editions until 1757 for the year 1758
Type of work: Almanac and maxim book

This work, an American institution, contains proverbs, maxims, poems, and anecdotes on how to achieve moral perfection.

Essentially *Poor Richard's Almanack* embodies all the themes of the *Autobiography* in a witty and accessible format. Franklin's literary influence on *Poor Richard's Almanack* comes in a variety of forms: Proverbs, epigrams, rhymes, and aphorisms abound in each edition, usually interspersed among the calendars, weather forecasts, and astronomical charts. Each edition opens with a letter from the almanac's alleged author, one Richard Saunders (another Franklin pseudonym). He was "excessive poor" but fascinated with the heavens. Influenced by his wife, who could not bear "to sit spinning in

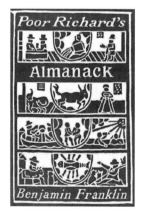

her Shift of Tow," he was compelled to publish his observations. Thus, Franklin presents to his readership "middling people" who had to work long and hard to save and prosper—one of their own, a man of humble means in search of moral perfection and its resultant prosperity.

Few of Franklin's sayings in *Poor Richard's Almanack* were original. He borrowed many of them from larger poetic works written within the preceding five or ten years; the poetic satirists Alexander Pope, John Dryden, and Jonathan Swift are heavily borrowed from but revised by Franklin to fit the needs and tastes of his readership. Many of these sayings have become oft-repeated foundations of American cultural heritage: "A true friend is the best possession"; "Don't misinform your Doctor nor your Lawyer"; "Don't throw stones at your neighbors, if your own windows are glass"; "Fish and visitors stink in 3 days"; "Haste makes waste"; "Eat to live, and not live to eat." Scholars point to the role that experience plays in the sayings found in *Poor Richard's Almanack*: It is not scholarly pursuits but wise, practical living that paves the road to virtue.

Although there were allusions to Deism ("Serving God is doing Good to Man, but praying is Thought an easier Service, and therefore more generally chosen") and the theories of Locke, Newton, and the essayist Francis Bacon, they were versed in language that indicated that such ideas could be acquired through experience—which includes, in the Lockean sense, observation. Thus, those colonists (and there were a great many) who did not have access to books could gain much contemporary philosophical and literary thought through Mr. Saunders's *Almanack*. Franklin's sayings, while not original in themselves, were revised to adapt to the emerging working class of the American colonies. Such an infusion of philosophical ideas dealing with equality helped give the American colonies the intellectual impetus for the Revolution that occurred less than twenty years after the last edition of *Poor Richard's Almanack* was published.

One final note as to the popularity of *Poor Richard's Almanack* concerns the Revolutionary War naval hero John Paul Jones, who waited for months in France for a refitted man-of-war promised to him by the French monarchy to aid the independence effort. Finally, Jones recalled a maxim from *Poor Richard's Almanack*. "If you'd have it done, go; if not, send," and he marched to Versailles and demanded the vessel. The resulting warship was christened *Bonhomme Richard* in appreciation of the influence of *Poor Richard's Almanack* on the indomitable Jones.

SUMMARY

George Washington and Benjamin Franklin are two of the many American colonial figures who have ascended to near-mythological status in the cultural heritage of the United States. Washington earned such stature by dint of his dominating, yet humble, leadership skills. Franklin, on the other hand, ascended primarily because of his intellectual accomplishments, which focused and adapted the philosophy of the century to the needs of a raw, colonial power. The American colonies were the epitome of the Enlightenment. Reasonable, rational, practical, and, above all, determined to assure liberty for all inhabitants, the Pennsylvania readership of *Poor Richard's Almanack* represented the realization of Franklin's belief in an ordered, modern society.

Richard S. Keating

BIBLIOGRAPHY

By the Author

NONFICTION:
"The Bagatelles," 1722-1784 (miscellaneous tales and sketches)
"Silence Dogood Essays," 1722
Dissertation on Liberty and Necessity, Pleasure and Pain, 1725
"The Busy-Body Essays," 1729
The Nature and Necessity of a Paper Currency, 1729
Poor Richard's Almanack, 1732-1757

"On Protection of Towns from Fire," 1735

"Self-Denial Not the Essence of Virtue," 1735

An Account of the New Invented Pennsylvania Fire-places, 1744 (science)

"Old Mistresses Apology," 1745 (also known as "Advice to a Young Man on the Choice of a Mistress")

Plain Truth, 1747

"The Speech of Polly Baker," 1747

Proposals Relating to the Education of Youth in Pennsylvania, 1749

Idea of the English School, 1751

Experiments and Observations on Electricity, 1751-1754 (3 volumes; science)

Observations on the Increase of Mankind, People of Countries, &c., 1751 (science)

"Physical and Meteorological Observations," 1751 (science)

"The Kite Experiment," 1752 (science)

Post Office Instructions and Directions, 1753 (state papers)

Some Account of the Pennsylvania Hospital, 1754

Treaty of Carlisle, 1754 (state papers)

Albany Plan of Union, 1754 (state papers)

Poor Richard Improved, 1757 (includes previous 2 titles; also known as *The Way to Wealth*)

The Interest of Great Britain Considered, 1760

Narrative of the Late Massacres, 1764

Cool Thoughts on the Present Situation of Our Public Affairs, 1764

Memorandum on the American Postal Service, 1764 (state papers)

Examination of Dr. Franklin by the House of Commons Concerning the Stamp Act, 1766 (state papers)

An Edict of the King of Prussia, 1773

Rules by Which a Great Empire May Be Reduced to a Small One, 1773

The Ephemera, 1778

Treaty of Amity and Commerce Between the United States and France, 1778 (state papers)

Political, Miscellaneous, and Philosophical Pieces, 1779

The Whistle, 1779

Dialogue Between Franklin and the Gout, 1780

The Handsome and the Deformed Leg, 1780

Treaty of Peace Between the United States and Great Britain, 1783 (state papers)

Remarks Concerning the Savages of North America, 1784

"On Smoky Chimneys," 1785 (science)

The Art of Procuring Pleasant Dreams, 1786

"Observations Relative to the Academy in Philadelphia," 1789 (science)

On the Slave Trade, 1790

Memoirs de la vie privée ecrits par lui-même, 1791 (*The Private Life of the Late Benjamin Franklin,* 1793; *Memoirs of the Life,* 1818; best known as *Autobiography*)

Writings of Benjamin Franklin, 1905-1907 (10 volumes.; Albert H. Smyth, editor)

Treaties and Other International Acts, 1931-1948 (state papers; 8 volumes; Hunter P. Miller, editor; also known as *Miller's Treaties*)

DISCUSSION TOPICS

- What experiences of his early life prepared Benjamin Franklin for the composition of *Poor Richard's Almanack?*

- How does Franklin's version of Enlightenment philosophy differ from that of Thomas Jefferson?

- Which of the virtues in Franklin's list in his *Autobiography* does he owe to religious tradition, which to his rationalistic philosophy? Do any partake of both?

- How does Franklin's sense of humor contribute to works such as *Poor Richard's Almanack* and the *Autobiography?*

- What are the chief ingredients of Franklin's prose style?

- Develop support for the following assertion: Franklin's writings illustrate a strong interest in both theoretical and applied science.

The Record of American Diplomacy, 1947 (state papers; Ruhl J. Bartlett, editor; also known as *Bartlett's Records*)
The Papers of Benjamin Franklin, 1959-2002 (36 volumes; Leonard W. Labaree et al., editors)

About the Author

Anderson, Douglas. *The Radical Enlightenments of Benjamin Franklin.* Baltimore: Johns Hopkins University Press, 1997.

Block, Seymour Stanton. *Benjamin Franklin, Genius of Kites, Flights, and Voting Rights.* Jefferson, N.C.: McFarland, 2004.

Brands, H. W. *The First American: The Life and Times of Benjamin Franklin.* New York: Doubleday, 2000.

Campbell, James. *Recovering Benjamin Franklin: An Exploration of a Life of Science and Service.* Chicago: Open Court, 1999.

Durham, Jennifer L. *Benjamin Franklin: A Biographical Companion.* Santa Barbara, Calif.: ABC-Clio, 1997.

Isaacson, Walter. *Benjamin Franklin: An American Life.* New York: Simon & Schuster, 2003.

Locker, Roy N., ed. *Meet Dr. Franklin.* Philadelphia: Franklin Institute, 1981.

Murrey, Christopher J., ed. *Benjamin Franklin: Biographical Overview and Bibliography.* New York: Nova Science, 2002.

Schaaf, Gregory. *Franklin, Jefferson, and Madison on Religion and the State.* Santa Fe, N.Mex.: CIAC Press, 2004.

Schiff, Stacy. *A Great Improvisation: Franklin, France, and the Birth of America.* New York: Henry Holt, 2005.

Wood, Gordon S. *The Americanization of Benjamin Franklin.* New York: Penguin Press, 2004.

PHILIP FRENEAU

Born: New York, New York
    January 2, 1752
Died: Freehold, New Jersey
    December 18, 1832

Although he was an indefatigable journalist and political propagandist, Freneau earned the title "poet of the American Revolution" because of his sincere patriotism and his satiric treatment of royalist attitudes.

BIOGRAPHY

Philip Freneau's family heritage was French Huguenot (Protestant). His father's family migrated to New York in 1705, became members of the city's respected and influential Huguenot community, and established a profitable agency for wines imported from Bordeaux, France, and from the Madeira Islands. Pierre Fresneau (Philip would change the spelling of the family surname) carried on this business with his brother, but upon his marriage to Agnes Watson he commenced his interest in the dry goods business. Philip Morin Fresneau was born on Frankfort Street in New York, on January 2, 1752; he was the first of his parents' five children. Later in the same year, the family moved to the hamlet of Mount Pleasant, near present-day Matawan, New Jersey, which was centrally located for the crucial New Jersey campaigns of the War of Independence at Trenton, Princeton, and Monmouth.

When Philip was fifteen, his father died, and the future poet inscribed at the end of Pierre's letter-book, "Here ends a book of vexation, disappointments, loss, and plagues that sunk the author to his grave short of 50 years." Philip's father left the family in unenviable financial straits. Philip's education, however, had not been jeopardized as his father's financial situation deteriorated. He had been sent to a Latin school in Penelope, New Jersey, headed by the Reverend Alexander Mitchell, a friend of John Witherspoon, the newly appointed president of the College of New Jersey (now Princeton University), subsequently one of the signers of the Declaration of Independence.

Although it was intended that Philip should prepare for a vocation in the church, his associations at Princeton (where he was admitted as a sophomore) militated against such a serene career. He was a roommate of James Madison; he became a close friend of Hugh Brackenridge, a future novelist; and he heard numerous sermons by Witherspoon, a leading theologian, philosopher, and rhetorician, who was to write much in favor of the Revolution. Freneau and Brackenridge were joint authors of "The Rising Glory of America," a long poem read at their commencement in 1771.

After graduation, Freneau taught school briefly, studied for the ministry desultorily, toyed with Deism, and penned several satires of British manners and administration before (early in 1776) sailing for the West Indies, where he was briefly a privateer. His "A Political Litany," written in 1775, is hardly above doggerel level, but the sentiments are genuine. In eight stanzas, the poet asks the Lord to deliver his countrymen from sixteen pestilences that range from Lord North and Admiral Montagu to bishops and slaves. His poems that resulted from his West Indian experiences are generally more socially significant, less petulant, and better composed: "The Beauties of Santa Cruz" is one.

Perhaps feeling embarrassed by his absence from North America during the tempestuous days of the infant revolution, Freneau returned to New Jersey in July, 1778, just after the Battle of Monmouth. He enlisted as a private in the militia but saw little action, though he was in the coastal patrol infantry. He was promoted to the rank of sergeant, was wounded in the knee, and ended his military service on May 1, 1780.

Shortly thereafter, aboard the privateer *Aurora,*

bound for the West Indies, he was captured by a British frigate and incarcerated in a prison ship, HMS *Scorpion,* and later in a hospital ship in New York Harbor for six weeks. Immediately upon his release, he returned to his family home in Mount Pleasant and wrote in prose *Some Account of the Capture of the Ship "Aurora"* (not published until 1899) and in verse "The British Prison-Ship" (1781), which detailed his detention in six hundred lines of heroic couplets. Canto 3 ("The Hospital Prison-Ship") describes the conditions on board with poignant phrase and vivid image:

On the hard floors these wasted objects laid,
There tossed and tumbled in the dismal shade,
There no soft voice their bitter fate bemoaned,
And Death strode stately, while the victims groaned.

This tribulation cast Freneau as an implacable enemy of the British and as an earnest and prolific propagandist for the revolutionary cause; henceforth, it was universally acknowledged that he wrote only with unquestioned sincerity.

After a brief recuperation, Freneau went to Philadelphia, where he worked for about a year as a printer and assistant editor of *The Freeman's Journal,* becoming a prolific contributor to the periodical. In 1786, Francis Bailey, editor of *The Freeman's Journal,* published *The Poems of Philip Freneau,* and two years later *The Miscellaneous Works of Mr. Philip Freneau.* Meanwhile, Freneau had worked as a clerk in the Philadelphia post office, translated Abbé Claude Robin's *New Travels Through North-America* (1784) from the original French, shipped to Jamaica as a deckhand aboard the *Dromelly* (and almost drowned in a hurricane), and became master of the *Monmouth, Industry,* and *Columbia,* which sailed between New York and Philadelphia and southern and Caribbean ports. He retired from the sea in 1789.

In March, 1790, Freneau took a position on the staff of the *Daily Advertiser* in New York, and a month later he married Eleanor Forman, daughter of a well-established Monmouth County family of Scots background, at Middletown Point, New Jersey. Within the following years, the first of the couple's four daughters was born, and Freneau (on the urging of James Madison) accepted an appointment as clerk for foreign languages to Thomas Jefferson at a minuscule salary. While working in Philadelphia, Freneau inaugurated the *National Gazette,* a twice-weekly publication that endorsed Thomas Paine's philosophy and the French revolutionists.

Soon Alexander Hamilton attacked the *Gazette* and proposed that Freneau was merely a front for Jefferson; both men publicly denied the charge. Jefferson declared Freneau to be the person who "saved our constitution, which was fast galloping into monarchy," while George Washington and the Federalists referred to him as "that rascal Freneau." Toward the end of 1793, Philadelphia saw an outbreak of yellow fever; Freneau resigned his clerkship, closed his *Gazette,* and returned to New Jersey, where he edited the *Jersey Chronicle* for a short time, issued a unique *Monmouth Almanac,* and published his *Poems Written Between the Years 1786 and 1794* (1795).

Freneau missed the "polite taste" and political environment of Philadelphia in Monmouth County, to which he had once referred as a "crude and barbarous part of the country." Freneau soon headed once more for the seas, briefly—none of his vocations seeming to be capable of significant endurance. After a decade of acting as a sea captain, Freneau retired in 1807, largely because of the effects of the Embargo Act. Thereafter he returned to his New Jersey home and worked as an occasional laborer and tinker, contributed essays to the *Aurora* (under the pseudonym Old Soldier), published poems and essays in the *True American* in Trenton, and issued two collections of new poems (in 1809 and 1815). His home burned down in October, 1818, so he moved to a farm near Freehold. Freneau died in a blizzard on December 18, 1832.

ANALYSIS

As an undergraduate poet, Freneau imitated the standard British poets; in his *Poems* (1786), he conveniently dated many of his compositions, so one can see his progression of interest from John Dryden and Alexander Pope to John Milton as models in both subject matter and technique. One of his best early lyrics, "The Power of Fancy" (dated 1770), suggests a conscious imitation of Milton's "L'Allegro" and "Il Penseroso" in its use of tetrametrical couplets, variously iambic and trochaic, although Joseph Warton's poem of the same title, written in 1746, may well have been an inspiration.

"The Power of Fancy" is a long poem for a beginning poet, though its 154 lines hardly exceed the limitation Edgar Allan Poe would impose in his theory of verse composition, for it can, with ease, be read at a single sitting. The poem is noteworthy for its fusion of the elements of the classical (in form and allusions) with those of the Romantic writers, whose philosophy and technique were not yet enunciated. There is praise for fancy as a transforming force; there is the introduction of dreaming as a device; there is the use of the distant and hence exotic; and there is a pervasive mood of melancholy. Furthermore, Freneau offers in this poem an early glimpse of his slowly developing Deist (or Unitarian) tendencies, which are perhaps most clearly stated in his poem "On the Uniformity and Perfection of Nature," one of his last. None of his other early poems has similar interest or quality.

In "The American Village," Freneau imitates the British poet Oliver Goldsmith's "The Deserted Village" (which had been published two years earlier), but whereas Goldsmith's poem is melancholy, Freneau's is optimistic and confident of the future of America and speaks of "this land with rising pomp divine" and "its own splendor." Thus, by 1772 Freneau was expressing his regional chauvinism; he was already displaying his special attachment to his American homeland.

Before long, Freneau's poems expressing simple pride and faith in the American colonies gave way to somewhat bellicose political verse, to statements of the theme that the North Americans valued the "godlike glory to be free" (a phrase in his "American Liberty"). By 1778, Freneau was writing the verse that earned for him the title "poet of the American Revolution": "American Independence" likened King George III to Cain, Nero, and Herod. In couplets that must have reminded some readers of the work of Thomas Gray, Freneau wrote: "Full many a corpse lies rotting on the plain,/ That ne'er shall see its little brood again." Here the juxtaposition of images of the battlefront campaigns and the violated domestic tranquillity shows Freneau at his most brilliant achievement as a patriotic and propagandistic poet.

The poet was somewhat ambivalent about engaging in the military conflict himself, and, in his "The Beauties of Santa Cruz," written during his privateering period, he both urged his fellow colonials to leave "the bloody plains and iron glooms" for "the climes which youthful Eden saw" and praised those who remained to "repel the tyrant who thy peace invades." Similarly, within the poem he vacillates between viewing the island of Santa Cruz as an edenic refuge and seeing it as a source of evil—slavery, avarice, indolence, and the annihilation of the native inhabitants.

From 1780 to 1790 Freneau produced some of his most commendable and lasting verse, both political and lyric. "The British Prison Ship," occasioned by the poet's capture and imprisonment in New York Harbor aboard the British ships *Scorpion* and *Hunter*, has the immediacy of a personal cri de coeur yet also offers detailed and reliable eyewitness evidence of the maltreatment of his fellow prisoners. It closes with a rousing appeal for revenge. No less rousing are the poems that memorialize the victory of John Paul Jones over the British warship *Seraphis* (September 23, 1779) and to the memory of those who fell in the action of September 8, 1781, under General Greene in South Carolina. In the first poem are the lines,

> Go on, great man, to daunt the foe,
> And bid the haughty Britons know
> They to our thirteen stars shall bend.

The second poem praises the "conquering genius," General Greene, and commends to "A brighter sunshine of their own" the "patriot band" who fought with him.

"The House of Night," written while Freneau was in the West Indies, was initially published in 1779 in seventy-three six-line iambic pentameter stanzas; it was subsequently expanded to 136 stanzas (816 lines). In an "Advertisement" (an authorial statement), Freneau indicates that the poem was founded upon Scripture ("the last enemy that shall be conquered is death"); he sets the poem at midnight in a solitary place that was once "beautiful and joyous"—perfectly suited for "the death of Death." The poem concludes, he notes, "with a few reflexions on the impropriety of a too great attachment to the present life." Throughout his life, Freneau toyed with the poem, adding lines and removing stanzas until, in its 1786 version, the death of Death was totally expunged. This remarkable composition was the first significant American poem to be written on the abstraction Death. It anticipates Poe in its pervasive Romanticism, its tone and atmosphere, though it is also in a direct line of descent from the "graveyard poets" of Britain of the immediately preceding years.

Several "reform" poems were written in the same decade; of them, "To Sir Toby," which describes and condemns the practices of slave owners in Jamaica, is a good example. "If there exists a hell," Freneau opens, "Sir Toby's slaves enjoy that portion here." Branding, whipping, chaining, imprisonment, and starvation—all the indignities and punishments inflicted upon the "black herd" are listed and condemned. "On the Anniversary of the Storming of the Bastille" is another of the poems that resulted from Freneau's intense interest in reform causes, but it is somewhat more philosophical and indicates a developing serenity in the poet's disposition.

That serenity became more apparent when Freneau took as subject matter the themes of nature, transience, and personal identity; it gave rise to some of his most pleasing lyrics, poems truly personal in essence, informed by a genuine rather than a spurious religious concern, and demonstrating his highest gifts in imagination and statement. Among those must be included "The Wild Honey Suckle"—generally agreed to be his most accomplished lyric—"The Indian Burying Ground," and "On the Uniformity and Perfection of Nature." Hardly inferior are "To a Caty-did" and "On a Honey Bee Drinking from a Glass of Wine and Drowned Therein," in which there is an unaccustomed levity to be found within the generally austere and mordant lines.

From the trenchant critic of the status quo before the American Revolution, Freneau became the true voice of the stalwarts of the rebellion. Toward the end of his life he again became evangelical—but for the status quo ruled over by Nature rather than by Britain. "No imperfection can be found/ in all that is, above, around," he wrote, and concluded that in the dominion of Nature, *"all is right."* In this conclusion he predated Robert Browning.

"ON MR. PAINE'S *RIGHTS OF MAN*"

First published: 1791 (collected in *Poems Written and Published During the American Revolutionary War*, 1809)
Type of work: Poem

The monarchy is inconsistent with the rights of the common person, and the new republic in North America will be the guardian of such rights.

This poem, which is sometimes published under the title "To a Republican, with Mr. Paine's *Rights of Man,*" was written immediately after the publication of Thomas Paine's great and influential book in defense of the French Revolution. It was later included in Freneau's *Poems* (1809). In many ways, the poem is uncharacteristic of Freneau: While trenchant in its criticism of monarchy and enthusiastic in its endorsement of Paine's thinking, it is neither overtly satiric nor especially lyrical, though it does make reference to the laws of Nature and to personified Virtue. As might be expected, it makes no allusion to God: It is, therefore, essentially a rationalist-Deist poem on the morality of the national polity.

Further, the structure of the poem is a departure from the usual forms that Freneau used: The fifty lines are divided into four stanzas of ten, fourteen, ten, and sixteen lines of iambic pentameter that are end-rhymed—that is, in closed couplets. The first three stanzas bemoan the ugly fate of the "sacred Rights of Man" as they have been travestied by monarchs; the final two celebrate the great plan for the enunciation and protection of the natural rights of the common person that was contained in Paine's treatise and was being worked out in the new Constitution of the United States, which is addressed as "Columbia."

Just as "A Political Litany" and "To Sir Toby" are characterized by catalogs of deficiencies and shortcomings, so too is "On Mr. Paine's *Rights of Man.*" Kings are presented as the source of discord, murder, slavery, knavery, plunder, and—worst of all—the restraint of freedom and "Nature's law reversed." The indictment is detailed and extensive. For example, after complaining that ships are or-

Philip Freneau

dered to sail the distant seas on royal orders, Freneau states that the benefits of these voyages, the proceeds of the "plundered prize," are used not to benefit humankind but "the strumpet," or they serve "to glut the king." These abuses of royal prerogatives are neither unusual nor passing: The reader is invited to scan the record of history for confirmation, for the poet is sure that he will be inflamed "with kindling rage" to see human rights aspersed and freedom restrained. The "manly page" of Paine and the reasoned argument of his treatise will not fail to convince any reader of the soundness of his thesis.

Then comes the bifurcation in the poem: In rather traditional Enlightenment manner, Freneau, having presented the present condition, offers a glimpse of the corrections to be obtained by pursuing the course proposed by Paine. Though the final stanza has sixteen lines, it is in the form of a rather loosely constructed sonnet. It opens with an apostrophe to Columbia and then lists some of the future's great boons: Without a king, the colonists—now American citizens—will peacefully and profitably till the fields to their own advantage. They have already "traced the unbounded sea," and they have instituted the rule of law, which is honored by one and all.

Freneau does not conclude with a listing of the immediate advantages of the new social order, however; he offers a list of responsibilities for the newly independent Americans. These include the restraint of the politically ambitious and the propagation of a few basic truths: that rulers are vain, that warfare inevitably brings ruin to a republic, and that monarchies subsist by waging war.

Then, in the concluding four lines, Freneau offers a magnificent view of the goals and future of the United States in language of undoubted sincerity. There is no suggestion of cliché or slogan, no inflated or bombastic vocabulary, no circumlocution or literary idiom—only the simple language of the new citizen of the new republic enunciating the rights of everyone to such things as life, liberty, property, and the pursuit of happiness:

> So shall our nation, form'd on Virtue's plan,
> Remain the guardian of the Rights of Man,
> A vast Republic, famed through every clime,
> Without a king, to see the end of time.

"THE WILD HONEY SUCKLE"

First published: 1786 (collected in *The Poems of Philip Freneau, Written Chiefly During the Late War,* 1786)
Type of work: Poem

The wild honeysuckle growing in the country grieves the poet because its beauty is so short-lived.

Although "The Wild Honey Suckle" is now the most frequently reprinted and quoted of Freneau's poems, it was seldom reprinted in the poet's lifetime. The consensus both in the United States and abroad is that this is the poet's best lyric and is perhaps his most accomplished verse composition. It is a comparatively short poem: It has only four six-line stanzas of iambic tetrameter arranged in the quite traditional rhyme scheme *ababcc*. The first two stanzas sing of the joys of growing in the country ("this silent, dull retreat"), where no careless bypasser will threaten the flower's gentle existence, its comeliness in the gentle shade of the woods. The poet stresses that this secluded location is "Nature's" design: The shade is to guard the plant, which is to "shun the vulgar eye"; that is, it is personified and admonished to assume an attitude of modesty despite its beauty.

The third stanza develops the image introduced in the penultimate line of the second stanza, that "quietly the summer goes." That is, an analogy is proposed between the life and death of the honeysuckle and the life and death of humankind; in both, one can see existence "declining to repose" (death). As if to place the death of the individual flower in perspective, Freneau suggests that even the flowers that bloomed in the Garden of Eden—which were no more beautiful than the native flower of the North American countryside—were killed off by the "[u]npitying frosts" of autumn. Of Eden's flowers there is no vestige; of the wild honeysuckle, also, there will be no trace.

The concluding stanza offers the traditional philosophical observation, or resolution of the situation presented in the preceding stanzas. It notes that the flower had its origins in morning suns and evening dews, developing from a pre-Edenic void. It will have its death knell from the same natural moisture and light—the ultimate paradox of life. Further, to place the life span of flower or person in perspective, the poet concludes with admirable logic that because the flower came from nothing, it can have lost nothing at death. It (and human-kind) moves only from void to void, and "[t]he space between is but an hour"—the twinkling of an eye of "[t]he frail duration of a flower."

Decay and death are immutable and universal, are irreversible, yet the disappearance of a thing of beauty, whether a wild honeysuckle or a beautiful young woman, is a melancholy phenomenon. In fact, the tone of the entire poem is one of melan-choly; the use of personification (which is used in even the opening apostrophe, "Fair flower," and continues unabated throughout the poem) makes the analogy between flower and individual inescap-able. The poet goes further, however, and makes the particular universal: The wild honeysuckle ap-propriately represents all the unseen, unacknowl-edged things of beauty that have ever existed and have died.

The poem has more than the traditional sense of the loss of beauty to recommend it, however. It has a serenity, a sense of awe and loss that is rare, and it combines native subject matter with the poet's personal philosophy of the transience of all human experiences without being circumscribed by the language of the English pre-Romantics such as William Collins and Thomas Gray and the great Scottish poet Robert Burns.

SUMMARY

Satiric verse that is inspired by temporary or pa-rochial concerns is seldom able to outlive the spe-cial circumstances that occasioned it: This is the reason for the almost total exclusion from antholo-gies today of Freneau's vitriolic verse of the Revolu-tionary years. Undoubtedly he was one of the most popular poets of his time and place and deserved his title, the "poet of the American Revolution." With the passage of time, however, his lyrical po-ems, in which he sang of the beauties of nature with the feeling and intensity of the British Romantic poets, are those that have remained of interest to readers. Some half-dozen beautiful lyrics represent a praiseworthy accomplishment and assure Fre-neau of a small but permanent place in American literature.

Marian B. McLeod

DISCUSSION TOPICS

- In what ways does Philip Freneau's poetry reveal his admiration for British poetical achievements?
- By what techniques does Freneau attempt to translate his patriotic fervor into po-etry? How successful is he in this effort?
- What are the objects of Freneau's satire? What satirical techniques does he chiefly employ?
- What structural devices are found in the poem "On Mr. Paine's *Rights of Man*"?
- Compare Freneau's practice of adding philosophical reflection to his nature po-ems with the same tendency in Ralph Waldo Emerson's poetry.

BIBLIOGRAPHY

By the Author

POETRY:
"The Rising Glory of America," 1772 (with H. H. Brackenridge)
The American Village, 1772
"The British Prison-Ship," 1781
The Poems of Philip Freneau, Written Chiefly During the Late War, 1786
A Journey from Philadelphia to New-York, by Robert Slender, Stocking Weaver, 1787
Poems Written Between the Years 1786 and 1794, 1795
Poems Written and Published During the American Revolutionary War, 1809

Philip Freneau

A Collection of Poems . . . Written Between the Year 1797 and the Present Time, 1815
The Poems of Philip Freneau, 1902-1907, 1963 (3 volumes; F. L. Patee, editor)
Poems of Freneau, 1929 (H. H. Clark, editor)
The Last Poems of Philip Freneau, 1946 (Lewis Leary, editor)

LONG FICTION:
Father Bombo's Pilgrimage to Mecca, 1770

NONFICTION:
Letters on Various Interesting and Important Subjects, 1799, 1943
Some Account of the Capture of the Ship "Aurora," 1899

MISCELLANEOUS:
The Miscellaneous Works of Mr. Philip Freneau Containing His Essays and Additional Poems, 1788
The Prose of Philip Freneau, 1955 (Philip M. Marsh, editor)

About the Author

Andrews, William D. "Philip Freneau and Francis Hopkinson." In *American Literature, 1764-1789: The Revolutionary Years,* edited by Everett Emerson. Madison: University of Wisconsin Press, 1977.

Elliott, Emory. "Philip Freneau: Poetry of Social Commitment." In *Revolutionary Writers: Literature and Authority in the New Republic, 1725-1810.* New York: Oxford University Press, 1982.

Leary, Lewis. "Philip Freneau." In *Major Writers of Early American Literature,* edited by Everett Emerson. Madison: University of Wisconsin Press, 1972.

Pearce, Roy Harvey. "Antecedents: The Case of Freneau." In *The Continuity of American Poetry.* Princeton, N.J.: Princeton University Press, 1961.

Ronnick, Michele Valerie. "A Note on the Text of Philip Freneau's 'Columbus to Ferdinand': From Plato to Seneca." *Early American Literature* 29, no. 1 (1994): 81.

Tichi, Cecelia. *New World, New Earth: Environmental Reform in American Literature from the Puritans Through Whitman.* New Haven, Conn.: Yale University Press, 1979.

Wertheimer, Eric. "Commencement Ceremonies: History and Identity in 'The Rising Glory of America,' 1771 and 1786." *Early American Literature* 29, no. 1 (1994): 35.

ROBERT FROST

Born: San Francisco, California
March 26, 1874
Died: Boston, Massachusetts
January 29, 1963

Although he was nearly forty when his first book was published, Frost came to be acknowledged within his lifetime as one of America's greatest poets.

Library of Congress

BIOGRAPHY

Famed as a New England poet, Robert Lee Frost was actually born in San Francisco on March 26, 1874, and named for a great Confederate general. His father, William Prescott Frost, Jr., was a footloose journalist who, as a teenager, had tried to run away from his Lawrence, Massachusetts, home and join the Confederate Army. After he died in 1885, his wife, Isabelle Moodie Frost, brought their young son, Rob, and daughter, Jeanie, back to Lawrence, where her late husband's parents still lived.

Frost's poem "Once by the Pacific" demonstrates that the West Coast did help shape the poet's imagination, but he grew to maturity in Lawrence, where he graduated second in his high school class, behind Elinor Miriam White, in 1892. Shortly thereafter the two became engaged.

After briefly attending Dartmouth College, Frost took a series of odd jobs, which included newspaper reporting and teaching in a school run by his mother. In 1894, he published his first poem, "My Butterfly," in a periodical called *The Independent*. He gathered this poem, along with four others he had composed, into a little book called *Twilight*, which he presented to Elinor White as a preview of what he hoped would be substantial success as a poet. He married Elinor in 1895 and was already a father when he entered Harvard College as a special student in 1897. Although he again

failed to graduate and, in fact, later boasted of walking away from two colleges, Frost was a good student in his two years at Harvard, and what he learned of classical poetry certainly furthered his poetic development.

The Frosts' early married years were difficult ones. Their first son died in 1900, but four other children were born between 1899 and 1905. While continuing to write poetry, Frost supported his family by farming in West Derry, New Hampshire, teaching at nearby Pinkerton Academy and accepting financial assistance from his paternal grandfather, who left him a generous annuity when he died in 1901.

After more than a decade of this modest and obscure life, Frost made a momentous decision in 1912. He decided to move his family to England, where, benefiting from the promotional efforts of his fellow American expatriate Ezra Pound, Frost published *A Boy's Will* (1913) and *North of Boston* (1914). He also developed friendships with other writers, particularly the English poet Edward Thomas. When the Frosts returned to the United States in 1915, he was finally gaining recognition as a poet.

Frost still hoped to combine farming and poetry and lived for several years after his return in Franconia, New Hampshire, and in South Shaftesbury, Vermont, but increasingly he played the role of a gentleman farmer. His 1923 volume, *New Hampshire: A Poem with Notes and Grace Notes*, which won the Pulitzer Prize the following year, made much of "the need of being versed in country things."

Having gained access to the literary and aca-

811

demic worlds, however, he undertook at this point three years as a poet-in-residence at Amherst College and two more at the University of Michigan. He later taught at both Amherst and Harvard, one of the colleges from which he had failed to graduate. His favorite activity became the performing of his own poems before chiefly academic audiences. Developing a chatty, informal style of discussing his poems that proved highly popular, he gained the reputation as he grew older, of a cheerful, homespun philosopher—a pose that is belied, however, both by his poetry and by the conflicts of his personal life.

A number of poems in his 1928 book *West-Running Brook*, among them "Bereft," "Acquainted with the Night," and "Tree at My Window," reflect a troubled spirit. Frost sensed in himself a precarious mental balance and feared a breakdown such as the one that led to the institutionalization of his sister, Jeanie. Later his son Carol committed suicide, and his daughter Irma had to be confined for a mental disorder. There were other tragedies—the deaths of his daughter Marjorie of puerperal fever in 1934 and of his wife in 1938, which devastated him.

His career, however, continued in high gear. His *Collected Poems* (1930) earned for him another Pulitzer Prize, as did *A Further Range* (1936), though critics disputed whether Frost's title could justly be regarded as an allusion to the extension of his poetic range or simply to another range of New England mountains. In the 1930's, when arguments raged over whether a poet ought to articulate a social commitment, Frost continued to write about solitary and rural figures, but "Departmental" wryly examines the subject of bureaucracy, and "Provide, Provide" twits those who would depend on the social legislation of Franklin D. Roosevelt's administration for their security.

In the 1940's Frost published two new books of poems, *A Witness Tree* (1942) and *Steeple Bush* (1947), as well as two masques—short dramatic works—on "reason" and "mercy," respectively. By the time of *Steeple Bush*, Frost was seventy-three; his output slowed to a trickle, but honors flowed in. Both the Universities of Oxford and Cambridge made him a doctor of letters in 1957; he was named American poet laureate in 1958, and he read a poem at the inauguration of President John F. Kennedy in 1961.

The last year of his long life proved to be a capstone. He brought out a final book of poems, *In the Clearing* (1962), and in late summer of that year he visited the Soviet Union as a goodwill ambassador. The trip proved an ordeal for the eighty-eight-year-old poet, however, and soon afterward his health declined rapidly. In December, he entered Peter Bent Brigham Hospital in Boston; he died on January 29, 1963.

ANALYSIS

Frost is that rare twentieth century poet who achieved both enormous popularity and critical acclaim. In an introductory essay to his collected poems, Frost insists that a poem "will forever keep its freshness as a metal keeps its fragrance. It can never lose its sense of a meaning that once unfolded by surprise as it went," an observation that applies to most of his three hundred-odd poems. Once his work came into circulation, its freshness and deceptive simplicity captivated audiences that shied away from more difficult poets such as T. S. Eliot and Wallace Stevens, while astute critics came to recognize the subtlety of thought and feeling that so often pervade these "simple" poems.

North of Boston ranks among the most original books of American poetry. Its title suggests its locale; one of the titles Frost originally proposed for it, "Farm Servants," indicates its typical subject matter. Most of its best-known poems—"Mending Wall," "The Death of the Hired Man," "Home Burial," "The Wood-Pile"—are in blank verse (unrhymed iambic pentameter). The language consists of everyday words, Frost having discarded the "poetic" vocabulary that he had occasionally used in *A Boy's Will*. None of these features was new in poetry, but in combination they result in strikingly innovative poetry.

The works in this volume represent the conscious application of a theory which Frost set forth most directly in several letters to a friend named John Bartlett. He aimed to accommodate what he called "the sound of sense" to blank verse. He noted that many casual utterances of the people among whom he lived fell into a basically iambic rhythm: "She thinks I have no eye for these," "My father used to say," "Never you say a thing like that to a man," and so on. Writing poetry involved listening for and adapting to meter—what Frost called "sentence sounds." In this way Frost created poems that did not only talk about rural New Englanders but also enacted them. Ten of the sixteen poems in *North of Boston* consist almost entirely of dialogue, one is a monologue, and several others incorporate colloquial lines. Many readers do not even notice that the poems all "scan" according to the rules of iambic meter, but it is there, a firm substratum to Frost's "sound of sense."

To Frost's credit, he refused merely to repeat the effects of this book in subsequent work. While he continued from time to time to base poems on dialogue—especially between husband and wife—dialogue does not dominate any of his later books. *Mountain Interval* (1916), his first book to appear originally in the United States, offers much greater variety in form: sonnets, poems in four- and five-line rhymed stanzas, poems written in short lines, and others in patterns made up of lines of different lengths. Several, including "The Road Not Taken" and "The Sound of Trees," are reflective poems that raise deep questions and provide teasing or ambiguous answers in a fashion that delighted Frost. They also remind the reader that many of life's important questions do not have answers both simple and unfailingly satisfying.

A number of Frost's poems celebrate encounters with nature. The first poem in his first book, "Into My Own," and the last poem in his final book, an untitled one beginning "In winter in the woods alone," depict a solitary person entering the woods, while in the long stretch between those poems the one that may be his best known of all, "Stopping by Woods on a Snowy Evening," portrays the desire to do so. On one level, Frost can be seen as simply continuing the love affair with the wilderness so common in American mythology, whose literary manifestations include such classics as James Fenimore Cooper's Leatherstocking Tales (1823-1841) and Mark Twain's *Adventures of Huckleberry Finn* (1884). On another level, the woodsman—independent, defiant of urban artificiality, at one with nature—is one of Frost's conceptions of himself. These poems convey a number of themes and even more attitudes. The woods can be a place for restoration of the spirit through vigorous activity and communion with nature, the locus of deep and sometimes sinister psychic forces, or a happy hunting ground for analogies of the human condition generally. Frost portrays both the perils and joys of isolation.

A considerable portion of Frost's poems are set

either in winter or at night or both. These are the times that tend to isolate people, to throw them on their own resources, to encourage reflection. Those readers who think that Frost's reflections are always mild and cheerful have not read his poems carefully enough. In *West-Running Brook*, a group of poems gathered under the epigraph *"Fiat Nox"* ("let there be night") suggests something of Frost's nocturnal range. These poems include "Acceptance," "Once by the Pacific," "Bereft," "Tree at My Window," and "Acquainted with the Night."

Frost is also a daylight observer of ordinary people and their ways. The relationships of husbands and wives interested him particularly, and his range is wide, from the telepathic harmony of a couple in "The Telephone" to the marital disintegration of "Home Burial." Perhaps no other poet has portrayed the give-and-take of marriage so variously and so vividly. His world is also one of neighbors, passing tramps, and even garrulous witches.

Neither children nor sophisticated adults appear very often in his poetry. Rooted in the countryside, his writing focuses on simple things and people. He used language with the same economy and precision his characters display in their use of the scythe, the axe, and the pitchfork. Demonstrating how much can be done by the skillful application of simple tools, Frost has left to an increasingly industrialized and impersonal society a valuable legacy of poems celebrating basic emotions and relationships.

"HOME BURIAL"

First published: 1914 (collected in *North of Boston*, 1914)
Type of work: Poem

Under the strain of their child's recent death, a young couple try vainly to communicate.

"Home Burial" is an intensely dramatic poem about a bereaved and increasingly estranged married couple. The husband has just returned from burying their young son in a family plot of the sort that served northern New Englanders as cemeteries for generations. He mounts the stairs toward his wife "until she cowered under him." What follows is a bitter exchange. The wife, unable to understand his failure to express grief vocally, accuses him of indifference to their loss; he, rankled by what he considers a groundless charge, tries blunderingly to assure her, but they fail to comprehend each other. At the end of the poem she is threatening to leave and find someone else who can console her, while he threatens, "I'll follow and bring you back by force. I will!—"

The poem is nearly all dialogue except for a few sections of description which work like stage directions in a play, serving to relate the couple spatially and to underline by movement and gestures the tension between them. Although the poem does not require staging, it is easily stageable, so dramatically is it presented. The reader surmises that the two really do love—or at least have loved—each other and that the difficulties between them have resulted not from willful malice but from clashes of temperament and different training. The man is expected to be stoical, tight-lipped in adversity. Having learned to hide his feelings, he is unable to express them in a way recognizable to his wife, with her different emotional orientation.

She has watched with a kind of horror his energetic digging at the gravesite; he has made the gravel "leap up . . . and land so lightly." She cannot understand that he has converted his frustration into a relevant and necessary physical activity, as men have traditionally learned to do. Nor does she realize that a seemingly callous remark of his about the rotting of birch fences may well constitute an oblique way of referring to the demise of the child that he has helped make. Instead she draws the conclusion that, because he does not grieve overtly as she does, he has no feelings. Because he is inexpert at oral communication, he cannot say the kind of thing that might alleviate her grief.

The poem becomes a painful study in misinterpretation that is in the process of leading to the disintegration of a marriage. The poem is also a brilliant example of Frost's success at unobtrusively adapting a vignette from life to the formal requirements of blank verse. In the early twentieth century, avant-garde poets were strongly resisting traditional verse poems, but Frost had his own way of escaping the tyrannizing effects of meter.

Although "Home Burial" and the other blank verse poems in *North of Boston* look conventional on the page, and although the poet's firm iambic support for the dialogue is readily apparent to well-versed readers, it is easy to forget that something such as the wife's "There you go sneering now!" followed by his "I'm not, I'm not!" is a more or less regular pentameter line as well as an easily imaginable bit of argument between two disaffected people. Frost showed that ordinary people could inhabit a poem, could talk and argue and move convincingly within a medium that William Shakespeare and John Milton in the sixteenth and seventeenth centuries had tended to reserve for aristocrats and angels.

Unlike a play, Frost's dramatic poem has no resolution. Will the wife leave, as she threatens? If so, will he restrain her by force as he threatens, or will he resign himself to the status quo, as he has before? It is not Frost's intention to solve this marital problem. He had known conflict in his own marriage and observed it in other marriages; he certainly knew the ways in which spouses might resolve, or fail to resolve, their conflicts. What he chose to do was provide an opportunity to eavesdrop on a bereaved couple at an agonizing moment and feel their passion and frustration.

"THE ROAD NOT TAKEN"

First published: 1916 (collected in *Mountain Interval*, 1916)
Type of work: Poem

A traveler through life reflects on a past choice of route "that has made all the difference."

The first poem in Frost's book *Mountain Interval*, "The Road Not Taken," has long been a popular favorite. Like many of his poems, it seems simple, but it is not exactly straightforward, and even perceptive readers have disagreed considerably over its best interpretation. It looks like a personal poem about a decision of vast importance, but there is evidence to the contrary both inside and outside the poem. Frost has created a richly mysterious reading experience out of a marvelous economy of means.

The first significant thing about "The Road Not Taken" is its title, which presumably refers to an unexercised option, something about which the speaker can only speculate. The traveler comes to a fork in a road through a "yellow wood" and wishes he could somehow manage to "travel both" routes;

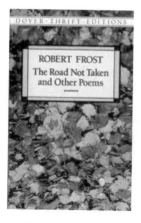

he rejects that aspiration as impractical, however, at least for the day at hand. The road he selects is "the one less traveled by," suggesting the decision of an individualist, someone little inclined to follow the crowd. Almost immediately, however, he seems to contradict his own judgment: "Though as for that the passing there/ Had worn them really about the same." The poet appears to imply that the decision is based on evidence that is, or comes close to being, an illusion.

The contradictions continue. He decides to save the first, (perhaps) more traveled route for another day but then confesses that he does not think it probable that he will return, implying that this seemingly casual and inconsequential choice is really likely to be crucial—one of the choices of life that involve commitment or lead to the necessity of other choices that will divert the traveler forever from the original stopping place. In the final stanza, the traveler says that he will be "telling this with a sigh," which may connote regret. His choice, in any event, "has made all the difference." The tone of this stanza, coupled with the title, strongly suggests that the traveler, if not regretting his choice, at least laments the possibilities that the need to make a choice leave unfulfilled.

Has Frost in mind a particular and irrevocable choice of his own, and if so, what feeling, in this poem of mixed feelings, should be regarded as dominant? There is no way of identifying such a specific decision from the evidence of the poem itself. Although a prejudice exists in favor of identifying the "I" of the poem with the author in the absence of evidence to the contrary, the speaker may not be Frost at all. On more than one occasion the poet claimed that this poem was about his friend Edward Thomas, a man inclined to indecisiveness out of a strong—and, as Frost thought, amusing—habit of dwelling on the irrevocability of decisions. If so, the reference in the poem's final stanza to

"telling" of the experience "with a sigh/ Somewhere ages and ages hence" might be read not only as the boast of Robert Frost, who "tells" it as long as people read the poem, but also as a perpetual revelation of Thomas, also a fine poet.

What is clear is that the speaker is, at least, a person like Thomas in some respects (though there may well be some of Frost in him also). Critics of this poem are likely always to argue whether it is an affirmation of the crucial nature of the choices people must make on the road of life or a gentle satire on the sort of temperament that always insists on struggling with such choices. The extent of the poet's sympathy with the traveler also remains an open question.

Frost composed this poem in four five-line stanzas with only two end rhymes in each stanza (*abaab*). The flexible iambic meter has four strong beats to the line. Of the technical achievements in "The Road Not Taken," one in particular shows Frost's skill at enforcing meaning through form. The poem ends:

> Two roads diverged in a wood, and I—
> I took the one less traveled by,
> And that has made all the difference.

The indecision of the speaker—his divided state of mind—is heightened by the repetition of "I," split by the line division and emphasized by the rhyme and pause. It is an effect possible only in a rhymed and metrical poem—and thus a good argument for the continuing viability of traditional forms.

"THE OVEN BIRD"

First published: 1916 (collected in *Mountain Interval,* 1916)
Type of work: Poem

In the call of a forest bird, the listener discerns the theme of diminishment.

"The Oven Bird" is an irregular sonnet that explores in various ways the problem of "what to make of a diminished thing." The poet does not refer to the bird directly by its other common name of "teacher bird" (based on the resemblance of its reiterated call to the word "teacher") but attributes to the bird an instructive discourse about diminishment, the downward thrust of things. In the middle of summer, this bird reminds one of the fall (specifically the petal fall) that is already past and of the fall to come.

Like many of Frost's poems, this one is built on paradox. This bird can be said to sing, but it is not particularly tuneful. Its repeated call in a trochaic, or falling, rhythm does not have the upward lilt that humans generally consider cheerful or merry. The bird is a twentieth century teacher—not the old-fashioned lecturer but the modern one who contrives to induce the students to teach themselves. Like the teacher, the bird "knows," and in knowing frames the kind of question that is intended to provoke thought, although without any guarantee of easy resolution. Paradoxically, the process of learning becomes one of discovering that some questions must be struggled with unendingly. Like the teacher bird, the poem supplies no answers.

Literally, the "diminished thing" of the poem is the weather and the natural year. The sonnet is full of words and phrases such as "old," "early petal-fall," "down in showers," "dust is over all," and "the bird would cease," that suggest decline in the natural order. Knowing that people persist in interpreting nature in human terms, the poet can safely assume that the poem will be read as referring to the diminishment of human hopes, of life itself. Frost reinforces his theme by using a proportion of diminishment: "for flowers/ Mid-summer is to spring as one to ten." As expectations turn into past events and remaining possibilities steadily diminish, any thoughtful person must ponder "what to make" of that which is left.

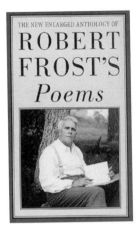

Frost also enforces his theme rhythmically. He crosses the usual iambic rising rhythm with trochaic words, those with first-syllable accents. "Singer," "flowers," "summer," "petal"—in fact, all the two-syllable words of the poem—carry this accent. These words, nevertheless, are all placed in positions that contribute to an iambic movement which might be taken as suggesting that, despite the declines and falls, both the cycle of seasons and human hopes endure.

The typical English sonnet ends in a rhymed couplet which often sums up or tops off the poem and gives a feeling of finality. This poem does have two couplets, but neither is at the end. It seems to be part of Frost's strategy to avoid any sense of completeness or finality. Whatever continues, continues to diminish, but while the process continues, something always remains. The only regular quatrain (the sort of rhyming unit one expects to find in a sonnet three times before the couplet) is the four lines that fall at the end. What to make of this feature is one of the persisting questions about this haunting poem.

"BIRCHES"

First published: 1916 (collected in
Mountain Interval, 1916)
Type of work: Poem

The tension between earthly satisfactions and higher aspirations emerges from the recollection of a childhood game.

In "Birches," the speaker's attention is first caught by a cluster of bent birch trees that he knows were bowed by ice storms. The sight reminds him of his boyhood sport of swinging on birch trees, although such an activity does not permanently bow them. Swinging on birches is a form of play that can be done alone, the competition strictly between child and tree. It is a sport requiring poise and good judgment; for a safe and satisfactory ride, one must climb to the very top of the tree and "launch out at just the right moment. A country boy might expect to master all the birches on his father's land."

The speaker dreams of swinging on birches again. From the perspective of adulthood, he envies his childhood capacity for launching out anew, making a new beginning on a new tree. In his mind, the game has become a way of escaping from earth, where life sometimes seems to be a "pathless wood"—but he knows that such a game is not a permanent escape from earth and that part of the fun is "coming back," for life is not always a pathless wood, and the earth from which he contemplates escaping is "the right place for love." The mature man thus recognizes a symbolic value that he could not have consciously realized when he was young enough to be a swinger of birches.

The poem consists of fifty-nine easily flowing blank verse lines. Though "Birches" has no formal divisions, it can be separated into three, almost equal parts: the observation and description of trees bent by winter storms, the recollection of the techniques of birch-swinging, and the grown man's dream, energized by his awareness of the claims of both "earth" and "heaven." Each part leads casually to the next: "But I was going to say" to the second part, "It's when I'm weary of considerations" to the third.

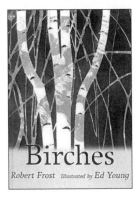

The poem is marvelously vivid and concrete in its descriptions of both ice storms and child's play. The stir of the trees after acquiring their load of ice "cracks and crazes their enamel"; casting their load off, they leave "heaps of broken glass." The reader is made to see the boy "kicking his way down through the air" and the man "weeping/ From a twig's having lashed it [his eye] open." Black and white are used suggestively and, as often in Frost, somewhat ambiguously. The white birches are first seen against the background of "straighter darker trees." The sun shining on the ice coating of the tree trunks turns them prismatic. The boy climbs "black branches up a snow-white trunk/ *Toward* heaven" ("toward" being significantly italicized, for heaven is not attainable), the white intimating the pure and heavenly aspiration, the black, the necessary physical, earthly steps, the "going and coming back."

Far from being the simple reminiscence of a sentimental adult, the poem not only acknowledges that returning to the birch-swinging of childhood is a "dream" but also assesses the significance of the game from a mature viewpoint. Part of maturity is coming to understand and articulate the profundity of early experience.

"DUST OF SNOW"

First published: 1921 (collected in *New Hampshire*, 1923)
Type of work: Poem

A small event on a winter walk unexpectedly changes a person's day for the better.

Frost was proud of his small, compact poems that say much more than they seem to say; his 1923 volume *New Hampshire* gathers several of these, including "Fire and Ice," "Nothing Gold Can Stay," and one of the shortest of all, "Dust of Snow." One sentence long, it occupies eight short lines and contains only thirty-four words, all but two of them monosyllabic, and all of them part of even a young child's vocabulary.

> The way a crow
> Shook down on me
> The dust of snow
> From a hemlock tree
>
> Has given my heart
> A change of mood
> And saved some part
> Of a day I had rued.

Much of the effect of this poem derives from its paradoxes or seeming contradictions, the first of which is in the title. Although the phrase "a dusting of snow" is common in weather reports, dust usually calls forth notions of something dirty and unpleasant, quite unlike the dust of snow.

It is also paradoxical that the speaker's mood is initially so negative on a presumably fine winter day after a fresh snowfall, that he has so far rued this day. Even more paradoxically, the agent responsible for provoking a change for the better is a bird normally contemned: the large, black, raucous crow. Even its important function as a devourer of carrion does not summon forth a favorable image. In medieval times the crow often symbolized the devil, and its larger cousin, the raven, was employed by Edgar Allan Poe and other writers to create a sinister or melancholy mood. This crow, however, rescues the speaker from his previously rueful mood.

One paradox that Frost did not intend occurred to a woman who heard him read "Dust of Snow" and responded, "Very sinister poem!" When the puzzled author asked her why, she replied, "Hemlock—Socrates, you know," alluding to the poison that the Greek philosopher was required to drink after his trial. Frost had intended no such suggestion, and it contradicts the effect of the poem as a whole. Socrates' hemlock was quite a different thing from the tree inhabited by Frost's crow, and the woman's misinterpretation exemplifies an important point: Not all the possible suggestions of a word or image are necessarily applicable in a given context. Frost depends on his reader to use imagination responsibly and to exclude meaning that will not make sense in a poem.

The rhyme and meter of this short poem contribute much to its effect. The firm iambic beat is established in the first three lines, but Frost knew exactly when to vary the rhythm to avoid a singsong effect; thus there is an extra syllable (in a different place) in each of the next two lines, and after two more regular lines, the last line consists of two anapests. Furthermore, the rhyming words are important ones, and the most surprising one, "rued," is reserved until the end. The reader is left with a memorable impression of an unexpected boon from an unlikely source. To be "saved" by a crow, because of its unexpectedness, is more delightful than being saved by a song sparrow.

"TREE AT MY WINDOW"

First published: 1928 (collected in *West-Running Brook*, 1928)
Type of work: Poem

A person who has known trouble recognizes a kindred spirit in the tree outside his window.

"Tree at My Window" differs from most of Frost's nature poems in its locale. Instead of being out in the fields or woods, the speaker is looking out his bedroom window at a nearby tree. He closes his window at night, but out of love for the tree he does not draw the curtain. This is an unmistakably modern nature poem. Whereas the transcendentalists of the nineteenth century had regarded nature as profound, the speaker here specifically denies the possibility of the tree speaking wisdom. Instead, he compares the conditions of human and tree. He has seen the tree "taken and tossed" by storm, and if the tree can be imagined as having looked in at him asleep, it has seen him "taken and swept/ and all but lost." That which brought them together is styled "fate"—but an imaginative fate, because of their respective concerns with "outer" and "inner weather."

He sees the tree not as an instructor but as a comrade, a fellow sufferer. Between Frost and the transcendentalist faith in nature as a teacher lies a scientific revolution that denies the possibility of "sermons in stones," and it is clear that the tree is physically, the person only metaphorically, storm-tossed. This metaphor, an old contrivance of poets, remains a potent one when used as freshly as it is here. The speaker's storm is only a dream, but dreams can be deeply disturbing; psychologists insist that they may be very significant.

"Inner weather" reflects a recurring theme in Frost, who in his personal life had to grapple with the maintenance of psychic balance. Inner doubt and conflict dominate a number of poems from Frost's middle years including, in his 1928 book *West-Running Brook*, "Bereft" and "Acquainted with the Night"; "Desert Places," in his next book, *A Further Range*, describes personal fear. In "Tree at My Window," the kinship with nature is even more therapeutic and steadying than it was in the earlier "Birches." Both tree and man have been "tossed" but survive. Frost would reassert nature's steadying influence in later poems such as "One Step Backward Taken" and "Take Something Like a Star," both in the 1947 *Steeple Bush*.

"Tree at My Window" has a distinctive form. First glance reveals it to be a neat, compact poem which uses the *abba* rhyme scheme made famous by Alfred, Lord Tennyson in his long poem *In Memoriam* (1850). The first three lines of each quatrain are tetrameter lines, while the last line has either two or three strong beats. The rhythmical variations, however, are quite unusual. Frost once observed that there are only two meters in English, strict iambic and loose iambic. This poem is definitely the latter. Out of the sixteen lines, only two—both short ones—are indisputably regular. Frost worked extra unstressed syllables into most of the lines. Again, Frost found a way to be rhythmically innovative without losing the sense of a traditional poetic structure.

"DEPARTMENTAL"

First published: 1936 (collected in *A Further Range*, 1936)

Type of work: Poem

Observing the funeral of an ant leads to a recognition of the strengths and weaknesses of human institutions.

"Departmental," a Frost poem of the 1930's, typifies its author in several ways. It is playful, full of clever rhymes, and closely observant of a natural scene that mirrors aspects of human life. In this Depression-era poem, Frost focuses on the popular theme of social organization. It is almost a fable, though it implies, rather than states, its moral.

To follow an ant on a tablecloth, the poem says, is immediately to see dutiful and specialized behavior. "Departmental" focuses on ants' way of dealing with death. If a particular ant finds a dead moth, its only obligation is to report the moth to "the hive's enquiry squad." Even when it encounters the body of another ant, it merely informs the proper authorities, who arrange for a "solemn mortician" to bring the body back home and give it a dignified burial, while the rest of the colony continue about their business: "It couldn't be called ungentle./ But how thoroughly departmental."

As observed, the ant colony excludes a host of what one considers human reactions. There is no "surprise" at death, no pausing to mourn or reflect on its meaning. The ant does not slow down, is not at all "impressed." Other than a formal report, there is no talk, no standing around and staring, as one expects at the scene of a fatal accident. Everything is routine, designated behavior and prescribed ritual. Ants are efficient; they eschew all the impractical reactions of human beings. Frost's ants are not cruel, but they are unfeeling and robotic in their reactions to death, as though it has been decreed that death is, after all, a commonplace event that should not be allowed to interrupt duty or waste the time of the populace.

Thus Frost calls attention to a basic difference between ants (at least as humans perceive them) and humans. The fact that death is common does not, for humans, negate its profundity. Human reactions are often not profound and seldom "useful," but they betoken the human way of experiencing life. The ceremony of a funeral, moreover, brings together in common cause people who otherwise may have few opportunities to socialize; such differences hover in the background of Frost's poem.

The differences between ant and human conduct, however, also call attention to the bureaucratic or "departmental" likenesses. The ant world of Frost's poem has been constructed with frequent analogies to specialized human institutions: janissaries, commissaries, courts, and the "state" funeral of a deceased dignitary. Ant behavior cannot be described successfully, it seems, without reference to concepts totally beyond the range of ants. Unlike ants, who do it instinctively, human beings have to learn to be efficient and impersonal. Because humans are capable of modifying their social norms, they run the risk of damaging specifically human ideas and feelings when they adopt the modes of social insects. Ants must be "departmental"; people do not have to be. Like an ancient fable, the poem amuses, then challenges its reader by comparing human conduct to that of other branches of the animal kingdom.

The lines are iambic trimeter, with a liberal sprinkling of anapestic feet. Rhymes are prominent, chiefly in couplets, occasionally triplets, with one quadruplet. A number of them— "any" and "antennae," "atwiddle" and "middle," for example— are the sort of feminine rhymes that often serve to reinforce humor. It was axiomatic with Frost to convey inner seriousness with outer humor. "Departmental" shows him avoiding the sugar-coated pill by blending the "sugar"—the delight—and the "pill"—the enlightenment—in a poem that appears light and droll but that slyly satirizes a prevalent human weakness: a tendency to design human institutions inhumanely.

"DESIGN"

First published: 1936 (collected in *A Further Range,* 1936)

Type of work: Poem

The question of whether there exists a comprehensible plan or design in nature is a baffling one.

"Design" was completed for the 1936 volume *A Further Range,* but Frost had completed an earlier version of the poem as far back as 1912 without attempting to publish it. In the tradition of New England Puritanism, it details closely a small event in nature and attempts to interpret its meaning for humanity. Since the revolution in scientific thought stimulated by Charles Darwin's *On the Origin of Species* (1859), however, poetry of this sort has been less likely to underline a received article of Christian or other transcendent faith. Frost's poem is a questioning one in the form of an Italian sonnet whose octave, or first eight-line unit, is balanced against the closing six-line sestet.

The speaker comes upon "a dimpled spider, fat and white" that has captured and killed a moth against the background of a white flower called a heal-all. The octave describes the scene, which is all "in white" (to quote a phrase not in the poem that stood as Frost's original title for it). The description is ironic: The disarmingly attractive spider and the moth are "characters of death and blight/ Mixed ready to begin the morning right." The spider is also compared to a snowflake, and the very name of the flower suggests the opposite of "death and blight."

The sestet asks three questions, the third of which seems to answer the first two but is then qualified in the last line: Why did the killing take place on a white flower, what brought the spider and moth together, and was the event part of a sinister design? The final line of the sonnet then implies another question: Can such a small event of nature properly be considered as part of any design, either good or evil?

The answers to these questions hinge on the meaning of "design." Before Darwin, the idea that the processes of nature, both generally and in particular, reveal a great design of the Creator prevailed in the Western world; overwhelmingly, this design was viewed as benevolent. A sparrow "shall not fall on the ground without your Father," Jesus told his disciples. A few dissidents might have argued that God was malign or that the devil had gained control, but even they would take for granted a designing intelligence.

Nineteenth century scientific thought changed all this by dispensing with design and the necessity of a designer in favor of concepts such as Darwin's "natural selection." Frost's poem shows the influence of the late nineteenth century American philosopher William James, who, while rejecting the simple Christian affirmation of a designer involved in every detail of creation, sought to retain the concept of design as a "seeing force" rather than a "blind force." Frost appears to be mocking the idea of design in "small" events such as the confrontation of an individual spider and moth, but he characteristically leaves his most important questions unanswered.

The pattern of the poem is that of a traditional sonnet: descriptive octave followed by reflective sestet. Because of what he has been taught, the observer of the spider's triumph both sees and reflects differently from a person of any earlier time. The poem dramatizes the impossibility of maintaining a view of God and nature similar to the one that satisfied people of past generations. At the same time, it embodies the difficulty of reinterpreting nature in a satisfactory way.

SUMMARY

The poetry of Frost has accomplished a feat rare in the twentieth century: It has received both critical acclaim and widespread popular acceptance. His poetry expresses common emotional and sentient experiences so simply and directly that its authenticity affects readers without expertise in reading poetry; the subtlety of his thought and the sublimity of his art are appreciated by those who ponder his work. The rural character or meditative speaker in a Frost poem represents not merely a person the poet has met or a mood he has felt but humanity in the process of being itself or discovering itself.

Robert P. Ellis

BIBLIOGRAPHY

By the Author

POETRY:
A Boy's Will, 1913
North of Boston, 1914
Mountain Interval, 1916
Selected Poems, 1923
New Hampshire: A Poem with Notes and Grace Notes, 1923
West-Running Brook, 1928
Collected Poems, 1930
A Further Range, 1936
Collected Poems, 1939
A Witness Tree, 1942
A Masque of Reason, 1945
Steeple Bush, 1947
A Masque of Mercy, 1947
Complete Poems, 1949
How Not to Be King, 1951
In the Clearing, 1962
The Poetry of Robert Frost, 1969

DRAMA:
A Way Out, pb. 1929 (one act)

NONFICTION:
The Letters of Robert Frost to Louis Untermeyer, 1963 (with commentary by Untermeyer)
The Record of a Friendship, 1963 (Margaret Bartlett, editor)
Selected Letters of Robert Frost, 1964 (Lawrance Thompson, editor)
Selected Prose, 1966 (Hyde Cox and Edward C. Lathem, editors)
Elected Friends: Robert Frost and Edward Thomas to One Another, 2003 (Matthew Spencer, editor)

DISCUSSION TOPICS

- What is simple and what is complex in Robert Frost's poetry?
- Consider "Home Burial" as a poem about communication failure.
- What evidence is there in individual Frost poems that the "I" of the poem does not necessarily represent the poet himself?
- Frost wrote exclusively in meter, chiefly in iambic meter. How prevalent are variations and irregularities in the meter, and what do they accomplish?
- What examples of humor reinforcing seriousness can you find in Frost's poems other than "Departmental"?
- Doubts and fears are often expressed or implied in Frost's poetry. Give several examples.

About the Author

Bloom, Harold, ed. *Robert Frost*. Philadelphia: Chelsea House, 2003.

Burnshaw, Stanley. *Robert Frost Himself*. New York: George Braziller, 1986.

Faggen, Robert. *Robert Frost and the Challenge of Darwin*. Ann Arbor: University of Michigan Press, 1997.

Galbraith, Astrid. *New England as Poetic Landscape: Henry David Thoreau and Robert Frost*. New York: Peter Lang, 2003.

Gerber, Philip L. *Robert Frost*. Rev. ed. Boston: Twayne, 1982.

Lathem, Edward Connery. *Robert Frost: A Biography*. New York: Holt, Rinehart and Winston, 1981.

Meyers, Jeffrey. *Robert Frost: A Biography*. Boston: Houghton Mifflin, 1996.

Poirier, Richard. *Robert Frost: The Work of Knowing*. New York: Oxford University Press, 1977.

Potter, James L. *The Robert Frost Handbook*. University Park: Pennsylvania State University Press, 1980.

Pritchard, William H. *Frost: A Literary Life Reconsidered*. New York: Oxford University Press, 1984.

Thompson, Lawrance Roger, and R. H. Winnick. *Robert Frost: A Biography*. New York: Holt, Rinehart and Winston, 1982.

AP/Wide World Photos

CHARLES FULLER

Born: Philadelphia, Pennsylvania
March 5, 1939

*One of the leading playwrights of his generation,
Fuller was the second African American to win the
Pulitzer Prize in drama.*

BIOGRAPHY

Charles Henry Fuller, Jr., was born in Philadelphia on March 5, 1939, the son of Charles Henry and Lillian (Anderson) Fuller. The son of a printer, Fuller was educated in Philadelphia, attended Villanova University, then served in the U.S. Army from 1959 to 1962. In 1962, he married Miriam A. Nesbitt, and they had two children, Charles III and David. He resumed his studies at LaSalle in Philadelphia from 1965 to 1967 and went on to become the cofounder and codirector of the Afro-American Arts Theatre in Philadelphia from 1967 to 1971. In 1982, LaSalle awarded him an honorary degree after the stage success of *A Soldier's Play* (1981). Honorary degrees than followed in 1983 from Villanova University and in 1965 from Chestnut Hill College as Fuller became one of Philadelphia's most famous writers. He was appointed professor of African-American studies at Temple University in Philadelphia.

Fuller's plays began to appear during the late 1960's. In 1968, his two-act play *The Village: A Party* was produced in Princeton, New Jersey, in October; in March of 1969 it was produced in New York City as *The Perfect Party*. In 1972, a collection of six of Fuller's one-act plays was produced in New York City under the title *In My Many Names and Days*. Other plays that followed in 1974 included the one-act *First Love*, the two-act *In the Deepest Part of Sleep*, and the three-act *The Candidate*. In 1976, his three-act play *The Brownsville Raid* was produced in New

York City by the Negro Ensemble Company, and in 1978, his two-act musical *Sparrow in Flight* was produced in New York. Another two-act play, *Zooman and the Sign*, won an Obie Award.

In 1980, Fuller completed the teleplay for Ernest J. Gaines's *The Sky Is Gray*, based on Gaines's short story about an African American farm boy learning about his place in the world. In 1981, Fuller's two-act *A Soldier's Play* was produced by the Negro Ensemble Company to high critical acclaim and went on to win the Pulitzer Prize in drama. It was later adapted to the screen by Norman Jewison, who invited Fuller to write the screenplay. *A Soldier's Story*, the film that resulted in 1984, went on to capture Academy Award nominations for Best Picture, Best Adapted Screenplay, and Best Supporting Actor. In 1987, Fuller wrote a screenplay for *A Gathering of Old Men*, a television adaptation of a Gaines novel.

In 1988, Fuller produced *Eliot's Coming* and the first two parts of a play series titled *We* (titled *Sally* and *Prince*). The year 1990 saw the production of part 3 (*Jonquil*) and part 4 (*Burner's Frolic*). *Zooman and the Sign* appeared as a Showtime television production called *Zooman* in 1995, as did a segment from *The Wall* in 1998 and the film *Love Songs* in 1999.

Fuller has earned a number of grants and awards besides the Obie Award in 1981 and the Pulitzer Prize in drama in 1982. Also in 1982, he won the Audelco Award as best playwright. That same year, *A Soldier's Play* won the New York Drama Critics Circle Award, the Outer Circle Critics Award, and the Theatre Club Award. The film adaptation, *A Soldier's Story*, won the Edgar Allan Poe Mystery Award for 1985. Fuller had grants from both the National

Endowment for the Arts and the Rockefeller Foundation in 1976. He was named a Guggenheim Foundation fellow for 1977-1978. He has also been active in the International Association of Poets, Playwrights, Editors, Essayists, and Novelists (PEN), the Writers Guild of America, the Dramatists Guild, and the Dramatist Guild Foundation.

ANALYSIS

Fuller has written a number of tough, uncompromisingly honest plays that can be disturbing to both black and white audiences. His works deal with such controversial issues as miscegenation, racism, reverse racism, and ruthless inner-city violence. He has shown an unflinching determination to scrutinize the consequences of easy liberal solutions to human problems that might occur in the black community and that need to be carefully examined. His plays address the issue of racial justice, to be sure, but he is also keenly aware of the rights of the individual.

The Brownsville Raid, for example, is a three-act play based on a historical incident that occurred in 1906, when a U.S. Army regiment was dishonorably discharged after the black soldiers refused to confess to inciting a riot in Brownsville, Texas. There was no evidence that the men were responsible for the riot, and the men's records were cleared some sixty-six years later when the Army reexamined the case and determined that a gross injustice had been committed. In the play, career Army Sergeant Mingo Saunders has faith that the Army will protect his men, but that faith is betrayed.

Fuller's interest in the conflict between people and institutions is also evident in his other, more widely recognized work in a military setting, *A Soldier's Play*. The play is mainly about justice, military justice and racial justice, but it also concerns integration in an army that is moving toward the last months of World War II. Integration is not to be achieved, of course, for at least another decade, but Fuller's play is historically accurate in suggesting that initial goals of civil rights were achieved in the military, in advance of society at large. The irony of *A Soldier's Play* is that the black soldiers win the right to fight—and then die in combat in Germany.

Fuller pushes the envelope of integration in *The Village: A Party* by focusing upon the issues of racially mixed couples working to achieve a utopian social experiment, an experiment that works until

the leader of the community falls in love with a woman of his own color and becomes a threat to the experiment. In this play, a relationship based upon love cannot succeed unless the colors of the partners are properly matched. The idealistic participants in this experiment do not account for the irrationality of human emotion.

Fuller has never glorified African Americans simplistically, for he is painfully aware of the problems that beset the black community. *Zooman and the Sign*, for example, dramatizes the consequences of ghetto violence by portraying the death of a twelve-year-old girl who is killed by a stray bullet in a neighborhood gang fight. In the play, the father of the dead girl confronts the same fear and apathy that one might expect to find in any neighborhood of any city. Frightened citizens fear becoming involved, even for the good of their neighborhood. When the father posts a sign on his front porch begging neighbors who witnessed the killing to come forth, he is ostracized by cowards who accuse him of "bringing the neighborhood down."

Part of the problem is a reluctance of blacks to cooperate with the police, but this cultural sticking point could also be considered an excuse to avoid taking action. This is a discomforting play that takes on openly such problems as armed teenagers on the streets. Zooman himself, the murderer, is a brutal fifteen-year-old thug, but he is also a victim of his environment. He is depicted as something besides merely a heartless villain.

Fuller turned to the reality of the streets for *Zooman and the Sign* and to the reality of history for *The Brownsville Raid*, but he made a significant dramatic advance with *A Soldier's Play*. The work reflects the atmospheric "reality" of black troops serving in the Deep South during World War II. It also takes the form of an American tragedy, with two potentially tragic protagonists, Sergeant Waters and Private First Class Melvin Peterson, both of whom have absolute notions of what constitutes proper behavior for African Americans in charge of a black company.

Waters hates ignorant "geechies" who perform for whites in expected ways which he considers demeaning and embarrassing. He is obsessed with changing such behavior. He believes that the only way for a black person to succeed in a white world is to adapt white ways, to imitate white speech and assimilate white ambition. He is profoundly embarrassed by country blacks and by black culture in general, as he has spent his life attempting to escape from it.

Waters attempts to change a good-natured country black named C. J. Memphis, but he ends up driving the man to suicide. For this, Waters is hated by his soldiers, two of whom, Peterson and Smalls, encounter him on a country road and shoot him dead. Peterson, the assassin, kills Waters because he cannot condone Waters's behavior. At one point, he asks Waters, "What kind of colored man are you?" He challenges Waters, and the two of them fight at one point, but in fact Waters, who beats Peterson in the fight, also respects him for his spunk and courage.

Peterson, however, despises the sergeant and feels no remorse. Both men are dehumanized by their idealism, but Waters is forced to understand his error in judgment in his treatment of C. J. and therefore reaches a moment of discovery, thus fulfilling a part of the classic Aristotelian tragic formula. He ruins his life and is made to understand why this has happened. His fate is tragic before his death. Even before his abuse of C. J., Waters is presented as being desperately unhappy. The most perceptive reading of his character comes from the unschooled C. J., who says of him, "Any man ain't sure where he belongs must be in a whole lotta pain."

As critics were quick to notice, the play is a tragedy disguised as a mystery that also explores the dynamics of racism. *A Soldier's Play* won the Pulitzer Prize in drama in 1982, no doubt because it represents an advance in both form and substance. In 1984, it was transformed into a motion picture that earned three Academy Award nominations for Best Picture, Best Supporting Actor, and Best Adapted Screenplay.

The film opens up the play and makes a few changes, the most substantial of which are the removal of a bitterly ironic final monologue by Captain Davenport, the investigating officer, and the fact that in the film both Peterson and Smalls are captured, giving Davenport a final opportunity to confront the murderer with the following words: "Who gave you the right to judge? To decide who is good enough to be a Negro, and who is not?" These questions drive home the nature of the tragedy and also the similarity between Peterson and the man he kills.

The film is excellently crafted and wonderfully acted; it both simplifies and clarifies the meaning of the original play. The film was made at a cost of $6 million and earned more than $30 million at the box office, becoming a runaway crossover hit. It set a significant precedent and marked the beginning of the 1980's renaissance of serious black films.

Fuller played a significant role in bringing about that renaissance. He earned an Obie Award for *Zooman and the Sign* as well as the Pulitzer Prize and other awards for *A Soldier's Play*. It is particularly surprising, therefore, that by the early 1990's, only one of his plays remained in print. He is surely one of the most gifted playwrights of his generation, regardless of color, and a major theatrical talent.

THE VILLAGE: A PARTY

First produced: 1968
Type of work: Play

Idealists living in a racially mixed community as a social experiment turn upon their leader when he wavers in his principles.

The Village: A Party is a two-act play that was first produced in Princeton, New Jersey, in 1968, then produced five months later in New York City in 1969 under the ironic title *The Perfect Party*. It is an important early play for Fuller because it raises questions of black awareness that resurface in *A Soldier's Play*. The cast consists of ten characters: five couples, husbands and wives who have founded an integrated, racially mixed community. They come together to celebrate the birthday of their charismatic leader—who, it turns out, has fallen in love with a black woman and wants to leave the white woman he has married.

The other couples are shocked. They see their interracial experimental community as an apparent success, and they are afraid of what will happen to the community's image if they allow their leader to defect from his dream and betray the principles upon which the community was founded. To protect the purity of the experiment, the other couples murder the leader at the birthday party, then insist that his white widow marry another black man.

The play questions the ideal of integration as a

realistic solution to the problem of race by suggesting that integration can, in fact, magnify emotional tension. The individual is made subservient to the community in this play, and the idea of a marriage based upon love is replaced by the notion that one must sacrifice all to satisfy the ideal of integration; the individual will is not to be tolerated. As in *A Soldier's Play*, some characters are attempting to force others to live by their notions of what may be considered right.

As Dan Sullivan wrote in his review of the Princeton production for *The New York Times* (November 13, 1968), "Utopia has become not just a ghetto but a cell-block." The play was controversial in what it had to suggest about miscegenation and also in what it suggested about ideologues so determined to change the world by their example that the life of an individual was deemed inconsequential. In this play, Fuller demonstrated a courageous tendency to question ideals that might be disturbing to both white and black audiences.

Zooman and the Sign

First produced: 1980 (first published, 1982)
Type of work: Play

A decent, working-class family seeks revenge for the death of their twelve-year-old daughter, who has been struck down by a stray bullet in a gang shooting.

The play, set in Philadelphia, begins with a rapping monologue delivered by the jive-talking "Zooman," Lester Johnson, a teenage thug who has just killed a little girl in a gang shootout. "She was in the wrong place at the wrong time," he says, expressing no remorse for having killed the twelve-year-old. Zooman's monologues continue to punctuate the action, but the main dramatic focus is upon the angry and grief-stricken family of Zooman's victim.

Reuben Tate (a bus driver who has been estranged from his wife because of an affair with another woman) and his wife, Rachel, are mourning the death of their child Jinny; they are joined in their grief by Uncle Emmett and their fifteen-year-old son, Victor. Emmett is a hothead who argues for revenge, "an eye for an eye," but Reuben is

more restrained, exclaiming, "We're not head hunters!" Rachel wrongly blames herself for having allowed the child to play outside. Victor says nothing in this argument but asks his friend Russell if he can find him a gun, which Russell agrees to do.

When a neighbor, Donald Jackson, stops by to offer condolences, the audience learns that Reuben had been a light-heavyweight boxer and something of a local celebrity of one time. Jackson tells Reuben that no one on the block would tell the police that they had seen anything. The Tate family knows that there were, in fact, witnesses, and they are disturbed by their neighbors' silence.

In his second monologue, Zooman confesses that "I shot the little bitch 'cause I felt like it!" The audience learns that Zooman and his friend Stockholm served time for raping a schoolteacher, a crime that Zooman claims they did not commit. It is later revealed that Zooman has committed other crimes as well, including armed robbery, and that he is a hard and brutal case. He seems to be the egotistical personification of evil.

Meanwhile, Reuben has attempted to contact the neighbors to find a witness to the shooting, but they are all afraid to come forward. Ash Boswell, a family friend, explains that "black people don't like to deal with the police." The family frustration is heightened because Reuben had been seeing another woman, and Rachel knows about this. For the present, however, they are united in their grief.

Jinny wanted her parents back together. Ironically, her death has given them a common purpose, but the parents do not agree upon what course of action should be taken. Rachel wants to move to another neighborhood, but Reuben knows they cannot afford such a move and seems determined to improve their present neighborhood. They are devastated that neighbors they have known for fifteen years will not come forward to help them identify Zooman as the shooter. Victor has heard rumors that Zooman did the shooting. Reuben has a sign made to hang on his porch, a sign that reads: "The killers of our daughter Jinny are free on the streets because our neighbors will not identify them." The sign proves to be controversial; many of the neighbors are offended.

In act 2, Russell advises Victor not to go after Zooman. He tells Victor that the neighbors are angry about the sign because "it brings the whole neighborhood down." Russell regrets having given

Victor the weapon and is reluctant to provide ammunition. When neighbors begin throwing bricks at the family's front door in protest, Victor brandishes the gun, but his mother disarms him. Reuben and Emmett return from a bar, where they have been in a fight over the sign. Emmett has apparently broken his arm in the fight and needs to be taken to the hospital.

At the funeral service, some people write threats about the sign in the register, and tension builds. The Tates suspect that Jackson or his wife might have witnessed the killing. Jackson denies this but tells Reuben some of the neighbors are organizing a march to tear the sign down. The police call to say that one of the culprits, the fifteen-year-old Stockholm, has been apprehended, adding that he has confessed and named Zooman as the murderer. Rachel tells Reuben that she wants him to leave if he will not take the sign down. Finally, Zooman comes to take down the sign himself and is shot through the window by Uncle Emmett.

Justice is done, perhaps, and Zooman no doubt deserves his fate, but the point is made that his death will not bring Jinny back to life. The play also makes it clear that Zooman himself was a victim of his environment; all that sets him apart from Jinny's brother, Victor, is that Victor has had a stronger home life. The play ends with another sign. "Here, Lester Johnson was killed. He will be missed by family and friends. He was known as Zooman." Hence violence breeds violence. The killing has continued, and the neighborhood has not really been improved.

A SOLDIER'S PLAY

First produced: 1981 (first published, 1982)
Type of work: Play

At first, A Soldier's Play *seems to be a murder mystery in a military setting, but the play is, in fact, both a modern tragedy and a commentary on racist attitudes in the United States.*

A Soldier's Play is set on an Army base at Fort Neal, Louisiana, in 1944, near the end of World War II. A black soldier, Master Sergeant Vernon C. Waters,

has been murdered at night on a country road near the base. The black soldiers and their white officers believe that the killing was racially motivated and probably the work of the Ku Klux Klan. In order to avoid tension between the black soldiers on the base and the local civilians, Colonel Nivens, the base commander, has not ordered a full investigation; the murder is not given the same kind of attention it would have been if a white soldier had been the victim. Captain Taylor, his subordinate, believes justice should be served, however, and he has reported the killing to Army headquarters. Consequently, an officer is sent from Washington, D.C., to investigate the murder.

The Department of the Army dispatches a bright Howard University-trained military attorney, Captain Richard Davenport, who happens to be an oddity for the time, a black officer. Both Colonel Nivens and Captain Taylor are worried about how local whites will react to Davenport. Nivens is convinced that the killers were white, and he assumes that Davenport will go after these racist murderers with a vengeance, causing problems in the white community. Nivens, however, does not understand the man Washington has sent.

Davenport's investigation is thorough, meticulous, and fair. He discovers that Waters was a hard taskmaster, feared by most of his men and despised by some of them. The story is revealed in flashbacks in which Waters alienates his men by picking on a well-liked, good-natured country boy named C. J. Memphis, whom he sends to the brig on a trumped-up charge. C. J. is held there and intimidated by the sergeant. Waters is embarrassed by C. J. and his Uncle Tom ways. C. J. is a gifted musician and also the best batter on the company's baseball team; he is a walking, talking stereotype of a talented, self-deprecating black man, and Waters hates the type. He frames C. J. to get him thrown into the brig so he can intimidate him and change his ways.

Yet the physically strong C. J. is psychologically weak. Driven to desperation in prison, C. J. commits suicide. Waters, who has a conscience after all, suffers guilt for what C. J. has done and turns to drink. His presumption is his tragic flaw; it causes his downfall and, ultimately, his death.

Gradually, Davenport begins to suspect that Waters might have been murdered by his own men, who blamed him for the death of C. J. The team falls apart and loses its chance to be the first all-black team to play the New York Yankees during an exhibition. Waters loses the respect of his men and then his own self-respect. Although Davenport suspects that Waters might have been murdered by his own men, Captain Taylor is pressing him to prosecute two white officers, Lieutenant Byrd and Captain Wilcox, who were placed at the scene of the crime shortly before the killing took place.

The issue becomes one of justice, not race, though the theme of racial justice is an important secondary one. Davenport is a good and dedicated lawyer who follows the evidence to where it takes him, discouraging though that may be. By the end of the play, one of the culprits has been apprehended; in a final monologue, the audience is told that the murderer will be captured a week later in Alabama, leaving the impression that justice will be done in military circles.

Yet there are other, larger social problems that are left unresolved. As Davenport's final monologue makes clear at the end of the play, the entire all-black company is doomed, even though they have won the right to fight the Germans in Europe. Davenport explains at the conclusion that the men of the company, the "entire outfit—officers and enlisted men—was wiped out in the Ruhr Valley during a German advance."

Moreover, Sergeant Waters is honored as a hero; he is believed to be the first black soldier from his hometown to die in action, because his death was wrongly reported. Thus, although the play celebrates a victory for the black soldiers, who win the right to fight for their country, the story ends with an ironic denouement that is devastating. The moral victory and the resolution of justice are made to seem hollow by the final monologue, which was removed from the film version. Fuller was given the opportunity to reinvent his drama for the screen and, in doing so, managed to clarify the message, even though the tone of the conclusion was substantially changed.

SUMMARY

Fuller's probing examinations of the corrosive effects of racism have earned him the admiration of critics and the attention of a wide audience. The popular success of his best-known work, *A Soldier's Play*, in both its stage and film versions demonstrates that serious—even disquieting—literature need not be the exclusive province of academics and the avant-garde. Fuller has transcended the limitations implied in such labels as "black playwright" to earn recognition simply as one of America's most accomplished dramatists.

James M. Welsh

BIBLIOGRAPHY

By the Author

DRAMA:
Sun Flowers, The Rise, pr. 1968 (one acts)
The Village: A Party, pr. 1968 (pr. 1969 as *The Perfect Party*)
In My Many Names and Days, pr. 1972
The Candidate, pr. 1974
First Love, pr. 1974
In the Deepest Part of Sleep, pr. 1974
The Lay Out Letter, pr. 1975
The Brownsville Raid, pr. 1976
Sparrow in Flight, pr. 1978
Zooman and the Sign, pr. 1980, pb. 1982
A Soldier's Play, pr. 1981, pb. 1982

Sally, pr. 1988
Prince, pr. 1988
Eliot's Coming, pr. 1988 (pr. as part of the musical revue *Urban Blight*)
We, pr. 1989 (combined performance of *Sally* and *Prince*; parts 1 and 2 of planned 5-part play series)
Jonquil, pr. 1990 (part 3 of *We* play series)
Burner's Frolic, pr. 1990 (part 4 of *We* play series)

SCREENPLAYS:
A Soldier's Story, 1984 (adaptation of his play)
Zooman, 1995 (adaptation of his play)

TELEPLAYS:
Roots, Resistance, and Renaissance, 1967 (series)
Mitchell, 1968
Black America, 1970-1971 (series)
The Sky Is Gray, 1980 (from the story by Ernest J. Gaines)
A Gathering of Old Men, 1987 (adaptation of the novel by Gaines)
Love Songs, 1999

DISCUSSION TOPICS

- In Charles Fuller's plays, military justice sometimes turns out to be military injustice. Give examples.

- What accounts for the reluctance of African Americans to cooperate with police in *Zooman and the Sign*?

- What are the arguments for and against Fuller's recommendation that African Americans imitate the speech habits of white Americans?

- What is reverse racism? Trace this theme in Fuller's plays.

- Aside from his authorship of plays, what important contributions has Fuller made to the cinema and the theater?

About the Author

Anadolu-Okur, Nilgun. *Contemporary African American Theater: Afrocentricity in the Works of Larry Neal, Amiri Baraka, and Charles Fuller.* New York: Garland, 1997.

Banham, Martin, ed. *The Cambridge Guide to World Theatre.* New York: Cambridge University Press, 1988.

Baraka, Amiri. "The Descent of Charlie Fuller into Pulitzerland and the Need for African-American Institutions." *Black Literature Forum* 17 (Summer, 1983): 51-54.

Draper, James P., ed. *Black Literature Criticism.* Vol. 4. Detroit: Gale, 1992.

Fuller, Charles. "Pushing Beyond the Pulitzer." Interview by Frank White. *Ebony* 38 (March, 1983): 116.

_____. "When Southern Blacks Went North." Interview by Helen Dudar. *The New York Times*, December 18, 1988, p. C5.

Harriot, Esther. "Charles Fuller: The Quest for Justice." In *American Voices: Five Contemporary Playwrights in Essays and Interviews.* Jefferson, N.C.: McFarland, 1988.

Kuner, Mildred C., and Christian H. Moe. "Charles Fuller." In *Critical Survey of Drama*, edited by Carl Rollyson. 2d rev. ed. Pasadena, Calif.: Salem Press, 2003.

Savran, David. *In Their Own Words: Contemporary American Playwrights.* New York: Theater Communications Group, 1988.

WILLIAM GADDIS

Born: New York, New York
    December 29, 1922
Died: East Hampton, New York
    December 16, 1998

Gaddis's innovative uses of dialogue in fiction and his sharply barbed satires of American society have confirmed his standing as a major American novelist.

© Marion Ettlinger

BIOGRAPHY

William Thomas Gaddis was born in New York City on December 29, 1922, the only child of parents who were divorced when he was three years old. His mother soon moved to Massapequa, Long Island, where Gaddis was raised in a house that would eventually serve as a model for the Bast house in his second novel, *JR* (1975). On his mother's side, Gaddis's family were Quakers, but he was brought up in a strict Calvinist tradition upon which he would draw for his first novel, *The Recognitions* (1955).

An intensely private man, Gaddis granted few interviews, and little is known about his life. He always preferred that his novels speak for themselves. It is known, however, that between the ages of five and thirteen, he was educated at a boarding school in Berlin, Connecticut, and that he later attended Farmingdale High School in Long Island. These experiences appear to have provided material for the vividly anguished recollections of his fictional character Jack Gibbs in *JR*, who cynically laments a lonely and emotionally unsatisfying childhood. Indeed, in Gaddis's novels much of the alienation, disorder, and strife that sets the narratives in motion and besets the characters has its beginning in the absence or death of the protagonists' fathers.

While in high school, Gaddis contracted a rare disease, erythema grave, upon whose symptoms of high fever and delusions he draws for Wyatt Gwyon, the protagonist of his first novel. Though easily cured with modern drugs, a kidney disorder that was a side effect of his treatment left Gaddis unfit for military service in World War II. Throughout the war he was a student at Harvard University. Enrolling in September, 1941, Gaddis majored in English literature, joined the staff of the *Lampoon* (a satirical campus magazine) in 1943, and then, beginning in September, 1944, took over the prestigious post of *Lampoon* president. This work provided Gaddis his first outlet for publication. His early pieces covered a wide range of forms: reviews, verse parodies, essays, short fictions, and satires of such forms as the scientific report.

Gaddis's Harvard career was cut short in his senior year. He and a drinking companion tangled with the Cambridge police, word of it came to the college dean, and both students were asked to resign. Gaddis then took up residence in New York's Greenwich Village and for two years worked as a fact checker at *The New Yorker.* Years later, he noted how this otherwise boring job taught him the virtue of paying close attention to details of reference and allusion. Late in 1947, Gaddis left New York and began a five-year sojourn through Mexico, Central America, and Europe, working his way as a machinist, briefly carrying a rifle during a civil war in Costa Rica, and beginning work on his first novel—through it all, he occasionally returned to the family residence on Long Island. Again these events were transmuted into fiction: they provide the experiences of Otto and Wyatt in *The Recognitions.*

The year 1950 found Gaddis in Paris writing radio scripts for United Nations Educational, Scientific, and Cultural Organization (UNESCO) broadcasts. There he briefly put *The Recognitions* aside to publish his first magazine work, a humorous article about player pianos for *The Atlantic Monthly.* On returning to the United States in 1951, he resumed work on the novel, secured a publisher's advance that allowed him to work full-time on what was becoming a very long manuscript. He also fell in with the Beat Generation writers—Jack Kerouac, Gregory Corso, Chandler Brossard, and others then residing in Greenwich Village. Gaddis finished *The Recognitions* in 1954; it was published in March, 1955, after some in-house disputes about whether the book should be cut or should be published at all.

Reactions to *The Recognitions* were greatly disappointing to Gaddis, as reviewers seemed rarely to have gotten beyond its length and difficulties of plot and reference. Still more disappointing were the sales figures. In hardcover and paper, the novel would sell fewer than seven thousand copies in its initial run, would top those figures only slightly with a 1962 re-release, and for years thereafter would be known among a limited group of writers and critics as a darkly satirical novel that brilliantly forecast the black humor fictions of the 1960's.

During this time (he was once classed among "ten neglected writers"), Gaddis nevertheless remained very active. He occasionally supported himself by writing for business and industry. When awarded a National Institute of Arts and Letters grant in 1963, he had a play and several novels either written or in progress, including another long novel, a satire of American finance that eventually became *JR.* Scholarly essays analyzing his first novel also began to appear, and when *JR* was published in 1975, it was to universal acclaim. This novel, another long and trying fiction that one critic called "a masterpiece of acoustical collage," won Gaddis a National Book Award in 1976. Further compensation for the years of relative neglect came in 1982, with the award of a prestigious MacArthur Foundation "genius grant" as well as with the first widespread scholarly attention to his writing.

During the 1970's and 1980's, Gaddis taught literature and creative writing at Bard College, published several more magazine pieces, and completed his third novel, *Carpenter's Gothic* (1985), which uses as its setting the Victorian house Gaddis owns in Piermont, New York. More accessible than his previous novels because of its brevity, *Carpenter's Gothic* is nevertheless as difficult in its collage methods and as dark in its satire as either of Gaddis's earlier fictions.

A fourth novel, *A Frolic of His Own,* was published to great critical acclaim in 1994, earning him a second National Book Award. He became a member of the Academy of Arts and Letters in 1989. William Gaddis died on December 16, 1998, as a result of prostate cancer and other illnesses. The semi-autobiographical novella *Agapé Agape* was published posthumously in 2002.

ANALYSIS

In "The Rush for Second Place," an April, 1981, essay for *Harper's* magazine, Gaddis spelled out the central concern of his fictions. "The real marvel of our complex technological world," he writes, is "that anything goes right at all." Events seem to follow a law of entropy: The more complex the system or message, the greater the chance for disorganization or error. Thus, in a United States grown hugely complex, there is "failure so massive," Gaddis argued, that no one is accountable, and few things seem "worth doing well" any more. From these convictions spring some of the main difficulties in reading Gaddis's works. The initial difficulties are of style, and they chiefly involve the complex allusions woven into the fabric of his dialogues and brief descriptive passages. They also involve Gaddis's experiments with dialogue.

The allusiveness of Gaddis's writing was a notable trait from the beginning. *The Recognitions* quotes and makes other forms of indirect reference to a wide range of texts: Snippets of T. S. Eliot's poetry appear alongside other literary allusions, but the principal field of reference is that of religious myth and mysticism. Gaddis draws from secondary works of scholarship such as Robert Grave's *The White Goddess* (1948) and James Fraser's massive *The Golden Bough* (1890-1915), as well as from an impressive range of primary texts by the Catholic Church fathers (Saints Clement and Ignatius), and other sources such as the Qur'ān, *The Egyptian Book of the Dead,* and books on occult beliefs and practices.

For his second novel, *JR*, Gaddis once more cast a wide net, bringing into play allusions to pre-Socratic philosophy, the poetry of Alfred, Lord Tennyson, and Germanic mythology—especially as it was popularly embodied in Richard Wagner's operatic cycle *Der Ring des Nibelungen* (wr. 1848-1852; *The Ring of the Nibelung*). Initial reviews of *The Recognitions* were perhaps harshest in judging these seemingly overdone scholarly tendencies in Gaddis's writing. Nevertheless, a first-time reader of Gaddis's novels does well to keep in mind that this allusive quality serves his aim of satirizing the uses of Western knowledge; a number of the allusions mouthed by characters are drawn from dictionaries of quotations and clearly participate in Gaddis's broad satire of those who pretend to learnedness.

Taken at a distance, the allusions to world mythologies are also crucial to Gaddis's great theme. They evoke a technologized, modern world in which meaning has shattered into "sound bites" or fragments of political and social dogma or even into mere errors. It is a world in which individuals long, often nostalgically, for totalizing messages, for the very stuff that myth provides.

The second stylistic difficulty of Gaddis's writing springs from his experiments with dialogue. Along with James Joyce, and especially American authors such as Donald Barthelme and William Burroughs, Gaddis has stripped his characters' direct speech of any conventional markers. He eliminated not only the quotation marks (which is the first thing the reader notices) but also markers such as speakers' names, details about voice inflections, gestural counterparts, or contextual details identifying the localities of speech.

All such narrative particulars may still he embedded in the characters' direct discourse (or, as well, they may not be). A Gaddis novel thus demands a much more active reader to reconstruct these ordinary signs of narrative art; eventually, in fact, one begins to know the voices by means of identifying tics, such as Jack Bast's expletives or J. R. Vansant's repeated exclamations ("Well holy!") in *JR*. The result is an auditory performance of human speech, in all its fragmentariness, as if recorded by some omnipresent instrument. From these minimal but very potent semblances of speech, one is able to imagine a world, including the knotted woof of the characters' pasts as they are criss-crossed by the accelerated and very noisy warp of present events.

Gaddis began to develop these rapid-fire dialogues in *The Recognitions*, with chapters set in the crowded and artistically pretentious nightclubs of Greenwich Village. These scenes of his first novel, composing a minor percentage of the text, are among its most memorably ludicrous for their disconnectedness and qualities of humorous counterpoint. In *JR* and *Carpenter's Gothic*, the technique has virtually taken over. Gaddis's second novel even dispenses with conventional markers of scene and time change, traditionally handled in fiction by chapter endings and beginnings or by the descriptive interventions of an omniscient narrator. Instead, across its several months of story time and 726 pages of text, *JR* is one seamless, nonstop ride on the babbling tongues of Americans in the year 1971. To block out chronologically separate scenes, chapter divisions were restored in *Carpenter's Gothic*, but they disappear again in *A Frolic of His Own*.

After his death, Gaddis became a central figure in an ongoing debate on the value of ambitious literary fiction versus conventional fiction. In the 2002 essay "Mr. Difficult," novelist Jonathan Franzen expressed his ambivalence for the postmodern novel—Gaddis's work in particular—and the demands that it places on readers, provoking a firestorm of controversy in the literary world.

In large measure, the boldness of Gaddis's techniques may be gauged by remembering that he was, foremost, a satirist. In traditional narrative satire, it is the function of omniscient intervention both to point out clearly and to judge plainly the exemplars of folly and vice. Gaddis refused to do this. He did, however, weave into each fiction a voice that points the finger and unceremoniously judges; such are the characters named Willy in *The Recognitions*, Jack Gibbs in *JR*, and McCandless in *Carpenter's Gothic*, who variously served as Gaddis's outraged mouthpieces. Yet theirs were merely other voices among the din, so the lack of an omniscient standpoint still left the task of moral judgment to the reader. It was only with the posthumous *Agapé Agape* that the reader was addressed directly by the narrator, a fictional stand-in for Gaddis himself. However, the conclusions that the narrator reached in this highly demanding final work still leave the reader unsure of what judgment to make, what lessons to learn.

Doubtless, this is exactly the point. As immensely complex "messages" in narrative, and charged as they are on the hyperspeeds and incompletions of contemporary technological culture, Gaddis's novels ask the reader to confront forms of "failure so massive" that they would initially seem to defy order or meaning. Having confronted them, though, the reader's next task is to begin tracing lines of organization and eventually to see that someone can indeed be held "accountable." In *The Recognitions*, Gaddis holds up before readers a massive indictment of fakery in all reaches of American culture; in *JR*, his target is the failure of democratic capitalism as an American ideal; in *Carpenter's Gothic*, his subject is the degrading of American millennial ideals by popular media, religions, and politics; and in *A Frolic of His Own*, it is the abuses of the American legal system under the false pursuit of justice. Defined by thematic intentions such as these, Gaddis's novels make literary claims of major importance.

THE RECOGNITIONS

First published: 1955
Type of work: Novel

An artist searches for authenticity and order in a culture defined by its myriad counterfeits and its decline into disorder.

The Recognitions takes its title from a third century theological romance inscribed by Saint Clement, whose story concerned a neophyte's search for true religious experience in the midst of a corrupted empire. Set in the 1950's in the United States, and mainly in New York City, Gaddis's novel nevertheless finds parallels (as one character notes) with "Caligula's Rome, with a new circus of vulgar bestialized suffering in the newspapers." Across 958 densely written pages, the text narrates the story of Wyatt Gwyon's maturation, both aesthetic and spiritual.

Like most of Gaddis's novels, this one begins with contested lines of descent. From the side of his mother, Camilla (who wanted to name him Stephen), Wyatt has inherited an artistic temperament. From his father, a Calvinist minister, he inherits a severe sense of the damnation of humankind and of his own guilt in particular. During a sojourn in Spain, Camilla dies mysteriously when Wyatt is three, and later the raging fevers of a mysterious childhood illness (drawn from memories of Gaddis's bout with erythema grave) seem to confirm what he has been taught as a Calvinist.

It is Wyatt's gift for drawing, however, that seems to pull his spirit back to health. Wyatt opts for divinity school, as had his father, but he paints in secret and eventually leaves the United States for Europe to study painting. There Wyatt is oblivious to styles of modernist art, and his best works are "recognitions" of the Flemish masters of the late middle ages. Disparaged by fashionable critics for this work, Wyatt gives it up, returns to the United States, and settles for draftsmen's work and a mindless marriage.

Lapsing into cynical despair over his failures, Wyatt is discovered by an art dealer, Recktall Brown, who proposes to employ the young man's talents in creating almost faultless forgeries of the Flemish masters, which he moreover proposes to have "authenticated" by his associate, a corrupted art critic named Basil Valentine. The circle of this plan closes when Wyatt's canvases bring spectacular prices and, indeed, even a perverse recognition of his talents. Plunged into the relentless work demanded of him by this counterfeiting ring, Wyatt also falls into the pretentious bohemian demimonde of Greenwich Village. These chapters provide Gaddis opportunities for some of his most corrosive satires of an art world driven by egotism and profit motives. In this middle portion of the novel, Wyatt is virtually surrounded by frauds: Frank Sinisterra, a counterfeiter; Otto Pivner, a failed playwright who fakes a war injury, and whose only artistic motive is pecuniary gain; and Agnes Deigh, an overweight matron of the art world who encourages artists by feeding their conflicting physical and spiritual needs.

Increasingly depressed because of his corruption by money and the semblances of fame in this society, Wyatt considers resuming his divinity studies. The break finally comes after he witnesses Brown's ludicrous death, in a fake suit of medieval armor. He also causes—or so he mistakenly thinks—the death of Basil Valentine. Wyatt flees America once again, on the same boat which had evidently brought his father home from Spain after

Camilla's untimely death. Wyatt eventually winds up at the same Spanish monastery, at Estremadura, where his mother is buried. Here Wyatt closes a different kind of circle. Not only does he change his name to Stephen, as his mother intended; he also leaves behind the seemingly ceaseless guilt about the conflict of matter and spirit which is his inheritance from his father.

Wyatt resumes a relationship with a Spanish mistress from his first European trip and commits himself to raising a child of that union. He also resumes his theological studies. He accepts the need for earned income, yet he continues with the painting which had been so corrupted by greed. The novel thus ends with tenuous assertions of balance, though on a very small scale. Wyatt/Stephen, his tiny family, their meager belongings, and few paintings suggest a balance achievable only in minimalist forms—a recurring theme in Gaddis's later work.

Wyatt/Stephen's solution stands opposite the enormously detailed world that Gaddis realized in this very large tapestry. Gaddis's satirical target was a society in which, as Frank Sinisterra notes, "Everything's middlemen. Everything's cheap work and middlemen wherever you look. They're the ones who take the profit." Elsewhere, Recktall Brown (whose name fixes his identity, as do the monikers given to other characters) plans "a novel factory, a sort of assembly line" for fictions that will be patchworked from other texts, for (as he asks), "What hasn't been written before?" The dialogue of Otto Pivner's play is plagiarized from Wyatt's abstruse bar-room speeches, themselves bursting with quotations and allusions. Wyatt's quest is to get outside these vicious circles. In his last scene, he stands within his monastery room and releases a bird from his cupped hands. The confused creature momentarily flutters before Wyatt's most recent painting—a work that has given up the apparently ceaseless mirroring of other artworks to become, instead, like a window. This is the most that Gaddis's dark novel will provide by way of positive values.

JR

First published: 1975
Type of work: Novel

A sixth grader fed promises absurdly builds a megacorporation which spins toward catastrophe and nearly pulls an artist down with it.

In *JR*, the society of "middlemen" has spread, virus-like, and the resulting depreciation of all values is Gaddis's main theme. The characters' desires for commercial and aesthetic success highlight a crisis in values: Artistic significations (words and musical sounds, for example) are conflated with money, and a monetized culture further governed by the principal of usury (the extracting of "interest") diminishes things all around. In this novel, therefore, money almost literally talks—and does so in relentless, rapid-fire sentences that threaten to drown out meaning. Edward Bast, the artist figure of this novel, must struggle relentlessly to free himself from these conditions. Mostly he struggles with a vastly institutionalized usury that drives him, at novel's end, into a feverish delirium (brought on by exhaustion and pneumonia) that recalls Wyatt's at the beginning of *The Recognitions.*

JR opens in the Long Island home of Bast's two aging aunts, who are engaged with a lawyer in discussing the settlement of the estate of Thomas Bast—their brother, Edward's father, and the owner of a business that manufactures player piano rolls. Thomas has died intestate, and thus, as in Gaddis's first novel, the constituting theme is inheritance. Edward's appears to be a purely financial legacy, but the characters' dialogues unfold complications: Thomas's first wife bore him a daughter, Stella, with claims on the estate; it also becomes evident that Thomas's second wife, Nellie, may have conceived Edward during an adulterous affair with Thomas's brother, James. Edward might therefore lay claim to the Bast wealth through either, or both, of these potential fathers. The overriding question, however, is whether he will choose to inherit the gifts of art or money.

Enter J. R. Vansant, a sixth grader at the Long Island school where Bast has been hired to teach music—absurdly, he is teaching Wagner's *The Ring of the Nibelung* for an upcoming performance. JR's part of the opera is, significantly, that of Alberich, the grotesque gnome who renounces love for money and sets out to enslave men by possessing the golden ring of the Nibelung. Having just returned from a field trip to a Wall Street brokerage house, JR is filled with dreams of unlimited financial success.

A bit of epithetic advice proferred by one of the cynical brokers—"buy for credit, sell for cash"—inspires JR. Scanning the newspaper want ads, working from a phone booth, and aided by an unwitting Edward Bast, JR purchases (on credit) four-and-a-half million surplus picnic forks from the U.S. Air Force, and as quickly sells them (for cash) to the Army. His ventures burgeon from that point, as JR acquires bankrupt companies, empty mining claims, an entire bankrupted New England mill town full of pensioned employees, a chain of nursing homes that services the pensioned millworkers (and is tied to another chain of funeral homes), as well as the Bast family company. In sum, "The JR Family of Companies" (as it is eventually known) balloons around the empty, the incomplete, the aged, and the dead. Yet it is wildly successful. By novel's end, when JR's enterprise comes crashing down, it triggers a national financial crisis.

JR functions as the consummate middleman in a society of cynical dealers. Along the way, Gaddis's satire took aim at Wall Street, at government, and especially at school administrators driven by chances to profit at the same kinds of "business tie-ins" that JR finagles. The novel's most consistent voice for this corrosive satire is Jack Gibbs, a science teacher at JR's school. He first appears in the text while trying to teach students the concept of entropy, which predicts the ultimate thermodynamic degradation of any closed system. This theory sets forward a crucial analogy in Gaddis's novel: in the closed (adulterous and nearly incestuous) system of the Bast family, entropy has seemed to lay their entire estate to waste, and that result is duplicated in the equally closed "family" of JR's companies, or indeed throughout the economy of which JR's ventures are simply a part. Gibbs rages against these abuses, and he tries (and in the course of the novel fails) both to love and to write. Thus, he exits the novel an impotent, sickly figure who cannot arrest the general decay, a failure he shares with a swarm of would-be artists around him.

Bast's story is more suggestive, however. Although plunged into the chaos of JR's school and business dealings, Bast struggles to compose a vastly orchestrated opera. Frustrated and broke, he barters his services on Wall Street by agreeing to write the musical accompaniment to a documentary film. Failing at both of these—in short, failing at both art and moneymaking—Bast begins limiting his artistic work. In succession he starts, and leaves aside, a cantata and then a suite. His frantic involvements as JR's "financial manager" drag him down until, exhausted and feverish in the hospital, he composes a brief solo work for cello. Initially he tosses this work in a hospital trash can but, leaving the hospital, he rescues the composition for the simple reason that a deceased roommate had liked the "idea" of Bast's music.

As in *The Recognitions*, Gaddis ended his second novel with suggestions that his artistic hero has, at last, managed to get "outside" the social contradictions hemming him in and has done so chiefly by working in a minimalist form. Even so, Gaddis gave his Alberich, JR, the last word. JR is a celebrity now, working the college lecture circuit, appearing in parades and on talk shows, and even contemplating writing a book. His business emerges from the chaos just as recuperated as Bast's aesthetic spirit. Gaddis's satire thus turned darker: His artist exits the novel a shambling and harried figure, as money triumphs over all.

CARPENTER'S GOTHIC

First published: 1985
Type of work: Novel

A nexus of political, journalistic, and religious affiliations spin the United States uncontrollably toward a nuclear holocaust in Africa, aided by a Vietnam War veteran.

Gaddis's third novel in as many decades, *Carpenter's Gothic* was also his bleakest satire. Its style, as well as its theme of cultural entropy in a civilization where meaning and value are utterly degraded in a complex "media-scape," are consistent developments for him. While no plot summary can succeed in conveying the rich tapestry of characters, events, and cultural detailing in his work, this novel is not only briefer (at 262 pages) but also more focused—and therefore more readable—than either of Gaddis's prior works. For many readers, it therefore constitutes the best door into the writer's work.

The story centers on the last four weeks in the life of Elizabeth Vorakers Booth, a former debutante and the daughter of a mineral tycoon. Her father's suicide, nine years earlier, had been a desperate attempt to block the U.S. Senate's investigation of various briberies, manipulations of the media, and monopolistic dealings in Africa that assured his company's success. Liz's husband, Paul, a Vietnam War veteran, transacted F. R. Vorakers's bribes; he met (and seduced) Liz while testifying before the Congress after her father's death.

The novel thus opens, as did Gaddis's prior works, with complications resulting from a father's will or lack thereof. Desperately frustrated that fortunes are either tied up in lawsuits or manipulated by a network of self-serving associates, Paul Booth rages against his fate, meanwhile goading Liz into pursuing any available tidbits the estate lawyers might give up and prodding her further into a lawsuit he has brought against an airline responsible (he claims) for his loss of Liz's "marital services" when she was injured four years previously in a plane crash. Meanwhile, he has attached himself as a "media consultant" to the Reverend Ude, a fundamentalist preacher whose South Carolina television ministry is rapidly burgeoning into an influential social and political force.

Paul and Liz are verging on bankruptcy. She approaches their ruin with a pathetic resignation, but Paul drunkenly schemes and rages either at Liz, at the morning newspaper, or at the incessantly ringing telephone, in dialogues that unfold entirely within the Booths' Hudson Valley rental house, the curiously pieced-together "Carpenter's Gothic," which they have rented from a Mr. McCandless.

With McCandless's entry into the novel, events begin to close in on the characters, as always happens in a Gaddis novel. McCandless, a sometime geologist, teacher, and writer, had surveyed the very southeast African mineral fields in which the Vorakers Reserve Company had consolidated its fortunes years ago, and in which the Reverend Ude is now building missions for a great "harvest of souls" expected during "the Rapture," or anticipated Second Coming of Christ. McCandless is being pursued by both the Internal Revenue Service for back taxes and the Central Intelligence Agency (CIA) for information about those African territories. He arrives one autumn morning to gather some papers from a locked room. A shambling, weary man, an incessant smoker and an alcoholic, McCandless is nevertheless a romantic mystery man to Liz, who straightaway takes him to bed.

Occasionally bursting into the claustrophobic and chaotic spaces of the novel is Liz's younger brother, Billy, a curious mix of cynicism and idealism. He is so taken by McCandless's drunken tirades against the nexus of American media, government institutions, and popular religions that he goes off to Africa himself, where he is killed when his plane is gunned down by terrorists. Events spin toward catastrophe. The Reverend Ude is under investigation for bribing a senator to grant a new television license, and the media skewer Ude for drowning a boy who had presented himself for baptism. In southeast Africa, civil war erupts. Liz learns that all of her stored personal belongings, her final links to family and tradition, were auctioned off.

The end comes on several fronts at once. McCandless, having accepted a CIA offer (or bribe) for his papers, simply exits the narrative after failing to persuade Liz to leave with him. She dies of a heart attack, the warning symptoms of which Gaddis has planted from the novel's beginning. While doubtless symbolizing an absolute loss of empathy and love in this fictional world, even Liz's heart attack is ironized when it is erroneously identified as having taken place during a burglary. Paul wastes no time in moving to claim any inheritance due Billy and Liz, and he exits the novel using the same seductive approach on Liz's best friend that he had used on Liz nine years earlier. In Africa, political events explode: U.S. forces are poised to strike in protection of "national interests"; indeed, apocalypse looms as senators and media commentators laud the use of nuclear weapons—a "10 K 'DEMO' BOMB OFF AFRICA COAST," as one headline puts the news.

With this novel, Gaddis brought his satire toward a kind of limit. There is nothing darker or more bitter in his work than McCandless's ragings against the failures of American democracy. Other than the cynical exits of Paul and McCandless, there seems no way out of this novel's dilemmas, and there is no generative artwork either, however minimal. Yet this novel clarified how Gaddis's great subject had always been the United States: the crushing weight of its mass society on the individual, the corruption of its civic institutions, the monetization and hence the counterfeiting of all values, and therefore the loss of its cultural inheritance. These remain the great themes of his satire.

A FROLIC OF HIS OWN

First published: 1994
Type of work: Novel

The law becomes a powerful weapon that backfires on a highly litigious man whose life is falling apart.

This novel is set thematically by the opening line, "Justice?—You get justice in the next world, in this world you have the law." Justice is conceptual and as an abstract ideal can be perfect, while law is about language and is limited, ambiguous, bound by context. The ideal is often invoked, while the practical application is used and abused by the greedy and self-important. The novel's title itself is a legal term, referring to a contracted worker who does something not specified in his contract and in doing so injures himself: The example used is of someone blinding himself by shooting paper clips with rubber bands at the office.

College professor Oscar Crease's life seems to be a constant frolic of his own: Readers first meet him in the hospital, having run himself over when he hot-wired his own car. He intends to sue the car company, Sosumi, and is in the middle of another lawsuit: Oscar claims that a vulgar, best-selling film plagiarized his play about the Civil War (based on Gaddis's own unpublished play). Returning to the deteriorating house where he grew up and contin-

ues to live, Oscar is cared for by his current girlfriend, Lily, and his sister Christina, who is suffering a strained relationship with her husband, Harry. As in other Gaddis novels, a good deal of action occurs offstage and certain characters never appear but loom heavily over those readers come to know. Oscar and Christina must deal with their father, a controversial judge whose ruling on a case involving a dog caught in an abstract steel statue has stirred a frenzy in the local community.

As lawsuits proliferate, so do documents—newspapers, transcripts, screenplays, legal rulings—all of which are parodied by Gaddis for their idiosyncratic use of language. If the flow of dialogue in a Gaddis novel is meant to reflect the thought processes of human beings, then the written documents are more insidious for being more consciously crafted and thus manipulated in unusual ways. Humor is mined when dialogue and the written word clash, and Gaddis infuses a great deal of aesthetic criticism and allusions into the documents that litter the novel: Judges make elaborate references to literature, while lawyers debate philosophical issues—all, it seems, in the service of the law, all mere fodder to the dehumanizing interaction of frivolous legal arguments.

Freed from justice, the law in *A Frolic of His Own* swings back and forth: Rulings are held in the balance, decided in favor of one side, reversed. Fortunes also swing in more literal fashion as the Creases, apparently affluent, are beset by bills that they cannot pay, with Oscar counting on lawsuits ruling in his favor for future income. The familial and legal dysfunctions unite gracefully when Oscar wins his suit against the film: The decision in his favor seems to have been molded by his estranged father, who dies soon afterward but has at least made this strange rapprochement with his son. It quickly becomes a Pyrrhic victory, however, as the producers claim that no actual profits have been made, while the estate that Justice Crease leaves behind for his children is little else but the expensive, deteriorating house. By the end, Harry is also dead (his life insurance paid to his law firm), and the Crease orphans are broke. The novel closes with Oscar tickling Christina until she cannot breathe, both of them reduced to a powerless infantilism.

Agapé Agape

First published: 2002
Type of work: Novel

A dying man makes his last statement about the history of the player piano and its relevance to modern culture.

Surrounded by the documents and papers accumulated over the course of his life, the dying man who narrates *Agapé Agape* is desperate to convey what he can of his work. The title is a pun: *agapé* is a Greek word referring to unconditional brotherly love and community, now most commonly used by Christians. For such love to be agape may mean that it has been torn apart, or caught off-guard and surprised. Indeed, in tracing the history of the player piano to other developments in the modern world—including the rising use of binary (which in turn led to the computer age), as well as changing attitudes about the individual's relationship to art—the narrator is filled with frustration at how the significance of his work is not appreciated by the world at large.

There is a strong autobiographical element to the narrator, as Gaddis was also aware of his impending death and had decades of notes regarding his own history of the player piano. The writing is dense and intimidating. The syntax is more complex than any previous Gaddis harangue, with no paragraph breaks in the novella to help guide one's reading. There are frequent lapses into other languages, as well as a constant stream of historical and artistic allusions. As an example, the narrator returns again and again to the philosopher Jeremy Bentham's famous observation that pushpin (a pub game) is as good as poetry if the amount of pleasure is equal, and from there tends to link the word "pushpin" to Pushkin, referring to the Russian poet Alexander Pushkin.

The narrator compares himself to his own documents, his skin parchment thin from medicine and held together by staples. His only refuge is the work that he is trying to complete: "hallucinations took place in the head, in the mind, now everything out there is the hallucination and the mind where the work is done is the only reality." The novella ends much as it began, but the very act of communicating—the direct address to the reader, something Gaddis never attempted in his earlier novels—becomes its own message, its own grasp at hope and continuity in the face of bitter finality.

Summary

It has often been noted that a satirist functions as the infuriated conscience of his or her national culture. The novels of Gaddis attest the accuracy of that statement. Gaddis's principal subject concerns the terms of failure in America. Like F. Scott Fitzgerald, Mark Twain, or Herman Melville, Gaddis took issue with the democratic ideal that success in great things shall come to all Americans who simply work hard for it. Throughout his writing runs the counterconviction that even small successes come only through hard-fought moral, aesthetic, and spiritual struggles.

Steven Weisenburger; updated by Ray Mescallado

Bibliography

By the Author

LONG FICTION:
The Recognitions, 1955
JR, 1975
Carpenter's Gothic, 1985
A Frolic of His Own, 1994
Agapé Agape, 2002

NONFICTION:
The Rush for Second Place: Essays and Occasional Writings, 2002 (Joseph Tabbi, editor)

About the Author

Bloom, Harold, ed. *William Gaddis: Bloom's Modern Critical Views*. Philadelphia: Chelsea House, 2003.

Comnes, Gregory. *The Ethics of Indeterminacy in the Novels of William Gaddis*. Gainesville: University Press of Florida, 1994.

Johnston, John. *Carnival of Repetition: Gaddis's "The Recognitions" and Postmodern Theory*. Philadelphia: University of Pennsylvania Press, 1990.

Knight, Christopher J. *Hints and Guesses: William Gaddis's Fiction of Longing*. Madison: University of Wisconsin Press, 1997.

Kuehl, John, and Steven Moore, eds. *In Recognition of William Gaddis*. Syracuse, N.Y.: Syracuse University Press, 1984.

Moore, Steven. *A Reader's Guide to William Gaddis's "The Recognitions."* Lincoln: University of Nebraska Press, 1982.

_____. *William Gaddis*. Boston: Twayne, 1989.

Wolfe, Peter. *A Vision of His Own: The Mind and Art of William Gaddis*. Madison, N.J.: Fairleigh Dickinson University Press, 1997.

DISCUSSION TOPICS

- Parse a William Gaddis monologue or dialogue, tracing the strands of thoughts that develop. What does this exercise tell about communication and how people relate to one another?

- Gaddis was a scathing critic of capitalism but also believed that it is the best system humankind has created. Explore how this tension is expressed in his work, showing both capitalism's excesses and its advantages.

- Consider the role of inaction in a Gaddis novel. What characters resist acting? What are the results? Is action always the best option? Why or why not?

- Explore anger and frustration as the defining mood of Gaddis's work.

- Gaddis often uses puns and wordplay in his books. Explore specific examples of this and how they serve the story thematically.

- Discuss techniques of transition in Gaddis's work, such as the telephone in *JR* or passages marking time in *Carpenter's Gothic*. How do they influence the reading of his work? How are they unique stylistic choices?

ERNEST J. GAINES

Born: Oscar, Louisiana
January 15, 1933

Gaines is celebrated for his simple but poignant and intensely sympathetic depiction of poor African Americans in rural Louisiana.

© Jerry Bauer

BIOGRAPHY

Ernest James Gaines, the first son of African American parents Manuel and Adrienne Gaines, was born on January 15, 1933, in Oscar, Louisiana, a small town a few miles northwest of Baton Rouge. He grew up in former slave quarters on River Lake Plantation where for six years he attended a one-room elementary school before enrolling in the Augustine Catholic School in nearby New Roads.

At the end of World War II, his mother moved to California to join her second husband, Raphael Colar, a merchant seaman, leaving Gaines behind to be reared by his invalid aunt, Augusteen Jefferson, who had a formative influence on the boy. Although she had never walked in her life, she had extraordinary resiliency and great faith, and Gaines credits her with teaching him fundamental values, above all about suffering with courage and dignity.

Like so many rural black people, after school and over the summer Gaines worked in the sugarcane and cotton fields, but many of his evenings were given over to reading and writing for his aunt and her illiterate acquaintances. From them he derived a strong sense of a native, oral tradition and his own heritage.

In 1948, when Gaines was fifteen, he moved to Vallejo, California, to live with his mother and stepfather. The move was traumatic for Gaines, who has dwelled on his departure from the quarters and who later returned in his depiction of characters with experiences paralleling his own.

Prompted by his stepfather's fear that he might fall in with bad company, Gaines spent long, lonely hours in the public library, reading voraciously while trying to cope with his yearning to return to Louisiana. He made his first serious attempt at fiction, writing the initial draft of what eventually became *Catherine Carmier* (1964), his first novel.

After completing high school and beginning college, Gaines was drafted into the Army, serving in the Pacific from 1953 to 1955. After his discharge, he entered San Francisco State College to study English. While there, he published his first story, "The Turtles," which helped to win a Wallace Stegner Creative Writing Fellowship for graduate study at Stanford University. Strongly influenced by the writing of Ivan Turgenev, James Joyce, and William Faulkner, at Stanford Gaines began bringing into focus his own artistic vision.

That vision became sharper in 1962 when he returned to Louisiana and strengthened his desire to write about the places and people of his boyhood years. He hoped to write from an honest but sympathetic perspective that no white writer of the rural South had been able to assume. His first novel, *Catherine Carmier,* contained several of the themes that would characterize his later work. This novel, generally considered to be of uneven quality, was not a critical success. He followed it by abortive attempts to write about his adopted San Francisco culture. Thereafter, he wisely turned again to writing about Louisiana, about the people and places in his heart.

In 1966 Gaines was awarded a National Endowment for the Arts grant, and over the next two years he published a novel, *Of Love and Dust* (1967), and a collection of short stories, *Bloodline* (1968), one

839

of which, "A Long Day in November," was also published separately as a children's story in 1971. Thereafter, he began garnering considerable acclaim and several awards, including a California Commonwealth Gold Medal Award (1972), the Louisiana Library Award (1972), a Guggenheim Fellowship (1974), and an honorary doctorate from Denison University (1980).

While writer-in-residence at Denison, he published his best-known novel, *The Autobiography of Miss Jane Pittman* (1971). It was followed by *In My Father's House* (1978) and *A Gathering of Old Men* (1983), which, like *The Autobiography of Miss Jane Pittman*, was adapted as a television play and helped to introduce his work to an expanding international audience.

During the 1980's, Gaines won a number of awards, including three more honorary doctorates and, in 1989, the Louisiana Humanist of the Year Award, presented by the Louisiana Endowment for the Humanities in recognition of his dedication both to his craft and to his teaching. Fame also brought him travel and lecturing obligations; after a hiatus of ten years, he was able to finish his long-awaited novel *A Lesson Before Dying* (1993). This novel won the National Book Critics Circle Award, was nominated for a Pulitzer Prize, and later was a selection of Oprah Winfrey's Book Club. In 1993, Gaines was awarded a "genius grant" by the John D. and Catherine T. MacArthur Foundation. In 2000, President Bill Clinton awarded him the National Humanities Medal.

In 1983, Gaines was appointed writer-in-residence at the University of Louisiana at Lafayette, about sixty miles from his birthplace, where he was recognized as a distinguished teacher. At that time, he also maintained homes in San Francisco and Florida. He retired from active teaching in 2003 with a lifetime appointment as writer-in-residence emeritus. He purchased land in Oscar, near the plantation where he had worked as a boy, and made his home near the town of his birth.

Gaines's collection of essays and short fiction *Mozart and Leadbelly* was published in 2005. Work on his novel *The Man Who Whipped Children* was interrupted by Hurricane Katrina in September, 2005, when he opened his home to relatives from flood-stricken New Orleans. He is married to Diane Saulney, an attorney.

ANALYSIS

Gaines is a raconteur of the agrarian South, specifically of the black experience in rural Louisiana during the three decades following World War II. His chief setting, former slave quarters located near the town of Bayonne, closely mirrors the actual surroundings of Gaines's boyhood: the quarters on River Lake Plantation and the town of New Roads. This world, remote for most readers, becomes in Gaines's novels a literary microcosm, inhabited principally by blacks, Creoles, and Cajuns, all treated with a simple honesty and direct style that are the hallmarks of his fiction.

Prevalent themes in Gaines's fiction often originate in his own experience. His male characters search for an identity at a time when change was hard-won and self-esteem required the courage to reject a demeaning place in a world in which wealth, prestige, and power belonged exclusively to white people. In those turbulent years of the mid-twentieth century, escape from poverty and racial servility often involved flight to the North or West, but at great emotional cost and with a deep sense of alienation and loss. In contrast to the stance of more militant African Americans who, writing during the 1960's, were advocating confrontation and even violence, Gaines has defined courage in the young black male as the power to endure with dignity the injustices of a racist society ("The Sky Is Gray" and *A Lesson Before Dying*).

Gaines's work reveals that the younger African Americans of his generation had few choices; the life that their parents and grandparents had known was disappearing. Slowly but relentlessly, black people who had eked out an impoverished but dignified living from the land were being pushed into the soggy bottoms, onto land unfit for serious cultivation. The inheritors, mostly Cajuns (that is, white people of French ancestry) were swallowing up the good lands, farming for profit with mechanized equipment, tearing down the houses of poor black people, and plowing over their graves.

Less deracinated by these events, the black women in Gaines's novels, especially the older ones, are more adaptable. Most of them cling tenaciously to their Christian faith, drawing strength from the church, which many young black men, like Jackson Bradley in *Catherine Carmier*, come to abandon. The women endure in part because the conditions do not so deeply erode their sense of purpose or identity. They can live a bare, frugal existence because they gain much strength from their community and the extended families that they strive to hold together. The younger black men, their prodigal sons, either set out on solitary quests for a new source of pride and dignity or succumb to an early defeat, even a violent death.

Against this background, Gaines spins highly personal stories of individuals and families profoundly affected by change and exacerbated racial tensions, a complex problem because of miscegenation and the existence of a large Creole and mixed-race population. The separatist attitude of Creoles, like Raoul in *Catherine Carmier,* is often as intransigent as that of many bigoted white people.

Remarkably, the bitterness that might surface in this world is usually muted. Although omnipresent and insidious, the racial caste system is not something its principal victims dwell upon or use as a psychological crutch. For most, the system is a fundamental fact of life, and though they dream of change, they are pragmatists, finding dignity despite the system and summoning moral strength to confront it.

There are few real villains in Gaines's fiction, even among the persecutors. The worst of men, such as Luke Will, the redneck bully in *A Gathering of Old Men,* are mindless and craven. Most, such as Fix Boutan from the same novel, are bound to a familial and racial code, however misguided, by a strong sense of honor. They, too, are victims of caste, for they cannot see that they are morally bankrupted by their blind arrogance and hate.

Such characters play only secondary roles, however, for Gaines's avowed purpose is to focus on poor black people, not their persecutors. To that end, Gaines has evolved a disarmingly plain and direct style, a "voice" to match the simple, unsophisticated lives of his principals, most of whom have no hope of sharing the white people's bounty. Inspired by the rhythm and phrasing of blues musicians, the harangues of Pentecostal preachers, and recorded interviews of former slaves, Gaines uses short sentences, colloquial cadences, and unpretentious diction with a lyricism that is both insistent and intense. He prefers monosyllabic, ordinary words of everyday speech, and his progress through a tale is seldom encumbered by elaborate description or extensive introspection by his characters. It is a style that he has mastered, and with it he evokes both humor and pathos.

It is also a style suited to Gaines's realistic, uncomplicated plots, which often focus on the impact of one critical event or relationship in the experience of simple people who live uneventful, even placid lives. With the exception of *The Autobiography of Miss Jane Pittman,* which covers a span of roughly one hundred years, the plot time frame is narrow, as in *A Gathering of Old Men* and *A Lesson Before Dying.* Gaines builds the real story in the event's uncertain, soul-searching aftermath.

Frequent characters in Gaines's fictive world are a young, educated black man, seeking purpose while impaled on the horns of a moral dilemma, and an older, righteous black woman, urging him toward the harder, self-sacrificing choice. They are Jackson Bradley and Aunt Charlotte in *Catherine Carmier,* Gaines's first novel, and Grant Wiggins and his aunt, Tante Lou, in *A Lesson Before Dying.* Younger counterparts to this pairing are James and his mother Octavia in "The Sky Is Gray." In one guise or another, they appear in much of Gaines's fiction. Primarily through such characters, the author has struggled with the fundamental ambivalence toward his own heritage. This personal spiritual odyssey has been responsible for the author's reputation as one of the most humane and compassionate novelists in the United States.

"THE SKY IS GRAY"

First published: 1963 (collected in *Bloodline,* 1968)
Type of work: Short story

A young African American boy learns a lesson in pride and endurance from his mother.

James, the eight-year-old narrator of "The Sky Is Gray," lives with his mother, Octavia, his aunt, and three younger brothers in rural Louisiana. Because James's father has been called to the army, the family lives a marginal existence, supported only by the mother's fieldwork. James, knowing that there is no money for a dentist, suffers in silence with an agonizing toothache. When his aunt reveals the child's misery, Octavia takes James to town on the bus. The action of the story occurs in one day.

The irony is achieved through the narrative position of the child who observes events he cannot comprehend but must accept. The rural town of Bayonne is rigidly segregated, with the warm restaurants and shops reserved for white people. The dentist is an inferior practitioner who accepts black patients. The black people must eat "back of town" and are not welcome in the white-owned stores. Octavia constantly corrects James, reminding him that he is the oldest son and must behave like a man. He understands that, no matter how intense his suffering, he must not cry or complain. The reader may view Octavia as hard and uncompromising, but James respects and loves her without reservation. Octavia is a realist who is preparing her son for his dangerous life as a black man in the rural South.

The gray landscape and the pervasive cold are central to the atmosphere of the story. After being turned away by the dentist's nurse and told to return later, James and his mother walk to the back of town to take shelter from the freezing cold. When they return, an elderly Cajun woman with an invalid husband invites them into the back room of her store for warmth and food. She insists that the boy work for his meal, instructing him to move two empty garbage cans from the back of the store to the front.

After the meal, Octavia asks to buy a piece of salt pork for twenty-five cents. The storekeeper cuts a generous piece, but Octavia will accept only half; this transaction preserves the dignity of both women. The storekeeper telephones the dentist, arranging for him to take James immediately, an act of kindness that Octavia accepts with equanimity.

A familiar theme in Gaines's work is the endurance and strength of the black woman contending with the harsh racism of mid-twentieth century America. The compelling details of Southern rural life, seen through the eyes of the keenly observant child, invite the compassion of the reader. The author, while acknowledging the tragedy of segregation, transcends oversimplification of racial issues to find hope in the strong bonds of pride and empathy in the brief encounter between the two women.

At the conclusion, when James turns up his collar for warmth, Octavia makes him turn it down, saying "You not a bum. . . . You a man." Mother and child must make their way with dignity in a world that, like the gray sky, is indifferent to their suffering. One biographer reports that the events in the story closely parallel an incident in the author's childhood.

THE AUTOBIOGRAPHY OF MISS JANE PITTMAN

First published: 1971
Type of work: Novel

A resourceful, engaging black woman survives a century of adversity and little joy to become a strong moral presence in her community.

The Autobiography of Miss Jane Pittman remains Gaines's best-known work, partly because of Cicely Tyson's portrayal of Jane in the 1974 televised adaptation of the novel. It is Gaines's most panoramic and episodic book, tracing the long life of its protagonist from her youthful emancipation to her old age in the 1960's.

The novel purports to be the recorded history of the protagonist herself, leading many to conclude that she was a real person, but she is actually a composite portrait Gaines drew from several inspirational sources, including his aunt Augusteen Jefferson. Miss Jane's narrative threads through historic events, providing a backdrop of well-known names and dates against which, through adversity and triumph, Jane grows in stature from an ignorant young slave to a wise old woman.

Her saga begins with no inkling of geographic reality, merely the desire to find the Union soldier who, in dubbing her "Jane Brown," had removed her stigma as a slave. She quickly learns that freedom means that she must forage for herself, not an easy task in a land full of marauding white people bent on exterminating black vagrants.

She teams up with Ned, a younger boy whose mother has been slaughtered, and together they follow her elusive dream. With the end of Reconstruction and the onset of the Jim Crow era, Ned migrates to Kansas, committed to helping his fellow black people, who have been forced once again into economic subjugation. Jane enters into a common-law marriage with Joe Pittman, a sharecropper and the great love of her life. They move near the Texas border, where Joe has a job breaking horses, but after Joe is killed, Jane settles near Bayonne, the epicenter of Gaines's fictive world.

Ned returns to Louisiana, rekindling in Jane a hope that had dimmed with Joe Pittman's death. Teaching the need for justice and change, he is soon marked for death. Within a year, Ned is gunned down by a Cajun assassin, Albert Cluveau, who, ironically, had befriended Jane.

In the final parts of the narrative, Jane's focus shifts from episodes in which she is the main participant to stories of other people living on the Samson plantation, her last home. She describes the various teachers who come to the one-room black school, including Mary Agnes, a Creole who inspires an ill-fated love in Robert Samson, the son of the white plantation owner. Jane also reflects on black heroes, including Joe Louis and Jackie Robinson, and other public figures, including Huey Long. Her main focus, however, is on Jimmy, who, like Ned before him, goes away to be educated, returns to preach against segregation, and is killed by lawless white people. It is his spirit that lives on in Miss Jane, who, at the novel's end, plans to carry on against racial injustice.

In Miss Jane, Gaines etched a compelling literary character who penetrates socially sanctioned wrongs with brash innocence. Yet her attraction lies less in that than in her wonderful earthiness and irrepressible determination to survive. She is an authentic, poignant, and engaging character who has left an indelible imprint on American literature.

A GATHERING OF OLD MEN

First published: 1983
Type of work: Novel

A group of elderly black men, defying tradition, reveal unprecedented courage when they gather to protect another man whom they believe has shot and killed a Cajun farmer.

Unlike *The Autobiography of Miss Jane Pittman* with its epic sweep, *A Gathering of Old Men* limits its primary action to a single day and to locales in and around

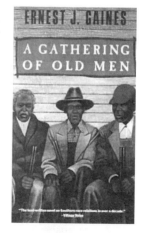

the plantation quarters near Bayonne. It is only in Lou Dimes's last narrative, a sort of epilogue, that the reader is carried past the climactic day on which a group of old black men gather to protect their friend, Mathu. They assume that Mathu has killed Beau, a white farmer and son of a powerful Cajun patriarch, Fix Bouton.

The old men congregate at Mathu's house, each carrying a shotgun and confessing to the crime. They have an ally in a young white woman, Candy, who has prompted the gathering. She also claims to have shot Beau, fearing that Beau's killer, once identified, will face brutal retribution. The men hold to their charade, braving the abuse of Sheriff Mapes and frustrating all of his attempts to intimidate them. Although he believes that only Mathu is capable of the act, Mapes slowly gains grudging respect for the men because they have dared to defy him.

Candy, too, must face the implications of the men's stand. As her friend Lou Dimes tells her, Mathu is now free of her, free of her protection, which, however well intentioned, in its way has been as demeaning for black people as the brutal intimidation of men such as Mapes and Beau. The black men are finally able to stand alone, with dignity and pride, beholden to nobody.

Complications in the novel introduce two other white men with sharply contrasting attitudes about what should be done to avenge the death of Beau. Gil Bouton, brother of the victim and a star football player at Louisiana State University, counsels restraint; Luke Will, an ignorant redneck, tries to flame bigotry into action against the old men. Although Fix is chagrined by his son's views, he declines to act. Disgusted, Luke leads a party of his friends to the quarters in an attempt to force Mapes into handing Mathu over to them. Mapes is wounded in the ensuing gunfight, and Luke and Charlie Biggs, who actually shot Beau, are both killed, ending the crisis.

The novel is narrated from the viewpoints of fifteen different characters, including several of the old men, whose accounts are full of good-natured ribbing in an engaging folk idiom. These men, with memorable nicknames such as Cherry, Dirty Red, Chimley, and Rooster, lend broad humor to the novel, so that its grim events, even the gunfight, have a seriocomic cast. That humor, at times self-deprecating, simply counterpoints their increasing sense of pride, for at the end they clearly stand triumphant, taller than they ever had before.

A LESSON BEFORE DYING

First published: 1993
Type of work: Novel

Enjoined by others to help another black man to face his impending execution with dignity, a teacher struggles with his own loss of faith and sense of purpose.

A Lesson Before Dying is set in the late 1940's, in the former slave quarters of the Marshall plantation and the town of Bayonne. Gaines takes his reader back to a time when racial segregation was both legal and endemic in the South, a time when black people could barely hope for recognition of their humanity, much less find justice in a court of law.

It is in this world that a dirt-poor, semiliterate black man, Jefferson, is accused of murdering a white liquor-store owner. In the Bayonne courthouse, Jefferson is quickly condemned to death by an all-white jury. Although he is innocent, the verdict is never in doubt. Even his attorney characterizes Jefferson as subhuman, claiming that electrocuting him would make no more sense than electrocuting a hog.

Jefferson's godmother, Miss Emma, aided and abetted by Tante Lou, prevails upon Tante Lou's nephew, Grant Wiggins, to help Jefferson face death like a man, with dignity. Grant, the teacher in the quarters where Jefferson lived, is very reluctant to undertake the task, but the women and Grant's girlfriend Vivian convince him that he has no choice but to try.

Grant's initial efforts are disappointing. Jefferson has accepted his lawyer's depiction of him as a hog, and he resists all attempts to help him break through his self-loathing. Furthermore, in order to help Jefferson, Grant must cope with his own doubts about his role, both as man and teacher. The task also puts his own pride at grave risk, as he must seek the cooperation of white men such as Henri Pichot and Sheriff Guidry, who want to stifle his "smartness."

Lashed by the righteousness of Tante Lou and the Reverend Ambrose, his chief tormentor, Grant persists and finally succeeds in befriending Jefferson, largely through simple kindness. He bolsters Jefferson's courage, helping him to face Gruesome Gerty, the portable electric chair, with unflinching dignity.

The novel thus ends with hope, both for Grant, the protagonist, and for the South. Grant has learned that his teaching is not in vain, that his education has given him the power to help others discover their humanity. He has also earned the respect and potential friendship of a young white deputy, Paul, who holds out the promise for a future racial harmony.

Except for a few segments in which *A Lesson Before Dying* subtly slips into a third-person point of view and the section in which Jefferson speaks through his diary, the novel is presented in the first-person voice of its protagonist, Grant Wiggins. The reader thus closely audits Grant's own progress from doubt and moments of self-hatred to an honest confrontation with his feelings of anger and bitterness, love and shame. His growth parallels that of Jefferson, who, by facing death bravely, at the end has become his teacher's teacher.

SUMMARY

The author has continued to receive many honorary doctorates and awards from American universities, as well as international acclaim such as the French Chevalier of the Order of Arts and Letters in 1996. The four works discussed above have been adapted as television films, reaching viewers who may not have read his fiction. His work is frequently taught in high school and college classes, evidence of its appeal to a generation largely unfamiliar with the history of segregation and racial discrimination. Gaines holds a respected position as one of the most influential voices in contemporary African American literature.

Gaines's award of the MacArthur Foundation genius grant in 1993 was a testimony to his selfless contributions to humankind as a writer and teacher. His works are strong indictments of bigotry and inhumanity that offer quiet pleas for sanity, for racial harmony and understanding. More than that, they are testimonies to the strength of the human spirit, not only in African Americans but in all people. Finally, they are works of great humor and compassion, rich in the folklore of oral tradition, told through the voices of ordinary people, with masterful skill.

John W. Fiero; updated by Marjorie J. Podolsky

BIBLIOGRAPHY

By the Author

LONG FICTION:
Catherine Carmier, 1964
Of Love and Dust, 1967
The Autobiography of Miss Jane Pittman, 1971
In My Father's House, 1978
A Gathering of Old Men, 1983
A Lesson Before Dying, 1993

SHORT FICTION:
Bloodline, 1968
A Long Day in November, 1971

MISCELLANEOUS:
Porch Talk with Ernest Gaines, 1990
Mozart and Leadbelly: Stories and Essays, 2005

DISCUSSION TOPICS

- Why do you think Ernest J. Gaines's fiction appeals to high school and college students?

- Find examples of strong black women characters who hold the moral center in much of his fiction.

- How does the author's portrayal of racism in the United States function as a lesson to readers unfamiliar with this history?

- Using examples from his fiction, discuss the author's skill in portraying the essential humanity of characters whose actions are intrinsically evil.

- Does the author take a political position on the issue of capital punishment in *A Lesson Before Dying?*

- Some have criticized Gaines's work for not expressing a strong enough protest against racism. Do you agree?

- Films of Gaines's fiction are available in schools and libraries. Compare one of these films with the original text and discuss whether it fits your own interpretation.

About the Author

Babb, Valerie Melissa. *Ernest Gaines.* Boston: Twayne, 1991.

Beavers, Herman. *Wrestling Angels into Song: The Fictions of Ernest J. Gaines and James Alan McPherson.* Philadelphia: University of Pennsylvania Press, 1995.

Carmean, Karen. *Ernest J. Gaines: A Critical Companion.* Westport, Conn.: Greenwood Press, 1998.

Davis, Thadious M. "Ernest J. Gaines." In *African American Writers: Profiles of Their Lives and Works,* edited by Valerie Smith, Lea Baechler, and A. Walton Litz. New York: Macmillan, 1991.

Doyle, Mary Ellen. *Voices from the Quarters: The Fiction of Ernest J. Gaines.* Baton Rouge: Louisiana State University Press, 2002.

Gaudet, Marcia, and Carl Wooton. *Porch Talk with Ernest Gaines: Conversations on the Writer's Craft.* Baton Rouge: Louisiana State University Press, 1990.

Lowe, John, ed. *Conversations with Ernest Gaines.* Jackson: University of Mississippi Press, 1996.

Simpson, Anne K. *A Gathering of Gaines: The Man and the Writer.* Lafayette: Center for Louisiana Studies, 1991.

© Allison Harris

MAVIS GALLANT

Born: Montreal, Quebec, Canada
August 11, 1922

Admired as an exacting stylist and a supreme ironist of the short-story form, Gallant focuses on complex social expectations in her native Montreal and expatriate dislocation in her adopted France.

BIOGRAPHY

Mavis Gallant was born Mavis Young in Montreal, Quebec, Canada, on August 11, 1922. Her father, who died when she was ten years old, was Anglo-Scottish; her mother, who soon remarried, was American. At age four, Gallant was sent to a French convent school and subsequently attended a number of boarding schools, completing her education at a New York high school, where she had been sent to live with a guardian.

After returning to Canada, she married John Gallant in 1943 and got a job as a feature reporter with the *Montreal Standard*, where she worked for six years. She began writing and publishing short stories in Canadian journals during this period, which she has called her apprenticeship. Although she has said she liked the life of a reporter, her goal was to move to Paris before she was thirty and write nothing but fiction. In 1948, she and her husband were divorced; she moved to Europe in 1950.

Gallant began her lifelong association with *The New Yorker* in 1950, rather insecurely. As she tells the story, she procured the services of an agent in the United States, because she knew she was going to be traveling around in Europe. She sent the agent several stories, all of which he said he was unable to place. It was only when she was destitute in Madrid in 1952 that she happened to see a copy of *The New Yorker* with one of her stories in it. She contacted the magazine and found out that her agent did sell the stories to *The New Yorker* and other magazines, giving a fictitious address for her in Europe and keeping the money. Gallant has said that the feeling of dismay she experienced when she believed every story she sent was a dead failure never really left her. *New Yorker* editor William Maxwell signed Gallant to a "first refusal" contract, and she subsequently published well over a hundred stories in *The New Yorker*, about half of which were collected in *The Collected Stories of Mavis Gallant* in 1996.

Although Gallant has traveled and lived in many places in Europe, she has spent most of her life in Paris, where she found much more "openness to women." Because her first schooling was in French, she has always felt comfortable speaking the language, although she says her fiction arrives in her mind in English. She has suggested that one of the most important influences on her life and ironic style of writing has been the fact that her knowledge of both French and English left her with two systems of behavior, "divided by syntax and tradition."

Gallant's first collection of *New Yorker* stories was *The Other Paris* (1956), in which she explored the displacement and dislocation of several North Americans living in France after World War II, a theme she continued to examine in her second collection, *My Heart Is Broken* (1964).

Between 1960 and 1965, Gallant made several trips to Germany, while working on the stories for *The Pegnitz Junction: A Novella and Five Stories*. The title novella, about a dreamlike journey symbolizing the problems of postwar Germany, which Gallant has said is her favorite story, has been called her most experimental piece of fiction.

Gallant's stories were not well known in Canada until her 1981 collection *Home Truths* won the Governor General's Award for fiction and she was made an officer of the Order of Canada. Her play *What Is to Be Done?* was produced in Toronto in 1983 and won the Canada-Australia Prize.

Gallant was writer-in-residence at the University of Toronto during 1983 and 1984. During the 1990's, she continued to publish short stories in *The New Yorker*, to collect them in book form, and to win prestigious awards, including several honorary doctorates. Her *Collected Stories* is out of print—an example of the failure of her work to gain a wide audience. Her admirers, mainly of whom are writers, were therefore encouraged when *Paris Stories* was published in 2002, with an introduction by Canadian author Michael Ondaatje, and a companion volume, *Varieties in Exile*, about life in Canada, with an introduction by American author Russell Banks, was released in 2003.

ANALYSIS

Like her Canadian colleague Alice Munro, Gallant has always given her primary literary allegiance with the often-unappreciated short-story form. In her preface to *Collected Stories*, Gallant insists that short stories are not chapters of novels and should not be read one after another as if they were meant to follow along. Although a number of her stories focus on the same characters as they develop over time, it would be exhausting to read a great many of Gallant's stories one after another; with their careful and precise style, each demands close reading.

Gallant is often referred to as "a writer's writer," an epithet suggesting an author whose writing is so polished that it is best appreciated by other authors. On the other hand, this label can suggest someone whose work is seldom read by anyone but other writers. Gallant is not widely enough read for any of her stories to be considered well known. Her stories are often irresolute and seemingly plotless. When she was writing a weekly column about radio for the *Montreal Standard* in the late 1940's, she once described one writer's plays as being unlike the usual radio play because they did not come to a traditional fictional climax. She further defended this practice by arguing that real problems are not always resolved in tidy ways and that if stories seem incomplete, that is because they may be true. However, in spite of this seeming allegiance to the ragged nature of reality rather than to the neat pat-

terns of art, Gallant claims in one of her essays that style is intentional and inseparable from structure.

Indeed, all of Gallant's stories reflect this apparent paradox. Whereas they seem relatively artless—simple sketches of minor characters caught in impasses of their own making—they are carefully crafted and highly stylized structures of rigid social patterns. Gallant has described her method of getting something on paper as a painfully precise play with the language. In discussing her "outrageous slowness," Gallant says that she sometimes puts aside parts of a story for months, even years. The story is finished when it seems to tally with a plan she has in mind but cannot describe, or when she believes that it cannot be written satisfactorily any other way. It is precisely this kind of care for the individual word and sentence that has led to Gallant being referred to as a writer's writer.

Although Gallant has been compared to Henry James and Anton Chekhov, she is probably more similar to Jane Austen. Gallant poses a problem for readers expecting stories that seem to have a clear point, a metaphoric texture, or a sense of closure. Rather, Gallant's stories seem to be so forthrightly focused on the everyday lives of her characters that there is little to say about them. They certainly do not appear to need interpretation, the only mystery about them being the mystery of what they are about. However, this seeming simplicity of Gallant's writing is an illusion, for her stories are carefully structured, highly stylized creations of character interrelationships. In one of her better-known essays, "What Is Style?" collected in the anthology *Paris Notebooks* (1986), Gallant claims that style is part of whatever the writer has to say, concluding—as Henry James might well have—that content, meaning, intention, and form make up a unified whole that must have a reason to be.

Of course, both James and Chekhov were also accused of presenting little slices of life, or huge chunks of verbiage, that were really little to do about not very much. However, Gallant's stories do not have James's convoluted syntax, reflecting the complexity of his characters' minds; nor do they seem to have Chekhov's calculated conciseness, suggesting that more is left out than put in. In fact, Gallant's characters do not seem very complex at all, at least self-consciously, and Gallant appears to say everything that needs to be said about them.

Instead of moving toward some explicit or implicit, patterned intention, as readers have come to expect in the modern short-story form, Gallant's stories seem as if they could go on and on, creating a novelistic "feel" that violates the reader's usual expectation that short stories will meaningfully lead somewhere. Trying to find out where the meaning lies or how meaning is communicated in a Gallant story is not so much challenging as apparently beside the point. Careful readers get so caught up in the creation of character and milieu that they do not care what the story means; inattentive readers may tire of the seemingly inconsequential nature of the story and just stop reading.

Like Austen, Gallant presents characters within a circumscribed social world, going about their usual manners and morals business without obvious conflict, analytical self-doubt, or troublesome introspection. The comedy of manners which results is a form that seems usually too leisurely and too detailed for the relatively short space of the short story. For example, the stories of the Carettes, because they focus on significant points in the life of one Montreal family, are typical of the novelistic tendency of Gallant's technique. However, upon reading the stories carefully, one soon realizes that if Gallant had put together enough stories about this family to fill a book, the result would still have been a collection of short stories rather than a novel. The reason for this distinction between novel and short story derives from Gallant's selectivity of focus and detail as well as her ironic style. On closer analysis, the reader begins to realize that her stories are not quite as realistically inconsequential as they first appear.

"Bernadette"

First published: 1964 (collected in *The Collected Stories of Mavis Gallant*, 1996)
Type of work: Short story

"Bernadette" is the story of Nora and Robbie Knight, an educated, liberal Montreal couple who have been married for sixteen years, and their servant Bernadette.

Nora has discovered her husband, Robbie, in extramarital affairs three times, and each time, like the articulate but emotionally distant couple they

are, they have talked the matter out and gone on with their relationship.

Bernadette, their French-Canadian servant, is a simple woman who never quite understands what her terrifying, well-meaning employers want. The story begins with Bernadette's knowledge that she is pregnant, having had several casual sexual encounters with strangers she met in town on her days off. Bernadette reflects little about life and asks for no more than a place to live and a job to do.

The Knights give Bernadette books by writers such as D. H. Lawrence and André Gide, which she puts in a drawer for a few days and then returns. However, Nora, blithely unaware, brags about Bernadette's elevated reading habits to guests at a party she gives. When Nora finds out Bernadette is pregnant, she suspects Robbie and is shocked when she realizes she is mistaken, for it undercuts her moral superiority. The Knights remain in their usual emotionally detached state, considering it their responsibility to pay for Bernadette having the baby at a home for unwed mothers in the United States.

The story ends with Bernadette sitting in a movie theater, watching a musical comedy, which she enjoys because she believes in uncomplicated stories of love. When she feels her baby move, she thinks of the child as alive, something to be given a name, to be clothed, fed, and baptized. However, because of her own lower-class background, she feels sure that the baby will die; all she can hope for is an angel of her own to pray for her in heaven.

"Thank You for the Lovely Tea"

First published: 1981 (collected in *Home Truths*, 1981)
Type of work: Short story

An American woman tries to ingratiate herself with her boyfriend's daughter.

This story perhaps reflects Gallant's sense of distance and disconnection as a result of spending much of her childhood in boarding schools. The central character in the story is Ruth Cook, a boarding-school student, who, while waiting for Mrs. Holland, her father's new, American girlfriend, to come pick up her for an afternoon tea, writes on the top of her desk "Life is Hell." Ruth, resigned to her boarding-school life, seems to have been conditioned to a passive, unemotional attitude. As her school's influence suggests, being emotional is being American, which is something worse than bad taste.

The tea, primarily an effort by Mrs. Holland to ingratiate herself with Ruth, is made even more uncomfortable by the fact that two of Ruth's friends, May and Helen, are invited along. Helen comes from a half-literate family with several children. Her dearest wish is to remain at the school as long as possible, to move from student to staff with no gap in between. May, who has been separated from a twin sister who goes to another school, feels split from a mirror half of herself but maintains the discipline learned at the school.

The conservative influence of the school is also symbolized by the fact that Helen cries whenever reminded of the recent death of King Edward and Rudyard Kipling, signaling a "year of change." However, things do not seem to change for the girls. The only issue pursuant to the tea is whether the girls remembered to thank Mrs. Holland. Ruth is left wondering if she will ever care about anyone, as she smiles placidly and breathes on the window, drawing a heart shape and watching it fade.

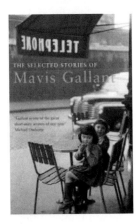

"1933"

First published: 1987 (collected in *Across the Bridge,* 1993)
Type of work: Short story

This very brief story introduces the Carette family, whose adventures will continue in subsequently written works.

A year after the death of her husband, Mme. Carette, with her two daughters, Berthe and Marie, has been forced to move to a smaller apartment. Although the new apartment is near the old one, the two girls, worried about the adult mysteries of change, death, and absence, stay awake at night, frightened about ghosts in the house.

The strict social conventions of the middle-class Carette family are revealed by the fact that the daughters never see their mother wearing a bathrobe and that the only English Mme. Carette thinks her daughters need to use are the phrases: "I don't understand," "I don't know," and "No, thank you." The most telling statement in the story is the mother's insistence that the children never refer to their mother as a seamstress but must say instead, "My mother was clever with her hands."

The children are often looked after by the landlord, M. Grosjean, and his Irish wife, who live downstairs. The story communicates the inarticulate fear and loneliness of the Carette family because of the loss of the husband and father; its artistry lies in the subtle way Gallant conveys that fear and loneliness.

"THE CONCERT PARTY"

First published: 1988 (collected in *The Collected Stories of Mavis Gallant,* 1996)
Type of work: Short story

A college professor looks back on the end of his marriage.

"The Concert Party" begins with the first-person narrator named Burnet, a Canadian academic, identifying with a colleague named Harry Lapwing while they are both graduate students in France. Lapwing and his wife, Edie, and Burnet and his wife, Lily, become a social unit, attending dinners and parties together. The concert party of the story's title is given by a man named Watt Chadwick, a novelist who is trying to figure out a way to socially elevate his nineteen-year-old, part-time gardener, David Ogdoad, a pianist, to the position of being his lover.

The situation at the party becomes complicated when David is attracted to Lily, and another Canadian named Fergus Bray, a playwright, is attracted to Lapwing's wife, Edie. During the party, Bray invites Edie to leave Lapwing and come to live with him in Madrid. When Lapwing humiliates Edie at the party, she decides to go. In a parallel action, Lily goes off to London with David.

Burnet knows that he romanticized the experience in France. If he had said that Lily had left for Detroit and Edie for Moose Jaw, leaving him and Lapwing stranded in a motel, they would have seemed foolish. However, the words "Madrid" and "London" and the fact that the event involved a musician, a playwright, and a novelist tinges the story with fiction and gives it an alien glow, making him and Lapwing appear as actors in a Technicolor film. However, he recognizes that the story is really that of men's humiliation, "bleached and toneless."

"ACROSS THE BRIDGE"

First published: 1991 (collected in *Across the Bridge*, 1993)
Type of work: Short story

An ironic and comic treatment of a family's efforts to play matchmaker for its daughter.

"Across the Bridge" begins with the narrator, Sylvie, walking across a bridge in Paris with her mother, who carries the invitations to her wedding in a leather shopping bag. When Sylvie tells her mother that she does not love the man her parents have chosen for her to marry, her mother says that loving a man takes "patience," like practicing scales. When Sylvie says she has thoughts of throwing herself off the bridge if she is forced to marry

the family choice, Arnaud, and not allowed to marry her own choice, Bernard, her mother dumps the invitations off the bridge. The rest of the story is an ironic and comic treatment of the family's efforts to match Sylvie up with Bernard, who, it turns out, in spite of Sylvie's romantic idealizations, has no interest in her at all.

The story ends with Sylvie falling in love with her family's original choice after all. The key scene in the story is a dinner engagement Sylvie has with Arnaud in which their future life together is presaged. When Sylvie cannot eat the flan because the restaurant has mistaken it for a piece of quiche and put parsley on it, Arnaud scrapes off the parsley and begins to eat the flan for her—a gesture that convinces Sylvie that he must love her. The story ends in romantic poignancy as Sylvie takes the long way home after seeing Arnaud board his train, for she thinks it unfair to arrive home before he does. She says she will never tell anyone about this, that it will remain a small and insignificant secret that belongs to the "true life" she is almost ready to enter. This is the bridge crossing reflected by the title of the story, for these small and seemingly insignificant secrets are what give Gallant's stories life.

SUMMARY

Gallant's stories have been called an acquired taste, delicate constructions that seem to be artless vignettes rather than carefully patterned stories. Gallant's characters do not seem significant in the large scheme of things, but as Gallant says in one of her essays, no life is more interesting than any other; what really matters is what is revealed and how.

Charles E. May

BIBLIOGRAPHY

By the Author

LONG FICTION:
Green Water, Green Sky, 1959
Its Image on the Mirror, 1964 (novella)
A Fairly Good Time, 1970

SHORT FICTION:
The Other Paris, 1956
My Heart Is Broken: Eight Stories and a Short Novel, 1964 (pb. in England as *An Unmarried Man's Summer*, 1965)
The Pegnitz Junction: A Novella and Five Short Stories, 1973

The End of the World, and Other Stories, 1974
From the Fifteenth District: A Novella and Eight Short Stories, 1979
Home Truths: Selected Canadian Stories, 1981
Overhead in a Balloon, 1985
In Transit, 1988
Across the Bridge, 1993
The Moslem Wife, and Other Stories, 1994
The Collected Stories of Mavis Gallant, 1996
Paris Stories, 2002
Varieties of Exile: Stories, 2005

DRAMA:
What Is to Be Done, pr. 1982

NONFICTION:
The Affair of Gabrielle Russier, 1971
The War Brides, 1978
Paris Notebooks: Essays and Reviews, 1986

About the Author

Canadian Fiction Magazine 28 (1978). Special issue on Mavis Gallant.
Essays in Canadian Writing 42 (Winter, 1990). Special issue on Mavis Gallant.
Gadpaille, Michelle. "Mavis Gallant." In *The Canadian Short Story.* New York: Oxford University Press, 1988.
Grant, Judith Skleton. "Mavis Gallant." In *Canadian Writers and Their Works,* edited by Robert Lecker, Jack David, and Ellen Quigley. Toronto: ECW Press, 1989.
Keith, William John. "Mavis Gallant." In *A Sense of Style: Studies in the Art of Fiction in English-Speaking Canada.* Toronto: ECW Press, 1988.
Kulyk Keefer, Janice. *Reading Mavis Gallant.* Toronto: Oxford University Press, 1989.
Schaub, Danielle. *Mavis Gallant.* New York: Twayne, 1998.
Simmons, Diane. "Remittance Men: Exile and Identity in the Short Stories of Mavis Gallant." In *Canadian Women Writing Fiction,* edited by Mickey Pearlman. Jackson: University Press of Mississippi, 1993.
Smythe, Karen. *Gallant, Munro, and the Poetics of Elegy.* Montreal: McGill-Queen's University Press, 1992.

DISCUSSION TOPICS

- How does Mavis Gallant explore the themes of rootlessness, dislocation, and alienation in her fiction?

- Why do you think Gallant's fiction is so highly admired by other writers but has never been widely popular with general readers?

- What is it about Gallant's stories, even those that deal with the same characters, that makes them read like short stories rather than chapters of novels?

- Is there anything particularly "Canadian" about Gallant's Canadian stories?

- How might Gallant's early experiences of being brought up in various boarding schools affect her themes and concerns in her fiction?

- How do Gallant's stories combine both humor and despair?

- Gallant once said in an interview that short-story readers are a special kind of reader, like readers of poetry. How do Gallant's stories support this idea?

JOHN GARDNER

Born: Batavia, New York
July 21, 1933
Died: Susquehanna, Pennsylvania
September 14, 1982

Believing that literature should make a serious contribution to human life, Gardner combined philosophical and moral concerns in fiction that emphasized the complexities of everyday existence.

© Joel Gardner

BIOGRAPHY

John Gardner's father was a dairy farmer and part-time preacher; his mother was a high school literature teacher. From these two, Gardner inherited and combined down-to-earth realism, life-affirming moral vision, and the belief in the power of art not only to reflect the human condition but also to affect it.

Gardner learned early the redemptive power of art. When he was twelve years old, he accidentally killed his younger brother by running over the boy with a tractor used on the family farm. In response to this tragedy Gardner turned to art—first music and then writing; he would later explain his serious, almost religious devotion to literature in terms of this early experience, when writing was his salvation.

Gardner received his bachelor's degree from Washington University in St. Louis. Recognized for his intellectual brilliance and promise, he was named a Woodrow Wilson fellow at the University of Iowa, and he earned his M.A. there in 1956, his doctorate in 1958. Although Iowa was widely known for its creative writing program—and Gardner did participate in it—his degree was in classical and medieval literature, and his earliest publications were primarily scholarly, rather than creative.

Yet while Gardner was teaching at various schools across the United States and publishing ac-

ademic articles on Old English texts and early classics such as the works of the Gawain Poet and the Wakefield cycle of mystery plays, he was also diligently writing his own fiction—more than diligently, in fact, because Gardner was compulsive in his need to write. He would complete more than twenty volumes during his relatively short life.

His novels were rejected by numerous publishers at first, and Gardner became dismayed at the state of contemporary literature, which he believed to be populated by superficial, nihilistic writers who shirked art's essentially moral responsibilities. Largely out of response to this, and to avoid dejection—the redemptive power of art again—he began work on a manifesto of his artistic creed. When it was eventually published, after Gardner's acclaim, it would cause considerable turmoil and even damage his reputation.

In the meantime Gardner persevered with his efforts, and was at last successful in 1966 with *The Resurrection*, his first published novel, which, however, drew little attention. *The Wreckage of Agathon*, his second novel (1970), was only slightly better received. It was his third effort, *Grendel* (1971), which retold the Beowulf saga (c. 1000 C.E.) from the monster's point of view, that first won for Gardner critical and popular recognition. Significantly enough, it was also the first of his novels to be illustrated, a device that he would retain throughout his career.

In 1972, Gardner published *The Sunlight Dialogues*, a massive philosophical novel which used ancient Mesopotamian myth and modern American complexity to comment upon universal themes of law and justice, the rights of the individual, and the needs of society. Although recognized as a work of daring originality and philosophical speculation, *The Sunlight Dialogues* was nominated for no major literary awards, which caused some furor and discussion in the literary world. Partially in response to this, but more in recognition of its considerable merits, Gardner's 1976 novel, *October Light*, won the National Book Critics Circle Award, perhaps the most respected of all American literary honors.

The prolific Gardner wrote in every genre: criticism, novels, short stories, biography, children's books, libretti for operas (*Frankenstein*, 1979, is his most notable attempt, but there were several others), poetry, translations, and academic studies. His two-volume biography and critical study of Geoffrey Chaucer raised the question, mainly in academic circles, of possible plagiarism: Had Gardner cited his sources fully enough, or had he merely adapted earlier scholarship without proper credit? Gardner himself freely admitted that he had drawn on earlier scholars, pointing out that he was essentially a popularizer—shown by his technique in the Chaucer biography, which included novelistic touches.

Even more of a controversy was stirred with the publication of *On Moral Fiction* in 1978. As noted, the book was largely written while Gardner was unpublished and frustrated, and, as he said, "I was furious, just enraged, at those guys with big reputations, and I wrote a vituperative, angry book. Most of it I got wrong." What he did not get wrong, according to many perceptive readers, was the insistence that art has a moral function—moral in the sense that it must affirm life by addressing serious issues in a serious (but not necessarily solemn) fashion. The book's message was much in keeping with traditional Western views of literature, but Gardner's willingness to question the accepted authors of modern American writing stirred great bitterness in the literary establishment. A number of the negative reviews which his subsequent books received were generated by this controversy, which lasted until the end of his life.

Gardner's personal life, which often seemed secondary to his artistic one, was turbulent and unsettled. Often at odds with authority, he scorned academic tweed to roar about campus on his motorcycle, wearing a black leather jacket and blue jeans. He had problems with drinking, a bout with cancer, and a running feud with the Internal Revenue Service over unpaid taxes. He was twice married and twice divorced. With Joan Patterson, whom he married in 1953, he had two children, Joel and Lucy; Joel took the photographs that illustrated Gardner's last book, *Mickelsson's Ghosts* (1982). Gardner's second marriage was to Elizabeth Rosenberg, an English professor and cofounder with Gardner of the publication *MSS*, which specialized in discovering new literary talent.

On September 14, 1982, only four days before he planned to marry again, Gardner rounded a curve near his home and lost control of the Harley-Davidson motorcycle he was riding. He was killed in the accident.

ANALYSIS

For Gardner, art, and in particular literature, was more than a career: It was, in almost the religious sense, a vocation, a calling of a chosen individual. He believed that art has a profound and lasting impact on those who receive it, whether they are watchers of plays, listeners to music, viewers of paintings, or readers of novels. For these reasons, reinforced by his personal experience, Gardner felt that art was essentially serious—although it could be playful—and that true art, art that is valid and lasting, must therefore be moral art.

By moral art he meant art that affirms and reinforces all that is best in human nature. Literature in particular has a special place, because among all the arts it has the possibility of being the most vivid and closely felt, and so has the greatest impact. In his own novels and short stories, Gardner sought to embody this artistic philosophy, and his book of criticism, *On Moral Fiction*, is an outspoken and uncompromising defense of the kind of writing he considered worthwhile and an unsparing assault on that which he considered merely facile, trivial, or downright harmful.

Gardner's touchstone of good writing was a standard easy to articulate but difficult to execute: It must create a "vivid and continuous dream" for the reader. Mere verbal dexterity, adherence to fashionable but pointless literary trends, or any technique or device that obscured the artist's ability to perceive and re-create the truth of human existence destroyed such a dream. In his brief book *On*

Becoming a Novelist (1983), Gardner gives a summary of the characteristics of true writing:

It is "generous" in the sense that it is complete and self-contained: it answers, either explicitly or by implication, every reasonable question the reader can ask. It does not leave us hanging, unless the narrative itself justifies its inconclusiveness. It does not play pointlessly subtle games in which storytelling is confused with puzzle-making. It does not "test" the reader by demanding that he bring with him some special knowledge without which the events make no sense. In short, it seeks, without pandering, to satisfy and please. It is intellectually and emotionally significant.

In his own novels, Gardner attempted to achieve such goals by concentrating upon his characters and by entering into the mind and heart of each of them so that he could present their points of view to the reader. These presentations were made without overt judgment, even with characters whose moral nature might be questionable or whose motives and ends were warped or distorted. Such intrusive judgments would, Gardner felt, have prejudiced the reader's vision and interrupted the dream. His view was summed up in the quotation from the *I Ching* found at the beginning of *The Sunlight Dialogues*: "The earth in its devotions carries all things, good and evil, without exception."

So, in *Grendel*, Gardner tells the story from the point of view of what most would call a monster, an inhuman beast who yet, when seen clearly, has something of a soul and the aspirations of a poet. In his two "pastoral novels," *Nickel Mountain: A Pastoral Novel* (1973) and *October Light*, Gardner moves among the various characters, filtering the story through each of their perceptions in turn, and so allowing a comprehensive and generous vision, not only of individuals but also of a community, to emerge. No single person has a monopoly on the truth, so the only valid vision—other than God's—must be a communal vision.

This sense of community is a powerful and recurrent theme in Gardner's fiction, and characters who find themselves in despair, without purpose, or acting in ways that even they sense are evil, are those who have cut themselves off from their societies. Thus James Page, in *October Light*, descends into bitterness, drunken rage, and nearly murder when he rejects his community. In a similar but not quite as dramatic fashion (although she does attempt to kill her brother), Sally Page Abbott, James's sister, suffers significant moral decline when she locks herself in her room, literally isolated. Significantly, Sally's moral deterioration is hastened by her reading a cheap, trashy novel, the kind whose bleak and cynical vision Gardner despised as being truly immoral art.

The positive power of community, on the other hand, is pervasive in Gardner's novels, where it is frequently linked with the concept of the natural world as a kind of moral center; the two, community and nature, are joined by the power of art. For Gardner, art does not necessarily mean the creation of beautiful objects but includes the honest observation and appreciation of the world. Henry Soames, the central character of *Nickel Mountain*, becomes such an artist during the course of the novel, discovering the enduring values of the Catskill Mountains and the people around him. In doing so, Henry actually saves his own life, drawing away from a self-imposed early death from compulsive overeating and resulting heart problems.

In Gardner's novels, a condition such as Henry's weakened heart is both actual and symbolic. Gardner's fiction is crammed with images and situations that carry far more than their literal meaning and create a multilayered and complex structure which suggests more than it states. Gardner is also a master of metaphor (for Aristotle, the supreme test of an artist) and uses it in very effective fashion, making the natural world a vast array of symbols without detracting from its concrete presence or tangible existence—without disturbing what the philosopher William James called, in words Gardner often cited, "the buzzing, blooming confusion."

High moral seriousness, a deep interest in philosophy and its relationship to everyday life, and everyday life itself as lived by fully realized, completely human characters: These are the hallmarks of Gardner's fiction. In his novels, he has re-created a world where the individual and the community exist in the special order of nature, mediated by the saving power of true art.

GRENDEL

First published: 1971
Type of work: Novel

The Beowulf legend is retold by the monster, who muses on the meaning of human life and art.

In *Grendel*, Gardner takes one of the mainstays of Western literature, the Old English epic *Beowulf*, and gives it a dramatic new vision by telling it from the point of view (and through the words) of the monster. In this way Gardner is able to present the story anew but also to make telling comments on his enduring theme, the place and power of art in human life.

Beginning the novel as a brute, barely articulate figure, Grendel is exposed to art and its powers by two competing forces. On one hand, there is the human he calls the Shaper, the blind poet of the mead hall; allied with the Shaper is Wealtheow, the beautiful queen. These two are embodiments of the positive power of art to raise human beings—or even creatures such as Grendel—beyond the pointless round of mere existence. Yet Grendel is profoundly troubled by them and by the power they wield and comes to prefer their opposite number. The Old Dragon represents another aspect of art, its negative side, as he holds the universe to be meaningless, a random collection of events without purpose, its creatures without dignity.

There is thus a truly philosophical dimension to the novel—as is always the case with Gardner's fiction—and in Grendel, Gardner has composed a satirical portrait of the noted modern philosopher Jean-Paul Sartre, whose theory known as existentialism posited a meaningless world, a vision close to the Dragon's bleak theories. In accepting this view, Grendel closes himself to the effects of what Gardner termed "moral fiction"—that is, literature that transcends limitations, makes sense of life, and is redemptive in an almost religious sense.

Lacking this view, Grendel attempts to force meaning upon the world by violence: He ravages the lands of King Hrothgar, kills his soldiers, wastes his crops, and defiles his queen, Wealtheow. In the end, however, Grendel is overcome by an unnamed hero—Beowulf—who is not only physically powerful but also morally superior, precisely because he has accepted and can use the art which Grendel fears and rejects.

The novel operates on several different levels. On the surface it is an exciting adventure, a literary tour de force. Below that it is a serious meditation on the power and place of art in human life. To signal these layers, Gardner employs numerous symbols and recurring thematic devices throughout the short book, and these give *Grendel* power and resonance greater than its length suggests.

Christian imagery and Norse mythology are mingled throughout the novel, most frequently in scenes where Grendel encounters trees: hiding in them, being caught in their branches, hanging from them. The chief god of Scandinavian myth, Odin, is closely associated with trees and with sacrifice by hanging from a tree; closely parallel to this are Christian beliefs in the sacrificial death of Christ on the cross, often referred to as a tree. Repeated use of such symbolism gives the novel a complexity and density more like poetry than fiction, as each word is capable of having several different meanings.

The structure of the novel is ingenious as well. Each of the twelve chapters is dominated by a symbol of the Zodiac, starting with the ram (Aries) and progressing through the year to the sign of the fish (Pisces). Once again there are the references to Christianity—the lamb and the fish are both signs of Christ—and a natural movement through the year, from spring to fall. The number twelve crops up repeatedly in the novel, a unifying technique which Gardner adopted from early English literature.

In the end, however, despite the intricate cleverness with which the novel is written, its main power lies in two points: its brilliantly evocative use of language, especially in the creation of Grendel as a character, and the battle between two powerful views of art and human life—one negative, the other positive.

John Gardner

THE SUNLIGHT DIALOGUES

First published: 1972
Type of work: Novel

During the course of a police investigation, two men with greatly differing philosophies debate the meaning of human life and morality.

The Sunlight Dialogues was Gardner's first major success in his writing career—a best seller for a number of weeks and a critically acclaimed serious novel of ideas. A long novel, it has a considerable amount of action, but it also contains extensive passages of discussion and debate on moral and philosophical issues, which is characteristic of Gardner's fiction, always deeply concerned with how abstract matters translate into the everyday human situation.

The novel centers on the confrontation between representatives of two differing points of view. One is a chief of police, the other a "magician," and their dispute concerns law and order, the universe, and humanity's place in that universe. The police chief, Fred Clumly, and the magician, known for most of the novel only as the Sunlight Man, thus are not only individuals but also representatives of much more.

The Sunlight Man is actually Taggert Hodge, member of a prominent local family now in decline. Taggert, who had fled the town of Batavia, New York, sixteen years previously, has returned for his own version of revenge and redemption. Clumly is drawn into this against his will, but once entered into the pursuit of the Sunlight Man, he becomes caught up in an even larger chase, that of the elusive truth. In a sense captive to his strange relationship with the Sunlight Man, Clumly allows his life and work to collapse, worrying his blind wife, Esther, and angering the mayor and city council, who eventually fire him. He joins the Sunlight Man for a final meeting at Stony Hill, the family home of the Hodges, now in decline, and the two men come to a half-spoken agreement. Later the Sunlight Man tries to surrender to the police; by mistake he is killed, shot (significantly enough) through the heart.

To express the search for meaning and order in which the Sunlight Man and Clumly engage, Gardner fashions his work around four dialogues between Clumly and the Sunlight Man in which far-ranging moral and philosophical issues are discussed. Using the contrast between ancient Babylonian and Jewish cultures, Gardner outlines the differences between justice and law, freedom and order, the individual and society. While Clumly and the Sunlight Man seem opposites, they actually have much in common. Both are disfigured physically (hairlessness for Clumly, fire burns for the Sunlight Man), each has a handicapped wife (the sheriff's is blind, his opponent's, mentally ill) and both are isolated from their fellow human beings, cut off from the larger community. The dialogues between the two are partially their fumbling, only partially conscious attempts to break through this isolation.

A vast novel with a multitude of characters, *The Sunlight Dialogues* is carefully constructed, filled with parallels of character and plot. The main supporter of order, Chief Clumly, pursues a criminal and has discussions with him; Will Hodge, another proponent of law, has a series of his own "dialogues" with a counterculture character named Freeman. Walter Boyle, a small-time thief who has an alternate identity (and thus is in one person a contrast between law and outlaw, order and disorder) has another set of confrontations with the boarder who seduces his wife. In this fashion, Gardner reemphasizes the impact that ideas and ideals can have on actual human life.

Two themes are emphasized in *The Sunlight Dialogues*. The first is one Gardner uses in several of his novels, the need to establish meaning for life in the face of death. This theme flows from his first published novel, *The Resurrection*, through his last, *Mickelsson's Ghosts* (1982), and is a central component of *The Sunlight Dialogues*. Here, as in the other works mentioned, Gardner resolved the conflict by the union, or at least acceptance, of seeming opposites through the power of love.

A second theme is the conflict between order and anarchy, society and the individual, law and justice. Clumly champions the first, a heritage Gardner identifies with ancient Jewish culture. The Sunlight Man speaks for the second, which is linked with the Babylonian world. While Gardner's novel suggests that these two widely divergent viewpoints may be combined in some fashion, it is also realistic in admitting that they might simply be ignored or forgotten by an indifferent world: At the end of the novel the Sunlight Man is dead, Chief Clumly is fired, and the events are soon relegated to the past. Still, Gardner insists, the effort is worthwhile, and true art is that effort to reconcile what seems irreconcilable.

The Sunlight Dialogues is the centerpiece of Gardner's works. It is his most ambitious and successful novel, filled with well-created, memorable characters in a believable setting. Its publication brought him his first popular recognition and firmly established his standing as a novelist who could handle ideas, realistic description of action, and the creation of distinct individuals.

NICKEL MOUNTAIN

First published: 1973
Type of work: Novel

By showing love and compassion to an unmarried mother and her son, a man regains his sense of community and accepts the natural world.

Although *Nickel Mountain* was published in 1973, it was begun when Gardner was nineteen years old. Despite numerous revisions, therefore, the novel is among the author's earliest works, and it shows clearly that the basic themes of his fiction were present from the start: the need for love and compassion, the ability of the true artist to adopt the point of view of others, and the need to affirm all that life contains.

The story in *Nickel Mountain* is that of Henry Soames, the three-hundred-pound owner of the Stop-Off Café, a little eatery deep in the Catskill Mountains of New York State. Henry, gnawed by vague despair, given to heart problems—both literally and metaphorically—receives a new chance at life when he marries Callie Wells, a sixteen-year-old waitress left pregnant by her boyfriend. The novel follows Henry, Callie, and their son, Jimmy, through a year of life and the lives of their neighbors in a small, agricultural community. Although a number of highly dramatic incidents occur, including accidental deaths, other tragedies, and a devastating drought, the core of the plot is how

Henry comes to accept life and love again; he becomes, in a sense, what Gardner would term a true artist.

In counterpoint to Henry's growing acceptance of the world are the characters Simon Bale and George Loomis. Both men are soured and embittered by the world. Bale's wife died when their house burned, and Loomis was wounded in Korea, jilted by a Japanese prostitute, and has lost an arm in a farm accident. The symbolically named Simon Bale has become a religious fanatic, but his faith brings no joy, only frustration and gloom. He wishes to be a disciple of the Lord (hence the "Simon," reflecting the original name of the Apostle Peter), but his influence is harmful (baleful). Henry Soames, who is frequently compared to Jesus, takes Bale into his house but is unable to bring love into the man's soul. In the end, Bale dies—perhaps by accident, perhaps by disguised suicide—by falling down the stairs at Henry's house. Twisted faith has killed the man, and he ends up literally twisted and crushed at the bottom of the steps.

George Loomis also withdraws from the world, retreating into his sense of the past. He lives in a house which has been in his family for more than two hundred years, and he derives his greatest pleasure from fondling the family heirlooms. Things, rather than people, have become his life. Early in the novel George has the opportunity to marry Callie—in fact, Henry himself makes the suggestion—but he rejects it, a symbolic rejection of the world outside his dark and shuttered prison. Like Simon Bale, George Loomis represents an alternative which Henry Soames wisely rejects.

Nickel Mountain is subtitled *A Pastoral*, and through the subtitle Gardner is indulging in a characteristic multilayered use of language. On one hand, the novel is literally a pastoral in the sense that it fits into the requirements of a particular literary genre that stretches back to classical Greece: The action takes place in the countryside, the characters are farmers and their families, cities are seen as embodiments of evil, while nature is the only source of goodness and true morality. All of these elements are present in *Nickel Mountain*.

On the other hand, the novel is "pastoral" in a religious sense. Henry Soames is the pastor, or good shepherd, of his small family, and by extension, of the entire community around Nickel Mountain. Numerous comparisons between Henry and

Jesus are made in the book, most notably to Christ's willingness to be crucified for the sake of humanity. In the novel's climactic scene, the members of the farming community gather at the Stop-Off to wait for the rain they desperately need, and they sing "Happy Birthday" to Henry.

The reader will sense the parallel between Christ's birth—which ensured salvation—and Henry's, which in a sense redeems his neighbors. Simply by singing the song they feel better, and later it does indeed rain. Still, *Nickel Mountain* does not advocate any particular religious doctrine or specific beliefs. Rather, it emphasizes that belief itself is important and that the varieties and particularities which individuals may select should all be tolerated, respected, and encouraged as long as they aspire to moral goodness and love.

OCTOBER LIGHT

First published: 1976
Type of work: Novel

The feud between an old man and his sister reenacts the American Revolution and depicts the conflict between changing values.

Published in 1976, *October Light* was in one sense Gardner's bicentennial novel, a symbolic retelling of the American Revolution through the lives of two elderly Vermont residents, James Page and his sister, Sally Page Abbott. The struggle between the two recapitulates, in miniature, the conflict between the colonists and Great Britain, while the small New England community where they live comes to represent the United States—its past and its promise.

On another, deeper, level the novel focuses on a theme which Gardner found compelling and which is the basis for his pastoral novels: the power of nature to act as a moral force and become the positive center for human life, strengthening that which is best and serving as a guide. Nature cannot accomplish this alone but needs to be mediated by art, and that art, as *October Light* makes explicit, must be moral art—moral fiction.

Fiction must be moral because fiction is powerful, capable of affecting lives and societies. In *Octo-*

ber Light this power is displayed in two fashions. First is the hostile, visceral reaction James Page has to modern media, especially television. The feud between Page and his sister starts when he blows apart her television with a blast from his shotgun. Later, enraged by the shows he sees in a bar, Page gets drunk, violent, and destroys his truck in a crash on a winding mountain road.

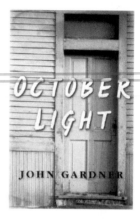

The second fashion through which Gardner shows the power of literature is by his device of a novel within the novel, a cheap crime/science-fiction thriller called *The Smugglers of Lost Souls' Rock*. Sally finds this trashy paperback after she has taken refuge in her room, and as she reads its tawdry tale of sex, violence, and crime, her view of life and her perceptions are coarsened and debased. Eventually she plans, with cold-blooded but fortunately inept determination, to kill her brother. This attempted murder, Gardner implies, is caused as much by the book she was reading as by the situation in which Sally finds herself.

The conflict between James Page and his sister operates on several levels simultaneously. On one, as noted, there are the parallels between them and the American Revolution. Some of these are specific, as when James Page destroys his sister's television, thereby depriving her of freedom of speech. Numerous other connections, more or less explicit, are scattered throughout the book. There is also the struggle between the old America and the new, in which the older sibling (Sally, who is eighty) ironically represents the future: She watches television, approves of nuclear power plants, and supports the Equal Rights Amendment to the Constitution. James finds all these abhorrent, perversions of traditional American values. Through careful modulation of his plot and a gradual softening in the positions of these two characters, Gardner suggests that there is room—and need—for compromise.

The "immoral fiction" of the antinovel embedded within the book rejects this, for it represents a United States where compromise has been rejected and all values, past and present, have been rejected as well. Quoting an imaginary review, *The Smugglers of Lost Souls' Rock* is "a sick book, as sick and evil as life in America." Gardner believes that such indeed would be the state of an America that could neither maintain its worthy traditions from the past nor recognize new strengths of the future.

Finally, there is the resolution of the conflict between James and Sally, past and present, America and Britain, through the power of nature as interpreted by art. *October Light* contains some of Gardner's most lyrical and evocative descriptions of the landscape and the patterned order of rural life, and this sets the characters within a world where healing is possible through nature's power and within the confines of a shared community of human beings. This community is symbolized in the novel by a party held to reconcile Sally and James. Although neither attends in person, the bond it calls forth works on them, and reconciliation is achieved. As is always the case in Gardner's fiction, isolation within one's self leads to despair; rejoining the larger community brings strength and joy. In *October Light*, the community envisioned becomes as close as a family and as widespread as the United States.

MICKELSSON'S GHOSTS

First published: 1982
Type of work: Novel

Disillusioned and despairing, a philosopher sets about restoring an old house and, at the same time, his life.

Recognized throughout his career as a philosophical novelist, fascinated with abstract ideas and how they are embodied in specific characters, Gardner returned explicitly to this kind of fiction in the final novel he published during his lifetime, *Mickelsson's Ghosts*. It is literally the story of a philosopher, Peter Mickelsson, and his attempts to restore meaning and purpose to his life—intellectually, morally, and emotionally.

Mickelsson is a professor of philosophy at the State University of New York, Binghamton, the school where Gardner was teaching at the time of his death. Significantly, Mickelsson's specialty is ethics, but neither ethics nor intellect stirs him anymore. Separated from his family, hounded by the Internal Revenue Service, drinking too much and too often, and wandering the streets alone at night, unable to sleep, his personal life is a shambles. While on one of his aimless nocturnal rambles, Mickelsson savagely kills a dog which startles him. Surprised at his descent into violence, he decides to move to the country, hoping to regain some order and purpose to his life.

Mickelsson buys a run-down farmhouse in the Endless Mountains, just across the border in Pennsylvania, and begins to restore it, but he finds this harder than he anticipated, just as he finds it difficult to bring clarity back to his own life. The nearby town of Susquehanna (again there is the echo of Gardner's own life) may be the site of an illegal toxic waste dump; the countryside is infested with sinister, mysterious Mormons. Mickelsson further complicates his own life by his dual affairs with Jessica Stark, a fellow Binghamton professor, and Donnie Matthews, a young prostitute in town. The farmhouse turns out to be haunted, and Mickelsson begins having windy debates with spirits, including the shades of famous philosophers.

Mickelsson reaches a crisis when he accidentally kills a man—an old, fat bank robber whose money Mickelsson needs to pay for Donnie's abortion. With this death and Donnie's subsequent flight from town, Mickelsson has reached bottom, and he can at last begin to put his life truly in order. At the novel's end, he returns to Jessica Stark, and they have sex in a scene of ambiguous but hopeful resolution.

In many ways *Mickelsson's Ghosts* returns Gardner to his first published novel, *The Resurrection*, which was also about a philosopher trying to get his life in order; in a sense, the book rounds out Gardner's career with the concerns that occupied him in all his writings: the need for community, the search for truly human values, and the place of art as a guide. The book is autobiographical in many aspects, set in the same locale where Gardner lived, and with Peter Mickelsson facing many of the same troubles that dogged John Gardner. The combination of these two forces, artistic and personal, and the fact that *Mickelsson's Ghosts* was Gardner's final novel, give the book a particular poignancy.

This poignancy is reinforced by the symbolic device of ghosts, which figures so prominently in the book. In a sense, Mickelsson himself is a ghost, a man who has died, not yet literally but intellectually and emotionally. As is the nature of ghosts, he wanders through the world able to see and be seen but unable to touch or make full human contact. In all of Gardner's fiction, process is a vital element, and in *Mickelsson's Ghosts* the basic process is the one whereby its hero regains his humanity.

The key element in that process is the power of love, mediated by art. Art in this novel takes two forms: Mickelsson's study of philosophy and his restoration of the old farmhouse. Both are initially useless, because Mickelsson attempts them in isolation; it is only when he admits others into his life—Donnie, Jessica, the townspeople—that art and love can perform their true function and make Peter Mickelsson more than a ghost.

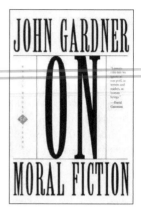

ON MORAL FICTION

First published: 1978
Type of work: Literary criticism

This summary is also a spirited defense of the intellectual and philosophical principles of Gardner's own writing.

On Moral Fiction is actually two books: One is a philosophical and aesthetic study of literature—in fact, of all forms of art—which attempts to define its purpose, explain its effects, and establish its values. In maintaining that fiction is at its basis serious and important, Gardner's work is squarely in the tradition of texts as old as Aristotle's *De poetica* (c. 335-323 B.C.E.; *Poetics*, 1705) and Sir Philip Sidney's masterpiece of English Renaissance prose and thought, *The Defense of Poetry* (1595).

The second book, which is much shorter and is actually a series of illustrative examples, consists of Gardner's evaluation of contemporary American writers, nearly all of whom he brusquely dismisses as having failed to adhere to the moral and artistic standards that he champions. In examining the work of such highly regarded authors as John Barth, John Updike, Norman Mailer, and E. L. Doctorow, Gardner is unsparing in his criticism and perhaps intemperate in his tone. It was this aspect of *On Moral Fiction*—especially its polemical style—which caused such controversy about the book and which clearly damaged Gardner's reputation with many in the literary establishment.

The philosophical and artistic arguments of *On Moral Fiction* are certainly not new, and while they might strike some readers as old-fashioned, they are clearly within a Western literary tradition that is thousands of years old, dating back to the ancient Greeks. True art, according to Gardner, is moral art, moral in the sense that it affirms and reinforces the dignity and purpose of human life, without falling into the trap of easy sentimentality. In the face of inevitable death—of individuals, civilization, perhaps of the world itself—true art finds and celebrates that which is worthwhile. Gardner maintains that in doing this, art is didactic—that is, it teaches its beholders to become better human beings. Once again, his line of reasoning follows traditional thought, and in this case the line reaches back to Aristotle and his theories of the effects of art on the spectator.

In Gardner's words, "Art rediscovers, generation by generation, what is necessary for humanness." In the process of rediscovery, art conveys the necessary information as elegantly as possible to those who hear it, see it, or read it. Art teaches while it entertains. In one sense art, especially literature, can be seen as exhausted, because there are no new stories, no truly original characters left; however, Gardner spurns the despair some of his contemporaries have over this fact because it is basically unimportant. The real value of art is in its restatement of essential and timeless truths which should never be forgotten but which, ironically, would be if not for art:

> Insofar as literature is a telling of new stories, literature has been "exhausted" for centuries; but insofar as literature tells archetypal stories in an attempt to understand once more their truth—translate their wisdom for another generation—literature will be exhausted only when we all, in our foolish arrogance, abandon it.

Gardner's most trenchant and even vitriolic criticism of his fellow writers was based upon this very premise: They had abandoned traditional writing—traditional not necessarily in the stylistic sense but traditional in its central concerns. The two aspects, however, content and technique, are linked, because Gardner believed that writers as different as Barth and Donald Barthelme, or J. P. Donleavy and William Gass, had become enamored of language for its own sake, neglecting its fundamental role as a vehicle for the presentation of character and archetypal truths. Gardner dismissed the vast majority of modern American writing as "toy fiction," and in doing so, he incurred the wrath of the cultural establishment that had accepted and validated the writers and works he attacked.

Gardner's conception of what constituted moral art in practice, however, almost required such an unsparing critique as he made in *On Moral Fiction*. In his view, the essential method of literary art had been abandoned. That method was the process of art: As the writer comes to understand his or her characters, their values, their points of view, then truth is revealed. In this way, the real artist breaks through the illusion of isolation and subjectivity which has weakened so much of modern writing.

"Nothing in the world is universal anymore; there is neither wisdom nor stability, and faithfulness is dead." So laments a despairing character in Gardner's novel *The Sunlight Dialogues*. This is the point that Gardner claims far too many modern writers have accepted. Their response has been to trivialize literature, to make it only a game of words and word play, irony for its own sake. Gardner rejected this view, and in *On Moral Fiction* he set forth a philosophical and artistic program for the redemption of literature, a program that would affirm not only art but what art itself affirms: human life.

SUMMARY

The key to all of Gardner's work was summed up in the title of his book *On Moral Fiction*. Gardner believed, with passionate intensity, that art was absolutely vital to human life and that it had a powerful and profound influence upon both those who created it and those who received it. In Gardner's view, moral art affirms and reinforces that which is best in human nature: understanding of others, compassion, and love. It does not pretend to resolve the terrible complexities and tragedies of the human condition into simplistic answers or a single point of view. Rather, it embraces the "buzzing, blooming confusion" of the world and helps make sense of it.

Michael Witkoski

BIBLIOGRAPHY

By the Author

LONG FICTION:
The Resurrection, 1966
The Wreckage of Agathon, 1970
Grendel, 1971
The Sunlight Dialogues, 1972
Nickel Mountain: A Pastoral Novel, 1973
October Light, 1976
In the Suicide Mountains, 1977
Freddy's Book, 1980
Mickelsson's Ghosts, 1982
"Stillness" and "Shadows," 1986 (with Nicholas Delbanco)

SHORT FICTION:
The King's Indian: Stories and Tales, 1974
The Art of Living, and Other Stories, 1981

DRAMA:
The Temptation Game, pr. 1977 (radio play)
Death and the Maiden, pb. 1979
Frankenstein, pb. 1979 (libretto)
Rumpelstiltskin, pb. 1979 (libretto)
William Wilson, pb. 1979 (libretto)

POETRY:
Jason and Medeia, 1973
Poems, 1978

NONFICTION:
The Construction of the Wakefield Cycle, 1974
The Construction of Christian Poetry in Old English, 1975
The Poetry of Chaucer, 1977
The Life and Times of Chaucer, 1977
On Moral Fiction, 1978
The Art of Fiction: Notes on Craft for Young Writers, 1984
On Writers and Writing, 1994 (Stewart O'Nan, editor)
Lies! Lies! Lies! A College Journal of John Gardner, 1999

CHILDREN'S LITERATURE:
Dragon, Dragon, and Other Tales, 1975
Gudgekin the Thistle Girl, and Other Tales, 1976
A Child's Bestiary, 1977
The King of the Hummingbirds, and Other Tales, 1977

TRANSLATION:
Gilgamesh, 1984 (with John Maier)

EDITED TEXTS:
The Forms of Fiction, 1962 (with Lennis Dunlap)
The Complete Works of the Gawain-Poet, 1965
Papers on the Art and Age of Geoffrey Chaucer, 1967 (with Nicholas Joost)
The Alliterative "Morte d'Arthure," "The Owl and the Nightingale," and Five Other Middle English Poems, 1971

DISCUSSION TOPICS

- John Gardner believed in the importance of striving to understand others' points of view. What are the effects of his very unusual assumption of a monster's point of view in *Grendel*?

- Christian imagery in *Grendel* is said to give it "power and resonance." Locate instances of this imagery. How would you justify this claim?

- What, according to Gardner, are the responsibilities of a novelist?

- For Gardner, authentic art is moral art. Is there such a thing as immoral art?

- Gardner makes severe criticisms of a number of novelists of his time. What is the essence of his charges against them? Could the same criticisms be justly leveled against his own work?

- What is an antinovel? How does the one said to be imbedded in *October Light* function?

About the Author

Henderson, Jeff. *John Gardner: A Study of the Short Fiction*. Boston: Twayne, 1990.
_____, ed. *Thor's Hammer: Essays on John Gardner*. Conway: University of Central Arkansas Press, 1985.
Howell, John M. *John Gardner: A Bibliographical Profile*. Carbondale: Southern Illinois University Press, 1980.
_____. *Understanding John Gardner*. Columbia: University of South Carolina Press, 1993.
Morace, Robert A. *John Gardner: An Annotated Secondary Bibliography*. New York: Garland, 1984.
Morace, Robert A., and Kathryn Van Spanckeren, eds. *John Gardner: Critical Perspectives*. Carbondale: Southern Illinois University Press, 1982.
Morris, Gregory L. *A World of Order and Light: The Fiction of John Gardner*. Athens: University of Georgia Press, 1984.
Silesky, Barry. *John Gardner: Literary Outlaw*. Chapel Hill, N.C.: Algonquin Books of Chapel Hill, 2004.
Thornton, Susan. *On Broken Glass: Loving and Losing John Gardner*. New York: Carroll & Graf, 2000.
Winther, Per. *The Art of John Gardner: Instruction and Exploration*. Albany: State University of New York Press, 1992.

WILLIAM H. GASS

Born: Fargo, North Dakota
July 30, 1924

Although Gass is a distinguished philosopher of language, he is known primarily for his original and experimental short stories and novels.

Joyce Ravid/Knopf

BIOGRAPHY

William Howard Gass was born in Fargo, North Dakota, on July 30, 1924, the son of William and Claire (Sorensen) Gass. With two brief exceptions, Gass has spent most of his life in the Midwest, the place most frequently evoked in his works of fiction. From 1943 to 1946, he served in the U.S. Navy, principally in China and Japan. He left the Navy in 1946 with the rank of ensign, and in 1947 he finished his undergraduate studies at Kenyon College in Ohio. He then enrolled in graduate studies in philosophy at Cornell University in New York, specializing in the philosophical analysis of language, a preoccupation that would become the central focus in his works of fiction.

While working on his Ph.D. in philosophy at Cornell, Gass supported himself by working as an instructor of philosophy at the College of Wooster (in Wooster, Ohio) from 1950 to 1954. On June 17, 1952, he married Mary Patricia O'Kelly, with whom he had two sons and one daughter. In 1954, he received the Ph.D. from Cornell and immediately took a new teaching position as a professor at Purdue University, where he taught until 1969. The period at Purdue was an especially productive one for Gass. During this time, he published his highly original first novel, *Omensetter's Luck* (1966), and a critically acclaimed book of short stories, *In the*

Heart of the Heart of the Country, and Other Stories (1968). In 1968, Gass also published an important novella, *Willie Masters' Lonesome Wife*, which appeared in the pages of *TriQuarterly* magazine. In 1969, he married again, to Mary Alice Henderson, with whom he had two daughters.

In 1969, Gass also began a long and fruitful association with Washington University in Saint Louis, Missouri, a period marked by a flood of publications having to do with his philosophy of language and general theories of fiction. He also wrote a prodigious number of reviews and critical articles on contemporary and classic works of fiction. Gass was writing regularly for such influential publications as *TriQuarterly*, *The New York Review of Books*, *The New York Times Book Review*, *The Nation*, and *The New Republic*. These scholarly articles and reviews became the basis for his important works of nonfiction and often served as chapters in such books as *Fiction and the Figures of Life* (1970); *On Being Blue* (1975), his most famous and frequently quoted work of nonfiction; *The World Within the Word* (1978); and *The Habitations of the Word: Essays* (1984).

The collective importance of these works of nonfiction for the student of Gass's work cannot be overstated; in them, Gass created his own complex theory of fiction as an end in itself, thus establishing himself as one of the chief practitioners and theoreticians of the New Fiction, a style practiced by such writers as Donald Barthelme, Richard Coover, John Barth, and John Gardner, among others.

Gass's work in all these arenas—teaching, literary creativity, and scholarly publication—began to attract more and more attention as well as many coveted awards, prizes, and honorary positions. In

William H. Gass

1965, he won the Standard Oil Teaching Award at Purdue University, followed by Sigma Delta Chi Best Teacher Awards at Purdue in 1967 and 1968. The _Chicago Tribune_ also recognized Gass in 1967, giving him an award for being one of the best Big Ten university teachers. In 1969, he was awarded a prestigious Guggenheim Fellowship, and in 1974, he received the Alumni Teaching Award from Washington University.

The awards were not limited merely to Gass's teachings skills, outstanding though they were. His fiction and essays began to receive more and more national recognition, as suggested by the following honors: The National Institute of Arts and Letters Prize for Literature (1975) and the National Medal of Merit for Fiction (1979). He won the National Book Critics Circle Award an unprecedented three times: in 1985 for _Habitations of the Word_; in 1996 for _Finding Form_; and in 2003 for _Tests of Time_. In 2000, Gass won the PEN/Nabokov Lifetime Achievement Award, which he called his "most prized prize." Gass was asked to serve as a member of the Rockefeller Commission on the Humanities from 1978 to 1980 and as a member of the literature panel of the National Endowment for the Arts from 1979 to 1982. Gass has also been awarded honorary degrees from Kenyon College (1974), George Washington University (1982), and Purdue University (1985).

ANALYSIS

Anyone who has read the first page of Gass's famous _On Being Blue_ must recall the dazzling, virtuoso performance of the author, who manages, in the first few paragraphs, to evoke every possible connotation of the word "blue," including the blues and such phrases as blue laws, blue stockings, blue blazers, and blue pencils. This playfulness with language, this delight in turning words around and examining them as if they were resplendent prisms or baffling puzzle cubes, is characteristic of Gass's fiction.

Again and again, one is struck by the fact that Gass's short stories and novels, however enticing and entertaining they may be, somehow evade the standard storytelling function of most narratives. Gass's stories are not so much about something as they are explorations of how to look at something, how to discover the multiple possibilities inherent in the simplest moment or action. In a real sense,

Gass is a proponent of art for art's sake. He is not interested in delivering a familiar moral or preaching a popular message, and he is rarely interested in realism as such.

A typical Gass story makes relatively few historical or chronological references to the everyday world. His narrative plots tend to be spare and minimal, even though a great deal seems to happen in each story. The reader thus may be hard put to summarize or encapsulate a Gass story, yet that story will leave its audience with an indelible sense of having experienced a richly imagined world—or a sense of having lived in the mind of an unforgettable character. Much of Gass's fiction is focused on the choices and thought processes of such characters. Gass often creates a kind of stream of consciousness in which every perception, doubt, dream, fear, or memory of a character bursts upon the page in a rushing torrent of words. Once again, it is the individual word, with all of its associations and musical reverberations, that becomes the principal unit of composition.

In a real sense, then, Gass's language-oriented technique is his basic theme. Everything he writes in some way reflects on his fundamental notion that words do not merely create reality; they are, finally, the only reality. This technique does not, however, absolutely exclude other interpretations or thematic possibilities. Words fail the narrator in Gass's novel _The Tunnel_. Although Professor Kohler has written an entire book seeking to discover the truth of _Guilt and Innocence in Hitler's Germany_, he is no closer to it at the end than he was at the beginning. In fact, he finds it necessary to add even more misinformation to justify his viewpoint. He is equally unable to discover the truth of his own life through words. Gass is certainly moved by the theme of human loneliness and alienation; he is fascinated by the spectacle of individuals cut off psychologically or socially from the rest of society. He is equally fascinated by the impossibility (or near impossibility) of arriving at any fundamental truth in human life. His works often suggest that ambiguity, misunderstanding, and confusion tend to be the norm.

This skepticism on Gass's part may well result from his professional training as a philosopher in general, or from his specific attention to the philosophy of language. After all, one of the most important philosophers of the twentieth century, Ludwig

Wittgenstein, theorized that language is a game that people learn to play by virtue of their humanity. The rules of the language game are arbitrary, for words can mean anything the speaker wants them to mean, as Lewis Carroll's Alice, for example, discovers on her confusing journey through Wonderland.

Despite his spare plots, general themes of uncertainty and misunderstanding, and love of individual words (a kind of poet's attention to craftsmanship), Gass does not leave the reader in a sort of literary vacuum, a minimalist universe with only bare outlines and skeletons. In fact, he provides one of the richest textures of detail in contemporary American fiction. His fictions positively bristle with details about weather, facial appearances, architectural details, slang terms, odd names, nicknames, bits of song and poetry, and passages from the Bible. In *The Tunnel*, he also uses different font styles, drawings, and cartoons. Perhaps the secret of Gass's success is that he invites the reader to make a fresh interpretation or reordering of the wealth of details always present in his narratives.

Therefore, what Gass provides most consistently is an overwhelming sense of the richness and complexity of day-to-day life. The subject most frequently evoked by that rich detailing is Gass's native Midwest, the region where he has spent most of his life. Midwestern weather, snowstorms, sunsets, fields, flowers, trees, farm buildings, and turreted Gothic mansions abound in his fiction. For all his avant-garde experimentation, Gass always keeps his attention on what he calls the "heart of the heart of the country."

Gass has always maintained a kind of love-hate relationship with the Midwest. On one hand, its pastoral beauties and traditional patterns of social life have fascinated him and provided him with the raw material for his experimental storytelling. On the other hand, however, he has utterly rejected the small-mindedness, bigotry, and cultural conservatism that often characterize small-town life in the heartland. One might observe that Gass's literary experimentation and philosophical independence might not have occurred in the first place if he had not experienced a kind of artistic claustrophobia in his youth.

In "A Revised and Expanded Preface," written in 1981 for the second edition of his classic work *In the Heart of the Heart of the Country, and Other Stories* (originally published in 1968), Gass speaks passionately and sometimes bitterly about his origins. Racial slurs ("nigs, micks, wops, spicks, bohunks, polacks, kikes") were spoken abundantly in his hometown. Gass's response to this poisonous atmosphere (which he described in many of his later works) was to seek refuge in art. He read widely and deeply, developing a taste for the works of modern writers such as Franz Kafka, James Joyce, Marcel Proust, Thomas Mann, and William Faulkner—in short, all the masters of twentieth century literary experimentation. In the process, Gass determined to become a writer himself and to define himself as an artist with "a soul, a special speech, a style." For Gass, there is no discontinuity between his life as an artist and the rest of his existence; the two are inseparably intertwined. "I was born somewhere in the middle of my first book," he explains. The rest of his life can be seen as a brilliantly successful process of self-discovery through one artistic creation after another.

"THE PEDERSEN KID"

First published: 1968 (collected in *In the Heart of the Heart of the Country, and Other Stories*, 1968)
Type of work: Short story

An adolescent boy survives a blizzard in the Midwest and thereby finds his own identity.

On the surface, at least, "The Pedersen Kid" is a relatively simple tale. A Scandinavian family, the Jorgensens, are trying to keep warm during a howling blizzard that has virtually rendered them snowbound. The family consists of Ma (Hed), a kindly, self-effacing woman, and Pa, a boorish, drunken lout who hides his whiskey bottles all over the house and expresses his displeasure by dumping the contents of his chamber pot on the heads of his victims. Jorge, their son and the narrator of the tale, fears and despises him, as does Big Hans, the hired hand who works for the family and lives in the house with them. It is Big Hans who finds the Pedersen kid, half-buried in a snowdrift in front of the Jorgensen farmhouse.

Although he first seems to be dead (the first of many ambiguities in the story), Ma revives the young child (his exact age is another ambiguity—he could be two or even four years old) with the help of Big Hans and Jorge. Pa awakens, fuming as always, but eventually he, Big Hans, and Jorge determine to visit the Pedersen family to notify them of the child's rescue—and to verify if they have been killed or put in the cellar by a mysterious character called "yellow gloves" by the Pedersen kid.

The bulk of the narrative is taken up by their visit to the Pedersen farm in the midst of the blinding blizzard, itself a kind of symbol for the confusion and ambiguity of the entire situation. Pa drops his whiskey bottle in the snow, and Jorge finds a dead horse, which they realize does not belong to Pedersen. They all conclude, without any real evidence, that the dead horse must have been ridden by the murderer of the Pedersens, although even the fact that the family has been murdered has not been established. The entire meaning of the story is revealed at that juncture, because Jorge (on whose point of view the reader is forced to rely) speculates that the horse may be the murderer's, or it may belong to Carlson or Schmidt—nothing is clear.

Pa and Big Hans dig a tunnel to the barn, and finally all three of them stumble toward the house, but Jorge thinks that rifle shots have been fired, killing Big Hans and Pa. In any event, they fall behind in the snow, and Jorge makes no attempt to rescue them or to check on their condition, preferring the relative warmth of the Pedersen cellar (which contains no corpses) and the empty house. The story ends there, with Jorge riding out the storm, uncertain of his fate or that of his companions, because at any moment he could be eliminated by "that fellow."

Like other precocious and highly imaginative narrators—Huck Finn and Holden Caulfield readily come to mind—Jorge invents a complex and often contradictory universe. Yet that world is always thrilling and vivid precisely because of its uncertainty. Like Jorge, the reader will want to thank the mysterious "yellow gloves" for the "glorious turn" he has given to what would have been a hopelessly ordinary little world.

OMENSETTER'S LUCK

First published: 1966
Type of work: Novel

A harness maker named Brackett Omensetter arrives in the isolated town of Gilean, Ohio, and immediately becomes an object of curiosity and gossip.

Omensetter's Luck is a highly complex and original novel which enchants and mystifies the reader on nearly every page. The novel actually takes the form of three closely related tales, the last two progressively longer than their predecessors, all somehow dealing with the mysterious central figure of the book. The three tales (subdivided into chapters) include "The Triumph of Israbestis Tott," "The Love and Sorrow of Henry Pimber," and "The Reverend Jethro Furber's Change of Heart." Just as in "The Pedersen Kid," Gass places his story in the familiar terrain of the Midwest, in Gilean, a small, imaginary community on the Ohio River at the turn of the twentieth century.

The broad details of the story are simple enough: Brackett Omensetter, a dark, burly harness maker, arrives in Gilean during a season of drought, rents a home from Henry Pimber, and takes a job with Mat Watson, the blacksmith. A flood arrives, and the Omensetter house survives in spite of its perilous location near the river. The myth of Omensetter's luck begins. Omensetter's reputation as a kind of magician or possessed man (a fiction created by the half-demented and jealous Reverend Furber) is enhanced when he cures Henry Pimber of lockjaw by using a poultice made from ordinary beets. Henry Pimber later hangs himself in a tall oak tree, Omensetter's recently born son contracts diphtheria, and Omensetter finds Henry's body at the same time that he refuses to seek a doctor's help for his son. The novel concludes with the departure of both the Reverend Furber and the

Omensetter family. Amos, the Omensetter infant, miraculously survives his diphtheria, and "Omensetter's luck" is forever established as a kind of catchphrase in the inbred community of Gilean.

Gass employs a number of literary techniques in this novel, another story of ambiguity and misunderstanding. Omensetter's luck is merely a projection of the town's superstitions and insecurities. The literary technique that Gass uses most frequently to bring this town and its unique residents to life is the device of the catalog or list of items, a technique used as far back as the ancient poetry of Homer. In Gass's novel, the catalog is used to show how people literally create reality by piling one piece of data atop another. In Gilean, the world is made up of lists.

Israbestis ("Bessie") Tott, the ancient postmaster of Gilean, is a kind of living historian, carrying lists of people's possessions (the opening scene of *Omensetter's Luck* is an auction). Henry Pimber will make a detailed list of Omensetter's possessions on the day of his arrival in town. The Reverend Furber makes lists of flowers, mourners at a funeral, and jars of preserves on a shelf. Names, though, constitute the primary data in this list-making process.

In his famous preface to *In the Heart of the Heart of the Country*, Gass admits that he collected names as the germs or catalysts for stories, including names such as Jethro Furber, Pelatiah Hall, George Hatsat, and Quartus Graves. It is not surprising, then, to see some of those names (such as Jethro Furber) figure prominently in his later work, nor is it strange to read the catalog of names supplied by the oddly named Israbestis Tott at the beginning of the novel, including May Cobb, Kick Skelton, Hog Bellman, and Madame DuPont Neff. For Gass, the world is made up of words, as suggested by the title of his book of essays, *The World Within the Word* (1978). Words possess the magical power of invocation: They can call things into being. Names are the most powerful of all words, able to call forth the whole town of Gilean, Ohio.

"In the Heart of the Heart of the Country"

First published: 1968 (collected in *In the Heart of the Heart of the Country, and Other Stories*, 1968)
Type of work: Short story

A frustrated lover and poet makes a detailed and documented journal of life in a small Indiana town.

In "In the Heart of the Heart of the Country," Gass not only makes short lists of names and objects, but he also creates the very structure of the tale from his ingrained habit of list-making. The story, in brief, becomes a list of lists. There is no regular story line or even normal paragraphing but rather a series of journal-like entries, each one with its appropriate subtitle such as "People," "Weather," or "Place." There is only one voice, that of the unidentified poet-narrator, who is living in the dismally boring town of B. . . , Indiana (identified in the preface to the whole volume, *In the Heart of the Heart of the Country*, as Brookston, Indiana).

As in *Omensetter's Luck*, the texture of the world is composed of words and, particularly, of words turned into poem-like lists. There is again the preoccupation with names, including Mr. Tick, the narrator's cat, and such hilarious names as "Gladiolus, Callow Bladder, Prince and Princess Oleo, Hieronymous, Cardinal Mummum, Mr. Fitchew, Spot." The narrator also lists all the possessions of an old man in Brookston, a kind of pack rat who has saved everything, even the steering tiller from the first, old-fashioned car he owned.

The narrator is a saver of things, too, a poet without a lover or a job who painfully plods through each day, examining the minutest details of his environment (clouds, trees, buildings) until they become a kind of poetry. This process of saving things through documentation is especially evident in the entries marked "Data," which culminate with a magnificent list of all the social clubs and civic organizations in Brookston, from the Modern Homemakers to the Merry-go-round Club. One theme that emerges clearly in this story is the idea that something can be so boring that it actually becomes interesting—if one has the artist's eye and the ability to have "intercourse by eye." Another theme is the loneliness and isolation (often self-imposed) of the American artist. In the preface, Gass observes, "The contemporary American writer is in no way a part of the social and political scene."

Thus this famous story, for all of its well-articulated pain and loneliness, is ultimately a celebration of the power of art to elevate and transform even the plainest elements of a little Midwestern hamlet. "In the spring the lawns are green, the forsythia is singing, and even the railroad that guts the town has straight bright rails which hum when the train is coming," the narrator says.

THE TUNNEL

First published: 1995
Type of work: Novel

A middle-aged history professor tries to write the introduction to his major work, Guilt and Innocence in Hitler's Germany, *but instead writes the story of his life and a meditation on the writing of history.*

The Tunnel is told in the first person by Professor Kohler, who is seized by some strange paralysis of the soul when he tries to finish his book and instead writes the contorted story of his own embittered life. Kohler realizes that he is engulfed with rage, and he is determined to mine his past in an attempt to expiate it. He is the only child of a disappointed mother whose dreams center on her sulky, obstinate son and an angry, bigoted father.

Time in the novel loops back and forth between personal history and world history as Professor Kohler (whose name means "miner" in German) becomes obsessed with his experiences in Germany in the 1930's. Kohler finds his colleagues contemptible and taunts Herschel, a Jewish professor at the college, about Nazi motives. Because of a student's harassment charges, his colleagues convene a faculty meeting to discuss Kohler's lechery. They bicker peevishly while he alternately lies and confesses. Kohler's colleagues find him a problem, not only because of his behavior but also because of his earlier book, *Nuremberg Notes.*

As he tunnels deeper into himself in an attempt to come to terms with his relationship to history, he begins to dig an actual tunnel in the basement of the home that he shares with his wife, Martha. A long interior monologue detailing his failed relationship with Martha leads to a meditation on the quarrels that erupted into World War II and other international conflicts. This sets the pattern for the novel: long sections of stream-of-consciousness narration interspersed with stories of the characters told with a more detached viewpoint by the narrator. The novel is not broken up into chapters, but the stories often have titles, such as "Learning to Drive," "Aunts," and "Do Mountains."

True to his midwestern background, Gass sets the novel in Indiana. A visit to an abandoned country farm with Martha and his two children segues into memories of the country drives of his childhood with his disapproving father. His thoughts drift to the failure of his marriage, his own young adult children who disappoint when they do not disgust him, and his father's death. His father brings back thoughts of his student days in Germany and his relationship with Magus Tabor, the charismatic professor whom Kohler worshipped. Tabor, who is entranced by the glorious sweep of history, is indifferent to individual death, falsifies historical facts, adores the German fatherland, despises truth and Jews, and loves conquest. Kohler recalls tossing bricks during the infamous *Kristallnacht* of November, 1938, and smashing the windows of Jewish shops. He adds a long defense of Adolf Hitler to his history of Germany and returns to excavating the tunnel, the debris of which he dumps into Martha's collection of antique bureaus and sideboards. At the end of the novel, Martha discovers the debris and dumps a drawer full of it on the manuscript lying on Kohler's desk. In some ways, *The Tunnel* is a long meditation on the difficulty of determining historical truth through language.

SUMMARY

In a marvelous book called *The Fabulators* (1967), the distinguished critic Robert Scholes suggested that the best writers of the late twentieth century were not realistic storytellers so much as artists who were motivated by the embellishments and multiple possibilities in any story. He called this process "fabulation" and identified the work of Kurt Vonnegut and John Barth as prime examples.

Like such fabulators, Gass has entertained and edified his readers by showing them the story behind the story—and the unending possibilities of meaning contained in even the simplest of words. Like all true geniuses, he took an established form, narration, and made something new and beautiful with it, something that no one had yet anticipated.

Daniel L. Guillory;
updated by Sheila Golburgh Johnson

DISCUSSION TOPICS

- Language is a preoccupation in William H. Gass's work. How does language help or hinder Professor Kohl in *The Tunnel*?

- How does Gass use names of characters (Omensetter, Kohler, Tott) to develop themes in his fiction?

- In Gass's fiction, it is often difficult to determine exactly what happens. Is this true to life as people experience it?

- Gass's individual characters sometimes hold contradictory views. Does this often happen in real life?

- Gass's work has often been called "experimental." In what ways can his novels and stories be called experimental?

BIBLIOGRAPHY

By the Author

LONG FICTION:
Omensetter's Luck, 1966
Willie Masters' Lonesome Wife, 1968
The Tunnel, 1995
The Cartesian Sonata, and Other Novellas, 1998

SHORT FICTION:
In the Heart of the Heart of the Country, and Other Stories, 1968
The First Winter of My Married Life, 1979

NONFICTION:
Fiction and the Figures of Life, 1970
On Being Blue: A Philosophical Inquiry, 1976
The World Within the Word: Essays, 1978
The Habitations of the Word: Essays, 1985
Finding a Form, 1996
Reading Rilke: Reflections on the Problems of Translation, 1999
Three Essays: Reflections on the American Century, 2000 (with Naomi Lebowitz and Gerald Early)
Tests of Time: Essays, 2002
Conversations with William H. Gass, 2003 (Theodore G. Ammon, editor)

EDITED TEXTS:
The Writer in Politics, 1996 (with Lorin Cuoco)
Literary St. Louis: A Guide, 2000 (with Cuoco)
The Writer and Religion, 2000 (with Cuoco)

William H. Gass

About the Author

Bellamy, Joe David, ed. *The New Fiction: Interviews with Innovative American Writers.* Urbana: University of Illinois Press, 1974.

Hix, H. L. *Understanding William H. Gass.* Columbia: University Press of South Carolina, 2002.

Holloway, Watson L. *William Gass.* Boston: Twayne, 1990.

McCaffery, Larry. *The Metafictional Muse: The Work of Robert Coover, Donald Barthelme, and William H. Gass.* Pittsburgh: University of Pittsburgh Press, 1982.

Saltzman, Arthur M. *The Fiction of William Gass: The Consolation of Language.* Carbondale: Southern Illinois University Press, 1985.

Unsworth, John. "Against the Grain: Theory and Practice in the Work of William H. Gass." *Arizona Quarterly* 48, no. 1 (Spring, 1992).

Vidal, Gore. *Matters of Fact and Fiction: Essays, 1973-1976.* New York: Random House, 1977.

KAYE GIBBONS

Born: Nash County, North Carolina
May 5, 1960

In her novels, Gibbons has created memorable female characters who use unique voices to tell their stories and validate their incredible life experiences.

John Rosenthal

BIOGRAPHY

Bertha Kaye Batts Gibbons, born on May 5, 1960, in the rural community of Bend of the River, Nash County, North Carolina, was the third child of Charles Batts, a tobacco farmer, and Alice, a housewife. Gibbons's childhood came to an end in March, 1970, when her mother committed suicide. The nine-year-old girl then had to find a new home, first attempting to live with her abusive, alcoholic father, then shifting from the home of one relative to another. Eventually, she found comfort with her older sibling. Many of the experiences from Gibbons's early life fueled *Ellen Foster* (1987), her first novel.

In 1978, Gibbons graduated from Rocky Mount High School and enrolled at North Carolina State University. While at North Carolina State, she became familiar with the work of Louis Rubin, a well-known professor of southern literature at the University of North Carolina at Chapel Hill (UNC). She later transferred to UNC, where her dream of studying with Rubin became a reality; she enrolled in one of his courses in 1985. In Rubin, Gibbons found a mentor and an active supporter of her creative writing. The previous year, Batts had married Michael Gibbons. The chronic illness of their daughter, Mary, would cause Gibbons to leave UNC without taking a degree. Around that time, her manic-depressive disorder was diagnosed.

Ellen Foster, encouraged by Rubin and published by Algonquin Books, the company Rubin had founded, was met with much critical praise. Writers Eudora Welty, Walker Percy, and Alice Hoffman commended both the novel and Gibbons's skill as a writer. More validation came with the award of the Sue Kaufman Prize for first fiction from the American Academy and Institute of Arts and Letters and a citation from the Ernest Hemingway Foundation. The book was chosen as a selection of the Oprah Winfrey Book Club in 1997.

Fueled by the success of *Ellen Foster*, Gibbons published several novels in the following decade. In 1989 came *A Virtuous Woman*, which would also became an Oprah Winfrey Book Club selection. Also in 1989, Gibbons won a grant from the National Endowment of the Arts to write a third novel.

The 1990's brought a mixture of success and struggle to Gibbons. Her third novel, *A Cure for Dreams*, was published in 1991 and heralded with the 1990 PEN/Revson Award for the best work of fiction published by a writer under the age of thirty-five and the Nelson Algren Heartland Award for fiction from *The Chicago Tribune*. Gibbons followed up with *Charms for the Easy Life* in 1994, *Sights Unseen* in 1995, and *On the Occasion of My Last Afternoon* in 1998. However, her personal life was tumultuous. She divorced Michael Gibbons, moved to New York City, and switched publishers. Compounding these changes were a second marriage, to attorney Frank Ward, two stepchildren, and a return to Raleigh, North Carolina.

In addition, Gibbons continued to battle manic-depressive illness. Her novel *On the Occasion of My Last Afternoon* was reportedly written in a manic stage, taking only three months to complete, with Gibbons sometimes working forty- to sixty-hour periods. She candidly discusses her battle with this disease in her 1995 autobiography, *Frost and Flower: My Life with Manic Depression So Far.*

Despite other personal setbacks, her divorce from Ward, and several moves, Gibbons has continued to write. In 2004, she released *Divining Women.* A sequel to *Ellen Foster, The Life All Around Me by Ellen Foster,* was scheduled for publication in early 2006. Gibbons currently lives in Raleigh with her three daughters.

ANALYSIS

Gibbons begins her novel *A Cure for Dreams* with this quotation from W. T. Couch, regional director of the Federal Writers' Project: "With all our talk of democracy it seems not inappropriate to let the people speak for themselves." This philosophy marks Gibbons's novels; she lets the characters, particularly the female characters, speak for themselves. With first-person narrators, Gibbons's novels are driven mainly by voice. Language is well used. The characters do not always use all the correct forms of verbs and pronouns; however, their words carry weight. These words reveal and enliven the characters, who give life to the words. Gibbons loves language; it is apparent in the way she uses it to empower her characters who would otherwise have no resources.

Both *Ellen Foster* and *A Cure for Dreams* feature female first-person narrators. *Ellen Foster* is told from the point of view of ten-year-old Ellen. Forty-seven-year-old Marjorie Polly Randolph opens and closes *A Cure for Dreams,* but the voice of her mother, Betty Davies Randolph, makes up the majority of the narrative. These voices are undeniably southern, full of idiom and slang and influenced by the southern tradition of storytelling. This is seen clearly in *A Cure for Dreams* as Marjorie allows Betty's voice to show the audience what kind of woman Betty was— and Betty shows the audience by relating anecdotes from her life. Oral history comes alive through the filter of Marjorie. Through this storytelling, Betty validates who she is and who her mother was, and, consequently, who Marjorie is. Likewise, in *Ellen Foster,* the otherwise powerless Ellen validates her experiences through her own voice, a voice that Gibbons so realistically creates; it is both naïve and knowing, much as is Ellen.

While the voices of Gibbons's characters may be destinctively southern, her themes are not limited to such regional designation. For instance, a theme that shows up in both *Ellen Foster* and *A Cure for Dreams* is self-reliance. This concern is tied to some of the other major ideas that appear in these works. For instance, Ellen, the product of an abusive environment, learns to fend for herself. With a sick mother who eventually commits suicide and an alcoholic, volatile father, she must often feed herself, get herself ready for school, and learn to survive in her harsh environment. After Ellen's mother dies, Ellen learns to intercept the money her uncle leaves in the mailbox each month. She saves some of it for food and bills and then puts a small amount aside for her father. In this way, she proves to be rather mature and resourceful for a ten-year-old.

For Christmas, Ellen even buys, wraps, and hides her own gifts to "find" on Christmas morning, realizing that no Santa Claus will mysteriously provide her with presents. On the following Christmas, she again acts as her own Santa Claus by delivering herself to the home of her new mother, her foster mother. She had previously been able to get herself out of everyday dangerous and unpleasant situations. In the act of approaching a local woman known to foster needy children, Ellen provides for herself on a much larger scale. She displays an incredible ability to use her wits to persevere.

Self-reliance is also a major theme in *A Cure for Dreams,* particularly as illustrated by Lottie O'Cadhain Davies, Betty's mother and Marjorie's grandmother. Lottie, like Ellen Foster, learns early in life that men cannot be counted on for comfort or protection. Lottie had seen her own mother stay in a marriage to an alcoholic man, raising several children mostly on her own and running a household as well as a farm. When her husband expects her to assume an equal share of farm work, she withdraws from him and makes a life for herself and Betty. She then creates a community of other women in the Milk Farm Road area. They gather at a local store, play cards for money, share stories, and generally support one another. As the community struggles through the Great Depression, these women do what they can for one another, Lottie often leading the way. In fact, Lottie's self-reliance serves as a model to many of the women in the group, and they, especially Betty, become more self-sufficient as a result.

Another theme shared by these two novels is suicide, a subject with which Gibbons is familiar.

Like Alice Batts, Gibbons's mother, Ellen Foster's mother commits suicide and leaves her young daughter to be raised by an alcoholic father. Ellen sees her mother take the overdose of heart medication, and she is even with her mother as she takes her last breath. Her attempts to save her mother have been thwarted by her father's cruel threats and intimidation. With the death of her mother, Ellen is left alone in the world, yet she learns to survive.

In *A Cure for Dreams*, Charles Davies, Betty's father, kills himself when the Depression threatens the success of his farm and gristmill. This act does not, however, send Betty and Lottie into deep mourning or serious financial difficulties; rather, it is almost liberating for Lottie, as she no longer has to argue with her husband over trivialities. He had long stopped being a companion to her, and he was never a loving, active father to Betty, so his death merely serves to highlight the power that women can find in themselves and in one another.

Overall, because of the abuse they suffer from or the hardships they face, Gibbons's female characters are survivors. Certainly their lives are not easy, yet they are able to build networks of support or discover inner strength and overcome adversity. Both Ellen and Lottie live in worlds where they essentially have no voice. Ellen is too young to matter, in a sense, and Lottie, a woman in the rural South of the 1920's, is constrained by her gender. This is where Gibbons gives these characters their voices. Only through them can readers learn about their lives. Readers become witnesses to events, told by the people who know them best.

ELLEN FOSTER

First published: 1987
Type of work: Novel

Ten-year-old Ellen watches her mother commit suicide, then struggles to find a new place to call home, finally finding security with her "new mama."

Ellen Foster, Gibbons's first novel, actually began as a poem written from the point of view of an African American girl (this girl would eventually become

Starletta, Ellen's best friend in the novel). After showing this poem to Louis Rubin, professor of southern literature at the University of North Carolina, Gibbons was encouraged to flesh out the work. It evolved into a novel, with many of the details taken from Gibbons's own childhood.

The novel, told exclusively from the point of view of ten-year-old Ellen, immediately reveals that the narrator has had a less-than-idyllic childhood: "When I was little I would think of ways to kill my daddy." This opening line sets the tone for the entire novel; Ellen, though now living in the comfort of her foster mother's home, has had to grow up too fast. She is far wiser than most ten-year-old girls, and this maturity comes as a result of all that she has seen in her life thus far.

The opening line also serves to take the reader back to the past, to illustrate the events that have led Ellen to the place where she is today. Looking back two years, she shows readers the terrible existence she and her mother led, mainly resulting from Ellen's father's alcoholism. Ellen then weaves past and present together in the rest of the novel, subtly contrasting that old life with the life she now leads in the secure home of her foster mother, the home where she decided to take "Foster" as her surname.

As Ellen recounts the events of her life, the picture of a true survivor emerges. She watched her mother, who suffered from a heart condition, endure the mental abuse inflicted upon her by her husband, Ellen's father, with the worst of it coming as both he and Ellen see Ellen's mother overdose on her heart medication. Though Ellen desperately wants to seek help for her mother, her father threatens to kill both of them if she does so. All Ellen can do is lie with her mother in bed as she takes her last breaths. This act leaves Ellen alone with her father for a while, yet she learns to survive on her own.

Later, Ellen leaves her father's house after a particularly harrowing night and bounces around from relative to relative. Eventually, she takes it upon herself, on Christmas Day, to place herself in the home of a woman she had seen in church, someone her cousin had referred to as "the foster family." Many of these events mirrored what went on in Gibbons's life as she, too, lost her mother to suicide, lived for a short time with her abusive, alcoholic father, and then went in and out of temporary homes until a suitable home with a foster mother (her older sibling) was found.

Despite Ellen's turbulent life, there were two constants: her optimism and her friend Starletta. Through all of the hardship, Ellen was always able to take care of herself, and she had faith in her ability to be self-reliant. Additionally, Starletta and her family always provided some refuge and stability. However, for most of the novel, Ellen is unable to embrace the beauty of Starletta completely because Starletta is African American, and Ellen is the product of a culture that has always insisted that no matter the economic status, Ellen is "better" than Starletta. Finally, at the end of the novel, when Ellen is given unconditional love by her "new mama," a woman who has no problem with letting an African American child spend the night in her house, Ellen can love and appreciate her dear friend fully. She opens her heart and her mind and admits that she has been mistaken all along—there is no shame is deeming Starletta her best friend.

A CURE FOR DREAMS

First published: 1991
Type of work: Novel

Betty Davies Randolph recounts the story of her and her mother's lives in a rural North Carolina community during the years of the Great Depression.

A Cure for Dreams, Gibbons's third novel, was written with the help of a grant from the National Endowment of the Arts. In preparing for writing this novel, Gibbons read transcripts from the Federal Writers' Project of the Great Depression and found much inspiration in the voices of the common, average men and women. Voice, then, becomes the centerpiece of *A Cure for Dreams*, with three extraordinary women characters sharing their stories.

The primary narrator is Betty Davies Randolph, but the reader gets to her voice only through the frame of her daughter, Marjorie Polly Randolph. Marjorie opens the novel, and she ends it. Marjorie provides the perfect segue for Betty's narrative as she says, "Talking was my mother's life." Then, the majority of the novel is told through Betty, with an occasional intrusion by Lottie O'Cadhain Davies, Betty's mother.

The southern art of storytelling, as well as reverence for the past, is alive in this novel, for Betty immediately acquaints the audience with the details of her mother's heritage and the stories surrounding her mother and father's courtship and marriage. For the most part, what seemingly emerges is the portrait of a typical southern woman who will acquiesce to her husband's wishes as Lottie follows her husband from Kentucky to North Carolina, but the picture quickly changes. When Lottie realizes that Charles merely wants a companion in the fields, she asserts her own will and draws more inward; the arrival of Betty then allows her to form a new bond which leaves her husband out. From this point on, the relationships between mothers and daughters, and among women in general, become the focal point of the novel.

As the story progresses, Lottie grows more distant from her husband and closer to her daughter and eventually to other women in the small community of Milk Farm Road. Lottie and Betty are practically inseparable, and their adventures include instigating card games in a local store, holding political discussions with other women, and helping other women in need. At Lottie's side, Betty learns how important it is to have such a network of women to depend upon, yet she also learns to be somewhat self-reliant. For the most part in Gibbons's work, men seem rather incapable of understanding women or contributing to their growth. For instance, Betty's father never has an active relationship in the Davies household, and his suicide seemingly frees the women to engage in life more fully. Also, when Betty attempts to live in New

York for a short time, the man she dates introduces her to drugs, and only when she returns home to her nurturing community is she able to find happiness.

Betty does eventually marry, but her husband immediately goes off to war, so she is left again to find support and comfort (and await the birth of her first child) with women, her mother, and Polly Deal, the local midwife. All throughout this novel, the steady voice of Betty remains constant. She is an ordinary woman, yet she recounts the details of a rather extraordinary life.

SUMMARY

The driving force behind Gibbons's work is voice. The characters and their stories become fully formed because they have words with which to give these notions life. Gibbons imbues her characters with a rich oral capacity; they do tell their stories because they can tell their stories. In this way, language almost becomes a theme, ranking in importance with self-reliance and community.

Michele D. Theriot

DISCUSSION TOPICS

- Which parallels can be drawn between Kaye Gibbons's life and the events in *Ellen Foster*?

- Does Ellen appear to be a dynamic character (one who changes in the course of the narrative)? What evidence can be presented to justify this opinion?

- What is the effect of the first-person narrators in *Ellen Foster* and *A Cure for Dreams*? Would the stories change significantly if told from another point of view? How is the theme of self-reliance evident in both of these novels?

- What does Gibbons seemingly have to say about the function of men?

- How can language, or the use of language, be seen as empowering in both of these novels?

BIBLIOGRAPHY

By the Author

LONG FICTION:
Ellen Foster, 1987
A Virtuous Woman, 1989
A Cure for Dreams, 1991
Charms for the Easy Life, 1993
Sights Unseen, 1995
On the Occasion of My Last Afternoon, 1998
Divining Women, 2004

NONFICTION:
Frost and Flower: My Life with Manic Depression So Far, 1995

About the Author
DeMarr, Mary Jean. *Kaye Gibbons: Critical Companion*. Westport, Conn.: Greenwood Press, 2003.
Gretlund, Jan. "'In My Own Style': An Interview with Kaye Gibbons." *South Atlantic Review* 65, no. 4 (2000): 132-154.
McKee, Kathryn. "Simply Talking: Women and Language in Kaye Gibbons's *A Cure for Dreams*." *Southern Quarterly: A Journal of the Arts in the South* 35, no. 4 (1997): 97-106.
Makowsky, Veronica. "Kaye Gibbons." In *The History of Southern Women's Literature*, edited by Carolyn Perry and Mary Louise Weaks. Baton Rouge: Louisiana State University Press, 2002.
Tappmeyer, Linda. "Writing and Rewriting: Stories in Kaye Gibbons' *Ellen Foster*." *Publications of the Missouri Philological Association* 25 (2000): 85-91.

WILLIAM GIBSON

Born: New York, New York
November 13, 1914

Gibson dramatized much of the life of Helen Keller and authored two very successful Broadway plays.

Kevin Sprague/Shakespeare & Company

BIOGRAPHY

William Gibson was born in the Bronx, New York City, on November 13, 1914. His father, a mailroom clerk and a talented amateur pianist, died during Gibson's childhood, and his Irish Catholic mother had to work as a scrubwoman to support the family. *A Mass for the Dead* (1968) is a heartfelt chronicle of Gibson's childhood and adolescence. Emulating his father, Gibson learned to play the piano as a child and in his early writing days worked as a piano teacher and as a performer to supplement his income. His lifelong interest in music is reflected in his work on the libretto for the operetta *The Ruby* (1955) and the text for the 1964 musical *Golden Boy*. By the time he was sixteen, Gibson had graduated from Townsend Harris Hall, a Manhattan public high school for gifted boys, and had begun work at what later became known as City College of the City University of New York. Gibson did not like college, however, and dropped out after two years.

In 1940, at twenty-six, Gibson married Margaret Brenman, a psychoanalyst, whose work with the Menninger Clinic had led them to Topeka, Kansas. At the Topeka Civic Theatre, Gibson had his first plays performed, a one-act verse drama about the Apostle Peter, *I Lay in Zion* (1943), *Dinny and the Witches* (1945), and *A Cry of Players* (1948). *Dinny and the Witches* was revised and produced Off-

Broadway in 1959 but was panned by critics and closed after only twenty-nine performances. *A Cry of Players* was also produced in New York City at Lincoln Center in 1968 but enjoyed only moderate success.

In the 1940's, however, Gibson had not settled on being a playwright. He was also writing short stories and poems and won the Harriet Monroe Memorial Prize for a group of poems published in *Poetry* in 1945. He also published, through Oxford University Press, a collection of poems titled *Winter Crook* in 1948. Eventually, he wrote a novel, *The Cobweb* (1954), which he sold to Metro-Goldwyn-Mayer film studios, earning enough to buy a home in Stockbridge, Massachusetts, where his wife had taken a new job.

In Massachusetts, Gibson turned again to drama and in 1956 completed the play that would launch his meteoric Broadway career. *Two for the Seesaw* (1958) is the story of a brief love affair between a Nebraska lawyer separated from his wife and a New York dancer down on her luck. The play was completed with the encouragement of Arthur Penn and appeared on Broadway with established star Henry Fonda playing Jerry Ryan and Anne Bancroft, then a newcomer, portraying Gittel Mosca. The play was a huge success, running for 750 performances and grossing more than two million dollars in its two-year run. Though the work drew critical praise, Gibson considered the four-year process "the most odious experience of my life" because commercial pressures had forced him to alter the script drastically. He records the story of the writing, casting, rehearsal, and production of the play in *The Seesaw Log: A Chronicle of the Stage Production* (1959); his unflattering portrait of Henry Fonda remains striking and controversial. Touring companies took the play around the world, a film version of the play appeared in 1962, and a musical version of the play was mounted on Broadway in 1973, rewarding Gibson with a considerable amount of money for his aggravation.

Before 1959 was over, Gibson already had another Broadway hit. *The Miracle Worker* (1959) treats the amazing true story of how Annie Sullivan helps the deaf and blind Helen Keller to acquire language at the age of six, despite Helen's inability to experience anything outside her own mind except what she can touch. The script had originally been a teleplay, appearing on CBS's *Playhouse 90* anthology series and winning the Sylvania Award in 1957 as the year's best television drama. Gibson rewrote the play for the stage, and it appeared on Broadway in 1959 with Anne Bancroft as Annie Sullivan and Patty Duke as Helen Keller. *The Miracle Worker* was Gibson's second great success, running for close to two years and then, like *Two for the Seesaw,* enjoying a transformation to the screen in 1962. In a few short years in the late 1950's, William Gibson had become a significant new playwright.

Thereafter, Gibson's career slowed significantly. The Off-Broadway version of *Dinny and the Witches* (1959) was not a success. In 1964, after the death of his friend Clifford Odets, Gibson was hired to complete the book for the musical version of Odets's *Golden Boy,* which was only moderately successful on Broadway despite the bravura performance of Sammy Davis, Jr. In 1966, Gibson cofounded the Berkshire Theatre Festival in Stockbridge, which in 1969 produced his *John and Abigail,* a play based on the letters of John and Abigail Adams, but Gibson eventually considered the play a disaster. It was remounted in 1971 in Washington, D.C., under the title *American Primitive.* In the 1970's and 1980's a number of plays followed—*The Body and the Wheel* (1974), *The Butterfingers Angel* (1974), *Golda* (1977), *Goodly Creatures* (1980), *Monday After the Miracle* (1982), *Handy Andy* (1984), and *Raggedy Ann and Andy* (1984)—but none achieved the success of his earlier plays.

Monday After the Miracle, a sequel to *The Miracle Worker,* premiered in South Africa and was featured at the Spoleto Festival in Charleston, South Carolina, before being mounted in New York City, but on Broadway it was not received well by either the critics or the public. Interest in the Helen Keller story as told by Gibson would continue, however.

Monday After the Miracle was filmed for television in 1998; *The Miracle Worker* was made into a teleplay in 2000.

ANALYSIS

Gibson's literary career is noteworthy partly because he worked successfully in a very wide variety of literary forms and has added to American popular literature a most unusual investigation into the nature of human love.

The diversity of Gibson's literary efforts includes poetry (*Winter Crook*), a novel (*The Cobweb*), screenplay adaptations of his own works (*The Cobweb, The Miracle Worker*), the teleplay version of *The Miracle Worker,* an operetta (*The Ruby*), a Broadway musical (*Golden Boy*), and numerous nonfiction pieces: *The Seesaw Log, A Mass for the Dead, Shakespeare's Game* (1978), and *A Season in Heaven: Being a Log of an Expedition After That Legendary Beast, Cosmic Consciousness* (1974). The diversity within his nonfiction corpus is also striking. The last title, for example, is an account of a visit to the Maharishi International University in La Antilla, Spain, where Gibson studied transcendental meditation with the Maharishi Mahesh Yogi and regained the Catholicism of his youth, while *Shakespeare's Game* is an exercise in practical criticism, with Gibson demonstrating how William Shakespeare's plays fit Gibson's personal theory of drama. Gibson's theatrical work is no less diverse, ranging from the fantastical quality of *Dinny and the Witches* (in which a trumpet player and Central Park witches stop the passage of time) to the domestic realism of *The Miracle Worker* and the ritualism of the liturgical passion play *The Body and the Wheel.* The most consistent format in which Gibson has worked has been biographical drama, but the range of materials and treatment even in that area has been wide as well, ranging from *A Cry of Players,* where Gibson focuses on the youthful Shakespeare and works with very sparse historical materials, to *Golda,* where Gibson writes during Golda Meir's lifetime about the famous prime minister of Israel and the Arab-Israeli Yom Kippur War.

On the other hand, there is a remarkable consistency in Gibson's subject matter, as many of his works are investigations into the complex nature of human love. *The Cobweb,* set in a mental institution, explores the emotional bonds between members of the psychiatric staff and their patients, with the imagery of the novel's title suggesting ways in which these complex relationships can be as treacherous as they are supportive. *A Mass for the Dead* is an attempt to come to terms with the complex love Gibson felt for his parents, and *A Cry of Players* hypothesizes about how a rocky marital love between the young Shakespeare and his older bride, Anne Hathaway, might have led to Shakespeare's theatrical career in London.

Perhaps Gibson's most provocative treatment of love comes in *Monday After the Miracle*, the sequel to *The Miracle Worker*, where he investigates a complex emotional triangle. In this play, Helen Keller is twenty-three years old and Annie Sullivan is thirty-seven. Twenty-five-year-old John May enters the household to help edit Helen's publications, and both women fall in love with John. John marries Annie, but his presence alters forever the love between the two women, and the play ends with the marriage's failure, with John turning to drink and leaving, and with Annie and Helen launching a new and highly profitable venture—an exhausting series of lecture tours for Helen—that brings Helen and Annie back together in the kind of relationship they had before John arrived.

The resolution of the action is not satisfactory even for Helen and Annie. In the last scene, Helen recites for Annie, her "Teacher," a poem that sums up her life: "Teacher. And once again, Teacher. . . . it will be my answer, in the dark. When death calls." Helen has her new work, but she may never know love with a man. Annie has Helen again but not her life as wife and mother, and it is fairly clear that both Annie and Helen have taken the energy they have for human love and sublimated it into their work, substituting work for the special intimacy that comes with marriage. John's stark summary captures the bleakness of the play's resolution:

> Love. John loves Teacher. Teacher loves Helen. Helen and Teacher love John, and John loves Helen and Teacher. John and Helen and Teacher are one huge love-turd. . . . Yes. It's next to murder, isn't it. Love.

Given the bleakness of this resolution, it is not surprising that *Monday After the Miracle* was not a commercial success. Most audiences demand a clear uplift at the end of a play, not the kind of stark examination that Gibson offers, provocative as it might be.

THE MIRACLE WORKER

First produced: 1957 (first published, 1959)
Type of work: Play

Helen Keller, blind, deaf, and unaware of the connection between words and things, learns to talk with the help of Annie Sullivan.

In *The Miracle Worker*, Gibson dramatizes the first month of Helen Keller's life with Annie Sullivan. By the age of six, the blind, deaf, and silent Helen is a savage child, gobbling food with her hands off any plate that she wants to invade around the family dinner table, even wrestling a young playmate to the ground and attacking her with scissors. Helen's family, the Kellers of Tuscumbia, Alabama, indulge nearly all of Helen's demands until they hire Annie Sullivan from the Perkins Institute for the Blind to be Helen's teacher and companion.

Herself only twenty years old and formerly blind, Annie insists upon civilizing Helen's behavior, much to the consternation of the family, who see Annie's treatment of Helen as brutally strict. Annie insists that the family's tenderness is misguided pity rather than love, that a superior love for Helen will respect her potential and demand that she live up to it. After a protracted struggle over Helen's table manners, for example, Annie is able to teach Helen to fold her napkin and use a spoon rather than her hands to eat from her own plate; however, the willful Helen returns to her more savage ways whenever she senses the family's indulgence, so Annie insists that she be permitted to teach Helen in isolation for two weeks.

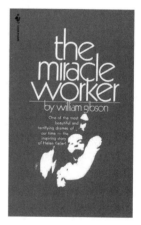

In a garden house behind the family dwelling, Annie succeeds in calming Helen somewhat and teaches her a "finger-game," spelling words into Helen's palm, even though Helen does not understand that the words correspond to things in the world outside her. The family is satisfied with the progress, but Annie insists that Helen is capable of more, that she cannot be fully human until she understands the connection between words and things and begins using language. In an emotional last scene, Helen regresses at the dinner table and empties a pitcher of water on her teacher. When Annie forces Helen to fill the pitcher from a pump in the back yard, the miracle occurs: Helen feels the water cascading over her hand, feels Annie spelling the word into her palm, and says, "Wah. Wah." Within minutes, Helen is clambering around the backyard, demanding to know the names of things. Finally, she spells "teacher" and identifies the word with Annie. As the play ends, Annie embraces Helen and whispers a sentence that she will eventually be able to spell into Helen's palm, "I, love, Helen. Forever, and—ever."

A play of power and eloquence, *The Miracle Worker* is still often revived by regional and amateur theater groups. In the story of Helen Keller and Annie Sullivan, Gibson creates an image of the indomitable human spirit and the power of language while suggesting that love includes discipline and is based more on respect for a person's potential than on indulgence of a person's weakness or handicaps.

TWO FOR THE SEESAW

First produced: 1958 (first published, 1959)
Type of work: Play

A brief romance between a Nebraska lawyer and a New York dancer ends with the lawyer returning to his estranged wife.

Two for the Seesaw is about an eight-month romance between a thirty-three-year-old Nebraska lawyer who has left his wife and an aspiring New York dancer of twenty-nine. Jerry Ryan has come to New York to escape a stifling marriage poisoned by a father-in-law whose money and influence makes Jerry feel dependent and trapped. While Jerry's wife awaits the divorce, Jerry wanders the New York streets and museums, going to films and living on the five hundred dollars he brought from Nebraska. Then he meets Gittel Mosca. Young, vivacious, but unsettled as she pursues her illusory

hope of becoming a famous dancer, Gittel's romantic entanglements have always been brief and superficial until she meets Jerry. Their romance, though tempestuous, is intense and appears potentially redeeming for both.

After becoming Gittel's lover, Jerry takes a job in a law office and plans to reassume his legal career in New York, while Gittel rents a loft and gives dance lessons, with Jerry eventually moving in and sharing Gittel's apartment. After Jerry's divorce becomes final, however, his wife decides that she wants to attempt again to make the marriage work, and Jerry decides to leave Gittel and return to Nebraska. He will try to resurrect his marriage under terms that do not involve dependence on his father-in-law. Jerry and Gittel part as friends, thankful for what they have gained from each other.

The original title of *Two for the Seesaw* was *After the Verb to Love*, which Gibson used as a curtain line for the end of the play: "After the verb to love, to help is the sweetest in the tongue." With Gibson, love is not the clichéd, windswept passion of Hollywood or the soap operas. The prosaic concern for another's well-being and the desire to aid is, for Gibson, a more concrete and realistic way to define love. Gibson is also precise about what he means by "help." Jerry received one kind of help from his father-in-law, but it was not love because the help created a feeling of dependence and inferiority. The help to which Jerry refers is what Jerry and Gittel helped each other learn through their relationship. Gittel helped Jerry regain his sense of independence and self-esteem, while Jerry helped Gittel gain the self-respect she needed to insist on real romance rather than shallow, exploitive relationships.

Gibson's conclusion, however, does not strike the audience or the reader as particularly uplifting, despite what the dialogue asserts. The play remains unsettling because after Jerry returns to his wife, Gittel is left behind with no prospects—a realistic but not particularly comforting or uplifting conclusion. Although Gibson attempts to soften Jerry's departure with Gittel's proclamation that the relationship has done her "a world of good," the sense of Gittel's abandonment is perhaps a vestige of Gibson's original script. In the original script, Gibson intended Jerry to be a much more ruthless character, a "taker" rather than a "giver," and in *The Seesaw Log* Gibson relates how Henry Fonda, who played

Jerry, and Arthur Penn, the director of the Broadway production, demanded that Jerry be made more sensitive and sympathetic. Whether the final script is superior or inferior to the script with which Gibson began remains unsettled, but it is clear that Gibson retained even in the final script the disturbing portrait of the failure of love rather than its success.

Terry Nienhuis

BIBLIOGRAPHY

By the Author

DRAMA:
I Lay in Zion, pr. 1943, pb. 1947
A Cry of Players, pr. 1948, pb. 1969
Dinny and the Witches: A Frolic on Grave Matters, pr. 1948, pb. 1969
The Ruby, pb. 1955, pr. 1957 (libretto; as William Mass)
The Miracle Worker, pr. 1957 (televised), pb. 1957, pr. 1959 (staged), pb. 1959
Two for the Seesaw, pr. 1958, pb. 1959
Golden Boy, pr. 1964, pb. 1965 (musical; adaptation of Clifford Odets's play; music by Charles Strouse, lyrics by Lee Adams)
John and Abigail, pr. 1969
American Primitive, pr. 1971, pb. 1972 (revision of *John and Abigail*)
The Body and the Wheel: A Play Made from the Gospels, pr. 1974, pb. 1975
The Butterfingers Angel, Mary and Joseph, Herod the Nut, and the Slaughter of Twelve Hit Carols in a Pear Tree, pr. 1974, pb. 1975
Golda, pr. 1977, pb. 1978
Goodly Creatures, pr. 1980, pb. 1986
Monday After the Miracle, pr. 1982, pb. 1983
Handy Dandy, pr. 1984, pb. 1986
Raggedy Ann and Andy, pr. 1984 (also as *Rag Dolly* and *Raggedy Ann*; music and lyrics by Joe Raposo)
Golda's Balcony, pr., pb. 2003

SCREENPLAY:
The Cobweb, 1954 (adaptation of his novel)

LONG FICTION:
The Cobweb, 1954

POETRY:
Winter Crook, 1948

NONFICTION:
The Seesaw Log, 1959
A Mass for the Dead, 1968

DISCUSSION TOPICS

- What dramatic techniques has William Gibson employed to bring biographical subjects to the stage?

- What incidents in *The Miracle Worker* best exemplify Annie Sullivan's "get tough" policy with the young Helen Keller?

- Publishers and producers often insist on changing author's titles. Would Gibson's original choice of a title for *Two for the Seesaw—After the Verb to Love*—have been more apt?

- The success of a play depends largely on the audience. Is the relative failure of *Monday After the Miracle* primarily a result of an imperceptive audience or of an unfortunate choice of incidents and subject matter by the author?

- How does Gibson's career illustrate the advantages and disadvantages of writing for the Broadway stage?

A Season in Heaven, 1974
Shakespeare's Game, 1978

About the Author

Atkinson, Brooks. "The Theatre: *Two for the Seesaw.*" Review of *Two for the Seesaw,* by William Gibson. *The New York Times,* January 17, 1958, p. 15.

Moe, Christian H. "William Gibson." In *Contemporary Dramatists,* edited by James Vinson. 4th ed. New York: St. James, 1988.

Moran, Michael, and Thomas J. Taylor. "William Gibson." In *Critical Survey of Drama,* edited by Carl Rollyson. 2d rev. ed. Pasadena, Calif.: Salem Press, 2003.

Richards, David. "Holiday Pageantry." Review of *The Butterfingers Angel,* by William Gibson. *The Washington Post,* December 2, 1989, p. C2.

Simon, John. *Uneasy Stages.* New York: Random House, 1975.

WILLIAM GIBSON

Karen Moskowitz

Born: Conway, South Carolina
March 17, 1948

As the best-known author of cyberpunk, Gibson explores how rapidly developing technology influences the way humans understand themselves and their roles in a changing society.

BIOGRAPHY

William Ford Gibson was born on March 17, 1948, in Conway, South Carolina. His father was in construction and helped build the Oak Ridge, Tennessee, facilities where the first atomic bomb was built. In 1968, at the height of the Vietnam War, Gibson fled to Canada to avoid the draft. He attended the University of British Columbia, earning a bachelor's degree in English. Settling in Vancouver, Gibson began publishing science-fiction stories with "Fragments of a Hologram Rose" in 1977.

In 1984 Gibson's first novel, *Neuromancer,* a noir thriller about cyberspace and artificial intelligence, became an instant cult classic and earned three major science-fiction awards: the Nebula, the Philip K. Dick, and the Hugo. The book inextricably linked Gibson to the cyberpunk movement, which was a group of writers who dealt with the rising influence of the Internet and the growing integration of advanced technology to everyday life.

Neuromancer was the first in Gibson's Sprawl trilogy, named after the megalopolis that dominates the United States East Coast. *Count Zero* (1986) followed, then *Mona Lisa Overdrive* (1988). Several short stories in the collection *Burning Chrome* (1986) also take place in the Sprawl, most notably "Johnny Mnemonic" and "New Rose Hotel"—both of which were later made into movies, for the former of which Gibson wrote the screenplay.

After the Sprawl trilogy, Gibson collaborated with fellow cyberpunk Bruce Sterling on a "steampunk" novel, *The Difference Engine* (1990). The novel used real-life historical figures to imagine a world where primitive computers came into being in the mid-nineteenth century. In 1992, Gibson experimented with a multimedia poem, "Agrippa (A Book of the Dead)." This autobiographical meditation on memory was published on a disk that would play the poem once and then destroy itself. Almost immediately, the disk was hacked and its contents made available without self-destructing.

Gibson returned to cyberpunk with *Virtual Light* (1993), the first of the Bridge trilogy, named after the Bay Bridge in San Francisco. In the story, it is seized by the homeless after a major earthquake. While the Sprawl trilogy is set in a near-future dystopia where cyberspace is firmly established, the Bridge trilogy is set in a nearer future—what Gibson calls an "alternate present"—deeply changed by earthquakes in Japan and California and overrun by an omnivorous media. *Virtual Light* was followed by *Idoru* (1996), featuring a Japanese artificial intelligence pop idol who seeks to become human, and *All Tomorrow's Parties* (1999).

The present may have caught up with Gibson—as many have observed, in the modern world technology grows by leaps and bounds. Nevertheless, it was surprising when Gibson set his novel *Pattern Recognition* (2003) in modern-day reality, using the destruction of the World Trade Center as a key plot point. Cayce, the novel's heroine, is an instinctive expert on marketing who tracks down the source of a mysterious series of film footage that has been released on the Internet and has developed a cult following.

Gibson has written for films and, notably, for television's *The X-Files* (1993-2002). He has donned a journalist's hat for venues such as *Wired* magazine. Married and a father of two, he was not personally familiar with the Internet when he first coined the term "cyberpunk," and he remained indifferent to computer technology for much of his career. However, Gibson now has an official Web site and maintains a blog, further proof that his fictional future has rapidly become the living, breathing now.

ANALYSIS

Gibson may have helped spark the cyberpunk movement in science fiction, but the concept—and Gibson's writing—has its roots in previously established forms. This includes the science-fiction New Wave of the 1970's, represented by such novelists as Philip K. Dick, J. G. Ballard, and postmodern writers who dealt with technology but were rarely labeled science fiction, such as Thomas Pynchon. A particularly important influence on Gibson is William S. Burroughs, whose hallucinatory visions of contemporary life and keen understanding of the human body's fragility can be traced in cyberpunk.

Stylistically, Gibson owes as much to the hard-boiled detective noir style as to science fiction. The typical Gibson hero is a descendant of Dashiell Hammett and Raymond Chandler's private detectives: loners outside of the system, hired to handle problems which conventional methods cannot solve. He has used femme fatales, such as the razorgirl Molly, and often employs MacGuffins—plot devices which move a story forward but whose real significance is miscalculated or unknown by the story's characters—such as the title sunglasses in *Virtual Light*.

Noir is often paranoid, especially about organizations that wield great authority but are essentially corrupt. Combining this notion with the science-fiction dystopia—a future world of chaos and disorder—Gibson often explores the workings of what may be called "corporate feudal states." While countries exist and national borders are observed, the true arbiters of power are organizations that do business across national borders or beneath legal codes of conduct, whose brand names and manipulation of the media are more influential than any political edict. As a result, Gibson envisions consumerism as the engine that drives the world—a

desire to follow the latest fashions, to own the latest technology, to know the most celebrity and pop-culture references. He often parodies this mania, perhaps most succinctly in *Pattern Recognition*'s brand-allergic heroine, Cayce.

Given the technologies about which Gibson writes, he handles the thematic concern over the mind/body division with striking clarity. He does not endorse a complete separation of mind and body—each is dependent on the other, and problems arise when characters refuse to admit this. This construct raises questions, however. If one's mind is the true source of identity, then what purposes can the physical body serve? And how reliable is memory if it is simply another construct? If intellect is a mechanical function, does a re-created mind (such as the Flatline Dixie in *Neuromancer*) count as a living being? Do the various artificial intelligences that pop up throughout Gibson's work?

Where technology ends and the human begins is often unclear, and a person's true identity is what emerges from this melding. Gibson imagines different possibilities. For console cowboys who control cyberspace, bodies are worthless appendages ("meat") that get in the way of their true calling. In "Johnny Mnemonic" the brain is used as secure information storage that can be rented out. A "victimless" form of prostitution involves women becoming "meat puppets" as their bodies are used for sex, but they have no memories of what transpired. Cybernetic enhancement of beauty or lethality is an everyday occurrence. In such a world, the body is (to use Burroughs's term) a "soft machine," and memory is merely another form of storage. As Gibson shows, in such a culture it takes a special act of will, a humane level of insight, to see humans as more than that.

NEUROMANCER

First published: 1984
Type of work: Novel

A broken cyberspace console cowboy has his abilities restored in order to help an artificial intelligence evolve into a higher life-form.

The title's significance is revealed late in the book, but the word itself is evocative: taken from necromancer, magic involving the dead, neuromancer is magic involving the human nervous system. Henry Dorsett Case's neuromancy is his ability to jack into cyberspace and navigate through the matrix of a computerized online world. Once a highly skilled console cowboy—someone who navigates through cyberspace (also known as the matrix) and breaks ICE, security measures that protect information— he stole from a client and had his jacking abilities physically destroyed as punishment.

Now based in Chiba, Japan, Case finds out from his lover Linda Lee that a client of his, Wage, wants him dead. Confronting Wage, Case learns that Linda's claim was merely a ruse so she could steal a RAM from Case and fly home. However, Case *was* being tailed by Molly, a cybernetically enhanced bodyguard. Molly introduces Case to her boss,

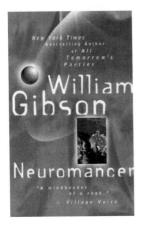

Armitage, who offers to surgically restore his console abilities if he will perform an assignment with those skills. Later, at an arena with Molly, Case witnesses Linda's murder.

After Case undergoes his operations in Chiba, he, Molly, and Armitage head to Paris, then to the Sprawl, a megalopolis covering the eastern United States. Thrilled to be able to jack into the matrix again, Case gets to work. With the help of Molly's associate Finn and the Modern Panthers gang, Case simstims through Molly—that is, jacks into her sensory experiences—while she steals a construct housing a copy of legendary console cowboy McCoy "Dixie" Pauley's intelligence. Later, the group finds out Armitage is controlled by Wintermute, an artificial intelligence (AI) owned by the Tessier-Ashpool corporation. Finn recalls an earlier encounter with another Tessier-Ashpool AI, Rio. With the Flatline Dixie's help, Case discovers Armitage is a personality imposed on Willis Corto, a soldier of Screaming Fist, Russian military special forces which helped develop ICE-breaking techniques. Throughout, Wintermute repeatedly contacts Case, often assuming the form of past Chiba associates, and eventually confesses to killing Linda to push Case forward.

Molly, Finn, Case, and Armitage go to Istanbul, where they join with a holograph artist, Pete Riviera. Finn stays on Earth, while the other four go to Freeside, an orbiting satellite city. Through Zion, Freeside's Rastafarian fringe community, Case's group is given use of the ship *Marcus Garvey* and the help of its captain, Maelcum. The plan is to infiltrate Straylight, the fortress home of the Tessier-Ashpool clan.

Attending dinner at the Vingtieme Siecle, the group watch a holographic performance by Riviera dedicated to 3Jane Tessier-Ashpool, who is in the audience. Riviera uses Molly's likeness to re-create a traumatic incident she once lived, forcing her to leave dinner and prepare alone for the raid. Case discovers that Molly has paid for her razorgirl transformation by being a meat puppet, a person who lends her body out for prostitution but has her consciousness turned off during sex acts. When her company made her use her razorgirl abilities during those acts, she lapsed back into consciousness and murdered her client, a senator, and was forced to go underground.

Case is arrested in his hotel room by Turing agents for conspiring to augment an AI—that is, to free Wintermute from the limits placed on his growth. Wintermute kills the agents guarding both Case and Armitage, and they proceed in different ships to Straylight. With the help of Dixie, Case deploys the virus Kuang, Mark Eleven on the Tessier-Ashpool ICE in the matrix, while Molly physically invades Straylight to activate a terminal that will complete the mission. When Armitage goes insane and recalls his life as Corto, he is also killed by Wintermute.

In cyberspace, Case is caught unaware and finds himself alone with Linda Lee in a deserted cyberoasis. Later the AI Rio—also known as Neuromancer—makes his presence known. Neuromancer is playing against Wintermute and tempts Case to stay with the construct Linda forever. With the help of Maelcum's Zion dub music, Case escapes Neuromancer's realm, returning to the physical world to complete the mission.

Case and Maelcum travel to Straylight and confront a traitorous Riviera, 3Jane Tessier-Ashpool, and Hideo, 3Jane's vat-grown yakuza bodyguard. 3Jane has Hideo kill Riviera, but Molly already got him with a slow-acting poison. 3Jane gives them the word to activate the physical terminal: Wintermute and Neuromancer combine into a new entity which soon dominates the matrix. Molly return to Chiba with Case, but she soon disappears. Case returns to the Sprawl to work as a console cowboy and once, in the matrix, sees Wintermute/Neuromancer with constructs of Linda Lee and himself.

"JOHNNY MNEMONIC"

First published: 1981 (collected in *Burning Chrome*, 1986)
Type of work: Short story

An idiot savant who stores other people's information in his brain changes his life after being hunted down by a Yakuza assassin.

Johnny Mnemonic is an idiot savant: He stores other people's secure information in his brain, though he cannot consciously access that information himself. Ralfi Face, a client, wants him dead. To fight back, Johnny goes low-tech by creating an old-fashioned gun. The story's central theme is that superior technology does not defeat one's enemy; what is needed is the best use of the technology one chooses.

Ralfi catches Johnny offguard despite the gun, but razorgirl Molly intervenes on Johnny's behalf. Ralfi explains that the information in Johnny turned out to be stolen from the yakuza, who do not want anyone else to obtain it through squids, a program that cracks idiot savant security. When Ralfi is killed by a vat-grown yakuza assassin posing as a tourist, Molly takes Johnny to Nighttown and the Lo-Teks, a gang who have forsaken high technology for more primitive means. For blackmail purposes, they unlock the yakuza information through Jones, a drug-addicted dolphin with cybernetic enhancements. Molly then confronts the assassin on the Lo-Teks' ritual Killing Floor: The two perform dancelike moves until the assassin falls to his death, as Molly "killed him with culture shock."

A year passes as Johnny and Molly live with the

Lo-Teks, working with Jones to draw old client information from Johnny's head and use it for profit. Now realizing the emptiness of his past life, Johnny hopes to clear out all that information eventually and retain only his own memories. Though this story ends well for Johnny, his later death at the hands of another assassin is recounted by Molly in *Neuromancer.*

"NEW ROSE HOTEL"

First published: 1981 (collected in *Burning Chrome*, 1986)
Type of work: Short story

A corporate spy causes a leading researcher to defect from one major corporation to another, only to have the woman he loves betray the plot.

From the New Rose Hotel outside Narita airport, the unnamed narrator describes the events which brought him to Japan, still yearning for his lover Sandii, whose gun is his last remaining souvenir of her. The hotel's rooms are coffin-sized capsules, making plain his desperation and imminent death.

A corporate spy, the narrator and his partner Fox arrange the defection of radical genetic research scientist Hiroshi Yomiuri from Maas Biolabs GmbH to Hosaka, the most powerful zaibatsu (conglomerate) in Japan. To do this, the pair have Sandii, the narrator's lover, seduce Yomiuri. Sandii is mysterious, making up different versions of her childhood and claiming each is the truth. The night before the defection, the narrator finds a strange disk in Sandii's purse.

The defection proceeds successfully, Fox and the narrator are rewarded by Hosaka, and the narrator looks forward to a rendezvous with Sandii in Tokyo. However, the double-crossing Sandii allows Yomiuri and most of Hosaka's other research scientists to be killed through a Maas-created virus—a situation the narrator suspected but could not accept. Fox is killed by Hosaka, and the narrator hides from the zaibatsu at the New Rose, still hoping to see Sandii again.

VIRTUAL LIGHT

First published: 1993
Type of work: Novel

A stolen pair of virtual-reality glasses bring together a bike messenger, a freelance security agent, and a Japanese student in post-earthquake San Francisco.

In Gibson's Bridge stories, media permeates lives in unexpected ways. For example, IntenSecure security guard Sublett has left Reverend Fallon's cult, which is centered on watching television in order to discover God. Criminal identification is more efficient by means of Separated at Birth, which lists what celebrities a person looks like. The reason Berry Rydell decides to become a police officer is the television show *Cops in Trouble*.

Unfortunately, Rydell was quickly fired when, playing with a homemade weapon, he killed a fellow officer. His case was picked up by *Cops in Trouble*, and Rydell was taken to Los Angeles by the lawyers Wellington Ma and Karen Mendelsohn (who seduced him). Abandoned by the show and his lover when a better story came along, Rydell becomes a security guard for IntenSecure and a partner of Sublett. The two get in trouble when hackers fool them into raiding a house which had no real emergency, merely to expose a cheating wife.

Faced with unemployment, Rydell agrees to freelance for IntenSecure on a case in San Francisco, acting as a driver for freelancers Lucius Warbaby and Freddie. The freelancers, in turn, consult with a pair of homicide detectives of Russian descent. The case is gruesome: Hans Blix, a courier, had his virtual-light (VL) glasses stolen and was found dead in his hotel room. VL glasses provide a virtual-reality medium which conveys to the wearer information on whatever he or she gazes. Rydell must track down the bike messenger who is considered the top suspect in the murder, though what the others really want is to retrieve the VL glasses.

Chevette Washington was the one who delivered a package to Blix and then stole the glasses out of spite, recalling Blix's rudeness at a party. Chevette lives on the Bridge with Skinner, an old man who helped establish the Bridge as a haven for outcasts after the Little Grande earthquake and construc-

tion of an underground tunnel rendered it useless. Skinner himself is the subject of a case study by Shinja Yamazaki, a researcher documenting the Bridge as an example of useless but fascinating urban monuments.

When IntenSecure agents seek her out, Chevette tells her friend Sammy Sal what she has done. Sammy goes back to the Bridge with Chevette, who prepares to throw the glasses from the roof of Skinner's shelter. Sammy shows her how they work, however, and Chevette uses the VL glasses to see plans for a radically changed map of San Francisco. Yamazaki arrives then, forced at gunpoint by Loveless, who demands the glasses. Chevette leads Loveless down the tower and fights him off with the help of Sammy, but Loveless shoots Sammy off the bridge. Chevette seeks the help of her boyfriend, Lowell.

Meanwhile, Rydell is sent to the Bridge to find Washington. He arrives as a storm brews, trailing Chevette and about to pick her up, when the Russian homicide detectives take over. Rydell senses something amiss with the homicide detectives, the two IntenSecure freelancers, and Loveless, who Chevette claims killed her friend. When another friend attacks the police, Rydell takes advantage

of the chaos and escapes with Chevette and the VL glasses.

Rydell and Chevette are on the run but are caught by Loveless, who confesses to killing Blix. They are told that the VL glasses reveal plans to rebuild San Francisco with the same nanotechnology being used in Tokyo, reshaping the city and giving insiders a chance to invest in a real-estate bonanza. They manage to escape Loveless and meet up with Sublett, who has returned to Fallon's cult to care for his ailing mother.

Rydell finally takes advantage of this situation by coordinating a plan with the Republic of Desire, masters of the still-developing cyberspace, to recreate the same sort of prank that got him fired from IntenSecure in the first place. Using their jobs as messenger and security guard, Chevette and

Sublett go to Mendelsohn's apartment to deliver the VL glasses and the nanotech plans to rebuild postquake San Francisco. Rydell has the Republic of Desire hack into the Death Star, the Los Angeles Police Department's spy satellite, to depict the five men pursuing him and Chevette—the Russian cops, Warbaby, Freddie, and Loveless—as terrorists with explosives and hostages. Thus, Rydell's pursuers are captured by the Los Angeles Police Department SWAT team. Loveless is killed. The producers of *Cops in Trouble* film Rydell and Chevette's story, financially and legally supporting their actions.

Yamazaki has been caring for Skinner in Chevette's absence and learns about James Shapely. Now a Christ-like martyr, Shapely had contracted a mutated version of the acquired immunodeficiency syndrome (AIDS) virus, which became the basis for a vaccine, but was killed by militants who considered him an abomination. Deciding to join in the Shapely followers' rituals, Yamazaki is no longer a student of the Bridge but one of its denizens, embracing the meanings and community outsiders cannot understand. He also discovers Sammy Sal was found alive after the storm.

SUMMARY

Science fiction is not so much a fantasy of the future as a heightened reflection of contemporary concerns. Gibson, understanding this, built a body of fiction which captures the most immediate fears and ambitions of cutting-edge technology in modern life.

While Gibson imagines horrific consequences of technology's abuse—especially by organizations whose size and influence allow them to abandon moral codes with ease—he also sees technology as a source of redemption and self-definition. It not

DISCUSSION TOPICS

- How is life defined in William Gibson's novels, and how does it connect to intelligence? In turn, how do these notions relate to the more abstract concept of humanity?

- How does *Neuromancer* work as a romance, especially regarding Case and the women with whom he becomes involved? Is it a believable romance?

- Examine the noir strategies in a particular Gibson novel: How does he deploy familiar motifs, and how does he change them to fit the particular need of the cyberpunk genre?

- Compare and contrast the Bridge stories to the Sprawl stories. Examine the levels of technology, the way language is used, and the key fictional events that mold each universe.

- In what ways did Gibson get the future wrong? What social concerns and cultural trends were off the mark from how the real world developed?

only redefines a society in mechanical ways, Gibson claims, but it also creates new cultures (such as cyberspace) and reinterprets the body's relationship to human identity. In this way, technology is a means to discover and define oneself, exemplified by the AIs and luckless heroes in his stories.

Ray Mescallado

BIBLIOGRAPHY

By the Author

LONG FICTION:
Neuromancer, 1984
Count Zero, 1986
Mona Lisa Overdrive, 1988
The Difference Engine, 1990 (with Bruce Sterling)
Virtual Light, 1993

William Gibson

Idoru, 1996
All Tomorrow's Parties, 1999
Pattern Recognition, 2003

SHORT FICTION:
Burning Chrome, 1986

SCREENPLAY:
Johnny Mnemonic, 1995 (adaptation of his short story)

TELEPLAYS:
Kill Switch, 1998 (*The X-Files* episode; with Tom Maddox)
First Person Shooter, 2000 (*The X-Files* episode; with Maddox)

MISCELLANEOUS:
Agrippa: A Book of the Dead, 1992 (multimedia; with Dennis Ashbaugh)
No Maps for These Territories, 2000

About the Author

Cavallaro, Dani. *Cyberpunk and Cyberculture: Science Fiction and the Work of William Gibson.* New Brunswick, N.J.: Athlone Press, 2000.

Easterbrook, Neil. "The Arc of Our Destruction: Reversal and Erasure in Cyberpunk." *Science Fiction Studies* 19, no. 3 (November, 1992): 378-394.

McCaffery, Larry, ed. *Storming the Reality Studio: A Casebook of Cyberpunk and Postmodern Science Fiction.* Chapel Hill, N.C.: Duke University Press, 1991.

Olsen, Lance. *William Gibson.* San Bernardino, Calif.: Borgo Press, 1992.

Slusser, George, and Tom Shippey, eds. *Fiction 2000: Cyberpunk and the Future of Narrative.* Athens: University of Georgia Press, 1992.

Tabbi, Joseph. *Postmodern Sublime: Technology and American Writing from Mailer to Cyberpunk.* Ithaca, N.Y.: Cornell University Press, 1995.

ALLEN GINSBERG

Born: Newark, New Jersey
June 3, 1926
Died: New York, New York
April 5, 1997

Ginsberg was a visionary poet of American English whose singular use of language, rhythm, and subject made him a major figure in the cultural, political, and literary life of the United States.

George Holmes/Courtesy, Harper & Row

BIOGRAPHY

Irwin Allen Ginsberg was born in Newark, New Jersey, the second son of Louis Ginsberg, a lyric poet and teacher, and Naomi Levy Ginsberg, a teacher and political activist. His family moved to Paterson, New Jersey, in 1929, the year his mother was hospitalized for mental stress for the first time, and Ginsberg attended primary school in Paterson. He published two pieces in the Easter issue of the Central High School magazine, *The Spectator,* his first public work, in 1941.

When he transferred to Eastside High School, he became president of both the Debating Society and the Dramatic Society before he graduated in 1943. He entered Columbia University as a pre-law student, hoping to pursue a career in labor law, and he studied with Lionel Trilling and Mark Van Doren, who were partially responsible for shifting his focus toward literature. His schoolmates at Columbia included Jack Kerouac, and he met William Burroughs in New York City during his first year there. With Kerouac and Burroughs, among others, Ginsberg formulated a philosophical discourse which they called "The New Vision," a precursor of the Beat generation precepts he exemplified in his later work.

At Columbia, he edited a humor magazine called *The Jester,* was on the debate team, and helped run the literary society. In 1945, he was suspended from Columbia for permitting Kerouac to stay in his room overnight, and he worked temporarily as a welder, dishwasher, assistant at the Gotham Book Mart, and apprentice seaman in the merchant marine. He was readmitted in 1946 and became assistant editor of the *Columbia Review,* in which he published poems, stories, and book reviews. Ginsberg spent the summer of 1947 traveling to Colorado to visit Neal Cassady, the model for Kerouac's Dean Moriarty character in *On the Road* (1957), and he graduated with a B.A. from Columbia in 1948. Later in that year, he had a vision of the English Romantic poet William Blake speaking to him directly—partially a product of Ginsberg's fairly extensive experimentation with hallucinogenic substances, partially an expression of his intense literary and philosophical considerations of the nature of the cosmos.

Although he had no intention to break the law, Ginsberg became involved in several quasi-criminal activities as a part of an underground (or as Kerouac called it, "subterranean") existence, and, following the counsel of several teachers at Columbia, he committed himself to an eight-month stay in Columbia Presbyterian Psychiatric Institute as a means of avoiding prosecution. During his stay he met Carl Solomon, the man to whom "Howl" (1956) is addressed, recognizing immediately a fellow enthusiast for avant-garde art and an unconventional life pattern.

After moving in with his father and stepmother in 1950, he sent a letter and some poems to William Carlos Williams, who was living nearby in Rutherford, New Jersey. Williams provided guidance and encouragement, and while Ginsberg traveled to Mexico and Europe during the early 1950's, he continued to work on his poetry. In 1953, he moved to the Lower East Side of Manhattan, which was to become his home ground for the following five decades, and worked as a copyboy at the *New York World-Telegram*. He spent much of 1954 living in Mexico and then San Francisco, where he worked briefly as a market researcher and met Lawrence Ferlinghetti, the poet and publisher of City Lights Books, which would issue Ginsberg's poetry for the following quarter century. In 1955, Ginsberg moved to Berkeley, California, where he wrote his tribute to Walt Whitman, "A Supermarket in California" (1956), and organized the now-legendary landmark reading of October 13 at the Six Gallery, where he joined Gary Snyder, Philip Lamantia, Michael McClure, and Philip Whalen to read "Howl" in public for the first time. There, also, he was introduced to Peter Orlovsky, who became a close friend and sometime lover, a relationship that endured, while becoming progressively contentious, for many decades. His mother, Naomi, died in 1956, the year that *Howl, and Other Poems* was published, and Ginsberg spent the following two years traveling extensively, promoting the work of friends, defending the *Howl* volume against charges of obscenity, and working on "Kaddish," his celebration of his mother, published in 1961.

The media had discovered the artists whom they grouped under the title "Beatniks" in the late 1950's, and Ginsberg began to appear in magazines and films as an exemplar and proponent of this literary movement. Ginsberg continued to travel widely, reading and discussing the books that he and his friends—Gregory Corso, LeRoi Jones (later Amiri Baraka), Herbert Huncke, Diana di Prima—were trying to publish. He and Orlovsky visited Burroughs in Tangier in 1957, where he took part in a group effort to pull together Burroughs's huge "word hoard" as *Naked Lunch* (1959). He spent time in South America and India in 1961 and 1962, before traveling to Great Britain where he met and performed with the Beatles (as well as Bob Dylan) in a now-legendary concert at London's Albert Hall.

He revived his friendship with Cassady when a bus driven by Cassady carried Ken Kesey, author of *One Flew over the Cuckoo's Nest* (1962), and the Merry

Pranksters across the United States to New York in 1964. In 1963, he published his third collection of poems, *Reality Sandwiches*, as well as an exchange of letters with Burroughs (*The Yage Letters*) on their experiences with the liquid mind-altering substance yage. His interest in the use of materials such as this led him to form LeMar (Organization to Legalize Marijuana) in 1964 with the poet Ed Sanders. In 1965, he appeared in a proto-music video of Dylan's "Subterranean Homesick Blues."

Because of his often critical comments about politics in the United States, the Communist governments of Cuba and Czechoslovakia invited Ginsberg to visit under the mistaken assumption that he would approve of their repressive regimes. In 1965, Ginsberg visited Cuba and was expelled when he challenged the totalitarian aspects of Cuban society, unsettling the puritanical Communist regime with rampant erotic invitations. He then visited Prague, where he was chosen "King of May" by a hundred thousand Czechs before being expelled for his "unusual sex politics dream opinions," as he put it in the poem "Kral Majales."

At the same time that he was becoming increasingly specific about his differences with the U.S. government about its policies in Vietnam, Ginsberg was also becoming a patron of sorts in forming the Committee on Poetry, a nonprofit foundation to assist other writers. In 1967, he was arrested at an antidraft demonstration; he also interviewed Ezra Pound, the most influential Modernist poet in American literature, in Spoleto, Italy. Ginsberg published *Planet News* in 1968, a volume including all the poetry he had written in the 1960's, and he was directly involved in the massive political protests at the Democratic National Convention in Chicago in the summer of 1968, acting as a strong voice for nonviolent expression amidst the increasing chaos of the demonstrations and police retaliation that disrupted the political program. He testified for the defense in the notorious trial of the "Chicago Seven" following the convention.

As the 1960's drew to a close, Ginsberg was becoming recognized more widely as an important figure in American literature. In 1969, he was awarded a National Institute of Arts and Letters grant for poetry, and in 1971, he served as a judge on the National Book Awards panel for poetry. In the early 1970's, he spent some time on a farm in upstate New York and published *The Fall of America:*

Poems of These States, 1965-1971 (1972), poems written during the previous six years. His interest in Buddhism, going back to his visit to India which was presented in *Indian Journals: March 1962-May 1963* in 1970, culminated in an acceptance of the teaching of Buddha under the instruction of Chögyam Trungpa, a religious figure from Tibet who initiated him with the name "Lion of Dharma." In 1974, *The Fall of America* won the National Book Award, and Ginsberg began to teach at the Naropa Institute in Boulder, Colorado, in a school he named "The Jack Kerouac Disembodied School of Poetics."

Continuing to work in areas not traditionally associated with conventional literary expression, Ginsberg joined Bob Dylan's Rolling Thunder Review as a percussionist-poet in 1975 and recorded much of his own work, as well as some poetry by Blake, with various types of musical accompaniment. In 1978, he published *Mind Breaths* and joined a protest at the Rocky Flat nuclear trigger factory, an activity that led to the composition of his "Plutonian Ode." As the decade closed, Ginsberg's increasing celebrity and accomplishment were honored by a gold medal from the National Arts Club Academy and induction into the American Academy of Arts and Letters.

Ginsberg continued to travel, teach, and perform during the early 1980's, publishing poems written during the preceding three years in *Plutonian Ode: Poems, 1977-1980* (1982) and then achieving stature as a major figure in American letters with the publication of his *Collected Poems, 1947-1980* in 1984, a volume received with wide attention and respect by both academic critics and the national media. In 1986, he was appointed distinguished professor at Brooklyn College, and then Professor at the Graduate Center of City University, and published *White Shroud*, an epilogue to "Kaddish" plus other poems from the early 1980's. In 1987, he appeared in several segments of the Public Broadcasting Service (PBS) *Voices and Visions* series on American poets; as the decade drew to a close, he began a collaboration with the composer Philip Glass that led to a release in 1990 of a chamber opera called *Hydrogen Jukebox* (a phrase from "Howl"), which placed many of his well-known poems in inventive musical settings. In 1993, he was awarded the medal of Chevalier de l'Ordre des Arts et Letters by the French minister of culture.

Ginsberg died of liver cancer in his apartment in the East Village of lower Manhattan on April 5, 1997. His death drew an exceptional outpouring of praise from many prominent members of the American cultural community, as well as some typical disparagement from those who decried his undeniable influence on American letters. Ginsberg, no longer considered a wild madman of language, was recognized as a vibrant force in American culture, successful during his last years in the preservation of the legacy of the Beat writers, whose work he taught, promoted, and celebrated. The tributes that appeared on the occasion of his death were both a testament to his work and an acknowledgement by a wide spectrum of the American cultural community of his exceptionally generous support of other artists and his consistent encouragement of all those who were trying to sustain the humane values that he advocated in his life and art.

ANALYSIS

When "Howl" was published, Ginsberg sent a copy to his former teacher at Columbia University, Lionel Trilling, a man widely regarded as one of the foremost professors of American literature. Trilling, who was fond of Ginsberg and wanted to encourage him, wrote in May, 1956, "I'm afraid I have to tell you that I don't like the poems at all. I hesitate before saying that they seem to me quite dull . . . [but] I am being sincere when I say they are dull." The significance of Trilling's reply is not simply that he was unable to appreciate an exceptional poem but that he was unprepared to recognize the qualities of an entire tradition in American literature. Trilling's training and experience had prepared him to respond with intelligence and insight to poems which the academic critical establishment regarded as important. The influence, however, of the New Critics—the writers who followed the teaching of such men as Cleanth Brooks, Robert Penn Warren, and John Crowe Ransom—left a line of poetic expression from Walt Whitman through Ezra Pound and on to Charles Olson, Marianne Moore, William Carlos Williams, and now Ginsberg essentially invisible.

When Ginsberg finished "Howl," many poets outside the academic and publishing network of power were extraordinarily enthusiastic (Kenneth Rexroth said that the poem would make Ginsberg famous "bridge to bridge," meaning across the entire American continent), but many critics and professors attacked it as formless and haphazard, the work of an uneducated buffoon. This particularly angered Ginsberg, who expected some misunderstanding but was especially disappointed that his own careful analysis of poetry in the English language and his efforts to find an appropriate structure for his thoughts had been so completely missed.

In addition to Trilling, Ginsberg sent a copy to his old mentor William Carlos Williams with a letter pointing out "what I have done with the long line," his basic rhythmic measure, a unit of breath which replaced the more familiar meter as a means of organizing the images of the poem. He believed that this "line" had what he called an "elastic" quality that permitted "spontaneity" and that its "rhythmical buildup" would lead to a "release of emotion," a human quality which he believed had been removed from the formal and often ironic stance taken by twentieth century poetry.

Although Whitman obviously was one of his models in his attempt to reclaim the life of an ordinary citizen as a subject as well as for his characteristically long-breath lines, Ginsberg also mentioned American poet Hart Crane and English Romantic poets Percy Bysshe Shelley (citing his 1821 volume *Epipsychidion*, in particular) and William Wordsworth ("Tintern Abbey") as influences. While Ginsberg was describing his modernist method of composition as "observing the flashings on the mind" and casually dismissing most editing by issuing the dictum "First thought, best thought," he also insisted on pointing out his lifelong familiarity with the traditional "bearded poets of the nineteenth century" that he had read in his father's home.

This solid background with conventional poetry was missed at first by critics who were overwhelmed by the originality of Ginsberg's writing and by his insistence on including all of his primary concerns—his amalgam of religions (Jewish/Buddhist/Hindu), his homosexuality, his radical politics, and his particular current literary enthusiasms—in his writing. When Ginsberg spoke of "compositional self exploration," he was challenging the idea that the poet worked everything out beforehand and selected an approved form to contain his thoughts. Ginsberg was, instead, one of the first proponents of Charles Olson's well-known

definition that "form is never more than an extension of content," seeking to "graph the movement of his own mind" without the limitations of grammatical, syntactical, or quasi-literary conceptions about what was and was not poetic.

Ginsberg's intentions were ultimately to remake or restore American poetry, "to open the field" to its fullest dimensions. The mass media's misguided view of Ginsberg as a somewhat pathetic jester was obliterated by Ginsberg's *Collected Poems, 1947-1980*, which made it clear just how much a part of the main current of American poetry Ginsberg had become. It was not a matter of Ginsberg's ideas replacing previous orthodoxy as a dominant mode but rather of a recognition that the approaches and ideas upon which Ginsberg insisted must be given the serious attention they require. From the sequence of what Ginsberg called "strong-breath'd poems," one might also derive a kind of counter-strain of lyrics which would not be "peaks of inspiration" in the most profound sense, but which exhibit Ginsberg's zany, Keatonesque comic spirit and his heartfelt commingling of sadness and sweetness.

They also demonstrate his extremely sharp eye for detail amid the intricate landscape of American culture and his consistently inventive use of contemporary American speech on all levels, mixed with a classic English-American diction. The poems included in this mode begin with "A Strange New Cottage in Berkeley" and "A Supermarket in California," which Ginsberg describes as one poem in two parts that he wrote to satisfy his curiosity about whether "short quiet lyrical poems could be written using the long line." The poignance of Ginsberg's lament in "A Supermarket in California" for the promise of an earlier America still alive among symbols of contemporary American decay, and his homage to Whitman in the poem's conclusion, in which he addresses Whitman as "lonely old courage-teacher," evoke a mood of lyric innocence that is sustained by poems throughout his career.

The comic nature of Ginsberg's work, often using his poetic persona as the source and object of the joke, is evident in poems such as "Yes and It's Hopeless" (1973), "Junk Mail" (1976), "Personals Ad" (1990), and especially in "I Am a Victim of Telephone" (1964), where his reveries are constantly interrupted by the telephone, which demands he respond immediately because "my husband's gone my boyfriend's busted forever my poetry was/ rejected." Because Ginsberg is essentially serious, however, his use of comic situations tends to underscore and to temper his earnestness so that when he vows in "America" (1956) that "I'm putting my queer shoulder to the wheel," his humor works as both a defense against a hostile world and as an expression of his modesty beneath his almost epic claims. In addition, the comic moods of his poems are often a product of his sheer delight in the weirdness of existence, another aspect of his ultimately optimistic and even exuberantly enthusiastic response to the world.

A major part of Ginsberg's world has always been his friends and literary companions, and they, too, figure prominently in his poetry. Cassady, Orlovsky, Kesey, and Burroughs are mentioned in various poems and dedications to collections, but the poem that unites generations of artists with a similar sensibility is "Death News" (1963). Ginsberg, upon learning of William Carlos Williams's death, recalls an earlier occasion when he, Kerouac, Corso, and Orlovsky sat "on sofa in living room" and asked for "wise words." Williams's wisdom— "There's a lot of bastards out there"—moves Ginsberg toward a celebration of the older poet in which he recognizes Williams's ability to retain humaneness in his life and art even though he is aware of the "bastards." From this lesson, Ginsberg proceeds to a series of reconciliations, including the theological (conflicting religious backgrounds), the local with the eternal, and most important in this context, the generational, as there is a mutuality of feeling and respect between the poets of two ages.

A similar Whitmanic generosity of spirit is displayed in "Who Be Kind To" (1965), a poem in which Ginsberg goes beyond the sympathy he extends to his friends to offer love to an often hostile environment. The community of underground artists with whom Ginsberg began his writing has broadened to include many members of the more traditional cultural enclaves, but there is still a very destructive force at large in the United States that Ginsberg has always opposed; in poems such as "Bayonne Entering NYC" (1966) or "Death on All Fronts" (1969), the ugliness and lethal pollution of the world is presented as a sickness to be challenged with the mind-awakening strength of the soul. This is what Ginsberg always tried to do in his poetry, beginning with "Howl," which identified and described the psychic disaster, on through all the other poems that have uncovered and examined fears and desires denied and repressed and have then demanded that these impulses be accepted as a part of the totality of human experience.

"HOWL"

First published: 1956 (collected in *Howl, and Other Poems*, 1956, 1996)
Type of work: Poem

The poet laments the loss of sensitive young people destroyed by society, castigates the forces behind the destruction, and concludes in a spirit of affirmation.

When Ferlinghetti heard "Howl" for the first time, he wrote Ginsberg a note asking for the manuscript so that he could publish it and repeated Ralph Waldo Emerson's words to Walt Whitman upon the publication of *Leaves of Grass* in 1855: "I greet you at the beginning of a great career." Many others shared his enthusiasm.

The tremendous energy that Ginsberg had generated with his images and gathered with his rhythmic structure was impossible to avoid, but while those who were open to all the possibilities of "language charged with meaning" (in Ezra Pound's famous phrase) were excited and inspired by the poem, a very strong counterreaction among academic critics and others frightened or appalled by Ginsberg's subject matter and approach produced some very harsh criticism.

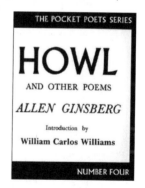

Norman Podhoretz attacked "Howl" for "its glorification of madness, drugs and homosexuality, and . . . its contempt and hatred for anything and everything generally deemed healthy, normal or decent." Ginsberg felt that the poem spoke for itself in terms of his ideas and attitudes, but what bothered him was how the poetic qualities behind its composition seemed to have been overlooked in the furor. Even if he saw himself as a poet who, in the ancient sense, was a prophet who offered insight which could guide his race, he was, initially, a poet. Therefore, it was his "craft or sullen art" (as Dylan Thomas put it) which he offered as his proclamation of intention, and when it was misunderstood, Ginsberg explained or taught the poem himself.

His work prior to 1955 had consisted primarily of imitations of earlier poets or variations on early modernist styles. Then, in a crucial moment of self-awareness, he decided "to follow my romantic inspiration—Hebraic-Melvillian bardic breath." His plan was to write down (or "scribble") images flashing across his perceptual circuits in an overview of his entire life experience. From the famous first line, "I saw the best minds of my generation . . . ," Ginsberg compressed or condensed the life stories of his acquaintances—students, artists, drop-outs, madmen, junkies, and other mutants deviating from the conventional expectations of the muted 1950's into what he called "a huge sad comedy of wild phrasing." He used the word "who" to maintain a rhythmic pulse and to establish a base from which he could leap into rhapsodic spasms of language:

> angelheaded hipsters burning for the ancient
>   heavenly connection
> to the starry dynamo in the machinery of night,
> who poverty and tatters and hollow-eyed and high
>   sat up smoking
> in the supernatural darkness of cold-water flats
>   floating
> across the tops of cities contemplating jazz.

When he realized that it would be difficult to sustain such a long line, he juxtaposed disparate items and elements in a kind of verbal associative collage. He likened his technique to a haiku that involved a clash of images which maintained an element of mystery while putting "iron poetry back into the line." The first part of the poem was designed to be a lament for what Ginsberg felt were "lamblike youths" who had been psychically slaughtered by American society, and it was conceived in a "speechrhythm prosody to build up large organic structures."

In the second section, Ginsberg identified "an image of the robot skullface of Moloch," which he used as a symbol for the devouring power of every destructive, inhuman, and death-driven feature of American life. His plan was to use a version of a stanza form, which he divided further by inserting and repeating the word "Moloch" as a form of punctuation; within each stanzaic unit, he defined the attributes of Moloch in order to form a picture of what he called "the monster of mental consciousness." Ginsberg builds this section to a climax of exclamation before temporarily releasing some of the accumulated tension in a vision of a breakdown or breakthrough where the social contract can no longer bind the diverse impulses of energy into any coherent arrangement. The lingering effect of the section is that of a ritual of exorcism, an incantation that develops a spell of sorts through the effect of a chant that alters consciousness.

Part 3 takes as its subject Carl Solomon, an old friend of Ginsberg from the time he spent in the Columbia Psychiatric Institute, who is the conspectus of all the "best minds" of part 1, a victim/hero of modern American life to whom Ginsberg pledges a unity of spiritual allegiance in his incarceration in Rockland Mental Hospital. Ginsberg took the form of this section from Christopher Smart, whose poem "Jubilate Agno" ("rejoice in the lamb") of the eighteenth century used a statement-counterstatement stanza which Ginsberg appropriated so that "I'm with you in Rockland" is followed by "where . . ." in a "litany of affirmation."

Ginsberg described the third part as "pyramidal, with a graduated longer response to the fixed base," and the last image of the poem depicts Solomon at the door of Ginsberg's "cottage/ in the Western night." The poem does not end with a period, however, suggesting the almost utopian hopes for a better future which Ginsberg maintained. Even if the poem now seems almost overwrought in spots, it contains the central concerns of Ginsberg's work: the intense interest in sound appropriate to a poet firmly in the oral tradition, a fierce condemnation of the worst of American politics, a commitment to an explicit statement of erotic intention, and a rapturous reaction to the wonder of the universe akin to religious ecstasy.

"KADDISH"

First published: 1961 (collected in *Kaddish, and Other Poems, 1958-1960*, 1961)
Type of work: Poem

The poet offers the traditional Jewish prayer for the dead as a celebration of his mother's life and his feeling for her suffering.

One of the central formative experiences of Ginsberg's life was the decline into mental illness of his mother, Naomi, a wrenching psychic ordeal that he internalized for the first four decades of his life before confronting his feelings in the poem "Kaddish," which he composed in bursts of confessional exhilaration from 1958 through 1961. The trigger for the central narrative section of the poem, a biographical recollection of his mother's life, was a night spent listening to jazz, ingesting marijuana and methamphetamine, and reading passages from an old Bar Mitzvah book.

Ginsberg then walked out into New York City, and with his mind racing with the rhythms of the Hebrew prayers, he found himself covering the same ground his mother had known in her early youth. As his thoughts turned to her life, and to his inability to talk to her directly as an adult, he remembered that she had been buried three years before without the traditional Kaddish, the prayer for the dead. Determined to honor her memory before God, to face his own doubts about death and about his relationship with his mother, and to come to terms with his life to that point, Ginsberg began with a direct exposition of his feelings, "Strange now to think of you, gone," and withheld nothing as he re-created the full emotional depth of their life together.

"Kaddish" is both an extended elegy and a dual biography. For the poet himself, it is a "release of particulars," the "recollections that rose in my heart," which he views with a mixture of lingering nostalgia for childhood and a dread of how details apprehended in innocence take on a darker cast when seen in terms of the course of a person's life. His own journey from early youth to his present middle age is a parallel to the path that Naomi took from a youthful beauty, "her long hair wound with flowers—smiling—playing lullabies on mandolin," to Naomi "At forty, varicosed, nude, fat, doomed." Her mental illness and paranoia, which baffled and frightened him in his youth, are now a lurking threat to his own mental stability, especially as he has experienced visions and hallucinations of awesome power. The direction of their lives, of everyone's life, is toward "the names of Death in many mind-worlds," and it is this awesome certainty that has driven Ginsberg to open the paths to his subconscious. Rebuked by his mother's madness in life, and by her silence now, the poet thinks with gratitude of his mother no longer suffering, but he realizes that he will not find any kind of peace because he still has not "written your history."

The central incident in the second section concerns the trip that the twelve-year-old Ginsberg took with his mother on a public bus to a rest home. The awful implications of unpredictability and confusion in the presence of one who is supposed to provide stability turn the child into a quasi-adult but one without guidance or education. While not blaming himself for his inability to handle the situation, he knows (even at the age of fifteen) that an inescapable incursion of the chaotic has been planted in his mind. In this lengthy narrative, carried along image by image through the power of Ginsberg's language, the world in which the poet developed his mind and began to shape his art comes into focus. It is a picture of American life in the late 1930's and early 1940's, and as Naomi retreats into mental illness, Ginsberg recalls how his political ideals, nascent poetic instincts, and sense of himself grew toward the poet who is writing this psychic history.

As the section concludes, Ginsberg turns his complete attention to his mother, indicating her madness by the seemingly logical but disjointed fragments of her conversation that he reproduces and using the power of very graphic physical details of the body's collapse as a metaphor for the decay of the mind. The extreme frankness with which Ginsberg describes his mother in a state of increasing deterioration is jolting in its candor, but it also functions as a seal of authenticity, implying an overall veracity, as the most painful of memories have been reconstructed.

The long decline that his mother suffered is so stunning that the poet is moved to prayer in the face of his helplessness, introducing the literal Hebrew words of the Kaddish, providing the prayer that the world withheld at her death. His own contribution, though, is not only to create a context of appropriateness for the ancient words but also to supply in language his own appreciation of his mother's best qualities. As the long second section moves toward a conclusion, Ginsberg employs a familiar poetic motif, setting the power of language in celebration of the beautiful against the agony of circumstance. Returning to some of the more traditional features of the elegiac mode (modeled on Shelley's *Adonais*, 1821), which he has held in reserve, Ginsberg declares:

> holy mother, now you smile on your love,
> your world is born anew, children run naked in the
> field spotted with dandelions,

and sings,

> O glorious muse that bore me from the womb,
>   gave suck first mystic
> life & taught me talk and music, from whose pained
> head I first took Vision—

and concludes:

>   Now wear your naked-
> ness forever, white flowers in your hair, your marriage
>   sealed behind the sky
> —no revolution might destroy that maidenhood—
>   O beautiful Garbo of my Karma.

The closing lines of this part quote a letter that Ginsberg received from his mother only days before her final stroke, in which she tells him "the key" is "in the sunlight in the window." The image of light immediately precedes her salutation, "Love,/ your mother," that Ginsberg ratifies, "which is Naomi—" as an acknowledgment of his own love.

The last section of the poem is called "Hymmnn," and it is divided into three parts. The first is a prayer for blessing that examines the "key" image, the second a recapitulation of some of his mother's attributes in a catalog of her characteristics, and the third what Ginsberg called "another variation

of the litany form" in which the poem ends in waves of "pure emotive sound" varying the words "Lord lord lord" and "caw caw caw." The poem is not really complete for Ginsberg, as he added a reflection on it in "White Shroud" (1983) and suggested that other parts might appear as well. It is not a really difficult poem, but it is not a comfortable one either, and in resisting all the temptations to use centuries of sentimental associations with motherhood, Ginsberg has placed an archetypal relationship in a vivid and original light, reaching depths of feeling rarely touched except in the most powerful art.

"KRAL MAJALES"

First published: 1965 (collected in *Kral Majales*, 1965)
Type of work: Poem

In accepting the Czechoslovakian honor of "King of May," Ginsberg attacks the evils of both communism and capitalism and extols the life-giving powers of art.

Among the links in the "chain of strong-breath'd poems," "Kral Majales" contains some of Ginsberg's strongest affirmations of human love as a force sufficient to overcome the powers of evil. The poem was written in May, 1965, after Ginsberg had been "sent from Havana" when his hosts found that he was not sympathetic to their suppression of unconventional behavior, and then "sent from Prague" when the authorities became nervous that a hundred thousand Czech citizens were deliriously cheering a bearded, anarchic American poet who was advocating action directly opposed to the political workings of their drab dictatorship. Ginsberg had been chosen as King of May by students and intellectuals in an ancient custom that had endured centuries of upheaval and conquest by foreign empires.

The poem begins as a comic rant juxtaposing the foolishness of capitalists who "proffer Napalm and money in green suitcases to the Naked" with his disappointment in the actuality of a communist government after hearing his mother "reading patiently out of Communist fairy book." Instead of a worker's paradise, the Communists "create heavy industry but the heart is also heavy."

After a balance of images condemning the idiocy of both sides, Ginsberg shifts the tone of the poem completely; he sets against the darkness of modern industrial decay at its most deadly the life-giving properties of the office with which he has been honored and which he honors in the poem. In a great list, he describes the King of May—himself, in this current incarnation—as a mythic savior who offers the powers of art, love, invention, true religion, and the excitement of language in action. Using the phrase "I am" to keep the beat, his long line pulses with energy; the method of juxtaposition utilized in "Howl" is even more concentrated and direct:

And I am the King of May, which is the power of
 sexual youth,
and I am the King of May, which is industry in
 eloquence and action in amour,
and I am the King of May, which is long hair of
 Adam and the Beard of my own body
and I am the King of May, which is Kral Majales in
 the Czechoslovakian tongue,
and I am the King of May, which is old Human
 poesy, and 100,000 people chose my name.

Ginsberg goes on to cite his other qualifications, including an inclusive, ecumenical vision of religion, labeling himself a "Buddhist Jew/ who worships the Sacred Heart of Christ the blue body of Krishna the straight back of Ram/ the beads of Chango the Nigerian singing Shiva Shiva in a manner which I have invented." "Kral Majales" concludes with the almost breathless excitement of the poet arriving at "Albion's airfield" still vibrating with the excitement of the poem's composition.

"ON CREMATION OF CHÖGYAM TRUNGPA, VIDYADHARA"

First published: 1987 (collected in *Cosmopolitan Greetings*, 1994)
Type of work: Poem

The poet evokes a mood of spiritual transcendence in his description of the ritual cremation of the teacher who guided him on a journey of philosophical exploration.

Allen Ginsberg's poem celebrating the life and teachings of Chögyam Trungpa, "On Cremation of Chögyam Trungpa, Vidyadhara," was written as a heartfelt tribute to his spiritual guide on the occasion of the burial ceremony conducted in Vermont by friends and students. Ginsberg's description of the events of the afternoon is designed to convey the inspirational effect of his teacher's life in the evocation of the exuberant mood of the gathering. Using a characteristic signature phrase similar to those in other well-known poems, "I noticed . . . ," Ginsberg adopts the position of a keen-eyed commentator, both involved and able to maintain a perspective with sufficient distance to acknowledge the power and providence of Trungpa's wisdom and example.

Beginning with a view of the terrain ("I noticed the grass, I noticed the hills"), the poem is structured as an inward spiral, moving steadily closer to the ceremony, as the poet becomes a part of the celebration. He moves among the spectators arriving, their dress and appearance indicative of the diverse population that was drawn to the guru. Then, the poet tightens the focus, highlighting the distinctive details that form the image-pattern of the poem. Color ("amber for generosity, green for karmic works"), texture ("silk head crowns & saffron robes"), and sound ("monks chanting, horn plaint in our ears") create an ambience of reverence and respect, charged with the energy practically pouring from the devotees, their families and friends. The poet registers the force of the celebration in his physical response to the myriad stimuli ("I noticed my own heart beating"), a full-body experience that is fused with his intimations of the eternal, expressed in a reversal of narrative direction back toward the outer edges of the scene, with the enduring elements of the natural world ("a misted horizon, shore &/ old worn rocks in the sand") leading toward a feeling of ecstasy, as the poem concludes with an exultant "I wanted to dance."

Allen Ginsberg

"FUN HOUSE ANTIQUE STORE"

First published: 1992 (collected in
Cosmopolitan Greetings, 1994)
Type of work: Poem

*The poet relishes the "minute particulars" of
the moment, exemplified by the unique and
appealing objects he finds in an antique shop on
a roadside near Washington, D.C.*

Recalling the catalogue of abundance that begins "A Supermarket in California," "Fun House Antique Store" conveys a similar feeling of excitement at the marvels available to an American citizen among the fundamental things of the American nation. In this poem, it is the apparently mundane objects of life along the road that Ginsberg, in the tradition of Walt Whitman and Jack Kerouac, sees with delight as he has been "motoring through States" on the way to an event at the nation's capital. No longer the "isolato" (as Whitman described himself) of the time in 1955 when he was about to publish "Howl" and enter the consciousness of his country, Ginsberg is now prominent enough to be traveling "through Maryland to see our lawyer in D.C.," but he has retained his ability to recognize the manifestations of the warmly human amid a bleak and forbidding environment, something he did regularly in poems such as "Bayonne Entering NYC."

Applying his sharp eye for the telling detail, Ginsberg evokes the feeling of an old dwelling made inviting by the accumulation of objects and devices that represent the substance of countless lives. Admiring the "old-fashioned house," Ginsberg leads the reader on a tour, beginning with an entry past "Flower'd wallpaper, polished banisters/ lampshades dusted, candelabra burnished" that sets the location within the flow of time's passage. Then, in a profusion of images that extend and deepen the mood of the house, he presents item after item as they appear: "washbowls beside the French doors/ embroidered doilies & artificial flowers/ ivory & light brown on mahogany/ side tables, a brass bowl for cards,/ kitchen with polished stove cold ready/ at Summer's end to light up with split/ wood & kindling in buckets beside/ the empty fireplace, tongs & screen/ in neat order."

The second floor is presented with similar attention to detail, until the poet is so overcome with the pleasure of contemplation that he declares, "I wished to make a speech," and while his praise is not readily acknowledged ("attendants conferred/ minds elsewhere"), one person "applauded our appreciation," perhaps a figure for the often limited but discerning audience that the poet finds and for which he is grateful even now, somewhat famous, with his "party on its way to the postmodern Capital."

SUMMARY

Ginsberg worked in the tradition begun by Walt Whitman, in which the poet is not only a master of language and literature but also a singer whose voice carries the spirit of a nation's speech and thought. A self-proclaimed "poet as priest" whose congregation was his country's citizenry, Ginsberg never lost sight of his initial vision of a cosmos where the full range of human possibility can be made manifest through the unrestricted explorations of the mind and body. In opposition to the evils of the modern age, Ginsberg tried to create a kingdom of love leading toward a utopian universe that is alive in his poetry. Like Whitman, the "dear father graybeard" who guided him, he never lost the courage to proclaim his heart's truth in his poetry.

Leon Lewis

BIBLIOGRAPHY

By the Author

POETRY:
Howl, and Other Poems, 1956, 1996
Empty Mirror: Early Poems, 1961
Kaddish, and Other Poems, 1958-1960, 1961

The Change, 1963
Reality Sandwiches, 1963
Kral Majales, 1965
Wichita Vortex Sutra, 1966
T.V. Baby Poems, 1967
Airplane Dreams: Compositions from Journals, 1968
Ankor Wat, 1968
Planet News, 1961-1967, 1968
The Moments Return, 1970
Ginsberg's Improvised Poetics, 1971
Bixby Canyon Ocean Path Word Breeze, 1972
The Fall of America: Poems of These States, 1965-1971, 1972
Iron Horse, 1972
The Gates of Wrath: Rhymed Poems, 1948-1952, 1972
Open Head, 1972
First Blues: Rags, Ballads, and Harmonium Songs, 1971-1974, 1975
Sad Dust Glories: Poems During Work Summer in Woods, 1975
Mind Breaths: Poems, 1972-1977, 1977
Mostly Sitting Haiku, 1978
Poems All over the Place: Mostly Seventies, 1978
Plutonian Ode: Poems, 1977-1980, 1982
Collected Poems, 1947-1980, 1984
White Shroud: Poems, 1980-1985, 1986
Hydrogen Jukebox, 1990 (music by Philip Glass)
Collected Poems, 1992
Cosmopolitan Greetings: Poems, 1986-1992, 1994
Making It Up: Poetry Composed at St. Marks Church on May 9, 1979, 1994 (with Kenneth Koch)
Selected Poems, 1947-1995, 1996
Death and Fame: Poems, 1993-1997, 1999

NONFICTION:
The Yage Letters, 1963 (with William Burroughs)
Indian Journals, 1963
Indian Journals, March 1962-May 1963: Notebooks, Diary, Blank Pages, Writings, 1970
Gay Sunshine Interview, 1974
Allen Verbatim: Lectures on Poetry, Politics, Consciousness, 1974
Visions of the Great Rememberer, 1974
To Eberhart from Ginsberg, 1976
As Ever: The Collected Correspondence of Allen Ginsberg and Neal Cassady, 1977
Journals: Early Fifties, Early Sixties, 1977, 1992
Composed on the Tongue: Literary Conversations, 1967-1977, 1980
Allen Ginsberg Photographs, 1990

DISCUSSION TOPICS

- When Allen Ginsberg asserted in "Howl" that he would be describing the "best minds of a generation," he was establishing a set of criteria for individual experience that challenged some familiar and generally accepted standards for personal behavior. What are some of the more prominent values that his work supports? What are some of the personal preferences that drew particularly virulent criticism from some cultural commentators?

- One of the most appealing aspects of Ginsberg's poetry is his comic capacity. He often regards himself as a figure of fun, even in serious statements. Locate and identify examples of his comic sense, and consider how they operate in the creation of an aesthetic sensibility.

- In "A Supermarket in California," Ginsberg depicts two poets dreaming of "the lost America of love." What are some of the most significant attributes of this "nation" that Ginsberg mentions and elucidates in his poetry?

- Ginsberg explained that "Wales Visitation" was a poem written to convey the essence of the psychedelic experience. How does Ginsberg use images to express the dimensions of his psychological mood? How does this correspond to the kind of visionary mental condition that he admires in poets such as William Blake?

- One of the most important factors in Ginsberg's development as a poet was his relationship with his parents. How does he describe and attempt to come to a resolution of tension with his mother's life in "Kaddish" and other poems?

- Among other terms, Ginsberg described his religious inclinations as a "Buddhist Jew." What are some of the religious precepts and principles which can be drawn from his poems?

Allen Ginsberg

Snapshot Poetics: A Photographic Memoir of the Beat Era, 1993
Journals Mid-Fifties, 1954-1958, 1995
Deliberate Prose: Selected Essays, 1952-1995, 2000
Family Business: Selected Letters Between a Father and Son, 2001 (with Louis Ginsberg)
Spontaneous Mind: Selected Interviews, 1958-1996, 2001

EDITED TEXT:
Poems for the Nation: A Collection of Contemporary Political Poems, 2000

MISCELLANEOUS:
Beat Legacy, Connections, Influences: Poems and Letters by Allen Ginsberg, 1994

About the Author

"Allen Ginsberg." In *The Beats: A Literary Reference,* edited by Matt Theado. New York: Carroll & Graf, 2004.

Hyde, Lewis, ed. *On the Poetry of Allen Ginsberg.* Ann Arbor: University of Michigan Press, 1984.

Kashner, Sam. *When I Was Cool: My Life at the Jack Kerouac School.* New York: HarperCollins, 2004.

McDarrah, Fred W. *A Beat Generation Album.* New York: Thunder's Mouth, 2003.

Miles, Barry. *The Beat Hotel: Ginsberg, Burroughs, Corso, Paris: 1958-1963.* New York: Grove Press, 2001.

_____. *Ginsberg: A Biography.* New York: Simon & Schuster, 1989.

Molesworth, Charles. "Republican Objects and Utopian Moments: The Poetry of Robert Lowell and Allen Ginsberg." In *The Fierce Embrace.* Columbia: University of Missouri Press, 1979.

Morgan, Bill, ed. *The Works of Allen Ginsberg, 1941-1994: A Descriptive Bibliography.* Westport, Conn.: Greenwood Press, 1995,

Morgan, Bill, and Bob Rosenthal, eds. *Best Minds: A Tribute to Allen Ginsberg.* New York: Lospecchio, 1986.

Mottram, Eric. *Allen Ginsberg in the Sixties.* London: Unicorn Press, 1972.

Portuges, Paul. *The Visionary Poetics of Allen Ginsberg.* Santa Barbara, Calif.: Ross-Erikson, 1978.

Raskin, Jonah. *American Scream: Allen Ginsberg's "Howl" and the Making of the Beat Generation.* Berkeley: University of California Press, 2004.

Schumacher, Michael. *Dharma Lion: A Critical Biography of Allen Ginsberg.* New York: St. Martin's Press, 1992.

NIKKI GIOVANNI

Born: Knoxville, Tennessee
June 7, 1943

Giovanni is best known as one of the most enduring of the 1960's black revolutionary poets, but she has continued to grow in importance and esteem during subsequent years.

© Jill Krementz

BIOGRAPHY

Nikki Giovanni was born Yolande Cornelia Giovanni, Jr., in Knoxville, Tennessee, on June 7, 1943, the younger of two daughters of Gus and Yolande Giovanni. As a child, Giovanni moved with her parents to the black middle-class suburbs of Cincinnati, Ohio, where her mother worked as a supervisor for the Welfare Department and her father worked as a social worker. Some of her most memorable times, however, were the summers she spent back in Knoxville with her maternal grandparents, John Brown and Louvenia Terrell Watson. Many of these experiences figure importantly in some of Giovanni's poems, most notably "Knoxville, Tennessee" (1969).

As a young girl, Giovanni began to display certain traits that would characterize her and her poetry after she became an adult—brashness, assertiveness, and outspokenness among them. These traits can perhaps be seen most clearly in Giovanni's fierce determination to protect her older sister, Gary, whom she idolized. Furthermore, these traits may have been inherited from, or at least encouraged by, her grandmother, Louvenia Watson, herself assertive and outspoken, as one learns in Giovanni's autobiographical statement, *Gemini: An Extended Autobiographical Statement on My First Twenty-five Years of Being a Black Poet* (1971). As Giovanni grew older, these traits merged into the one which brought her to the attention of both the literary world and the political establishment during the 1960's: militance.

Upon graduating from high school in 1960, Giovanni entered Fisk University, a historically black college located in Nashville, Tennessee, but was dismissed from the school in February, 1961, because her attitude was not consistent with that expected of Fisk women. She returned to Fisk in 1964, where she excelled as a scholar, became active in student literary circles, and became involved in campus politics, soon establishing at Fisk a chapter of the SNCC (Student Nonviolent Coordinating Committee), a prominent organization in the Civil Rights movement. This was the first display of the revolutionary spirit for which she would become well known in the following years.

Also at Fisk, Giovanni became editor of *Élan*, the campus literary publication, and participated in the Fisk Writers' Workshop. This workshop for younger writers was directed by John Oliver Killens, an important African American novelist and critic. Through such activities, Giovanni began to develop her feelings and talents as a poet of intense sensitivity. Further, her interest in the various struggles of black people for social, political, cultural, and economic liberation became much more pronounced.

Giovanni graduated from Fisk magna cum laude with a bachelor's degree in history during the winter commencement exercises held in early February, 1967. Following graduation she returned to Cincinnati but within a few weeks received the news of her beloved grandmother's death in Knoxville. This event profoundly affected Giovanni, immediately making her ill and also triggering a more far-reaching and longer-lasting anger that would characterize the majority of her early poetry.

From her grandmother's death, Giovanni became more aware of the plight of powerless people in the United States. Her grandmother had been forced to move from her home at 400 Mulvaney Street when an urban renewal project relocated her neighborhood to make way for new commercial development. Although the new house had more amenities—a bigger back yard, the reader is told in *Gemini*—Louvenia Watson was never happy because the house was not "home." She had simply had to leave behind too many memories, and she withered and died as a result of this displacement.

During the late spring and early summer of 1967, Giovanni became involved in organizing Cincinnati's black community and established the first Black Arts Festival in that city. Through this activity her black awareness became more keenly pronounced, and though she would have preferred to continue her activities in the black community, Giovanni's mother, supported by her father, delivered the ultimatum that she either go to work or go to graduate school. Neither option was attractive to Giovanni at the time, but she entered the School of Social Work at the University of Pennsylvania. Later she attended Columbia University in New York and began teaching at Queens College, also in New York. During this period, Giovanni received several grants, notably from the Ford Foundation and the National Foundation for the Arts.

In 1968, Giovanni published *Black Feeling, Black Talk*, her first book of poems. This was followed by *Black Judgement* (1968), which was combined with its predecessor into a single volume, *Black Feeling, Black Talk, Black Judgement* in 1970. These poems are mostly characterized by Giovanni's black revolutionary ideas and spirit, and they quickly established her as one of the most able spokespersons of the Black Arts cultural movement. Another event that underscored Giovanni's new independence and her revolutionary stance was her decision to have a child, though yet unmarried, an unpopular choice even during the turbulent 1960's. Her son, Tommy, was born in Cincinnati on August 31, 1969, while Giovanni was visiting her parents during Labor Day vacation. Tommy soon became the center for most of the poet's artistic and spiritual concerns.

In 1970, Giovanni published her third book of poems, *Re: Creation*, which continued in the revolutionary vein, and followed in a rather rapid succession the combined volume of her first two works, her autobiographical statement, *Gemini*, and a book of poems for children, *Spin a Soft Black Song: Poems for Children*, both issued in 1971 and both dedicated to her son.

Giovanni's national reputation and popularity were further established in 1971 when the record album *Truth Is on the Way* was released; it featured Giovanni reading her poems to the background of black gospel music, itself an up-and-coming art form, sung by the New York Community Choir under the direction of Benny Diggs. The album was a monumental success, and Giovanni began to be in great demand throughout the country, especially on college campuses. In addition, she was recognized in many national magazines, including *Ebony*, *Jet*, and *Mademoiselle*, and was awarded numerous distinctions, including the key to the city of Gary, Indiana. In April, 1972, an honorary doctorate degree was conferred upon her by Wilberforce University in Ohio, the nation's oldest historically black college.

Also in 1972, the immensely popular book of poems *My House: Poems* appeared, and its enthusiastic reception further enhanced the poet's reputation. In 1973, Giovanni issued a new collection of poems for children, many previously published, under the title *Ego-Tripping, and Other Poems for Young People*. This book increased Giovanni's popularity among younger readers and gained for her continued respect among other readers as well.

During 1973 and 1974, the transcriptions of two important exchanges between Giovanni and older established black writers were published. The first, a conversation with James Baldwin, the novelist and essayist, had actually taken place late in 1971. It was published in 1973 as *A Dialogue: James Baldwin and Nikki Giovanni* and was a spirited exchange of ideas between the two writers on a number of topics of interest to black people, including black male/female relationships, black literature and the black liberation movement, and religion and the black community.

The second exchange was with the poet and novelist Margaret Walker, published in 1974 as *A Poetic Equation: Conversations Between Nikki Giovanni and Margaret Walker*, and it contained much more intense and heated discussions on the present and future states of black people in the United States and the role of black literature in the black liberation movement, among other topics. Giovanni emerged from these discussions as the clear spokesperson for new trends in black literature; she gained, in addition, much admiration and respect from an older generation of writers.

Giovanni continued publishing her steady stream of poetry collections into the twenty-first century, which saw the publication of *The Collected Poetry of Nikki Giovanni, 1968-1998* (2003). She also published books of essays and other prose as well as several more collections of poetry for children, including *Just for You! The Girls in the Circle* (2004).

Giovanni is a perennial favorite on the college lecture circuit and delights in sharing her thoughts and insights with others, especially the young. In addition, she is in great demand as a teacher, having taught at a number of colleges and universities, including Rutgers University and Virginia Polytechnic Institute.

Her awards include numerous honorary doctorates as well as the Jeanine Rae Award for the Advancement of Women's Culture (1995); the Langston Hughes Award (1996); the National Association for the Advancement of Colored People Image Award (1998 and 2003); the Tennessee Governor's Award (1998); the Virginia Governor's Award for the Arts (2000); and the first Rosa Parks Woman of Courage Award (2002). A University Distinguished Professor at Virginia Tech since 1999, she continues to write, speak, and publish regularly and is one of the most popular poets of her generation.

ANALYSIS

Giovanni's poetry is largely the chronicle of the development of a black poet, and each volume reflects her concerns and sensibilities at various phases of her development. The poems are always written in free verse and employ plain, simple, direct language with a strong rhythmic sense and an often playful, yet meaningful, manipulation of words. All of these are characteristics of the revolutionary black poetry of the 1960's and 1970's that sought to speak directly to the black community to motivate black people to become liberated.

Giovanni's first two books of poems, *Black Feeling, Black Talk* and *Black Judgement*, both published in 1968 (and combined into a single volume in 1970), contain poems that speak primarily from a revolutionary stance. The poems, like their author,

are young, angry, and assertive, and their very titles are often suggestive of their subject matter. "Black Separatism," "Black Power," "Of Liberation," "Revolutionary Music," and "Beautiful Black Man" are examples of some of the more revolutionary poems of Giovanni's early period. The two poems that show her at her most bitter point are "Poem (No Name No. 2)" and "The True Import of Present Dialogue, Black vs. Negro." These poems point to Giovanni's rejection of safe, comfortable middle-class values in favor of the revolutionary values associated with black liberation. These and other poems written in a similar vein brought Giovanni to the forefront of the Black Arts cultural revolution of the 1960's, and she became one of its most ardent and celebrated spokespersons.

While Giovanni's early poems tend to fall into the revolutionary category, from the beginning she has also been concerned with family, love, childhood, experiences, and friendship. Poems such as "Nikki-Rosa" and "Knoxville, Tennessee" speak of the importance of family but also insist on the importance of self-definition, another concern that is found often in Giovanni's work. This self-definition, or concern for the individual, having been announced in the early collections and developed more fully in *Gemini*, is at the center of the 1972 collection *My House* and figures importantly in each subsequent work—most notably in *Cotton Candy on a Rainy Day* (1978) and *Those Who Ride the Night Winds* (1983).

In her prose works, particularly the autobiographical statement *Gemini* and a later volume of miscellaneous essays titled *Sacred Cows... and Other Edibles* (1988), Giovanni employs the characteristic crisp, direct, simple language and the often playful style and conversational tone that are found in her poems. In fact, her poems are often so prosaic and her prose so poetic that if one were to hear instead of read Giovanni's work, one would hardly be able to tell the difference in genre.

Whatever mode of expression Giovanni elects to use, the thing that is the most obvious is the artist's sincerity. Giovanni not only believes in her ideas, but she also is fiercely committed to her craft; moreover, she wants her readers to believe and be committed as well. Thus, reading Giovanni is often like reading a big sister or a best friend—one trusts her judgment, shares her vision, and appreciates her wisdom and concern.

"The True Import of Present Dialogue, Black vs. Negro"

First published: 1968 (collected in *Black Feeling, Black Talk, Black Judgement*, 1970)
Type of work: Poem

The speaker in the poem challenges black people to reject complacency for revolution.

"Nikki-Rosa"

First published: 1968 (collected in *The Collected Poetry of Nikki Giovanni, 1968-1998*, 2003)
Type of work: Poem

The poet reflects on what it means to grow up black.

"The True Import of Present Dialogue, Black vs. Negro" challenges black people to reject their middle-class complacency and adopt an angry revolutionary spirit in the quest for liberation of the black community. The title establishes the polarization of opposing attitudes among black people during the Civil Rights movement of the 1960's—on one hand, "Black," or those of a more revolutionary bent and, on the other hand, "Negro," or those with a more bourgeois mentality. Here Giovanni insists that the revolutionary approach is the only one that will guarantee a meaningful future for black youth, who will be the beneficiaries of their efforts to liberate the black community from domination and possibly annihilation.

How does one adopt a revolutionary stance? By becoming angry enough to kill, according to Giovanni, but while the possibility exists for literally killing someone, what she really means is killing in the sense of rejecting values, habits, and actions that have kept black people enslaved. These include certain religious practices, economic habits, and behavioral characteristics that black people must "kill" if they are to be free from continued oppression by the white majority.

The poem is effective in its badgering repetition of "Can You Kill"; similarly, the harsh, often revolting language underscores the urgency of the poet's message, which she states succinctly in the last two lines: "Learn to kill niggers/ Learn to be Black men."

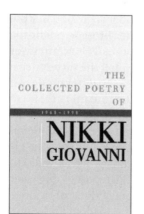

THE COLLECTED POETRY OF NIKKI GIOVANNI

"Nikki-Rosa," like many of Giovanni's poems, is full of the poet's personal experiences. This poem talks about growing up black and the pleasures and pains inherent in the process. The poem was perhaps prompted by the tendency of white biographers of black people to point out only what seems to be wrong in black families and in black communities. The tone is reflective and critical but not bitter, although Giovanni very matter-of-factly observes that

> I really hope no white person ever has cause
> to write about me
> because they never understand.

Giovanni flatly rejects white interpretations of black life because they come from different frames of reference with different values and simply are incapable of truly assessing what it is to grow up as a black child in a black family in a black community. Giovanni concludes:

> Black love is Black wealth and they'll
> probably talk about my hard childhood
> and never understand that
> all the while I was quite happy.

Here Giovanni establishes her reverence for black folk culture. Furthermore, in addressing a number of realities for poor people, ranging from alcoholism and domestic violence to having no indoor toilets to bathing in galvanized tubs, Giovanni asserts that "it isn't poverty that concerns you/ . . . but only that everybody is together." The theme of the communal nature of black communities as something to be celebrated and preserved resounds in much of Giovanni's work.

"MY HOUSE"

First published: 1972 (collected in *My House*, 1972)
Type of work: Poem

The poet stresses individuality and self-expression.

"My House" is the title poem of Giovanni's 1972 book of poems and concludes the collection with a forthright statement of the poet's freedom to live by her own rules. Furthermore, she is willing and capable of accepting the responsibilities for her choices, as is clear when Giovanni asserts that "i run the kitchen/ and i can stand the heat."

On the surface, "My House" seems to be hodgepodge, a haphazard collection of comments on everything from love to individuality to the inadequacy of the English language to express emotions. A more careful reading, however, uncovers a more conscious blend of seeming incongruent parts, akin to the quilting motif used in the poem, into a bold statement of independence. This concern for individual worth and self-expression that characterizes the poems in *My House* becomes even more pronounced in subsequent works, For example, in "My House," Giovanni adopts a stance shared by many later feminists, that of challenging the idea of the male as name-giver. This challenge is evident when the speaker asserts:

> i mean it's my house
> and i want to fry pork chops
> and bake sweet potatoes
> and call them yams.

Precisely put, since this is her house, she will accept no compromise; thus, she asserts the validity of a female name-giver, and, by extension, the validity of an Afrocentric perspective in American culture (varieties of what are commonly called "sweet potatoes" in American culture are known as "yams" in African cultures). Here again, Giovanni offers a revolutionary interpretation of black life in the United States. She underscores this interpretation emphatically as she vows to

> smile at old men and call
> it revolution cause what's real
> is really real.

"My House" is one of Giovanni's most popular poems and shows her at once at her most playful and most serious self.

"I WROTE A GOOD OMELET"

First published: 1983 (collected in *Those Who Ride the Night Winds*, 1983)
Type of work: Poem

The speaker is delightfully confused after a wonderful experience with love.

"I Wrote a Good Omelet" also shows Giovanni at her playful best. The speaker has had a spectacularly jolting encounter with love and has everything confused. She tells the reader, "I goed on red . . . and stopped on green . . . after loving you." In short, things were never the same but were filled with ecstasy, passion, and delight.

Stylistically, "I Wrote a Good Omelet" is representative of the entire collection *Those Who Ride the Night Winds*. In this book, the poems are longer, more prosaic, and frequently punctuated with ellipses. Furthermore, they mark a continued growth in the poet, at once becoming more introspective and showing an even more pronounced spirit of the individual than previous poems.

GEMINI

First published: 1971
Type of work: Autobiography

Giovanni presents memories and observations of the first twenty-five years of her life.

Gemini, so titled because of the sign of the zodiac under which Giovanni was born, is subtitled *An Extended Autobiographical Statement on My First Twenty-five Years of Being a Black Poet*. As such, *Gemini* is not a strictly chronological autobiography in the usual sense; rather, it is a collection of carefully selected and arranged recollections and observations that helped her develop into the black revolutionary poet that she was at the time of its writing. Published when Giovanni was twenty-eight, most of the pieces had indeed been written several years earlier, when she reflected on having turned twenty-five.

The book is divided into thirteen sections and covers everything from a history of her grandparents, John Brown and Louvenia Watson, to an appreciation of actress, singer, and black icon Lena Horne to an appraisal of the early black novelist and short-story writer Charles Waddell Chesnutt to a review of a book on black music by black writer Phyll Garland that Giovanni finds severely limited. Through these comments, and especially in the last section, "Gemini—A Prolonged Autobiographical Statement on Why," Giovanni grapples with various aspects of her thoughts and feelings in an attempt to explain and justify her stance as a revolutionary. She is never apologetic; rather, she speaks her mind very matter-of-factly in the characteristic Giovanni manner.

One important revelation in *Gemini* is her commitment to preserving family history. This is established in the first section of the book, "400 Mulvaney Street," a short account of her maternal grandparents with a special emphasis on the grandmother, Louvenia Terrell Watson, herself something of a revolutionary, who influenced Giovanni tremendously. Giovanni intimates later in *Gemini* that her grandparents migrated to Knoxville, Tennessee, from Georgia to escape the consequences of her grandmother's outspokenness, but as she reflects on how Mrs. Watson lived and died, Giovanni resolves that "Tommy, my son, must know about this. He must know we come from somewhere. That we belong."

Another section of *Gemini* that is especially important is "Don't Have a Baby till You Read This," about Giovanni's decision to have a child without being married and the accompanying responsibilities and adjustments. Family had always been important to Giovanni, and while she concluded that marriage was an unattractive prospect, she did want to experience motherhood—thus the decision to have a child, born Thomas Watson Giovanni in 1969. The numerous adjustments the entire family must make are often comic, but more important, Tommy becomes the absolute central focus of Giovanni's life and occupies an important station in the larger family as well. Giovanni's devotion to her son is admirable.

Gemini alternates between superficial observation and whimsical comment on one hand to deep philosophical analysis on the other. Like her poems, though, *Gemini* contains the same unquestionable sincerity, the same clarity of vision, and the same precision of statement. Most important, *Gemini* goes a long way toward explaining the revolutionary psyche and simplifying many of the artistic complexities of a fine poet.

SUMMARY

Giovanni has been aptly called a child of the 1960's and a woman of the 1970's; however, the most frequent title bestowed upon her is the Princess of Black Poetry. From articulating concerns of the black liberation movement to championing the individual, Giovanni has emerged as a keen interpreter of modern times.

Warren J. Carson

BIBLIOGRAPHY

By the Author

POETRY:
Black Feeling, Black Talk, 1968
Black Judgement, 1968
Black Feeling, Black Talk, Black Judgement, 1970
Re: Creation, 1970
Poem of Angela Yvonne Davis, 1970
Spin a Soft Black Song: Poems for Children, 1971, revised 1987 (juvenile)
My House, 1972

Ego-Tripping, and Other Poems for Young Readers, 1973 (juvenile)

The Women and the Men, 1975

Cotton Candy on a Rainy Day, 1978

Vacation Time, 1980 (juvenile)

Those Who Ride the Night Winds, 1983 (juvenile)

Knoxville, Tennessee, 1994 (juvenile)

Life: Through Black Eyes, 1995

The Genie in the Jar, 1996 (juvenile)

The Selected Poems of Nikki Giovanni, 1996

The Sun Is So Quiet, 1996 (juvenile)

Love Poems, 1997

Blues: For All the Changes, 1999

Quilting the Black-Eyed Pea: Poems and Not Quite Poems, 2002

The Collected Poetry of Nikki Giovanni, 1968-1998, 2003

Just for You! The Girls in the Circle, 2004 (juvenile)

NONFICTION:

Gemini: An Extended Autobiographical Statement on My First Twenty-five Years of Being a Black Poet, 1971

A Dialogue: James Baldwin and Nikki Giovanni, 1973

A Poetic Equation: Conversations Between Nikki Giovanni and Margaret Walker, 1974

Sacred Cows . . . and Other Edibles, 1988

Conversations with Nikki Giovanni, 1992 (Virginia C. Fowler, editor)

Racism 101, 1994

The Prosaic Soul of Nikki Giovanni, 2003 (includes *Gemini, Sacred Cows,* and *Racism 101*)

EDITED TEXTS:

Night Comes Softly: Anthology of Black Female Voices, 1970

Appalachian Elders: A Warm Hearth Sampler, 1991 (with Cathee Dennison)

Grand Mothers: Poems, Reminiscences, and Short Stories About the Keepers of Our Traditions, 1994

Shimmy Shimmy Shimmy Like My Sister Kate: Looking at the Harlem Renaissance Through Poems, 1996

Grand Fathers: Reminiscences, Poems, Recipes, and Photos of the Keepers of Our Traditions, 1999

DISCUSSION TOPICS

• Contrast the depiction of the setting in Nikki Giovanni's poem "Knoxville, Tennessee" with that of the same city in James Agee's *A Death in the Family* (1957).

• By what strategies does Giovanni unify "My House"?

• "Negro" is a Latinate word denoting "black." What is the basis of Giovanni's objection to "Negro"?

• Giovanni is known for a particularly free-verse form and informal, conversational diction. What is specifically poetic about her work?

• Cite several lines or phrases in Giovanni's poetry that seem to be calculated to shock the reader into thoughtfulness.

• Given her preoccupation with African American life and issues, what aspects of Giovanni's writing entitle her to the wider distinction of being judged "a keen interpreter of modern times"?

About the Author

Beason, Tyrone. "Survival of the Baddest: Poet and Activist Nikki Giovanni Keeps Her '60s Spirit Intact for a New Generation." *The Seattle Times,* January 15, 2004, p. C1.

Davis, Arthur P. "The New Poetry of Black Hate." In *Modern Black Poets: A Collection of Critical Essays,* edited by Donald B. Gibson. Englewood Cliffs, N.J.: Prentice-Hall, 1973.

Fowler, Virginia C. *Nikki Giovanni.* New York: Twayne, 1992.

Jago, Carol. *Nikki Giovanni in the Classroom: "The Same Ol Danger but a Brand New Pleasure."* Urbana, Ill.: National Council of Teachers of English, 1999.

Josephson, Judith P. *Nikki Giovanni: Poet of the People.* Berkeley Heights, N.J.: Enslow, 2003.

"Nikki Giovanni." In *Her Words: Diverse Voices in Contemporary Appalachian Women's Poetry,* edited by Felicia Mitchel. Knoxville: University of Tennessee Press, 2002.

Washington, Elsie B. "Nikki Giovanni: Wisdom for All Ages." *Essence* 24 (March, 1994): 67.

ELLEN GLASGOW

Born: Richmond, Virginia
April 22, 1873
Died: Richmond, Virginia
November 21, 1945

With her ironic juxtaposition of moral idealism and unflinching realism, Glasgow is considered the founder of the modern southern literary tradition.

Library of Congress

BIOGRAPHY

Ellen Glasgow was born in Richmond, Virginia, on April 22, 1873, to Anne Jane Glasgow and Francis Thomas Glasgow, manager of Tredegar Iron Works. Ellen was the eighth of ten children. During her childhood, she was particularly sensitive to the nervousness and depression from which her gentle, aristocratic mother suffered, undoubtedly the result of Anne Glasgow's almost incessant childbearing. This experience was to motivate Ellen's later work for women's rights and was clearly reflected in her fiction.

Ironically, in temperament, Glasgow was more like her father than her mother. Even though she rejected her Calvinistic faith, she retained a strong ethical sense, which is evident throughout her works. Furthermore, her own fierce independence of thought and rebelliousness of spirit were the very qualities which had motivated her Presbyterian ancestors in their defiance of monarchs.

In lieu of formal instruction, Glasgow was educated by relatives and, perhaps even more important, was allowed to choose books at will from her father's extensive library. When she was still a child, she began to write. Although later she accused her family of lacking sympathy for her ambitions, Glasgow was probably exaggerating their unkindness. Always delicate, always aware of her mother's unhappiness, Glasgow seemed destined to develop a sense of alienation. Even while she was flirting and dancing at the innumerable balls to which a young lady of a good Richmond family would be invited, she was becoming more and more convinced that her real interests were creative and intellectual.

Guided by George Walter McCormack, the husband of her sister Cary Glasgow McCormack, Ellen read the works of philosophers, economists, playwrights, and novelists. She also continued to write. When she was eighteen, she took a novel that she had written to a New York agent, but when he made advances to her, she was so angry that she destroyed the manuscript. When Glasgow was twenty, she was so shattered by her mother's sudden death from typhoid fever that she destroyed the manuscript of another novel. Fortunately, after two years had passed, she reconsidered and reconstructed the work. This novel, her first full-length work to be published, *The Descendant*, appeared anonymously in 1897.

With its illegitimate, politically radical hero and its independent, art-student heroine, both southerners in New York, *The Descendant* was a marked departure from the sentimental, nostalgic novels which had come to be expected from southern writers. The book was well received and sold well. It was followed in 1898 by *Phases of an Inferior Planet*, which took another young southern woman, in this case a singer, to New York and explored her doomed relationship with another intelligent, alienated hero. Partly because of inherent flaws, partly because of her publisher's failure to advertise it, *Phases of an Inferior Planet* was unsuccessful.

For the setting of her third book, Glasgow wisely turned back to her native Virginia. *The Voice of the People* (1900) is significant because it is the first of a series of novels that analyze Virginia society rather than simply voicing Glasgow's anger with the social and religious expectations which threatened her freedom. In later works, Glasgow viewed her society from various angles. In *The Battle-Ground* (1902), she turned back to the Civil War period for her story, and in *The Deliverance* (1904), she wrote about the Reconstruction era. In neither book was there any regret for the loss of what she saw as a social structure based on repression and one that had condemned its women to frustration and despair.

Despite problems with her hearing, which were to culminate in total deafness by the time she was forty, Glasgow later called the period between 1899 and 1905 the happiest of her life. Her works were best sellers, as well as critical successes. She was being compared with such literary giants as American writers Hamlin Garland, Stephen Crane, and Theodore Dreiser. Furthermore, she was involved in the great love affair of her life. Although her lover was married, Glasgow and he met for romantic intervals, such as the summertime rendezvous in the Swiss Alps which she described so rhapsodically in her autobiography.

When the relationship ended in 1905, she was shattered. The books that followed, *The Wheel of Life* (1906), *The Ancient Law* (1908), and *The Romance of a Plain Man* (1909), lack the energy of Glasgow's later works. Her three-year engagement to the Episcopal minister Frank Ilsley Paradise, which was broken in 1909, did not assuage her grief over the loss of her illicit lover.

There were other losses for Glasgow during this period. In 1909, her brother Frank committed suicide. Within a year, her beloved sister Cary developed cancer; her death was slow and agonizing. After Cary died, Glasgow fled from Richmond to New York, where she lived for five years. The novels published during that period, *The Miller of Old Church* (1911) and *Virginia* (1913), indicate that she had regained her former creative energy.

After her father's death in 1916, Glasgow moved back to the family home in Richmond, where she spent the rest of her life. On the surface, her situation seemed ideal. With the money she had inherited, she could live well and travel whenever she liked; she was not dependent on the success of her literary works. She was entrenched in Richmond society, and, perhaps more important to her, she had made numerous friends in the literary world.

In 1918, however, Glasgow attempted to commit suicide. She was evidently distraught by the involvement of her fiancé, the prominent Richmond lawyer Henry Watkins Anderson, with Queen Marie of Romania. This episode, along with Glasgow's general depression about World War I and its aftermath, resulted in a period of unimpressive literary output.

With *Barren Ground* (1925), it was evident that Glasgow had recovered. During the decade that followed, most of her best novels were published: *The Romantic Comedians* (1926), *They Stooped to Folly* (1929), *The Sheltered Life* (1932), and *Vein of Iron* (1935). During this period, she won many honors. Perhaps her most significant achievement, other than her novels, was her leadership in the first Southern Writers Conference, held in 1931 at the University of Virginia, over which she presided.

At the end of the decade, Glasgow's health declined, and once again her works reflected the diminution of creative energy. Even though it won a Pulitzer Prize, *In This Our Life* (1941) is less impressive than Glasgow's earlier works. On November 21, 1945, Glasgow died. She left in manuscript an autobiography, later published as *The Woman Within* (1954), which, though it appears to have many factual errors, provides important insights into the psychological makeup of an important southern realist.

ANALYSIS

Throughout her life, Glasgow considered herself to be a searcher for truth, and it was this quest that motivated her writing. As she frequently pointed out, her novels began with ideas. Over a long gestation period, those ideas became embodied in character and scene and finally coalesced into a plot. Then the actual writing process would begin, and during that process, the world Glasgow was creating became more real to her than the actual world in which she lived. When each book was finished, she felt a sense of deprivation, almost a death; the only remedy was to begin another novel.

This summary of her creative process makes it clear that to Glasgow, fiction was indeed an imitation of reality; however, she was not interested in presenting a mere slice of life. Her works always had an intellectual basis. That fact accounts for the artistic failure of early works such as *Phases of an Inferior Planet*, in which characters do not achieve a real existence but merely illustrate ideas.

For example, the heroine of *Phases of an Inferior Planet*, Mariana Musin, is the daughter of a Presbyterian father and a Catholic mother, whose religious differences eventually destroy their love for each other. After she goes to New York to become an opera singer, Mariana meets, marries, and parts from a teacher, Anthony Algarcife, who later goes into the priesthood and becomes the most famous preacher in New York. Algarcife is noted for his brilliant essays in rebuttal to a series of antireligious articles, which he himself is actually writing. Despite the novel's portrayal of romantic love, grinding poverty, the death of a baby, and final reunion, the characters never become real enough to inspire sympathy; they are pasteboard symbols of alienation, illustrating the evils of institutional religion.

By the time she wrote her third novel, *The Voice of the People*, Glasgow had learned to let her characters come alive and to suggest her ideas through those characters. From her own life, Glasgow could draw on very real conflicts, but she no longer protested shrilly; she was able to examine the ironies which were so evident in her culture. One of Glasgow's major themes is her view of southern history as a conflict between two traditions, that of the pleasure-loving cavalier and that of the rigidly righteous but strong Calvinist.

In *The Voice of the People* and in *The Deliverance*, she shows how people of her mother's aristocratic stock live upon lies, embracing an illusory past. In *Vein of Iron*, on the other hand, the heroine discovers that neither the past, nor even love, can get one through life—only strength of character can. In the South, Glasgow stresses, that strength came not from the cavaliers, who are far more appealing, but from the rigid and dour Scots-Irish Calvinists.

Another theme that pervades Glasgow's work is the conflict between the Old South and the New South. In her Civil War novel, *The Battle-Ground*, Glasgow described the dying society, as well as the war which doomed it, realistically, not sentimentally. At the end of the book, the survivors seem to be relieved that they no longer are burdened by the past. The same conflict is treated comically in *The Romantic Comedians*, which follows the protagonist,

a gentleman of the old school, from shock to shock as he moves forward in time into a world that he does not understand.

A third major theme of Glasgow's work involves the conflict between the expectations for women, as the objects of male chivalry, and their need for independence. In her first two novels, women rebel by leaving the South for New York, where they pursue careers and live bohemian lives. In later books, however, women fight their battles on the South, on home territory. In *The Battle-Ground*, Betty Ambler has learned her own worth through hardship. When the man she loves returns from war, it is clear that he will never be able to imprison her again by referring to the code of chivalry.

Although Glasgow's themes change little from work to work, her tone varies greatly from novel to novel. It is amazing, for example, that a work as grim as *Barren Ground* should have been followed by two comedies of manners, *The Romantic Comedians* and *They Stooped to Folly*, and then by a work that is only somewhat more serious, *The Sheltered Life*, which was followed by the near-tragedy of *Vein of Iron*. Immediately before she wrote *Barren Ground*, the founder of southern realism had even participated in the writing of a romance, but as her collaborator was Henry Anderson, her fiancé, that lapse may be understandable.

Throughout all of her work, whatever the tone, Glasgow is a careful plotter and scene builder, as well as an expert in revealing character through the spoken and the unspoken word. Her skill is illustrated in the initial scene of *The Romantic Comedians*, which takes place at a grave on Easter Sunday. At the beginning of the scene, the widower, Judge Gamaliel Bland Honeywell, is moaning a sentimental formula for his grief, while vainly attempting to remember his wife's face. At the end of the scene, he leaves the cemetery, almost simultaneously musing about his dislike of old women and contemplating the virtues of the old social system, which women of his generation support. It is spring.

At the end of the book, after the judge has very nearly died as a result of his disastrous marriage to a young girl, Glasgow repeats the elements of that first scene—the judge's conservatism, his antipathy to old women of his own age, his consciousness of spring, and finally, his response to a young woman. Even though Glasgow stressed the intellectual content of her works, this level of writing illustrates the fact that she had worked hard to become a superb craftswoman. From her third novel on, her readers expected artistry from Glasgow as well as challenging ideas.

BARREN GROUND

First published: 1925
Type of work: Novel

For thirty years, Dorinda Oakley vainly seeks happiness through human love but finally discovers contentment in her relationship with the land.

Barren Ground, Glasgow's favorite among her novels and the most autobiographical of them, is the story of Dorinda Oakley, a woman who spends her life in the pursuit of happiness, only to discover that happiness comes through the rejection of human relationships. The book was written after Glasgow's suicide attempt; it is significant that she sent her unfaithful fiancé a copy of the book, which concludes with Dorinda's statement that she is happy to be finished with love.

Barren Ground is set in the Shenandoah Valley of Virginia, where there are few aristocrats, and the chief distinction among men is their stewardship of their farms. James Ellgood, for example, is a fine stock farmer, and his family prospers accordingly. On the other hand, a doctor in the neighborhood has let his large farm go to ruin because he spends his time drinking instead of taking care of it. The case of Dorinda's father is somewhat different: Although he is a hard worker, he is a poor white, raised in poverty and ignorance, fearful of change, and therefore unable and unwilling to improve his land. His children seem doomed to live as he lived—in misery and frustration. Seeing him as he is, Dorinda's mother hates the man she married for love (marrying below herself), and she hopes that she can persuade Dorinda not to make the same mistake.

Unfortunately, Dorinda is aware that she will never again be so young and pretty as she is at twenty, and despite her mother's warnings, she believes that she must use her power to win a hus-

band. The young man she chooses to charm is the doctor's son, who, beneath his sophisticated exterior, is actually as weak as his father. After proposing to Dorinda, he leaves town; when he returns, he has been persuaded to marry someone else. The betrayal devastates Dorinda. She turns against the God who was her mother's consolation, and she turns against men. From that time on, she is barren ground, incapable of response. Although in her preface, Glasgow praises Dorinda as a character who has learned to live without hope or joy—merely to endure life—the reader is likely to find Dorinda's denial of love and even of sex a tragic denial of life.

Ironically, after she has lost the capacity to love, Dorinda is courted by several men who, unlike her first love, are strong, unselfish, and responsible. The first of them is a young doctor, whom she meets in New York, where she has been living and working after her flight from home. He senses her frigidity, but he hopes eventually to win her love. It is clear that Dorinda must fight to deny her emotional self; when she attends a concert, she is intensely moved. If there is a chance for love, however, it is thwarted by fate. Dorinda is called home because her father has had a stroke and her mother needs her help.

Actually, Dorinda is not unwilling to return home. During her stay in New York, she has been reading books on agriculture, and she has an idea that the farm could be made profitable. More than that, Dorinda muses, she can dare to give her heart to the farm; because it is not human, it will not betray her.

After both of her parents have died, worn out from poverty and hard work, she agrees to marry the storekeeper Nathan Pedlar, an intelligent, resourceful man who has always been devoted to her. Dorinda has only one condition: that it will be a marriage in name only. Nathan and Dorinda are happy together; in a sense, Nathan does eventually win Dorinda, but he must die to do it. In a train wreck, he saves the lives of many passengers but sacrifices his own. Now a hero, now no physical threat, he is given what love Dorinda has to give. Her first love was an illusion; her last love is a mythical figure.

In an attempt at a happy ending, Glasgow gives Dorinda a peculiar revenge. When her former lover, the doctor's son, now ruined and destitute, is about to be sent to the poorhouse, Dorinda chooses to take him in and to see that he is cared for until his death. The fact that, although she is kind, her former lover must realize that she is completely indifferent to him gives her great pleasure.

In her conclusion, Glasgow has Dorinda realize that a woman can be happy without love as long as she has a spirit of adventure. Presumably that is the spirit that enabled Dorinda to try new ideas on the farm. It is clear to the reader, however, that in reality Dorinda's contentment derives simply from the knowledge of her own strength. This revelation, which comes to Dorinda at the age of fifty, is exactly the bleak conclusion that Glasgow herself had reached in her forties, when she began to write the novel.

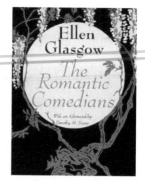

THE ROMANTIC COMEDIANS

First published: 1926
Type of work: Novel

A widower in his sixties spurns the woman who has spent her life waiting for him in order to marry a twenty-three-year-old, with disastrous results.

The Romantic Comedians was the first of Glasgow's comic novels—written, she said later, to amuse herself. The pleasure she had in writing it was shared by her readers; *The Romantic Comedians* was one of her best-selling novels.

Like *Barren Ground*, *The Romantic Comedians* deals with the conflict between men and women in a society that defines their roles and their relationships. While *Barren Ground* was tragic in tone, however, *The Romantic Comedians* is comic. The protagonist of *Barren Ground* was a woman who could find contentment in life only by denying her natural feelings. The central character in *The Romantic Comedians* is a man who, despite the disastrous results of his marriage to a young woman, at the end of the book is still pursuing happiness and the opposite sex.

Interestingly, although the tone of the earlier novel is tragic, Glasgow obviously considers the ending a happy one, while in the second novel, although the tone is comic, it is suggested at the end

of the book that the next young woman with whom the protagonist becomes involved will probably be the death of him.

In *The Romantic Comedians,* as in all Glasgow's other fiction, the conflict between the sexes is an integral part of the conflict between an old world, which is dying, and a new world, which is coming into being. Despite his pride in what he considers enlightened views, the protagonist of the novel, sixty-five-year-old Judge Gamaliel Bland Honeywell, lives by the standards of the Old South and is appalled at the moral decay that he perceives all around him.

In his world, women of good family adhered to rigid rules and were rewarded for good conduct with the respect and protection of the men in their class. As an example of proper conduct, the judge need look no further than the memory of his late wife, Cordelia Honeywell. After her death, Queenborough society expects the judge to marry another exemplary lady, Amanda Lightfoot, who had been his fiancé until a foolish quarrel severed the engagement; she has remained unmarried, cherishing her love for him and spending her time in good works during the thirty-six years of his marriage to Cordelia.

If Cordelia and Amanda represent the ideal of the Old South, the impoverished widow Bella Upchurch represents the reality. Unlike Amanda, who never had to worry about money, Bella does not intend to suffer for love; instead, she will use the weakness of men to get the money she desperately desires. She decides to play her highest card and expose the judge to the charms of her twenty-three-year-old daughter, Annabel Upchurch, who is inexperienced enough to think that there is no more to marriage than pretty clothes and compliments, and who is devoted enough to be generous to her mother, who will then not have to be burdened with another husband.

There is yet another major woman character in Glasgow's comedy—Edmonia Bredalbane, the judge's twin sister. While Bella and Annabel play the parts of the helpless southern ladies, Edmonia flaunts her freedom. As she comments to her brother, while he spent his life doing his duty and living up to the ideal of the Old South, she devoted hers to pleasure. Edmonia has caused scandal on two continents, used up four husbands, and acquired considerable wealth. Back in Queenborough (Glasgow's fictional name for Richmond), Edmonia is completely open about her past; it is clear that it is age, not morality, that has prevented her from continuing her hedonistic lifestyle.

The judge will not listen to the advice of Edmonia, who is fond of him and concerned about his vulnerability. As a realist, she understands that her brother is too old to change his way of thinking, to abandon the chivalric code by which he has lived. Therefore, Edmonia urges her brother to marry someone who will share his standards and make him comfortable in his declining years. The still-attractive Amanda is the obvious choice. When Edmonia sees the judge's infatuation with Annabel, she foresees disaster, and she begs him to break off the relationship; however, the judge insists on marrying youth, in the person of Annabel.

The central portion of the book proves that Edmonia was right. At first, all is harmonious. Then Annabel becomes bored with mere possessions. There are quarrels about their lifestyle. The judge has limited energy, while Annabel's is limitless. When she gives in to him, she is bored and petulant; when he gives in to her, he is crotchety and becomes ill. Eventually, Annabel becomes involved with a man of her own age and leaves the judge.

At the end of the book, he considers taking the sensible course of action and returning to Amanda. In the final pages, however, the proverbial sap is rising again, and the judge is eyeing his young nurse. The female protagonist in *Barren Ground* became wiser as she became older, but the male protagonist of *The Romantic Comedians* never does achieve self-knowledge or an understanding of the real world in which he lives.

VEIN OF IRON

First published: 1935
Type of work: Novel

Surmounting disappointments and hardships, a strong woman perseveres to find happiness.

Vein of Iron stresses one of Glasgow's dominant themes: that only the strong can make it through the hardships of life. As in many other Glasgow novels, including *Barren Ground*, the most obvious of these hardships is the lack of money. Ada Fincastle, the protagonist of *Vein of Iron*, has been aware of her family's precarious financial situation from her earliest years.

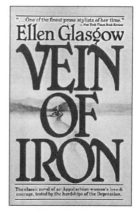

Her father, however, unlike Dorinda's father, is an educated man; indeed, his intellectual gifts have been his downfall. A Presbyterian minister, he had published a brilliant but unconventional book; as a result, he lost his church and his profession, and he had to move back to his Appalachian home, where he lives with his mother, attempting to support the household on what he can make as a schoolmaster.

Ada's childhood is summed up by her disappointment when her father brings her a cheap doll for Christmas instead of the one with real hair on which she had set her heart. Her character is summed up by the comment made at that time—that the child has a single heart. Although that singleness of affection means that Ada will never be happy with the wrong doll, in later life it enables her to cling to her love for Ralph McBride until together they find happiness.

The love story of Ada Fincastle and Ralph McBride begins in their childhood, when they are schoolfellows. By the time Ada is twenty, she knows that she is in love with Ralph, who is then a young law student. After a quarrel, however, Ralph gets involved with another young woman; when he is found in a compromising situation, he is forced by her parents to marry her. Years pass; Ralph goes into military service during World War I. When he returns home on leave, separated from his wife but not yet divorced, he and Ada spend some idyllic days together in a mountain cabin before Ralph returns to his unit.

When Ada's pregnancy becomes known, the devout Christians of her community treat her like an outcast. Eventually, Ada, her father, her aunt, and her little son move to Queenborough, where Ada

Ellen Glasgow

DISCUSSION TOPICS

- How does Ellen Glasgow's early work illustrate the difficulty of managing a satisfactory relationship between ideas and characters in a novel?

- What traits of southern society depicted in Glasgow's novels provoke her theme of women's rebellion?

- To what extent does *Barren Ground*—and especially its conclusion—relate to Glasgow's own problems of middle age?

- In what ways did Glasgow influence later southern writers?

- What raises *Vein of Iron* above a mere attempt to exploit the success of *Barren Ground*?

- Glasgow was interested in the conflict of the "Old South" and the "New South." What sorts of issues are involved in this distinction?

can find a job in a store, while her father again turns to teaching. Although this is a very difficult period for Ada, she endures. When Ralph at last finds her and the son he did not know he had, it seems that her trials are over.

Yet the pattern repeats itself. Ralph is injured in an accident. Ten years of savings go for his medical care. Then, just as the family is getting back on its feet, the Depression bursts upon them. The plight of the McBrides, who have always worked hard and saved what they could, only to lose their jobs and their savings, is repeated over and over. Ironically, Ralph and Ada show a strength in adversity that is

lacking in Ada's once-wealthy kinfolk, who formerly snubbed her and now must accept her generosity.

At the end of the novel, Ralph and Ada move back to their old Appalachian home. Even though they will probably always be poor and even though the first glow of love is gone, they realize that they have found happiness in their love for each other. The comparison with *Barren Ground* is obvious. In *Vein of Iron*, the protagonist's first love is basically a man of character (although he has his weaknesses) who never ceases loving her. In turn, she retains her capacity to love and, though it brings her heartaches, in the end that openness gives her contentment.

Although much in the two plots is similar—the disappointment in love, the illicit sexual relationships resulting in pregnancy, the unstable and unhappy family situations, and the haunting poverty—the heroines, though both strong, react in very different ways to life's hardships. Where Dorinda denies her emotional being, Ada draws strength from it. Not only her ancestry but also her willingness to love gives her the iron to endure.

SUMMARY

Whether in serious works or comic, satirical novels, Glasgow's primary goal is to show life as it is. Like the southern realists who followed her, Glasgow invents plots full of missed chances and chance decisions that lead to alienation and tragedy. Her characters often destroy themselves by deluding themselves; by the time they attain self-knowledge, it is often too late to salvage their lives. Furthermore, Glasgow presents the societies in which her characters live as repressive and hypocritical, particularly in their treatment of women, whom they pretend to revere but actually enslave.

Rosemary M. Canfield Reisman

BIBLIOGRAPHY

By the Author

LONG FICTION:
The Descendant, 1897
Phases of an Inferior Planet, 1898
The Voice of the People, 1900
The Battle-Ground, 1902

The Deliverance, 1904
The Wheel of Life, 1906
The Ancient Law, 1908
The Romance of a Plain Man, 1909
The Miller of Old Church, 1911
Virginia, 1913
Life and Gabriella, 1916
The Builders, 1919
One Man in His Time, 1922
Barren Ground, 1925
The Romantic Comedians, 1926
They Stooped to Folly, 1929
The Sheltered Life, 1932
Vein of Iron, 1935
In This Our Life, 1941

SHORT FICTION:
The Shadowy Third, and Other Stories, 1923
The Collected Stories of Ellen Glasgow, 1963

POETRY:
The Freeman, and Other Poems, 1902

NONFICTION:
A Certain Measure: An Interpretation of Prose Fiction, 1943
The Woman Within, 1954
Letters of Ellen Glasgow, 1958

About the Author

Godbold, E. Stanly, Jr. *Ellen Glasgow and the Woman Within.* Baton Rouge: Louisiana State University Press, 1972.

Goodman, Susan. *Ellen Glasgow.* Baltimore: Johns Hopkins University Press, 1998.

McDowell, Frederick P. W. *Ellen Glasgow and the Ironic Art of Fiction.* Madison: University of Wisconsin Press, 1960.

Matthews, Pamela R. *Ellen Glasgow and a Woman's Traditions.* Charlottesville: University Press of Virginia, 1994.

The Mississippi Quarterly 49 (Spring, 1996).

Rouse, Blair. *Ellen Glasgow.* New York: Twayne, 1962.

Scura, Dorothy M., ed. *Ellen Glasgow: New Perspectives.* Knoxville: University of Tennessee Press, 1995.

Taylor, Welford Dunaway, and George C. Longest, eds. *Regarding Ellen Glasgow: Essays for Contemporary Readers.* Richmond: Library of Virginia, 2001.

Wagner, Linda W. *Ellen Glasgow: Beyond Convention.* Austin: University of Texas Press, 1982.

SUSAN GLASPELL

Born: Davenport, Iowa
July 1, 1876
Died: Provincetown, Massachusetts
July 27, 1948

A pioneering and prolific American feminist novelist, journalist, short-story writer, and Pulitzer Prize-winning playwright, Glaspell advocated freedom of expression and was cofounder and codirector of the influential Provincetown Players.

BIOGRAPHY

Mystery surrounds the birth date of Susan Glaspell. Both 1876 and 1882 have been given. Glaspell always asserted that the latter date was correct, and it was often used in past studies. Recent evidence suggests, however, that the earlier date is accurate. Why she would deny a linkage to the nation's centennial and make herself appear younger has never been explained. Susan was born to Elmer S. and Alice Keating Glaspell in Davenport, Iowa. Her father's family was among the first of the Davenport settlers. Her father was solidly middle class with some affluence, but he was not a wealthy man. Her parents instilled in their daughter a love of the region that she would retain to the end of her life.

Glaspell was educated in the public schools of Davenport. She then went to Des Moines, Iowa, to attend Drake University. She graduated in 1899 with a Ph.B. degree, having studied literature, classics, and the Bible. By all accounts, she was popular; she was also noted for her storytelling abilities and gained experience as a writer. Her first job after graduation was as a reporter for the *Des Moines Daily News*. While there, she met and befriended Lucy Huffaker, who became an influential and lifelong friend.

Glaspell worked at the paper for two years, became expert at political writing, and had her own column, "The News Girl," which began with politi-cal commentary and then strayed to fictional forays and personal observations. The column's success prompted Glaspell to quit her job at the newspaper in 1901, return to Davenport, and begin earning a living as a freelance writer. The "Freeport" stories, twenty-six in all, based on the city of Davenport, were escapist and romantic works filled with local color and unexpected plot twists.

The turning point in her private and literary career occurred in 1907, when she met George Cram Cook, a charismatic man. Nicknamed "Jig," he opened Glaspell's eyes to new forms of literary expression, especially in the theater. They married six years later, on April 14, 1913, in Weehawken, New Jersey. Both Glaspell and Cook had become involved with several free-thinking, nontraditional groups, most notably the Monist Society and the Liberal Club. Between the time they met and married, Glaspell published her first novel, *The Glory of the Conquered: The Story of a Great Love* (which Cook heartily disliked) in 1909; a second novel, *The Visioning*, in 1911; and *Lifted Masks*, a collection of short stories, in 1912.

In 1915, two years after their marriage, Glaspell and Cook cofounded the Provincetown Players at the Wharf Theatre in Provincetown, Massachusetts. They had summered there the year before and had put on some amateur theatricals. Now the new little group, patterned after the New Theatre movement in Europe, began a quest to produce works by new playwrights.

Many artists became attracted, and attached, to the Provincetown Players. Some of the most notable were Robert Edmond Jones, John Reed, Edna St. Vincent Millay, Edna Ferber, Theodore Dreiser, Djuna Barnes, and, most important, Eugene O'Neill. In 1916, the Provincetown Players, which also took on the name "The Playwright Theater" at O'Neill's request, opened in New York City in Greenwich Village. The playbill included Glaspell's best short play, *Trifles*, and O'Neill's *Bound East for Cardiff*, the first of his "S.S. Glencairn" quartet. The Provincetown Players, which continued as an organization until 1929, became an important theater laboratory that took creative risks with budding playwrights, actors, and designers.

On March 22, 1922, Glaspell and Cook, having recently dropped their association with the Provincetown Players (now led by O'Neill, Jones, and Kenneth Macgowan), moved to Greece. Cook had always dreamed of moving to Delphi and creating theater where classical drama had once flourished. Less than two years later, on January 24, 1924, Cook died in Delphi and was buried there.

Glaspell returned to Provincetown to resume her professional literary career as a novelist. She married writer Norman Matson in 1925 (they divorced in 1931) and collaborated with him on several works, most notably a play, *The Comic Artist*, in 1927. A year earlier, she had published *The Road to the Temple*, a loving biography of her first husband. Glaspell was awarded the 1931 Pulitzer Prize in drama for her play *Alison's House* (1930), produced by Eva Le Galliene. Three years later, she was briefly appointed Midwest Director for the Federal Theater Project. Glaspell remained in Provincetown writing novels, the last of which was *Judd Rankin's Daughter* (1945), until her death from pneumonia on July 27, 1948.

ANALYSIS

Glaspell had a remarkable literary career that spanned almost five decades. It was as an experimental playwright that she found her own distinctive and innovative style, which would win her fame and a permanent place in American dramatic literature. Throughout her long literary career, Glaspell remained consistent, always dealing with midwestern themes and attitudes and employing unusual women as her leading characters. Her earliest short fiction, published at the turn of the twentieth century, reveals her talent for local color, a trait that made her work admirably suitable for

such popular women's magazines as *Good Housekeeping, Ladies' Home Journal,* and *Harper's Bazaar.*

The stories had certain recurring qualities. They were primarily escapist reading, perennially optimistic, and sentimental in nature. Glaspell often included last-minute plot switches or humor to offset saccharine sentiment. Romance and romantic problems appear in many, with obstacles to true love (usually young) removed at the last moment. In her early short fiction, Glaspell never attempted to shock or moralize to her readers.

Glaspell's best short fiction was written between 1916 and 1919. Two of her best stories, "Finality in Freeport" (1916) and "The Escape" (1919), are set in Freeport, a fictional place modeled after her hometown, Davenport. In the first, she pokes fun at the city's bluestockings who attempt to censor literature because of some new ideas, underscoring the conflict between freedom and morality.

In "The Escape," a free-thinking, pacifist woman refuses to be caught up in the jingoistic fervor of World War I. Glaspell's entire output of short fiction, with one exception, was written for popular magazines of the day and reflects the editorial demands and public expectations of such entertainment. The single exception, now considered a classic, is "A Jury of Her Peers," which was adapted from her earlier one-act play *Trifles* and concerned an Iowa woman accused of killing her husband. Its depiction of the locale is realistic and demonstrates a complete unity of plot, characters, and conflict.

Trifles was the second play Glaspell wrote after she collaborated with Cook on *Suppressed Desires* (1915). In all, she wrote fourteen plays. Unlike in her short stories, which had a predictable framework, in her plays Glaspell experimented with the dramatic form despite her lack of dramatic experience or training. She wrote short dramas and comedies before switching to full-length plays. The one-act plays, eight in all, appear to be tentative efforts. She seemed more comfortable writing satiric or comic sketches rather than serious ones; her serious works sometimes come across as vague, and the idealism behind them at times seems ill-defined.

Glaspell found a stronger dramatic voice and greater confidence switching to full-length drama, but her experiments in the shorter form paid off handsomely with *Bernice* (1919). As in *Trifles*, the main character is never seen (Bernice dies before the play opens); it is her death and its impact on the main characters that fuels the play. Glaspell creates a play of little dramatic action, strong mood, and interesting people. Her second play, *Inheritors* (pb. 1921), is a historical piece covering the lives of three generations. Against a midwestern college background, the heroine supports independence of thought against narrow-minded provincialism, which is represented by faculty and students.

Glaspell's next play, *The Verge* (1921), is perhaps her most difficult to comprehend. The heroine, Claire, is a wife and mother who rejects all societal restraints and murders her lover; the play builds to a shocking conclusion. After two less than satisfactory plays—*Chains of Dew* (1922) and *The Comic Artist* (1928)—she wrote *Alison's House*, produced in 1930. The play is based loosely on the life of poet Emily Dickinson; the title character is already dead, and her life and work are shown through the eyes of family, friends, and strangers.

Glaspell's major weakness as a playwright is one of too much intellect. She sometimes creates static, "talking" drama, with characters who cannot articulate their feelings or emotions. Yet she also creates a strong modern drama populated with fascinating people, particularly strong-minded women. Her plays are experimental, treating topical themes, and contain strong idealism. Unlike her contemporary and friendly rival, O'Neill, Glaspell never strays from her American heritage, and she successfully merges American beliefs and ideas with mysticism and a oneness with the eternal.

Glaspell's nine novels, published between 1909 and 1945, can be neatly categorized within three distinct periods. Despite the wide separation of time, all of them take place in the Midwest and contain a melodramatic situation, with strong women (who are often artistic) searching for fulfillment and coming into harmony with the universe. The first period (1909-1916), like her early short fiction, used romantic love to heal and unify. The best play from this period is *Fidelity* (1915), in which a Freeport woman runs off with a married man to Colorado, returning home eleven hours later to face family, friends, and society. Love does not conquer all here, as Glaspell's heroine follows her own principles instead of society's; the author compares and contrasts early midwestern veracity with its later prudishness.

The second period (1928-1931) produced Glaspell's least interesting work. The novels in question—*Brook Evans* (1928), *Fugitive's Return* (1929), and *Ambrose Holt and Family* (1931)—focus away from love and deal with individuals battling society. Her faith in the midwestern tradition permeates the work, as do her political liberalism and Christian ethics.

Glaspell's last cycle of novel writing (1940-1945) offers a clearer, more coherent vision of her life and art. Her last and best work is *Judd Rankin's Daughter* (1945), in which three main characters represent different aspects of the Midwest. The book reveals Glaspell's major strengths as a regional novelist who captures the pioneering spirit, the physical beauty, and the colorful characters of midwestern life.

"A JURY OF HER PEERS"

First published: 1917
Type of work: Short story

In an Iowa farmhouse, investigators gather evidence against a woman charged with murder, but two visitors discover the truth and sympathize with the accused.

Most critics agree that Susan Glaspell's "A Jury of Her Peers" is, by far, her best short story. First published in *Everyweek* on March 5, 1917, the work is a faithful adaptation of her play *Trifles*, produced the year before by the Provincetown Players. Cook had decided to stage two one-act plays for the company. He already had O'Neill's *Bound East for Cardiff* (wr. 1913-1914, pr. 1916, pb. 1919) but needed another, and he told Glaspell to write one. She protested because of her lack of experience as a dramatist and the pairing with O'Neill. Reaching into her past as a courthouse reporter in Iowa, she remembered covering a murder trial and her impressions of entering the

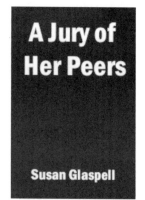

A Jury of
Her Peers

Susan Glaspell

kitchen of the accused. She had meant to write about the experience as a short story but had never gotten to it.

> So I went out on the wharf . . . and looked a long time at that bare little stage. After a time the stage became a kitchen—a kitchen there all by itself. I saw just where the stove was, the table, and the steps going upstairs. Then the door at the back opened, and people all bundled up came in—two or three men, I wasn't sure which, but sure enough about the two women, who hung back, reluctant to enter that kitchen.

The play was a big success for Glaspell and the Provincetown Players. It is considered one of the finest short pieces written for the American theater and is frequently anthologized.

Glaspell had only to make minor changes in adapting *Trifles* to a short story. As with some of her other literary work, the main character is never seen. The setting is the Iowa farm of Minnie Wright. Minnie has been charged with murdering her husband. Her guilt in committing the crime is never questioned. Three men—a sheriff, a county prosecutor, and a neighbor—have come to gather evidence to support the prosecution. Two women—wives of the sheriff and neighbor—accompany the men. Their purpose is to pick up effects for Minnie.

Glaspell skillfully shows how the men and women look at the household differently. While the men seek evidence to convict the accused, the two women come across trifles such as a disordered household, an irregular quilting pattern, and a strangled canary. They conclude that such details are indicative of Minnie's motivations for the murder. The women gossip openly about Minnie's abusive and authoritarian husband and discuss why they sympathize with her desperate act. Glaspell creates a courtroom in that Iowa farmstead, and the women become jurors who decide that Minnie is not guilty. They base their judgment not on legality but on simple humanity and compassion. The women decide not to reveal their evidence to the male investigators out of respect for Minnie's long suffering.

ALISON'S HOUSE

First produced: 1930 (first published, 1930)
Type of work: Play

The survivors of a famous poet must decide whether to publish her poems about her unfulfilled love for a married man.

Alison's House, the last produced play by Glaspell, was first presented at the Civic Repertory Theater in New York City on December 1, 1930. The production, produced and directed by Le Galliene, ran for forty-one performances and won for Glaspell the 1931 Pulitzer Prize in drama—a decision that outraged some critics who disliked her play and thought it too literary.

Alison's House concerns a noted fictional poet, Alison Stanhope, who has been dead for eighteen years when the curtain rises. Her poetry, published after her death, has brought her posthumous fame. The play begins on December 31, 1899, in the library of the Stanhope estate. John Stanhope, Alison's brother, is selling the property, and there is much confusion as family members gather to say goodbye and pick up keepsakes. One of the recently arrived relations is Elsa, Alison's niece and John's daughter, who had scandalized the family some years earlier by running off with a married man. A Chicago newspaper reporter, Ted Knowles, has also come to do a story on Alison; he is curious to know if all Alison's poetry has been published.

Slowly, the dark secret buried inside the house comes to life. Alison's family has withheld some of her poetry. Agatha, Alison's spinster sister and close friend, decides to burn down the mansion to destroy the papers and bury the secret. Failed in her attempt, she gives Elsa the unpublished poetry and dies shortly after of a heart attack. The final act takes place in Alison's old room. Alison's secret is revealed: She was in love with a married man, but unlike Elsa, she sublimated her secret passions into poetry. The play ends with Elsa planning to publish Alison's lost poetry because it belongs to the world and the new century.

Glaspell based the play loosely on the life of the New England poet Emily Dickinson; she moved the setting to Iowa. Unable to use Dickinson's poetry, Glaspell freely borrowed from the work of Ralph

Waldo Emerson. She again used one of her favorite literary devices; the title character is never seen, but her presence is felt through the other characters. The newspaper reporter Knowles sums it up best:

> You know, I think all your family have something of the spirit of Alison Stanhope. . . . Yes, coming in fresh, I can tell better than you. It's as if something of her remained here, in you all, in—in quite a different form.

The dramatist ends the play on the note of rebirth and love. The play is tightly constructed and adheres to the classical dramatic unities. Through the various characters, Alison becomes a reality, an ideal who brings hope and regeneration.

JUDD RANKIN'S DAUGHTER

First published: 1945
Type of work: Novel

Midwestern beliefs and values clash and coalesce through the dynamically different personalities of conservative Judd Rankin, his liberal daughter Frances, and her nonconformist cousin Adah.

Judd Rankin's Daughter was the last of Glaspell's nine novels. The final three—*The Morning Is Near Us* (1940), *Norma Ashe* (1942), and *Judd Rankin's Daughter*—were written close together; each of the three features a memorable heroine seeking to rediscover her midwestern heritage in order to better understand the present. In the first two of these books, the protagonists must struggle through the corruption and dissipation of their early idealism to a gradual reawakening in themselves. *Judd Rankin's Daughter*, which is not representative of most of Glaspell's work, delineates a much more complex and interesting heroine involved with the major problems of modern life.

Judd Rankin's Daughter is about three wonderful people: Judd Rankin, a lovable old Iowa farmer and philosopher who has finally written a book about people living in the Midwest; Frances Rankin Mitchell, his liberal daughter, who is living in Provincetown, Massachusetts, and who embodies both midwestern and eastern values; and Cousin Adah Elwood Logan, a nonconforming sophisticate whose love lives on long after her death.

The novel opens with the anticipated death of Cousin Adah. She lived a rich and happy life, had lovers before and during marriage, and kept a salon where writers and workers met. Frances is present as witness to the death of someone she loved, someone who symbolized freedom and a piece of the pioneering spirit of women. A young soldier arrives at the deathbed, wishing to speak to Cousin Adah about the meaning of life. Frances tries to comfort him and warns against following ideologies. Her adoption of this spiritual son brings Frances to understand her biological son, Judson, who has returned from World War II's Pacific theater of operations. He now hates his parents, particularly his father, whom he believes helped to provoke the war.

Frances is forced to reexamine her beliefs. Her husband hates Judd for his conservative, isolationist views. Her friend, a left-wing writer, is slowly turning into a fascist. Her best friend reveals herself to be anti-Semitic. Her son's accusations about her husband's politics combine with Frances's other concerns to shatter her complacency. She visits Judd, her father, in Iowa to help pull her life together and to seek his help with her son. Judd writes a powerful letter to his grandson that changes Judson's mind, and Frances's dearest wish is realized on New Year's Eve, when her father, husband, and son are reunited.

Glaspell's last literary work is marked by a mature fluidity of style that reveals her as an artist of integrity. She offers up a prevailingly hopeful picture of honest people and grass-roots wisdom, and she does so in a pleasant, witty, and thoughtful manner. *Judd Rankin's Daughter* reveals the faith in the American heritage, particularly the midwestern tradition of common sense, that suffuses Glaspell's art.

SUMMARY

Glaspell was a truly prolific writer. During her lifetime, this remarkable feminist wrote fourteen plays, nine novels, forty-three short stories, numerous essays, a biography, and a children's tale. Although successful in a variety of literary genres, Glaspell is best known for her dramatic works. The

Pulitzer Prize-winning playwright created a new theatrical voice and dealt with contemporary issues. Glaspell is also remembered as the inspirational force behind the founding of the Provincetown Players and for her continuous encouragement of new playwrights, particularly Eugene O'Neill.

Terry Theodore

BIBLIOGRAPHY

By the Author

DRAMA:

Suppressed Desires, pr. 1915, pb. 1917 (one act; with George Cram Cook)

Trifles, pr. 1916, pb. 1917 (one act)

The People, pr. 1917, pb. 1918 (one act)

Close the Book, pr. 1917, pb. 1918 (one act)

The Outside, pr. 1917, pb. 1920 (one act)

Woman's Honor, pr. 1918, pb. 1920 (one act)

Tickless Time, pr. 1918, pb. 1920 (one act; with Cook)

Bernice, pr. 1919, pb. 1920

Plays, pb. 1920 (includes *Suppressed Desires, Trifles, Close the Book, The Outside, The People, Woman's Honor, Tickless Time,* and *Bernice*)

Inheritors, pr., pb. 1921

The Verge, pr. 1921, pb. 1922

The Chains of Dew, pr. 1922

The Comic Artist, pb. 1927, pr. 1928 (with Norman Matson)

Alison's House, pr., pb. 1930

Plays by Susan Glaspell, pb. 1987 (C. W. E. Bigsby, editor; includes *Trifles, The Outside, The Verge,* and *Inheritors*)

LONG FICTION:

The Glory of the Conquered: The Story of a Great Love, 1909

The Visioning, 1911

Fidelity, 1915

Brook Evans, 1928

Fugitive's Return, 1929

Ambrose Holt and Family, 1931

The Morning Is Near Us, 1940

Norma Ashe, 1942

Judd Rankin's Daughter, 1945

SHORT FICTION:

Lifted Masks, 1912

NONFICTION:

The Road to the Temple, 1926

CHILDREN'S LITERATURE:

Cherished and Shared of Old, 1940

DISCUSSION TOPICS

- How specifically did Susan Glaspell's education prove beneficial to her career as a writer?

- Generally speaking, Glaspell's best short stories were written early in her career and her best novels later, a situation not uncommon among fiction writers. What might account for this tendency? Life experience? Artistic maturity? Something else?

- What is the theme of Glaspell's play *Trifles*, and how does she modify it in her story based on it, "A Jury of Her Peers"?

- What did the great playwright Eugene O'Neill owe to Glaspell?

- What are the "classical dramatic unities" and how are they exemplified in *Alison's House*?

About the Author

Ben-Zvi, Linda. "Susan Glaspell's Contributions to Contemporary Women Playwrights." In *Feminine Focus: The New Women Playwrights*, edited by Enoch Brater. New York: Oxford University Press, 1989.

Bigsby, C. W. E. Introduction to *Plays by Susan Glaspell*. New York: Cambridge University Press, 1987.

Dymkowski, Christine. "On the Edge: The Plays of Susan Glaspell." *Modern Drama* 1 (March, 1988): 91-105.

Goldberg, Isaac. *The Drama of Transition: Native and Exotic Playcraft*. Cincinnati: Stewart Kidd, 1922.

Makowsky, Veronica A. *Susan Glaspell's Century of American Women: A Critical Interpretation of Her Work*. New York: Oxford University Press, 1993.

Noe, Marcia. *Susan Glaspell: Voice from the Heartland*. Macomb: Western Illinois University, 1983.

Ozieblo, Barbara. "Rebellion and Rejection: The Plays of Susan Glaspell." In *Modern American Drama: The Female Canon*, edited by June Schlueter. London: Associated University Presses, 1990.

_____. *Susan Glaspell: A Critical Biography*. Chapel Hill: University of North Carolina Press, 2000.

Papke, Mary E. *Susan Glaspell: A Research and Production Sourcebook*. Westport, Conn.: Greenwood Press, 1993.

Waterman, Arthur E. *Susan Glaspell*. New York: Twayne, 1966.

MEL GLENN

Born: Zurich, Switzerland
May 10, 1943

With unparalleled productivity and commercial success, Glenn, a career educator, reinvigorated young adult poetry, experimenting with the free verse monologue as a vehicle to reveal character and investigate difficult dilemmas facing contemporary adolescents.

Courtesy, ASIJ

BIOGRAPHY

Although most associated with Brooklyn, Mel Glenn was actually born in Switzerland to an American father studying medicine and an Austrian mother. When Glenn was three, the family returned to the United States and settled in Brooklyn, near Coney Island. As a child, Glenn relished the escape provided by books. He matriculated at New York University, initially in pre-med. Finding the curriculum unappealing, Glenn opted ultimately to pursue an English degree. He wrote, principally about sports, for the campus newspaper, deciding finally that journalism would be his field. After graduating in 1964, however, Glenn, fascinated as a child by the exotic ports he had studied in geography, volunteered for the Peace Corps and for two years taught English and history at a tiny Methodist missionary school in Sierra Leone. Despite its impoverished circumstances, the school taught Glenn important lessons on the dedication and enthusiasm that children bring to education. Returning stateside in 1967, he completed a master's degree in education at New York's Yeshiva University and taught junior high briefly until he accepted a position on the English faculty of Abraham Lincoln High School in Brooklyn, the same school he himself had attended. He would teach there for more than thirty years, retiring in 2001. Following his retirement, Glenn became a tireless promoter for reading and creative writing in schools.

His writing career—one of the most prolific and successful among contemporary young adult writers—did not begin until Glenn was thirty-seven. After being asked to review a colleague's manuscript intended for submission as a young adult novel, Glenn confided to his wife that the manuscript was quite bad; she then challenged him to write his own. As a New Year's resolution, Glenn did just that, finding in free verse form access to what had compelled him since his Peace Corps days: his fascination and respect for kids. Drawing on his background in journalism, he put himself on a schedule: one poem a day. After years of teaching and listening to students and their anxieties, joys, traumas, and dreams, Glenn had material sufficient to shape his first collection, *Class Dismissed! High School Poems* (1982). Patterned on Edgar Lee Masters's 1915 *Spoon River Anthology, Class Dismissed!* presented free-verse poems, each in an agreeably colloquial cadence, in which individual students at an inner-city high school voices what troubles them: problems with parents, grades, love and sex, friends, violence, poverty, and racism. The success that greeted the book, including a Best-of-the-Best Books 1970-1982 citation from the American Library Association, encouraged Glenn to continue the series in two sequels, *Class Dismissed II: More High School Poems* (1986), which earned a prestigious Christopher Award, and *Back to Class* (1988). Although Glenn would publish three young adult novels during the 1980's, his reputation and his success came from his poetry, rare in the young adult field where poetry is often a career sidelight.

However, Glenn was restless with the snapshot

923

structure of his works. With 1991's landmark *My Friend's Got This Problem, Mr. Candler,* Glenn moved into a more deliberate structural plan: interconnected, free-verse monologues that together create a novel-like plot, allowing voices to recur within the narrative, not only creating suspense but also allowing characters to reveal more of themselves across a number of entries. He would again explore the genre in *Who Killed Mr. Chippendale?* (1996), a murder mystery involving the shooting of a popular English teacher; *The Taking of Room 114* (1997), a look at school violence in which a history teacher holds a terrified classroom hostage; the critically acclaimed *Jump Ball* (1997), a sports narrative that follows a high school basketball team's championship season; *Foreign Exchange* (1999), a tense murder mystery involving racism and class bigotry; and *Split Image* (2000), a taut psychological study of a beautiful Asian student who, pressured by her academic success and her reputation as a model student, leads a dangerous, nocturnal double life in bars and who ends up committing suicide. The books found a wide appeal, feted with awards for excellence in the field of young adult writing and regularly taught in classrooms by teachers happy to find poems that are both accessible and relevant to their students.

Such recognition testifies to work that challenges young adult readers. As a body of work, Glenn's poetry ultimately treats the intricate problem of perception. In his defining works, Glenn juxtaposes monologues to explore how understanding any character is an imprecise act of imperfect perception. The truth of any situation in Glenn's story lines emerges only from the unintended and often ironic collision of these voices. Drawing on Glenn's background in journalism, where witnesses must unintentionally work together to produce a sense of an event, these works ask the reader to play a collaborative role, sorting through the voices to assemble a coherent version of a difficult truth, a sort of truth-enough.

ANALYSIS

As a Brooklyn public school teacher for more than thirty years, Glenn found sources for poetry in the materials most readily at hand—the voices of the thousands of kids that surrounded him every day in hallways and classrooms. Understanding how that material has been shaped into poetry be-

gins with three influences Glenn readily acknowledges: the country music that played on the family radio while he was growing up, the journalism that first defined his writing style, and the folk music he discovered during its heyday in 1960's New York. From country music, Glenn learned to appreciate the impact of stories and sharply drawn characters, how voices give immediacy to stories, and how the most unpromising lives are rich with unsuspected drama. Journalism honed Glenn's observational skills and his curiosity as well as his keen ability to listen and record events around him. It also nurtured his enduring fascination with those materials. The folk song movement instilled in his poetry not only its inviting colloquial ease but also its fierce populism, its steady, if underplayed, outrage over the problems facing contemporary culture (specifically, for Glenn, adolescents). Like folk music, Glenn's poetry does not endorse street-level activism but rather exercises language to reveal, illuminate, and dissect significant issues and problems that can be addressed only after they are first acknowledged.

Glenn revitalized young adult poetry, recognizing that young people often approach poetry with dread and find traditional poetry dense, inaccessible, and requiring lengthy classroom analysis and the often condescending "help" of teachers. Glenn's characters, however, speak in an accessible voice unadorned by stylized language or poetic conventions. His poetry does not deploy the intricacy of irony or elaborate symbolism, difficult ambiguities, or involved wordplay. The poems happen in the ear—they are, after all, essentially voices. Rendering the street language of high school kids is hardly simple transcription—Glenn has often cited his revision process, weighing each word for its pitch-perfect aptness to achieve the sonic rhythm of unforced music. The poetic form itself, however, never obscures Glenn's driving interest in story and character. Indeed, his voices draw out the implications of familiar high school types—the nerd, the tramp, the jock, the underachiever, the poor kid, and the isolated minority. Without trivializing adolescence with the condescending voice-over of an adult author or sentimentalizing the period with simplistic nostalgia, Glenn's oeuvre speaks of the terrifying loneliness at the heart of the adolescent experience, the confusion—both anxious and exhilarating—of defining an "I" within a context of uncontrollable circumstances. Glenn's "ordinary" speech invites reader identification and sympathy; each voice is given individuality and importance, thus creating a rich immediacy. In elevating the dilemmas of the threshold experiences of adolescence into verse, Glenn recovers these everyday pressures into the music of language, giving high school experiences the traditional privileges of literature.

MY FRIEND'S GOT THIS PROBLEM, MR. CANDLER

First published: 1991
Type of work: Poetry

One by one, high school students "speak" to their guidance counselor and reveal concerns in plainspoken free-verse monologues.

"I'm here/Like always." Thus closes Mel Glenn's 1991 collection of interrelated poems. The lines are spoken by the overworked, if infinitely patient, high school guidance counselor, Mark Candler. It is Friday afternoon. Just as Mr. Candler is about to close the office for the week—and take his car in for a muffler repair and himself to the dentist—a student has appeared at his doorway, and the dedicated Mr. Candler quietly understands that his own errands, indeed his own life, must wait a bit. Here is another student whose crisis deserves airing, whose voice deserves to be heard.

Mr. Candler's generous response defines Glenn's own democratic vision, born of his long commitment to the classroom: the conviction that every adolescent voice deserves an audience. The name Glenn selected for his guidance counselor—Candler—provides some insight. It suggests a profession that provides illumination, here the counselor's patient ear. No student problem presented in the collection is resolved; the therapy here is honest confrontation rather than treatment. Because each voice speaks in monologue, because the voices never directly speak to each other, Glenn creates an unnerving sense of distance, underscoring the unsettling isolation of adolescence with voices that never receive an answer. These are unsettling poems that raise dilemmas without quick-

fix remedies. Indeed, the voices emerge, speak, and then dissolve back into the narrative text, never to be heard again. It is the impact of their collective voice that creates the work's emotional impact—the steady accumulation of dilemma that reveals the angst, confusion, joys, and fears of adolescence.

For more than one hundred pages, Glenn's reader listens to students who might otherwise pass unnoticed in the overcrowded halls of any urban high school, students coaxed into confession by an appointment with the guidance counselor. Each is rescued from anonymity, given a name that serves as the poem's title. In five chapters, each given over to a single day's appointments in a single work week, the poetry creates vignettes as each student, in turn, makes a complicated, often painful turn to the mirror. Although some adults speak (usually anxious or frustrated parents), the voices are largely students, struggling against their own reticence, against their own distrust of revelation. With slice-of-life honesty and a journalistic immediacy, the teenagers voice what bothers them and indirectly reveal the degree of their pain. They speak of their teachers' indifference, of breakups and the confusion of new infatuations, the dread of exams, troubles with parents, struggles with poverty, and, most poignantly, of their dreams of success and the heartbreaking ease with which dreams become hard choices, the awful finality of the road never taken.

Structurally, Glenn's poems, seldom more than twenty lines, favor a sonnetlike closing, a kicker that draws out the fullest—and more unsettling—implications of the character's revelation. For instance, a character still terribly hung over from his first drinking experience closes by anticipating the weekend, the lesson of such dead-end excess apparently unlearned; in another, a girl is tormented by the sexual harassment she is receiving in the card store where she works and assumes "real work" cannot be like that; in another, a girl relishes shopping with her father's new girlfriend but closes by confessing she could never call her "mother," foretelling a complicated emotional showdown. Coherence comes from the device of the guidance counselor as audience, the listener who never interrupts, never lightens the anxiety with patronizing platitudes. We simply listen, reading itself becoming a gesture of compassion and a strategy of inevitable identification. Such realism is heightened by the accompanying black-and-white photographs of Michael J. Bernstein (a colleague of Glenn's), each an unposed, unretouched headshot, a teen staring unnervingly into the camera lens. The text thus becomes a multimedia experience in which initially voices, abstract and intangible, are recovered into form (the poetry) and then revitalized into people (the photographs).

JUMP BALL: A BASKETBALL SEASON IN POEMS

First published: 1997
Type of work: Poetry

A diverse collection of voices, including players, coaches, fans, teachers, and family, records the triumph and turmoil of a high school basketball program during a single dramatic— and ultimately tragic—championship season.

Glenn discovered the drama of prep sports in the early 1990's when Lincoln High School felt the impact of Stephon Marbury, a point guard of considerable talent who guided Lincoln to a state championship and would go on to an All-Star career in the National Basketball Association. Most obviously, *Jump Ball* draws on the roller coaster emotions of that experience—the Tigers of fictitious Tower High School ride the talents of point guard Garrett James to position themselves for a run at a state title. Among the voices of the Tower players and fans, Glenn juxtaposes broadcast accounts of pivotal games, providing not only a linear thread to the anthology but exploiting as well the pulsing suspense inherent in any championship season. The reader is caught up by the persuasive tension of the unfolding season. Here, voices recur as the season plays out, and characters are given nuance. For instance, readers follow a hopeless crush that a female student manager has for one of the players; one player's ill-advised decision to play despite a bad heart; a player's struggle to conceal the depths of his family's poverty and his own homelessness; and the aching loneliness of a coach's wife.

Glenn deploys his characters to assess the cult of the jock that arguably has come to challenge academics in high school education. He explores the

mental stamina and emotional register of the athletes themselves; the pressure to win despite the clichés that sports is not about the score; the jealousy that star players generate not only among students but also among teammates; the distaste some teachers feel for the glorification of game playing; and the dreams that such success engenders in lesser others who see the single talented star as validation that dreaming is not unrealistic. More dra-

matically, in stepping inside the heads of gifted players, Glenn anatomizes the magic of sports itself, the thoughts of those who so effortlessly work the visual spectacle of sports performance. Glenn explores what it means to be "alone, alive, above the rim, above the arena."

However, *Jump Ball* is not content to be a sports book, although it does bring a human dimension to issues that are typically scrutinized by media covering prep sports. Early on, amid the monologues of players and fans, teachers and coaches, the reader is given disturbing voices that speak of a catastrophic mid-winter bus accident: a bus in upstate New York skids on an icy country road and crashes through a guardrail with significant casualties. Even as we are swept up into account of the games, the reader begins to realize that the bus is in fact the Tigers' team bus on its way at season's end to the state championship game. Such a realization casts a troubling shadow across the Tigers' march to the championship—indeed, each voice that is part of the accident account and the massive rescue effort is printed on a page that is itself backgrounded with an ominously shaded oval. Thus, what Glenn brings to his sports poetry is the hard reality of the real world that unfolds outside the tidy lines of the basketball court. The bus accident represents the difficult world of chance and misfortune that does not follow rules, that does not play fair, that does not add up. The narrative moves toward the only logical closing—not an account of a state championship but rather a hospital accident report that, in stark unrhymed prose, simply lists those who survived the accident and those who did not. Glenn thus compels his young adult reader to accept what is most difficult at that age (and any age)—the precariousness of every moment, the fragile structure of life, the harsh unpredictable intrusion of death. It is only after the initial reading that such irony can be fully felt, the doom that lurks in the most casual remarks. Thus, finishing the book leads the reader to a complex moment of beginnings: the characters so dramatically affected by the accident must now begin to address that impact, a beginning suggested by the title itself that recalls the moment of initial play in a basketball game. Glenn, an enduring optimist whose years as a public educator only convinced him of the resilience of the human spirit, is certain of recovery; the volume closes with a resident of the town nearest the crash site grimly surveying the accident scene but refusing despair, "Hope we get no more snow/ I'm looking forward to spring."

SUMMARY

By reinvigorating the genre of young adult poetry, Mel Glenn has provided a significant body of work that depends on the ear-friendly rhythms and the accessible diction of free verse to explore difficult issues facing contemporary high school students. Glenn's belief in the importance of every voice as well as his careful reproduction of the colloquial speech of young adults encourage a profound respect for the dilemmas of adolescence. Not compelled by an agenda to fix these problems, Glenn deploys poetry to do what important literature has always done: illuminate rather than solve complex dilemmas.

Joseph Dewey

DISCUSSION TOPICS

- What makes a more appropriate metaphor for the poet: a guidance counselor or a teacher?

- Mel Glenn's poetry raises problems of adolescence without offering solutions. In what ways does this strategy affect the reading experience?

- How do Glenn's character-voices avoid becoming stereotypes?

- What is the role of the poet, and the poet's own experiences and feelings, in poetry that depends on created voices?

- How does the technique of free verse affect the reading experience? Do the poems have the feel of traditional poetry? Would more traditional poetic forms work with Glenn's characters?

- Glenn's poetry represents a distinctly urban world. Would this type of poetry succeed in a rural setting?

- Glenn has often spoken of how his poems speak to the "kid" inside everybody. Define that inner child.

- What does Glenn's technique of cooperative monologues reveal about the nature of truth and the reliability of appearances?

BIBLIOGRAPHY

By the Author

LONG FICTION:
One Order to Go, 1984
Play-by-Play, 1986
Squeeze Play: A Baseball Story, 1989

POETRY:
Class Dismissed! High School Poems, 1982
Class Dismissed II: More High School Poems, 1986
Back to Class, 1988

Mel Glenn

My Friend's Got This Problem, Mr. Candler: High School Poems, 1991
Who Killed Mr. Chippendale? A Mystery in Poems, 1996
Jump Ball: A Basketball Season in Poems, 1997
The Taking of Room 114: A Hostage Drama in Poems, 1997
Foreign Exchange: A Mystery in Poems, 1999
Split Image: A Story in Poems, 2000

About the Author

Children's Literature Review, pp. 84-95. Detroit: Gale, 1999.

Copeland, Jeffrey S. *Speaking of Poets: Interviews with Poets Who Write for Children and Young Adults.* Urbana: University of Illinois Press, 1993.

Lesesne, Teri S. "Mel Glenn." In *Writers for Young Adults,* edited by Ted Hipple. Supplement 1. New York: Scribner, 2000.

"Mel Glenn." In *Contemporary Authors: New Revised Series.* Vol. 127. Detroit: Gale, 1989.

"Mel Glenn." In *Twentieth-Century Young Adult Writers.* Detroit: St. James Press, 1994.

Mel Glenn Web site. www.melglenn.com.

Thomas, Joseph T., Jr. "Mel Glenn and Arnold Adoff: The Poetics of Power in the Adolescent Voice-Lyric." *Style* 35, no. 3 (Fall, 2001): 486-497.

LOUISE GLÜCK

Born: New York, New York
April 22, 1943

James Baker Hall/Library of Congress

As a poet, Glück has addressed complex issues of loss, irreconcilable relationships, and rebirth in deceptively simple and direct language; her style combines elements of the classical and the confessional.

BIOGRAPHY

Born in New York City on April 22, 1943, Louise Glück is the daughter of Daniel and Beatrice Glück. Their first daughter died before Louise was born, an event that would affect the poet profoundly and has influenced the themes of loss and grief in her works. Another daughter was born after Louise's birth.

Glück had a solid knowledge of the Greek myths by the age of three. Her father, who wanted to be a writer but eventually decided to go into business with his brother-in-law, and her mother, who admired creative gifts and appreciated the arts, encouraged Glück and her sister to develop any inclinations or talents they had in such areas.

As an adolescent Glück developed anorexia nervosa, a condition she has described as a manifestation of the ravenous need for control and an independent self as well as a hunger for praise. Her anorexia eventually became so severe that she withdrew from high school in her last year to begin psychoanalytic sessions, which would last seven years.

Having graduated from Long Island's Hewlett High School in 1961 and attended Sarah Lawrence College, Bronxville, New York, in 1962, Glück studied at Columbia University during 1963-1966 and 1967-1968. She enrolled in a poetry workshop where poet and teacher Stanley Kunitz significantly influenced her. In 1966 Glück won the Academy of American Poets Prize, and in 1967, the same year that she married Charles Hertz, Jr., a Rockefeller

Foundation Fellowship. In 1968 Glück's first book, *Firstborn*, was published, followed by her receipt of a National Endowment for the Arts grant in 1969.

In 1970, Glück was a visiting teacher at the Fine Arts Work Center in Provincetown, Massachusetts. This was followed by a position as artist-in-residence at Goddard College in Plainfield, Vermont, 1971-1972. She served as a faculty member at Goddard College, 1973-1974. In 1975, she received a Guggenheim Fellowship, and her second book, *The House on Marshland*, was published. Glück spent 1976-1977 as a visiting professor at the University of Iowa while also serving as a faculty member and member of the M.F.A. Writing Program board at Goddard College; this position lasted until 1980, the same year that her book *Descending Figure* was published. In 1977 Glück married her second husband, John Dranow, and then accepted a position as professor of poetry at the University of Cincinnati in the spring of 1978, with a visiting professorship at Columbia University in 1979.

In 1980, Glück began a four-year term as a faculty and board member of the M.F.A. program for writers at Warren Wilson College in North Carolina. She received an award from the American Academy and Institute of Arts and letters in 1981. In 1982 and 1983 respectively, Glück served as Holloway Lecturer at the University of California at Berkeley and as Scott Professor of Poetry at Williams College. From 1984 to 2004, Glück was senior lecturer in English at Williams.

In 1985, Glück received several awards from the National Book Critics Circle, *The Boston Globe*, and the Poetry Society of America for *The Triumph of*

Achilles, her fourth book. She won the Sara Teasdale Memorial Prize from Wellesley College, her mother's alma mater, in 1986. This was followed by another Guggenheim Fellowship, 1987-1988, and a National Endowment for the Arts Fellowship, 1988-1989.

In the same year that she was appointed Phi Beta Kappa Poet at Harvard University, 1990, Glück's fifth book, *Ararat*, won the Bobbitt National Prize. This was followed by the Pulitzer Prize and the William Carlos Williams Award from the Poetry Society of America for her sixth book, *The Wild Iris* (1992). Her book of essays on poetry, *Proofs and Theories* (1994), won the Martha Albrand Award for nonfiction from PEN. *Meadowlands* was published in 1996, and Glück was appointed special consultant to the Library of Congress in 1999.

Having received the Bollingen Prize in 2001, a year after her former professor Stanley Kunitz received it, Glück went on to receive awards from *Boston Book Review* and *The New Yorker* for her book *Vita Nova* (1999). Her eleventh book of poems, *The Seven Ages* (2001), was nominated for the National Book Critics Circle Award in poetry. In 2003, she was appointed as the Library of Congress's twelfth poet laureate consultant in poetry. In 2004, the year she published *October*, Glück became writer-in-residence at Yale University.

ANALYSIS

Glück's career is marked by a pursuit of truth and authenticity. The subjects that some critics have described as grim and austere in her work, such as loneliness, isolation, grief, and ambivalence in relationships, she sees as the challenges in life that one strives to transcend in order to reach a higher spiritual level. This struggle, she believes, is the essence of art—the continual desire to capture that which is always just out of reach. Glück's poetry shows this movement toward spiritual enlightenment in an approach that embraces not only what can be articulated but also that which cannot. While the poems have closure in a sense that they often end with dramatic images or revelations about the relationships and observations they have described, these epiphanies are portrayed as cumulative, moments of perception that are enlightening but do not transform in themselves.

In fact, Glück raises more questions in her later poems, which are written in a more conversational style, than she does in her earlier work, which is more surreal, imagistic, and fragmented. Glück has described her own struggle with the need for perfection and its manifestation in a battle with anorexia starting in her high school years. The death of her sister before she was born has also left her with questions which she has addressed, if not answered, in her poetry. Two marriages that ended in divorce raised other questions about relationships and whether they can last without the people in them sacrificing who they are in some way. Throughout her career, Glück's goal has been to grow as an artist and continually to strive toward articulating that which is most difficult to articulate, or what William Faulkner described as "the human heart in conflict with itself."

Glück's first four books of poetry, *Firstborn, The House on Marshland, Descending Figure*, and *The Triumph of Achilles*, display her progression from surreal imagery showing the often disturbing irony and absurdity of perceptions versus reality to exploration of philosophical questions relating to how one exists in the world with this irony. In *Firstborn*, the speakers of the poems seem to observe what could otherwise be considered ordinary and even ritualistic events, such as a ride on a Chicago train and Thanksgiving dinner, as if they were apart from them, looking upon an almost comical display of human frailty and vulnerability, where images are distorted as if in a carnival funhouse, and those in the midst of them are oblivious to their absurdity.

The speakers also implicate themselves and their failures to grasp the import of such events at the times they occurred and the way they replay these events over and over in their minds, helpless to change what is now in the past and resigned to put the fragments together in some way. *The House on Marshland* shows a movement from exterior images toward the interior psyche. Although these poems still contain the images that help readers connect the exterior to the interior, they are more mythological and religious than scenes from daily life. In poems such as "All Hallows," "Gretel in Darkness," and "Nativity Poem," Glück builds her poems around natural, folkloric, and biblical elements to show the interconnectedness of these three profound influences on identity.

In *Descending Figure*, detachment returns as a thread running through the poems, yet rather than the comic irony of Glück's first book of poems, these works take a more intellectually ironic stance in their apparent detachment of emotions from observations. This is true of "The Drowned Children" and "Epithalamium," a poem that predicts the end of a marriage as it describes the beginning. The poems of *The Triumph of Achilles* portray the detachment in relationships and the desire to connect despite the limitations of communication, such as in "Metamorphosis," where the speaker describes her frustration at her father for apparently forgetting her as he approaches death, and "The Mountain," where the speaker describes struggling to convey to her students the Sisyphean effort that art takes and the rewards that make the hardships worthwhile.

In *Ararat, The Wild Iris, Meadowlands,* and *Vita Nova,* Glück shows a more conversational style, writing in sentences rather than phrases, and asking questions. These questions are either rhetorical or directed to a person to whom the poem is addressed, as are the statements that Glück makes in the more colloquial but not casual poems in these later books. In poems like "A Novel," "Mount Ararat," and "Appearances," she primarily addresses family dynamics and the ways in which families can deceive themselves as well as those outside the family. "The Untrustworthy Speaker" specifically addresses the illusion of self-knowledge as well as how actual self-deception is dishonest to others and undermines credibility.

In poems like "The Wild Iris," "Lamium," and "Violets," Glück uses flowers, plants, and other elements of nature as metaphors for the human need for spiritual illumination and darkness in order for growth to occur. *Meadowlands* is distinguished by several parables which raise rhetorical questions about things people take for granted, such as vocation in "Parable of the Hostages" and relationships in "Parable of the Swans." Rather than containing a moral, as conventional parables do, Glück's parables question how perceptions change and cause humans either to stay or leave situations. The poems of *Vita Nova* explore the longing for security and the vulnerability of love, or "the desire to be safe and the desire to feel" as described in "Aubade." In poems often written from the first- or second-person perspective, Glück captures the desire of lovers to communicate with one another and their inability to say exactly what they mean.

In *Proofs and Theories,* Glück has articulated her poetic philosophy in essays such as "Education of the Poet," "Against Sincerity," "The Forbidden," and "Disruption, Hesitation, Silence," referring to the work of poets she admires as examples of these concepts. This collection also includes essays on writers T. S. Eliot and Stanley Kunitz.

"THE SCHOOL CHILDREN"

First published: 1975 (collected in *The First Four Books of Poems,* 1995)
Type of work: Poem

Glück explores the complex relationships among mothers, children, and teachers, symbolized in the offering of apples.

"The School Children," from *The House on Marshland,* contains fragmented imagery and phrasing to show the disconnection of the children to both their mothers and their teachers, despite the ritual of the mother giving the apple to the child, who then gives it to the teacher. The children, the speaker says, "go forward with their little satchels," innocent yet businesslike. The mothers who "have labored to gather the late apples, red and gold" are the agents who smooth the way for their children to develop relationships with their teachers.

The teachers "wait behind great desks . . . to receive these offerings" and perhaps pass judgment on them, as they do the students' work. The next line, "How orderly they are" at first appears to refer to the teachers but is then found to describe "the nails on which the children hang their overcoats of blue or yellow wool." The blue and yellow, along with the red apples, convey the primary colors associated with childhood.

The children are further disconnected from the teachers who, the speaker says, "shall instruct them in silence," while the mothers "scour the orchards for a way out." Here the image of the detached teacher is contrasted with the desperation of the mother who perhaps lives vicariously through her children and the success she desires for them. This is further shown in the description of the "gray limbs of the fruit trees bearing so little ammunition," as if the apples are not only offerings but

Louise Glück

weapons against those who the mothers believe hold their children's destinies in their hands.

"THE DROWNED CHILDREN"

First published: 1980 (collected in *The Descending Figure*, 1980)
Type of work: Poem

In a matter-of-fact tone, a speaker observes children who have drowned and speculates about what death must be like for them.

In "The Drowned Children," from *The Descending Figure*, an onlooker comments on children who have fallen through the ice of a pond and drowned. With the cool detachment of the ice cracking, this speaker addresses the reader directly, describing how the children "have no judgment. So it is natural that they should drown." The "ice taking them in" and "their wool scarves floating behind them as they sink" convey the experiences of the children being swallowed by the water. Nevertheless, the pond lifts the children "in its manifold arms," keeping them buoyant at least temporarily.

The speaker determines that "death must come to them differently, so close to the beginning," as though not much time had elapsed since the children had been "blind and weightless," like babies. The images of "the lamp, the good white cloth that covered the table, their bodies" symbolize the light, warmth, and purity associated with children.

By describing how the children "hear the names they used like lures slipping over the pond," Glück refers to the children hearing their names called by their parents or calling one another's names on a day that demands nothing more than the simple pleasure of fishing. The voice at the end of the poem which asks what the children are waiting for and beckons them to "*come home, come home*" is silenced in an image of the children "*lost in the waters, blue and permanent.*"

"DESCENDING FIGURE"

First published: 1980 (collected in *The First Four Books of Poems*, 1995)
Type of work: Poem

The speaker describes her sadness for a sister who died and her own loneliness as a result of her sister's absence.

In a meditative tone, "Descending Figure" chronicles the grief process of the speaker, who longs for her dead sister.

The first of three sections, "The Wanderer" describes the persona going into the street at twilight. The contrast of the sun which "hung low" and "the iron sky, tinged with cold plumage" underscores the speaker's sense of dislocation, her longing to fill "this emptiness." She describes playing with her "other sister, whom death had made so lonely." The speaker's question, "Why was she never called?" emphasizes the idea of this sister being left out.

In the second section, "The Sick Child," the images of stars shining above a wooden chest and the child relaxing in her mother's arms are at first soothing, but the next line describing how "the mother does not sleep" but "stares fixedly into the bright museum" introduces a disturbing note, which is then confirmed by the statement, "By spring the child will die." The speaker decides that it is "wrong, wrong to hold her" and pleads with the mother, "Let her be alone, without memory."

The third section, "For My Sister," also begins on a hopeful note, with the speaker describing how her sister is "moving in her crib" but then adds a note of troubling surrealism with the next line: "The dead ones are like that." The speaker speculates that if her sister "had a voice, the cries of hunger would be beginning," and she concludes that she should go to her sister. The ending image of her sister with "skin so white, her head covered with black feathers" echoes the image of the sun's plumage against the iron sky in the first section of the poem.

"A Fantasy"

First published: 1990 (collected in *Ararat,* 1990)

Type of work: Poem

This work critiques the funeral as a ritual designed to help mourners cope with grief.

The title of this poem has a double meaning: the fantasy that a funeral can provide closure to grief plus the fantasy of moving backward to a time before the death of a loved one.

To set a tone to demystify death and destroy the illusion of mortality, the speaker begins the poem in a straightforward manner: "I'll tell you something: every day people are dying. And that's just the beginning." The "new widows" and "new orphans" who are born "sit with their hands folded," as if trying to stay calm in the midst of chaos, "trying to decide about this new life."

This state of disorientation and indecision continues as the mourners are described as "frightened of crying, sometimes of not crying." Someone has to "lean over" and tell them "what to do next." At the reception, the house is ironically described as "suddenly full of visitors," with the widow receiving the respects that the other mourners pay to her and bravely finding "something to say to everybody." She "thanks them, thanks them for coming," while secretly wanting them to leave so that she can go back to a previous time and place, to the cemetery, the "sickroom," and the hospital, traveling back in time "just a little, not so far as the marriage, the first kiss." This implies that the widow does not necessarily long for the marriage but a time when she did not have to decide what to do next with her life.

"The Wild Iris"

First published: 1992 (collected in *The Wild Iris,* 1992)

Type of work: Poem

This poem describes the experience of being buried and coming back to life through the metaphor of the wild iris.

"The Wild Iris" compares human suffering and finding a voice to the growth of the wild iris or any plant or flower that makes a "passage from the other world" underground despite the difficulty of breaking through. In the image of the wild iris, the explosion of color symbolizes new life.

The speaker describes a door which she sees "at the end of [her] suffering" and implores the reader/listener, "Hear me out: that which you call death I remember." Hearing the "branches of the pine shifting" as "the weak sun flickered over the dry surface" of the earth, this soul is only conscious of being "buried in the dark earth" alive, then feeling "the stiff earth bending a little." The image of "birds darting in low shrubs" underscores the movement from underground to aboveground and the vantage point of the speaker as she emerges from the earth. As she "returns from oblivion . . . to find a voice," she sees a "great fountain" with "deep blue shadows on azure seawater" gushing forth, not only as a wild iris appears but also as the voice does when it bursts into song or eloquent speech.

This theme of struggling to find a voice is a consistent one for Glück, who has gone through periods of more than a year without writing but then experienced periods of great productivity. She has described the liberation she felt after realizing that she could not write according to a schedule and would have to wait until the time felt right to her.

"Parable of the Hostages"

First published: 1996 (collected in *Meadowlands,* 1996)

Type of work: Poem

A speaker wonders whether soldiers are actually eager to go home after a war.

Set during the Trojan War, this poem describes "The Greeks sitting on the beach wondering what to do when the war ends." The speaker states that they do not really want to go home to their relatively mundane lives after the excitement and unpredictability of fighting at Troy.

Still, the soldiers realize that their "excuse for absence" will not be accepted because fighting a war is considered a better reason to stay in a place away from home than is "exploring one's capacity for diversion." Nevertheless, they do miss their families "a little." They begin to wonder: "What if war is just male version of dressing up, a game devised to avoid profound spiritual questions."

The soldiers feel not only the call of war but also the call of the world and its beauty, like "an opera beginning with the war's loud chords and ending with the floating aria of the sirens," or mermaids, who, with their beautiful, haunting voices, lured men to their doom. The temptation to stay in Troy is so strong that they calculate ten years as the time needed to get back to Ithaca. Hopelessly, the Greeks are hostages, "already enthralled," some by "dreams of pleasure, some by sleep, and some by music," and the longer they delay their journey, the more tightly they are caught in the "insoluble dilemma" of "how to divide the world's beauty into acceptable and unacceptable loves."

"VITA NOVA"

First published: 1999 (collected in *Vita Nova*, 1999)
Type of work: Poem

In images from childhood and a scene from a relationship that has ended, a rebirth or new life (the literal translation of "Vita Nova") is described.

In a poem which begins and ends her book of the same name, Glück describes a past relationship that causes the speaker to reconsider her life by looking back at her childhood, when she remembers "laughter for no cause, simply because the world is beautiful" or "because the air is full of apple blossoms." In such images of spring, as well as images of courtship ("young men buying tickets for the ferryboats" and "a young man [who] throws his hat into the water"), Glück describes "the mo-

ment vivid, intact" that causes her to wake "hungry for life, utterly confident." Still, she recognizes her own mortality in the spring appearing "not as a lover but a messenger of death." The message is "meant tenderly," however, as a gentle reminder to seize the day.

The "Vita Nova" that ends the book recreates a scene from the failed relationship, with the couple arguing over who will get custody of their dog, Blizzard. The woman explains to the dog, as if he is a child, that "Daddy" is leaving "Mommy" because the kind of love he wants, she, "too ironic," cannot give him.

After a surreal image of the dog growing into a poet, she concludes that "Life is very weird, no matter how it ends, very filled with dreams" and promises that she will never forget the image of her dog with his "frantic human eyes swollen with tears." She thought her "life was over" and her "heart was broken." Whether this is from the failed relationship, losing custody of the dog, or both is unclear, but she moves to Cambridge where, it is implied, she begins a new life.

"EARTHLY LOVE"

First published: 1999 (collected in *Vita Nova*, 1999)
Type of work: Poem

The speaker describes a recently ended relationship, noting the ways in which happiness therein was illusory, but states that she has no regrets about the experience.

The first line of "Earthly Love" comments on a couple and how "conventions of the time held them together." This notion, combined with the title of the poem, makes the speaker seem to be looking down on earth from above, commenting on the awkwardness of mortals as they navigate the challenges of relationships. "The heart once given freely" says the speaker, is now "required as a formal gesture."

The second stanza shifts to the first-person plural perspective, in which the speaker comments, "Fortunately we diverged from these requirements," reinforcing with her smug tone how her complacency was destroyed when her life shattered. In stating "We are all human," the speaker shows how people can protect themselves as well as deceive themselves, "even to the point of denying clarity." Ironically, she says, "within this deception, true happiness occurred." She states that this happiness, which may or may not have been built on illusion, "has its own reality" and will end no matter what. The speaker seems to be saying that true happiness is such a rare and fragile state that it cannot last and that the illusion of happiness cannot last because illusions must be destroyed.

SUMMARY

Known for her precision of language in declarative sentences rather than description, Glück has shown that poetry need not have its own vocabulary to be poetry. Her poems are not designed to call attention to words but to images, statements, and questions about the motivations of humans and why they keep performing certain rituals, no matter what the potential loss, perhaps because that is what makes them human. Through continual experimentation and practice of her craft, Glück has achieved a transparence in her poetry that lets the truth shine through.

Holly L. Norton

BIBLIOGRAPHY

By the Author

POETRY:
Firstborn, 1968
The House on Marshland, 1975
Descending Figure, 1980
The Triumph of Achilles, 1985
Ararat, 1990
The Wild Iris, 1992
The First Four Books of Poems, 1995
Meadowlands, 1996
The First Five Books of Poems, 1997
Vita Nova, 1999
The Seven Ages, 2001
October, 2004

NONFICTION:
Proofs and Theories: Essays on Poetry, 1994

About the Author

Diehl, Joanne Feit, ed. *On Louise Glück: Change What You See.* Ann Arbor: University of Michigan Press, 2005.
Dodd, Elizabeth. "Louise Glück: The Ardent Understatement of Postconfessional Classicism." In *The Veiled Mirror and the Woman Poet: H. D., Louise Bogan, Elizabeth Bishop, and Louise Glück.* Columbia: University of Missouri Press, 1992.
Harrison, DeSales. *The End of the Mind: The Edge of the Intelligible in Hardy, Stevens, Larkin, Plath, and Glück.* New York: Routledge, 2004.
Upton, Lee. *Defensive Measures: The Poetry of Niedecker, Bishop, Glück, and Carson.* Lewisburg, Pa.: Bucknell University Press, 2005.
_____. "Fleshless Voices: Louise Glück's Rituals of Abjection and Oblivion." In *The Muse of Abandonment: Origin, Identity, Mastery in Five American Poets.* Lewisburg, Pa.: Bucknell University Press, 1998.

DISCUSSION TOPICS

- How would you describe the voices of the speakers in Louise Glück's poems? In what tones do you imagine them speaking?

- In Glück's poems featuring children, how does she avoid the sentimentality that is so often associated with portrayals of children?

- What words would you use to describe the romantic relationships in Glück's poems? How do they compare to conventional images and descriptions of romantic love?

- What characteristics of parables do Glück's parable poems have? How do they differ from classical parables?

- How does Glück uses images from nature to relate to human nature?

Mary Gordon

Born: Far Rockaway, New York
December 8, 1949

Gordon is a brilliant stylist whose fiction explores human love and its limitations and the familial, religious, and cultural legacies impinging upon modern Americans and their communities.

Eileen Barroso/Columbia University

BIOGRAPHY

Mary Catherine Gordon was born in Far Rockaway, New York, on December 8, 1949. Her mother, Anna Gagliano Gordon, was the daughter of Italian and Irish immigrants and a devout Catholic. David Gordon, her father, was born in Ohio. He converted from Judaism to Catholicism in the 1930's.

As a young child, Gordon was cared for by her father, who stayed at home with her while her mother supported the family by working as a legal secretary, despite the crippling effects of childhood polio. David Gordon, a lively and literate man, who was educated at Harvard University, enthusiastically fostered his daughter's intellectual development. Although he died when she was seven, he had already begun to teach her French, Greek, and philosophy and had transmitted to her his devotion to Catholicism.

After her father's death, Gordon attended Holy Name of Mary School in her predominantly Catholic working-class neighborhood in Valley Stream, Long Island. She had literary aspirations quite early. While in grade school, she dreamed of becoming both a poet and a nun. At Mary Louis Academy, a Catholic girls' school in Queens, Gordon rebelled against the Church, but she continued her literary efforts. In 1967, Gordon won a scholarship to Barnard College of Columbia University, where she knew she could escape from the sheltered Catholic community in which she had been reared. She has stated that her experiences at Barnard, especially in the novelist Elizabeth Hardwick's creative writing course, changed her life. At the time Gordon was writing nothing but poetry; Hardwick advised her to switch to prose. She did so. After graduating from Barnard in 1971, Gordon enrolled in the writing program at Syracuse University. She received her M.A. in 1973 and remained at Syracuse in the English Ph.D. program. During that period, she met James Brain, a British anthropologist, whom she married in 1974.

Between 1975 and 1988, Gordon published some sixty-five short stories, reviews, and other articles. Twenty of her short stories were reprinted in the volume *Temporary Shelter* (1987). Many of those stories address themes that recur in her novels, human love and loss, parent-child relationships, and the Irish immigrant experience in the United States.

From 1974 to 1978, Gordon was an instructor of freshman composition at Dutchess Community College in Poughkeepsie, New York. In 1975, she began writing her first novel, *Final Payments*. It was rejected by several publishers, even though she rewrote the novel a number of times. Finally, Hardwick suggested that Gordon change the narration from the third person to the first. After Gordon did so, Random House accepted the novel. It was published in the spring of 1978. Like her subsequent novels, *Final Payments* was a critical and popular success.

Gordon's first marriage ended in divorce. In 1979, she married Arthur Cash, an English professor, and moved to New Paltz, New York. She began teaching at Amherst College in Massachusetts. She also began work on her second novel, *The Company of Women*, which was published in 1980. *Men and Angels*, her third novel, appeared in 1985, and *The Other Side*, her fourth, in 1989. In 1988, Gordon had begun teaching courses at Barnard College. She had two children, Anna Gordon and David Dess Gordon. Gordon has acknowledged a number of influences on her work. Among the earliest were the language of religious devotions, the language and structure of the Roman Catholic Mass, which she attended daily, the small world of Roman Catholicism in which she grew up, and stories of saints' lives, which afforded vivid images of heroic women who were not dependent upon men for their identities. She has cited James Joyce's *Dubliners* (1914), Simone Weil's *Attente de Dieu* (1950; *Waiting for God*, 1951), and the novels of Virginia Woolf, Margaret Drabble, and J. F. Powers as major influences on her fiction. Among Catholic writers, she especially admires Georges Bernanos, the author of *Journal d'un cure de campagne* (1936; *Diary of a Country Priest*, 1937), which she considers the greatest of all religious novels.

ANALYSIS

To categorize Gordon as simply an American Irish Catholic novelist is too narrow. She is also a feminist, a lyrical realist, an astute diagnostician of human relationships, and a brilliant prose stylist. Yet her ethnic and religious heritage figures prominently in her fiction as both source and subject.

Just as Gordon addresses her own background in much of her fiction, so all of her major characters try to come to terms with their pasts. Concern with one's past, especially one's childhood, has been a salient feature of Western literature and society at least since the late eighteenth century. In the twentieth century, this concern was closely connected with the predominant schools of modern psychology, particularly the Freudian. Mary Gordon is rare among modern novelists in that she does not embed her explorations of human life in psychological theory at the expense of its spiritual and theological dimensions. Indeed, Scripture, rather than psychological theory, is frequently her reference point.

Gordon does not equate art, including the art of fiction, with religion or even with morality. She has written:

An experience to be properly religious must include three things: an ethical component, the possibility of full participation by the entire human community and acknowledgment of the existence of a life beyond the human. Art need do none of these things, although it may.

These three dimensions of religious experience emerge as implicit or explicit concerns in all of Gordon's novels.

The strongest ethical component in her works is their close examination of human love. She has commented that "love is the source of any moral vision that's worth anything." She effectively dramatizes the dynamics of love between friends and between parents and children, as well as the challenges posed by those people who are apparently unlovable. She has been criticized for delineating romantic and marital relationships sketchily in her first three novels, but the marriage of Ellen and Vincent MacNamara in *The Other Side* is presented vividly and in depth.

Gordon's depiction of communities is a natural extension of her treatments of individual relationships. *The Company of Women* and *The Other Side* are especially remarkable as detailed and realistic examinations of the ways in which communities succeed or fail and of their influence upon children. Gordon pays particular attention to figures who attempt to dominate their communities—Father Cyprian and Robert Cavendish in *The Company of Women*, for example, and Ellen MacNamara in *The Other Side*. The religious ideal of "full participation by the entire human community" remains largely unrealized in Gordon's novels, as their characters typically endeavor to protect their identities by excluding others. This ideal of full participation is always implicit, however, and is frequently dreamed of by Gordon's characters.

Most of Gordon's major characters acknowledge the existence or at least ponder seriously the possibility of a life beyond the human. Those characters, raised as traditional Catholics, struggle with questions that are closely related to faith in a supreme being. How best can one know God? Who or what is authoritative, in a world where the authority of the Church is weakened or absent? Part of Gordon's project as a novelist is, it seems, to dramatize individuals in the context of their subjectivity. Consequently, one narrative convention that she consistently avoids is that of the omniscient narrator who speaks in a morally normative voice. Instead, she has the reader listen to her characters' first-person voices or to their interior monologues as they strive to see life steadily and wholly, while limited in their vision by ideological, psychological, or circumstantial blinders.

Gordon's prose style, in its solidity of physical detail, its abundance of metaphors and similes, militates constantly against what she has called the "twin dangers of the religious life," dualism and abstractionism. One thinks, for example, of the wealth of detail about Catholic schooling in the first two novels and about Vincent MacNamara's work on the New York subways in *The Other Side*. The fact that Gordon's most engaging characters tend to be witty reveals a lively appreciation of life in the physical human world. In *Final Payments*, for example, Liz assesses Isabel Moore's disastrous hairstyle thus: "Who did your hair? Annette Funicello?" Isabel reflects, "It was a miracle to me, the solidity of that joke. Even the cutting edge of it was a miracle. And our laughter was solid. It stirred the air and hung above us like rings of bone that shivered in the cold, gradual morning."

In her fiction, Gordon strives to find images to render "the highest possible justice to the visible world." She is eager, she says, "to get the right rhythm for the inner life, and the combination of image and rhythm to pin down an internal state is terribly important to me. At least as important as any sort of moral report of the world."

FINAL PAYMENTS

First published: 1978
Type of work: Novel

A young woman comes to terms with her past after the death of her father, an invalid whom she nursed for eleven years.

Final Payments begins and ends with its central character and narrator, Isabel Moore, contemplating the death of her father. For eleven years before his death, she cared for him in his illness. Now, at age thirty, she is determined to invent a life for herself. Before she can embrace life fully, however, Isabel

must learn to acknowledge and accept the risks it poses and must come to terms with the legacy she has inherited.

This legacy is cultural, philosophical, emotional, and material. Isabel was raised in a conservative Irish-Catholic neighborhood in Queens, New York. Motherless from age two, she spent her childhood intensely influenced by her father, Joe Moore, a brilliant and opinionated professor vehement in his traditional Catholicism, and by Margaret Casey, their unattractive, life-denying housekeeper, whose jealous devotion to Isabel's father was as strong as her dislike and disapproval of Isabel, who came to return such feelings. Isabel's intelligence, wit, elegance, and even her disdain for housework were cultivated in calculated opposition to Margaret's ways.

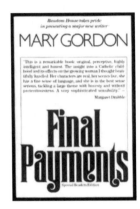

Behind Joe Moore's authority stood the authority of the Church and its educational system, from which Isabel inherited her intellectual legacy. Entailed in this legacy are a respect for authority and a valuing of love as synonymous with life. Isabel learned to love her father in part because he was so certain he was right. Such authority, however, breeds rebellion and courts betrayal. At nineteen, Isabel betrayed her father by having an affair with David Lowe, his favorite student. Three weeks after finding the couple in bed together, Joe Moore suffered a stroke, and for the following eleven years Isabel lived a life of expiation, nursing him and keeping house.

Isabel knew that she had violated the moral standards of both her father and the Church. She comes to confront the conflicts that arise between other-worldly spiritual imperatives and earthly needs. Isabel is perplexed by her desire for pleasure. Is pleasure a good? If not, why does it exist? Is it something for which one must always pay in the end? Isabel has been taught that love is self-sacrifice and that it is the key to identity. How, then, can one live, if the only way to have an identity is to sacrifice one's very being? Throughout the novel, Isabel contemplates Jesus's paradoxical dictum that one must lose one's life in order to save it.

Her father's death leaves Isabel free but stunned and confused. She is as yet unable to acknowledge the full import of losing him, and at his funeral she does not weep. The middle chapters of *Final Payments* chronicle her first attempts to move forward. She is aided by two women friends, Eleanor and Liz, whose love and support contrast significantly with Joe Moore's unbearable emotional demands. Isabel buys new clothes, sells the house she inherited, sets up her own apartment, and secures a job investigating home health care for the elderly. She reflects constantly about the needs of the people with whom she works.

In most of her relationships, Isabel has felt cheated in the act of giving and guilty in the act of getting. Her years of nursing her father left her feeling that she had given up her life for him. Her guilt-inducing relationship with David Lowe is repeated in kind after her father's death. First she humiliates herself by having sex with Liz's husband. After Liz forgives her, Isabel proceeds to fall in love with a married man, Hugh Slade. When Hugh's wife finds out about the affair and confronts her, the guilt-ridden Isabel embarks upon yet another course of expiation.

Isabel chooses the life of a martyr, believing that it will be her salvation. She goes to live with Margaret Casey, devoting herself to the one person she is least capable of loving. She suffers Margaret's insults and ingratitude; she sacrifices her own beauty by overeating and gaining an enormous amount of weight and by acquiescing to Margaret's malicious suggestion that she get her beautiful long hair cut and styled unattractively. Depressed, she spends most of her time sleeping. At this low point, Isabel is aided by what is best in her past: her friends and her Catholic habits of mind. Her old friend Father Mulcahy warns her that she is sinning by killing herself slowly. Clearly, losing one's life in order to find it is not to be equated with destroying oneself, body and spirit.

The import of her own self-destructiveness comes to Isabel in a way that is full of saving ironies. Jealous about Isabel's visit from Father Mulcahy, Margaret insinuates that Isabel has been behaving improperly with the priest. In the raging quarrel that ensues, Isabel is reminded of a Gospel passage: "The poor you have always with you: but me you have not always." She interprets these words of Jesus as meaning that the pleasures of life must be taken, because death will deprive a person of them soon enough. She realizes that she has been trying to second-guess death, to give up all she loves so that she will never lose it. On Good Friday, she comes to acknowledge in Christ' death the mortality of everyone she has loved. Only now is she able to weep for her father. She realizes that "the greatest love meant only, finally, the greatest danger." In accepting the danger of loss, Isabel affirms life and love.

Isabel then makes her final payment to her past, losing her old life to find renewal in relinquishing her material legacy. She gives Margaret a check for twenty thousand dollars, the money she received from the sale of her father's house. She rejects strict orthodoxy and returns to her friends. In doing so she preserves the spiritual core of her past; from her Catholic legacy there emerges a Christian redemption.

THE COMPANY OF WOMEN

First published: 1981
Type of work: Novel

A girl raised by a company of Catholic women and their spiritual adviser searches for "ordinary human happiness."

The New York Catholic upbringing of Felicitas Taylor, the central character in *The Company of Women*, is in one respect a near photographic negative of that of Isabel Moore in *Final Payments*. While Isabel was motherless and raised by her widowed father, Felicitas's father is dead, and she has not only a mother but three godmothers as well. Each of these four women has been independent of a husband for many years. The practical and wise Charlotte Taylor has worked as a secretary to support Felicitas ever since her husband's death, just six months after Felicitas was born. Good-humored Mary Rose is a motion-picture theater usher, whose husband has been confined for thirty years to an insane asylum. Clare, an elegant, independent-minded woman, manages a Manhattan leather-goods store. Elizabeth, fragile and impractical, is a schoolteacher, full of imagination and a love for poetry. Hovering in the shadows, never really one of this company of women, is Muriel, who is reminiscent of both the bitter uninvited godmother in "Sleeping Beauty" and the jealous housekeeper, Margaret Casey, in *Final Payments*. These women came to know one another through Father Cyprian, a conservative Catholic priest, whose retreats for working women they attended during the late 1930's. Father Cyprian is like Joe Moore in *Final Payments* in his respect for the Church, his anger at modern society, and his role as an authority figure over the women in his life.

Part 1 of the novel is set in 1963. Its narrative weaves in and out of the minds of these various characters. Love, community, and continuity between generations are crucial themes. Felicitas is the central focus of concern; at fourteen, she is seen by Father Cyprian and the company of women as their hope for the future. Father Cyprian makes her his protégée, teaching her theology , as well as skills such as carpentry, which one would not expect a woman to know. Felicitas sees that Cyprian is bullheaded, dictatorial, and self-centered. These weaknesses distress Felicitas, but even so, she becomes enveloped in his love and determined never to leave him.

Leave him she does, however, when, in part 2 of the novel, dated 1969-1970, Felicitas enrolls at Barnard College to study classics. She has rebelled against her upbringing: She has discarded her faith; secretly she has even been attending peace marches. At Barnard, Felicitas discovers the counterculture. She becomes infatuated with Robert Cavendish, her handsome and charismatic political science professor, who takes her first to bed and then to live at his apartment, which he shares with two young women and a small child who was named Mao, as a tribute to the Chinese Communist leader. Clearly Felicitas's life with Robert and his friends is meant by Gordon as a deliberate contrast to her childhood. Robert is a parodic, shallow version of Father Cyprian; both men surround themselves with women that they can dominate.

What Felicitas seeks consistently is what she calls "ordinary human happiness." She senses that in the context of human community, love is the key to such happiness. However, Robert's commune proves itself as false and inadequate a community as Robert is a lover. Spurning an exclusive relationship, he goads Felicitas to sleep with someone else. Finding herself pregnant and unsure of who fathered the fetus, she seeks an abortion, which in 1970 was an illegal procedure. Horrified at seeing a woman being hustled out of the backstreet clinic, ill and bleeding, Felicitas rushes home to her mother.

Part 3 of the novel is set seven years later, in 1977. Felicitas and her mother are living in western New York near Father Cyprian's retirement home. Elizabeth, Clare, and Muriel live nearby. The hopes of the group are now focused on Felicitas's daughter Linda. Felicitas's own plan is to prepare Linda for ordinary human life, in contrast to the way she was trained by Father Cyprian, who wanted her to be extraordinary. Felicitas intends to marry Leo, a local hardware store owner, in order to give Linda a father and a normal home. True to her name, Felicitas tries to pass on her hope for happiness to her daughter.

This section of the novel is a series of interior monologues by the major characters. However, while in the earlier part of the novel Gordon used the third-person point of view to present the perspectives of various characters, now she changes to first-person narration. In this way, she gives each character a chance to present his or her own last word, completely unmediated. Appropriately, the closing monologue is given to Linda, who represents the future. In it, she muses about love and wonders what happens to it after death. Her final words are, "We are not dying." Like those words, *The Company of Women* offers a qualified affirmation of life on earth, celebrating its possibilities and recognizing its limitations.

MEN AND ANGELS

First published: 1985
Type of work: Novel

The need to give and receive love is dramatized through the tragic relationship of a professional woman and the mentally disturbed babysitter of her children.

In *Men and Angels*, Gordon continues her examination of human love and its limitations and of female identity. She explores these issues in the contexts of work, friendship, motherhood, and male-female relationships. Set in the 1980's in the fictitious small college town of Selby, Massachusetts, this novel dramatizes, in alternating chapters, the sharply contrasting perspectives of two women, Laura Post and Anne Foster. Although in this novel Gordon moves beyond the world of New York Irish Catholicism, she gives this complex and compelling novel a well-defined religious perspective. Its title and epigraph are the words of Saint Paul: "Though I speak with the tongues of men and of angels, and have not charity, I am become as sounding brass, or a tinkling cymbal."

At the outset, neither Laura Post nor Anne Foster fully understands Saint Paul's words; neither has come to terms effectively with her own needs to love and to be loved. The spiritual conditions of both women fail to empower them: Laura's spirituality is diseased, while Anne's is undeveloped. Their relationship proves to be a fatal combination.

Rejected cruelly in childhood by her mother and neglected by her father, twenty-year-old Laura Post has drifted into the byways of fundamentalist and charismatic religious cults. She has come to address the absence of human love in her life by convincing herself that the Holy Spirit has summoned her to teach children that such love—especially family love—is unimportant. Armed with her Bible, from which she has gleaned texts that seem to reinforce this conviction, Laura comes to Selby, where she meets Anne Foster, who, despite some misgivings, hires her as a live-in babysitter for her children, Peter, age nine, and Sarah, age six.

Laura soon becomes enamored of Anne. She imagines that the Holy Spirit is calling her to save Anne's soul by freeing her from her family so that she can live alone with Laura, who will lead her to the Lord. On the surface, Laura is reliable and diligent in her babysitting and household chores, but Anne distrusts her and finds her unlikable and intrusive. One day Anne discovers that her suspicions were well founded: Laura endangers the children's lives by leading them onto thin ice. Enraged, Anne immediately fires Laura. In despair, Laura takes revenge by carving Anne's name on her wrists and bleeding to death in the bathtub. She leaves the water running, and Anne and her children return home to find a pool of bloodied water in the living room. It is Peter who discovers Laura's dead body.

The chapters that are narrated from Laura's point of view powerfully dramatize the workings of an unbalanced mind obsessed with terrible memories and longings. Laura's thoughts are rendered in sentences whose syntactical simplicity conveys her inability to reason effectually. She is haunted by biblical passages and stories whose sense she passionately contorts. By contrast, Anne's chapters are more deeply reflective than Laura's. One dimension of Anne's experience that broadens and deepens her perspective is her work. Anne is an art historian who is studying the work of Caroline Watson, a neglected but brilliant twentieth century artist. She discovers that Caroline neglected and discouraged her son Stephen, a frustrated artist, who killed himself. Caroline's efforts to forge a career for herself lead Anne to reflect upon her own professional life. Although she is determined not to sacrifice her children to her career, there are some similarities between Laura's suicide and that of Stephen.

Although Anne believed at first that her anger in firing Laura was justified, and although Laura was indeed more dangerous than she could have suspected, Anne is left understanding that, Laura's madness notwithstanding, in her failure to love Laura she is at least partly responsible for her death. Anne has indeed proved capable of loving others, her friends, her husband, and her children, and that love has been returned, even if, as in the case of her marriage, imperfectly at times. Laura, however, was seemingly unlovable; even after her death, Anne can mourn for her but does not find that she loves her, and she is perplexed by this limitation. She is perplexed as well by her new understanding of the ways in which mother love, supposedly the strongest of human bonds, is limited. She realizes that no matter how fervently she may love her children, she cannot protect them from the world's ravages or from their own mistakes.

THE OTHER SIDE

First published: 1989
Type of work: Novel

Four generations of an Irish American immigrant family struggle with their emotional legacies of love and anger.

Gordon's fourth novel is one of the most vivid presentations in American fiction of the experiences of Irish immigrants in the twentieth century. Centering on the life histories of Vincent and Ellen MacNamara and depicting the lives of their children, grandchildren, and great-grandchildren as well, *The Other Side* is also an intricate and perceptive examination of the dynamics of familial relationships.

Unlike the conventional generational sagas of popular fiction, *The Other Side* is not linear in structure. The novel focuses on a single day in August, 1985, at the home in Queens Village, New York, in which Ellen and Vincent MacNamara have lived since 1922. The extended family has gathered to welcome the eighty-eight-year-old Vincent home from his long stay in a nursing home, where he has been recovering from a broken hip he suffered when Ellen, a stroke victim suffering from mental disorientation, knocked him to the floor. Although Vincent prefers the friendly community of the nursing home, he is returning home to fulfill a promise he made to Ellen sixty years ago, that he would let her die in her own bed, with him there, rather than among strangers. Moving back and forth in time through the inner reflections of diverse family members, Gordon pieces together a patterned whole whose configurations resemble those of an elaborate patchwork quilt.

The novel is divided into five long sections. Sections 1, 3, and 5 shift in focus from one character to another; their variety of viewpoints balances section 2, told from Ellen's perspective, and section 4, told from Vincent's.

Vincent is motivated primarily by love—for his wife, for his children and grandchildren, for his friends, and for life itself. He seeks genuine enjoyment for himself and for those he loves, and although he is a very old man, he is hungry for life. Vincent's problem is that he can no longer afford Ellen any enjoyment beyond her satisfaction, which she probably will be unable to communicate to him and indeed may never be able fully to feel, of knowing that he has kept his promise not to abandon her. In the final sentence of the novel, as Vincent enters Ellen's room, the reader finds that "he believes that she can see him, but he's not quite sure." Vincent's power of loving is a power of protectiveness, a crucial issue in Gordon's fiction.

Paradoxically, the emotion that has ruled Ellen's life was, in its inception, also protective in kind, even though most of the results have been de-

structive. Ellen has lived most of her life in passionate anger. As a child in Ireland, she was enraged by her father's abandonment of her mother, who was driven half mad by a series of failed pregnancies. Eventually her rage empowered her to leave Ireland for America, on "the other side" of the Atlantic Ocean, and to find a new life, but she never put this rage behind her. Despite her husband's protective love and his integrity, she diffused her rage toward other targets—priests, employers, politicians, her daughters, even Vincent himself. Ellen's anger comes down hard upon the succeeding generations of MacNamaras, for Vincent's love proves insufficient as a shield. Her rage is almost palpable in its active force, while Vincent's love is relatively passive. The power to wound, Gordon implies, is stronger than the power to heal.

The other sections of the novel show how the rest of the family has fared. Ironically, John, the only child of hers whom Ellen could love, died in World War II. Her daughter Magdalene suffers from agoraphobia and alcoholism. Theresa, her other daughter, tries to hide her malice and anger at her mother's failure to love her behind a facade of charismatic religiosity. All the descendants of Ellen and Vincent are scarred in some critical way. Two of them, however, emerge as potential survivors, Dan and Cam, the grandchildren whom Ellen took into her home and fostered.

Cam has inherited her grandmother's energy, but it has emerged not as rage but as resourcefulness in the face of difficulty. Despite childlessness, a sexless marriage, and a selfishly domineering mother, Cam has succeeded in defining a satisfying life for herself. She has a lover who cherishes her, professional fulfillment, and the personal strengths of self-respect, keen intelligence, and lively wit. Dan, her cousin and partner in law practice, reveals tenderness and reflectiveness that are like his grandfather's: "He sees the wholeness of all life, the intricate connecting tissue. It is this, this terrible endeavor, this impossible endeavor. Simply to live a life." Dan's response to his family and even to his clients is that he "would like to embrace them all. He would like to say: You must believe this. I understand you all." This same faith, vision, understanding, and compassion are implicit throughout *The Other Side*; they are the essence of Gordon's outlook.

PEARL

First published: 2004
Type of work: Novel

A daughter's determination to sacrifice her life for a cause brings her mother and her mother's best friend to reexamines their lives and their values.

Mary Gordon's novel *Pearl* begins with a phone call on Christmas night, 1998, from the American embassy in Dublin, Ireland, to Maria Meyers in New York. To her horror, Maria learns that her twenty-year-old daughter Pearl, who had gone to Ireland to study the Irish language, has chained herself to the embassy flagpole, evidently as a protest for peace. Pearl has not eaten for six weeks, and because she has now begun to refuse water as well as food, she is near death from dehydration. In desperation, the embassy has telephoned Maria, hoping that her appearance will convince Pearl to relent.

Maria arranges to take the next plane to Dublin. Before she leaves, however, she telephones her oldest friend, Joseph Kasperman, in Rome, knowing that he will come to Dublin to offer whatever aid he can. Kasperman grew up with Maria; his mother was hired as a housekeeper for the Meyers family after Pearl's mother died. Pearl's affection for him is evident in that one of the letters she had written in anticipation of her death was to Kasperman; the other, of course, was to her mother. In the letters, Pearl admits that she knows her death will cause them pain, but she hopes that they will understand.

Although the novel is written in the third person, the perspective is always a limited one. Sometimes it is that of Pearl, often that of Maria, and at other times that of Kasperman. Pearl has finally been unchained and taken to a hospital, where she lies, sedated, her hands tied to prevent her from removing the tubes that keep her alive. Through her thoughts, the author gradually reveals the events

that brought Pearl to her decision, among them her feelings of guilt for calling a mentally challenged boy "stupid," which she thinks caused him to be run over some time later.

On their way to Dublin, both Kasperman and Maria relive the past. After their arrival, since for some days they are forbidden to see Pearl, they continue this process. Though she was reared as a devout Catholic, in the 1960's Maria became a convert to the radical Left. Even her daughter's very existence symbolized Maria's new faith; Pearl's father was a Cambodian doctor who returned to his country certain that he would be killed. Although Maria was unable to get arrested, she exhibited her principles by making Pearl attend an inner-city school, where she was bullied and poorly taught. Maria now sees that she set Pearl on her present path by teaching her that principles were more important than people. Ironically, Kasperman now sees that he made the same mistake. By making his wife's musical career the sole purpose of their life together, he ignored their human needs and doomed their marriage.

In the end, all three characters realize that in becoming slaves to abstract principles, they have denied their humanity and that of others. What is essential, they now know, is not a grand gesture of self-abnegation but a life in which every day one loves and forgives others and, just as important, forgives oneself.

THE SHADOW MAN: A DAUGHTER'S SEARCH FOR HER FATHER

First published: 1996
Type of work: Memoir

In her attempt to find out who and what her father was, the author discovers a great deal about her family and herself.

The Shadow Man: A Daughter's Search for Her Father is a true story. Because he died when she was seven, Mary Gordon's father was indeed no more than a shadowy presence in her life. Her image of him was derived from her limited memories and from the scraps of his writings that she had in her possession.

Gordon had used her impressions of him in creating fictional characters, and she also had written meditations about his death. However, in her middle forties, she still did not know who he really was. Gordon could not obtain any information from her mother, who was in a nursing home, her memory largely gone. However, as a skilled researcher, Gordon knows how to search out facts. This memoir is the account of her search.

The book is divided into five sections. "Knowing My Father" is a collection of her recollections. Gordon begins with his death and a description of the changes that took place in her own life as a result of it. She then moves on to what she calls "films," fragments that show him with his daughter, taking her places, talking with her. Unfortunately, she is no longer sure about the accuracy of these memories, and therefore she does now know whether her father really was the man she thinks she remembers.

One way to solve the mystery, Gordon realized, was to read what her father had written. She knew that he could translate Vergil; she believed that he had gone to Harvard and then immersed himself in bohemian life in Paris and in London. Years before, she had found his articles and poems in some of the premier publications of his time. She also knew that in the 1920's he had published a pornographic magazine. Rereading his other articles, however, she finds something much more troubling: that at the very time the Nazis were bent on exterminating the Jews, her father, himself of Jewish ancestry, was mocking his own people and justifying the Holocaust. Against this shocking discovery, Gordon must balance the tender letters that her father wrote to her while he was on his deathbed.

In "Tracking My Father: In the Archives," Gordon discovers that her father had lied about the date and place of his birth, that he never went to Harvard and never traveled abroad—in short, that he was not the person he pretended to be. In the next section, "Seeing Past the Evidence," Gordon attempts to reconcile these upsetting truths with her faith in her father's love for her. Finally, in "Transactions Made Among the Living," she fits what she now knows of her father with what she can guess about his life with her mother. She knows that he was never accepted by his wife's family. It troubles Gordon that he was buried with them. She decides to have his remains moved to a cemetery that she often passed when she was with him.

The reburying of her father is in a sense also a resurrection. After losing her faith in him and in her loving memories, the author forgave him, and in that way she has regained him. Like many of Gordon's novels, *The Shadow Man* thus ends with the insistence that only charity, in the Christian sense, can give one hope for the future.

SUMMARY

From *Final Payments* to *Pearl*, Gordon's literary technique has become increasingly complex and experimental, especially in her approach to structure and point of view. Her outlook on life broadens, deepens, and darkens. The fact that life is chancy and perplexing becomes successively more apparent in her fiction. While her characters' futures appear less and less promising, those individuals nevertheless remain affirmative of human life on earth, as does their author. In the course of Gordon's novels, the world of organized religion becomes less and less central, but the author's religious perspective becomes more subtly implicit.

Eileen Tess Tyler;
updated by Rosemary M. Canfield Reisman

BIBLIOGRAPHY

By the Author

LONG FICTION:
Final Payments, 1978
The Company of Women, 1980
Men and Angels, 1985
The Other Side, 1989
Spending: A Utopian Divertimento, 1998
Pearl, 2004

SHORT FICTION:
Temporary Shelter, 1987
The Rest of Life: Three Novellas, 1993

NONFICTION:
Good Boys and Dead Girls, and Other Essays, 1991
The Shadow Man: A Daughter's Search for Her Father, 1996
Joan of Arc, 2000
Seeing Through Places: Reflections on Geography and Identity, 2000
Conversations with Mary Gordon, 2002 (Alma Bennett, editor)

About the Author

Bennett, Alma. *Mary Gordon.* New York: Twayne, 1996.

Gordon, Mary. "Getting from Here to There: A Writer's Reflections on a Religious Past." In *Spiritual Quests: The Art and Craft of Religious Writing,* edited by William Zinsser. Boston: Houghton Mifflin, 1988.

Juhasz, Suzanne. "Mother Writing and the Narrative of Maaternal Subjectivity." In *A Desire for Women.* New Brunswick, N.J.: Rutgers University Press, 2003.

Labrie, Ross. *The Catholic Imagination in American Literature.* Columbia: University of Missouri Press, 1997.

Leonard, John. "Mary Gordon's Father Runs Away from Home." In *When the Kissing Had to Stop.* New York: New Press, 1999.

Mahon, Eleanor B. "The Displaced Balance: Mary Gordon's *Men and Angels.*" In *Mother Puzzles: Daughters and Mothers in Contemporary American Literature,* edited by Mickey Pearlman. Westport, Conn.: Greenwood Press, 1989.

Mahon, John W. "Mary Gordon: The Struggle with Love." In *American Women Writing Fiction: Memory, Identity, Family, Space,* edited by Mickey Pearlman. Lexington: University Press of Kentucky, 1989.

Sheldon, Barbara H. *Daughters and Fathers in Feminist Novels.* New York: Peter Lang, 1997.

Smiley, Pamela. "The Unspeakable: Mary Gordon and the Angry Mother's Voices." In *Violence, Silence, and Anger: Women's Writing as Transgression,* edited by Deirdre Lashgari. Charlottesville: University Press of Virginia, 1995.

DISCUSSION TOPICS

- What evidence is there in Mary Gordon's work of her Roman Catholic background?
- How do the themes of guilt and redemption appear in Gordon's works?
- How does the theme of forgiveness function in Gordon's works?
- How does Gordon characterize a good marriage? A destructive marriage?
- What difficulties does Gordon point out in the relationships between mothers and daughters?
- Gordon's novels often show a close relationship between a well-meaning but domineering man, perhaps a father or a priest, and a younger girl or woman. To what extent are these relationships beneficial? When do they become destructive?
- Gordon's novels are often open-ended. What do you think would happen to her characters in the future?

JOHN GUARE

Born: New York, New York
February 5, 1938

Smith & Kraus

A New York born-and-bred dramatist, Guare writes increasingly sophisticated farces about the impact of the American Dream on lives shaped by contemporary cultural forces.

BIOGRAPHY

John Guare was born in Manhattan on February 5, 1938, to John Edward and Helen Clare (Grady) Guare. Shortly after his birth, his parents moved to Forest Hills, Queens, where he attended St. Joan of Arc Parochial School and, when old enough, was taken to mass every day by his mother.

Guare's father worked on Wall Street and had in earlier years been employed as office boy for George M. Cohan. Guare speaks of his very bright and unhappy parents, of listening to constant arguments between them and of hearing stories about his Hollywood uncle, Billy Grady. He heard stories about his uncle's having secretly signed Elizabeth Taylor to star in *National Velvet* (1944) and about Grady's managing the careers of Ruby Keeler, W. C. Fields, and Will Rogers. Exposed early to religion and Hollywood, he learned from direct experience about "Catholicism and show biz," which he referred to as "full of dreams and phoney promises."

Guare graduated from Georgetown University in 1961 and went on to receive his M.A. in English at Yale University in 1963. He was a fellow at Yale's Saybrook College from 1977 to 1978 and adjunct professor from 1977 to 1981. He lectured, as well, at New York University and City College of New York.

His serious interest in the theater emerged following a series of experiences that included service with the Air Force Reserve, a job with a London publisher, and extensive hitchhiking through Europe that concluded in Cairo, Egypt. While in the service, he stopped going to Mass. In Rome, he read newspaper accounts of the pope's impending visit to New York in 1965, and in Cairo, he received a letter from his parents about the pope's ride through Queens on his way to speak at the United Nations. The letter pushed into perspective the events of his own life in a Joycean epiphany. He fell to imagining his mother's reaction to the visit and "was suddenly intensely in touch with myself and my past." He returned to New York in July of 1966, having written act 1 of his first New York success, *The House of Blue Leaves* (1971). In its completed form, the play is crowded with images of his life up to 1965.

Unable to finish the play because of the death of his father shortly after his return, he did accede to having the first act staged at the O'Neill Playhouse in Connecticut. He became active in the protests against the Vietnam War and was once knocked unconscious by a kick from a policeman's horse. Troubled by the fact that there were decent people on both sides of the protests, Guare once more left for Europe, where he finished *The House of Blue Leaves*, returning home in 1970 to enjoy its production at the Off-Broadway Truck and Warehouse Theater in New York in 1971. The play was then successfully revived in 1986 at the prestigious Lincoln Center Vivian Beaumont Theater, which soon became Guare's stage home in New York. His other

946

two major plays, *Six Degrees of Separation* (1990) and *Four Baboons Adoring the Sun* (1992), were produced there as well.

His lesser plays include *Muzeeka* (1967), the musical *Two Gentlemen of Verona*, for which he wrote the lyrics (1971), *Marco Polo Sings a Solo* (1973), *Rich and Famous* (1974), *Landscape of the Body* (1977), *Bosoms and Neglect* (1979), *Women and Water* (1984), and *Moon Over Miami* (1988). He has, as well, joined with playwrights Austin Gray, Romulus Finney, Jean Claude Van Itallie, Edward Albee, and Christopher Durang, each writing a segment of *Faustus in Hell* (1985) and with seven writers, among them David Mamet and Wendy Wasserstein, in adapting stories from Anton Chekhov in a production titled *Orchards* (1987).

Guare served as playwright-in-residence at the New York Shakespeare Festival Public Theater in 1976 and 1977; his other activities include coeditorship of the Lincoln Center *New Theater Review*. He has received many honors for his plays, including a Tony Award, two Obie Awards, two New York Drama Critics Circle Awards, and an Award of Merit from the American Academy and Institute of Arts and Letters. For his screenwriting, he has been honored with the New York, Los Angeles, and National Film Critics Circle Awards. A fellow of the New York Institute for the Humanities and a member of the council of the Dramatists Guild, Guare lives in New York with his wife, the former Adele Chatfield-Taylor.

ANALYSIS

Guare's play titles are an important indication of the theatricality of his style, suggesting dynamism that is spectacular in its sensory and artistic images. In *The House of Blue Leaves*, there are the American icons of song, food, and a bomb. In *Six Degrees of Separation*, a double-sided Wassily Kandinsky painting; and in *Four Baboons Adoring the Sun*, an incredible massing of art and myth imagery: an Egyptian sculpture (from the Louvre) of four baboons staring blindly into the sun; a nearly naked, singing Eros, skirting the rim of the stage throughout; the assigning of mythical names to children; and, finally, the play's locale, archaeological digs in Sicily, to which a recently married couple have brought their nine children from previous marriages.

Images, musical and visual, are Guare's vehicles for messages involving the yearnings of his characters for material success and then for something spiritual beyond the disillusionments that contemporary values have either denied or provided them. In the first of Guare's trilogy of major plays, fame haunts Artie Shaughnessy but in the end denies him, and he is left with the ashes of his life. In the second, affluence and the good life are Ouisa Kittredge's, but she discovers them to be hollow. In the third play, Penny McKenzie takes Ouisa's questioning a step further in the form of a spiritual quest that includes all eleven members of her newly formed family.

With his strong academic background, Guare has gradually moved his latest characters beyond the borders of the United States and modern times to the time and space of mythical reality. In one play, realism and myth blend in an Icarus character who flies too close to the sun and falls to his death. Yet even in Guare's early plays, there is the Greek sense of lives haunted by the pursuit of truth and the eventual acceptance of the sometimes disastrous consequences of that search. Deaths occur in all three of his major plays.

In his portrayal of urban and suburban America, Guare paints with a highly theatrical brush. In his plays nuns maneuver to see the pope while a political activist plots to bomb him, even as domestic problems vie with national events for attention. Complacently affluent couples have their lives disrupted by an imposter posing as Sidney Poitier's son. Disrupted families seeking harmony in Sicily find not only that their pasts haunt them but also that their problems continue into the present.

Guare combines visual techniques with musical ones, an important aspect of his personal life. The dissonances in the Shaughnessys' lives are matched by the jangling ditties that Artie constantly plays and sings throughout *The House of Blue Leaves*. The soliloquies (like operatic arias) in *Six Degrees of Separation* function as Hamlet-like self-questionings. The antiphonal dialogues, the soliloquies, and the chants of Eros successfully fuse the dissonances into a music of life in *Four Baboons Adoring the Sun* as in no other of Guare's plays.

Structurally, his plays reflect the techniques of absurdist theater, with disconnected plots unhindered by logic or chronology. Guare abandoned the episodic structure of the two acts in *The House of Blue Leaves* for a ninety-minute, intermissionless form in *Six Degrees of Separation* and *Four Baboons Adoring the Sun*. The results are dramas in which the themes are so sharply focused and images so crowded that their density and brilliance can be blinding if, like Guare's four baboons, one stares too long and too hard.

Like Chekhov's uses of the seagull and the cherry orchard and Tennessee Williams's uses of a glass menagerie and a streetcar, Guare's blue leaves and baboons provide him with images that reveal truths reaching into the lives of each character. His titular imagery is reinforced within the plays by his use of the arts. Music, important in Guare's life, is a natural part of his plays. A painting in one play and a sculpture in another may seem contrived to some. Yet in combination, domestic realism, myth, and art provide, respectively, emotional, intellectual, and visual rewards for those who choose to "stare into the sun."

Guare's overall theme is the American suburban family in all of its aspirations and losses. The dysfunctional Shaughnessy family—composed of a wayward son, an insane wife and mother, and a husband and father who works at a zoo and entertains Hollywood dreams—is bombarded by the media. The family in *Six Degrees of Separation* has realized its dream, only to undergo disturbing intrusions by those who have not enjoyed its affluence. In *Four Baboons Adoring the Sun*, two middle-class families—one headed by a university professor of archaeology and the other by a congressman—are the victims of divorces. In a marriage of two of the divorced parents, there is an attempt to unify the disparate experiences of each group of children, for whom there looms yet the marriages of the other two divorced parents, with further family relationships to be embraced or rejected.

Guare's comment on society reaches a sophisticated savagery in its portrayal of the supposed insularity of the successful family in *Six Degrees of Separation*. The same society contains a drug-and-crime culture to which the privileged have become so impervious that only the imposters can penetrate it. A struggling young couple, newly arrived in New York to make their way in the theater world, become innocent victims of the same scams made necessary, it would seem, by the insularity of wealth and fame.

Yet the largest truth in Guare's suburban universe is, perhaps, found in the questioning and the quest, respectively, of a Ouisa and a Penny in the hope of attaining some solution to the problems. Such solutions may ultimately be found only in the mythical truths, so old and yet so persistently relevant.

THE HOUSE OF BLUE LEAVES

First produced: 1971 (first published, 1971)
Type of work: Play

The collision of dreary middle-class reality with ideals of Hollywood success destroys the world of an untalented songwriter.

What happens in the lives of the family of a middle-aged zookeeper, Artie Shaughnessy, in Queens, New York, on October 4, 1965—the day of the Roman Catholic pope's journey through Queens—is the result of an explosive combination of a lifetime of dreams and realities. Blending historical and personal events, Guare describes the play in his introduction as "a blur of many years that pulled together under the umbrella of the Pope's visit."

Based on Guare's father (who referred to his Wall Street job as a "zoo"), Artie comes home from his job to an untidy house. At home, he devotes his time to playing and singing corny jingles that he has written, with dreams of Hollywood success constantly on his mind. His household consists of his insane wife, Bananas; his mistress, Bunny Flingus, who lives in the apartment below; and his eighteen-year-old son, Ronnie, currently a serviceman stationed in Fort Dix, New Jersey.

Artie, with the knowledge of Bunny, is in the process of making arrangements to put Bananas into an asylum. Ronnie arrives, unnoticed, with a box of explosives intended for the pope but which, in the course of the play's manic action, go off accidentally, killing three visitors, two nuns, and a visiting Hollywood actress. Ronnie, Bunny, and three visiting nuns maneuver to get as near the pope as they can, each for personal reasons. Among the frenetic events and images of the play, one of the most hilarious is that of the nuns, whose dreams of seeing the pope in person are thwarted; one ends up photographing another who is hugging the television picture of the pope.

The play's title derives from Artie's description of a tree near the asylum to which he plans to remove his insane wife. To get out of the rain, he walks under the tree, the leaves of which turn into birds "waiting to go to Florida or California." After the birds' flight to another tree, the bare tree bursts into blossom again. Like those unrealistic blue leaves, the fantasies of Guare's characters keep returning, their insistence suggesting a permanence denied them in the practical world.

Guare's style, that of the dream in which anything can happen, brings together in one rich, highly detailed tapestry the diverse color and strands of his own life—Catholicism, politics, and art. He points to Ronnie's childhood scene with Uncle Billy—the one member of his family whose Hollywood dreams have been realized—as "an exact word-for-word reportage" of a boyhood event. The image of Billy hovers over the play from start to finish, its destructive influence symbolized by Ronnie's bomb. Dedicating the play to his parents, Guare seems to exorcise their hold on him: "I liked them, loved them, stayed too long, and didn't go away." His comment is a perverse variation of a song written by his father for Guare's mother before Guare's birth.

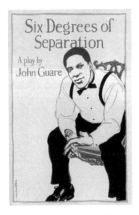

friend of the families' offspring enrolled at Ivy League universities.

Like Don Quixote of old, he sallies forth, but without the don's ideals. He goes so far as to stab himself before intruding at the home of Ouisa and Flan Kittredge, sophisticated and affluent dealers of art. When he appears, he is bleeding, pleads having been robbed, and invokes friendship with their children, Tess and Woody, including knowledge of a "double" Kandinsky painting that hangs on their wall. He exudes the kind of charm, knowledge, and manners expected of a son of Sidney Poitier. His success consists of acquiring the facade of a member of the social tribe to which the Kittredges belong. Furthermore, he whets the interests of his victims by posing the possibility of their appearing in a new film his "father" is in New York to cast (Guare's reinvention of a detail in *The House of Blue Leaves*) and by tales of how their children, away from home, freely discuss their parents.

Paul's downfall begins when he is discovered in Tess's bed with a male prostitute he has taken in off the streets. Other discoveries involve two families who had been similarly defrauded and, finally, a struggling Mormon couple from Utah, Rick and Elizabeth, who are in New York to study acting. This latter scam ends in Rick's suicide, and Paul eventually fails in his goals.

As in Greek tragedy, past events are the subject for a reevaluation of the present. The past is reenacted by means of short, abrupt, tension-creating lines of dialogue and by monologues delivered in asides directly addressed to the audience. Ouisa, in particular, as Guare's version of the Greek chorus, reveals moral questionings that throw her self-centered existence into a tailspin.

The play's title derives from Ouisa's ruminations about the comforting theory that only six "degrees"—six people—separate one from everyone else on the planet. The quandary is to find those six and thus to realize the connection. She experiences the dilemma, and her theory is the basis for Guare's simultaneously funny and searing exploration of modern mores and manners.

SIX DEGREES OF SEPARATION

First produced: 1990 (first published, 1990)
Type of work: Play

A confidence man posing as the son of Sidney Poitier causes chaos and moral self-questioning by his audacious invasions into the lives of privileged urban American families.

In *Six Degrees of Separation*, a young black man named Paul educates himself in order to pull off a daring scam. He enlists the aid of a high-school friend and accumulates the addresses of a number of wealthy New York families. He becomes familiar with the names of family members, their possessions, and customs. He is trained by the friend, now a student at the Massachusetts Institute of Technology (MIT), to speak the language of the upper class. Fully armed with a knowledge of upper-class tribal customs and rites, he passes himself off as a

John Guare

FOUR BABOONS ADORING THE SUN

First produced: 1992 (first published, 1993)
Type of work: Play

A recently married American couple bring to Sicily their nine children from previous marriages in an attempt to forge familial and individual identities beyond those offered by American culture.

The questioning of the rewards of success in the lives of Ouisa and Flan Kittredge in *Six Degrees of Separation* are again enacted in *Four Baboons Adoring the Sun*. Here, however, the couple—Penny and Philip McKenzie—and their children (ranging in age from thirteen to seven) are younger. Philip has left his successful "empire" as an archaeology professor at a California university, and Penny has severed her typical suburban existence "off Exit 4 of the Connecticut Turnpike" as wife of a congressman. Having realized the rewards of the American Dream, both need, more than anything, change and love, and they wish the same for their children.

In Philip's words, there are two universes—Universe A, which is "all facts and reasons and explanations," and Universe B, the universe of childhood, which is essentially mythic. It is this mythic level to which the play aspires. In no other play has Guare so richly invested the style and symbols of myth; for example, the family's children are given mythic names (the most important of which is Wayne's appellation of Icarus). The mythical ambience is created immediately with the appearance of Eros, Guare's version of the Greek chorus. As background to the action, Eros is onstage throughout, chanting aspirations and forebodings in the tradition of the chorus. Beyond Eros, there is a replica of a four-thousand-year-old granite Egyptian sculpture of four baboons who have stared at the sun until they are blinded. Wayne (Icarus), in a forbidden love with his new sister Halcy, feels trapped in a labyrinth his father has created. He climbs a nearby mountain and falls to his death.

The exotic myth imagery in the play blends with the poetically framed dialogue, in which realistic American speech is stylized in the manner of the stichomythia of classical drama. Realism and myth are one as the eldest children question the parents in incantatory lines:

Wayne: Did you hate Mom?
Halcy: Did you hate Dad?
Penny: No.
Philip: Yes.

The antiphonal nature of the questions and responses in which parents and children participate transforms the play into a ritual without diluting the realism of their respective situations. The play ends with Eros chanting about choices he offers and with parents and children choosing their futures. Penny, like Philip's Wayne, chooses to "leap into space." Philip, like Penny's Halcy, chooses not to leap, and he will return to his university.

SUMMARY

Guare was influenced by Chekhov and Henrik Ibsen in his younger years, and he acknowledges the existence, from Aeschylus on down, of what has been labeled in the twentieth century as the Theater of the Absurd. He goes on to say that "the absurd is that which generates music." In the ditties composed and sung by Artie Shaughnessy, in Ouisa Kittredge's poetic reachings for a reality beyond that she has known, and in the McKenzie family's realization of a mythic reality, Guare has caught the music of life in the suburbs of contemporary America, in its lofty aspirations and its phoniness—all exposed at some point to the harsh glare of the sun.

Susan Rusinko

BIBLIOGRAPHY

By the Author

DRAMA:
Universe, pr. 1949
Theatre Girl, pr. 1959

The Toadstool Boy, pr. 1960

The Golden Cherub, pr. 1962(?)

Did You Write My Name in the Snow?, pr. 1962

To Wally Pantoni, We Leave a Credenza, pr. 1964

The Loveliest Afternoon of the Year, pr. 1966, pb. 1968

Something I'll Tell You Tuesday, pr. 1966, pb. 1968

Muzeeka, pr. 1967, pb. 1969 (one act)

Cop-Out, pr. 1968, pb. 1969

Home Fires, pr. 1968, pb. 1969

A Play by Brecht, pr. 1969 (libretto; music by Leonard Bernstein; lyrics by Stephen Sondheim; adaptation of Bertolt Brecht's *The Exception and the Rule*)

A Day for Surprises, pr., pb. 1970

The House of Blue Leaves, pr., pb. 1971

Two Gentlemen of Verona, pr. 1971, pb. 1973 (with Mel Shapiro; music by Galt MacDermot; adaptation of William Shakespeare's play)

Marco Polo Sings a Solo, pr. 1973, pb. 1977

Optimism: Or, The Misadventures of Candide, pr. 1973 (with Harold Stone; adaptation of Voltaire's novel)

Rich and Famous, pr. 1974, pb. 1977

Landscape of the Body, pr. 1977, pb. 1978

Bosoms and Neglect, pr. 1979, pb. 1980

In Fireworks Lie Secret Codes, pr. 1979, pb. 1981

A New Me, pr. 1981

Gardenia, pr., pb. 1982

Lydie Breeze, pr., pb. 1982

Women and Water, pr. 1984, pb. 1990

The Talking Dog, pr. 1986, pb. 1987 (one act; based on a story by Anton Chekhov)

Moon over Miami, pr. 1988

Six Degrees of Separation, pr., pb. 1990

Four Baboons Adoring the Sun, pr. 1992, pb. 1993

The War Against the Kitchen Sink, pb. 1996

The General of Hot Desire, pr., pb. 1999

The General of Hot Desire, and Other Plays, pb. 1999

Lake Hollywood, pr. 1999, pb. 2000

A Book of Judith, pr. 2000

Lydie Breeze, pr. 2000, pb. 2001 (revision of *Lydie Breeze* and *Gardenia*)

Chaucer in Rome, pr. 2001, pb. 2002

Sweet Smell of Success, pr. 2001 (libretto; lyrics by Craig Carnelia; music by Marvin Hamlisch; adaptation of Clifford Odets's screenplay)

A Few Stout Individuals, pr. 2002, pb. 2003

SCREENPLAYS:

Taking Off, 1971 (with Miloš Forman and Jean-Claude Carrière)

Atlantic City, 1981

Six Degrees of Separation, 1993

DISCUSSION TOPICS

- Compare John Guare's visual imagery in two plays.
- Compare Guare's musical imagery in two plays.
- What are the thematic similarities of *The House of Blue Leaves*, *Six Degrees of Separation*, and *Four Baboons Adoring the Sun*?
- Compare Guare's treatment of dysfunctional families in two plays.
- What is Guare saying about Roman Catholicism in *The House of Blue Leaves*?
- How is show business a metaphor in *The House of Blue Leaves*?
- Is the theory of six degrees of separation merely a plot device, or is it central to the themes of *Six Degrees of Separation*?
- How is the 1980 film *Atlantic City* similar to Guare's plays?

John Guare

TELEPLAY:
Kissing Sweet, 1969

NONFICTION:
Chuck Close: Life and Work, 1988-1995, 1995

About the Author

Cohn, Ruby. *New American Dramatists: 1960-1990.* 2d ed. New York: St. Martin's Press, 1991.

Curry, Jane. *John Guare: A Research and Production Sourcebook.* Westport, Conn.: Greenwood Press, 2002.

DiGaetani, John L. *A Search for a Postmodern Theater: Interviews with Contemporary Playwrights.* New York: Greenwood Press, 1991.

Gillian, Jennifer. "Staging a Staged Crisis in Masculinity: Race and Masculinity in *Six Degrees of Separation.*" In *New Readings in American Drama: Something's Happening Here,* edited by Norma Jenckes. New York: Peter Lang, 2002.

Martin, Nicholas. "Chaos and Other Muses." *American Theatre* 16 (April, 1999): 26-29, 51-52.

Plunka, Gene A. *The Black Comedy of John Guare.* Newark: University of Delaware Press, 2002.

_____. "John Guare and the Popular Culture Hype of Celebrity." In *A Companion to Twentieth Century Drama,* edited by David Krasner and Molly Smith. Malden, Mass.: Blackwell, 2005.

Rose, Lloyd. "John Guare." In *The Playwright's Art: Conversations with Contemporary American Dramatists,* edited by Jackson R. Bryer. New Brunswick, N.J.: Rutgers University Press, 1995.

Slethaug, Gordon E. "Chaotics and Many Degrees of Freedom in John Guare's *Six Degrees of Separation.*" *American Drama* 11 (Winter, 2002): 73-93.

Zimmerman, David A. "Six Degrees of Distinction: Connection, Contagion, and the Aesthetics of Anything." *Arizona Quarterly* 55 (Autumn, 1999): 107-133.